GREAT CASES
OF SCOTLAND YARD

GREAT CASES OF SCOTLAND YARD

Selected by the Editors of
The Reader's Digest

The Reader's Digest Association
Pleasantville, New York
London, Montreal, Sydney, Cape Town, Hong Kong

The publishers gratefully acknowledge the cooperation they have received from the commissioner of the Metropolitan Police, Sir David B. McNee Q.P.M., and his predecessor, Sir Robert Mark G.B.E., Q.P.M.

The publishers also wish to acknowledge the ever-ready help and advice that they and the authors have received throughout the planning and preparation of this book from the following serving officers and members of the force: Deputy Assistant Commissioner Peter Walton, Mr. F. Athill M.B.E., Mrs. Linda Bell, Mr. W. F. Maxfield; also from the former public relations officer, Mr. G. D. Gregory O.B.E.

In addition, the publishers and authors would like to express their warmest appreciation to all the serving and former officers who so generously took the time and trouble to talk about—and to answer innumerable questions about—specific cases on which they had worked. The serving officers are Detective Chief Superintendent J. K. Slipper, Detective Superintendent R. Lawrence, and Detective Inspector J. K. O. Coote. The former officers are Mr. Colin MacDougall, Mr. Alistair Dent, Mr. James W. Marshall B.E.M., Mr. William Henry Rudkin, Mr. Ferguson Smith, and Mr. Wilfred ("Bill") Smith.

In particular, they would like to thank Mr. M. G. Down M.B.E., who made the progress of this book his own special responsibility.

Finally, the publishers owe a debt of gratitude to Mr. Nigel Morland, editor of *The Criminologist*, for his unfailing encouragement and assistance.

CONTENTS

INTRODUCTION

"I am Bucket of the detectives. I am a detective officer."

The speaker is an inspector from Scotland Yard. The year is 1853 and the novel in which the speech appears is *Bleak House* by Charles Dickens. It is the first recorded appearance in print of the word "detective" meaning what it means today.

More than fifty years were to elapse, however, before London began to feel that its plainclothes detectives could be trusted. As an early police commissioner noted sadly, the detectives were "viewed with the greatest suspicion by the majority of Englishmen."

Dickens could make Inspector Bucket a sympathetic character because he knew real Scotland Yard detectives, decent men doing their best to make a science of criminal investigation. In the minds of most of Dickens' fellow citizens, however, all detectives fell into one of two categories. If they were not the cunningly disguised successors of the corrupt and incompetent Bow Street Runners, then they belonged to a new corps of secret-police spies organized on the continental model as agents of political oppression.

Who could win against those odds? Indeed, even the best of policemen must have wondered in the end whether it was worth trying to do so. After all, failure was punished only with ridicule. The penalty for success could be more serious.

In 1860 a four-year-old boy was found stabbed to death in the garden of his parents' house. The family concerned was of the highest respectability. For the local police the prime suspect was the child's nursemaid. When, however, Inspector Whicher of Scotland Yard was called in to give his opinion, he deduced from the evidence that the murderer was the dead boy's sixteen-year-old stepsister, Constance Kent.

The idea of that nice, well-bred girl being accused of such a dreadful crime was so clearly absurd that, as soon as her family complained to the commissioner, he immediately fired Inspector Whicher. When, five years later, dear little Constance confessed to the murder, everyone was much surprised. However, nobody bothered to apologize to Whicher.

Small wonder that in his Sherlock Holmes stories of the 1880s Conan Doyle portrays the Scotland Yard detectives as amiable dullards. When

Queen Victoria, shocked by the Jack the Ripper murders, declared that more detectives were needed, the commissioner—an even sillier man than the one who had fired Whicher—ordered a field trial of bloodhounds. Unfortunately the trial took place on a foggy day and the hounds got lost. The newspapers picked up the story, and this time it was the commissioner who was fired. A period of reform at last began.

At that time, the only police force thought capable of conducting a serious criminal investigation was the French Sûreté. Its detective branch was headed by François Eugène Vidocq, a crook turned policeman, and its success had been based on its possession of inside information and a network of stool pigeons. Vidocq's more respectable successors compiled and used criminal records and invested them with the trappings of new technologies. It was the Sûreté's Alphonse Bertillon who evolved a system of criminal identification based on photography and the precise measurement of physical characteristics. Indeed, Scotland Yard was still debating the adoption of a modified "Bertillonage" when Sir Francis Galton published his treatise entitled *Finger Prints*. A little later, Sir Edward Henry, destined to become one of the Yard's great commissioners, devised the simple system of fingerprint classification still used by police departments all over the world.

Since Commissioner Henry's time the progress of Scotland Yard's Criminal Investigation Department has been continuous and for the most part successful. Identification by means of fingerprints was only the first of a series of technical innovations developed by the CID. Later they were to find the all-important answers, not only to the problems of using the new forensic sciences to trace and identify criminals, but also to those of persuading British juries to understand and to accept scientific findings as evidence.

It took a long time for the detectives of Scotland Yard to win the kind of public respect traditionally accorded to the uniformed branch. In the end, though, they won it by becoming obviously and exceptionally good at their jobs. Standards are high and mistakes, even those that can be forgiven, are rarely forgotten. Also well remembered is the case of Inspector Whicher. At Scotland Yard it is a long time since anyone has been fired for being right.

Eric Ambler

THE STEALING OF MURIEL McKAY

by
Clive Egleton

When Detective Sergeant Birch of Scotland Yard arrived at the McKay residence in the exclusive London suburb of Wimbledon, he found a house in some disorder, a worried husband, and not a single clue to the whereabouts of Muriel McKay. All that was known was that she was gone. But where? Then came the first phone call—a weirdly chilling communication from a person who identified himself as M3 and demanded a million pounds on threat of Mrs. McKay's life.

A borrowed Rolls-Royce, a case of mistaken identity, a cruel twist of fate; thus began a search that was to dominate headlines for six weeks—a race against the clock, with the skill and manpower of the Yard pitted against the elusive and ruthless M3.

Clive Egleton, author of *Seven Days to a Killing*, re-creates in graphic detail the harrowing fight to save the life of Muriel McKay.

CHAPTER 1

DETECTIVE SERGEANT BIRCH turned into Arthur Road and drove up the hill, keeping an eye out for the Panda car which had answered the call shortly after eight o'clock that evening. He didn't know the exact location of St. Mary House, but with the number twenty, it had to be somewhere near the top. Less than half a mile from the All England Lawn Tennis Club, this end of Arthur Road lay in the select section of the South London suburb of Wimbledon, where every house looked solid and prosperous.

The people who lived in this neighborhood were obviously successful, but even if they were financially well off, Birch knew that they still had their problems. Vandals frequently damaged their property, their houses were sometimes burgled, and it had been known for a husband to return home from work to find that his wife was missing, as was the case with Alick McKay.

Approaching a bend in the road, Birch spotted the Panda car standing in the drive of a large, red brick, mock-Georgian house, and turning off the road, he pulled in behind it. Although he personally had not been involved in the case, he was aware that St. Mary House had been burgled some three months back, and he thought he could see now why the thief had singled it out. Apart from the fact that its appearance suggested that the owners were wealthy, it was a good deal more isolated than many other houses in the immediate vicinity. Partially screened from the road by a tall wooden fence and largely hidden from the rectory next door by a row of trees, there was also a considerable gap between the house and the entrance to a school which separated it from number twenty-four, lower down the hill.

Birch got out of the car and walked toward the front door, reflecting that this could well be his last case if only because this was Monday, the twenty-ninth of December, 1969, and his retirement was less than a month away. Anderson, an inspector in the uniformed branch, who'd answered the call from Wimbledon Police Station over his car radio, was waiting for him on the doorstep.

Birch said, "I wouldn't turn a dog out on a night like this."

"Aye," said Anderson, "it is bitterly cold."

"And all for a missing person."

"I don't think it's that simple, Sergeant."

"So I gathered."

"It looks to me as if somebody might have forced his way into the house."

"Might have?" Birch echoed. "Is there some doubt?"

"I think you should form your own opinion."

"I intend to. Is there anything you can tell me about Mr. McKay before I meet him? I mean, what's his line of business?"

"He's in Fleet Street, on the board of the *News of the World*."

"Is he now?" Birch said thoughtfully.

It wasn't necessary to be a reader of that Sunday newspaper to know something about the recent history of the *News of the World*. Rupert Murdoch, a young, ambitious Australian news tycoon, had acquired it at the beginning of the year.

A tall figure came up behind Anderson, and Birch, moving past the inspector, stepped inside the porch.

"Mr. McKay, sir?" he said. "I'm Detective Sergeant Birch."

McKay shook hands. "My wife has gone," he said calmly, in a marked Australian accent.

"So I understand, sir." Birch was immediately impressed by Alick McKay's appearance and bearing. A handsome man with a

strong open face, he could have been any age between fifty and sixty.

"What has happened?"

"Try not to worry, sir," Birch said quietly. "We'll find out soon enough."

McKay appeared not to hear him. "Where has she gone?" he asked.

Going through the inside door, they entered a large, square hall. Birch saw that a pair of high-heeled shoes had been set tidily on the floor at the foot of the staircase. Just above, a black leather handbag lay open on the bottom step, its contents scattered up the next five steps. A white telephone, which obviously belonged on the writing desk opposite the staircase, lay turned over on the floor. Its wire had been yanked from the wall and the number disk removed from its dial. A pair of eyeglasses—which later proved to be Mrs. McKay's reading glasses—were lying on the floor beside the phone. There was a ball of thick twine on a hall chair, and a rusty billhook had been placed on top of the desk near photographs of the three McKay children. A strip of adhesive bandage, folded over itself, had been left on a small table near the door.

Birch took out his notebook. "I know you've been over this before with Inspector Anderson," he said, "but I'd like you to tell me again, in your own words, what you found and what you did when you returned home and discovered your wife was missing."

For a moment McKay seemed irritated. A man of action, he was now being asked to adopt a passive role. His wife was missing and he was convinced that she had been abducted, yet the police seemingly were not in a hurry to do anything positive about it, and time was pressing on. The frustration flared briefly and then died.

"I returned home at seven forty-five," he said, "a little later than usual because a meeting I'd attended had overrun. The chauffeur dropped me at the door and I told him to pick me up at the same time tomorrow. You see, Rupert Murdoch suggested I use the company Rolls-Royce while he's away on six weeks' holiday in Australia."

"Oh yes," murmured Birch.

"Well, then I pressed the bell and gave it three short rings and one long. Muriel and I have this private signal because the house was burgled last September and she was nervous about opening the door after dark. When she didn't answer, I tried the door. To my surprise, it was unlocked and the chain was hanging loose. When I opened the

Detectives examining the front door of the McKay home

inner door, I walked into this." McKay indicated the scattered objects in the hall.

He went on to describe how he had grabbed the billhook and, thinking that an intruder might still be in the house, had run upstairs, calling his wife's name. He went through all the bedrooms and bathrooms, but she was nowhere to be found. He then returned downstairs and looked into the sitting room at the back of the drawing room, which he referred to as the Snug. It was here that Mrs. McKay would wait for his return in the evening.

"The television set was on," McKay continued, "and one of the evening newspapers was open across the arm of Muriel's chair. Carl, our dachshund, was sitting on the floor in front of the fireplace. Though logs were still burning, the fire had been left unscreened, a negligent practice that Mrs. McKay had been particularly careful to avoid.

"I was getting seriously worried by this time and I searched all the other rooms on the ground floor and then went into the kitchen. I found Muriel's coat lying on a chair. Two steaks that were to be cooked for dinner had been set out on a plate by the stove. I came back into the hall and checked to see whether anything was missing from Muriel's handbag. The cash and some jewelry that she usually carried with her were gone. I suppose that's when I first saw the bandage and noticed that the inner door had been forced."

Birch looked at the door. The wood on either side of the housing had split, as if someone had put a shoulder to the door, forcing it open before the lug was fully engaged.

McKay continued. "I then went outside and searched the garden and outbuildings, and finding that Muriel's Ford Capri was still in the garage, I called on our neighbors to see if they'd heard anything. I used their telephone to ring the police."

"Is anything missing besides the things from the handbag?"

"Missing?"

"Jewelry, money, silver, stuff like that."

McKay looked surprised. "I don't know, I didn't think to look."

"Well, we ought to see if anything has been stolen."

Photo issued by police of kidnapped Muriel McKay

The search wasn't very conclusive. They found a drawer in Muriel's dressing table open, and a silver brocade pouch in which she kept some jewelry was missing, but apart from this there was nothing to suggest that the house had been ransacked. As far as McKay could tell from the rows of clothing in the fitted wardrobe, nothing seemed to be missing. To Birch it began to seem as if the disturbance in the hall had been artificially created, like a set for a stage production of an Agatha Christie mystery.

Although McKay was firmly convinced that his wife had been kidnapped, the fact remained that this type of crime was unknown in Britain. On the other hand, it was not unknown for a woman to leave home suddenly and without any prior warning. Within the boundaries of V Division, which embraced Wimbledon, the uniformed branch had an average of between five and six cases to deal with each week involving a missing person. Birch could recall instances where the missing woman had even staged a dramatic exit, as if anxious to draw attention to her disappearance.

In the dining room, over a whisky and soda, he began to question Alick McKay about his wife and family. The description of Muriel McKay which Birch took down in his notebook hardly did justice to the attractive woman in the photograph on the mantelpiece, but he wrote that she was five feet nine, medium build, dark complexion, dark brown hair, straight nose, green eyes, oval face and was fifty-five years old. He also added that at the time of her disappearance she was thought to be wearing a green jersey suit, a bracelet, a wedding ring and two diamond rings.

The McKays had been married for over thirty-six years and had two grown daughters and a son. The son, Ian, who was just a boy when the family came to England in 1957, had returned to Australia, where, like his father, he had gone into newspaper advertising. The two daughters, Diane and Jennifer, had both married and settled in England.

Birch said, "Don't you think you should call your daughters? Your wife might have spoken to them and perhaps they know something we don't."

McKay thought about it. "I don't want to worry them unnecessarily," he said slowly.

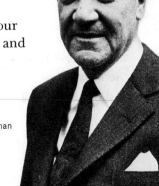

Alick McKay, husband of the missing woman

"Even so, I really do think you ought to telephone them."

"All right," said McKay. "I'll phone from the sitting room."

In the space of the next half hour or so, a number of telephone calls were made from the house in Arthur Road. McKay spoke to his daughters, Diane Dyer and Jennifer Burgess. Alarmed and upset, both were driving to Wimbledon immediately with their husbands. Detective Sergeant Birch called Detective Chief Superintendent Bill Smith, of Scotland Yard's V Division, at home. Smith listened carefully to what Birch had to say and, satisfied with the way he was handling the inquiry, advised him to keep him informed.

DETECTIVE SERGEANT WHITE, a night-duty Criminal Investigation Department officer, had the feeling that he was about to enter a three-ring circus. There were a number of cars parked both down the hill and around the corner from the house, and as he turned off the road into the drive, he passed a photographer and several reporters standing near the entrance. The police were also in evidence: a constable guarded the front door, and he could see others searching the garden and outbuildings; they were also inside the house, photographing the interior of the hall from every angle, measuring it up and making notes, while Birch hovered in the background.

White caught his eye. "Hello, Graham. How's it going?"

Birch shrugged his shoulders expressively. "To tell you the truth, Wally, I don't know what to make of it. We'd better go into the dining room; at least it's quiet in there and we can talk in private. Do you want a cup of tea, or a sandwich? I'm sure Mrs. Nightingale would be happy to make you something."

White shook his head. "Who's Mrs. Nightingale?"

"The home help; she's filled in some of the details for us. I've got a good idea now what Mrs. McKay did during the day."

White looked around the hall, frowning as he saw the billhook, the ball of twine, the handbag and shoes, the upturned telephone and the strip of adhesive bandage. "Odd," he muttered.

"You can say that again." Birch opened the door to the dining room, and then a telephone trilled. "There it goes again," he said morosely. "Hasn't stopped ringing all the time I've been here. Word has somehow got around that Muriel McKay is missing and the press wires are obviously humming."

"Are any members of the family here yet?"

"Diane Dyer and her husband; they're with McKay in the sitting room. The other daughter, Jennifer, should be arriving soon." Birch opened his notebook. "You know what really bothers me?"

"The family breathing down your neck?"

"No; they're just very worried and anxious, and you'd expect the atmosphere to be a little strained and tense. It's just that I can't help feeling that if she was taken by force, there ought to be some evidence of a struggle. Oh, we've got that mess out there in the hall all right, but it all looks a bit contrived to me."

"How did she get on with her husband?" White said quietly.

"McKay is adamant that they were very happy together, and so is the rest of the family." Birch rubbed his chin. "Me, I don't know what to think. Look, according to Mrs. Nightingale, Muriel McKay spent the early part of the morning helping her with the household chores. At midday she walked up to Wimbledon Village and did a little shopping before returning home to eat a light lunch. It seems she had a routine dental appointment in Central London this afternoon and she went up to town by car. Mrs. Nightingale says she then finished her work and sat down to watch television while she waited for Mrs. McKay to return, which she did at five o'clock. She then drove Mrs. Nightingale home, stopping on the way to buy two copies of the *Evening News*. Since Mrs. Nightingale arrived home at five thirty, we can assume Mrs. McKay was back here ten minutes later, which means that we've got a gap of two hours before McKay returned from the office and found that she had vanished. Incidentally, we

Interior of McKay home
after the kidnapping

found the black and white coat she'd been wearing draped over a chair in the kitchen."

White's fingers drummed on the table. "Is anything missing?"

"A few pieces of jewelry and the cash from her handbag. We think the whole lot is worth about six hundred pounds."

It made sense in some ways but not in others. If burglary was the motive, why abduct the woman? If it was a kidnap, why did they bother taking a few pieces of jewelry and the money? On the other hand, a woman deciding on the spur of the moment that she was going to leave home in a theatrical manner might just do that. And perhaps, at the last minute, she realized she would need some money if she was going to run off. It wasn't rational, but in White's experience, women in an emotional state often behaved oddly.

"Did Mrs. Nightingale notice anything unusual about her behavior today?"

Birch closed his notebook. "Not a thing, Wally. She seemed perfectly normal."

"And that's it?"

"Well, we've been busy making door-to-door inquiries and are checking with the hospitals in case she has met with an accident. And, of course, I've been keeping the Guvnor informed. Not that there has been much to report."

White pushed his chair back and stood up. "You'd better introduce me to the family," he said, "and then you can go off duty."

"Right," said Birch. "Let's get on with it."

IT WAS PAST MIDNIGHT when Jennifer Burgess and her husband arrived at the house, but even after he'd spoken to them at length, White was still groping in the dark. Like the other members of the family, Jennifer was unable to think of a single reason why her mother might choose to leave home of her own accord. So far, they had drawn a complete blank with the local hospitals, and from the various reports he'd received, it was very clear to White that none of the neighbors remembered seeing anything unusual either.

There had been no fresh developments, but White knew that the number of reporters outside the house had grown considerably since he had arrived. Some, no doubt, had been surprised to see Hugh Cudlipp, the chairman of the International Publishing Corporation, call at the house, but if so, White thought it probable that this was all the news they were likely to get that night.

The telephone rang again and David Dyer answered it, as he'd become accustomed to do ever since he'd arrived at the house with his wife, Diane. A frown creased his forehead, and then he frantically signaled his father-in-law as White, understanding the signals, ran into the kitchen and picked up the extension there.

A voice said, "This is Mafia Group 3. We are from America. Mafia M3; we have your wife."

White, racing to jot the conversation down, heard McKay say, "You have my wife?"

The caller said, "You will need a million pounds by Wednesday."

"What are you talking about? I don't understand."

A pause, and then, "Mafia. Do you understand?"

"Yes, I have heard of them."

"We have your wife. It will cost you one million pounds."

"That is ridiculous. I haven't got anything like a million."

"You had better get it. You have friends. Get it from them. We tried to get Rupert Murdoch's wife. We couldn't get her, so we took yours instead."

"Rupert Murdoch?" McKay said blankly.

"You have a million by Wednesday night or we will kill her."

"What do I do?"

"All you have to do is wait for the contact. That is for the money. You will get instructions. Have the money or you won't have a wife. We will contact you again."

There was another pause, followed by a clatter, and then a different male voice said, "Have you finished, caller?"

White said, "Hold it, who are you?"

"The telephone operator."

"Where?"

"At Epping. I put that call through from a phone box on Bell Common because the party had trouble dialing your number on standard trunk dial. I heard part of the conversation."

"In that case," said White, "let's have your name. We may want to talk to you later."

"Who's we?"

"The police."

"Oh, I see. Well, my name's Underwood. Terence Underwood."

White thanked him and hung up. He thought the man who called himself M3 had a curious voice. He couldn't quite place it, but to his ears it sounded not unlike a West Indian accent. Without a moment's hesitation, he lifted the phone off the hook and called Detective Chief Superintendent Smith.

CHAPTER 2

DETECTIVE CHIEF SUPERINTENDENT Bill Smith still retained traces of a Lancashire accent. Direct and blunt when the occasion demanded, he also happened to be a very resilient, experienced and able detective.

Smith now read through the transcript of the telephone conversation with Mafia M3 again and frowned. "We're dealing with a nut," he said, looking at White.

"Sir?" White made it sound like a question.

"A million pounds? It's not reasonable. Where would McKay get that kind of money? I wonder if they even realize what putting a million pounds together entails? You'd need a truck just to cart it around."

"The call came through at one fifteen," White said.

It was a fine point. Around one o'clock, a BBC newscaster had reported that "police in the London area have started a massive hunt for the wife of the deputy chairman of the *News of the World,* who was found to be missing from her home in Wimbledon last evening." Smith knew it would be stupid to ignore altogether the possibility that there might be a connection between the news bulletin and the subsequent telephone call. He said, "It might not tell us much, but we must treat this message as though it was not a hoax."

"I expect we'll get plenty of those before the day is out," his assistant, Detective Inspector John Minors, said quietly. "The news of her disappearance is bound to be in all the newspapers."

There was no need for any amplification. Once the public read about it, they would be inundated with telephone calls from decent people anxious

Detective Chief Superintendent Bill Smith

to help the police in any way they could, as well as from the other kind—the cranks, the sick in mind and the malicious. And there would be letters too, a trickle at first but swelling in volume by the hundreds as the days passed. To deal with all this they would need to create a crime index, a complex and meticulous filing system to cross-reference every piece of information they received, no matter how petty or irrelevant it might seem.

Smith turned to Minors. "All right," he said briskly. "I want a tape recorder plugged into one of the extensions so that we've got a record of all incoming calls to the house. We'll circulate her description to every police force in the country and follow it up with a photograph as soon as we've run off sufficient copies. We shall need question-and-answer papers printed, but nothing too elaborate at this stage. We just want people to say where they were between five thirty and seven forty-five yesterday evening. Limit the inquiries to Arthur Road and the adjoining streets; we can always enlarge the net later if we have to." He turned to face White. "Apart from the stuff in the hall, what else have you found?"

"Only a copy of *The People*. According to Mr. McKay, he found several pages blowing about in the drive when he came home last night. The rest of the newspaper was inside the hallway."

"And that's all?"

"Yes."

"Right. We'll go through the house again from top to bottom. I'll ask the daughters to look through her wardrobe, because I don't believe she left the house in her stocking feet and without a coat. And then I want the garden and outbuildings turned over until I'm satisfied we haven't overlooked anything. Got it?"

"Yes, sir."

"Another thing. I want all her movements during the day checked out. I'd like to know where she went shopping, who she saw, that sort of thing. Find out where she banks, whether the account is in her name or if it's a joint one. Either way, I want it stopped. Clear?"

"Yes," said Minors.

"Good. Well, I'd better have another word with the family before we start organizing the setup at Wimbledon Police Station." Smith raised a cautionary hand. "I think it's best to warn them."

"What about?"

"That they're bound to receive a number of obscene and abusive phone calls. The heavy breathers will be pretty active too."

"That figures."

"And then I shall have to inform them that we intend to take their fingerprints." Smith glanced at the writing desk in the hall. "We know that McKay handled that billhook, for a start."

THE WHEELS WERE gathering momentum now and Smith chose his team with care. In Detective Sergeant Parker he found the perfect man to handle the difficult and often tedious task of assembling the crime index. A patient and dependable officer, Parker also had a remarkable memory for detail which others, less gifted in this respect, might well overlook as the pressures increased.

The accommodation at Wimbledon Police Station was rearranged to make room for a special inquiry office. Rosters were changed; detectives reassigned to the case were instructed to shed their present work load, and were then briefed, given a specific task and sent on their way. Questionnaires were drafted. Extra telephones, installed by the post office, coped with the flood of incoming calls which had threatened to jam the switchboard.

Terence Underwood, the late-night operator at the Epping exchange, was interviewed but couldn't tell them much that Smith didn't know already. He agreed that the man who referred to himself as M3 had a deep, muffled voice, and judging by his accent, he thought the caller was either an American or a colored immigrant.

As the day wore on and the first reports started to come in from police officers on the ground, the crime index began to grow in size, and with it emerged a clearer picture of how Muriel McKay had spent the previous day. In the morning she had gone to the bank and cashed a check for twenty-five pounds. A few minutes later she'd entered a fashionable boutique and spent a happy half hour there while she selected a matching dress and evening coat that cost sixty pounds. She had left the outfit at the shop, saying that she would come for it later.

The first tape had arrived from the house in Arthur Road, and playing it back, Smith could appreciate just what sort of effect this constant stream of messages must be having on the family, McKay in particular. Some callers tried to be helpful, were well meaning and sympathetic; others, as he had warned, were abusive and obscene. There were cranks claiming to have extrasensory perception who, in a vision, had seen where Muriel McKay was being held captive. There were those who gave information which, because of its conflicting nature, was almost certain to be yet another false lead but which nevertheless could not be ignored.

THE TELEPHONE AT McKay's house was often engaged for twenty minutes at a time, but as the hours passed, there was still no further word from the kidnappers. Four o'clock came and went, four thirty, a quarter to five; the hands on the clock crept forward, marking the passage of time. At one minute to five, the telephone, which had rarely been silent all day, rang again. As David Dyer lifted the receiver off the hook, the tape started tracking to record a series of pips.

The coins went down in the box and then a deep, muffled voice said, "Your wife has just posted a letter to you. Do cooperate, for heaven's sake. For her sake, don't call the police. You have been followed. Did you get the message? Did you get the money?" And then the line was dead before Dyer could ask a question.

It was Tuesday, the thirtieth of December, and if M3 meant what he'd said in his previous message, they had just twenty-four hours to comply with the demand for one million pounds. And yet the fact remained that he had still failed to indicate how, when and where this ransom was to be delivered.

CHAPTER 3

SMITH HAD TRAVELED the route from Wimbledon Police Station to the house in Arthur Road so often now that he had no need to check the landmarks to know precisely where he was at any given moment in time. A short run up Queens Road before turning right into The Broadway, and then on up the hill for seven hundred yards before turning right again into Belvedere Drive. A quick turn to the left followed by one to the right into Arthur Road, and there was St. Mary's Church on the left. A mere five-minute journey from door to door, but time enough to reflect and wonder how he could establish a close rapport with the family.

They were under an intolerable strain. Anyone who had seen Diane Dyer's face yesterday evening, when she'd appeared during BBC's eight-fifty television news to appeal for the safe return of her mother, would know that. Perhaps anticipating an intensely sympathetic public response, more and more news reporters gathered outside the house. Smith felt that somehow he'd have to find a way to use the reporters for police advantage.

Alick McKay was waiting for him in the sitting room, looking tired and drawn but still in control of himself. Without saying much, he handed over the letter, which had arrived with the first post. The envelope indicated that the letter had been mailed at six forty-five p.m. in Tottenham North 17 on the thirtieth of December. The letter itself was written on blue-lined paper in a hand so shaky as to be almost unreadable. The words were crowded and ill matched, and the sentences fell away in a downward curve. Clearly, one section in particular had been written with great difficulty.

It read,

Alick Darling, I am blindfolded and cold. Only blankets. Please do something to get me home. Please cooperate or I cannot keep going. I think of you constantly and have kept calm so far. What have I done to deserve this treatment? Love

Muriel

Now that he was seeing it for himself, the letter made a far greater impact on Smith than when it had been read out to him over the telephone earlier that morning. The spidery handwriting emphasized her fear and bewilderment far more graphically than anyone could describe it in words.

Smith said, "You're satisfied she wrote it?"

McKay nodded. "I'd know her handwriting anywhere."

"Well, that makes them authentic."

"What?"

"The phone calls from M3 are genuine. They are holding your wife. Until now, we couldn't ignore the possibility that they were trying to obtain money by deception. It could still happen."

"What could?"

"The whole country knows that your wife has been kidnapped.

McKay with son, Ian, and daughters, Diane Dyer (left) and Jennifer Burgess

That being so, some petty criminal may decide to get in on the act. I know it's lousy," Smith said gently, "but I think we should be prepared for the eventuality."

"I wish I knew what to do. You feel so helpless just waiting for something to happen."

"We're doing everything we can."

"Yes." The doubt was in his voice, even if McKay hadn't expressed it in so many words.

"This letter may help," Smith said firmly. "Someone had to stick the stamp on and seal the envelope. We may find thumb and palm prints."

There was no point in telling him that they had already lifted a palm print from a page of *The People* they'd recovered from the house, because the Criminal Record Office (CRO) had been unable to match it with any they had on file. Smith hoped the letter would produce a lead, since it was logical to suppose that more than one person was involved in the kidnapping. One man would have to guard her while the other posted the letter and made the telephone call, but it was best not to say anything to McKay about this possibility until they had something definite to go on.

"My son, Ian, is arriving tomorrow from Australia."

"Well, he'd want to be with the family at a time like this."

"There must be something we can do. Maybe an appeal?"

To attract even more publicity was undoubtedly an unorthodox approach, but then there were no precedents for this particular case. Smith could see it would certainly help to promote a better understanding with the family if he went along with the idea. Handled properly, it might even draw M3 out into the open.

"Perhaps Mrs. Dyer should go on television again?"

"Diane?" McKay said blankly.

"This time on Independent Television. We can also hold a press conference with all the family present."

"When?"

"Tonight," said Smith. "I'll make the necessary arrangements."

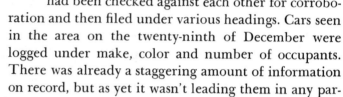

THE CRIME INDEX WAS GROWING like a hothouse plant as the telephone calls multiplied and the letters poured in by the hundreds. A description of the missing jewelry had been circulated, in case the kidnappers tried to pawn the rings and brooches or dispose of them through a fence. The billhook had been photographed and inquiries were being made to see if anyone could identify the manufacturer, who would be able to list the retailers.

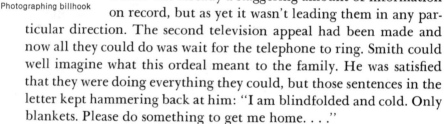

Photographing billhook

Statements brought back to the police station had been checked against each other for corroboration and then filed under various headings. Cars seen in the area on the twenty-ninth of December were logged under make, color and number of occupants. There was already a staggering amount of information on record, but as yet it wasn't leading them in any particular direction. The second television appeal had been made and now all they could do was wait for the telephone to ring. Smith could well imagine what this ordeal meant to the family. He was satisfied that they were doing everything they could, but those sentences in the letter kept hammering back at him: "I am blindfolded and cold. Only blankets. Please do something to get me home. . . ."

CHAPTER 4

SMITH STARED AT THE calendar. There was nothing very significant about the date except that it was Tuesday, the twentieth of January, and almost three weeks had gone by since the family had attended the press conference on New Year's Eve. David Dyer, addressing the reporters outside St. Mary House later that night, had issued a statement on behalf of his father-in-law. Aimed at the kidnappers, he'd asked them to say what McKay had to do to get his wife back.

The appeal had provoked a response of sorts from M3, who had telephoned the house on the afternoon of January 1, well past his deadline. He had spoken to Diane Dyer twice in rapid succession. Yet, despite a menacing tone, he'd been as evasive as ever. Nothing about how the money was to be paid over, just the chilling statement, "You

Search setting out from Epp

have gone too far; it has gone too far now." And Diane Dyer protesting, "What's gone too far? There's nothing gone too far," before being cut off in midsentence. A few minutes later, M3 had called again to instruct Diane. "They've got to get a million, a million pounds. I'll contact them tomorrow, and they have got to get it in fivers and tenners." And then, for some reason which passed understanding, M3 and his associates had simply lapsed into silence.

Day followed day with no word from them. But other people had been active. People like William Alexander Peat, an eighteen-year-old waiter, who had demanded five hundred pounds on Friday, the second of January, and who'd been arrested later that same evening by Detective Inspector John Minors when he'd stepped off the train at South Wimbledon Station to keep a prearranged rendezvous. And Roy Edward Roper, of Leytonstone, unemployed and a deserter from the army, who had sent a letter to McKay instructing him to leave two thousand pounds in the end cubicle of the public lavatories outside Stratford Station. Like Peat, he too walked into a reception party and was arrested.

Such peripheral events had been time-consuming and largely unproductive as far as Muriel McKay was concerned, but in retrospect, Smith believed that they had marked a turning point. McKay had been impressed by the way the detective had handled them, and this in turn helped to establish the rapport he'd been seeking. The foundations for this new relationship had been laid earlier, when Smith had shown that he was willing to try anything, even to the point of acting on information supplied by a medium, whose help had been

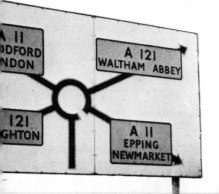

sought by a friend of the family's. The resultant search of an isolated house on the Essex-Hertfordshire border had proved totally abortive, as he had thought it would all along, but it had helped to reassure McKay that the police were doing everything in their power to find his wife.

Police and dogs searching Wimbledon Common

Like the palm impression on *The People*, the prints lifted from the envelope mailed in Tottenham North 17 had led them nowhere. Since M3 could not be identified by the CRO, Smith decided to try a different approach. Seeking to wrest the initiative from the kidnappers, a press conference had been held at St. Mary House, during which McKay, carefully primed as to what to say, had created the impression that Muriel's life might be endangered if she didn't get the drugs she needed. There was nothing seriously wrong with her health, but Muriel McKay suffered from arthritis and had been taking cortisone for it. The bait had been further reinforced by McKay in a television appearance on Friday, the ninth of January, but M3 hadn't fallen into the trap of obtaining the requisite drugs from a pharmacy. Instead, he sent a letter to the *News of the World*.

Marked "Personal and Urgent," the letter arrived the following day and was addressed to editor Stafford Somerfield. Written on lined paper which had been torn from a notebook, it stated that once McKay had gotten rid of the police, the writer would telephone him to tell him how the ransom money was to be collected. The writer specified that the million pounds was to be picked up in two installments of half a million each. There was also a near apology to the effect that the writer had tried to contact McKay at home but that the phone was always engaged.

Stafford Somerfield, of course, lost no time in hurrying to Arthur Road with the letter.

Just one letter after an interval of nine days. And then silence once more. But the hoaxers had been active and one at least had been very convincing.

In a case singularly devoid of humor, Smith could now see the funny side of the telephone call which had turned Detective Sergeant White into a drag artist. Diane Dyer had received instructions over the telephone on the twelfth of January, and White, disguised as Diane, in a miniskirt and wearing a head scarf over a blond wig, had caught the five-forty-five a.m. bus from Catford Garage. Two other detectives, disguised as workmen, were with him; following the bus was a bogus taxi with Detective Inspector John Bland of Scotland Yard's Flying Squad inside, and behind him, an unmarked car. Moving almost in convoy, the bus, the taxi and the backup car had crawled all the way from Catford to Stamford Hill without once seeing the car which was supposed to draw up behind the bus, flashing its head-lights to signal that White, posing as Diane Dyer, should get off at the next stop.

Then, on the fourteenth of January, just when it seemed there would be no further contact with the kidnappers, M3 telephoned the house again. In this, his sixth conversation with the family, he told McKay that he would get his wife back if he cooperated, assured him that Muriel was getting the drugs she needed, and then said that he would contact McKay again. And this time he had kept his word.

At his office, Smith punched the playback on the tape recorder and heard McKay's voice saying, "I am cooperating, but I can't cooperate with impossible demands. . . . Make it a reasonable sum of money. I can kill myself. That would solve the problem. . . . Take me instead. I can't give you what I haven't got. Nobody has got a million pounds and it is ridiculous to talk about it."

Minors looked up from the pile of reports on his desk. "McKay sounds pretty upset to me."

"Right. And he's doing most of the talking."

"Well, after all this time, you'd expect him to be strung up and on edge. He's getting desperate."

"Look, we've got thirty detectives working on this case; we've got thumb and palm prints we can't match and God knows how many statements which don't tie in anywhere. We've searched every park and open space for miles around. Tracing the billhook hasn't been exactly productive either; all we know is that it's thought to be pecu-liar to Hertfordshire, but just about every farm worker in the county seems to have one."

"So?"

"So we're stuck with M3. But we need to play him like a fish, and to do that we must have someone who can draw him out. Both the daughters and Alick McKay are too emotionally involved and no matter how well we brief them, they still tend to do all the talking." Smith's fingers drummed on the desk. "But Ian McKay, now he's different. He has what it takes to bring M3 out of his shell."

"Do you think the family will agree to the idea?"

"They will after I've had a word with them," Smith said.

IN APPEARANCE, IAN McKAY was not unlike his father. He had the same build, the same open face, but with a more prominent forehead emphasized by a receding hairline. More than anyone else he had held the family together during the long silence. He was rock calm, objective and shrewd; tough enough to play the role Smith had in mind, because he had shown that he could suppress his innermost feelings.

Smith said, "We're dealing with a greedy man who has little sense of reality. He's set on getting a million pounds and it's no use trying to convince him that you're unable to raise it."

"So we shouldn't try to make him see reason." It was a presumption, not a question.

"That's right, Ian, but you're going to put the pressure on him. You'll ask him for proof that he is holding your mother and is in a position to make a trade."

"I can see that."

There was something in his voice which led Smith to believe that Ian McKay suspected that his mother was already dead.

"We have to go for M3 and gradually push him into a corner. He may try to insist that we withdraw from the case."

"And what do I say to that?"

"That it's impossible. If necessary, tell him we even suspect that your father is implicated in some way."

"All right."

"It won't be easy."

"I don't suppose it will, but I think I can do it."

"Yes," said Smith. "I think you can too."

"I am blindfolded and cold. Only blankets. . . ." It was beginning to sound like an epitaph.

CHAPTER 5

THE GAMBIT WAS beginning to work. M3 had wanted the police to be withdrawn from the case, but had swallowed his objections when Ian told him that it was impossible to get rid of them because they now suspected that his father was involved. Yet, when he saw the two letters which had been posted at two fifteen p.m. on the twenty-first of January from Wood Green, together with a ransom note in the same envelope, Smith was filled with a sense of deep foreboding.

The one addressed to Alick McKay read,

> I am deteriorating in health and spirit. . . . Please cooperate. . . . excuse writing, I'm blindfolded and cold. Please keep the police out of this and cooperate with the Gang giving code number M3 when telephoning to you. . . . The earlier you get the money the quicker I may come home. . . . Darling, can you act quickly? Please, please keep police out of this if you want to see me.
>
> Muriel

The other was for Diane Dyer. In it Muriel McKay said that she had heard her daughter on television, and then went on to thank her for looking after her father. For the rest, there was the same plea that they should act quickly and with discretion. It was very clear to Smith that both letters had been written early on in Mrs. McKay's captivity and then held over. Obviously, Diane's dated back to either her appearance on BBC Television during the eight-fifty news bulletin on the thirtieth of December, or the screening on ITV which had followed twenty-four hours later. The note to Alick Mc-Kay confirmed this supposi-tion, and its contents led Smith to believe that it had been posted out of sequence. That M3 was the code name for the

Part of a letter from Muriel McKay to her daughter

kidnappers had been made very clear as far back as Tuesday, the thirtieth of December; yet in her second letter she was telling Alick McKay to expect a call from a representative of M3. Then, too, for the first time, she had repeatedly asked him to keep the police out of it, which was another indication that the letters had arrived in the wrong order.

If the letters painted a black picture, at least the ransom note was a step forward. It set a date for the delivery and gave directions where Alick McKay should go to receive further instructions, which would lead him to the final rendezvous. It also imposed certain conditions which Smith was anxious to have changed.

THE NUMBER OF reporters outside the driveway of St. Mary House had not decreased significantly over the weeks, and there was still an occasional foreign correspondent among the crowd of journalists. However, Smith's arrival at the house excited little interest; by now he had called on the McKays so often that his appearance in Arthur Road was no longer considered newsworthy.

The family were learning to live with the situation as best they could. A routine of sorts had long since been established, the daughters helping Mrs. Nightingale with the household chores while Alick McKay worked on papers brought to him from the office. But the shift system, which ensured that two policemen were always on duty day and night to monitor the incoming calls, was a visible reminder of the kidnapping. It was impossible for Smith not to experience the strain and tension the family felt the moment he entered the house.

If Ian McKay no longer had any doubts that his mother was dead, he kept his fears to himself. It was quite apparent that he appreciated the significance of the letters, but instead of discussing them, he concentrated on the instructions received from M3.

"We're getting somewhere now," he said. "At least they've set a date, and Sunday, the first of February, isn't so far away."

Smith rested his elbows on both arms of the chair and leaned forward. "Time enough for us to make the necessary arrangements."

"To obtain the money?"

"Well, we may want to borrow a few hundred to make it look good, but we'll provide the rest. I've got a printer who'll run them off for us. He's very good. You can take my word for it." A bland, almost conspiratorial smile appeared on Smith's face. "The Home Office and the Treasury will have kittens when they hear about it."

"Will they try to block it?"

Smith shook his head. "No. Our problem is M3. We've got to persuade him to modify his instructions."

"Oh? In what way?"

"The note says that your father is to come alone in the Ford Capri; we have to get him used to the idea of meeting you instead. Of course, one of my men will be impersonating you."

"Let's talk about that."

"There's nothing to discuss," Smith said firmly, "because neither you nor your father is going to keep that rendezvous. There's no telling what you might walk into, and I'm not prepared to put either of you at risk. Let's get back to M3. Making him accept you is just the first step; once we're over that hurdle, we'll see if we can't substitute the Rolls-Royce for the Ford Capri." Smith forestalled the unspoken question. "Yes, I could have someone lying on the floor of the Capri, but it would make life much easier if he knew the car was going to be driven by a chauffeur."

"He'll need a lot of convincing."

"I think we can do it if we bounce it on him at the last minute."

"And just how do we play him along in the meantime?"

"I think the time is coming when you should lean on him a little. I mean, he wants to make a trade, right?"

"And we're not in the market for buying damaged goods," Ian McKay said in a quiet voice.

It was out in the open now, a grave acceptance of the assumption that in all probability his mother was dead.

"You might try something along those lines," Smith said carefully.

THE CALL CAME through at ten thirty-seven in the morning, and answering it, Ian McKay heard the now familiar deep, muffled voice.

"This is M3. Did you receive the letter?"

"Yes, we have. We received it yesterday." Ian McKay hesitated a moment before deciding to take the initiative. "There's no proof that she's alive and well," he said flatly. "The letters could have been written weeks ago. We have the money, but why the hell should we give it to you unless we know she's alive?"

"I told you what she is wearing." Flustered now, M3's voice rose. "What do you want me to do?" he said excitedly. "Take her clothes off and send them in to you? We are in business and want to cooperate to sell good stuff. If you do not cooperate, you will get her dead on your doorstep. I'm asking you for the last time, I'm asking you if you want to cooperate, yes or no?"

"Of course we intend to cooperate, but first we want proof. . . ."

"Well, look, you're not going to get—"

"Because you haven't got her," snarled Ian McKay. "You've got a corpse, a corpse."

"We've got her," M3 said plaintively.

"You've got a dead person, you haven't got her at all. You know she's not alive, you're just trying to trick us."

"Look, if you want to stick, we have many jobs."

"How many kidnaps have you done then?"

There was a brief pause, almost as if M3 had been winded by the question, and then he was back again. "Never murdered anyone as yet, but there will always be a first time. You see now?"

"Okay then. But you don't get the money."

"I'm going to drop the phone on you."

The connection was severed, but slowly, in a way which suggested that M3 was reluctant to break it off. Yet Ian McKay couldn't help wondering if he had gone too far. The thought that it would be all his fault if they never heard from M3 again made him sick at heart.

A minute passed and then the telephone shattered the silence.

M3 said, "Look, either you cooperate or we shall proceed. Then we will not be needing the money and you will not be seeing your mum again."

Ian took a deep breath. "I want to hear her voice on tape."

"No, that's—"

"All right then, let me speak to her on the telephone."

"No, you don't seem to—"

"Okay, suppose you allow my mother to write another letter."

"No, we shall not be letting her write to you again."

M3 was blustering, but he was on the defensive and now the moment was ripe to hit him hard.

"Buy tonight's *Evening Standard* and get her to write out the headlines and the date in full."

"We don't have to cooperate with you—"

Ian cut in, his voice grating. "The headlines in tonight's paper," he snarled, "and the date in full, and I'm going to hang up on you. Goodby." He slammed the phone down for emphasis.

IT RANG AGAIN shortly after midday.

M3 said, "I've just spoken to her, your mum, I mean. . . . She asked why you had forsaken her. If you want her back, then you will have to follow instructions."

There was no stopping M3 now. A bond had been established between them and he wanted to talk and talk and talk. Confident that it was impossible to trace an STD call, his words flowed on like a river in full spate.

CHAPTER 6

TWO LETTERS ADDRESSED to Alick McKay arrived on Monday, the twenty-sixth of January, in the same envelope with a further ransom note and some pieces of material clipped from the suit, the reversible coat and the shoes which Diane and Jennifer had discovered were missing from the wardrobe. It was apparent from the serrated edges on the cloth and shoe leather that a pair of tailor's shears had been used to cut them out, and this information became part of the ever growing crime index, a tiny bit of the fragmented jigsaw puzzle from which the major pieces were still missing.

The ransom note contained a number of spelling errors and was both cheerful and plaintive in tone. In it, M3 expressed a hope that their business would be brought to a successful conclusion on Sunday, the first of February, while making it clear that they resented taking instructions from Ian McKay. "We give the order and you must obey," the final sentence had read.

Neither of the two letters provided the proof which Ian McKay had asked for. They contained no reference to the headlines in Friday's issue of the *Evening Standard*, or to any other subject which might lead them to hope that Muriel McKay was still alive. In one, the writing was indecipherable in parts; individual words and, in some cases, whole sections of a sentence tailed off in an ink blotch.

Just why M3 should choose to continue the operation, when he knew perfectly well that the police had not been withdrawn from the case, was beyond anybody's understanding. Any hardened and experienced criminal would have cut his losses long ago; yet, although nearly a full month had now elapsed, M3 still wanted to negotiate. By their own admission the kidnappers had seized the wrong woman, and not content with that, they had then compounded the blunder by sending the letters off in the wrong sequence. That at least one of their number didn't have a previous record lent added weight to Smith's contention that this was probably their first major crime. They might be amateurs enjoying a long run of good luck, but they were also cunning, and there was every chance that they could prove dangerous when finally they were cornered.

There were good reasons for assuming the rendezvous would be somewhere to the north of London, because every letter they had received had been posted from different boroughs in North London.

M3 might be a blundering amateur, but he was also crafty, and before disclosing the final rendezvous he would probably run a series of checks to make sure Ian McKay was not being followed. Whether they used the Rolls-Royce or the Ford Capri still depended on M3, but keeping either car under discreet surveillance was not going to be easy in those circumstances. In view of this and realizing that his own resources were inadequate for the task, Smith, supported by Commander Guiver, the CID area commander, decided to ask Scotland Yard and the Home Office for assistance.

Using a helicopter to maintain aerial surveillance would have posed certain difficulties, because M3 had already indicated that the rendezvous would take place after dark. So, to overcome this problem, the scientists at the Home Office were busy fitting an electronic bug to the suitcase to enable Smith to keep track of the kidnappers after the ransom had been collected from the drop. Experiments had shown that it was possible to monitor it accurately from a maximum separation distance of fifty miles.

Scotland Yard placed a total of one hundred and eighty policemen and fifty-six unmarked cars at Smith's disposal and also agreed that Commander Guiver should use their main operations room. This nerve center, equipped with Telex machines, large-scale maps, open- and closed-circuit telephones, would allow him to keep in touch with and, if required, provide additional support for Smith, in charge of operations at the rendezvous.

With so little to go on, it seemed prudent to organize the available manpower into three groups. Of these, one squad would be held in reserve at Wimbledon in case the operation moved away from North London; a second would track the Rolls or the Ford Capri; while the third would be deployed early on Sunday to cover the trunk routes leading north from the capital.

Smith also decided that Detective Inspector John Minors should go on the run, but whether he posed as the chauffeur or as Ian McKay had to be left open until the last moment. If M3 finally agreed that they could use the Rolls-Royce, then Detective Sergeant Street would accompany him and impersonate Ian McKay, because he was about the same age, height and build. Since both men would be at risk from the time they left St. Mary House, it was obvious that they and other officers would have to be armed.

The contingency plans having been made, the men allocated their tasks, and the counterfeit money under lock and key at the police station, all that remained was to wait for M3 to call again.

On Friday, the thirtieth of January, after a week of telephone silence, M3 called once more, and Ian McKay, schooled and rehearsed in what had to be put across, was ready for him.

He said, "We're prepared to cooperate in every way we can."

"Okay, so it will be the first, that's Sunday."

"Yes, and I'll bring the money with me." A brief pause now, because Ian McKay knew that he was approaching the crunch point and he wanted his proposals to sound natural and convincing. "Look," he said. "I can't bring the Capri because the press are sitting outside." He licked his lips. "It's been in the garage for five weeks and if it comes out, they'll take pictures of it."

"Oh, I see."

"So I'll have to come in the Rolls. I don't know the north of London very well and I've also injured my hand a bit, so I want to bring the chauffeur."

"Oh, I see." The same answer, as if M3 didn't know what to say now that he no longer had to urge them to cooperate.

Ian McKay rammed the point home. "Also, if I took the Rolls out on my own, they've never seen me drive it before and they'll guess what's going on."

"Yes."

A one-word capitulation because greed had overruled native caution and suspicion. M3 had swallowed the bait, hook, line and sinker.

CHAPTER 7

MINORS CHECKED HIS appearance once more and was satisfied that he looked the part. The borrowed chauffeur's uniform fitted him well enough and the revolver sat snugly on his hip without a telltale bulge. No one would spare him a second glance when they saw him behind the wheel of the Rolls-Royce, but Detective Sergeant Roger Street was going to be in the limelight each time he left the car to take a call from M3. Dressed in one of Ian McKay's suits, with his hair touched up at the edges, he bore more than a passing resemblance to him. It was going to be a dark night, and his arm resting in a sling might well be the clincher, for Ian McKay had told M3 that he had injured his hand. Show them the obvious and there was every chance the kidnappers would accept the impostor on sight, because they couldn't risk getting too close to Street.

Minors glanced at his wristwatch. "I think it's time we were on our way," he said quietly.

"I'm ready if you are."

"The two-way radio?"

Street patted the sling with his free hand. "In here."

"Good. Don't make a check call until we are well clear of the house. You never know, they could be watching us. I'll make sure we aren't being followed and then give you the word."

Street nodded. "Don't worry. I'll keep it short and sweet."

The Rolls was parked outside the front porch, facing the entrance. Minors, opening the door for Street, ushered him into the back and then got in behind the wheel. He pressed the starter button, and shifting into gear, he swept out of the drive, the headlights momentarily picking out a small knot of reporters clustered around a car. Five minutes later, when satisfied that the Rolls was not being followed, he told Street to make a radio check. Smith came through loud and clear.

They drove steadily through South West London, then crossed the Thames and picked up the North Circular Road. The streets were all but empty. Most people seemed to be indoors watching television behind drawn curtains. Display lights burned in shopwindows; the cinemas, bingo halls and pubs were open for business, but like any other Sunday night in midwinter, the city was more dead than alive. The buses were few and far between, and the traffic was very light compared with a normal weekday.

Minors left the North Circular at the A10 junction and turned into Great Cambridge Road, as they had been instructed to do in the first ransom note. The route through Edmonton was so clearly fixed in his mind that he knew just what to expect over this last mile. He drove past New Park Avenue, The Fairway and a long row of terraced houses, and then turned into Church Street. The call box was there on the corner and it was empty.

Minors pulled up to the curb and switched off the engine.

"We're here," he said.

"Yes. What's the time?"

Minors glanced at a clock over a store window. "Nearly ten."

"Then I guess this is it." Street opened the car door, stepped out onto the sidewalk and walked over to the phone box. There was none of the usual graffiti inside, just a dog-eared telephone directory with a torn cover and a few cigarette stubs on the floor. As he stared at the silent instrument, Street consoled himself with the thought that this couldn't be a wild-goose chase, because M3 had called St. Mary House earlier in the day to check that the deal was on. A minute passed like an hour and then the telephone rang and he snatched it off the hook.

A deep, muffled voice said, "Who's that?"

"Ian McKay," said Street, imitating an Australian accent.

"This is M3. These are your instructions. Proceed along the Cambridge road away from London. At the second set of traffic lights on the left is Southbury Road, with a telephone box on the corner. The number is 01-363-1553X. Go there and wait for another call from me. Any error will be fatal."

The caller gave him no time to ask any questions. Replacing the phone, Street left the kiosk and returned to the car.

Minors said, "Well, how did you get on?"

"We've been directed to another pay phone farther up the Cambridge road. Maybe they want to have a look at us to make sure we're not being followed."

Minors looked into the rearview mirror, saw that the road was clear behind and made a U-turn. Heading back to the traffic lights at the crossroads, he then turned left and rejoined the A10.

"Where did you say this other call box is?"

"On the corner of Southbury Road at the second set of lights."

"Is it far?"

"I've no idea."

"All right," said Minors. "Put out a call and let them know what's happening."

The road curved to the right and then straightened. They passed Harrow Drive and Bury Street and, continuing in a northeasterly direction, crossed the railway line and entered Enfield. When they reached the junction with Southbury Road, Minors was surprised to find that they had covered only one and a half miles.

The second call came through shortly after ten forty-five. From where he was parked, Minors could see Street talking into the telephone and was puzzled when his detective sergeant suddenly broke off the conversation to look down at his feet. There was a moment's hesitation before he stooped and retrieved something which was apparently lying on the floor. When he resumed the conversation, Minors noticed that he kept referring to a scrap of paper, which he had placed on top of the coin box. He surmised that they had left written instructions and that Street was now verifying the details with M3. A few minutes later the sergeant replaced the phone and returned to the car. "It gets better all the time."

"What does?" said Minors.

"Can you beat it? The directions for the rendezvous were on a sheet of paper tucked inside an empty packet of Piccadilly cigarettes. They were taking a bit of a chance, weren't they?"

Street was right, they had taken a risk. Somebody else could have gone into the box and picked up the packet. That somebody else could have crumpled it and thrown it away. On the other hand, there was no telling how long it had been lying there; perhaps M3 had only arrived there a few minutes ahead of them and possibly even now he was watching them from a side street.

"What happens now?"

Street looked at the sheet of paper, on which there was also a rough sketch. "We're supposed to continue on the road to Cambridge until we come to a village called High Cross."

Minors checked the road map. "That's in Hertfordshire," he said.

"After we pass through High Cross we're to look out for an Esso petrol station, and then a few hundred yards farther on we will come to a signpost on the left-hand side of the road which points to Dane End. They have left two paper flowers on the embankment above the road to mark the spot where we're to leave the suitcase."

"And then what?"

"We're to go back to the call box in Church Street and wait for M3 to tell us where to find Mrs. McKay."

Minors looked at the map again. High Cross was less than twenty miles away. Even if he kept their speed down to thirty, it would still only take them just over forty minutes to reach the rendezvous. Somehow he would have to spin out the journey to give Smith the time he needed to infiltrate the unmarked cars of the backup force into the area. Obviously there would have to be a time limit, otherwise his delaying tactics would arouse the suspicion of M3. Minors folded the map away. "Tell him that we'll drag it out as long as we can, but an hour is the most he should expect."

Street glanced at his wristwatch. "In that case, we'll be there about midnight."

"Give or take a few minutes," said Minors.

He turned the car around and drove back to the Cambridge road again. Sleet began to fall from the cold, leaden sky.

SMITH TOOK ONE look at the rendezvous and decided he didn't like it a bit. Dane End was flat and open, with only a few ditches and thin hedgerows offering any prospect of concealment. A light burning in one of the cottages situated diagonally opposite the dropping place might or might not be a problem. Unless his men were very careful, the occupants might well spot them as they moved into the adjoining field. Equally, anyone trying to take up a position on the grassy bank above the road would be in full view.

He had a small armada of cars to deploy in an area where there were very few lateral roads, and since there was not enough time to make a detailed reconnaissance on the ground, their positions would have to be chosen from the map. He thought Guiver, who was sitting back at the operations room in Scotland Yard, would be able to help him with this task, but it wasn't going to be easy. Of necessity, instructions would have to be passed over the radio, and as he knew only too well, the police wavelengths were not secure; anybody with a VHF set could tune in to their frequencies. Yet action had to be taken, and taken quickly; otherwise the buildup of road traffic in this lonely part of the countryside would begin to resemble the rush hour in London. The net would also have to be thrown far and wide if they were to fool M3 and remain undetected.

Smith found himself a quiet spot away from the rendezvous and began talking urgently, first to Guiver and then to each car in the backup force.

ONE BY ONE THE cars from the backup force overtook them and disappeared into the night. The headlights on the Rolls picked up a signboard with the words HIGH CROSS stamped on it in block capitals, but then, almost before they had time to digest this gratuitous piece of information, they were beyond the village. The tires swished over the wet tarmac taking them past an Esso petrol station and diner on the left-hand side of the road. Recognizing these landmarks, Minors eased his foot on the accelerator, and the speedometer needle fell back.

A bank gradually rose above the road in a gentle gradient and suddenly, right on the junction, they saw a tall, thin signpost pointing down a lane which led to Dane End. Minors, braking sharply, pulled into the verge and doused the headlights. A moment or two later he switched off the ignition.

Raising his eyes, he looked at Street in the rearview mirror. "We'd better make sure we've got the right spot."

"I'll take a look."

"I think I'll come with you," said Minors. "You'll never be able to lift that suitcase with one hand, it's too damned heavy."

There were two artificial flowers lying on the embankment, one orange, the other green. Both had been fashioned out of tissue paper and looked homemade.

It was quiet, almost too quiet. Just the rain dripping from the bare trees and falling onto the roof of the car, but as they placed the suitcase down, they heard something move. There was a faint rustle behind the hedgerow above them, as if someone had crawled forward through the damp grass to take a closer look.

Minors dropped his hand to the gun resting on his hip. "Get back to the car," he whispered, "and lock yourself in."

Street nodded and moved away. His heels clacked briefly on the road, a door opened and closed with a dull clunk, and then there was silence. Nothing moved, but Minors knew that somebody was watching him from the other side of the hedge. Someone with a balding head whom he recognized.

The tension melted away, but his heart was still thumping as he walked back to the car. He tried the door and was surprised when it wouldn't open. For a moment Minors was nonplussed, but then, remembering that he'd told Street to lock himself inside, he tapped on the glass and signaled him to release the catch.

Street said, "Who was it?"

"One of ours, O'Hara, Flying Squad."

Minors started the car and headed back to Edmonton.

THE LUMINOUS HANDS on the face of his wristwatch creeping toward two thirty confirmed his worst fears. For some time Smith had had a gut feeling that nothing would happen, but until this moment he had nursed a faint ray of hope. The suitcase was still sitting by the side of the road, but he was convinced now that no one was going to come near it.

In two and a half hours the number of cars passing the drop had amounted to no more than a dozen. With the exception of a mud-splattered Volvo 144, whose left-hand sidelights were not in working order, he had their license numbers together with a rough description of the occupants. Apart from the flowers on the embankment and the cigarette packet, this was all that one hundred and eighty men and fifty-six unmarked cars had to show for the night's work.

His thoughts turned to the McKay family. The bitter disappointment he felt was nothing compared to what theirs would be. Whether or not they believed she was already dead, their hopes must have been raised. But the news had to be broken to them quickly, just in case M3 decided to get in touch with them again.

MORNING, AND A mood of black despair hung over the McKays. Nothing Smith could say would dispel the conviction that they were now faced with a hopeless situation. Yet Ian McKay allowed himself to be coached once more for a telephone call, even though there seemed little point to it. After what had happened, no one really believed that they would hear from M3 again.

But they did.

M3 sounded angry. He said, "You tricked us."

"What?"

"We saw the police."

Ian McKay gripped the telephone. "Now look—" he said.

"No; you listen to me. You tricked us and that is bad."

"I give you my word. If the police were there it was without my knowledge."

"You didn't cooperate."

"But I did. I had no idea they were following me."

"I radioed the boys and they told me that the police were following the Rolls."

"Now look—"

"The boss laughed and said he had seen cars around the pickup spot."

"I tell you straight, the police were acting on their own initiative. We had nothing to do with it. I followed your orders. You do see that, don't you?"

"I don't know. I'm going to meet with the semi-intellectuals."

"Who?"

"The bosses. They're going to decide when your mum is to be executed, but I'm going to plead with them."

"Tell them we still want to cooperate."

"Yes, I will do that. I am fond of her—your mum—you know. She reminds me of my mum." His tone was quieter now, the anger gone from his voice.

"Will you call us again?"

"Perhaps, but I will not speak to you."

"Oh?"

"I do not trust you anymore. I will speak to your father and to no one else."

M3 had seen the hook, but incredibly, it appeared that he was still prepared to go for the bait.

CHAPTER 8

THE TAPE STARTED running and M3's voice said, "I radioed the boys and they told me that the police were following the Rolls." Smith stopped the recorder and looked at Minors. "Well?" he said.

"I think he's bluffing. I don't think he called anyone on the radio."

"Then how do you explain this? 'The boss laughed and said he had seen cars around the pickup spot.' "

Minors shrugged. "Who knows? Perhaps they did spot something."

"They're laughing at us."

"But they're still prepared to talk."

"Only to Alick McKay; they don't trust Ian anymore." Smith drummed his fingers on the desk. "No matter what Alick McKay thinks, one thing is certain: if we do get another crack, he's not going to meet them at the rendezvous. You'll go in his place."

Minors fingered his mustache.

"And you'll have to shave that off," said Smith.

"I guessed as much."

"Dane End was a mess, a real mess. Next time, if there is a next time, we're going to use fewer people. A hundred and eighty men, and what did we get? Two paper flowers, a cigarette packet and a list of car numbers."

Parker cleared his throat. "About those cars, sir."

"Yes?"

"I've been going through the crime index. We've got a report from a local resident stating that at ten to five on Monday, the twenty-ninth of December, he was driving from Wimbledon toward Putney when he overtook a muddy Volvo parked by the common. There were two men inside, one of whom he thought was an Arab."

It didn't add up. Smith was quite sure that M3 had a West Indian accent, but it would be foolish to ignore any lead. After all, a casual observer could mistake a West Indian for an Arab.

"Go on."

"Well, about ten minutes later he saw the same car turning into Church Street, which is only a stone's throw from Arthur Road. Detective Sergeant Stevens saw a Volvo 144 at Dane End early on Monday. Unfortunately he couldn't see the license number."

"This other Volvo, the one seen entering Church Street, was that also a 144?"

"The man didn't say."

"How many Volvos are there on the roads in Britain, Sergeant?"

"I checked," said Parker. "There are over thirty-three thousand."

Smith smiled. "Well, that narrows the field," he said. "You'd better get someone to have a word with this resident, see if we can't jog his memory a bit. Maybe he can remember the type and color. Let's try and halve the number; then it shouldn't take you more than three months to trace the owners."

Minors said, "Perhaps the Flying Squad will have better luck with their inquiries in Hertfordshire. I shouldn't think there are many West Indians living in that part of the world."

"No; they're basically urban dwellers. Still, you never know, they might uncover a few in Ware or Bishop's Stortford. Bishop's Stortford is a market town, but there's some light engineering which might attract an immigrant population."

"It's possible."

"We're looking for three, maybe four men. Four times out of five, it's the same man who makes the calls for M3."

"We've only heard one other voice," said Minors, "so perhaps there are only two men."

"Theorizing isn't going to get us very far," Smith said firmly. "We have to keep digging away until we hear from them again."

IF THE DANE END operation had been totally abortive, then as far as Smith could see, the follow-up had proved equally negative. Detectives from the Flying Squad, working in conjunction with the Hertfordshire police, had made extensive inquiries in the Ware–Bishop's Stortford area without uncovering a single positive lead. There were no West Indians and no Arab-looking

Dressed up as McKay, Detective Inspector John Minors checking the ransom money men in the area; however, the neighborhood search for likely hiding places did reveal a Pakistani farmer, living at Stocking Pelham, who drove a Volvo. But the detectives of the Flying Squad could find absolutely no evidence to show that the farmer, his German-born wife or his brother had criminal potential.

And yet Smith supposed they had made some progress since Sunday. The empty packet of Piccadilly cigarettes which M3 had left at the call box in Church Street, Edmonton, had yielded a thumbprint which matched the one on the envelope containing the first letter from Muriel McKay. The page from *The People,* the envelope and stamp and now the cigarette packet had all been handled by the same man. But he was still without a face.

The telephone rang. Smith lifted the receiver and answered it.

Minors said, "I'm at the house; we've had a call from M3."

"What did he have to say?"

"He's talking about making further arrangements for the payment of half a million."

"When?"

"I don't know yet, but we're expecting him to telephone again shortly. He wants Alick McKay and Diane Dyer to bring the money with them in two briefcases."

Smith said, "All right, I'm on my way. We'll have to give Alick McKay some guidance, because there's no way you can cram five hundred thousand into two briefcases. We'll have to use two suitcases."

THE SECOND TELEPHONE call came through a few hours later. M3 told Alick McKay that on the next day, Friday, the sixth of February, he and Diane would have to drive the Rolls to the same call box in Church Street, where they would receive further instructions. The rendezvous was set for four o'clock in the afternoon, leaving Smith less than twenty-four hours to make a plan and set the wheels in motion.

This time he was determined that there wouldn't be another Dane End. Instead of shadowing the Rolls-Royce, Smith decided to ask for assistance from the Hertfordshire CID. With their cooperation, he intended to deploy selected officers, drawn from the Flying Squad and the Regional Crime Squad, in an arc north of London to cover the A1, A10 and A11 trunk roads. As on the first occasion, command would have to be exercised from the operations room at Scotland Yard, but with one important difference: except in an emergency, they would use landlines to stay in contact. By imposing radio silence he would get maximum security, and whether M3 had been bluffing or not, this time they would be unable to pick up anything from the police VHF net.

The two suitcases containing the ransom money would have to be fitted with a homing device, and he thought there could be some advantage in having a helicopter ready to maintain aerial surveillance, at least during the hours of daylight. A small identification mark on the roof of the car would enable the pilot to recognize it in traffic.

Minors would impersonate Alick McKay, but he needed an experienced policewoman, used to undercover work, who could double for Diane Dyer. And someone else to hide in the trunk of the car who had firsthand knowledge of clandestine operations. As far as Smith was concerned, there was only one obvious choice: Detective Inspector John Bland, the Flying Squad officer who had shadowed Detective Sergeant White during his abortive bus journey on the twelfth of January and who had subsequently taken part in the Dane End affair.

It was a pretty impressive shopping list, but Scotland Yard met his every request. The girl they selected to take the place of Diane Dyer was Detective Constable Joyce Armitage.

CHAPTER 9

BLAND WAS FEELING cramped. He was slim and wiry and only five feet eight, but with a cylinder of oxygen to contend with, there was precious little room left for him in the trunk. The oxygen was for emergency use, a nice touch, in case he was poisoned by carbon-monoxide fumes. He was also equipped with a two-way radio so that Minors could let him know what was happening. Flexing his leg muscles, he shifted into a more comfortable position to ease the pressure on his hip. If the car were ambushed, he would have to leave the trunk in a hurry and not like an arthritic old man.

The uneven sound of two sets of footsteps reached him; one, quicker and lighter than the other, had to be Joyce Armitage. The doors opened and closed in quick succession, the starter whirred, the engine turned over, and the rich exhaust gases, eddying beneath the car, rapidly dispersed as the Rolls moved out of the drive. With a picture of the route fixed in his mind, Bland tried to chart their progress through South West London by dead reckoning.

They crossed the river and headed north through heavy traffic, making fitful progress. Lying there in the semidarkness, he got the impression that just about every light was against them; their speed was often reduced to a crawl, and he soon lost count of the number of times they ground to a halt before Minors turned onto the North Circular, where there was less density. Some minutes later the car turned sharply to the left and slowed to a stop. And then the long wait began.

MINORS LEANED A shoulder against the glass-partitioned wall and stared at the telephone, which had remained obstinately silent for the past forty minutes. Daylight was already beginning to fade, and with night fast approaching, he knew that very shortly Smith and Guiver would be forced to forget the helicopter. Aerial surveillance had never figured prominently in the plan, but without it they were even more naked.

And then, at last, the telephone rang.

A voice in his ear said, "Who's that?"

"It's me, Alick McKay."

"Is anyone with you, Alick?"

"Only my daughter Diane," said Minors. An accomplished mimic, his Australian accent seemed to reassure M3.

"Oh; well, this is M3."

"Yes?"

"You must go to the call box in Bethnal Green Road to receive further instructions."

"When?"

"Now," said M3.

The connection was broken, and Minors dialed through to the operations room at Scotland Yard and asked to speak to Commander Guiver.

Minors said, "We've been directed to another call box, in Bethnal Green Road."

Detective Inspector
John Minors

Detective Constable
Joyce Armitage

"They're making you dou-
ble back."

"So it would seem."

Guiver said, "We'll need
time to get our people into
position. You'd better take it
slowly."

"That won't be a problem," said Minors. "I'm not familiar with
that part of London."

Bland breathed on his hands and rubbed them together. The air
seeping through the gap between the lid and the floor of the trunk
was becoming decidedly chilly. There was a click on the two-way
radio and he heard Minors say, "Do you know how we get to Bethnal
Green Road from here?"

Bland suppressed a laugh. "Go back to the Cambridge road, John,
and turn right. You want to keep straight on the A10 until you come
to Shoreditch High Street and then turn left."

"Right."

"Sing out if you get lost."

The engine fired into life and Bland felt the exhaust fumes tickling
his nostrils. He just knew it was going to be one of those nights.

MINORS FOUND IT hard to believe that M3 knew what he was doing,
because the telephone kiosk they had chosen lay within a few yards of
Bethnal Green Police Station. Keeping the street under observation
would pose few problems for the police, but he thought that M3 had
landed himself with a well-nigh impossible task.

Unlike the rendezvous in Church Street, they only had to wait a
few minutes for the contact.

M3 said, "Is that you, Alick?"

"Yes."

"Well, these are your instructions. You are to leave the Rolls at
Bethnal Green Underground Station and take the Central Line to
Epping. You will find a phone box in the entrance hall at Epping
Station, where you will wait to receive further instructions."

"I understand."

"No error must be made. If the police are around this time, we will
execute Muriel and no one will ever see her again."

Detective Inspector John Bland in trunk
of car, and Minors, dressed as McKay

"I've already given you my word," said Minors.

"I want to speak to her."

"Who?"

"Diane, your daughter."

"Wait." Minors cupped his hand over the mouthpiece and looked at Joyce Armitage. "He wants to speak to you," he whispered.

She took the phone from him. "Hello," she said.

"Hello, Diane, is that you?"

"Yes."

"Have you got the money in the suitcases?"

"Yes, of course we have."

"Good. You and your dad must go to the nearest tube station, taking them with you. Take the tube down to Epping. This is your last chance and any error will be fatal for your mum. When you get to Epping, you will see a telephone box there. The number is 3077."

"Yes, I understand."

"You will be called there."

Joyce Armitage caught a warning look from Minors and sought to end the conversation. "Listen, I can't talk any longer, I'm too upset."

Minors removed the telephone from her grasp and said, "It's me again—Alick; we'll do as you say."

He rang off in a thoughtful frame of mind. Guiver and Smith wouldn't like it. The trail was leading them out of London again, and worse, they'd been instructed to leave the Rolls and go by train, taking the suitcases with them. When they boarded the train, there would be no one but Bland to back them up.

BLAND WAS LOSING all account of time. According to his wristwatch, he had been cooped up in the trunk of the Rolls for close on four hours. He came to the conclusion that he must have dozed off at some time or other, and he wondered if the exhaust fumes had made him drowsy.

The radio clicked again and Minors said, "Can you hear me?"

"Yes."

"All right, listen care-

fully. M3 told us to take the Underground to Epping from the nearest tube station—Bethnal Green—but to minimize the risk, it's been decided we should go from Theydon Bois instead. That's just one stop down the line from Epping."

"Right."

"Okay. Now, I want you to travel in the opposite end of the same carriage and then, when we get to Epping, go through the entrance hall and wait for us in the approach road. Got it?"

"Yes. What gives?"

"Joyce and I have got to wait at the station until we hear from M3 again."

Bland placed the two-way radio on the floor of the trunk. Seconds later the car pulled away from the curb.

BLAND GUESSED THAT Minors was dawdling because Smith needed time to deploy a backup team in Epping before they arrived. No matter which way he turned, the floor of the trunk was unyielding and it was impossible to find a comfortable position which lasted; within minutes of easing one ache, another would appear somewhere else.

The Rolls slowed to a crawl, completed a full U-turn, and halted briefly before reversing into what he assumed must be a parking space. The engine died, doors opened and closed, the trunk lid was raised, then Minors whispered, "All right, John, come out now."

Bland crawled out, brushed the dirt from his trousers, and tried to do something about his disheveled appearance. Still far from immaculate, he walked into the station, queued for his ticket, and passed through the barrier onto the platform. A minute or two later he saw Minors and Joyce Armitage, waiting about ten yards from where he was standing. Out of the corner of his eye he watched Minors lower both suitcases to the ground.

The train rattled into the station and squealed to a halt. There was a hiss of compressed air as the doors opened, and the compartment facing him all but emptied. Bland waited until Minors and Joyce Armitage had boarded the train before he entered the carriage. It would take them roughly four minutes to reach the end of the line, at Epping, and he knew that a lot could happen in four minutes.

But the journey was uneventful, almost an anticlimax. Surrendering his ticket at the barrier, Bland left the entrance hall and sauntered down the long, dimly lighted approach road until he found a sheltered spot near the end of the lane where he could observe the station and wait for Minors.

Minors put the suitcases down and, pulling open the door, looked inside the phone box. The light was not all that bright, but he could see the figures 3077 on the disk.

He turned to Joyce Armitage and said, "This is the one, all right."

She nodded. "How long do you suppose he'll keep us waiting?"

Minors shrugged his shoulders. "I wouldn't like to guess." He looked at the suitcases and hoped he wouldn't have to carry them very far, because each weighed close on ninety pounds.

Joyce Armitage folded her arms and stamped her feet. "God," she said, "it's cold."

"I think we could both do with a drink. I should have brought a flask with me."

"Never mind," she said. "Perhaps it will be over soon."

The clock in the entrance hall moved forward to seven thirty just as the telephone started ringing. Answering it, Minors heard a voice say, "Alick, are you there?"

"Who is that?"

"M3. I see you are being watched."

"Nonsense," Minors said firmly. "You're imagining it."

"Yes?"

"Look. I said we'd cooperate and we are. Nobody's watching us and we haven't been followed."

"Good. Now you must take a taxi and go to Gates Garage. It's on the outskirts of Bishop's Stortford. You will see a Minivan, UMH 587F, in the used-car lot. You are to place the suitcases on the sidewalk opposite this Mini. Then you must go back to Epping and wait for instructions. We will tell you where Muriel is. Do you understand?"

"Yes. What was the number of the Mini again?"

"UMH 587F."

"I've got it."

M3 said, "When you get into the taxi, Alick, I want you to place the suitcases on the back seat where I can see them."

"All right, I'll do that."

"If you do not drop the money, Muriel will be dead. You must trust M3. We deal with high-powered rifles and shotguns. If anyone tries to interfere with the cases, we'll let them have it."

"Surely you won't do that?"

"If anyone tries to stop us, we will use high-powered telescopic rifles and shotguns."

There was a moment of silence, then M3 broke the connection.

Minors turned to the Yellow Pages in the telephone directory and looked up a taxi firm. He made a note of the number and then decided he'd better call the operations room first. He imagined that Guiver and Smith might well have some reservations about using a taxi. They could be putting the cabdriver at risk, but he didn't believe there was an alternative. Like it or not, they would have to go along with M3.

BLAND WATCHED THEM place the suitcases inside the Ford Zephyr taxi, but waited until Minors had closed the door for Joyce Armitage and climbed in beside the driver before he moved out of the shadows. As the car came toward him, he was careful to make sure its headlights picked him out only at the last moment. Veering toward the curb, the taxi slowed down and came to a halt, the rear door swinging back on its hinges. Bland, dropping to his hands and knees, crawled inside and lay down on the floor, and then Minors reached back and closed the door behind him.

The taxi driver didn't like it. "Here," he said, "what's going on?"

"We're playing a joke on a friend."

The cabdriver glanced at the man in the fur hat sitting beside him. "Oh yes? What sort of joke?"

Minors said, "Suppose you just drive us to Bishop's Stortford."

THE COMMUNICATION SYSTEM was foolproof, because no information was passed over the air. When Smith heard his call sign broadcast over the radio, he simply contacted the operations room by landline and was given the location of the final rendezvous.

Gates Garage lay between the arms of a Y-shaped junction on the outskirts of Bishop's Stortford. Approaching it from the south, Smith took the left-hand fork, cruising past a row of houses opposite the used-car lot. Turning right at the next intersection, he rejoined the A11 and drove past the garage once more. On this third side of the triangle there was a piece of wasteland below the railway embankment, but it was thrown into sharp relief by the powerful lights of the garage.

As a result of this reconnaissance, Smith could see that keeping the Minivan under discreet observation posed problems, but he reckoned that it was possible to infiltrate two officers into the grounds of the taxation office next door to the car lot.

THE ZEPHYR APPROACHED the Y junction, forked left, then stopped opposite Gates Garage.

Minors said, "There's a house on the left, lying well back from the road. You'd better crawl inside the front garden, John, and get behind the hedge. You'll have a good view from there."

"Will you give me the nod when to move?"

"I'll do better than that."

Minors got out of the car and opened the rear door. Reaching inside the taxi, he lifted out both suitcases and then stood back to form a tunnel with his legs astride and a case in each hand. "All right. You can come out now. Crawl between my legs."

Bland slithered out of the car, crawled under Minors, wormed his way across the sidewalk, and slipped into the front garden of the nearest house.

The driver stared at Minors as he got back into the car. "You're not leaving those suitcases there, are you, guvnor?" he said. "They'll get pinched."

"Don't worry, it's just a joke."

"You're dead right. Where to now?"

"Back to Epping," said Minors.

FROM WHERE HE LAY behind the hedge, the suitcases on the sidewalk were almost within touching distance. Bland reckoned the temperature was down to freezing point and already the cold night air had chilled him to the bone. The minutes slowly ticked away what he guessed would be a long and lonely vigil.

At five past nine, a mud-spattered dark blue Volvo drove slowly past him and he noticed that its left-hand sidelights were not working. The driver stopped by the curb and, leaning across the passenger seat, stared at the suitcases on the sidewalk. He had long dark hair, large protruding ears and a youthful-looking face. Bland thought he was in his early twenties, and his coloring suggested that he was of East Indian extraction. For a moment it seemed as if he would leave the car, but he changed his mind when a car behind sounded its horn. A Volvo with defective left-hand sidelights had been seen at Dane End on Sunday, and as the car moved past, Bland noted that its license number was XGO 994G.

Shivering with cold, Bland continued the night watch. Ten, fifteen minutes dragged by and then, behind him, he heard a door open. Glancing back at the house over his shoulder, he saw a shaft of light coming from the porch and then a small dog scampered out into the garden. The animal circled the lawn, sniffing the grass and the rose-bushes, cocking a leg whenever the fancy took him. Suddenly the dog froze and pointed, and Bland thought it had picked up his scent. He waited, hardly daring to breathe. Then the owner called out and the dog trotted back into the house.

The Volvo made its second appearance, and this time it was heading away from Bishop's Stortford. The driver stared at the suitcases, hesitated and then drove on. The suitcases were an open invitation; they were in full view, and yet Bland had lost count of the number of people who had walked past without giving them so much as a second glance. Nobody, not even the driver of the Volvo, seemed interested enough to collect them.

But there he was wrong. One hour later the Volvo was back again for the third time. It was doing no more than ten miles an hour and there was a male passenger sitting beside the driver. The car slowed to a halt and Bland thought one of the men was going to open the door, but then he apparently had second thoughts, and the Volvo drove slowly away and disappeared into the night.

Other people began to take an interest in the cases now. A young couple stopped their car and got out to examine them closely. Presently a man walking his dog joined them, and Bland could hear snatches of their conversation. He lay there, hoping that they would move on, but as the minutes lengthened he realized he would have to do something.

"Go away," he hissed. "This is the police."

The trio looked up and down the street.

"The police," he repeated furiously.

The man and his dog went one way, the couple retreated to their car and drove off. Bland was tempted to call Smith on the two-way radio and advise him about the Volvo, but finally decided it was wiser to maintain radio silence. He thought other officers with access to a landline were bound to have made a note of it.

Bland was right. Smith already had the number of the Volvo and had telephoned it through to the operations room at Scotland Yard with the request that they check the owner's name and address. One hour later he had the answer; the records showed that it was owned by Mrs. Elsa Hosein, of Rooks Farm, Stocking Pelham.

It was late and his men were cold and exhausted. There was no point in searching the farm at this hour of the night with a different team, because Bland and the other officers who had been watching Gates Garage would have to be present to identify the occupants of the Volvo. They had spent nearly six weeks looking for M3, and Smith thought they could surely wait a few more hours. In the meantime, he would block off the lane leading to the farmhouse, and then move in when it was daylight and his men were fresh and there was no likelihood of anyone making a mistake.

"I am blindfolded and cold. Only blankets. . . ." The reckoning was at hand and the long manhunt was drawing to a close.

CHAPTER 10

THE POLICE CARS moved in convoy past the Cock Inn at Stocking Pelham and turned into the lane which led to Rooks Farm. Narrow, winding and lined with trees on either side, the potholed track passed between neglected fields and overgrown ditches until it came to a dead end at the house. Dating back to the seventeenth century, the house lay to the right of a cluster of farm buildings behind an L-shaped hedge. In front of the porchway, an elm tree leaned drunkenly to one side. A couple of Alsatians, locked inside one of the sheds, started barking as Smith and Superintendent Harvey of the Hertfordshire CID got out of the car and walked over to the house. Smith had to rap on the door twice before it was opened by a plump but attractive blonde.

"Mrs. Elsa Hosein?" he said.

"Yes?"

"We're police officers. I have a warrant to search this farm."

A slim dark man, wearing a maroon-colored jacket over a white polo-necked sweater and blue trousers, appeared at her side. "I'm Arthur Hosein," he said. "What can I do for you gentlemen?"

Smith stared at Hosein. He was about five feet six and affected a drooping mustache and sideburns. His black hair rose like a bush to crown a face that some women might find attractive.

"I'm Detective Chief Superintendent Smith and this is Chief Superintendent Harvey. We are looking for some jewelry which has been stolen from Mrs. Muriel McKay."

"Well, I know nothing about that." Hosein smiled. "I earn over a hundred and fifty pounds a week. I do not deal in stolen property, but you can look where you like."

"Good," said Smith. "Then you won't mind if I call in some of my men, will you?"

"Not at all. Perhaps you would like to make yourself comfortable in the lounge while they're looking."

The oak-beamed lounge was spacious. A large, semicircular cocktail bar, its shelves liberally stocked with spirits and liqueurs, had been installed in one nook. Arranged in front of it were three matching gilt and cream bar stools. The floor was fitted with a green pile carpet; a settee and two armchairs with chintzy, flowered pattern cov-

Arthur Hosein

Elsa Hosein

Nizamodeen Hosein

ers were grouped around the hearth angled toward a twenty-one-inch television set which dominated that corner of the room.

Hosein said, "You must have a drink, Mr. Smith. What would you like? I have everything."

"It's too early in the day for me."

Hosein glanced at the antique clock. "Yes, perhaps it is. A cigarette then?"

"I'll stick to my own cigars, if you don't mind."

"I am a wealthy man, Mr. Smith."

"Really?"

"Well, look around you. Any gentleman would be proud to own a place like this."

"How long have you been in this country?"

"I came here in 1955 from Trinidad."

So, though his origins were Pakistani, he came from the West Indies. It wasn't much to go on, and Hosein was very calm and self-assured. A team of detectives were busy searching the outbuildings and the house itself, but he remained quite unconcerned.

Bland opened a door and walked into a bedroom. A gangling young man, his hands stuffed into the pockets of his narrow trousers, was standing by the window with his back toward it. He was still wearing his pajama jacket, but it was his face that really interested Bland. The cheeks were pockmarked, the ears large and protruding beneath the lank hair, and the mouth slack and half open, as if he found it hard to breathe through his nose.

Bland said, "I know you. What's your name?"

"Nizamodeen."

"Come again?"

"Nizamodeen Hosein. Arthur's my brother; he calls me Nizam."

"Does he now?" said Bland. "Well, I tell you what, Nizam, suppose you come with me. I know someone who's going to be very pleased to meet you."

Smith looked at the green and orange artificial flowers which a detective had found in one of the children's bedrooms and knew that the world of Arthur Hosein was about to fall apart. Made out of tissue paper, they were identical to the ones which had been placed on the bank at Dane End to indicate the first ransom drop.

"Where did you buy these?"

Arthur Hosein shrugged. "I don't believe I've seen them before."

"I'm told there's a row of them in one of the bedrooms."

"Well, I don't know where they came from. Is it important?"

"I think so."

The door opened, and looking around, Smith saw Bland enter the room with another man.

"Who's this?" he asked Bland.

"Nizamodeen Hosein; he's the younger brother. It was him I saw last night at Gates Garage. He was driving the Volvo."

"Are you sure?"

"Positive," said Bland. "I'd know his face anywhere."

"Good. Let's have Detective Sergeant Quarry in here."

Arthur Hosein settled back in an armchair and crossed his feet, feigning indifference. Smith thought that no two brothers could be less alike—Arthur an extrovert, quick-witted, vain and conceited, while Nizam was dull and slow on the uptake. O'Hara had already found out in the local pub that he was the hired hand around the farm, earning eight pounds a week and his keep, while Arthur was the Walter Mitty dreamer who had boasted to the villagers that he was going to make a million and become an English country squire.

Quarry came into the lounge, and one look was enough. He had spent most of Friday night in the grounds of the local Inland Revenue Office keeping watch on the used-car lot, and the little dapper man in the armchair was very familiar. He glanced at Smith and then pointed to Arthur Hosein.

"I recognize this man," he said. "He was the passenger in the Volvo."

Police queuing up for refreshments at Rooks Far

It was a turning point. Now that both men had been identified, there was no longer any need to tread warily.

"Right," said Smith. "Let's call in the reserves and take this farm apart."

A SMALL ARMY WENT through the house and outbuildings. Upstairs in Nizam's bedroom they found an exercise book with blue-lined paper, the sort which had been used for the ransom notes. There was also a scrap of paper in the pocket of a pair of his trousers which bore the number of the Minivan at Gates Garage.

Bit by bit the evidence mounted against them. Another paper flower lay next to the front seat of the Volvo; two pairs of tailor's shears were discovered in the shed which Arthur used as a workshop, as well as a ball of twine. There was an empty tin of adhesive bandage on top of a radiogram and, in another bedroom, an empty packet of Piccadilly cigarettes similar to the one containing the instructions for the drop at Dane End. One detective unearthed a billhook in the kitchen which Arthur said he'd borrowed from a farmer to chop up a calf, while another policeman uncovered a sawed-off shotgun.

Smith said, "Who sawed the barrels off?"

"I did," said Nizam. "Arthur borrowed a neighbor's hacksaw."

"What were you playing at?"

"I wanted to shoot some rats."

Smith held out the truncated shotgun. "With this? Good God, you'd hit the man standing next to you." He looked at both men and then said, "I think you'd better come with me."

"Where to, Mr. Smith?" Arthur asked politely.

"London. You've got a lot of questions to answer."

All the way back to Wimbledon, Arthur Hosein kept up a one-way nonstop conversation.

"I am an extremely good tailor and a most successful businessman,"

he boasted. "Naturally, I am very well thought of in Stocking Pelham and I expect to be invited to join the local hunt. Of course, I come from a wealthy family, you know. My father is a holy man and I can tell you that he has great influence in high places. . . ."

FOR THREE DAYS and nights Arthur talked and talked without once saying anything incriminating. Of the two, Nizam seemed the more vulnerable, but every time the interrogation reached a decisive point, he withdrew into his shell, as if in a trance.

But when their fingerprints had been compared, it was found that Arthur's matched those on the stamp and the envelope containing the first letter from Muriel McKay, as well as those on the empty packet of Piccadilly cigarettes left in the call box in Church Street, and on the page from *The People* newspaper. On the strength of this, Smith now had enough evidence to charge both men and ask for a remand in custody. But this was only a beginning.

The forensic experts were able to raise indentations from the exercise book found in Nizam's bedroom that corresponded to the letter from M3 which had been received by the editor of the *News of the World* on the tenth of January. In part this had read, "A clue for him to know she is alive. Muriel said that Rupert Murdoch left for Australia [just before] Christmas . . . for six weeks. Seems he has not paid out for St. Mary House. . . ." In the letter, "out" and "St. Mary" had been inserted into the text above an arrow, and in the notebook it was these words and indentations which showed up under ultraviolet.

The rusty billhook left behind in St. Mary House was identified by a local farmer, who had lost it at Rooks Farm. Being left-handed, he had sharpened the blade on the reverse side. From samples taken from the brothers, experts were able to confirm that at least two of the ransom notes and the instructions in the packet of cigarettes had been written by Nizamodeen Hosein.

Piece by piece, Smith built his case. The flowers had been made by Mrs. Liley Mohammed, a girl friend of Nizam's. And then there was Michael Byers, an attendant at Gates Garage, who had seen the Volvo several times on Thursday, the fifth of February. On one occasion he had actually spoken to the driver, whom he now knew to be Nizamodeen Hosein.

Of equal significance was the fact that Elsa Hosein and the children

Head covered, one of the accused arriving
police station with Detective Chief Superintendent Sm

had only returned from Germany on the third of January, following a visit to her parents. On the night of the kidnap, therefore, the brothers had been alone at the farm.

There was one more link in the chain. On the nineteenth of December, Nizam had gone to the County Hall, Westminster, where he had seen a clerk in the vehicle-registration department. He said that he had been involved in a minor accident and wished to trace the owner of a Rolls-Royce with the license number ULO 18F. On the application form, he stated that he was Sharif Mustapha, and gave an address in Norbury, London, which was subsequently traced to a cousin of his. The Hoseins had thought the Rolls-Royce belonged to Rupert Murdoch, but all the clerk could tell Nizam was that it was registered in the name of the *News of the World* organization on Bouverie Street. Since they did not know where Murdoch lived in London, the brothers had decided to follow the Rolls when it left the *News of the World* building and, in so doing, had found Muriel McKay instead of Anna Murdoch.

Every woodland and field surrounding Rooks Farm was searched. Ponds were drained, hedges and ditches dug over; and as the weeks passed, the hunt was extended as far as the village of Brent Pelham. But there was no trace of either Muriel McKay or the missing jewelry.

ON MONDAY, THE FOURTEENTH of September, the trial opened before Mr. Justice Sebag Shaw at the Old Bailey. In addition to murder and kidnap, the brothers faced five other charges, including two of demanding one million pounds with menaces.

The trial was to last more than three weeks, but on the second day, Nizamodeen Hosein made a number of damaging admissions through his counsel which were intended to alleviate his own predicament. However, in admitting that he had applied for the ownership details of the Rolls-Royce, had placed the flowers at Dane End, had driven to Gates Garage to look for the ransom money, had written down the number of the Minivan in the used-car lot, he strengthened the case for the prosecution and placed his brother in an impossible position.

Confronted by the overwhelming scientific evidence against him, Arthur Hosein wove a fantastic story, alleging that on three occasions he had seen his brother in conference with the Mafia at the farm and that he was now being made a scapegoat for their crimes. Under cross-examination, his acting ability deserted him and at times he became hysterical with rage.

Even in the absence of a body, and without the introduction of the sawed-off shotgun, which, according to ballistics, had been fired after the barrels had been removed, the jury had no hesitation in finding them guilty on all seven charges. Arthur Hosein was sentenced to life imprisonment for murder and ninety-eight years on the other charges, Nizam to life and seventy-eight years, in both cases the sentences to run concurrently.

The judge praised Smith and his team for a brilliant piece of detective work in what had been a cold-blooded and abominable crime. Defiant and cocksure to the last, Arthur said, "Injustice has not only been done, it has been seen and heard by the gallery to have been done."

But no one remembering those words "I am blindfolded and cold" would agree with him.

NEILL CREAM, POISONER

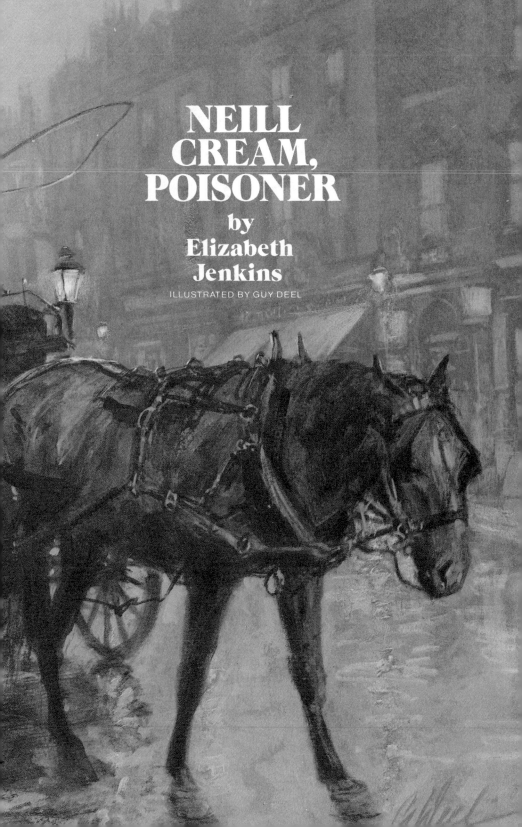

NEILL
CREAM,
POISONER

by
Elizabeth
Jenkins

ILLUSTRATED BY GUY DEEL

He was a strange-looking man—large, balding, with an odd cast to his eyes, yet very smartly turned out and a gentleman unquestionably, or so most people believed. Still, his habits were curious. He was a doctor, but he did not appear to practice his profession. Instead, he remained in his rooms most days, going out at night to wander down the back alleys of London's seamy East End. Could he have had anything to do with the rash of ghastly poisoning deaths suddenly attracting the concern of Scotland Yard?

The distinguished historian and biographer Elizabeth Jenkins re-creates London's gaudy, gaslit Victorian era and portrays for us one of the great archfiends in the annals of crime.

CHAPTER 1

ON OCTOBER 1, 1891, THE liner *Teutonic*, coming from America, docked at Liverpool. If any passenger aboard had been infectious from smallpox, cholera or typhoid, he would have undergone quarantine till it was safe for him to rejoin society. The arrangements for such a situation were excellent; for a still more deadly, but secret, unsuspected sickness, no precautions were possible and no quarantine system ever devised could protect society from the ghastly peril.

A passenger on the *Teutonic* was returning from Canada. His Scottish parents had taken him there at four years old, in 1854, and though he had come to London as a student and taken a course at St. Thomas's Hospital, he had not revisited England for fourteen years. Ten of those years had been spent in the state of Illinois, in jail. The long, weary, endless-seeming stretch of repression and emptiness had not altered his cast of mind or left it less avid for the pleasure it had once enjoyed. The death of his father before his release from jail had provided him with a small, comfortable fortune. The desires he had he could gratify. He was coming back to the area of London where he had found those keen enjoyments which, for all that wilderness of time, had stayed in his mind like phosphorescent fire on rotting wood.

OF THE THREE bridges spanning the elbow of the river Thames, Blackfriars Bridge, Waterloo Bridge and Westminster Bridge, the latter was the noblest and most important. On each side of it, on both the river shores, stretched the Embankment, lighted at dusk by pale globes of incandescent gas standing on wrought-iron pedestals wreathed with dolphins. Actually some twenty yards apart, the lamps appeared thrown together by distance to make a single shining string, their reflections diving down into the dark water in shimmering streaks.

Along the south shore, the Lambeth Palace Road ran past St. Thomas's Hospital. The greatest of the London teaching hospitals, with a distinguished medical staff, it had unsurpassed nursing standards, for these had been set up by Florence Nightingale herself, relentless and inspired.

At the corner of Lambeth Palace Road and Lambeth Road stood the fifteenth-century gatehouse, the entrance to the palace itself. As a carriage and pair approached it, the pale face of the occupant was sometimes seen, burdened with anxious thought, stately, splendid and agonized—the Most Reverend and Right Honorable Edward White Benson, Archbishop of Canterbury. Immediately opposite, across the river, rose the Victorian Gothic shapes, pinnacled and turreted, of the Houses of Parliament, where programs of social reform were attacking the forces of apathy, ignorance and vested interest; and facing them, on the other side of Westminster Bridge, was an imposing building that stood like a sentinel over the public safety.

THE DETECTIVE BRANCH of the Metropolitan Police had been reformed in 1878 and was now the world-famous Criminal Investigation Department (CID). It had previously occupied cramped quarters beside Charing Cross, at 4 Whitehall Place, on a site known since the thirteenth century as Scotland Yard, from its use by Scottish visitors to the English court. The police were in urgent need of more spacious accommodations, and in 1888 a building of romantic splendor was acquired for them by the government. A Colonel Mapleson had intended to build an opera house of international fame; the location on the Embankment had been acquired, a station opened at Westminster Bridge to convey the patrons, and the foundation stone laid by the Prince of Wales in 1875. But after these grand preparations the colonel's money had run out, and by 1890 the Metropolitan Police and the CID were installed in it. Colonel Mapleson's proposed decoration of Venetian marbles was replaced by one of Portland stone, quarried by convicts on the Portland Bill, but otherwise the exterior remained as the colonel had devised it—carnelian brick banded with white, great rounded turrets at the corners, a covey of dormer windows in the steep roof, and two soaring red-and-white striped campaniles. Known as New Scotland Yard, the scene was strangely at variance with the work of the clearheaded, quiet and very able men who now occupied it.

Scotland Yard, the Houses of Parliament, St. Thomas's Hospital, Lambeth Palace—law, government, medicine, religion, were represented by the great buildings, all very near to each other, all situated near Westminster Bridge; but a few hundred yards away the scene was very different. Streets of beautiful little eighteenth-century houses, grimy and sinking into decay, were broken up by factories and warehouses, noisy not only with cabs, drays and omnibuses, but with the roar of trains going over lofty railway bridges, under whose arches footsteps, wheels and horses' hoofs echoed loudly. Lambeth Road, Lambeth Palace Road and the streets about them were partly lined by little houses, some clean and comfortable, others in varying stages of neglect. In some places new buildings had intruded. In Hercules Road, at right angles to Lambeth Road, there was a modern block of tenements called Orient Buildings. Whether its occupants understood the term and connected it with the Moorish-shaped windows and the public entrances arched like a spade on a playing card was doubtful.

The appearance of most of the housing property was grim, if not decaying, but down the Westminster Bridge Road, under the thundering railway arch, you came to two music halls, the Canterbury on the right and Gatti's, farther down on the left. The Canterbury's name was four centuries old; an inn had once stood there, named for the archbishop, but it and Gatti's were of the present—raucous, brilliant, hot, lighted by great gasoliers with circles of glittering globes, their walls bright with brass and looking glass. Under a gilded proscenium arch, songs and turns were given throughout the evening by ribald, dazzling artists.

The music halls were overpoweringly successful because they provided everything the patrons could not get at home—warmth, gaiety, brilliant light and exciting company. The garish scene was hazed with smoke; the heat was torrid; the noise of talk and laughter that a comedian could only just bawl down, was so unceasing that nobody needed to think. To come in—with shoes soaked through and the clothes sticking to your back with rain—was to be feverishly glowing in twenty minutes, hair steaming and cheeks burning. It was a good place for the more presentable whores to pick up a client, and unaccompanied men came to look about them at women in tight jackets, leg-of-mutton sleeves, and hats whose brims were loaded with ostrich feathers.

THE EVENING OF October 6 was dark and very wet. Elizabeth Masters had come across Waterloo Bridge and up Fleet Street to Ludgate Circus. A railway bridge ran above the street, and beyond it, rising high in mist and rain was the great dome of St. Paul's Cathedral, dimly seen. The night was bad and her luck seemed out when she was accosted outside the King Lud public house by a tall, somewhat heavy man, solidly dressed against the rain in a caped mackintosh and a felt hat. He took her into the public house and gave her a glass of wine. He spoke with a strong but soft American accent, she thought, looking up at him. There was, too, something queer about his appearance, but she was so glad to be in harbor, she did not think twice about it. Presently he hailed a four-wheeler and they drove all the way to Orient Buildings, where Elizabeth lived. He seemed to take to her, because when they had been on her bed an hour or so, instead of paying her and making off down the stone staircase, he acted quite the gentleman and asked if she would like to come out for the evening. She suggested Gatti's, because she had arranged to meet her fellow lodger, Elizabeth May, there; she and May often worked together. Elizabeth Masters didn't as a rule stop to ask herself whether she liked a client or didn't, but she did rather like this one. Not that he wasn't strange to look at; he was not only bald in front, but his scalp showed through the hair at the back of his head, though his ginger mustache was very heavy, and behind his gold-rimmed spectacles he was cross-eyed. However, he had a quiet, powerful way with him, and his clothes were very good. The perfect freshness of his stiff collar, his snowy shirtfront, the good quality of everything he wore, was noted by her practiced eye.

Inside the doors of Gatti's a burst of warmth and light and noise met them. Elizabeth May soon picked them out, but after a drink

she went off on her own affairs. Later in the evening she rejoined them. The gentleman told Masters he would write to her when he was settled in lodgings. Then he said that he was taking a cab back to Ludgate Circus, as his hotel was in Fleet Street, and he would give them a lift if they wanted to go that way. Orient Buildings was not ten minutes' walk and Ludgate Circus was a long way from home, but instinct forbade Masters to leave the client before the client left her. So they went on to Ludgate Hill and had a drink at a public house. The rain had stopped and from Waterloo Bridge the reflections in the dark river were tranquil and golden; but by that time Masters had had a good deal to drink, she was tired and cross, and the prospect of the long walk home made her thoroughly bad tempered. When they were about to part for the evening, she and May flounced off without saying good night.

CHAPTER 2

THE HOUSES IN Lambeth Palace Road that were opposite St. Thomas's were respectable and much in request by students at the hospital. Number 103, run by Miss Sleaper, was very comfortable and convenient. Miss Sleaper kept it in apple-pie order, providing the lodgers with breakfast and with dinner if they wanted it. The lodgers had their latchkeys and, hardworking young men as they were, they came and went without disturbance to anyone. The one who at present occupied the two rooms on her first floor was as good a lodger as you could find. He was called Walter J. Harper, a slight, pale young man with a brown mustache, nice-mannered, quiet and a hard worker, just the sort Miss Sleaper liked to have. He had been with her while studying at St. Thomas's for the past two years, and she was sorry to think they would have to part when he qualified next April. His father, Dr. Joseph Harper, practiced in Barnstaple, and young Mr. Harper meant to take a practice in the same neighborhood.

As so many of her best lodgers had been medical men, Miss Sleaper was well disposed toward a man obviously well found and calling himself Dr. Neill, who came inquiring for accommodations on the morning of October 6. He had a bad cast in one eye and rather a horrid look to his head. You could see the scalp through his hair at the back, but he was solid, middle-aged and prosperous-looking. After a few minutes of her experienced observation, Miss Sleaper felt she would be justified in letting the second-floor front room to him. There was no second room to spare, but this one was spacious, with a pleasant outlook on the river. There was a built-in cupboard beside the hearth, and the wardrobe and the bed left plenty of room for a table in the window, a chest of drawers and two armchairs.

The lodger arrived next morning with a large portmanteau, a tin box and two trunks. When his clothes, of which he had a large supply, all new, were unpacked, the trunks were stood one on top of the other on the landing. He seemed satisfied, and prepared to make himself comfortable. He told Miss Sleaper that he was a postgraduate at St. Thomas's Hospital, but as day followed day, accustomed as she was to lodgers who followed a hospital routine, she did not think he was engaged in any course of studies, and he certainly did not receive patients at the house. Still, when he told her that he had been ill and had come to England for his health, this seemed natural. He had already consulted an oculist, Mr. James Aitchison, of 47 Fleet Street, who diagnosed hypermyopia, or extreme shortsightedness. Mr. Aitchison was not surprised to hear the patient complain of headaches and sleeplessness and to learn that he took heavy doses of morphine and cocaine. It was scarcely possible to control a doctor's treatment of himself, but Mr. Aitchison hoped that the spectacles he prescribed would lessen the cerebral strain by correcting the shortsightedness and the squint, and reduce the need for opiates. Two pairs were made, with handsome gold frames, and delivered to 103 Lambeth Palace Road. They added to the wearer's comfort very much, soothed the reeling sensation in his head and gave a new impetus to his hunt for pleasure.

ELIZABETH MASTERS HAD a letter delivered to her at Orient Buildings on the morning of October 9. It was written from 103 Lambeth Palace Road and said the writer would call on her between three and five that afternoon, and she must not be as cross as she had been the other evening. She was to be careful to keep the letter and the envelope and give them back to the writer. This degree of caution struck her rather disagreeably; everyone knew that you had to be careful, but this showed a lack of trust in other people. Still, he'd written, as he'd said he would. She went into the next room, where Elizabeth May was still in bed, half asleep. The bolster was in its bare ticking, the pillowcase was very dirty; it and the sheets and the thin blanket were all of the same dingy hue. No care, no style, May hadn't. Masters kept things much cleaner and more comfortable, but May did better. When she slid out of bed and came across to Masters' room, wearing a man's pea jacket over her crumpled nightdress, she looked like the farm girl she had once been. Masters was nothing like so fresh. She was jerky and irritable, but she wore a clean cotton Japanese kimono; and while she made herself a cup of tea from a small tin kettle on a rusty gas burner, May padded back to her room for a half-empty bottle of brandy and poured herself out a tumblerful. Masters was studying the letter and May leaned over her shoulder. Well, they would have everything shipshape by three o'clock.

So they had, and by that time they were sitting at Masters' window, looking down to the right onto Hercules Road. They had sat about half an hour when they saw him coming along the sidewalk toward Orient Buildings. He was differently dressed, wearing a black cloth overcoat and a tall silk hat, but they recognized him at once, and in that instant they saw something else. Ahead of him was a figure that they would not have noticed except as a mere passerby; and their gentleman, coming on at a steady pace, was following her. Matilda Clover was a young woman in their line of business whom they knew only by sight. When she wasn't dressed to kill, she didn't mind how she went out. Now she was walking along the sidewalk with a basket in her hand, and though her hat was on, she was wearing a white apron with crossed shoulder straps. She passed the entrance to Orient Buildings beneath them, and the gentleman, without a glance toward it, passed it too. With one impulse the watchers sprang to their feet. Masters cried, "Get your hat!" and seized her own. They rushed down the stone stairs and out through the Moorish arch. Turning to the left, they followed the pursuer and his quarry.

Where Hercules Road ran at right angles into Lambeth Road, they paused on the edge of the sidewalk. Across Lambeth Road and to the right was a row of houses, broken by the Masons' Arms. Almost opposite to where her two rivals stood, Matilda Clover had her hand on a front door. She turned and smiled at the follower, paused for a moment, then went into the house without shutting the door.

The man made his way into the house after her. The door was shut.

After a second's silence Masters darted across the road and studied the number on the door; it was 27. She and May determined to wait. They weren't taking this sort of thing lying down! They retired into the Imperial Wine Stores, a wedge-shaped, bowfront public house built on the corner of Hercules Road and Lambeth Road, and sat in its window as long as they could spin out two glasses of beer. At the end of half an hour no one had emerged from number 27, and they went back to Orient Buildings with plenty to say about it.

MATILDA CLOVER WAS twenty-seven; she had a slight, energetic figure, and the tight waists and full sleeves of her cheap, smart clothes showed it off. When dressed in her best, she wore a hat with a large bow in front of it tipped forward over her hard, harassed young face.

She had lived in Mrs. Phillips' house for three months. It did as well as anywhere else, better than some places would have done. She had her little boy of two with her, and when she had to be out at night, the maid, Lucy Rose, would listen for him, or sometimes Mrs. Phillips would. They were good-natured to her, and Matilda would often sit down, her head on her hand, and talk to Mrs. Phillips about the baby's father, a fair, slight young man called Fred, who thought rather a lot of himself. He had had a violent, shouting quarrel with Matilda four weeks ago, and Mrs. Phillips had heard him say that he would never come to that house or see Matilda again. When Matilda repeated this last quarrel, as she often did, word for word, she would speak with a dreary, stunned hopelessness. She had always been inclined to drink—it was the life that did it—but after Fred left she really took to it. More than once she was brought home late at night by some friend or friendly passerby, too drunk to stand, and they would all have to get her upstairs between them.

Matilda had several friends, and some of them had advised her, in this state, to pay into the club run by Dr. Graham in the neighborhood. For a very small but regular payment the members could have all the attention and the medicines they might need, without extra charge. Dr. Graham was shabby, overworked and kind. He understood and didn't blame you, but he told Matilda that she must stop drinking, or she'd never see her boy grow up. He gave her some medicine that was supposed to help the craving and soothe the burning sensation inside her. It did some good, making her satisfied with only beer; but without the support of brandy and gin she felt dull and mopish. Then a new friend, who seemed a gentleman and was certainly well-to-do, brought some interest into her life, even if he wasn't the sort she could have fancied. When she told him that Fred, her child's father, had deserted her, he gave her a strange look and said that Fred was his name too. For the next few days, besides visiting her at night, he went on outings with her in the daytime.

At 129 Westminster Bridge Road, Mr. Will Armstead had his photographer's business; the studio was on the ground floor, and he and his wife and a lodger occupied the premises above. Dr. Neill seemed fond of being photographed; he had some impressive studio portraits taken here. In one he was sitting, wearing a top hat and a dark cloth overcoat with a velvet collar, his right hand resting on the handle of his umbrella. His heavy mustache had the ends curled up, his gold-rimmed spectacles had improved the squint; really quite a good-looking man, you would say, and very well turned out, but there was something . . . something strange about his face.

Dr. Neill approved of Mr. Armstead's work and had another portrait taken, wearing this time a small-brimmed bowler; but the odd look was there again, something that made him look not quite like other people. However, he was a desirable client, and when he brought Miss Clover with him to be photographed among the urns of artificial flowers on plaster pedestals, Mr. Armstead made no bones, and posed Miss Clover freestanding, calling out encouragements to her from where he lurked behind the camera on its tripod, his head buried under the black velvet cloth. Matilda was not nervous; though the camera brought out an expression of defiance and despair, it was not the fact of being photographed that made her look like that.

CHAPTER 3

MISS SLEAPER HAD BEEN right in deducing that Dr. Neill had no settled occupation; but though his time was spent in social contacts of a humble and often dubious kind, he could, when he wished, appear to be the doctor he said he was. The wide thoroughfare of Whitehall, running down past the Admiralty, the Horse Guards and the War

Office, became Parliament Street before it reached Parliament Square, where the Houses of Parliament loomed above the river. In this street some shops of distinction were to be found.

Priest's, the pharmacy at 22 Parliament Street, with its ranges of glass-handled mahogany drawers, its eighteenth-century china jars and its delicious smell compounded of antiseptics, expensive soaps and orrisroot, was not only elegant, it was highly competent, run by an intelligent proprietor and his assistant, who were accustomed to serving the physicians of St. Thomas's Hospital. In the second week of October, a tall man in glasses, with a heavy mustache, very respectably dressed, presented himself and asked for an ounce of nux vomica. This being a restricted poison, the assistant, Mr. Kirkby, asked him to write down his name and address, with the required prescription for the drug. The customer wrote out: "Nux vomica, one ounce, ten to twenty drops, diluted in water." He signed it "Thomas Neill," adding, as the pharmacist had expected, "M.D." The address was 103 Lambeth Palace Road, and the customer explained that he was attending a course of lectures at St. Thomas's Hospital. Nux vomica, the liquid extracted from "the nut that causes vomiting," contains two alkaloid poisons: brucine, which is dangerous; and strychnine, which is deadly. Very useful in medicinal doses as a tonic, the lethal dose of strychnine brings on tetanic convulsions and an agonizing death. There is, of course, no danger in its use by a qualified doctor. For a sale across the counter to a physician, the pharmacist did not need to enter the transaction in his book. He complied with the law if he placed one of his shop's labels on the bottle and marked it POISON.

When Dr. Neill had left the shop and some waiting customers had been served and had departed, Mr. Kirkby seized a minute's leisure to consult the *Medical Register*. Dr. Neill's name was not there, but remembering the transatlantic accent, he assumed that Dr. Neill was the holder of an American degree. In any case, the reference to St. Thomas's was good enough.

A few days later, on October 12, Dr. Neill appeared in the shop again. He wanted some gelatin capsules, those which are in two parts, one half sliding over the other, and are used for administering medicines with a very nasty taste. The pharmacy had none in stock, but Mr. Priest told Kirkby to go to Maw, Son and Thompson, of Aldersgate Street in the City, wholesale pharmaceutical suppliers, and get a box of 100 twelve-grain capsules. When Dr. Neill came in again on October 13, he said they were too big; he wanted some for five grains, which would be less than half the size. That afternoon, at the first opportunity, Kirkby went to Maw, Son and Thompson again and came back with the five-grain capsules. They were packed in a round flat box covered with shiny black paper; the round white label on the lid was marked MAW, SON AND THOMPSON, WHOLESALE CHEMISTS, and a narrow purple label was stuck at the base of this, saying in gilt letters, PRIEST'S CHEMIST, 22 PARLIAMENT STREET. A day or two later Dr. Neill called again and accepted these capsules, thanking Messrs. Priest and Kirkby for their trouble.

He went out of the shop with a determined air and, going down Parliament Street, bore left across Westminster Bridge, leaving behind him the open, stately neighborhood, the Houses of Parliament on the right and the red-and-white building of Scotland Yard a little way down the Embankment to his left. When he had crossed the broad river, restless and sparkling under a keen breeze, he turned left again and made for the Waterloo Road. Here the scene changed to one of drabness verging on squalor, and his bearing changed with it. Walking along badly swept sidewalks and under reverberating railway bridges, he seemed to develop a new personality. His discreet, self-contained air gave place to a sharp, eager, curious look, with which he scanned the female passersby. A lurking, humorous enjoyment in his peculiar face gave him, in spite of his mustache, his spectacles and his top hat, the look of something inhuman. The Waterloo Road had numerous public houses, such as the Wellington and the Lord Hill, and though their trade was heaviest in the evening, at midday it was possible to meet a female companion there, to give her a glass of beer and a sandwich, discuss an assignation and find out her address.

The Waterloo Road, dingy as it was, was respectable enough, thronged with carriages, four-wheeled cabs, drays and omnibuses; the streets that led off it were another matter. The whores who came out of them at dusk, walking slowly, jauntily, hanging about the open doors of public houses from which light poured out, haunting the parapets of the great bridges, were so much a part of the city's life that they were spoken of in a poetic convention by journalists and other writers as "the nymphs of the pavement," "the wandering beauties of the night," "the legion of the lost." Dirty and draggled as they often were, sometimes so ill that their disease was patent, some of them were young, energetic, lively; they had an air both wild and approachable, utterly different from the women that men met anywhere else. In their company, shyness and inexperience ceased to matter, impulses could be given way to without a man's being either rebuffed or finding himself committed for life; what had been longed for as unattainable could be had without difficulty. They possessed Aladdin's lamp, that took the seeker, momentarily, into a cave of jewels.

ELLEN DONWORTH WAS sometimes called Ellen Linnell, because a young fellow named Ernest Linnell had been keeping her, quite regularly, only it ended. Ellen was nineteen, and her mixture of experience and youth might take her far, with luck. At present she had a room at 8 Duke Street, a dark and dirty little road off the Westminster Bridge Road. The place was cheap, and also very near the best hunting ground. Her friend Annie Clements, who lived in the same house, had a more laborious job than Ellen's, but Annie preferred it in spite of red, swollen hands and dirty, broken nails; she was a cleaning lady.

Early on the morning of October 13, Annie was going out to work when Ellen showed her a letter she'd just had by the first post; it was from a gentleman she'd met already; it told her to meet him that evening outside the York Hotel, in the Waterloo Road. He had added that she must bring the letter with her to prove that she'd received it. The girls didn't quite understand this, but after all, it was easy enough to do. Ellen said he was tall, bald and cross-eyed, but free with his money. Annie left her friend deciding between two high-necked muslin blouses, both worn out, and preening the wings of a vivid green bird that was fastened to her hat.

DARKNESS HAD COME down on the Waterloo Road and the gas lamps were haloed in the mist that was coming in from the river. The rumbling and commotion and shrieks of locomotives from Waterloo Station mingled with the uproar of the still heavy traffic, the endless procession of cabs, carts and vans. James Styles, a fruit vendor, had a stand in the New Cut, a road off the Waterloo Road, lined with secondhand shops and fruit and vegetable barrows. He was going home, and waiting on the curb opposite the Lord Hill, till the stream of vehicles should allow him to cross. As he stood, watching for his chance, he noticed a young woman with a green bird on her hat, leaning against the wall of the public house. In another moment she had fallen flat on her face. He darted across, under the nose of a trampling, clattering dray horse, and gained the sidewalk. The girl was still prostrate, and as he bent over her he found at his shoulder another vendor of his acquaintance, a man called Adams. They turned the slight body onto its back. The hat fell off, and the face in the gaslight was ghastly white.

"Where do you live, dear?" Styles asked urgently.

The girl's eyeballs rolled, catching the gaslight in a frightful way. "Eight Duke Street," she gasped.

"What's wrong, dear?" said Adams.

She trembled, shivered; then she said, "Pain, all over me." At that she became completely rigid, so that they couldn't lift her; then her spine arched backward; the convulsiveness of the movement, which made the body bounce on the sidewalk, and the utter stiffness of the limbs, as if she'd been turned to lead, were so extraordinary and so horrifying that the two men were staggered; but they had the strong camaraderie of the London streets, and they did not need to tell each other that they would take her home.

At that moment a policeman, Inspector Harvey of the Lambeth (L) Division, coming up the sidewalk, saw a small crowd outside the Lord Hill. It was the usual mixture, some anxious to help, some merely curious. Two decent-looking men were on their knees beside a woman. He stood over them and asked if they knew who she was and where she lived. They told him they'd got the address and would take her home. Did they want any help? No, they said. (You didn't want the coppers round at your place if you could help it.)

Inspector Harvey saw that they could carry her. He made a note of the address and told them that help could be summoned from the South London Medical Institute. On his return beat, in about an hour's time, he made his way through the ill-lighted neighborhood to 8 Duke Street, and when ushered up to the first floor of the dark little house, where only candles in tin holders gave light, he found a bedroom in a scene of frantic commotion. The lodgers had brought in their own candles, which burned in a row on the narrow mantel shelf. Two women and a man were holding down the arms, the shoulders, the feet of the girl on the bed, whose convulsive leaps and struggles were so powerful that they almost tore her out of their hands. On the iron bedstead the ornamental brass globes had long since split in two, and the halves rattled and jingled. The movements of the helpers made the floorboards spring and creak.

As Inspector Harvey came up to the bed, the frenzied movements died down. The girl, bathed in sweat, lay limp; the helpers moved aside and he bent over to question her. She was fully conscious and answered him weakly but coherently. A tall, dark, cross-eyed fellow had given her some white stuff to drink, out of a bottle, in the street. Did she know this man? asked Inspector Harvey in a low, compelling tone. Had she ever seen him before? Yes, she had met him before. She'd had two letters from him. When had the last one come? This morning. She stared at Inspector Harvey with a fixed gaze. Where are the letters? he asked. She'd given them back to him, she said. He had told her that he must have them back when they met this evening, and she'd taken them with her and given them to him. At that moment she began again to tremble and shudder; the fearful convulsions came on, and under their savage onslaught her spine bent backward like a bow. The bedstead jingled and rang, and her convulsive leaps, held down by the sympathizers, made a series of thuds on the mattress.

In the middle of this seizure, Mr. Johnson, sent by Dr. Lowe of the South London Medical Institute in answer to a summons, appeared in the room. He had come straight up, for the street door was standing open. He saw the spasms, the collapse into exhaustion, the pouring sweat. He decided that the symptoms were consistent with strychnine poisoning, and told Inspector Harvey that the girl must be got to St. Thomas's Hospital at once. A willing bystander ran out to summon a cab, and when it clattered up, he helped the inspector to carry her downstairs and into it. Then the jolting and the darkness and the passing gleams of light, the firm, supporting arm and the kind words, and the terrible shudderings that opened the gateway to the pain's coming back, the plunge into the abyss of agony, where the dreadful power shook her as if it were a ferocious dog and she a helpless rat, all died away in a blessed oblivion; and when the cab stopped at the hospital gates and a porter and a house physician, seeing a policeman get down, hurried forward, it was not a person they lifted out but a thing.

The mortuary at the hospital was lighted by gas lamps whose brilliant glare had a faintly greenish tinge. The assistants removed the clothes, which were clean, but scanty for autumn wearing. The thin, vigorous body was well washed, but the feet were dirty because the boots had let in rainwater. There was no mark of injury and no ascertainable cause of death, so a postmortem was necessary. This investigation found a quarter of a grain of strychnine in the stomach. The inquest, held at the hospital, was presided over by the coroner for East Surrey, Mr. George Percival Wyatt, and opened on the fifteenth of October; its progress was reported in the papers.

CHAPTER 4

DR. NEILL WAS AN omnivorous newspaper reader. When he went out he would return with several under his arm, and would sit at his table in the window, spending far more time in reading them than Miss Sleaper's other lodgers had leisure to bestow. He was always interested in anything of the sensational medical line, and he pored over the accounts, fragmentary and inconclusive as they still were, of the death of Ellen Donworth and of the inquest that was still going on. But though he seemed to have no settled occupation, he was a satisfactory lodger; he needed no meals except breakfast, at which he took only milk and a plate of toast, and an occasional dinner. Though he was a late riser and spent a long time in his room in the morning, reading and writing, he was out almost all the rest of the day, as well as coming in usually very late at night—early morning, often as not. But he was quiet, and it was only now and again that Miss Sleaper wakened in her bedroom at the back of the house to hear his weighty but soft footfalls creaking up the stairs.

THE INQUEST ON Ellen Donworth was a slow business and the work at the coroner's court was heavy. Four days after it had opened, Mr. Wyatt had a letter handed to him, addressed care of the court. It bore a signature unknown to him—"A. O'Brien, Detective"—and it said the writer could produce evidence that would lead to the arrest of the murderer of Ellen Donworth, alias Linnell. Someone clearly knew something about the girl and her fate, and as the writing, though curious, did not look uneducated, Mr. Wyatt read to the end with some attention. The final sentence, however, dashed his hopes, if he had had any: "Provided your Government is willing to pay me £300,000 for my services."

The stark insanity of the proposition showed that the letter had been written either by a mischievous practical joker or a lunatic. He filed it and, addressing himself to the final stage of the inquest, thought no more of it.

IT WAS WITHIN ten days of the end of October and darkness came on early. In the Waterloo Road, gas jets over the stalls and in the windows of shops imparted a theatrical air to the murky scene. A great number of the shops in the district were for secondhand clothing; LADIES' AND GENTLEMEN'S WARDROBES PURCHASED, said signs in their windows. The whores of the neighborhood bought almost all their clothes secondhand. The dresses, costumes and feathered hats were good value, but the boots were apt to be worthless, discarded because they had not been worth mending.

Matilda Clover was particularly pleased when her new friend said he would buy her a pair of brand-new boots. They went out one evening, down the Westminster Bridge Road to Lilley's Boot and Shoe Emporium, still open at eight o'clock. Matilda had been drinking and was distinctly tipsy, but she still knew what she wanted. She chose the boots herself and the gentleman paid for them. They were buttoned, the toe caps and heels of patent leather, the uppers of black cloth. The edge containing the buttonholes was scalloped; each button, fastened in the curve of a scallop, had a twinkling center. The boots did not look good quality, they did not look ladylike, but on Matilda's feet and ankles they looked very attractive. She was on the verge, where she could still be pulled back into sense and cleanliness and physical attractiveness, or could just as well be pushed over into the state of almost perpetual drunkenness, where all standards would collapse.

Her little boy, Fred, would even now have had a hard time if the little maid of all work, Lucy Rose, hadn't been so good to him. Lucy was supposed to come up and "sweep round" Matilda's rooms once in a while, and on the morning of October 20, while Matilda was out at the shops, Lucy saw a letter lying open on the table in the front room. The National School had taught Lucy to read very well. She stood and read the letter, leaning on her broom while the little boy clutched her skirts. The writer told Matilda to meet him outside the Canterbury at seven thirty that evening, and to bring the letter with her—"if you can come clean and sober," he went on, adding that when he'd bought her boots she'd been too drunk to speak to him. Those boots! Lucy had admired them very much, stylish and brand-new. It was a crying shame about the drink. She didn't seem able to help it, even with what Dr. Graham did for her. Lucy had seen others go like that.

Fred was now clutching her knees and burying his face in her skirts. He knew she was his great friend. She would come upstairs and feed him if she knew his mother was too drunk to look after him; poor little chap, she used to say. Not that she wasn't sorry for his mother too. The landlady's grandson, Edgar, a boy of nine, was living in the house, and sometimes little Fred was downstairs with him in the warm kitchen. Edgar came of people whose children had to start very early taking care of the little ones. The two would sit on the warm flags under the kitchen table, Edgar talking to him and Fred being very quiet.

It wasn't that Matilda wasn't fond of the child—she was devoted to him; it was just that she couldn't help herself. Of her two rooms, the front one, looking into Lambeth Road, had a large, reasonably sound sofa with cushions on it, and covered with an Indian-cotton spread, which was sometimes washed out. This was where clients were entertained. The back room had a large bed in it, but that was where she slept, with Fred beside her. Men didn't go in there. The rooms were lighted with candles, for there was no gas in the house, and the small hall was lighted by a hanging oil lamp. The wallpaper here was very old; it had been varnished, and in the dim light the pattern looked like plants massed together underwater.

On the evening of the twentieth, Matilda told Lucy that she was going out (at which Lucy lowered her eyelids, since she knew this and hadn't ought to have) and asked her to come up and help put Fred to bed, and listen for him. Lucy, tired as she was after her heavy day, never thought of refusing. She washed Fred's face and hands from the basin on the rickety little washstand, and settled him in bed with a cup of milk and a bit of bread and butter, while Matilda buttoned the boots and shrugged herself into her jacket. The hat with its big bow, which she would once have poised in a graceful, airy fashion, now had to go on anyhow. She was off, and Lucy, seeing Fred come over drowsy, kissed the top of his head, laid him down and went quietly out of the room, leaving the door ajar.

Sometime before ten o'clock she had to come up from the kitchen and open the front door. Matilda didn't always have her key with her; she hadn't tonight. When Lucy let her in, she was followed by a tall, stoutish man whose face Lucy couldn't distinctly see in the dim light, but she did see that he had a heavy mustache and wore glasses. He was very much the gentleman in appearance, with a tall silk hat and an overcoat with a cape to it. The couple went upstairs, and in a few moments Matilda came down again, slipping out to the Masons' Arms for some beer. Soon after her return the guest departed, and Lucy, at the foot of the kitchen stairs, heard Matilda say, "Good night, dear," as she let him out of the front door. Matilda herself went out shortly after that, but whatever her scheme had been, she would seem to have given it up, for she was in again by half past ten. Mrs. Phillips saw her go upstairs, and the house became quiet for the night.

Lucy's bedroom was at the back, immediately under Matilda's. She was, as usual by the time she got to bed, dead tired and, in spite of a lumpy mattress and thin pillows, sank at once into a deep restoring sleep from which it was difficult to wake her.

But at three o'clock the tearing screams did wake her, piercing her brain and stabbing her awake in amazement and terror. She jumped out of bed and in only her nightdress rushed across the landing to Mrs. Phillips' room and banged on the door. The shrieks had not reached Mrs. Phillips as soon as they had penetrated to Lucy, but they did so now, a series of sounds so appalling, so terrifying, that everyone was roused into full activity. Lucy tore upstairs ahead of Mrs. Phillips and burst into Matilda's bedroom. As she came in, the screaming stopped and was succeeded by deep, shuddering moans.

The bed stood at one side of the room, about a foot from the wall.

Matilda, in her nightgown, was lying across the end of it, her head having become wedged between the bedside and the wall in her last convulsive struggle. She lay still now, limp and gasping, and at the other end of the bed, sitting up against the pillows, there was Fred, sobbing with terror. Matilda, deathly pale but looking wide-awake, said weakly, "I'm glad you've come; I've been calling a long time."

Mrs. Phillips, in a purple flannelette dressing gown, with her hair in curlers, was now in the room. She lifted Fred up. He clung around her neck, screaming and sobbing, and while she comforted him, Lucy, bending over the bed, said, "What's happened to you, dear?"

Matilda was exhausted but quite coherent. She said, "That wretch Fred gave me some pills."

Lucy managed to guide her across the bed so that her head was on the pillow, and to pull the bedclothes from under her, so that they could be pulled up again to cover her. Mrs. Phillips said she'd take the child downstairs, he could go into Edgar's bed, and while she was out of the room with him, the fit came back. Matilda's limbs twitched as if they were on wires; the sweat poured off her ghastly face; she shuddered and trembled, and before Lucy could get the basin to her she was violently sick.

Lucy, hardly knowing what to do first, ran down to the kitchen for a pail of water and a cloth, and as she flew up, slopping the water on the stairs, the frightful screams began again. They had died down when Mrs. Phillips reappeared in her long coat and her hat. Saying she was going for Dr. Graham, she went downstairs and let herself out into the chill darkness and stillness of Lambeth Road.

Making her way the mile-long distance to Kennington Lane, under a starlit sky with no one to break the void of the silent street, Mrs. Phillips asked herself, as she trudged hastily along, what she had done to deserve this. When she had pealed and pealed at the doctor's night bell, a voice from above told her that Dr. Graham was out at a confinement. She got back to number 27 and, going upstairs, found things as bad as ever. There had been more seizures. Matilda was now lying in passive exhaustion, but Mrs. Phillips thought she looked near death.

Lucy, who was shivering, said, "If you please to stop here while I go and dress."

"Bring a cup of tea when you come," Mrs. Phillips said.

The girl was back in ten minutes with a cup of strong tea. They propped Matilda up and held the cup to her lips. She said in oppressed tones, "Something on my chest, in my throat. I'd be better if I could get it up."

When Mrs. Phillips had gone downstairs there was another fearful attack of vomiting, after which the patient lay shuddering and trembling, the sweat shining on her white face. Mrs. Phillips, who had not heard what Matilda had said about pills, was sure that this was the result of drink that had overtaken the girl, as Dr. Graham had warned her that it would if she didn't stop—delirium tremens, always spoken of as something dreadful, how dreadful a person couldn't know till they saw it.

By half past six further attacks had convinced Mrs. Phillips to go for the doctor once more. It was nearly light by the time she got to his office again. This time she did see Dr. Graham, untidy and unshaved; he had come back from the confinement, but he was going to it again; he could not possibly visit Matilda Clover, and told Mrs. Phillips to try Dr. McCarthy in the Westminster Bridge Road.

Dr. McCarthy was also out on a case, but his assistant, Mr. Coppin, agreed to come, to Mrs. Phillips' great relief. Mr. Coppin was well known in the neighborhood. He was not a qualified doctor, but his wide experience and his sense made him very useful. Mrs. Phillips hurried back to 27 Lambeth Road, and by half past seven Mr. Coppin was in the house. Lucy had tried giving the patient some milk and soda water, as easier to keep down than tea, but that had been vomited too. In one of the quiet spells Matilda had said, "I think I am dying. I should like to see my baby."

Lucy had gone downstairs and fetched Fred, who was asleep, out of Edgar's bed. The older child, who was awake, looked at her with silent apprehension. She carried Fred upstairs, and he woke as she brought him to the bedside. The smell of vomit and sweat was pungent, but the child only knew that this was his mother. Lucy lowered him toward her and she put her arms around him. Her face was like creased white leather. Then there was a terrible, fierce shaking, and he began to cry with fright. Lucy seized him up and was carrying him out of the room when Mrs. Phillips, followed by Mr. Coppin, came in.

Mr. Coppin knew that the patient had been treated by Dr. Graham for alcoholic poisoning, and the spasm before his eyes seemed to him entirely characteristic of delirium tremens—the shaking, the pains, the vomiting, the sweats. He hadn't heard about the pills, for Lucy was out of the room; or about the sense of oppression in the chest and throat. He faced only one of the seizures; he didn't observe the patient's perfect lucidity when the seizure passed. These symptoms might have warned him that the case was not one of delirium tremens. As it was, he had no doubts. Where he did judge correctly was in thinking that the girl was very near to death. He said he would prepare some medicine to help the vomiting, and Mrs. Phillips said her grandson should call for it at his office.

Edgar brought back the medicine, and Lucy administered a dose as the label ordered. The effects were shocking: a blackish color spread over the face and the eyes rolled wildly. Mrs. Phillips went off again to the doctor's office to beg Mr. Coppin to come back, but Mr. Coppin, having a great deal on his hands, and feeling sure that the patient was within an ace of death and that he could do no more, said that he could not come.

At some time after midday Dr. Graham arrived. When he was taken upstairs to the second floor, it was not only that the commotion and the crying out had stopped; there was a deep stillness over everything. The clear morning light filled the room, and Matilda lay on the soiled bed, motionless.

"About quarter to nine," Mrs. Phillips told him. "I wasn't in the room at the time."

"I was," said Lucy.

Dr. Graham had had a report from Mr. Coppin; it exactly confirmed his opinion that the woman had died of an epileptic seizure ending in heart failure, following the alcoholic poisoning for which he had been treating her. He told Mrs. Phillips where to register the death and where to find the parish authorities who would see to the burial. He wrote out the death certificate. "Delirium tremens followed by respiratory arrest." His exhaustion and his craving for sleep swept over him, blurring the small but vitally important space between the time, two days before the death, when he'd last treated her, and the death itself. He stated on the certificate that he'd attended the patient in her last illness.

The room was left to its silent inmate. They would try to clear up a bit before the laying-out woman came in from Lambeth Walk, but first Mrs. Phillips and Lucy took cups of strong tea, standing at the kitchen table. Meantime, there was Fred. Lucy dressed him and collected the rest of his little clothes in a parcel, and, Mrs. Phillips having been to the Lambeth Workhouse, they came from there and took him away. (The outcome was not altogether sad. A respectable family badly wanted a little boy, and they adopted him. At first he used to wake up in the night and cry and cry, but they were very kind, and it gradually got better and better, till it all faded away.) Some rent was still owing to Mrs. Phillips, to say nothing of consideration for wear and tear. There was nothing of Matilda's, about the rooms or in her tin trunk, that would fetch much, but Mrs. Phillips pawned the new boots. So ended the day of Matilda Clover's death, October 21, 1891.

CHAPTER 5

ON OCTOBER 22 THE inquest held at St. Thomas's Hospital on Ellen Donworth was concluded, the jury's verdict being death from poisoning by strychnine, administered by a person unknown. The case had become known locally as the Lambeth Poisoning Mystery, and as it had occurred in the red-light district, the interest of the local inhabitants who followed Ellen Donworth's way of life was acute and painful. Their fears were the more easily aroused since the unforgettable events of three years ago. Murders of prostitutes had not been, in the past, matters of public interest, but during the summer and early autumn of 1888 there had occurred six such murders, one after the other, so horrifying that they had aroused a national concern. The women had not only been murdered, but eviscerated, in a fashion of which the indecency was outweighed by its sheer ghastliness. All the killings had been in a small area of Whitechapel, a slum district, north of the river, it was true, but in circumstances which made them terrifying to prostitutes in every quarter. They had all been done under cover of darkness, with some so near to discovery that the murderer's agility and boldness were looked on as almost supernatural. No shred of evidence to say who or what he was had come to light, but the police had published facsimiles of a letter they had received whose writer claimed to be the murderer. He signed himself "Jack the Ripper," and the public at once adopted the name. Dimly lighted streets and dark entries had new alarms for women when they remembered it, and the murder of a prostitute now had a news value it would not have rated three years ago. The verdict of the coroner's inquest on Ellen Donworth was printed in several newspapers.

Dr. Neill found the story related at some length in three dailies and mentioned briefly in four more. He had all the papers on the table in his room; he scanned and scanned the paragraphs, going back to the ones he had already read. He was sitting at his window; when he raised his eyes from the newssheet he saw the wide, shimmering river and, beyond it, the Houses of Parliament. He looked like a wild animal occasionally lifting its head from the mass of entrails on which it was gorging.

The passion for cruelty which led to the act was equaled only by the devouring eagerness to hear people discuss it afterward, to gain a repetition of the sensation through realizing the impact the deed had made on others. This lust made him dissatisfied—irrational and absurd though it was—with the verdict: "person unknown." The burial would now be performed—had no doubt already been carried out—and the matter would sink into silence, uncompleted, unsatisfying. It must be made to yield something more; it must.

Though the terrain of Lambeth Palace Road and its neighborhood had a compelling fascination for him, it did not absorb all his attention. One evening toward the end of October, Dr. Neill made his way to the altogether grander region of Leicester Square, where, amid the streetlamps and lamps of carriages, an intensified cluster of lights showed the façade of the Alhambra Music Hall. This was a good many cuts above the Canterbury, especially as to the ladies of the night who paraded in its promenade in large black velvet hats and imitation diamonds.

Dr. Neill was preparing to pay his entrance fee and go in when a pert, elegant little piece, angling for his attention in the foyer, caught it very thoroughly. She was a girl of immense spirit, with the attractions of tameless energy. Her name was Lou Harvey, she said, and this was not true, for it was Louisa Harris; but she was living out at St. John's Wood with a young man called Charles Harvey, who had been a house painter, a glazier, a bus conductor, and was now subsisting comfortably on her earnings. The arrangement would break up when she was tired of him; meantime, he said, it was nothing to *him* how Lou got her living—who was he to order her about? She had made a real capture of this gentleman, and queer though he looked, she was pleased; he was very well dressed, had a quiet, experienced way with him and was ready to spend his money. They did not go into the Alhambra; there was no need to now.

He took her out to dinner at the St. James's Restaurant in Piccadilly, and then in a cab to a quiet little hotel in Berwick Street, off Oxford Street. There were numerous hotels in the West End where you could arrive without luggage and book a double room for the night, but you had to know which they were. The gentleman obviously knew his way about. Provided he was not eccentric, or ill, or mean, one client was very much like another, and Louisa had no objection to this one. ·

When she was putting on her clothes next morning, he took her face between his hands and said, "Those spots on your forehead—I'll give you something to clear them." He'd already told her he was a doctor at St. Thomas's Hospital, and she'd wondered what the other doctors would say if they could see him at that moment, but it was none of her business. He made an arrangement then and there to meet her that night at half past seven, down on the Embankment by Charing Cross underground station, when he would give her the medicine. She agreed, and in that instant a change seemed to come over his face, a look of smiling eagerness, keener than anything he had shown during the night—something . . . something she couldn't put a name to. This indefinable change caused her, unconsciously, to put a defense around herself. When he asked for her address, she said it was 55 Townshend Road, St. John's Wood, but actually it was 44. She wondered afterward why she'd given the wrong number; she supposed it was on account of her having lived there such a short time. Anyway, it didn't matter.

When she got home, about midday, and was having bread and cheese and beer with Charlie, she told him how she'd agreed to meet the gentleman that evening to get the medicine. Charlie paused with a hunk of bread and cheese halfway to his mouth. He was not decent, but he had sense. Taking medicine in the street off a man you didn't know might be all right—or it might not. Lou was his for the time being, and he determined to look after his property.

That evening, shortly after the appointed time, Lou and Charlie walked down Northumberland Avenue, the wide street leading from the Strand down to the Embankment, beside Charing Cross underground. On the left was the great railway bridge carrying the trains across the river into the Charing Cross main-line station; under it could be seen the next reach of the river, Waterloo Bridge lying across it; and beyond that, the great dome of St. Paul's, looming against rifts of dying light in the dark sky. All along the parapet of the Embankment the lampposts, their globes now glowing palely, marked the path to the right, leading to Westminster Bridge. Their light was enough to show where he stood against the low wall, in a caped greatcoat and a top hat, motionless, waiting.

Charlie, who had walked apart from her, now halted some yards away while Lou tripped forward. "I'm late," she said. She was never one to apologize.

"I've brought your pills," he told her.

"Am I to take them now?" she asked.

He caressed her upper arms. "Not till you've had a glass of wine," he said fondly. He took her by the elbow and led her toward the Northumberland Arms.

Inside, all was cheerful and noisy, bright with polished brass, and breathing out a rich spirituous smell. They had a glass of port each, and while they were drinking, an old woman in shawl and bonnet made her way about the saloon with a basket full of roses. "I would like some," Lou said, her bright eyes on the bunches.

"Certainly," he said gallantly. He paid for a bunch, and the woman handed it to her, saying, "Good luck, dearie."

Lou held the roses against the front of her jacket. She still had an inch of wine left in her glass, but he took her by the elbow again—she could feel him trembling—and led her out of the pub, down to the Embankment once more. Here a vendor was wheeling a barrow piled with pineapples and little round baskets of figs. The gentleman bought a basket and the vendor put it into a bag; he gave it to Lou and said she could eat the figs after she'd taken the medicine.

At the Embankment, he took the flowers and fruit from her and laid them on the parapet. Then he brought out of an inside pocket a little packet wrapped in tissue paper, from which he extracted two long capsules, which he put into her right hand. "Don't bite them, swallow them whole," he said.

In the half-darkness, concealed but not far off, Charlie, she knew, was standing. She cupped her right palm in her left and, opening her fingers, let the capsules drop into the lower palm. Then she covered her mouth with her right hand and made gulping, swallowing noises. The light was uncertain and his sight not good. He heard the sounds of her collecting saliva in her mouth, he saw the movement of her chin; he did not notice the two capsules drop from her left hand to the sidewalk, but some instinct of suspicion was roused in him. "Let me see your right hand," he said, and she held it out. "Now the left," he said. She showed that one—also empty.

There had been an arrangement that they should go on to the Oxford Music Hall, at the corner of Oxford Street and Tottenham Court Road; now he said he couldn't come with her after all, as he had an appointment at St. Thomas's Hospital at nine o'clock; but he gave her five shillings to cover her entrance money and a cab fare, saying he would meet her outside the Oxford at eleven o'clock and take her to the Berwick Hotel for the night. Now he'd find a cab and put her into it. Something about his face, very pale in the indistinct light, and his tall, batlike figure in the caped overcoat, roused her resistance. She had always been a girl who resented being pushed. She said tartly she'd get a cab for herself, and gathered up the roses and the fruit; so he said good night hurriedly and went toward Westminster Bridge, tall and made taller by his top hat, gradually disappearing down the long stretch of the lights and the shadows.

Charlie didn't want to go to the music hall, so she went by herself. She came out at eleven o'clock and scanned the foyer, but he wasn't there, so she went right out onto the brightly lighted sidewalk, where the traffic was passing. She darted her sharp glances all about, but she still didn't see him. She waited and waited, till half past eleven, but he didn't come, so she set out for St. John's Wood, with an eye to any adventure that turned up by the way.

HER CLIENT DID NOT enter St. Thomas's Hospital, but he did not go home either. His knowledge of the district was now so thorough, he could take his choice of ports of call, and sometimes visited two or three different places in one night. His voracious sexual appetite was not the only one he fed; he had on this night another secret delight. When he was at last nearing 103 Lambeth Palace Road, he gave himself up to it entirely. It was the imagining of Lou Harvey, in the middle of the music-hall audience, suddenly falling out of her seat, screaming, twitching in violent convulsions. As soon as her state was noticed among the general hilarity and the din, the bouncers would close on her, thinking she was drunk, and carry her out. In an interval of the trembling and sweating they could do this; during one of the seizures they'd have to put her down—on the dusty carpet of the foyer, perhaps. The uncontrollable screaming would frighten them and upset the customers; they'd have to get her away as quickly as they could. The useful bobby would be sent for, and a four-wheeled cab; he'd take her to one of the hospitals—St. George's in the Strand would be the nearest—and the inquest would be reported in the newspapers.

The excruciating pleasure of imagining these things was something so ravishing to his senses, it satisfied every secret want; but two ingredients were necessary before this feast could be enjoyed in perfection. One was that other people should talk over the matter with him, because repetition in his own mind, over and over again, made the pleasure pall, and to hear the topic discussed by someone quite unconnected with it gave it a fresh vitality, a new quality of stimulus. The other was a thrillingly delicious sense of approach to danger without being endangered, a sailing near the wind. It was something, on an adult scale of sensation, like a boy's game of runaway-knock, a loud tattoo that brought an exasperated householder to the door, which the boy could see opening from a safe distance down the street. These variations on the main theme filled his mind with piercing delights. He was exhilarated and satisfied, and would have been altogether content except for the still occurring headaches, which he had to damp down with opium; he had a prescription of his own, in which strychnine, cocaine and morphine were included, and which he claimed acted as an aphrodisiac. It worked well. He used to get it dispensed at Priest's every ten days or so.

The morning after his vision of Lou Harvey's death was too soon for a discussion with anyone; the corpse would be lying in marble stillness, as yet unexamined, in the mortuary of St. George's Hospital; but there were other enjoyments, stored up, each to be broached in turn.

Several days ago Matilda Clover had died, and as there was no word of an inquest in the press or among the local girls—and they would have been bound to know, with their instinct for danger like wild animals'—some doctor must have written a certificate saying she'd died of drink, as he himself had told her she would if she didn't stop. She would be buried by the parish—where, he didn't know, and it made no difference; but he wanted, avidly, to hear about those hours made vivid by agony. It was an enthralling mental spectacle, an indulgence into which he retreated, hour after hour, emerging from it with brain reeling. Then he would take a dose of his medicine and be prepared to mingle with the world again. But it wasn't enough that she should be quietly buried and that no accusations should point out the episode. That was waste—a losing hold of something brilliant, letting it sink overboard into the ocean of oblivion, of nothingness.

CHAPTER 6

TOWARD THE END of October, Miss Sleaper was in her sitting room on the ground floor; the door was open and she could be seen sitting at her little davenport, arranging bills and receipts. Dr. Neill, dressed for the street, his tall hat in his hand, paused in the doorway and Miss Sleaper looked up, her preoccupied expression changing to one of courteous attention. Dr. Neill came into the room with a very grave air and said, "Would you do me a favor, ma'am? You know the house, Twenty-seven Lambeth Road?"

"I don't actually know it," Miss Sleaper said. "I know whereabouts it must be."

"Then would you be so kind as to deliver a letter there, when I have written it?" Miss Sleaper was surprised. Why could he not take it himself?

"Who is it for?" she asked.

He came a step farther into the room and said, "I know a girl there, and I think she has been poisoned. I want to know if she is dead or not."

"Good gracious!" exclaimed Miss Sleaper. Then she said, "I really think you had better take it."

"Well, perhaps so," he said, and withdrew in a stately manner. At the door he turned. "I think," he said, "I think I know the person who poisoned her."

"Good gracious!" cried Miss Sleaper again. "Who do you think it was, then?"

He answered, "Lord Russell," and left the room, letting himself out at the front door.

Lord Russell! Good gracious! Since last May the newspapers had been full of this extraordinary case. Young Lord Russell had married a very pretty girl, but one whom anyone of Miss Sleaper's sense could have warned him not to choose. She had been living in a riverside villa with her mother, Lady Scott, the pair of them being, no doubt, on the catch for a young, wealthy, titled husband for the daughter. The couple had married last February, and in May, Lady Russell had petitioned for a judicial separation, urged on by Lady Scott, as wicked as an old witch. The case, based on the horrible accusation of homosexual vice, had completely broken down; the court had refused the countess's plea, but people in the know said that the poor young man hadn't heard the last of Lady Scott; so, indeed, it turned out. The matter was one of sensational interest, tempered only by the fact that it had gone on so long, and this amazing statement by Dr. Neill could not but startle Miss Sleaper's attention. She could scarcely credit it at first, but of course a great deal went on that ordinary people didn't get to hear about, and you never knew. The extreme respectability and impressiveness of Dr. Neill's appearance, the solemn way in which he'd spoken, made her sure he must have *some* grounds for what he'd said, but he might be mistaken and she hoped he was.

In any case, she could not deliver the letter; the rather peculiar neighborhood of Lambeth Road was uncomfortably near to Lambeth Palace Road as it was. Miss Sleaper earned her living as a respectable woman and she didn't want any dealings with the place. As she clipped her receipts together and put them tidily away in the desk, she wondered once again what Dr. Neill's occupation really was. Something took him out a great deal, sometimes keeping him out all night. Could he be a spy for the government, perhaps? She hardly knew the names of the mysterious callings, to one of which she vaguely supposed he might belong. Almost nothing, she now felt, would be too strange to be true about him. And look at this secret information he appeared to possess! Altogether, it was a little uncomfortable; but his payments were regular, he gave no trouble and his appearance was a credit to the house. Miss Sleaper was accustomed to lodgers who dressed respectably, but there was something about Dr. Neill's sleek black clothes and impeccable silk hat which marked him out even among crowds of men wearing the same sort of thing.

THE OUTER, CONVENTIONAL covering increased the acute pleasure which Dr. Neill felt in being able to go so near to danger protected by an impenetrable disguise. On Westminster Bridge, news vendors had their posters out, advertising the midday editions. He bought a paper at each end of the bridge, and another at the bottom of Whitehall; then he made his way slowly up Whitehall toward the Strand, and the restaurant where he often lunched.

The day was so fine that he thought he would first take a turn around Trafalgar Square, which lay before him, its fountains glittering in the sun. In the mood for a stroll, however, he first turned left down Cockspur Street. This was a street of superior buildings, leading to Pall Mall, where some of the most fashionable clubs were sited. As he walked on slowly, looking about him with interest, his eye was caught by a neat brass plate on an elegant doorway; it was engraved: G. CLARKE, PRIVATE ENQUIRY AGENT, 20 COCKSPUR STREET. A few paces farther on he retraced his steps and came into the square. The sunshine was so pleasant, he sat down on a bench at the foot of Nelson's column and opened one of his newspapers.

The editors were forever trying to attract public attention, and though the events they published might not always do this, certain topics were sure to appeal; these included the doings of persons much in the public eye, among whom was Mr. W. H. Smith, now, it was feared, in his last illness. This celebrated personage had become immensely rich by developing his father's stationery business and by securing the monopoly of railway bookstalls. He had entered Parliament, and when Disraeli made him First Lord of the Admiralty, Gilbert and Sullivan had lampooned him in *H.M.S. Pinafore* as Sir Joseph Porter, who became the "ruler of the Queen's Navy" without ever having been to sea.

His son, Mr. F. W. D. Smith, was in attendance at his father's bedside, and when, on November 6, a preposterous letter arrived addressed to him at W. H. Smith and Son's branch, 186 The Strand, it was opened by another director, Mr. Dyke Acland. The letter said:

"Ellen Donworth of 8 Duke Street, Westminster Bridge Road, was poisoned by strychnine. Two letters were found among her effects, incriminating you, which, if published, will surely convict you of the crime. If you employ me at once to act for you in this matter, I will save you from all exposure and shame, but if you wait till arrested before retaining me, I cannot act for you, as no lawyer can save you after the authorities get hold of these two letters."

The writer enclosed a copy of one of the letters. It read:

"I wrote and warned you once before that Frederick Smith, of W. H. Smith and Son, was going to poison you, and I am writing now to say that if you take any of the medicine he gave you for the purpose of bringing on your courses you will die. I saw Frederick Smith prepare the medicine he gave you, and I saw him put enough strychnine in the medicine he gave you for to kill a horse. If you take any of it you will die."

The covering letter said that if Frederick Smith wished to retain the services of H. M. Bayne, let him write accordingly on a slip of paper and paste it on a window at 186 The Strand.

Mr. Acland turned the letter over to the police, who asked him to exhibit a letter on the window, telling Mr. Bayne to call. This was done and a discreet watch kept on the premises, but no one answered the summons. The throng of passersby in the Strand was always considerable, and it was not noticeable that a tall, respectable, silk-hatted figure passed among them, stopping to glance, as many people did, at the paper pasted to the window, which was, after all, addressed to the public, and then walking on with a fleeting expression of avid amusement. It was not even noticeable that this figure repassed the window later in the day and then passed and repassed it again, as pedestrians frequently did in their day's concerns, and that each time he turned his head in the direction of Messrs. W. H. Smith and Son's.

THE LATE AUTUMN weather made walking in London very pleasant, especially in the West End, with its firm-surfaced dry roads and its white-flagged sidewalks scrupulously swept. One of Dr. Neill's walks along the Strand carried him across the top of Whitehall to the Mall, where he found before him the long, straight thoroughfare whose vista terminated in the stately rectangular block of Buckingham Palace. As he walked toward it he drew near, on his right, to Marlborough House, the London establishment of Edward, the jovial, formidable Prince of Wales, and his princess, the exquisitely lovely Alexandra. As he came level with the gates, a carriage and pair, the sun shining on harness and swiftly turning spokes, dashed up the Mall and turned into the courtyard. From the bustle at the great double doors, it was clear that the visitor was important. A lounger outside the palings, glad to show off his knowledge to the little group of loiterers, explained that this was Dr. W. H. Broadbent, one of the most distinguished of the London physicians. A member of the prince's household was down with typhoid fever, and Dr. Broadbent called every day to see the patient. His name was attached to the daily bulletin issued in *The Times.*

The top-hatted figure, moving away with stately gait, was one of the most respectable-looking among the small crowd of persons whom interest and loyal concern had gathered in front of Marlborough House. He walked down the Mall again in what amounted to a cloak of invisibility, but he was now assuming yet another defensive covering.

Dr. Neill's attitude to women, a merciless scrutiny that searched for what he desired, had operated a few days ago in a rather different manner. His encounter with the dark, pretty little woman with whom he'd got into casual conversation—an exchange so slight that it could have disappeared like foam on the tide, leaving her to go her way with barely a recollection of the tall, imposing stranger who had picked up the parcel she had dropped from among the many she carried as she entered Euston Station—had developed, taking delicate root, into a cup of tea in the Tea Room, over which Dr. Neill, as he introduced himself, regretted very much that the departure of her train for Berkhampstead would not allow her to stay and dine with him in the station's restaurant, the Pillar Hall.

Laura Sabbatini lived with her mother in Chapel Street, Berkhampstead, Hertfordshire, and came up fairly often to London, where she would do some extensive shopping, as she had been doing on this occasion. She was a dressmaker with a local but superior clientele, and she was beautifully turned out herself, with an elegance so quiet that it did not call attention to itself at first. She was a hard-working little creature, thirty years old; she had never had followers or suitors, being particular and liking to keep to herself. The magnetic, serious, not to say reverent attitude of this admirer made an impression on her that she had never felt before. When she had admitted that she was coming up to London again in two days' time to a concert at St. James's Hall, Piccadilly, and he had asked permission to meet her and accompany her, she told herself as the train bore her away into Hertfordshire that she did not absolutely expect to see him there, but of course it would be nice if he were to be.

He was; as soon as she entered the foyer he came forward, hat in hand, saying how much he'd looked forward to this, and that he'd got their tickets. During the hour and a half of Mozart, Weber and Berlioz, each was more interested in the other than in the music, though he could listen to music with pleasure and Laura really loved it. During the intermission and over the cups of tea which they again took in the Tea Room at Euston, she got to like him very much indeed, and he delighted her by asking, as he saw her into the train, when he might come down to Berkhampstead and call on her mother.

He continued to meet her on her visits to town, and the contrast between his outer life, with this charming and blameless element, and his inner life was made the stronger and headier. On a late afternoon he was walking, almost in a trance, down Regent Street. On the right hand a colonnade made the sidewalk a favorite resort for whores, to the annoyance of the superior shopkeepers, the glovers, milliners, habit makers and jewelers whose windows, behind the pillars, now glowed and glittered in the early dusk. As he paused on the curb before crossing Piccadilly, a pert face was lifted to his. Its owner, standing stock-still beside him, was clearly his for the asking. In a couple of seconds he was leading her to a public house in Air Street, the little turning off Piccadilly Circus. They had a glass of port and as they were coming out he began to suggest meeting her that night.

"Don't you know me?" she said.

He stared down myopically at her upturned face. "No," he answered. "Who are you?"

"You promised to meet me outside the Oxford Music Hall."

So many faces, with reddened mouths and hard, cold eyes, so many

provocatively perched hats with feathers and bows and flowers; in the last resort they were all the same. He said, "I don't remember. Who are you?"

She said, "Lou Harvey."

Lou Harvey! Impossible! The impish, smiling face seemed to carry an accusation, an impudent scoring off, impudent, dangerous . . . *dangerous.* He turned without a word and walked rapidly away, lost to sight in a moment.

Across the darkening sky the stars were coming out. Hanging overhead, traced in diamonds, the vast symbols silently asserted the connection between a character, good or bad, with the zodiacal sign rising at its birth. The sign of Gemini, under which he had been born on May 27, gave so much that could be forceful, exhilarating, attractive—a nervous nature that could enliven, a duality that could mean a double richness, an extraordinary power of living on the mental plane. This was the framework with which his mind had been endowed, and every asset played its part in the absolute dedication to evil. The resolute dwelling in a metaphysical state of thrilling sexual enjoyment made that state a reality. When he compared the fleeting impression of the figure he'd left in the lighted, noisy public house with the vision that had accompanied so many hours of his days and nights—of the girl shuddering and agonizing on the floor of the Oxford foyer and stretched out at last on a mortuary slab—the actual experience grew vague and pale. The further it receded in time, the less he believed it or even remembered it. Before long it had disappeared as though it had never been.

It was pleasant to have at this very time a harbor in the sweet, romantic friendship with Laura Sabbatini. His meetings with her became frequent—on shopping expeditions, at concerts and in her coming to tea in Lambeth Palace Road. He told her that owing to rather complicated legal business over a family inheritance, he called himself Thomas Neill, though his real name was Thomas Neill Cream. She understood that he possessed ample means, that he had a medical degree from McGill University, that he'd come to England partly on account of his health—to consult eye specialists—and partly from his deep respect for the teaching at St. Thomas's Hospital. He'd been a student there fifteen years ago and was now attending the medical school on a refresher course. It was not very long—in fact, it was barely a month from the time of their first meeting—before they became engaged. Laura had then thought him a little strange-looking. Now she had lost sight of that impression; in fact, she now hardly saw his outward form; she only recognized in him the purpose of her existence. His kisses did not mean so very much to her, but when she read his letters, signed, "Yours for ever, Neill," she felt she'd never lived till then.

His affection, such as it was, was sincere. In his letter to her after her acceptance of his proposal, he had said, "Your letter has brought a pleasure into my life that I have never before felt. May the giver [of] all good reward you, my darling, for the great happiness you have brought into my life, for I know not how to do so."

He enjoyed the feeling that she was in a completely different area of his mind from that occupied by others. Her charming little person, the freshness of her clothes, the perfect neatness of her small shoes and gloves, gave him great pleasure. She was touched by his admiring these points so much, not knowing the comparisons that made them so attractive. All this, and her unassailable respectability and complete innocence, not only made a delicious, refreshing contrast; they provided him with another ring of defense, making it possible for a man so accepted, so accounted for, to sail in still closer to the eye of the storm in perfect safety.

CHAPTER 7

When Dr. Broadbent, at his house, 34 Seymour Street, off Portman Square, came down to breakfast on November 30, the morning was so dark that the gas was lighted in the dining room. It shone on the Crown Derby breakfast service, all red and gold and indigo, and on the silver-plated covers keeping warm grilled bacon and mushrooms. He had not slept altogether well and had a heavy day before him. He glanced through the pile of letters beside his plate before putting them aside for detailed consideration—professional letters, checks, invitations, notes, advertisements—what was this?

"London, 28th November, 1891. Dr. W. H. Broadbent. Sir, Miss Clover, who, until a short time ago, lived at 27 Lambeth Road, S.E., died at the above address on 20th October (last month) through being poisoned with strychnine. After her death a search of her effects was made, and evidence was found which showed that you not only gave her the medicine which caused her death, but that you had been hired for the purpose of poisoning her." Some lunatic, who had got hold of his address. "You can have the evidence for £2500, and in that way save yourself from ruin. If the matter is disposed of to the police it will, of course, be made public by being placed in the papers, and ruin you for ever." Miss Clover—was the name an invention, too? "Now, sir, if you want the evidence for £2500, just put a personal in the *Daily Chronicle*, saying that you will pay Malone for his services, and I will send a party to settle the matter. If you do not want the evidence, of course, it will be turned over to the police at once and published, and your ruin will surely follow."

Dr. Broadbent laid down the letter momentarily while he reached for the ivory handle of the silver coffeepot. "It is just this—£2500 sterling on the one hand, and ruin, shame and disgrace on the other. Answer by personal on the first page of the *Daily Chronicle* any time next week. I am not humbugging you. I have evidence strong enough to ruin you for ever. M. Malone."

It was not the first time in a long career that Dr. Broadbent had received an insane letter. Usually such things were best ignored, but this one, since it contained an attempt, however preposterous, at blackmail, he thought it best to hand to the police. He sent his manservant with it and a covering letter to Scotland Yard. An inspector visited him the next day, and it was agreed that a personal announcement should be inserted in the *Daily Chronicle* and a watch kept on 34 Seymour Street to see if anyone called in answer to it. The announcement was published in the paper on December 4, and a watch kept on Dr. Broadbent's house for two days; when by midday on the second day no one had turned up, at Dr. Broadbent's own suggestion the watch was discontinued. He very soon forgot the episode of the absurd letter at his breakfast table.

BUT NOW IT WAS somebody else's turn. So far Lady Russell had failed in her petition for a judicial separation, but she and her mother were in a state of smoldering activity and it was understood that they were now considering an action for divorce. The papers, who felt that their readers could never hear too much of the countess's enthralling history, had reported that her ladyship was staying at the Savoy Hotel for the purpose of consulting her solicitors, the famous firm of Messrs. Lewis and Lewis. The first week in December she received a letter telling her that Lord Russell had been responsible for the death of a young woman called Matilda Clover, of 27 Lambeth Road, and offering to provide evidence of the deed. She was naturally surprised; and when—a beautiful apparition in her sable toque clasped with a jeweled aigrette, and her great sable muff—she next visited the senior partner of Lewis and Lewis, Mr. George Lewis himself, she brought the letter with her and gave it to him.

The case of *Russell* v. *Russell* was based on an attempt to convict Lord Russell of homosexual vice—difficult enough, in all conscience. A statement that he had murdered a young woman living in a dubious neighborhood would hardly assist Lady Russell and her advisers; but this apart, a lawyer of Mr. George Lewis's experience could see at a glance that the letter was valueless. He handed it back to Lady Russell, advising her to ignore it, and she restored it to the satin lining of her fragrant muff.

DECEMBER, WITH ITS opaque skies, its black frosts and cutting winds off the river, made most people spend as much time indoors as they could, but it caused no alteration in Dr. Neill's habits. He was still out for hours, day and night. He always had money to do what he wanted to do, but the funds left to him by his father were administered by trustees, and he was not satisfied with the scale on which they were being remitted to him. Letters of remonstrance received prevaricating replies; their demands were indefinitely postponed. A visit to the attorney's office in Quebec was the obvious remedy for someone who could afford the passage. A visit there, particularly in view of his approaching marriage, on the strength of which he could call for a large capital advance, would be a profitable undertaking, also a pleasant one. There were many memories of Canada, some enjoyable to relive for their own sake, some that would afford the always delicious sensation of having escaped from danger, which invested old haunts with an attraction that made the blood thrill.

His farewell meeting with Laura, to whom he explained the necessity for his departure, was tender and touching. He enjoyed it. He had drawn up a will, leaving her all his property, which he assured her was unalterable. She knew no more than most young women of legal matters and could not tell that no will was, or could be, so drawn as to be incapable of alteration. She valued this testimony of his love exceedingly. Other papers she kept in a little bureau in the drawing room; the will, with his letters, she kept at the back of the glove drawer in her bedroom chest, with the neat layers of kid gloves, exquisitely clean and smelling of violet sachets. He said he expected to return in about a couple of months; he promised to keep in close touch with her, and told her to write to him at Blanchard's Hotel, Quebec.

HE SET SAIL IN the *Sarnia* on January 7, 1892, and arrived in Quebec on January 20. What a host of impressions, past and present, rose up and occupied his mind! At first, however, none of this strange mental territory was apparent to the outside world. Dr. Cream seemed a visitor of impeccable respectability, a desirable guest for Blanchard's Hotel.

This was a well-run, comfortable establishment of a somewhat homely cast. Any visitors under its roof were inevitably thrown together by their use of the common sitting room. A visitor whose business brought him there at the end of February was Mr. John McCulloch of Ottawa, traveling salesman in coffee, spices, baking powder and extracts for the grocery firm of Messrs. Robert Jardine and Company of Toronto. Mr. McCulloch felt unwell a couple of days after his arrival, and Dr. Cream, whose acquaintance he had already made, took him into his own room to prescribe for him. Dr. Cream produced a suitcase which contained a number of bottles, and from these he gave McCulloch an antibilious pill and a blue pill. The effects were good. Their acquaintance developed, and Dr. Cream became quite confidential about himself, taking McCulloch on an expedition about Quebec to point out where he'd lived as a boy and where his father's place of business had been. That evening he showed McCulloch some indecent photographs. As he passed these to his companion he uttered a curious, mirthless laugh, a kind of bark. McCulloch had not lived to his present age without seeing such things, but he did not care for them and handed them back after a cursory glance.

The longer they were together, the more unwelcome the doctor's confidences became. It was not long before he told McCulloch that he practiced abortion. Although this was confessing to an extremely serious crime, punishable with a long term of imprisonment, Dr. Cream seemed to take it for granted that an experienced man of the world like McCulloch would see nothing in it but what was sensible and profitable.

One afternoon in March he asked McCulloch into his room to smoke a cigar. Once they were inside and lighted up, Dr. Cream drew out of his tin trunk a cashbox, and from this a widemouthed bottle, three inches long by one inch broad. One-third of it was filled with white crystals. "That is poison," he said.

"For God's sake!" exclaimed McCulloch. "What do you want with that?"

Cream said, "I give that to the women to get them out of the family way."

McCulloch stared at the bottle. "How do you do that?" he asked.

The doctor answered, "I give it to them in these." He took the lid off a round flat box of gelatin capsules. Because he put the lid aside, McCulloch could not see whose name was printed on the round white label or on a little purple one. While he was standing in dumb surprise, the doctor stepped back and drew something else out of the trunk. McCulloch for a moment couldn't imagine what it was—it looked like a torn bird's nest. Then he saw it was a large, bushy pair of false whiskers. "I use these," Cream said, "to prevent identification when operating." He gave an ogrelike smile.

The bedroom window was draped with thick white cotton lace. A cuspidor on a tripod stood in front of it. The chilly light of the afternoon made the scene more alarming than darkness would have done, or stage fire.

McCulloch was tough, and like many men he was prepared to put up with a good deal rather than come out into the open and find fault. But enough was enough, and when Dr. Cream began to say that for enjoying oneself with street women there was nowhere like the south of London, that he had sometimes had three in one night between ten p.m. and three a.m. and paid them no more than a shilling each, McCulloch grew first restive and then downright disgusted. Still, he did not refuse the doctor's society; that would have been difficult in a hotel with only one sitting room, and he was an interesting man if you could get him off the one topic. He seemed, for one thing, to know a good deal about musical instruments. He wanted to buy a violin, and McCulloch took him to a dealer. McCulloch realized, as he watched the negotiations for the purchase, that Cream handled the instruments with a knowledge and judgment altogether superior to his own.

They had some forthright talks about business. Dr. Cream had ordered a large supply of strychnine pills from the G. F. Harvey Company of Saratoga Springs, New York. He took strychnine and great quantities of opium and cocaine. When McCulloch said surely he was taking too much, Cream replied that he needed those amounts to keep his head quiet.

Since McCulloch was a salesman of spices and doing very well at it, it occurred to Cream that he himself might travel for the Harvey Company—be, in fact, their London agent. In an interview with his reluctant trustees, he told them that he should require some cash to set him up in this project, which would make a handsome return. But when he wrote to the Harvey Company with this proposition, they rejected it. They did not want a London agent. The refusal rasped him and put him in a frame of mind when he would, half in earnest, consider preposterous ways of making money.

On the evening of March 3 an American traveler came into Blanchard's to order dinner and book a room. Most of the clients were prosperous-looking, but this man had the unmistakable aura of wealth. His suitcases were of very fine leather. His heavy cloth overcoat was lined with mink, and a lynx-fur hat was pushed to the back of his head. Throwing down a scarlet-lined fur traveling rug on the counter, he took out a gold pocket pen to sign his name in the hotel register. He asked for a bottle of whiskey to be sent up to his room, and drew out his wallet. When the clerk told him civilly that everything should be put on his bill, he put it away again, but not before an onlooker had seen that it was stuffed with hundred-dollar bills. When the visitor was following his luggage upstairs, Dr. Cream said to the clerk, "Lot of money that gentleman carries about. Fifteen hundred dollars in that wallet, I reckon."

"All of that," said the clerk. "Two thousand, I guess. All right with us, not very safe in some places." The American guest departed next morning, and Dr. Cream, describing him to McCulloch, who had not seen him, ended by saying, "I ought to have had that man's money."

"How could that be?" McCulloch asked.

The other said, thoughtfully but with absolute conviction, "I could have given that man a pill and put him to sleep and his money would have been mine."

McCulloch said incredulously, "You would not kill a man for two thousand dollars, would you?"

Cream said, "I ought to have done it."

The words carried such weight of meaning, McCulloch was really frightened. Uttered in that tone by a man who traveled with poison in his suitcase, they made his blood chill. He slipped away, into the bar, and from there went up a back staircase to his bedroom. He had now made up his mind that he would avoid his fellow guest at all costs. He had only a day or two more to spend in the neighborhood, and he got away without any renewal of intimacy.

The rejection of his proposal by the Harvey Company and the disappearance, unscathed, of a man carrying two thousand dollars on his person set up an inflammation of resentment in Cream's mind. It needed some definite object to feed upon, and since having gained the advance from his trustees, he now turned his thoughts toward London and the dark enjoyments of which he had told McCulloch nothing, and devised a plan combining several satisfactions in one—namely, a plan to redress a grievance that had been inflicted some time before by a London hotel.

The Hotel Metropole, abutting on Trafalgar Square, was an expensive place with fashionable patrons; just at dinnertime its lounge and restaurant were always very busy, with guests streaming in and being conducted to the dining room. Many were going to the theater afterward—the men in evening dress, accompanied by women, tight-skirted, with sleeves puffed to enormous width, long white kid gloves, and sparkling ornaments quivering in their hair.

Between fetching drinks, seeing the diners to their tables and sending page boys for hansoms for those who had already dined, the waiters had no leisure to attend to the gentleman (not quite a gentleman) seated in the lounge, and his order for brandy and soda was answered with "In a minute, sir," by one waiter, who never came back, and ignored altogether by several more.

The sight of the parading throng, self-absorbed, chattering like parakeets, none of whom had so much as a glance to spare for the gentleman, was an impression that had not died. He thought very carefully and long, and finally he ordered five hundred copies to be printed of a leaflet, set out in the following terms:

Ellen Donworth's Death
To the guests of the Metropole Hotel.
Ladies and Gentlemen,
I hereby notify you that the person who poisoned Ellen Donworth on the 13th last October is today in the employ of the Metropole Hotel and that your lives are in danger as long as you remain in this Hotel. Yours respectfully, W. H. Murray.

As he had booked his passage to Liverpool on the *Britannic*, to sail on March 23, he had the circular dated London, April 1892.

HE HAD SEVERAL TIMES written to Laura and received her simple, affectionate, trusting replies. Among the pleasures alluring him to return to England, the prospect of seeing her was one—one, but not the keenest and most goading.

His passage being booked to Liverpool via New York, he took the opportunity to visit in person the offices of the Harvey Company in Saratoga Springs. He had drawn fourteen hundred dollars from his father's estate to finance him in setting up as a salesman for this firm, assuring the trustees that the appointment would bring in a substantial income; but the director who interviewed him repeated Mr. Harvey's original decision—he did not want the services of a London representative. However, it was agreed that he should receive a commission on any large orders for drugs received through him.

He had already, while in Quebec, bought from them through their Canadian agent a consignment of five hundred strychnine pills, and these had to be carried about in bottles in his suitcase; now, at the company's office, he saw and bought—although he was not to be their representative—a salesman's polished wooden sample case. It was divided into three sections; the middle one was upright and had on each side of it a row of twelve tubular bottles pushed through leather loops. The two other sections were flaps, each holding sixteen similar but slightly thinner bottles, also secured by loops. When closed, the side flaps folded up on the central double row of bottles and formed a neat, elegant container of beautiful workmanship. It might have been a jewel case. Of the fifty-six bottles ranged inside, seven contained strychnine pills, each weighing $\frac{1}{22}$ of a grain. These were medicinal doses. Eleven of them, making half a grain, might prove fatal; any number approaching twenty-two certainly would. Twenty of the pills could be stuffed into a five-grain gelatin capsule; of loose strychnine crystals, a capsule would hold five grains.

Dr. Neill regarded the case with great satisfaction. It was a most gentlemanly-looking affair, a nice thing to have among one's belongings, and as far as the purchase of strychnine was concerned, with the quantity he had laid in already, it would make him independent of chemists for a long time to come.

CHAPTER 8

THE LONDON AND North-Western Railway, carrying passengers from Liverpool to London, ran into its terminus at Euston Station. With a doubly interesting sensation, both of coming home and being about to embark on a new series of thrilling enjoyments, Dr. Neill came out under the station's enormous pediment supported on gigantic columns—erected in the 1840s during the short-lived fashion for "the sublime," of which the British Museum and the entrance to Euston Station were now the only reminders. Outside, the view dwindled to the shabby-genteel commonplace. In the rectangle misnamed Euston Square, Edwards' Hotel was already known to him. He engaged a room and dined, then he set out. When he crossed Euston Square he was lost to sight in the April dusk, made magically blue by the streetlamps and the lamps on hansoms and carriages.

He did not let Laura hear of his return immediately. This was April 2; two days, three days he must have, for retracing his haunts, forming new connections, scenting new quarries. He had told McCulloch of the pleasure grounds of South London—the Waterloo Road, Blackfriars Road, St. George's Road, Stamford Street. He retraced them all, with a prowling gait and an intent, businesslike air. It seemed easier than ever to take his pick—the throngs of young, healthful, stylish ones were so great. With some he went home; with others there were drinks and promises. Two attracted him particularly. They had come up from Brighton; they were both knowing and young—Alice Marsh was twenty-one and Emma Shrivell was eighteen. They all three got on very well over a glass of wine, and Alice Marsh wrote down their address for him—118 Stamford Street.

On the morning of April 7 he went out to Lambeth Palace Road and approached the front door of 103 with all the zest of a returned traveler glad to see old friends. He had not retained his room with Miss Sleaper, only said that he hoped she'd be able to accommodate him when he came back. She was not able to give him the same room, but one on the opposite side of the landing was available, and she was pleased—yes, pleased—on the whole, to have him again as a lodger. He arranged to come in with his luggage in two days' time.

Meantime, he paid the visit to Berkhampstead he had discussed last winter. The little terrace house in Chapel Street was just as he had expected it to be—small, neat, fresh, full of simple comforts. Mrs. Sabbatini, a pleasant, sensible old lady, had always wished to see her daughter married and felt sorry that Laura seemed to have no interest in the idea. She was prepared to welcome a fiancé, one who was mature and responsible, educated, reasonably well-to-do, it seemed, and who paid her the long-desired compliment of finding her daughter irresistible. At the same time Mrs. Sabbatini hoped they would not be in too much of a hurry to get married, and she was thankful to learn that he meant them to live in London, that he would not take Laura away to America or Canada. He was rather . . . rather strange-looking, but that did not matter, as Laura did not mind it.

In two days he became immediately, delightfully domesticated with them, relating to Mrs. Sabbatini a history of his parentage and the affairs of the family fortune which had made his recent journey to Quebec essential, and throwing out hints that he had sometimes been entrusted with commissions of a very confidential nature by the Home Office of the British government. He was not at liberty to say more at present, but the time would come when he would be able to explain himself completely. It all seemed, so far, solidly satisfactory with just a touch of mystery, which naturally appealed to Laura. A mother could not expect to control a daughter of Laura's age, nor did Mrs. Sabbatini feel any impulse to interfere.

While Laura played the piano, he sat listening with genuine pleasure. The mantelpiece above their little glowing hearth was festooned with crimson plush, bordered with ball fringe. In the middle of it stood a creamy alabaster statuette of the Virgin and Child under a glass shade. He occupied an armchair at one side of the hearth, and Mrs. Sabbatini one opposite. The air was full of the notes of one of Chopin's waltzes, very well played. The scene was one of both romantic and domestic comfort.

ON APRIL 9 HE arrived at 103 Lambeth Palace Road in a cab, with a pile of luggage. Within an hour he was settled in as if he had never been away, and his strange nocturnal habits also were resumed at once. At three next morning Miss Sleaper awoke at the sound of the front door's being shut, gently but with unavoidable shaking, and heard the heavy, cautious footfalls on her stair.

Stamford Street ran out of the Waterloo Road to join Blackfriars Road. It had once been an elegant thoroughfare, with a distant prospect of Westminster Abbey. Blocks of buildings now shut off that view, but the street still contained terrace houses, with front doors between fluted columns, and roundheaded windows whose glazing bars made pointed arches in the upper panes. Many of the houses showed peeling plaster and unwashed windows with dingy lace curtains behind them. The road surface was broken in places, so that wide puddles stood across it, and cabbage stalks, old newspapers and clotted rags lay in the gutters. It was not well lighted, the gas lamps being stationed at rather wide intervals. One of these stood immediately outside the door of number 118, on the right side of the street going toward the Waterloo Road.

At a quarter to two on the morning of April 12, Police Constable George Comley of the Lambeth Division was on a beat which led him through Stamford Street. As he came abreast of number 118, the front door opened and a young woman appeared in the dimly lighted interior. She was seeing someone out of the house, a tall, broadshouldered, middle-aged man, in a dark overcoat and a silk hat. The pallid light of the streetlamp showed him clearly. He had a heavy mustache but was otherwise clean-shaven, and he wore gold-rimmed glasses which caught the lamplight. After a murmured word the door closed and the visitor walked rapidly up Stamford Street toward the

Waterloo Road. No wonder he moved briskly, the constable thought; the early morning was very cold. The sight of a man leaving a house in that district in the early hours was common enough, and ordinarily the constable would not have thought of it again; but when his return beat brought him back down Stamford Street three-quarters of an hour later, he saw a four-wheeled cab standing outside number 118 and Constable Eversfield, also of the L Division, coming out of the house with a large bundle in his arms. Approaching, Comley saw that it was a girl—the girl he had seen bidding good night to the nocturnal visitor.

Constable Eversfield had been brought to 118 by the landlady's husband, Mr. Vogt, hurriedly dressed in trousers, overcoat and carpet slippers. At half past two he and his wife had been roused by terrifying screams outside their bedroom door. Alice Marsh, in her nightgown only, had come down for help and was now prostrate on the floor of the landing. Her limbs twitched in great leaps, she shuddered, the sweat poured off her; and as Mrs. Vogt leaned over her, wondering in the first panic-stricken moment what to do, wilder and more piercing screams sounded from above. She ran upstairs to the second floor, where the girls had rooms, and plunging after the frantic sounds, found Emma Shrivell not yet undressed, lying on the floor, her head against the end of the sofa. "Alice! Alice!" shrieked the victim, unaware that her friend could no longer help her.

Constable Eversfield, fortunately discovered in a few minutes, returned with Mr. Vogt, commandeering a cab on the way. Both made for the stairs but the policeman got up them first.

Alice Marsh's convulsions had ceased; she was lying face downward over the seat of a chair, but a fresh burst of screams was heard from the upper floor. Eversfield got up to Emma Shrivell's room. The dreadful jerkings, making the body inhuman, like a marionette, and the shrieks and moans lasted for a couple of minutes, during which time it was impossible to question her. When they died down and she lay in complete exhaustion, bathed in sweat, the constable bent over her and asked what she'd eaten. She gazed up at him, limp but clear-eyed, and whispered, "I had some supper, some tinned salmon and beer."

Eversfield said to Mrs. Vogt, "A glass of hot water with mustard in it, as quick as you can." The woman was back with the steaming glass in a few moments, and he held it to the girl's lips. She swallowed some mouthfuls; then a dreadful jump knocked the glass against her teeth. "See if you can get the other to take it," he said to Mrs. Vogt. When the girl was passive again, she told him that she had come up from Brighton and had been here three weeks. She and Alice had got to know a man called Fred; he was very bald on top of his head and wore spectacles and a silk hat. He had given her three long capsules.

Eversfield picked her up, carried her downstairs and into the cab. He placed her in a corner of the back seat. Comley appeared at that moment, and Eversfield said, "Another one inside, first floor. Quick." Comley strode upstairs and found Alice collapsed over the seat of a chair on the landing. Putting one of her arms around his neck, he heaved her up and carried her downstairs to where Eversfield stood beside the cab, waiting to take the girls to St. Thomas's. He deposited her on the woven rope matting of the cab's floor, leaning her against the seat, for it was obvious she could not hold herself in a sitting position. Then he leaned across and said to Emma Shrivell, "What have you had to eat?"

"Some tinned salmon and some beer," she said faintly. "And a gentleman gave us three pills each."

Comley said, "Was that the gentleman with glasses on, that you let out of the house at quarter to two?"

"Yes," she said, just above a whisper, but he heard her. "Long, thin pills," she said.

Eversfield got into the back seat of the cab with the two girls. There was no room for anyone else inside; Comley slammed the cab door and mounted the box beside the driver. With a lurch and a clatter of hoofs the cab started off down the cold, dark, silent street, above which the stars were shining. The distance up Stamford Street and York Road, across Waterloo Bridge, was not long and it was quickly covered, but Eversfield wished he could have had his colleague inside with him. Emma Shrivell gave shuddering gasps and moans, and fugitive gleams from streetlamps showed her white, rigid face shining with sweat. He was fearful of the spasms coming on again before they reached the hospital. Alice Marsh was quiet. No wonder. When the cab stopped at the hospital gateway, Comley jumped down from the box and opened the door, leaned in and drew her out. She was dead.

The helpers who now surrounded them took the responsibility from the young constables' shoulders. Alice Marsh was removed to the mortuary and Emma Shrivell carried to a ward. It was nearly three o'clock. Comley had mentioned the supper of tinned salmon, but he had also spoken about the long, thin pills. Dr. Wyman, the house physician, thought that the convulsions, the sickness and the sweating were consistent with poisoning by strychnine. He gave her an emetic and administered chloroform; this had been known in such cases to postpone the final collapse, but not to avert the end. It did not now; the eighteen-year-old girl died at eight o'clock; with brief intervals of respite, she had endured five and a half hours of agony.

Dr. Wyman said that an inquest must be held on both bodies. This was opened, but adjourned till the results of the autopsies should be received. *The Times* of April 13 carried a small announcement of the deaths of two girls lodging at 118 Stamford Street. The newspaper said that a police constable had taken them to St. Thomas's Hospital, that one had died on the way and one in great agony some hours later. It was thought that ptomaine poisoning from a tin of salmon might have been the cause of death.

Constable Comley had made his report to his superiors, and as a result Inspector Harvey had visited 118 Stamford Street, bringing away the empty salmon tin. The scraps of fish remaining in it were wholesome, so the theory of ptomaine poisoning had to be discarded; but the dying girl's reference to long, thin pills, and Constable Comley's description of the man he saw under the streetlamp in the small hours, were not discarded.

CHAPTER 9

MEANWHILE, EASTER CAME on; Easter Sunday, April 17, was bright and balmy, and 103 Lambeth Palace Road was springlike, with little bunches of flowers in Miss Sleaper's sitting room, open windows, and a soft breeze coming fitfully off the river. Early on Sunday afternoon Dr. Neill appeared in her doorway and asked for the loan of *Lloyd's Weekly*, a paper which he knew she took. He brought in so many newspapers himself—they were always lying about his room—that it was strange he should want to read other people's; but he said he wanted to see what *Lloyd's* said about the two girls who had been found dying in Stamford Street. He had heard they had an article on the case. Yes, Miss Sleaper said, she thought they had. She put the paper into his hand, and, thanking her, he said it had been a cold-blooded murder. Miss Sleaper was rather surprised; she didn't know it had been discovered to be murder, but, busy as she was, she made some vague, appropriate reply and went down to the kitchen.

Easter Monday was fine again. Young Dr. Harper was away over the Easter holiday, staying with friends in Bromley, and Miss Sleaper meant to give his rooms a special cleanup while he was out of the way. The cleaning woman swept the carpets, but Miss Sleaper did the dusting herself, very carefully, so as not to disarrange books or papers; and though he was leaving her so soon, she meant to give her usual polishing to his candlesticks and inkstand. His living room overlooked the river; sunlight poured through the two sash windows, and as she stood at his writing table, wiping delicately with a checked duster, she was calmly and contentedly employed.

Suddenly Dr. Neill came through the open door. She supposed he wanted something, and waited to hear, but he began walking casually around the room, examining it and asking questions about the occupant. What sort of a gentleman was Dr. Harper? Very quiet, she said. Very hardworking. Very pleasant. Dr. Neill looked closely at a row of medical textbooks. He was rather inquisitive, but she was there to see that nothing was interfered with. There were photographs of Dr. Harper's father and mother on the mantelpiece, and Dr. Neill said they looked a good class people. Miss Sleaper said the family photographed well; she had a very nice picture of young Dr. Harper himself in her album. She liked to have a photograph of everyone who stayed with her.

"Ah," said Dr. Neill, "you must let me see your album. I must give you a photograph of mine for it. Have you got it handy?"

Miss Sleaper said it was in her sitting room, if he liked to come downstairs. She went out, and in the act of following her he managed with uncanny swiftness to take in the heading and the signature of a note lying open under a glass paperweight with a colored view of Llandudno in its base—"Bear Street, Barnstaple . . . Your affectionate father, Joseph Harper." He was downstairs almost on Miss Sleaper's heels. The album lay on a beaded velvet mat on a small

table. "Here it is," she said. "I don't let it out of the room, it's got
so many old friends in it. But you're welcome to sit here and look
it through."

She left him with it. The photographs had names written under
them, in white ink on the dark pages. Walter J. Harper's likeness was
among the last, a serious-looking young man in a tweed jacket and a
straw boater hat, taken by a seaside photographer. He scanned it
avidly, pushing it upward with his thumb till it began to slide out
of the slot that held it. Not now, too risky. Reminded of the photograph, she might think of looking at it and find it missing. Presently,
when he could get access to the room again, it would be easy. After
some ten minutes of looking through the photographs, some in postcard form, of the royal family—the beautiful Princess of Wales in a
pearl-and-diamond dog collar, Queen Victoria driving to the Jubilee
Service at St. Paul's—and some of Miss Sleaper's own family, but for
the most part a procession of cheerful or solemn medical students,
he put the book back on its little table; and on hearing Miss Sleaper
come downstairs, he met her at the door and said the album was a
very nice memento.

The sight of so many photographs, most of them of undistinguished
young men, not worth the taking, reminded him of the Armsteads
and spurred him to a desire for some more studio portraits of himself. He had not seen the Armsteads since his return, and he determined to pay them a social call and book a sitting at the same time.
In their ground-floor living room behind the studio, opening into a
little greenhouse where pots of dry, dusty fern were kept, he found
Mrs. Armstead giving a cup of coffee to their lodger from upstairs.

John Haynes was not a man easy to place at first sight, rather ordinary, quite respectable. On closer acquaintance his calm, interested,
self-possessed air was seen to be consistent with his occupation—with
one branch of it, at least. His ostensible profession was engineering,
but he had sometimes been used by the government in minor aspects
of secret-service work. He had no employment at all at present, and
sat stirring his coffee in Mrs. Armstead's parlor in a frame of mind
that was on the lookout for something interesting.

The rather curious-looking visitor arrested his attention. The man
seemed disposed to be friendly, even confidential. Hearing that
Haynes had traveled in America, Dr. Neill volunteered that he him-

self was in London as an agent for the Harvey Company. The opportunities for meeting of two men living near each other, fond of company and masters of their own time, were frequent. Soon they were lunching together, dining together, in modest restaurants used by city clerks in Ludgate Circus, Fleet Street and the Strand; taking tea together at Mrs. Armstead's invitation; and spending some evenings in smoking and conversation in Dr. Neill's room in Lambeth Palace Road.

Haynes was half repelled, half interested by his new acquaintance. Dr. Neill seemed to be in an increasingly nervous state; he was extremely restless, continually shifting his legs even when sitting, always chewing tobacco or American gum, and pouring out anecdotes and reminiscences of a decidedly raw kind.

On the other hand, it was difficult not to believe, to a certain extent, in the man's presentation of himself as one of substantial means, an important executive, an experienced medical man; no doubt he was all that he claimed, but decidedly eccentric into the bargain.

As far as mere personal enjoyment went, Haynes would have been glad enough to receive no more of the doctor's overtures, but some vestigial professional instinct led him to keep up the intercourse, respond to conversations and accept suggestions for lunching or dining out together. With half his mind he thought the man interesting, and sometimes, in an odd way, companionable.

On April 20 Neill paid a pleasant visit of twenty-four hours to Berkhampstead. Laura's admiration, sympathy, devotion, were balm to him. On this occasion the Wednesday midweek service, a choral evensong, was held at the parish church, and she was charmed when her tentative suggestion that he should come with her was enthusiastically received. As she stood in the pew beside him, with his figure towering over her, she loved to hear his vibrant baritone and stopped singing to listen, till he gently shook her elbow, when she again produced her small, true soprano notes.

At home, the marriage plans were discussed warmly but vaguely. The wedding was to wait until his business as the Harvey Company's representative was fully established; that would be within the year at latest. Mrs. Sabbatini entered into Laura's prospects with affectionate warmth; she liked to hear her plans for a trousseau, but she was glad for her own sake that the event was not to be immediate.

Neill enjoyed every minute of the visit, but it was so charming, so innocent, so domestic, it sharpened his appetite for other pleasures. Four days after his return to London, on April 25, he sat at his window in Lambeth Palace Road, carefully writing a letter in his curious, thick black hand:

"Dr. Harper, Barnstaple. Dear Sir, I am writing to inform you that one of my operators has indisputable evidence that your son, W. J. Harper, a medical student at St. Thomas's Hospital, poisoned two girls named Alice Marsh and Emma Shrivell on the 12th inst., and that I am willing to give you the said evidence (so that you can suppress it) for the sum of £1500 sterling. The evidence in my hands is strong enough to convict and hang your son, but I shall give it to you for £1500 sterling, or sell it to the police for the same amount. The publication of the evidence will ruin you and your family for ever, and you know that as well as I do. To show you that what I am writing is true, I am willing to send you a copy of the evidence against your son, so that when you read it you will need no one to tell you that it will convict your son. Answer my letter at once through the columns of the London *Daily Chronicle* as follows:— 'W. H. M.—Will pay you for your services.—Dr. H.' After I see this in paper I will communicate with you again. As I said before, I am perfectly willing to satisfy you that I have strong evidence against your son by giving you a copy of it before you pay me a penny. If you do not answer it at once, I am going to give the evidence to the Coroner at once. Yours respectfully, W. H. Murray."

THE SMALL, EIGHTEENTH-CENTURY country town of Barnstaple, in Devonshire, on the estuary of the river Taw, was a very pleasant abode for an elderly doctor. Dr. Harper was happily settled there and looked forward to his son's arriving to take over a practice at Braunton, on the other side of the estuary, within easy driving distance in a dogcart. The son's science would be fresher than the father's, and the father's experience would be very useful to the newly qualified young man. He and his wife were thinking much of their son's coming when, on the morning of April 26, Dr. Harper opened a letter with a London postmark, addressed in an unknown hand. Besides the letter, the envelope contained newspaper cuttings. He first read the preposterous communication; then he examined the cuttings. One of them was from *Lloyd's Weekly*, with an account of the inquest then pending on Alice Marsh and Emma Shrivell; the others, from different newspapers, concerned an inquest on a girl called Ellen Donworth, who was found to have died by strychnine poisoning, "but how administered, there was no evidence to show."

Dr. Harper sat thinking for a few moments. As a doctor he was less surprised by this sort of letter than many of the laity would have been. The writing was peculiar; it was not uneducated, but the repetitiousness of the letter's wording showed that the writer was not cultivated. It was, on the face of it, an attempt at blackmail, but so ridiculous that it was scarcely worthwhile to trouble the police with it. He thought it unlikely that W. H. Murray would write again. If he did, and made himself a nuisance, that would be time enough to call the police in. He put the letter and its enclosures away, meaning to show them to his son when the young man came home.

Several days' issues of the *Daily Chronicle* were scanned by an eager searcher, without result. The bait which had been flung seemed to have lost itself without bringing in any hoped-for, delicious catch. The emptiness of the mental scene, giving a sensation of gnawing hunger and one of resentment, as of being snubbed and ignored by the family of the pale, superior-looking young man whose quietness Neill was now ready to ascribe to superciliousness, began to set up an inflammation in his mind which needed drastic action to allay.

ANOTHER VISIT, OF three days, to Berkhampstead on April 30 was soothing and deeply enjoyable, but Laura, delighted as she was to do anything for him, was surprised when he asked her to write some letters at his dictation, and still more surprised at what the nature of the letters turned out to be.

She sat at the little writing table in the sitting room and he stood behind her, dictating in his strong, soft voice, slowly but without a pause, and the effect was almost hypnotic. In her pretty hand, she wrote:

"London, 2nd May, 1892 [To Coroner Wyatt]. Dear Sir, Will you please give the enclosed letter to the foreman of the Coroner's jury at the inquest on Alice Marsh and Emma Shrivell, and oblige, Yours respectfully, Wm. H. Murray."

Her surprise turned to consternation as she took down the words of the second letter:

"To the Foreman of the Coroner's Jury, in the Cases of Alice Marsh and Emma Shrivell. Dear Sir, I beg to inform you that one of my operators has positive proof that Walter Harper, a medical student of St. Thomas's Hospital, and a son of Dr. Harper, of Bear Street, Barnstaple, is responsible for the deaths of Alice Marsh and Emma Shrivell, he having poisoned those girls with strychnine. That proof you can have on paying my bill for services to George Clarke, detective, 20 Cockspur Street, Charing Cross, to whom I will give the proof on his paying my bill. Yours respectfully, Wm. H. Murray."

The third letter was equally disturbing:

"To George Clarke, Esq., Detective, 20 Cockspur Street, Charing Cross. London, 4th May, 1892. Dear Sir, If Mr. Wyatt, Coroner, calls on you in regard to the murders of Alice Marsh and Emma Shrivell, you can tell him that you will give proof positive to him that W. H. Harper, student, of St. Thomas's Hospital, and son of Dr. Harper, Bear Street, Barnstaple, poisoned those girls with strychnine, provided the Coroner will pay you well for your services. Proof of this will be forthcoming. I will write you again in a few days. Yours respectfully, Wm. H. Murray."

Her exclamations as she wrote he quelled by saying, "Hush!" and continuing to dictate.

But as she wrote the last signature, "Wm. H. Murray," she raised her eyes and said, "But Neill! *Have* you got this evidence?"

"A friend of mine has," he answered darkly. "He is a detective."

"Why do you want the letters signed Murray?"

"Because that is his name."

"But—why do *you* have to write for him? What is it all about?"

He put his hand, fondly but with heavy pressure, on the nape of her neck, the little neck enclosed in a lace gorget, held up to her ears by tiny stays of transparent celluloid. "I'll tell you all about it someday," he said.

She believed fully that she would presently know about it all. She remembered those vague, mysterious statements he had made about himself. It all fitted in, and seemed to be leading to some dark, overshadowing event. She could almost have shivered, but to disobey him was impossible. He laid three envelopes before her and made her address them. "That's my good girl," he said. He collected letters and envelopes and, opening his coat, put them inside his breast pocket.

Dr. Wyman, the house physician at St. Thomas's who had received the dying Emma Shrivell and the dead Alice Marsh, had stated at the inquest on April 14 that in his opinion both deaths were due to strychnine poison and that in each case an analysis of the contents of the stomach must be made. The police remembered that strychnine, administered by some person unknown, had been said to have caused the death of Ellen Donworth, who had died last October. Inspector Harvey of L Division, who had seen her in agonizing convulsions on her bed in Duke Street and had heard some of the last words she uttered, was instructed to institute a house-to-house interrogation in the district, particularly those where prostitutes lodged, to see if anything could be found that would throw light on these three deaths, occurring within the past six months, all ascribed to this poison, administered by an unknown hand.

Harvey instructed several policemen to investigate the Lambeth district, and among them, Sergeant Ward returned with the report that Mrs. Robertson, of 88 Lambeth Road, now had in her service a maid of all work, Lucy Rose, who had previously been in service at 27 Lambeth Road, and knew something about a woman who had died there in great agony, but there was nothing mysterious about that death, she'd died of drink, as everyone had always said she would.

"Very likely," Sergeant Ward said, but he'd just inquire. Lucy Rose was not in the house that day, but they expected her back tomorrow. Sergeant Ward returned on April 27. This time he saw the straightforward, valiant little creature, and the report he carried back convinced Inspector Harvey that he must go himself to interrogate the girl.

The following day, April 28, he heard and took down everything Lucy Rose could tell him about the death of Matilda Clover. Lucy said Mrs. Phillips declared she'd heard nothing about poison; it was drink—what the doctor had told her she'd come to. She'd drunk a bottle of brandy that very evening; but Mrs. Phillips hadn't been in the room all the time, and Lucy, who had, heard the patient say that the man Fred had given her pills. Though Matilda Clover had been buried under a certificate saying she'd died in delirium tremens followed by respiratory arrest, this evidence made the certificate highly suspect. Inspector Harvey made a report to the Home Office, and an order was issued for the exhumation of Matilda Clover's body.

She had been buried in a parish grave in the parochial cemetery at Tooting, and several coffins were now deposited on top of hers. On May 5 the work of exhumation was carried out. From among others like it, her plain deal coffin, with a metal plate on it inscribed M. CLOVER, 27 YEARS, was heaved up to ground level by Lambeth Cemetery workmen and carried to the cemetery mortuary. The next day the lid was unscrewed and the shrouded body taken out and laid on a slab. The head was covered with plentiful brown hair. The face was much marred, but Matilda Clover's clothing was perfectly recognizable by the undertaker's foreman, who had made the coffin and put the body inside it. It was unpleasant work, naturally, but the men were accustomed to their work's being unpleasant.

Now it was the turn of two very different actors. Dr. Thomas Stevenson, lecturer on medical jurisprudence at Guy's Hospital and analyst to the Home Office, assisted by Mr. Dunn, senior demonstrator at Guy's Hospital, approached with their paraphernalia. In their shirt sleeves, protected by large rubber aprons, under the thickened white light of a skylight of ground glass, they made their incisions and removed brain, duodenum, liver, kidneys, spleen and heart. These organs were put into large-mouthed, stoppered glass jars, and the jars placed in a wicker basket padded with straw. The mortuary attendant brought two enamel basins and a large enamel jug full of hot water. The doctors took towels and pieces of carbolic soap out of their bags and washed their hands very thoroughly.

CHAPTER 10

THE EXHUMATION HAD BEEN carried out without any information to the public; canvas screens had been placed around the grave and there were apparently no loiterers in the grounds, but news of the matter traveled over Lambeth. Dr. Neill said to Miss Sleaper one morning that it was a good thing she hadn't gone to inquire after the girl who'd died at 27 Lambeth Road, as he had heard there was to be an inquiry into that matter. He said nothing more, but maintained what seemed meant to be an expressive silence. Miss Sleaper, however, did not ask any questions. She did not want to hear anything more about the matter.

A few days later, about May 8, Neill came in at the front door and walked straight in at the open door of her sitting room. He seemed in a state of great excitement, and exclaimed, "Do you know who poisoned those girls in Stamford Street?"

"No," she said, staring at him blankly. "Of course I don't."

He said, "If I tell you, you are not to tell anyone." Before she could reply, he went on. "It was Mr. Harper."

Miss Sleaper for a moment was pale and speechless with shock. Then the blood flowed back into her cheeks and she found her voice. "What a fearful accusation to make against anyone!" she cried. "How do you know?"

Dr. Neill replied somberly, "The police have proof of it. I have a friend who is a detective."

Miss Sleaper exclaimed that Dr. Harper was the last man in the world to do such a thing; but Dr. Neill said very gravely that the girls had had a letter, warning them that Dr. Harper meant to poison them, and that they must not take anything he gave them. This letter was in the police's possession.

Miss Sleaper put her hands to her temples. It must be all some horrible mistake—it must be! But she felt as if the walls were going around with her.

Dr. Neill walked impressively out of the room. Miss Sleaper wanted to cry; she felt helpless in the face of something obscure and frightening and cruel. What it was she could not say, nor what the right of it might be. She looked in a dazed way about the room, seeking comfort in its familiarity. A pile of *The Strand Magazine*s lay on the whatnot. One of her last year's young gentlemen had left them with her, saying that they had stories in them by a doctor which were having a great success, she'd be interested in them; but Miss Sleaper was not much of a one for reading, and they'd not been touched.

The stories were called "The Adventures of Sherlock Holmes." Dr. Conan Doyle had, for some reason, chosen to exalt his great detective at the expense of Scotland Yard. In the adventures, Inspector Lestrade of the Yard usually played a foolish part, to point up Holmes's brilliant qualities. However, in spite of the enormous popularity of the stories, the reputation of Scotland Yard with those who knew anything about its work stood extremely high.

John Haynes, whose career had often brought him into contact with the police, had some personal friends in the force, one of whom was Detective Inspector McIntyre of Scotland Yard. Haynes used now and then to stroll from Westminster Bridge Road across the bridge and enter the red-and-white striped building with the swelling turrets, to have a chat with his friend if McIntyre were not busy; and sometimes Inspector McIntyre, when off duty, would call on him at the Armsteads', when, as often as not, Mrs. Armstead would make tea for all the party. On one or two occasions they had discussed Dr. Neill. A rum stick, they all agreed. Inspector McIntyre, as was his way, listened, stirred his tea and said nothing.

CONSTABLE COMLEY HAD always felt that the significance of the man who was let out of the door of 118 Stamford Street, three-quarters of an hour before the girls there had been found in their death agonies, had not been pursued as it ought to have been. True, it was almost impossible to see how to proceed; to go about looking for him without a clue would be looking for a needle in a haystack. But the characteristics of his appearance were so definite and striking—the height, the build, the mustache, the spectacles, the rich, somber clothes, and something . . . something indefinable but immediately recognizable —that if Comley were ever to see him again, he was sure that he would know him instantly. Not only this; he was able to give such a graphic description to his superior, Sergeant Ward, that Ward was sure he, too, given half a chance, would recognize him.

On the evening of May 12, Constable Comley was on patrol in Westminster Bridge Road. The sky was now dimmed with dusk, but the illuminations outside the Canterbury Music Hall were already alight. On the sidewalk the patrons were converging toward the entrance, and in the road, just off the curb, a string of whores in differing degrees of elegance, shabbiness and dirt were hovering.

Comley, standing alone on the sidewalk on the opposite side of the road, inconspicuous among the crowd, stopped dead—then went very slowly on again. On the street outside the Canterbury was the man they were looking for. A felt hat, a caped evening overcoat, a pale face with a heavy mustache, and spectacles that glinted under the Canterbury lights; he was watching the women with an intent, avid stare, and from time to time prowling with slow step up and down the front of the music hall. When a woman approached, the man would scan her for a moment, then turn away. In half an hour's time he took himself off, going down the road in the direction of Westminster Bridge. It was quite dark now, and the constellation of lights over the Canterbury was brilliant. Comley hesitated whether to follow. This particular beat was apt to be rowdy and needed to be policed. He spoke to the man who stood outside the Canterbury to call cabs. Did he know the gentleman who was walking away? No, not to say *know*, the man said, but he saw him there often enough. So, Comley thought, they would know where to look.

The usual disturbance in front of the music hall now broke out, a jostling among a crowd who were tipsy. It would spread unless broken up. It was clear he couldn't leave the spot for the time being; but at nearly eleven o'clock a small urchin, barefoot, in ragged trousers and shirt, ran up to him and squeaked out, "You Constable Comley? Sergeant Ward wants for to see you, this end of the bridge." He started to run back, beckoning Comley on with a toss of the head.

"I'll find him," said Comley, advancing.

"Oh no you don't," cried the child shrilly. "He's to give me six-pence for to bring you." He ran on, stopping every so often to look back and make sure Comley was following.

They came out onto Westminster Bridge, dazzling on the dark water with lamps and surrounding lights. There stood Sergeant Ward by the left-hand parapet. He put sixpence into a grimy little paw, and the boy vanished as if into the earth. Ward pointed across the bridge to the public house that stood at the corner of Westminster Bridge Road and Lambeth Palace Road. "Do you see him?" he asked.

The play of lights at first made it difficult; then he saw that the man was there. "That's him," he said.

"I've seen him already tonight, outside the Canterbury."

"I was sure it was," Ward said, low-voiced.

As the man stood in a patch of light thrown on the sidewalk through the swing doors of the public house, twirling his walking stick and looking about him, a hard, bony, handsome creature with a feather boa around her neck and two red roses in her hat engaged him in talk. She then moved off with a jaunty step, and the tall, dark figure moved off after her, walking close behind her.

The two policemen swiftly and quietly joined the pursuit. It led them down Westminster Bridge Road into St. George's Road, a street of small but solid, respectable houses, off which five or six mean streets ran parallel with each other. Down one of these, Elliott's Row, the couple went, almost disappearing in the dark; but the watchers saw that they went into number 24 and the door closed behind them.

The policemen, almost blotted out in the deep shades of an ill-lighted street, stood a little apart from each other, waiting. A few hundred yards away lay Newington Causeway, with the famous public house the Elephant and Castle, its façade all over colored lamps, fronting it. Down the wide thoroughfare went a string of lamplit vehicles. The sky above reflected the lights of London. The night scene was nearly as bright and busy as the day, but in Elliott's Row, so near at hand, silence reigned, and almost total darkness.

The wait was very long, and now and again they moved softly to ease cramping muscles, but they felt no fatigue; a slow-burning excitement kept them alert. An hour and a half later the door of 24 opened on a crack of light and the unmistakable figure came out. They stood stone-still against a gatepost on the opposite side of the road, and when the quarry had reached the end of Elliott's Row, they started after him. In the hush of night his steps could be heard echoing on the flagged sidewalk; theirs were almost soundless.

The trail took them up St. George's Road into Lambeth Road, into Lambeth Palace Road, beside the slow-moving, darkly gleaming river, past the archbishop's palace, under the lee of St. Thomas's Hospital to a neat terrace and a small house, now closed up for the night. From the other side of the road they saw their prey stop, take out a key, ascend the steps and let himself in. A moment later they approached, and from the bull's-eye lantern hooked to his belt Sergeant Ward shone a beam on the brass figures above the brass knocker on the front door: number 103—103 Lambeth Palace Road.

CHAPTER 11

THE ARMSTEADS WERE sociable people, and glad to see any friends of Mr. Haynes's. Inspector McIntyre, they felt, was an addition to any circle, and as for Dr. Neill, well, he was too, in his own way, though Mrs. Armstead was beginning to feel that his presence was a little oppressive. He would sometimes sit like a statue, with an intent

look at you in those crossed eyes behind his spectacles; at other times he would shift about in his chair, or come all over trembling, as if he were going to be ill. She did not think the less of him for it—it added to his impressiveness—but it was sometimes disconcerting.

At eleven o'clock one morning about May 14, Mrs. Armstead was dispensing coffee, as she often did. She, her husband, Mr. Haynes and Dr. Neill were all in the ground-floor sitting room. As she passed the window that gave onto the Westminster Bridge Road, she noticed a man in a shiny blue serge suit, a celluloid collar and a brown billycock hat, leaning against a lamppost and gazing fixedly in her direction. "Will!" she said. "That man is watching the house, I'm sure."

Mr. Armstead went to the window and Haynes followed, looking over his shoulder. "It looks like it," he agreed. "Well, he's not doing us any harm."

Neill had also stood up to look out, but had sat down again. When he had left Lambeth Palace Road an hour ago, that loiterer had been leaning over the parapet, looking at the river.

The two men came back to the table. "Is it you he's after?" Haynes asked, not seriously thinking that it could be.

"Certainly not," said Dr. Neill in stately tones. Then, as if the words were released by a spring, he exclaimed suddenly, "What a dreadful murder that was of the two girls in Stamford Street!"

"Dreadful," said Mrs. Armstead. "But girls like that— What do they expect to happen to them, sooner or later?"

"Well, well," said Dr. Neill with a patronizing air. "I don't think poor Alice Marsh and Emma Shrivell deserved anything quite like murder."

"Did you know them?" demanded Mrs. Armstead, all agog.

"I knew them well," he answered solemnly. "They used to solicit up on the bridge of an evening."

When Haynes and Neill left the Armsteads' the man had abandoned the lamppost, but he was leaning against some railings a little farther down the street.

That night Haynes spoke to Detective Inspector McIntyre and asked him if the Yard were keeping his friend Dr. Neill under observation. McIntyre said prudently, not so far as he knew. He had better make inquiries in the Lambeth Division.

Next day, Haynes met Neill for lunch in a restaurant at Ludgate Circus. The air inside was filled with the rattle of dishes on marble-topped tables, the scraping of bentwood chairs with perforated wooden seats, and outside, with the clanging bells of trams and the shouts of newsboys hawking midday editions. Haynes said as soon as their plates were set before them, "Why didn't you tell me yesterday you were being watched? What is this all about?"

Neill said with portentous seriousness, "They are watching me because they've confused me with a doctor who used to lodge in the same house."

Then he began a narrative so extraordinary, so compelling, so convincing, that at last Haynes said, "Do you mind if I take down a few notes?"

Neill said, "I recommend you to, if you want to investigate the matter."

Haynes, in a dog-eared notebook with marbled covers, wrote down with a stub of indelible pencil:

Walter J. Harper, student at St. Thomas's, at one time well known among a low class of people, lived at time of murder at 103 Lambeth Palace Road; father an M.D. at Barnstaple (B. St.); been supplying son with ample means while in London, promising son partnership on account of W.J.H. got girl at Mutton's, at Brighton, in trouble some time back; procured abortion for her. Stamford Street girls aware of this. H. visiting them, they threatened him, blackmail, victims. W.J.H. weeks before tried to purchase strychnine, telling him of his trouble, asking what he could do under the circumstances, be well to get rid of them; person suspecting wrote girls warning, anonymous letter; is fairish, 5.8, slim, thick brown moustache, haughty and distant in manner, gentlemanly. Ask Sidney Jones, consulting surgeon, Thomas's. Issued invite to H. to wedding of daughter. Left day before inquest suddenly, leaving property behind, 118 Stamford Street, Mrs. E. Vogt. Did girls receive anon. letter before affair?

When Haynes had written this down feverishly, his notebook wedged between covered dishes and glasses of ale, he raised his head, gazing at his companion in a stupefied manner. Neill said with an air of authority, "And here is his photograph." He held it out across the table—a young, reserved, tranquil face under a straw boater. Watching his companion's look of amazement, Neill went on, "Wouldn't think so, would you? But those weren't his only victims. He was responsible for Ellen Donworth, Matilda Clover and Lou Harvey."

The names of Donworth and Clover were now familiar to Haynes, but who, he asked, was Lou Harvey? Neill said, "A girl he poisoned so that she fell down dead in a music hall—the Oxford, or the Royal, I don't remember which," he added carelessly. Then he said to his still astounded companion, "If you want to go into all this, I'll take you to where some of them lived and you can inquire." A devouring eagerness seemed suddenly to possess him. His finger joints began an uncontrollable tattoo on the table. "We'll go now," he said. "We'll pick up a cab." With fumbling eagerness he took out his purse and summoned the waitress.

In Ludgate Circus he hailed a four-wheeler and gave the address of 27 Lambeth Road. The girl who lived there, he said, had been poisoned with strychnine. She should be exhumed and the poison would be found. When they were put down, he said to Haynes, "Go and knock. Say to whoever comes to the door that you want to inquire about the young lady who lived here last autumn and was poisoned."

Mrs. Phillips had found that she couldn't let her two top rooms for months after Matilda Clover died. She had got a tenant for them at last, but it had been an anxious time. When a gentleman appeared on the doorstep saying he wanted to inquire about Matilda Clover, she was horrified. "Are you the newspapers?" she demanded faintly.

"No, madam, no," said Haynes courteously. "I only wanted to make a few inquiries for a friend of mine." She looked past him and saw a tall figure standing a few paces away on the sidewalk, looking at her intently.

"No," she said, "I've got nothing to tell you," and shut the door firmly.

"That is significant, is it not?" said Dr. Neill. "Now we will investigate St. John's Wood."

The District Railway took them to Baker Street, and from there, a cab skirting Regent's Park brought them up Wellington Street into St. John's Wood. They dismissed it at the corner of Acacia Road and

Townshend Road, where the houses were square ones of chalk-white stucco set among greenery. Number 55 Townshend Road was a charming, low-pitched one, with a French window on each side of the pillared door. It was clearly in very good hands. The visitors were surprised. Had they gone on to number 44, a block of peeling plaster with an untidy garden, they would not have been surprised at such a one as Lou Harvey occupying its ground floor back. At number 55, Neill stayed at the wrought-iron gate while Haynes went up the neatly graveled path.

The elderly lady who opened the door was at first uncomprehending, then alarmed, as she listened to Haynes's apologetic questions—a young lady, Miss Lou Harvey, last October, died by poisoning in a music hall. She saw a somewhat sinister figure standing beside her gate, tall, massive, motionless, staring through spectacles. Fright was succeeded by indignation. "I don't know what you're talking about!" she exclaimed, and shut the front door with a bang.

It was a nice day for a walk, and the two men strolled back toward Regent's Park. In spite of their having missed on both barrels, Haynes was convinced that there was something afoot, something serious. He said as they walked on, "Why don't you go to the police?"

Neill looked cunning. "That would be a fool's game," he said. "There's more money to be made down at Barnstaple."

Haynes was now really shocked. "Look here," he said. "You can't behave like that. If you don't go to the police, I shall."

Neill appeared to consider. "Very well," he said. "I can't prevent you. Give them the information about young Harper, but keep my name out of it."

The deaths of Ellen Donworth, Alice Marsh and Emma Shrivell had all, after postmortem analyses, been ascribed to poisoning by strychnine; the exhumation of Matilda Clover had been ordered, and the results were awaited. Now here was John Haynes with a statement that another young woman had met her death from poisoning, and that all the deaths had been brought about by a young doctor, newly qualified at St. Thomas's, now in practice in Devonshire.

SIR MELVILLE McNAUGHTON, the head of the Criminal Investigation Department at Scotland Yard, had all the available information pooled and at the disposal of himself and his personal assistants, but much of the work was done by detectives who had been instructed to pursue a particular line without having, for the time being, all the data in their hands, and these men were the backbone of the investigation.

The investigators wore civilian dress, usually of a shabby, commonplace kind, and were known as plainclothesmen. They looked as unremarkable as posts and paving stones. Their art was to mix with the crowds in pubs and street markets and to get up conversations at back doors and area entrances. They could not be seen to write down what they heard; it would have unmasked them immediately. They carried the information in their heads as they made their way back to headquarters by long, circuitous routes, stopping often to watch street sweepers' carts loading, or a string of barges going under a bridge.

When these men had told their seniors where information might be picked up, inspectors or police sergeants or constables would visit houses or localities and put questions with overt authority.

There was something about Detective Inspector McIntyre which invited confidence; he was pleasant to talk to. When Neill met him in Westminster Bridge Road, coming away from the Armsteads', as he himself was going to drop in on Haynes, Neill stopped him on the sidewalk. The visits the day before to 27 Lambeth Road and 55 Townshend Road had rekindled an unholy excitement that mounted as he saw the inspector. With an almost delirious impulse, he said that he had a complaint to make. He was, he said, a salesman for the products of the Harvey Company, and he was being followed by the police. It was some foolish mistake, of course, but it was injurious to him in his business, and he must ask Inspector McIntyre to look into the matter and release him from this annoyance. McIntyre said he was sorry to hear of the inconvenience, and undertook to make inquiries. He did so, and the inquiries he made about Dr. Neill of 103 Lambeth Palace Road brought in the information that Constable Comley of the L Division thought he was the man whom Emma Shrivell had let out of the house in Stamford Street three-quarters of an hour before she was taken with the pains of death, on the early morning of April 12.

Inspector Harvey of the L Division had been alerted to the Lambeth poisonings ever since last October, when he had found Ellen

Donworth lying on the sidewalk outside the Lord Hill. Chief Inspector Mulvaney of Scotland Yard proposed to Inspector McIntyre that they and Inspector Harvey should arrange an informal meeting with Neill over a drink in The Pheasant public house in Lambeth Palace Road.

This was easily brought about, and the three plainclothes policemen were pleasantly conversational with their strange-looking guest. The two others left most of the talk to McIntyre. As the subject of the meeting was Dr. Neill's complaint of professional injury, McIntyre suggested that, being so near his lodging, Dr. Neill should fetch his sample case, as a proof of his occupation. Neill agreed at once, and in a quarter of an hour was back again with the beautiful case in his hands. Mulvaney and Harvey looked at it and admired it, then, saying they were due elsewhere, finished their drinks and left McIntyre to conduct the interview.

"What makes you think, Dr. Neill," said the inspector, "that you are being followed by the police?" Neill almost started out of his chair with the dramatic energy of his reply. A few nights ago, he declared, he'd been stopped on Westminster Bridge Road by a "rip," using this transatlantic term for a streetwalker. She'd told him the police had set her to spy on him, because they suspected him of being connected with the Stamford Street poisoning cases. As these words burst out, McIntyre's usually inexpressive face showed complete amazement. He stood up, repeating that he would make inquiries, and adding that meanwhile he would keep in touch with Dr. Neill.

The latter was now in a state of strong excitement and pleasure, with a corresponding reversion to nervousness and fear. The observation had been put into more experienced hands, and he never again saw a figure unmistakably on the watch. But any man whom he noticed walking behind him, or pausing till he himself came up, or coming out of a side road across his path, caused him to shudder. The sense of alarm went with one of curious importance. He came out one afternoon and met Miss Sleaper in the hall. "The house is being watched," he told her.

"Then it must be you they are watching," she exclaimed.

"No," he said in a lowered tone. "They are watching Dr. Harper."

She could say nothing. Who would have thought that letting rooms could bring you into such a state!

As Dr. Neill sometimes gave a cup of tea to a visitor in his own room—Mr. Haynes, or his young lady, Miss Sabbatini—a little set of cheap Japanese tea things was kept up there, in the cupboard by the fireplace. Miss Sleaper used to put them away when they had been washed, and she was familiar with the look of the lower shelf. Among the objects on it were a notebook and a flat, round chemist's box. She had once opened this out of curiosity; it contained empty gelatin capsules. The next time she was in the room after the brief exchange in the hall, the cupboard door was ajar; it was apt to swing open again if not carefully shut. She went to close it and caught sight of the lower shelf. The notebook and the pillbox were not there.

Though now thoroughly disturbed, she continued her part as a good-natured landlady. His headaches had come on again and he was dosing himself heavily. He would swallow a pill in the middle of talking to her, and he kept a bowl of sugar in the cupboard, eating a lump after he had drunk tincture of opium from a medicine glass.

On May 24 he took to his bed soon after tea, and asked Miss Sleaper to leave a message at The Pheasant for Inspector McIntyre, saying Dr. Neill was not well enough to keep his appointment with him. The result of the message was that McIntyre came around to number 103, and saying to Miss Sleaper that he would just go upstairs and have a word with Dr. Neill, up he went, calm as a custard.

Neill was propped up in bed, bottles and medicine glasses on the small table beside him. Though he had tried to evade the appointment, he now seemed very eager to talk. He began almost at once, to say that "about a week before the inquest on Marsh and Shrivell—"

"That closed on May 5, I think," said McIntyre. "You are speaking of sometime about April twenty-eighth?"

"Yes," said Neill, brushing aside the interruption. He had been stopped on the sidewalk outside number 103, he said, by a man who said he was a detective, name of Murray. "He put me through a whole rigmarole of questions about young Harper's associations with women."

"But did you know anything about his associations with women?"

"Yes. I was entirely in his confidence. He used to come to me for advice. Murray showed me a letter that had come through the post, warning Marsh and Shrivell to be careful of Dr. Harper, or he would serve them as he had served the girls Clover and Harvey."

"What was this man like?" asked McIntyre impassively.

"About five feet eight inches in height, a heavy mustache, straggling gray hair."

"Well," said McIntyre, "I will inquire at headquarters. Meantime, will you oblige me with a specimen of your handwriting?" Without waiting for a reply, he took a sheet of writing paper from the table in the window, laid it on *A Handbook of Therapeutics* that lay there also, and placed the book on Neill's knees, at the same time giving him his own pocket pen. The latter wrote the address, 103 Lambeth Palace Road, and the date, May 24.

"Thank you," said McIntyre. "And now, Dr. Neill, if you would be good enough just to jot down for me a record of the places where you've been since you came to this country, and the dates, that's all I need to trouble you with at present."

"You shall have it tomorrow morning," Neill said.

Next morning, the servant who opened the door to McIntyre told him that Dr. Neill was still in bed. McIntyre went straight upstairs and, after a knock which he did not wait to have answered, found the patient in bed and Miss Sleaper writing at his dictation. She had just finished, for she was saying, "Will you sign it?"

He put on a cunning expression and said, "No, you will sign it for me."

When she had done this, McIntyre glanced it over. "Liverpool," it said, "London, Edwards' Hotel, the country, London, 103 Lambeth Palace Road 'where I still reside,' " and a scattering of dates.

McIntyre said, "You haven't said where you were when the Stamford Street poisonings occurred."

Neill said, "As soon as I am able to get out of bed and refer to a few dates, I will tell you. I think I was at Berkhampstead."

McIntyre took possession of the document and, with a courteous farewell to Miss Sleaper, told Neill he hoped he'd soon be on his feet, and left.

The invalid's recovery was indeed rapid, for next day McIntyre encountered him at the end of Lambeth Palace Road, almost at Westminster Bridge. Neill never shirked a meeting once he knew that it was unavoidable. He went boldly up to McIntyre and said, "I am going away, today, at three o'clock." Then he added, "Will I be arrested if I do?"

McIntyre was a little taken aback. He said, "I can't say, but if you will walk across with me to Scotland Yard, I'll make inquiries."

They walked onto Westminster Bridge. Facing them, on the right-hand bank, was the massive, steep-roofed, turreted building. The wide thoroughfare of the bridge led inexorably toward it, while the water rippled and a soft wind blew. Like an animal scenting danger, Neill stopped short with a wild movement of the head. He said, "I won't go any farther with you. I believe you are playing me double." He declared, with mounting indignation, that he would consult a solicitor, and turning around abruptly, retraced his steps without a good-by.

That afternoon Neill was in Haynes's company, on top of an omnibus riding down the Strand. The pair of horses, skillfully driven, took them at a smart pace, but the driver was obliged to pull up at a crossing. On the sidewalk below, newspaper sellers were shouting, "Arrest in the Stamford Street case!"

Neill jumped to his feet. "We must get off!" he cried. "I must get a paper." The horses were already moving.

"Sit down!" exclaimed Haynes. "We shall be at the station in a minute. You can get one there."

The omnibus drew up in the station yard, and Neill was down the stairs and off the platform almost before the omnibus was at a stand-still. A group of news vendors approached him, and he bought a Star, a News, a Globe, an Echo, an Evening Monitor; pushing them into Haynes's hands, he gasped, "Find the place, read it out!"

It was front-page news, easily discovered. But the Stamford Street Road to Ruin Case of enticement and robbery in a house of ill fame had nothing to do with affairs at number 118. Neill drew a great breath and left the papers on the station bench, but Haynes collected them, to enjoy a good read for once.

They boarded another omnibus, which took them down Whitehall and across Westminster Bridge; it carried a cheerful crowd on the top deck, cracking jokes with the conductor as he ran upstairs and downstairs with his jingling leather bag. No one gave a backward glance to where, on the left of the bridge, the Scotland Yard building stood on the river shore. Within its walls, at that very moment, Sir Melville McNaughton was instructing Detective Inspector Tunbridge to inquire into the Lambeth poisoning cases.

CHAPTER 12

A LETTER FROM Messrs. Waters and Bryan, solicitors, of East Arbour Street, off the Commercial Road, had reached the chief commissioner of police, stating that their client Dr. Neill was being impeded in his profession as a salesman of pharmaceutical products by the action of the police in keeping a watch on his movements. This letter was to be Inspector Tunbridge's ostensible reason for calling on Neill.

On an afternoon toward the end of May he presented himself at 103 Lambeth Palace Road and found that Dr. Neill was entertaining his fiancée, Miss Sabbatini. Her ladylike appearance—in dove color, and a straw hat with a lot of gauze about it—her pale face and somewhat anxious dark eyes, both surprised the inspector and impressed him very favorably. So far as she was aware, the visit was simply in answer to the complaint Neill himself had made. Since the latter had voiced it on the ground of being a salesman, Tunbridge asked to see his credentials, and Neill put the sample case into his hands. "What is in *this* bottle?" he asked. (Donworth, Marsh, and Shrivell, found poisoned by strychnine, no evidence to say by whom administered; Clover, exhumed, no verdict yet found. By what means had *she* died?)

"Pills containing one-sixteenth of a grain of strychnine," Neill said.

"Then there is a very large quantity of strychnine here!" exclaimed Tunbridge. "It would be very dangerous if this were to fall into the hands of the public."

Dr. Neill answered, "They are not sold to the public direct, only to chemists and doctors, who dispense them in the proper quantities required."

"I see," said Inspector Tunbridge.

Miss Sabbatini's anxious, wistful little face made him take leave with scrupulous politeness. He repeated his regrets that Dr. Neill should have been inconvenienced, and undertook to keep the matter under review.

THE OFFICIALS OF Scotland Yard were accustomed to getting letters sent, as they said, "by insane persons" or misguided humorists; it was exceptionally rare for such letters to be of any intrinsic value; but whatever they might be, they were kept. Now that the inquiry into the Lambeth poisonings had been placed in the hands of an investigator of Tunbridge's distinction, a search was made through everything that had been received since October last, after the death of the first victim, Ellen Donworth. This revealed five letters, in two different hands: one to Dr. Broadbent and one to Mr. F. W. D. Smith in one writing, the remaining three—to the coroner and the foreman of the jury at the inquest of Alice Marsh and Emma Shrivell, and to the private inquiry agent Clarke—in another.

Tunbridge had been provided with samples of Dr. Neill's handwriting by McIntyre—the specimen the latter had taken from Neill, and one from the records of Priest's pharmacy, traced by McIntyre from the label on a bottle by Neill's bed. This writing, peculiar and distinctive, was the one in which the letters to Mr. Smith and Dr. Broadbent had been written.

The next step in the investigation was to interrogate young Dr. Harper, so positively and circumstantially accused, and now practicing (as the secretary of St. Thomas's Hospital told the inspector) at Braunton in Devonshire.

Early on the morning of June 1, Tunbridge took a train, arriving in Braunton in the afternoon. He introduced himself in an apologetic manner to Dr. Harper, and the interview was thoroughly satisfactory. Dr. Harper had known nothing of his fellow lodger, did not even know him by sight, had only seen letters addressed to him lying in the hall; but he told Tunbridge of the preposterous letter his father had received.

"Your father has kept the letter?" said Tunbridge sharply.

"I am sure he will have done. Will you drive over to Barnstaple with me and we'll see?"

The doctor's gig took them over in less than an hour, and the elder doctor was at home. "The letter? Certainly I have it," said Dr. Joseph Harper. He opened a drawer in his desk and laid the letter in its envelope before Inspector Tunbridge. The latter scanned the contents with intense eagerness, but it was not so much the words that riveted his attention as the handwriting. The letter was signed "W. H. Murray," but the writing was Neill's.

The round-trip train journey took several hours, and Tunbridge was only back in London late in the evening. On June 3 he applied at Bow Street Magistrates' Court for a warrant for the arrest of Thomas Neill on the charge, merely, of the attempted blackmail of Dr. Joseph Harper.

At five twenty-five in the afternoon, the inspector saw in Lambeth Palace Road, coming toward him, the man he was looking for, in a dark suit and a silk hat. At a distance he appeared respectable, at close quarters sinister. The river, streaked with eerie light, was sliding by very fast. Tunbridge stopped him and showed him the warrant. The reply was, "You've got the wrong man; fire away!"

Tunbridge took out the letter. "This is the envelope you're accused of sending."

"That's not my writing," Neill said.

"And this is the letter," the inspector added. There was silence.

Tunbridge had been followed at a discreet distance by two constables. He signaled, and they came up with a cab. The journey through the fine evening covered ground that was a map of personal history—Waterloo Road, Waterloo Bridge, across the Strand, then into uncharted territory, Bow Street and the portals of the Magistrates' Court. By seven o'clock that evening it had led to Holloway Gaol, with its entrance in Victorian Gothic, like the gatehouse of a toy medieval castle. Being only on remand, the prisoner was allowed tobacco, writing materials, newspapers, food brought in from outside and his own clothes. He demanded to see his solicitors, Messrs. Waters and Bryan. "You can telegraph to them," said Tunbridge. "Here is a form."

The prisoner fixed him with a cunning stare. "I write nothing," he said. "*You* send it for me."

Next day, however, he wrote to Laura Sabbatini, explaining the ridiculous error, in which he was being detained in mistake for Dr. Harper. *She* knew his innocence! They would soon be reunited.

TUNBRIDGE HAD SEARCHED the room in Lambeth Palace Road, with Miss Sleaper, pale and shocked, standing in the open doorway. One of the discoveries was a baptismal certificate in the name of Thomas Neill Cream, and from henceforward the prisoner was so called. In one of the small drawers of the chest the inspector found an envelope; on it was penciled, "Oct. 19, M.C. Oct. 19; Oct. 13; Ap. 11, E.S., Apr. 11; Oct. 23, L.H. Oct. 23." It was not a consistent record.

"Oct. 13," the date of Ellen Donworth's death, was not followed by her initials. "Ap. 11 E.S. Ap. 11" had Emma Shrivell's but not those of Alice Marsh. "Oct. 23, L.H. Oct. 23" was out of chronological order, but—"L.H."? Was this the Lou Harvey—mentioned as one of the victims in a letter supposedly sent to Marsh and Shrivell, and spoken about to Haynes—the Lou Harvey for a record of whose death from unnatural causes the police had been searching all over London and utterly without success? Mystery still shrouded this crime, for, noted in that record, a crime it must surely be.

"OCT. 19, M.C. OCT. 19." Dr. Thomas Stevenson's report of the post-mortem had been received, and on the morning of June 22 the inquest on Matilda Clover opened in the Vestry Hall, Tooting. The coroner, Mr. Braxton Hicks, presided over a jury of twenty-three businessmen and shopkeepers, all looking awed and anxious. The bright light outside the narrow Gothic windows made the hall seem dark at first. It was filled with police, reporters and onlookers. Then, through a door at the back of the coroner's dais, between two warders, Thomas Neill Cream was brought in from Holloway Gaol.

The witnesses, marshaled by Scotland Yard, gave their testimonies one after another. Lucy Rose, Mrs. Phillips, Mr. Coppin, described the sweats, the tremblings, the agonies. It was natural that the prisoner should attend closely to what went on, but his intent listening was not anxiety only; it was a secret, devouring relish.

The proceedings went on, day after day, with one adjournment, for twenty-one days in all. Dr. Stevenson described his analysis of the organs of the body. He had extracted one-sixteenth of a grain of strychnine, which pointed to the administration of a lethal dose. The evidence of the witnesses who had described the symptoms was read over to him. The symptoms, Dr. Stevenson said, were not only consistent with poisoning by strychnine, they actually pointed to it.

Mr. Kirkby, the assistant from Priest's pharmacy, gave evidence as to the prisoner's purchase of nux vomica and gelatin capsules.

Dr. Broadbent, whom the prisoner now laid eyes on for the first time, appeared briefly. The prisoner, shifting himself slightly, gazed upon the severe, preoccupied face of the physician as if it were some enthralling book.

Dr. Broadbent testified that he had received the letter, now read aloud, on November 30, in the prisoner's handwriting and signed "M. Malone," which, although Matilda Clover had been buried under a certificate saying that she had died of delirium tremens followed by respiratory arrest, stated that her death was due to poisoning by strychnine, and demanded twenty-five hundred pounds for surrendering the proof of the doctor's guilt. Dr. Broadbent received the coroner's thanks for his attendance, and left the hall hurriedly for the street, where his carriage and pair were waiting.

Masters and May the prisoner would not have recognized with any certainty, but they had picked him out in a police lineup. They both swore that on the afternoon of October 9 they had watched him, from a window in Orient Buildings, following Matilda Clover down Hercules Road, and had seen him enter number 27 Lambeth Road in her wake.

Laura Sabbatini, in her demure little gray skirt and jacket, her white frilled blouse and black straw hat, was at first too frightened and unhappy to glance toward him. She admitted writing three letters at his dictation. She had given up to Inspector Tunbridge his letter proposing marriage and his will, both in his handwriting. Before she left the witness box she sent a look of agonized appeal in his direction.

The next day she received a letter from him which she was passionately eager yet afraid to open:

"I was perfectly safe till you swore against me. . . . You know, dear, you never saw me write a letter in your life, yet you went on the stand and swore that my will and my letter, which you gave to the authorities, were in my writing."

She could not, with her clear intelligence, overlook this absurdity, but she was totally committed to him; what he might have done, she did not ask herself—not what he was accused of doing, that was certain.

"The next time you are on the stand you must swear positively that you never saw me write, and that you cannot identify any of my writing. . . . For God's sake burn anything you have with my writing on. If you annoy me in any way or do me any injury in my time of trouble, you are going to get into terrible trouble, and I cannot save you from it; but my solicitor and I will protect you as long as you are true to me and do me no harm."

He was short of money till his next remittance arrived, and he asked her to lend him a few pounds. She sent ten pounds to the jail at once, with a letter reproaching him for threatening her. In his letter of thanks, he said:

"I shall never threaten you, my darling. All I ask of you, dear, is to say or do nothing that will hurt me, or annoy my counsel. I would not have written as I did, but I was afraid you would bring terrible trouble on your own head by your conduct."

Miss Sleaper's appearance in the box he viewed with intense, silent hostility. In a quiet way she was saying everything she could to injure him, not daring to look at him, of course. He sat rigid with a stony hatred; but this settled calm was broken up by the appearance of the next female witness.

That slender, tight-waisted figure, that pert, aggressive chin! Mrs. Louisa Harris—in other words, Lou Harvey! When she had read in the papers an account of the inquest, she wrote to the magistrate a letter full of high spirits and information:

"Met him same night opposite Charing X. Underground R. Station. Walked with him to the Northumberland Public-house, had glass of wine, and then walked back to the Embankment. Were he gave me two capsules. But not liking the look of the thing, I pretended to put them in my mouth. But kept them in my hand. . . ."

All this she related over again with buoyant energy, and then told of the subsequent meeting at the bottom of Regent Street. Neill had told Haynes that she was dead; Haynes had told McIntyre that she was dead; and McIntyre had alerted the police all over London to find the trace of her dead body. Like an impertinent ghost, she had risen up in the witness box, to the amusement and astonishment of all.

But even the impression of Lou Harvey was eclipsed by that of Lady Russell. In a mauve straw hat, heaped with lilacs, and carrying a diamond-studded lorgnette, all the countess had to say was that she *did* receive such a letter as the court described, accusing Lord Russell of poisoning Matilda Clover, but she had lost it. If it should turn up, she would certainly send it to Mr. Braxton Hicks; and amid the bows and thanks of the court, all eyes turning to follow her, she departed on a waft of heliotrope scent.

On and on, day following day, the sufferings and deaths of Ellen

Donworth, Alice Marsh and Emma Shrivell were recalled to show the pattern of Matilda Clover's fate. Then, while the minds of all present were concentrated on these dark and frightful scenes, there shot up an apparition like some hideous, comical, ghastly jack-in-the-box. Mr. Braxton Hicks said he had received a letter which he felt he ought to read to the court:

" 'Dear Sir, The man that you have in your power, Dr. Neill, is as innocent as you are. Knowing him by sight, I disguised myself like him, and made the acquaintance of the girls that have been poisoned. I gave them the pills to cure them of all their earthly miseries, and they died. Miss L. Harris has got more sense than I thought she had, but I shall have her yet. . . . If I were you, I would release Dr. T. Neill, or you might get into trouble. His innocence will be declared sooner or later, and when he is free he might sue you for damages. Yours respectfully, Juan Pollen, *alias* Jack the Ripper. Beware all. I warn but once.' "

Everyone present had been conscious all the time of the prisoner, even when not looking at him. It was clear that the proceedings must terminate in a coroner's verdict against him of willful murder; but when this letter was read aloud, an intensified charge of interest, of fearful curiosity, was directed against him. The letter was patently absurd, from yet another vilely irresponsible joker trying to upset the general equilibrium. Where could it have come from? The prisoner was proved to have a turn for sending curious letters, but he could not have sent this one, for he could not have got it out of Holloway Gaol, and its air of knowingness caused a creeping sensation in the assembled listeners. The coroner passed on to the evidence of Inspector Tunbridge, the backbone of the case, and then asked Neill if he wished to say anything. He was not being tried for the murder; if he had been, he would not have been allowed to speak in his own defense. He was here merely as a potential witness at the inquiry. If he had anything to say in his own behalf, let him say it. The prisoner refused to admit his name, refused to be sworn, refused to testify. He declared that his legal advisers had told him to say nothing. The jury retired, and in twenty minutes returned with the verdict that Matilda Clover died from the effects of strychnine poisoning, administered with intent to destroy life, by Thomas Neill Cream.

CHAPTER 13

BACK AT HOLLOWAY GAOL, Neill was visited by Inspector Tunbridge, who formally charged him with the murder of Matilda Clover. The prisoner replied, "All right." Then he said unexpectedly, "Is anything going to be done in the other cases?"

"Not at present," said Tunbridge, surprised.

Neill said, "You will be sure to let me know if anything is to be done."

THE HOT SUMMER weather was oppressive, the legal process was long-drawn-out. The prisoner, already in custody on the charge of blackmail, was returned to Bow Street, where on August 24 he was committed for trial for the willful murder of Ellen Donworth, Alice Marsh, Emma Shrivell and Matilda Clover; for sending to Joseph Harper a letter demanding money, with threats; for sending a similar letter to William Henry Broadbent; and for attempting to administer to Louisa Harvey a large quantity of strychnine with attempt to murder her. His trial was put down for the Central Criminal Court at the Old Bailey on October 17, at the Michaelmas Sessions.

These famous law courts had long been thought due for pulling down and rebuilding, but they still stood as they had for the last hundred and twenty years. Court number one was oak-paneled, lighted by sash windows in the daytime, by pendant gas globes at dusk. At ceiling height there was a gallery for spectators. In the iron-spiked dock was the head of a staircase leading down to a passage to Newgate Prison. The condemned man who went down those stairs, unless he were reprieved, was never seen in the world again. The ventilation of the court was notoriously bad, and its feverish miasma added to the tension of an important criminal trial, especially with such a judge as Mr. Justice Hawkins on the bench—who, if he began to sum up late in the day, would go on though he kept the court sitting till ten o'clock at night.

Sir Henry Hawkins, most famous of the Queen's Bench judges, was known to be one of the very few who had been appointed solely on merit. The rest, all admittedly able men, had been chosen by the government of the day according to whether their politics were conservative or liberal. Sir Henry Hawkins had no interest in politics whatever; he was interested only in the law. Hard and brilliant, fair-minded and severe, he was an excellent judge to be tried before if you were innocent, and an extremely formidable one if you were guilty.

The counsel briefed for their client by Waters and Bryan was Mr. Gerald Geoghegan, conscientious, nervous and humane. He knew that he faced an almost impossible task. His one chance would have lain in the charges' being restricted to the murder of Matilda Clover and in getting the evidence on the other cases ruled out. But the evidence had been allowed at the inquest, and because the other cases were held to show "a system," to the despair though not in the least to the surprise of Mr. Geoghegan, Mr. Justice Hawkins allowed it at the Central Criminal Court.

ON THE MORNING OF October 17, the court was filled from floor to ceiling. Spectators crammed into the gallery looked down on counsel, solicitors, police. The jurors filed in and were sworn. The Attorney General, Sir Charles Russell, who was to lead for the crown, appeared with his juniors; Mr. Geoghegan was there with his.

The prisoner was brought up into the dock between two warders. In the last three months he had grown a large, bushy brown beard. Since Constable Comley's extremely important identification would describe him as clean-shaven except for a heavy mustache, the jury was provided with a copy of one of Armstead's photographs. As the trial approached, Neill's behavior in Holloway had become obstreperous. He had abused the prison governor in foul terms, and had declared to his legal advisers and to the warders that at the Old Bailey he was going to "give it to Hawkins." Apprehension was felt, therefore, by all those who, however blameless, would be held to a certain extent responsible for any disturbance in the court.

Then the judge was ushered in and, returning the bows with which he was greeted, took his seat on the bench. The scarlet and ermine robes, the black sash and the horsehair wig were impressive, but not so impressive as the judge's face—a face of iron in which the eyes were like planets.

The opening speech for the prosecution, and the supporting witnesses, made it clear what a massively competent operation Scotland Yard had mounted. Friends of the dead women, relatives, landladies, house physicians, postmortem assistants, undertakers, cemetery keepers, the prisoner had seen in the coroner's court. But one now appeared whom he had never expected to see on this side of the vast Atlantic. John Wilson McCulloch, of Ottawa, had read Canadian newspaper accounts of the inquest in London at the close of which the Canadian doctor, Thomas Neill Cream, had been charged with murder by poison. "I identified him," said the witness, "as the person I knew." He had written to the police in Canada, and Scotland Yard had told Inspector Jarvis, who was already in America making inquiries about Cream, to get in touch with him. "I was subpoenaed to come here and give evidence," said McCulloch.

Then came all the story of the strychnine pills, the regret for not having poisoned the rich hotel guest; the tales of three women in a night for a shilling each in the morbid, dismal excitements of the streets about Waterloo Road, the terrain where his secret nocturnal footsteps had been followed with unremitting energy and were now exposed to the day.

But in spite of their activity, Scotland Yard incurred at one point Mr. Justice Hawkins's stern displeasure. It came out in Inspector Tunbridge's evidence that when they received from Dr. Broadbent the letter stating that Matilda Clover had died at his hands of strychnine poisoning at 27 Lambeth Road, no steps had been taken to inquire at the house. Inspector Tunbridge said they had regarded the sending of such a letter to Dr. Broadbent as the action of a lunatic merely.

"But," persisted the judge, "here is a real person, who actually lived at Twenty-seven Lambeth Road, and it is said this person was poisoned by strychnine. This information comes to Scotland Yard, within a quarter of an hour's walk of the place. How comes it that no one took the trouble to make an inquiry at Lambeth Road?"

"Well, it was not done, my lord," said the inspector resignedly.

The judge expressed his very great surprise, the force of his personality investing his words with such weight that, faced with the demonstration of Scotland Yard's efficiency at which they were all assisting, some of the people present felt this abrasive criticism to be unduly harsh.

In a carefully built up synopsis of events and scenes, the most emotionally charged passages of the evidence were those describing the agonies of the victims. As detail followed detail from the lips of Lucy Rose, Mrs. Phillips, Mr. Coppin, Mrs. Vogt, Constable Comley and Constable Eversfield, of the tremblings, the sickness, the sweats, the archings of the spine, the screams of pain of Matilda Clover and Alice Marsh and Emma Shrivell, a change came over the crowded audience. They had been quiet before, as the place demanded, but by degrees they fell profoundly silent, under a spell of compassion and horror. But there was one listener who was intent, not from horror but from deep-seated, sensual enchantment. The prisoner, in spite of the stresses, the acute fears of his situation, during these moments of recounting enjoyed in heightened form the pleasure he had sought. In this place—a place so public, so splendid—the telling, in his hearing, of what he had done was a gratification he had scarcely dreamed of. His bearing in the dock, said observers, was callous, like that of most murderers; but this utter immobility, this breathless attention, was not callousness.

During a trial of five days, the pitch of his feelings veered from fear to indignation, from approval and confidence to anger and dread. When Laura Sabbatini was brought in—so small, so elegant, so cast down—he did not look at her, but fixed his gaze on a region beside her head; nor, after the first appalled glance, did she look at him.

She answered the questions put to her with careful accuracy, though she had sometimes to be asked to raise her voice; it was worn with suffering, and the pace at which she spoke was slower than normal, the result of exhaustion. She might have been speaking of someone altogether removed from her in time and space, except that once it could be seen she had borne his commands in mind. The letter proposing marriage, and the will in his handwriting, were in the hands of the police, but when Sir Charles Russell asked, "Did you receive other letters or documents from him?" she made the reply, unusual in an engaged young woman, "Yes, but I have destroyed them. I am not in the habit of keeping letters."

The sympathy of the court was painfully engaged to this innocent creature who stood there, so sincere, so gentle, so worthy of respect, against a background of other women not so innocent, some who were nameless even.

Constable Comley related how he and Sergeant Ward, in the all-important expedition of tracing the prisoner, had followed him and a woman to 24 Elliott's Row.

"Do you know this woman's name?" asked counsel.

"No," Comley said.

"Do you know where she walks?"

"No."

"How often have you seen her?"

"I have seen her once since then."

WHEN THE COURT assembled on the morning of what was to prove the last day of the trial, Mr. Justice Hawkins said he was anxious to correct an impression he feared he had given, that Scotland Yard had not been thoroughly efficient. He thought that the conduct of the police throughout the case had been eminently praiseworthy. It was only over the matter of the letter to Dr. Broadbent that he felt more might have been done. "But," his lordship said, "I am satisfied now that all was done that I should myself have desired to be done."

Sir Charles Russell said, "I have no doubt that your lordship's public statement to that effect will be received with satisfaction."

At that point the clerk of the court felt able to put in that the jury in the Magistrates' Court had wished to commend Inspector Tunbridge and all the officers concerned in the case. The judge bowed his agreement.

The preceding days of the trial had all been an implied tribute to the efficiency of Scotland Yard, and their thorough and painstaking investigations were now the basis of the judge's charge to the jury.

In a lucid recapitulation, Mr. Justice Hawkins gathered up for them what had inevitably been an irregular and slow-moving progress. All through his summing-up, after one initial reference to Matilda Clover as an "unfortunate," there was nothing in the judge's manner of speech to show that she had been a whore. "A quiet, well-conducted young woman, following her calling," he said.

His concluding words, while reminding the jurors that the final decision was theirs, placed the series of proved facts before them with irresistible force: the prisoner had been seen in the woman's company, going with her into 27 Lambeth Road; the girl had died of poison; she had been buried with no suspicion of poison attaching

to her death; no man or woman knew that the poor creature had had strychnine administered to her except the person who administered it; the prisoner wrote to Dr. Broadbent, boldly accusing him of poisoning the girl with strychnine. The jurors recalled that the prisoner had in his possession a large quantity of pills containing strychnine.

The questions they had to answer were: did they believe that the girl died of strychnine poisoning; did they think the poison was administered, if administered at all, with intent to kill; looking at the whole of the circumstances which were before them, had they the conviction borne into their minds that the prisoner was the person who committed this diabolical crime—for a diabolical crime it was, by whomsoever committed. If they were not so convinced, the prisoner was entitled to be acquitted. But if they were satisfied that he was the man who did commit the crime, then it was their duty to say so. The judge rose, and withdrew through a door opened for him behind the bench. The jurors filed out. The duty imposed on them took them exactly ten minutes to perform. Almost before the disturbance of their retirement had subsided, they were back, the prisoner led into the dock again, the judge reseated.

"Guilty," the foreman said. The muscles of the warders were tense as the clerk of the court asked the prisoner if he had anything to say and why sentence of death should not be passed upon him. But he met the question with a total silence. Nevertheless, when the judge had spoken, in tones that left the hearers breathless, of the crime and its atrocious cruelty, and had pronounced sentence of death by hanging, those nearest the dock heard the prisoner say as he was led to the stairs, "They shall never hang me."

THE TRIAL BEING OVER and the case no longer sub judice, the prisoner's past history, gained from the liaison of Scotland Yard with the Canadian and American police, was now published. Astounding as it was, yet it fitted the course of his career in this country as the haft fits and forms one instrument with the blade of a knife.

In 1876 he had taken the degree of M.D. at McGill University, whose authorities had afterward removed his name from their roll.

In that year he had seduced Flora Eliza Brooks and performed an abortion on her. Her father had forced him to marry her. Neill had then left her and she had died eleven months later.

In that year, 1876, he had come to England and enrolled for a postgraduate course at St. Thomas's Hospital. He had failed the examination, but since his parents had emigrated from Glasgow, he had gone north to Edinburgh and gained the double certificate of the Royal Colleges of Physicians and Surgeons.

Returning to Canada, he began practicing in London, Ontario. The death from abortion of Kate Gardener, though the evidence was inconclusive at the subsequent trial, obliged him to leave the neighborhood. In 1880 he was arrested in Chicago on the charge of causing the death by abortion of Julia Faulkner. Again the evidence was not considered conclusive.

In 1881, Julia Stott, the pretty young wife of an elderly epileptic, came to Cream's office for a nostrum for the relief of epilepsy, which he was advertising. Cream seduced the woman and gave the husband a medicine laced with strychnine, one dose of which killed the patient in twenty minutes. The death was ascribed to an epileptic seizure. At this point the mania that was to prove fatal eleven years later showed itself. Cream wrote to the coroner, charging the pharmacist who had made up his prescription with negligence. When the coroner ignored the letter, Cream wrote, repeating the charge, to the district attorney, who had the body exhumed; at which time four grains of strychnine were found in the stomach. The woman turned against him and gave evidence for the prosecution at his trial, and he received a life sentence, to be served in the Illinois State Penitentiary. An agitation on his behalf after his father's death and the inheriting of his father's money resulted in a reduction of the sentence to seventeen years, which, with remissions for good conduct, brought about his release in July 1891. Three months later he had landed at Liverpool. Ten years in jail had taught him exactly nothing.

CHIEF WARDER SCOTT of Newgate Prison said afterward that the prisoner gave them no trouble. He did not even make the attempt at suicide which his words in the dock had led the prison authorities to expect. He talked incessantly, taking the warders into his confidence over spectacular passages of his past, but contradicting himself so often that they could not accept the revelations as matters of fact. The consistent element in what he told them was an almost religious sense of his own great importance and the dramatic nature of his experiences. He told Scott that he had put these girls to death—these and many others—out of pity for the sufferings which, as the victims of society, they were doomed to undergo. When Scott asked him gently how he could have tried to lay the guilt on an innocent young doctor, he said with an appearance of extreme surprise, "Surely they do not pretend that I tried to do that? Impossible!"

The last night, of moanings and pacings up and down, did not on the morning of November 15 leave him unmanned. His conduct in the execution shed was calm and docile; but as he stood bound, with his face covered, in the split second before the drop, the recollection of the letter in the coroner's court, saved perhaps for this moment, sent up one last flare of exhibitionism. The hangman, Mr. Billington, heard from behind the mask, "I am Jack—" before the rest was silence.

One year and one month had passed since he had entered on his adventures in the neighborhood of Lambeth—dark, secret adventures, yet all pursued within a stone's throw of Scotland Yard itself, of the Houses of Parliament, of St. Thomas's Hospital, of the palace of the archbishop of Canterbury.

"Do you know this woman's name?"

"No."

"Do you know where she walks?"

Beside Westminster Bridge, where, above, the vault of deepest sapphire trembles with the glitter of a myriad of stars, and below, the tide is full of dark ripples and broken lights.

THE CASE OF
STANLEY SETTY

The Case of
STANLEY SETTY
by
Andrew Garve
ILLUSTRATED BY DAVID BLOSSOM

By the standards of London's seedy used-car markets, Stanley Setty was a remarkable man. He was an Iraqi born in Baghdad; he was a financial wizard who had risen from obscurity to wealth by the time he was forty-five; and—strangest of all—he was kindly and generous in a business notorious for its sharp dealings. He was last seen alive on October 4, 1949, after receiving a thousand and five pounds in settlement of a car sale; on October 21 his headless, legless torso was discovered in one of the shallow salt flats along the Essex coast. Medical examination revealed the surprising fact that the body must have been dropped from a great height.

Thus began a bizarre case in which Scotland Yard detectives, technicians, and forensic pathologists teamed up with incomparable skill to unearth all the facts about a bloody but ingenious murder—and then watched in frustration as their case collapsed in court. Andrew Garve, famous for his novels of murder at sea such as *The Sea Monks* and *Death and the Sky Above*, turns his hand here to a true story in which the facts are indeed stranger than fiction.

CHAPTER 1

THE ENGLAND OF 1949 was a country recovering only slowly from the draining struggle against Hitler and his allies. Its people were weary, its cities were battered, and its resources were spent. The long process of turning swords into plowshares had barely begun. It would take many more than the four years that had elapsed to make good the ravages of World War II, and replace—if it ever could be replaced—the wealth destroyed and squandered in that war.

There were shortages of practically everything—and restrictions, regulations, and controls to match them. The continuing scarcity of food was what the populace felt most keenly. All the basic foods were still rationed by coupon, and the rations were small. Any change, up or down, was big news. An announcement that the meat ration would be increased from one shilling and fourpence to one shilling and sixpence (about twenty cents) a week for three weeks, and the bacon ration from three ounces to four ounces a week for four weeks, rated a front-page headline. The small quantities of unrationed foodstuffs had to be queued for, pleaded for, and often bribed for, by desperate housewives scratching around to feed their families.

Living space was naturally in short supply. In the county of London alone, seven hundred thousand dwellings had been damaged by bombs, and of these nearly a third had been totally destroyed. Wherever the damage was not too great, homes had been patched up, but as yet there had been little rebuilding in the areas cleared of rubble.

Many thousands of people were living in single-story prefabricated homes that had been set up almost overnight on the bombed sites.

Clothes, furniture, and household goods were all scarce and mainly of the utility type, mass-produced to basic standards. Coal was in short supply, and electric current liable to sudden blackouts. The petrol ration allowed the private motorist only ninety miles' travel a month—and if he were discovered with a trace of the pink commercial petrol in his tank, he could be jailed. The citizen was not forbidden to travel abroad—but if he did so, his allowance of foreign currency was only fifty pounds in any year. It was a time of tight belts, of economy, of austerity for all. Well, for *almost* all.

For the unscrupulous few the shortages brought opportunities. This was the heyday of the black marketer—the spiv, as he was called in England at the time. There were quick and easy profits to be made by anyone prepared to breach controls and flout the law. Business was brisk in smuggled American nylons, in forged or stolen petrol coupons, in war surplus goods dubiously acquired, in foreign currency otherwise unobtainable, and in many other things which in the sly euphemism of the day had "fallen off the back of a truck." It was a time, more than most, of shady deals and surreptitious cash transactions. Shortages do not create crime—but crime, like water, seeks the easiest channels. So the black markets flourished.

DESPITE THE DEARTH of petrol, one of the things in most insistent demand and in shortest supply at this time was any kind of motorcar that would run. During six years of war virtually no new cars had been built; and their manufacture for the home market was still well down in the order of priorities. With demand insatiable, the men in the business of buying and selling secondhand cars could expect to make a very satisfactory living if their sources and contacts were good.

In London the secondhand-car trade was concentrated in and immediately around Warren Street. This street is approximately one mile north of Piccadilly Circus. In outward appearance it has changed little in the past quarter of a century. It is a mean and narrow street, partially cobbled, and lined for most of its length with grimy and dilapidated two- and three-story terraced buildings of late Victorian vintage. Many of these had stables, which are now used as small garages each capable of holding two or three cars. Interspersed among the garages are the tiny ground-floor or basement offices of various small car-trading outfits, their windows listing cars for sale (unpriced) on chalked blackboards. The street has virtually no showrooms. Basically it is now, as it was in the immediate postwar days, an open-air market, with most of the wares displayed at the curbside.

In 1949, the year of our special interest, there were three hundred or four hundred traders who depended on Warren Street for their living. Some worked on commission for outlying garages; some bought and sold on their own account. The market was both flourishing and well organized. Much of the trading was legitimate—but some of it was not. The open market attracted all sorts of undesirable characters to the vicinity, ready for spot-cash transactions and no unnecessary questions asked. Spivs were drawn to the place—and not all the bargains made were concerned with cars.

ONE OF THE best-known and best-liked dealers in Warren Street was a man named Stanley Setty. He was a native of Iraq, born in Baghdad; the name he answered to was an anglicized form of Suliman Seti. At an early age he had been brought to England by his parents, along with other members of his family, and he had lived and worked there ever since.

At the time of our story Setty's age was around forty-five. He was a short, very fat man—no more than five feet six inches in height—but weighing roughly a hundred and ninety pounds. With his wide shoulders and heavy figure, his shape was somewhat bearlike. His head was long—rectangular rather than round. He had dark eyes, dark hair much receded from a high, square forehead, a large nose, and the swarthy complexion of a Levantine.

The known facts about his early career are sketchy. It would appear that his father was concerned in some way in the Lancashire textile trade, and at the age of fourteen young Setty was working in a Manchester cotton mill. But he was an ambitious lad, eager to get on and make money, and at sixteen he went into business with an elder brother. Together they had a trading capital of some eighteen hundred pounds; they described themselves as shipping merchants. They had acumen but little experience, and after two years the business failed for a considerable sum. Stanley, because he was still a minor, was not legally declared bankrupt. Four years later he had saved enough money to start up again in business on his own account—once more as a shipping merchant, though in fact he bought and sold wherever he could see the chance of a profit. Dealing was his first and second nature. A year passed, a year of struggle, and once again the business failed. The deficiency was large—around seven thousand pounds. Setty left Manchester, his creditors, and his inadequately kept account books and went off to Italy to try to raise money from his father, who was then living there. In this he was apparently unsuccessful. In a few months he was back in Manchester, penniless. He tried to mend his fortunes by gambling on horses and dogs, but merely acquired more debts. Meanwhile, he had been officially declared bankrupt.

He was soon in much worse trouble. At the age of twenty-four he was found to be in breach of the law. He was charged on twenty-three counts with offenses under the Bankruptcy Act and the Debtors Act, pleaded guilty, and was sentenced to eighteen months' imprisonment. His counsel urged that he should never again seek to be a master or employer—he had "evidently not the mentality to deal with sums of money or large quantities of goods."

After his release from prison Setty lived precariously for a while, buying and selling on commission for merchants, which brought him in only two or three pounds a week. Around the middle 1930s he moved to London, discovered Warren Street, and started to trade there. The open-air market, with its haggling and dealing, was his natural element, and he began to prosper. In 1938, having once more accumulated a little capital, he applied for his discharge from bankruptcy. The application was refused. The judge remarked grimly that Setty appeared to be planning to set up in business again "in a way which might or might not be for the benefit of the business community." So he remained an undischarged bankrupt, restricted by the rules of that financial limbo.

However, he was in no way deterred from trading, and he continued to make money. By 1949 very large sums of cash were passing through his hands. To deal as he did, the Warren Street fraternity reckoned, he must have had at least twenty thousand pounds behind him. It was not unknown, friends said, for him to buy ten cars at a thousand pounds each in a single day, and pay cash for all of them. As a bankrupt he could not write checks, so his pockets always bulged with notes. He became known as the unofficial banker of Warren Street. The banks might be closed, but Setty was never closed. He always had money about him in plenty, and he was always ready to oblige his fellow dealers—for a reasonable discount. Over a period of three years he was said to have cashed checks for one local merchant totaling thirty thousand pounds. He cashed, too, many small checks that proved worthless. Some of them he never presented. By 1949 he held more than fifty checks, for amounts from eighty to a hundred and twenty pounds, which were not worth the paper they were written on. This was not because he had been in any sense taken in. He regarded the checks as IOUs from less fortunate traders, to be honored as and when the money became available—or perhaps never. It was not surprising that he had the reputation in the street of being a good-natured and generous man, a man always willing to help a lame dog—a kindly man. No doubt it was a reputation that Setty took pride in.

He was living by now in some style, sharing with his sister, Eva Ouri, and her wealthy husband, Ali Arim Ouri, a luxury flat at Maitland Court, Lancaster Terrace, overlooking the green expanse of Hyde Park. He also had an office and garage in Cambridge Terrace Mews. A brother, with a working garage in the same mews, did a brisk business repairing and respraying cars.

Though his fortunes had so markedly improved, Setty remained, according to most reports, a man of modest tastes and steady habits who preferred the quiet life to the social whirl. His greatest interest was undoubtedly the conduct of his business. He liked to sit with his friends in the saloon bar of the Goat and Compasses in Warren Street, discussing deals over a glass of brandy and a cigar. He enjoyed a game of darts, at which he excelled. He was said to enjoy an occasional flutter on the dogs. He had no expensive hobbies. He owned—or partly owned—a motorboat, but not for reasons of exercise or recreation—only to "do it up" and sell it at a profit.

He had one other big interest. Much of his spare time was spent in the company of a young lady who had agreed to marry him. She was Miss Constance Palfreyman, an attractive twenty-nine-year-old clerk whom he had known for three years. The wedding date had not yet been fixed, but it was to be soon. Three or four times a week they would dine out together in the West End; sometimes they would go to the pictures. But there was no "hitting it up," no nightclub life, no dancing—for which, in any case, Setty had neither the figure nor the inclination. He just liked to be with his fiancée, quietly. He saw her almost every evening.

The evening of Tuesday, October 4, 1949, was an exception. On that day he had another engagement. Whatever the engagement was, he didn't return from it. On the night of October 4, Stanley Setty disappeared.

As LATER INQUIRIES showed, he had had a busy and rewarding day in and around the market. His activities and movements on October 4 can be pieced together as follows:

In the morning he was in his usual place among the dealers in Warren Street. He had for sale a Wolseley 12 sedan, and was prepared to wait for a good offer. Such cars didn't grow on trees.

Soon after midday he sat down at one of the tables in a small café where he was well known, and ate the lunch he had brought with him—a melon. At two fifteen, outside the café, he sold the Wolseley to a dealer from Blackpool, a man named Laurie Lewis, for the odd but satisfying sum of a thousand and five pounds. Lewis gave him a check in settlement. Setty said something about needing the cash to buy a three-and-a-half-liter Jaguar he had his eye on, and dispatched a long-standing friend of his, an Isadore Rosenthal, accompanied by Lewis, to the Yorkshire Penny Bank in Cheapside to get the check cashed. The money was paid to Lewis in five-pound bank notes. Lewis handed it to Rosenthal, who took it back to Setty. As Setty was known to have in his possession fifty pounds in fivers from a previous transaction, this meant that he would be carrying on his person a total of a thousand and fifty-five pounds in five-pound notes. In 1949 that was a lot of money.

That afternoon Setty paid a brief call at the flat in Lancaster Terrace. He left there around three o'clock in his distinctive car—a cream-and-yellow Citroën limousine with scarlet upholstery—and drove to his garage at Cambridge Terrace Mews. He told his brother about the car sale, showed him the wad of fivers, and said he was going off to Watford—a suburb some ten miles north of London—to buy another car, a three-and-a-half-liter Jaguar. He also told a friend, Bert Wright, about the Jaguar.

Some time later he telephoned his fiancée, Miss Palfreyman. He had mentioned to her the day before that he wouldn't be able to see her that evening because of the job he had to do. This call was to remind her, and to say hello.

He was busy on his affairs around the market for the rest of the afternoon. Wherever he went he was in his car. By chance he was seen by his sister, Eva, as he was driving along Osnaburgh Street toward the Euston Road with Bert Wright beside him. The time was then just after five. Setty stopped the car and spoke to her, reminding her that he wouldn't be home for dinner.

He was seen once more, at five fifty, by his cousin Jack Samuel Shashoua. Setty was driving along Great Portland Street with a man beside him whom Shashoua didn't recognize.

That was the last sighting.

THE ALARM WAS raised by Ali Arim Ouri shortly after midnight. He telephoned the police and told them that his brother-in-law had not returned home, and that he feared some injury might have happened to him. In different circumstances Ouri's action might have been thought precipitate, since Setty had said he would not be back for dinner and only a few hours had passed. But in Setty's case there were special considerations, which the police took seriously. He was, the Ouris emphasized, a man of regular habits, a man who could be completely relied on. He knew that he was expected home to sleep that night, and if he had found that for some reason he was going to be detained, he would undoubtedly have let the family know. The possibility of some accident may well have been uppermost in Ouri's mind, but there were other reasons for anxiety. In the light of Setty's association with Warren Street, a place of many unsavory characters, there could be a more sinister interpretation of his failure to come home—particularly as he had been carrying over a thousand pounds in cash on his person. In the classic phrase, foul play could certainly not be ruled out.

By morning there was still no word. No accident involving anyone of Setty's description had been reported. Fears for his safety mounted when around nine o'clock it was discovered that his cream-and-yellow Citroën car had been left outside his garage in Cambridge Terrace Mews. Neighbors in the mews had heard it being driven in at about eleven o'clock on the previous night and thought it strange that it had not been put away as usual. So did Setty's brother. Stanley, he said, would never have left his car outside the garage all night. Miss Palfreyman was equally emphatic. "I believe someone else left the Citroën near his office," she said. "If it had been Stanley, he would have phoned me."

The time had clearly come for Scotland Yard to put its missing-person machinery into full operation. An all-stations message was sent out by teleprinter, alerting the Metropolitan Police area. Setty's description and photograph were circulated to the press and widely published.

His clothes were described in detail. When last seen he had been wearing a navy-blue double-breasted pin-striped suit without a waistcoat, a cream silk shirt with collar attached, a navy-blue tie with a white leaf pattern, green socks, and brown shoes. It emerged later that he had also been wearing an oblong gold wristwatch with a crocodile-skin strap, and that he had been carrying three blank checks signed by Mrs. Ouri.

One possibility the police considered was that Setty might have been lured into making a journey to buy a fictitious car, and been murdered for his money. Inquiries in the Watford area had failed to turn up anyone who had been expecting to sell him a three-and-a-half-liter Jaguar. His friends were inclined to be skeptical about the whole trip.

Setty, it was known, had been a highly nervous person who took great precautions to guard himself and his cash. He would rarely get into anyone else's car, and would never go to a strange garage. He seldom left his Warren Street pitch to look a car over; cars had to be brought to him. For an unofficial banker, a walking till of cash, such precautions were obviously sensible. Why should he have made an exception on October 4? Especially since, as Bert Wright said, he never worked in the evenings. "It must have been a wonderful deal," Wright remarked, "to make him go to Watford."

There was another angle on this. According to Setty's garage hand, Charles Fryer, the Citroën had done only fifteen or twenty miles since he had checked the petrol the day before. Going to Watford would have involved a ten-mile journey each way, and Setty had already done a lot of running around in town during the afternoon. If

Fryer's estimate was correct, it seemed unlikely that the car had been as far as Watford. Yet Setty had said he was going there—not once, but several times, to several people. He had made quite a point of it. And if he hadn't been to Watford, where had he been? There was certainly a puzzle here.

CHAPTER 2

THE SEARCH, NOW well under way, was led by Detective Chief Inspector John Jamieson of Scotland Yard. It involved a vast amount of hard work, much patience, and many frustrations.

One of the first tasks had been to go over Setty's car for fingerprints. Chief Superintendent Fred Cherrill, the expert of the day, found eight good sets. This seemed promising, but when they came to be checked with records, none were identifiable except Setty's own. Later the Citroën was taken to the Yard and thoroughly swept. The sweepings, which included cigarette ash, fabric dust, and shoe scrapings, were put onto slides for microscopic examination. These also produced nothing helpful.

Meanwhile, people who had known Setty were being interviewed. On October 6 police spent two hours talking to Miss Palfreyman and the Ouris, trying to glean every scrap of information they could about Setty's life pattern, his contacts, his friends, his interests. Detectives made scores of inquiries among his business associates in Warren Street. The general view was clear. Setty had had many friends and no known enemies. The cash he carried must have been the reason for his disappearance.

The inquiry involved some extra legwork for the men on the beat. A search was ordered of all bombed buildings and blitzed sites where a body might have been dumped. Nothing was found.

The net was thrown wider when Eva Ouri mentioned that her brother had been planning a continental holiday by car just before his disappearance, and had taken out an international driver's license. Paris was to have been his first destination, and the Yard asked the French police if they could help in tracing the missing man.

As always happens during well-publicized searches, there were many reports of sightings by the public. A reward of a thousand pounds for any news of Stanley, offered by the family through their solicitor, may well have stimulated vigilance. All the reports had to be investigated. One of the more hopeful ones was that a man similar in appearance to Setty had been seen in Wallingford, Berkshire, where he had paid for lunch with a five-pound note before leaving in a Wolseley. But he wasn't Setty.

There was one curious episode early in the search. On the afternoon of October 7, Eva Ouri left the Lancaster Terrace flat, closing the door behind her and turning the keys in two mortise locks. When she returned with her husband at seven in the evening, the door was open. Someone had been in, but nothing in the sumptuously equipped flat had been taken or disturbed. The police were called— and they wondered. Had Setty secretly come back? Or was it an intruder who had got possession of his keys? If so, what had been the purpose of the visit? There were many questions, but no satisfactory answers.

That night a watch was kept on Setty's garage and office, since the keys to their locks had been on the same bunch as his flat keys. But nothing happened. The significance of the episode was never finally determined.

Throughout the search, one of the best hopes of tracing the missing man seemed to lie in the thousand and five pounds in five-pound notes which had been paid to Setty on the afternoon of his disappearance. In 1949 fivers were as rare in common use as twenty-pound bank notes today. Many families passed their lives without ever seeing one. They were engraved in black on beautifully watermarked white paper of great strength and quality, and they rustled crisply in the fingers. When a bank issued fivers, the numbers were always noted.

At an early stage in the inquiry the police had learned from the Yorkshire Penny Bank in Cheapside that the notes paid out on Lewis' check to Setty had been in consecutive serial numbers— M41 039801 to 040002. These numbers were circulated to the press, with a request from the Yard that the public—and especially such individuals as bookmakers and dog-track managers—should keep watch for them. If a single note turned up and could be traced back, the Setty mystery might well be on the way to a solution.

But the days went by, and nothing happened except continuing patient effort by the police. There were no fresh leads, no promising clues. Stanley Setty seemed to have vanished without leaving a trace. It began to look as though his disappearance might have to join others in the file of unsolved mysteries.

That was the position on October 21, some sixteen days after Ali Arim Ouri had first telephoned the police.

ALONG THE EASTERN coast of England, northward from the Thames estuary, a high seawall constructed of earth and clay and faced with concrete slabs runs without a break for many scores of miles. It is there to protect the rich cornland and pastures on the landward side from flooding by the high spring tides. The seaward shore is almost as flat as the farmland. At low water a vista of exposed brown mud stretches away in places for almost two miles before it is lapped by the sea. Alongside the wall, the flats have a gray-green fringe of tussocky grass and sea plants, cut by innumerable muddy rills, and varying in width from a few yards to half a mile or more. This is a special kind of marsh, known to the coastal community as the saltings. At spring tides the sea flows over them twice in every twenty-four hours; at neaps, when sun and moon are pulling different ways, the rills may fill, but the grass remains dry. Over stretches of many miles these bleak saltings are remote from habitation, accessible only by paths across fields, by muddy tracks, by foot along the wall, or by boat. They are given over to ducks and geese and curlews, to scuttling green crabs, to sea-pinks and sea lavender, and to larks trilling in the wide sky.

There are people who hate these flats for their lonely desolation; there are others who love them for their emptiness. Standing on the wall, with an unobstructed view in every direction, nobody needs to tell you that the world is round.

It was in such a place—to be precise, the Dengie Flats, which lie off the coast of Essex some fifteen miles to the northeast of Southend-on-Sea—that on the morning of Friday, October 21, a man was out in a duck punt, wildfowling. This man—though his small, slight figure and his owlish circular spectacles hardly suggested it—was tough. His name was Sidney Tiffin. He had spent most of his life fishing and fowling, the pursuits he most enjoyed. Now, at the age of forty-seven, he was a reluctant farm laborer, because that was the only way he could qualify for the council house he occupied. At present he was having his annual week's holiday, which for him meant taking to the water. His home was in the tiny old-world village of Tillingham, about three miles inland. He was an expert with a punt and a punt gun, and he knew the wilderness of the saltings—here extending seaward for nearly half a mile—intimately. During the war he had patrolled them as a coastguard.

The tides that day were coming up to springs. The rills would soon be full, the saltings covered. Around twelve thirty Tiffin saw what looked like a gray bundle floating in the shallow water some hundred yards from shore. He thought at first it was a target drogue dropped from a training plane—he had recovered several of them during the war—or possibly a bit of flotsam from a wreck. He was concentrating on his birds and paid little attention to it. But half an hour later he paddled over to see what it was. It wasn't a drogue. It seemed to be a blanket, bound up with string. He was curious, and cut the string, and undid the cloth. He saw now that the thing floating beside his punt was part of a human body. It was a headless, legless torso, clothed in a shirt and undershirt and the upper, cutoff section of a pair of trousers, with suspenders attached. It floated chest down on the quiet sea.

Tiffin was not an unduly squeamish man. It was reported later that he had come across at least ten bodies during his forty years around the marshes, particularly during the war. But this was something different, and the gruesome find was to prey on his mind for a long while afterward. At the time, however, he was concerned only with his duty—to report what he had discovered. What worried him was that the torso might float away on the ebb that had now set in. "I was in a tidy stew," he told newspapermen later. "I didn't want to lose it."

So he drove a stake into the saltings mud, tied a piece of rope around the torso's right arm, and secured it. Then he paddled ashore, walked two miles across the fields to the police station at Bradwell, and told of his find. As the tide receded, the body remained where it had been staked, and was seen there by the police whom Tiffin led directly to the spot.

At about ten o'clock next morning Detective Sergeant William Jackson, of the Essex constabulary's photographic department, returned to the saltings with other officers. He took three photographs to mark the position of the torso, and then conveyed it to the St. John's Hospital mortuary at Chelmsford. At about three thirty p.m. Superintendent G. H. Totterdell, of the Essex CID, arrived there, and an hour later he was joined by Dr. Francis Camps, with whom he had worked on several previous cases.

Camps was an outstanding pathologist of his day; a lecturer in forensic medicine at London Hospital; a cheerful pipe smoker, with a quizzically amused expression that seemed surprising in a man of his grim calling.

The police sergeant took possession of the material in which the torso had been wrapped—which appeared to be a felt of the kind that is put under carpets—together with the thin piece of rope that had been tied around it, and the bits of clothing. At ten forty-five Dr. Camps performed an autopsy on the trunk.

His conclusions were as follows:

The cause of death was shock and hemorrhage resulting from five stab wounds in the chest. They had been made by a two-edged weapon about one inch wide and at least four inches long. Cuts in the undershirt and shirt that had covered the torso coincided with the cuts in the flesh. All the wounds had been inflicted before death. Three of the blows had penetrated the lungs, and the man had probably died within a few minutes.

The head had been severed after death by cutting through the skin and tissues with a sharp instrument, presumably a knife, and by sawing through a neck bone with a close-toothed saw. The legs had been severed in a similar way: the flesh had been cut, then the bone sawed through, and then the flesh cut again, leaving a stump about five inches long in each case. The work had been carried out with dexterity but with no indication of medical knowledge. The neck, for instance, had been sawed right through one of the vertebrae, instead of between two of them.

There were other very extensive injuries to the torso, including ribs crushed on both sides and additional bone fractures. These had all been incurred after death. At the time there was no obvious explanation of them.

Judging by the state of decomposition of the body, Dr. Camps formed the opinion—though it was somewhat speculative—that the man had been dead for about forty-eight hours before being put in the sea, and had been in the sea for between sixteen and twenty-one days—estimates that were to prove remarkably accurate. He was to say later, "I think this body was cut up quickly. I give as a reason for saying that, that there are no marks on the body at all; and from experience in previous cases it has been accepted that if there are no marks at all, it indicates that the body has been cut up shortly after death." That was an important opinion, though one not susceptible of proof.

Superintendent Totterdell, noting the swarthy color of the skin, already had a hunch. "I think we've got Setty's torso here," he said. What was needed now was positive identification. Dr. Camps removed the entire skin of the hands, loose from immersion, by making an incision around the wrists and then peeling it off like a pair of rubber gloves. It was put into a jar, and Totterdell himself took it to the fingerprint department at Scotland Yard. Because of the long immersion it was not possible to take prints in the usual way, but by using sophisticated techniques Chief Superintendent Cherrill was able to get perfect prints and then identify them. "It's Setty all right," he said.

Even without the prints, there would soon have been evidence that the torso was Setty's. Eva Ouri was shortly to identify the once cream shirt (which had a laundry mark and the name of the maker on it), the undershirt, the portion of trousers, and the suspenders as belonging to her brother Stanley. All the same, it had been a mistake on the murderer's part not to detach the hands, which provided immediate and conclusive proof of identity. Either he had not known or had overlooked the fact that Setty had been convicted of fraud some twenty years earlier, and that his prints would be filed at the Criminal Record Office of Scotland Yard.

All in all, it had been a fruitful twenty-four hours' work for the police. Fruitful, too, for Sidney Tiffin. His morning of duck shooting was to bring him the best bag of his life—the Setty family's thousand-pound reward. And the chance to have a fishing boat again.

IMMEDIATELY AFTER THE identification, a conference was called at the Yard. Questions to be answered as soon as possible were how the torso might have got into the water in the Dengie Flats near Tillingham, and whether the missing head and legs were anywhere around. Deputy Commander Rawlings directed Superintendent Colin Mac-Dougall of the Murder Squad—who would henceforth be in charge of the case—and Detective Sergeant Neil Sutherland to go at once to Essex with Superintendent Totterdell and comb the saltings for any further clues.

On Sunday morning, October 23, the party—now including Dr. Camps and assisted by several local officers—set out for the Dengie Flats in two cars. The weather and the terrain were alike unhelpful. There was torrential rain and a high wind. The approach road petered out a mile from the seawall, and the cars had to be left in a barn. The detectives, wearing mackintoshes and borrowed Wellington boots and carrying planks to help them across the rills, trudged the rest of the way by muddy tracks and sodden fields to the wall. The tide was rising but still low, and the saltings were uncovered. Around the spot where the torso had been found, they searched every rill, every tussock of grass.

Two exhausting hours in the driving rain produced no trace of the missing portions of the body, nor any other clue. Soaked to the skin, the party returned to the barn, conferred there briefly, and then drove to their temporary headquarters in Chelmsford—having first had to manhandle their cars out of the mud.

One thing had been learned from the trip. Because of the difficulty of access, it seemed unlikely that the torso of this very heavy man had been dumped over the wall at that particular spot. It could have been carried there by boat, or it could have floated there from somewhere else. Experts in tides and winds were consulted—but since at this stage there was no certainty about when the torso had been put in the water, the help they could give was limited. As for the head and legs, the best hope seemed to lie with the people who lived and worked along the coast. The remains could be anywhere—in some desolate building, in one of the hundreds of small boats in the area, deep in a glutinous ditch in any of the numerous inlets along the shores of Essex. A yard-by-yard police search was clearly out of the question, but local boatmen, fishermen, coastguards, and farm laborers alerted by the publicity might well stumble across something as they went about their duties. Apart from that, there was little to be done on the spot, though the police launch *Vigilant,* brought up from Tilbury, in the Thames estuary, did make a search of the main rivers of the area—the Crouch, the Blackwater, and the Colne. It found nothing.

Once again, many reports relating to the case were being received from the public, and all had to be investigated. A strange car had been seen three times in the Tillingham district a week ago. That had to be looked into. A Tillingham builder, out shooting on the saltings on October 15, had noticed two men near the spot where the torso had been found, carrying guns and wearing camouflage. Was that significant? A resident at a seafront hotel at Westcliff-on-Sea, only a few miles away, told police that Setty, accompanied by a man and a woman, had had tea there three weeks earlier, on a Saturday or a Sunday. Was that a fact, and if so, who were the man and woman?

MacDougall himself spent some time investigating a report radioed to his car that a man had been seen being bundled into a sedan car in Victoria Circus, Southend, during the previous week. There was even a suggestion that Setty's pleasure boat, moored in the Thames, might have been involved in the case. That also had to be checked.

There were other, more productive police activities during these early days. At the time they went largely unpublicized. Much police work is necessarily secret, and the moment had not yet come for the press to be told what was going on.

Meanwhile, the newspapers were full of their own speculations about the crime. Now that Setty was known to be dead, there was quite a lot of theorizing. Some of the theories advanced at this time make interesting retrospective reading:

Item. Setty was murdered, possibly by a gang, for a large hoard of money he had salted away, and not for the fivers he was carrying.

Item. He was tortured with a stiletto before being killed, and probably finished off by a blow on the head. (A safe speculation, that one, since the head was missing!)

Item. He had been mixed up with some dubious associates in Southend, ready-money dealers and dog-track regulars, and had sometimes visited an all-night club which they frequented—subsequently raided and closed down. The implication was that these unsavory contacts might have had something to do with his death.

Item. He knew about a stolen-car racket and the men who had organized it, and this could very well have brought about his murder.

Item. He was a liaison man for an illicit-currency gang, and had arranged contacts in Paris for travelers who wanted more than their legal allowance of francs.

Item. He had had some secret political background, possibly connected with Palestine, which could have provided a motive for his murder.

Item. A search was going on for a missing blonde who *knew* the killers—and it was a race against time. If they found her hiding place, she would die.

None of these conjectures about the cause and circumstances of Setty's murder proved in the end to be true.

At the inquest on Setty, Mr. V. Durand, representing the family, said to the coroner, "I wonder if you will give me the opportunity of saying that Stanley Setty had been an honest trader for well over twenty years. It may be that if you look back in the past, digging deep enough, you may find something against this unfortunate man's name. It is a thousand pities that a man having lived perfectly respectably and honestly for well over twenty years should form the subject matter of large articles which are written purely for profit and are of no benefit to the public. It has hurt the relatives very deeply indeed."

That, of course, was hardly an impartial statement. But when the murder case eventually came to court, there was a robust exchange between Superintendent MacDougall, who had led the inquiry, and counsel for the defense. It went like this:

COUNSEL:	Would it be right to say that Setty was a well-known dealer in this black car market in Warren Street?
MacDOUGALL:	No, sir, I would say he was a well-known car dealer.
COUNSEL:	If he himself was not a dealer in what I call the tainted cars, he was closely connected with that market generally, was he not?
MacDOUGALL:	He had never been convicted of receiving stolen cars.
COUNSEL:	I am not suggesting that for a moment. I am suggesting he was in an environment which, shall I say, was a little dangerous.
MacDOUGALL:	He was looked upon as quite an honest trader. That's as far as I can go.

CHAPTER 3

FOR THE FIRST couple of days after the discovery of the torso, Superintendent MacDougall and his men were without any promising lead on the Setty murder. They still had no idea of Setty's movements after the last sighting in Great Portland Street on October 4; they had no idea where he might have been murdered; they had no certain evidence about where or how the body had been put in the water; and the head and legs had not turned up. The detectives were working hard—pursuing inquiries, as the phrase goes—among the dead man's associates in London and elsewhere, but they seemed to be making little progress.

Then, on October 24, they got a break. As events would show, they would in the end have reached the same point by another route, but the information they were now given undoubtedly shortened the investigation.

On Sunday, the twenty-third, the national press had splashed the story of the discovery of Setty's torso in Essex under huge headlines. On the twenty-fourth, Scotland Yard was contacted by a Mr. John Simpson, a director and chief engineer at the United Services Flying Club, Elstree, which is about ten miles to the north of London. Simpson, having read about the torso, had been pondering some curious matters, and had come to the conclusion that he might have some helpful information regarding the Setty affair. The police went at once to Elstree and, having talked to Simpson, started an investigation which in a day or two uncovered the following remarkable sequence of events:

Around midday on October 5, the day after Setty's disappearance, a member of the flying club named Brian Donald Hume had telephoned the club and booked a three-seater single-engine Auster aircraft, number G-AGXT, for the afternoon. He arrived at Elstree in a Singer self-drive car which he had hired, accompanied by his dog, Tony, half Alsatian and half sheepdog. He shut the dog up in the car, since he didn't expect to be away for very long. At the office he paid an outstanding club account of twenty pounds in five-pound notes. He had brought two bulky parcels with him in the car, which he transferred to the airplane, putting one in the pilot's seat and the other in the back. He then asked an aircraft fitter, William Davey, to "give him a turn" to start the engine. Davey told him that he was in the wrong seat—the copilot's seat. Hume got out and switched the parcel and himself. Davey asked him if he wanted the parcel strapped down, but Hume said it would be all right. He took off shortly after five o'clock, saying he was going to Southend. The weather was typical of an English October—hazy in the morning and evening, warm and sunny by day.

Hume landed at Southend Airport, a mere thirty miles from London, around six thirty. The trip had taken him well over an hour, though at a cruising speed of seventy-five miles per hour it should have taken less than half an hour. His arrival at Southend by no means went unnoticed, for he violated the landing regulations, and two red Very lights sent up to warn him didn't prevent him from setting down in the direct path of a four-engine freighter plane and narrowly avoiding a pileup.

On the airfield he encountered by chance a fellow member of the Elstree flying club whom he knew—a man named James Small, who happened to be staying at the Southend club. He told Small that he had lost his way in the gathering haze, and asked if Small would fly him back to Elstree in the Auster.

Small said he couldn't do that, as he was on holiday with his wife and family. What he did do was taxi the aircraft to the hangar for Hume and put it away. In a statement to the police Small recollected that Hume had had no parcels with him, and that there were none in the plane.

Hume later approached a taxi driver at the airport and asked him to drive him back to London. The driver, Owen Rawlings, who worked for a firm at Leigh-on-Sea near Southend, agreed to do so, and at the end of the journey was paid with a five-pound note from a roll which Hume took from his pocket. Sometime in the evening Hume telephoned the Elstree club, explained that bad weather had prevented his bringing the aircraft back, and asked that his dog, Tony, should be taken from the Singer car and exercised, which was done.

At nine o'clock next morning, October 6, Hume hired another taxi from a garage near his London home and had himself driven to

Elstree. There he collected the Singer he had left the day before, together with the dog, and returned home. Later in the day he drove the Singer—and the dog—to Southend Airport. At about four p.m. he was seen by an airport employee struggling to load a large and very heavy package from the car into the Auster aircraft. The employee offered to help him with it, but the assistance was declined. The Auster took off at seven minutes after four, ostensibly for Elstree.

Sometime later Hume landed in a field near Faversham, on the Kent side of the Thames estuary, having once again lost his bearings. He got directions from a local farmer and took off again. At five forty-five, in thickening weather, he landed at Gravesend Airport, which was only a short distance away.

James Rayfield, employed by the Essex Aero Club at Gravesend, was there when the plane landed. He said in a statement that Hume was carrying a traveling bag and a hearthrug, but there was no sign of any large package.

Once more Hume returned to London by taxi. The Auster was subsequently collected by an Elstree pilot, who reported on his return that he had found the port door damaged. Possibly it was the state of this door, together with the peculiar disappearance of the parcels, that led the director of the Elstree flying club to get in touch with the police.

THE MOMENT HAS come to take a preliminary look at Brian Donald Hume, his background, and his career. Donald Hume was born at Swanage in Dorset, a southwestern county of England, in the year 1920. His mother was a village schoolmistress. Her name alone appeared on the birth certificate, and Hume was never able to discover who his father was. From the age of three until he was about ten he was brought up in an institution which he always described as an orphanage.

He felt neglected and unloved, and later was to write bitterly about the cruelty of his mother in sending him away. His one-sided account of his childhood may well not be a fair picture of what happened, but it seems clear that these early years left him with a massive chip on his shoulder.

At the age of eleven he entered a local grammar school. His school reports show that he was a backward pupil. At fourteen or thereabouts he abandoned his lessons and rushed off into the world to earn his living. He had a succession of menial jobs—as kitchen boy, bootblack, and barman in various hotels—before leaving for London and finding work as an apprentice electrician.

He had been in London only a short time when war came—and with it, opportunity, the chance of adventure. The young Hume had a craving for excitement, for glamour, for fame. He was fascinated by airplanes, by flying. He had long dreamed of becoming a pilot. In 1942, at the age of twenty-two, he was accepted into the Royal Air Force for aircrew training. His career there was short. After he had had a few hours' instruction in flying, he crashed his training aircraft on a solo flight and suffered a severe concussion, followed by an attack of cerebrospinal meningitis. Soon after his discharge from the hospital in 1943 he was invalided out of the service, still an ordinary aircraftsman.

What aroused him to grief and fury later was the suggestion that he had failed his tests. "You have no right to say I failed," he shouted at prosecuting counsel in court. "I was never allowed to take them, because I had concussion."

He still saw himself as a pilot—and if he couldn't be one in fact, he could represent himself as being one. For the sum of five pounds he bought an RAF officer's uniform, complete with wings and the ribbon of the Distinguished Flying Medal, and showed himself off in West End clubs and officers' messes, "shooting a line" about his part in the Battle of Britain, and enjoying the prestige and good-fellowship that the uniform brought. It was a short-lived fantasy. Inevitably someone was bound to inquire about his squadron and his plane. Leaving Northolt Airport one day in his RAF trappings, he was stopped at the gate and questioned. Subsequently he was convicted at the Old Bailey of falsely representing himself as a member of His Majesty's forces, wearing an RAF uniform to gain admission to a prohibited place, and possessing a forged official document. Since it was wartime, he could well have faced more serious charges. But the court decided that he was no spy—that he was merely an impostor eager for the company of "flying types." He got off very lightly, being bound over in the sum of a few pounds to be of good behavior for three years.

To earn his living after his discharge from the RAF he had embarked on a variety of enterprises in line with his interests. He was keen on everything electrical, he had some practical and inventive skills, and he was bursting with initiative and energy. In partnership with a friend he started a company called Hume Electric Ltd. and opened an electrical and radio shop in London. He took over a small factory at a place called Hay-on-Wye, on the Welsh border with Herefordshire, and manufactured plastic electric-switch covers. He formed a company called Little Atom Electrical Products Ltd. and designed and sold, very profitably, large numbers of Little Atom toasters. He was enjoying a period of considerable prosperity, and he lived well on the profits.

Whenever he was in the money he was a lavish spender. His tastes were extravagant. He liked expensive clothes, rich living, smart hotels, and West End clubs. He also liked running around in his big American Cadillac.

The prosperity didn't last. There was a destructive fire at his Hay-on-Wye factory. A steady decline in his business profits led him, in the later 1940s, to look elsewhere for money. There were stories going around of large fortunes being made selling planes to Israelis and Arabs, and Hume tried to get a share of the traffic. He was too late for the fortunes, but he found some business as a go-between, and in June 1949 he made about six hundred pounds from the sale of two war-surplus Ansons in the Middle East. He also became involved in the Warren Street secondhand-car market. Here, in December 1947, when he was trying to sell a car in the market, he was introduced to Stanley Setty.

These sporadic deals in planes and cars formed only a part of his very varied activities and plans. It may have been in the hope of making money by flying an airplane that in 1949 he joined the Elstree flying club and gained a civilian certificate which permitted him to pilot a light plane solo in daylight. Or it may have been simply that he wanted to get in the air again.

In 1949 Hume was twenty-nine years old. He was a strong, well-built, rather stocky man. By most people's standards he was good-looking. He had an abundance of black curly hair, deep-set dark eyes burning with eagerness, a full mouth as shapely as a woman's, chubby cheeks—some called him baby-faced—and a fetching grin. He was a very sociable man, a good mixer, with a fund of entertaining stories, a quick wit, a ready tongue, and a taste for lighthearted banter. His accent was nondescript—not provincial, not cockney, not educated, yet not uncouth—but he could speak Oxbridge or barrow boy with equal facility if he wished. He had a great deal of boyish charm that appealed particularly to women. "You may think him *extremely* charming," prosecuting counsel was to say about him at the trial. And the records suggest that wherever he went he was liked and welcomed.

A year previously, in September 1948, he had married a girl named Cynthia. She was the daughter of a retired chief examiner of a Midlands savings bank, at that time settled with his wife in a small Herefordshire town. Cynthia had been for a term or two at a provincial university; then, at the age of nineteen, she had gone into the Women's Royal Air Force. She had made an unsuccessful marriage and become divorced. At the time of her marriage to Hume she was a secretary in a fashionable restaurant. She had soft dark hair, gentle eyes, a finely cut mouth, and an exceptionally beautiful, creamy complexion. Her voice was low-pitched and very attractive, her manner charming.

There were those who thought Cynthia "a lovely girl." There were those who were content to describe her as "smart and elegant." There were those who found her kind and tender, and those who sensed behind her languid feminine exterior a tough and shrewd personality of immense resolution.

By October 1949 the Humes had a three-month-old baby daughter, Allison. They lived in a rented flat on the top two floors of a four-story terraced Victorian building in Finchley Road, Golders Green, an outer suburb some seven miles northwest of Piccadilly Circus. They had a sitting room, dining room, scullery, and kitchen on the lower floor, and a bedroom, nursery, and bathroom above. The place was furnished in neat middle-class style—the sitting room with a three-piece suite, a picture, bookshelves, a large carpet, a floor lamp, and a coffee table. A touch of originality was that the upper parts of many of the walls were covered with photographs of airplanes and aviators. The books on the shelves dealt largely with flying and adventure.

The flat below was rented by a schoolmaster, and below that there was a greengrocer's shop. Access to the Hume flat was by a side door near the shop entrance, and then up a steep, narrow, and winding flight of stairs. Finchley Road, which the sitting room looked out on, was a main road, a busy traffic artery, but from the domestic point of view it had the advantage of being an excellent shopping center, with general stores, pharmacies, cleaners, banks, and garage all close at hand, and a bus stop right outside the front door.

A convenient and conventional setting, one might think, for a recently married, not too well off young couple with a small child. Less conventional, perhaps, was the fact that Cynthia Hume—as she was later to say in court—knew little of her husband's private life, or how he was making ends meet. He had told her that he was earning his living by flying airplanes, and this, apparently, she was happy to accept without curiosity or question.

CHAPTER 4

THE YARD DETECTIVES, collecting statements as they went along, had followed Hume's two-day odyssey with mounting interest and suspicion. Except for the transport of large parcels, his hectic journeys and hazardous flights in poor weather seemed purposeless. And the parcels had vanished. Vanished on two successive days, and while he was in the air. In the air, moreover, not far from where Setty's torso had been found. Some explanation by Hume was clearly called for. All the more so because one of Setty's consecutively numbered fivers had been traced to a Southend taxi firm. All the more so because on October 25 Dr. Henry Holden, director of the Metropolitan Police Laboratory, had gone to Elstree, examined the Auster aircraft that Hume had used, and found a smear of blood immediately behind the copilot's seat.

At seven forty-five a.m. on October 26, Detective Chief Inspector John Jamieson and Inspector Evan Davies, of D Division, called at the Hume flat—the usual precautions having been taken to guard against any attempted escape out the rear. In fact, Hume was in bed, and was asked to dress. Jamieson told him, in the polite and formal language customary on such occasions, "We are police officers inquiring into certain serious matters in connection with which I think you can help."

Hume said, "What's it all about?"

Jamieson said, "I don't think this is a convenient place to discuss the subject. It would perhaps be better if we went to the police station." Cynthia Hume was present at the time—and detectives usually prefer their questioning to be done in private.

Hume said, "All right, I'll come with you." When they were in the police car outside, he said, "Can't you tell me more about it now?"

Jamieson said, "Our inquiries are in connection with the murder of Stanley Setty, who disappeared on fourth October this year."

"Oh, I can't help you with that," Hume told him. "I know nothing about it."

At Albany Street police station, Jamieson began the interrogation: "I would like you to account for your movements on fourth and fifth of October this year."

Hume said, "That's going to be difficult."

Jamieson asked, "Do you own a motorcar?"

Hume said, "No."

Jamieson asked, "When did you drive a car last?"

Hume replied, "About three or four months ago."

Jamieson said, "I have good reason to believe that on the afternoon of fifth October you drove a car to Elstree airdrome and there took two parcels from the car and put them into a plane which you had hired."

Hume replied, "I hired a plane that day to go to Southend, but I had no parcels with me. I only had my coat. I hired a car that day and drove myself to the airdrome."

At that stage Superintendent MacDougall arrived at Albany Street and took over the questioning. He said, "I am a police officer making inquiries into the murder of Stanley Setty, who disappeared on October fourth and part of whose body was found on the Essex coast on twenty-first October."

Hume said, "I can't help you. I can't see where it has anything to do with me. Setty has not been to my place."

MacDougall said, "I understand you hired an airplane at Elstree airdrome on fifth October on which you loaded two parcels, and took off for Southend at about five p.m."

Hume said, "It's a lie. I put no parcels on the plane. All I had with me was my overcoat."

MacDougall, with a whole sheaf of statements to back him up if necessary, said, "I have evidence to prove that you put two parcels into the plane before you took off that day, and that the following day you put a heavy parcel in the same plane at Southend."

For a few moments Hume was silent. Finally, burying his head in his hands, he said, "I'm several kinds of bastard, aren't I?" He then volunteered a statement, which was taken down in writing by Detective Sergeant Neil Sutherland, in the presence of MacDougall and Jamieson, and was subsequently read to Hume and signed by him.

It was one of the longest, most detailed, and most extraordinary statements ever recorded in a British police station.

HUME'S STORY BEGAN in 1946, when he bought an Allard car. It was new when he bought it. After he had had it for about four months he sold it to two traders in partnership in Warren Street, William Mansfield and Roy Salvadori. He was paid twelve hundred pounds for the car in five-pound notes. There was a bit of trouble later about his selling the car in breach of his purchase contract, but no civil action was taken against him over the deal.

Early in 1949 he had another car for sale—his 1940 Cadillac. He sold it to Salvadori for seven hundred pounds, which was paid in cash. As a result of these and other transactions he became friendly with Salvadori, his brother Oswald, and Mansfield. In the course of a civil action in which he was concerned as a witness, he also got to know several other dealers in Warren Street. Since then he had visited the street a number of times, and when he was there he always called in at Salvadori's office. He told Salvadori, Mansfield, and other traders that he could fly an airplane. He admitted romancing to them about his capabilities as a pilot.

On Friday, September 30, 1949, he was in Salvadori's office in the afternoon. He could be definite about the date because it was the Friday before "the man Setty" disappeared. The office was in a basement, and on leaving it and getting to the top of the stairs he encountered a man whom he had met only briefly and whom he knew as Mac or Max.

This man was about thirty-five years of age, five feet ten or eleven in height, heavily built, clean-shaven and fresh-complexioned, with fair hair parted in the center and brushed right back. He wore suede

brogues and had a ring with a large red stone, which—Hume noticed later—he continually polished on his coat.

Mac, who was alone, asked Hume if he had any cars to sell. Hume told him he hadn't. Mac then said, "Are you the Flying Smuggler?" Hume agreed that that was a name he was known by in Warren Street. Mac asked him how his business was going, and Hume said not so well. Mac then asked him if he had dollars or anything else for sale, and Hume told him he had ninety dollars; but he refused to sell them at the price offered. Mac then invited Hume for a cup of tea.

They went together to a café on the corner and Mac led the way to the far part of the room, where a man was sitting at a table. Mac said to the man, "This is him." Hume hadn't seen the man before, and Mac introduced him. He was variously known, it appeared, as Gree or Greeny or G. He was dark-complexioned, with a thin black mustache divided in the middle, and black hair cut in the Boston fashion with the distinct rounded hairline at the neck. From the way he spoke and looked, Hume judged him to be a Cypriot. He was wearing green-colored trousers, a heavy, belted light brown overcoat, plain suede shoes, and no hat. While he talked he cut his name with a penknife.

Mac told Gree that Hume's business was not very good. Gree said to Hume, "You would like to make some money? I can put you on to a deal if you can keep your mouth shut."

Mac said, "How can we get hold of you?" and Hume gave them his name, address, and telephone number. Mac said, "They tell me you can get hold of and use airplanes." Hume said that was correct. Mac said, "How about getting hold of a plane that will carry five or six people without worrying about the customs?" Hume, not taking the suggestion very seriously, said he could.

Gree said, "How about one for Monday?" Hume said it might be arranged, but it would cost a lot of money. Mac asked him if he knew Roy Salvadori well, and he said he did.

After some general conversation about motorcars, Mac said he had a deal on and would be getting in touch. Hume then left them. This first meeting had lasted about half an hour.

Two days later, on Sunday, October 2, Mac telephoned Hume at home during the morning. He said, "You are not messing us about over these airplanes?"

Hume said, "If you want an airplane you will have to find some money first." He added that if Mac wanted a plane, it would have to be a single-engine one.

Mac said, "I don't care how many engines it's got as long as we can come."

Hume said, to put him off, that he didn't think it would be easy to go abroad, because of the necessity of obtaining trip tickets and other formalities. He said, "I can only take one passenger, although it is a three-seater."

Mac said, "So you are messing us about after all." He asked how long it would take to get a single-engine plane, and Hume told him that before he could get the plane he would have to have some money. Mac said, "If we don't want to go abroad, will it be necessary to get these papers?" and Hume said not if the flying was in England. Mac then said he would speak to his mates about it, and rang off.

The next day, Monday, October 3, Mac telephoned Hume again at about nine thirty a.m. He said, "I can do with the single-engine plane." Hume again told him he would have to have some money, and Mac said, "I will fix all that. I want it for today. I will ring you back in a short while and tell you what I want." Soon afterward he rang again and said, "I don't want a plane for today."

Hume said, "You are the one that's messing me about."

Mac then said, "Have you got a motorcar?"

Hume said, "What type did you want to buy?"

Mac said, "I don't want to buy one, but you can drive?" He added, "I'm not messing you about, I'll fix you up with a deal."

On the morning of Wednesday, October 5, at about ten o'clock, Mac phoned Hume once more. The deal was definitely on, and for that day. "We will call round and see you," Mac said. "We want that plane." On the strength of this, and on the promise of money, Hume called up the United Services Flying Club at Elstree around midday and booked a single-engine aircraft. Either before or after booking the plane he went to a nearby garage, Saunders Ltd., and hired a self-drive car for twenty-four hours.

Sometime between two and three o'clock that afternoon, Mac and Gree appeared at Hume's house and rang the front doorbell. Hume went down and let them in. They had with them a third man, who was introduced as Boy. He was about thirty-five years old and five

THE CASE OF STANLEY SETTY

feet nine or ten in height. He was of medium build, clean-shaven, with brown hair receding from his forehead. He was later seen, Hume said, to be wearing a pair of steel-rimmed glasses. His shoes were a bright-colored brown, with buckles, and Hume believed he was wearing a raincoat.

Gree and Boy were each carrying a parcel. They went upstairs with Hume to the flat.

On arriving there, Mac said, "As you know, we wanted to go abroad. It will be good for you, now we have started doing deals with you, if you can keep your mouth shut." Hume told them he could do that all right. Mac then spoke about forged petrol coupons and said he had been making them and wanted to get rid of the plates, or presses. He said they wanted to get them dumped in the English Channel, and added that they were "hot." The three men implied that the plates, or presses, were in the parcels they had brought.

Hume said that dumping in the sea was an expensive way of getting rid of the parcels, and offered to hide or to bury them. The men discussed this but seemed not to like the idea, and finally insisted that Hume should drop them from his plane. They debated among themselves the desirability of one of them going with Hume to make sure the parcels were thrown out, but Hume assured them they could trust him. "I'll throw them out all right," he said.

Gree said, "You're getting paid for what you're doing, you're not dealing with poofs from Hyde Park." As he said this, he put one of his hands into his coat pocket and showed Hume a pistol or revolver.

An agreement was finally made. Hume was to be paid a hundred pounds for the job. Boy pulled a roll of notes out of his pocket. Gree produced an even bigger bundle. Hume would have liked the whole hundred pounds paid in advance, but this was refused. Boy, now wearing his steel-rimmed spectacles, counted out ten five-pound notes as payment on account. Mac said that the three of them would call around again at about eight o'clock that evening to pay the second fifty pounds. Hume said they should meet outside, as he didn't want them coming up to the flat when his wife was there.

Before the men left, one of them impressed on Hume that the parcels had been done up properly, and that it would be unwise for him to interfere with them.

The parcel that Boy had brought was a Heinz baked-beans cardboard box, about fifteen inches square, almost completely covered with cardboard and securely roped. Hume pushed his foot hard against it, and it was firm. The other parcel was about two feet six in length, and about two feet thick, and round. The outer cover was corrugated paper, and the whole parcel was securely tied with thick cord. When Hume squeezed it with his fingers it had a soft feeling, and when he lifted the parcel it did not bend or sag. It was fairly heavy. He put the parcels in a cupboard in the kitchen of his flat. He didn't think his wife knew the men had been to the house, and he couldn't be sure whether or not he had told her. He certainly didn't tell her the arrangements he had made with the men regarding the disposal of the parcels.

At about three thirty that day he carried the bundles downstairs and put them in the back of the self-drive Singer he had hired from Saunders. He then drove with his dog to Elstree Airport. On arrival there, he took the parcels and went to the airport office, where he saw his former instructor, a Mr. Keats, who told him his aircraft was ready. He had a cup of tea in the canteen and afterward left the motorcar, with the dog inside, near the airport office, expecting to be back later that day. One of the ground staff carried one of the parcels, and he carried the other, to the airplane, and placed them both inside the cabin. Before taking off, he paid the cashier twenty pounds in four five-pound notes to settle an outstanding account. He couldn't be sure whether any of the five-pound notes were those he had got from the three men.

He took off from Elstree Airport at about five p.m., flew toward Southend, reached the pier, went straight out to sea, and continued on for a quarter of an hour toward the Kent coast. Just before he turned, he opened the door on the pilot's side of the plane with both hands, holding the controls with his knees. He got the door open, held it against the air resistance, and threw both parcels into the sea. He was then flying at about a thousand feet, and reckoned he was about four to five miles from Southend Pier. He flew back to Southend Airport and landed at about six twenty. Officials of the airport spoke to him about his flying after he had obstructed a large freight plane—a Halifax, he thought—on landing. He left the plane on the airfield outside the clubhouse and went in and saw Mr. Small, whom he knew. He asked Small if he would fly him back to Elstree, as he knew the way, but Small declined because he was on holiday. He offered to taxi the plane to the hangar, and in fact did so.

After the plane had been put away, Hume made inquiries about getting a car to take him back to Golders Green by eight fifteen p.m., to meet the three men as arranged. He managed to hire a car at the airport. He remembered he asked the driver to leave the meal he was eating in order to get away quickly, on the promise that he would buy him a meal in town. He had a quick cup of tea and they left the airdrome about a quarter to seven. On the way to London the driver had trouble with his car lights and called at three garages to try to get them put right. He still had trouble, and was pulled up by police at Southgate.

As a result of these delays they didn't arrive at Golders Green until about a quarter to nine. The driver set Hume down close to his flat and Hume paid the four-pound charge with a five-pound note, inviting the driver to keep the change.

After leaving the car he went toward his flat, and when he got to the street door Mac came up and said, "You are really late." Hume told him he had dumped the parcels in the Channel. He didn't say it was between Southend and the Kent coast that he had dropped them, but he did tell Mac about leaving the plane at Southend and about the troubles he had had. Before this conversation took place, Mac asked him to cross the road to a stationary car—a Humber, Hume thought—where Gree was sitting in the front nearside seat and Boy on the nearside at the back.

Hume noticed that in the back beside Boy there was a bulky package, on the floor and leaning against the seat. He told Mac he had already spent about thirty pounds, and because of this he would only have about seventy pounds for himself.

Mac said, "We are going to give you a chance to earn another fifty pounds tonight."

Hume asked how, and said, "How about giving me the other fifty pounds first?"

Mac said, "We will give you the hundred tonight. We want you to drop another parcel in the sea tonight."

Hume said, "The airplane is at Southend. I haven't done any night flying, and I can't do it."

Gree said, "We can take you to Southend, it will be on our way."

Hume again told them he could not fly at night. They then showed him the big parcel in the back of the car. Hume said, "I don't think it will fit in an airplane."

Mac said, "You've started the job, you've got to finish it."

Boy said, "You won't get any more unless you do finish it."

Hume then said, "If you take the parcel out to Elstree, I can put it in the back of my car, bring it back here, and take it to Southend tomorrow." The Three refused to go to Elstree.

Boy took some money out of his pocket and said, "Here is the hundred pounds. I'll give it to you now and you can arrange to keep the bundle upstairs until tomorrow, when you can take it down at your own convenience."

Hume had another look at it and said, "I still don't think it will go in the plane." However, he agreed to take it to Southend the following day and dump it in the sea. Boy gave him ninety pounds in five-pound notes and ten one-pound notes. Mac and Boy then took the package out of the car and carried it into Hume's flat and put it in the far cupboard in the kitchen. Hume said, "One of you must come out tomorrow and give me a hand to put it into the car."

One of them said, "We will be busy tomorrow and cannot do it; you will be able to get someone to help you." Hume asked them what the package contained and they said, "The same as before," or words to that effect. By this time Hume was afraid of the three men, and because of this he agreed to carry out their instructions.

The following morning, October 6, he left for Elstree Airport in a chauffeur-driven car he had hired from Saunders. He got there about nine thirty. He collected his self-drive car, with his dog, and drove back to the flat, after telling one of the mechanics, "I will bring the plane back from Southend tonight."

He parked the Singer outside the house, and around lunchtime, with the help of a Saunders garage employee, he got the heavy parcel downstairs and put it in the car. While they were taking it down, it made a gurgling noise. Hume thought it was a human body, that of a small or a young person. It crossed his mind that the package might contain Setty's body, as he had read in the papers that morning that he was missing. He knew Stanley Setty because he had sold him a Pontiac two years ago for two hundred pounds, having been introduced to him by Roy Salvadori.

Hume described the package. It was about four feet long and about two feet six inches across and about two feet deep. It was wrapped up in what he thought was an army blanket, brownish gray in color. It was secured by a rope or cord tied crossways and end to end. The blanket must have been folded over and sealed by sewing, as there were no loose ends protruding. It was not a solid, hard bundle but had a give to it. It was very heavy, and it was all he could do to lift it.

In the afternoon he drove to Southend, arriving there, he thought, at about three. He parked the car close to the Auster and man-handled the package into the copilot's seat. Then he took off and flew out to sea until he was about the same distance from Southend Pier as on the previous day.

When he tried to drop the parcel he had difficulty, but by pushing it against the door he managed to get the door open. He let go of the controls, and the plane went into a vertical turn and the parcel fell out into the sea. He then lost his way and landed in a plowed field at Faversham, Kent. Someone gave the propeller a swing for him, and he took off again and landed at Gravesend Airport. He left the plane there, as it was now too dark to fly, hired a taxi, and arrived back home about eight.

The next morning, October 7, he went to Elstree—he thought by bus—and tried to get a plane to Southend. He was unsuccessful, but one of the mechanics working on the airfield offered to take him to Southend on the back of his motorbike. They arrived there between two and three p.m. Hume picked up the Singer and drove home and returned the car to Saunders garage.

That same day, having seen in the newspapers the numbers of the five-pound notes that were reported to have been in Setty's possession when he disappeared, Hume checked the numbers with those on the notes given to him by Boy. He found that four of the notes were identical with four of the five-pound notes reported to have been obtained by Setty from the bank.

He disposed of the hundred and fifty pounds he had obtained from the Three in the following manner: he gave eighty pounds in five-pound notes to his wife, half of which she put into the baby's post office savings account and half into her own bank. He couldn't remember how he had disposed of the other notes, apart from the four he had mentioned. One of these he had paid at Fortnum and Mason's for a telephone-address pad; one at a shop in Burlington Arcade for a set of scissors in a leather case, and the other two to a tobacconist's in the Edgware Road.

On Sunday, October 23, he read in the newspapers that part of Setty's body had been found in Essex tied up in a blanket. At about eleven o'clock that morning the telephone had rung, and it was Boy at the other end. Boy asked Hume if he had read the Sunday papers, and said, "I hope you are not getting any views about getting squeamish and claiming any reward. You have a wife and baby."

Hume said, "I am in it, I presume, as deep as you are, for a hundred and fifty pounds at that." There was a lot more said, which he couldn't now remember.

He had not seen any of the three men since the night of October 6, and had not heard from any of them since Sunday, October 23, when Boy rang.

Asked to account for his movements on the evening of October 4, when Setty had disappeared, he said that as far as he could remember he had met at approximately six o'clock a Mr. Douglas Muirhead, who lived somewhere in the Belsize Park area and with whom he had made an appointment in the morning. Both of them were interested in a zip-fastener invention. They had arranged to meet outside the Shepherd public house in Shepherd Market, and they did meet there. They went into the saloon bar, and Hume stayed there for about three hours drinking with Muirhead and then went home, arriving about ten.

That, in summary, was Hume's story. Later he would disavow an item or two, despite the fact that he had signed the statement at the time, but there would be no major retractions. At the trial the statement would become his defense to the charge of murder.

IN THE POLICE VIEW, Hume's story was true only as to the facts which at the time he knew they could prove, and about which it would therefore have been folly to lie. These included the details of the flights and the dropping of the parcels from an aircraft—which incidentally explained the postmortem bone fractures of the torso that Dr. Camps had noted. What the detectives wholly disbelieved was the story of the Three, whom they regarded as a pure invention. It was not lost on them that the descriptions given by Hume were in many respects remarkably similar to the appearance of the three officers chiefly concerned in the inquiry—MacDougall, Jamieson, and Sutherland!

Still, disbelief was not evidence, and the Yard spared no effort to try and trace Mac, Gree, and the Boy. Working from a special room in Albany Street equipped with many telephones, MacDougall and his officers conducted a conscientious and intensive search. The detailed descriptions of the Three were circulated to the press and widely published. Criminal records were combed. Hume, who was still being detained at Albany Street, was taken to the Yard and shown photographs from the rogues' gallery. He was unable to pick out anyone as Mac or Gree or Boy.

MacDougall twice sought Hume's further help. On October 27 he saw him at Albany Street and said, "Can you tell me anything more about the three men you mention in your statement?"

Hume said, "No, I have told you all I know about them."

Next day the detective again saw Hume and said, "Have you been able to remember anything further about the three men you described, as I have had many inquiries made and they cannot be identified."

Hume said, "No, I have been thinking hard, but I can't tell you anything more about it. You should be able to pick them up in Warren Street."

Detectives had already made exhaustive inquiries in Warren Street and its surroundings. Traders they had interviewed at the time of Setty's disappearance had been seen again and asked about the Three. By October 30 some two hundred people had been questioned. Such names as Mac and Green and the Boy were not wholly unknown in the world of spivvery, and several trails were followed. One "Green" was tracked down, but was found to be wholly dissimilar from Hume's Gree. Another man, vaguely answering to one of Hume's descriptions, was cleared of any connection. Because of the publicity, members of the public were writing to the police, and the search soon embraced the whole country. But in the end, no one, it seemed, could provide any solid information about Mac or Gree or Boy. Not a trace of any of them could be found.

Other inquiries were proving more positive.

The Setty five-pound note that Hume had passed at Fortnum and Mason's had been tracked down and satisfactorily identified by a shop clerk—because of some peculiar serrations—as the one Hume had produced.

The half alibi that Hume had advanced for the evening of October 4, the evening of Setty's disappearance, had been found to be without substance. When the police came to check with Mr. Douglas Muirhead, he denied that he had seen Hume that evening. He agreed he knew Hume, and said that from time to time they had met at the Shepherd public house for an evening drink—but not on October 4. That evening he had left work between five thirty and six o'clock, gone home, and stayed there. The Yard men were able to confirm this. So there was no alibi—only a potential boomerang.

The detectives had also made inquiries about Hume's financial position just before the Setty disappearance. They had found that he had been overdrawn at his bank, had had some checks returned, and had recently pawned some clothes and jewelry.

Hume's activities and movements on the morning of October 5, before his first plane flight, had been closely investigated, with many interesting results. It had been, the Yard men discovered, an extremely busy morning for Hume. He had called at his bank and paid in some money. He had bought some floor stain for his flat. He had had a conversation with the baby's doctor. He had visited a pharmacy and had a prescription made up for sleeplessness, from which—perhaps not surprisingly—he was suffering. He had called at the garage to hire a car, and had telephoned Elstree to book the Auster. Nor was this all. That morning, the police learned, he had taken his sitting-room carpet to a nearby cleaner's, and asked that it should be dyed a dark green. And he had taken a carving knife to be sharpened at Saunders garage. On the twenty-eighth MacDougall asked him about the knife. "Yes," Hume said, "I got it sharpened for the joint." He had also, it transpired, shut himself up in his kitchen for nearly an hour on that same October 5, after giving instructions that he was on no account to be disturbed.

At six thirty p.m. on October 28, MacDougall saw Hume again. He said, "As a result of inquiries made, I am going to charge you with murdering Stanley Setty between fourth October and fifth October, 1949"—and cautioned him.

Hume said, "No, I didn't kill him. I am not guilty." Next morning he was taken to Bow Street police court, charged before the magistrate with Setty's murder, and remanded in custody.

ONE OF THE MOST painstaking investigators in the week that followed was Dr. Henry Holden, the Scotland Yard forensic scientist who had found the spot of blood in the Auster plane.

On October 29 he went to the Hume flat and took possession of the sitting-room carpet, the one that had been dyed. On examination he found a stain, approximately fourteen inches by nine inches, toward one corner of it on the underside, and on this he carried out some tests. First he took a number of fibers from the stained area and extracted their content in sterile water. He then introduced this extract into a series of test tubes, in each of which there was a test serum. These test serums had been prepared to give a reaction against various types of blood—human, ox, sheep, pig, rabbit, fowl, and so on. He got a positive reaction to human blood and a negative reaction to all the others. Largely because of the cleaning and dyeing, he was not able to group the blood.

On October 31 he returned to the flat and took up some of the floorboards in the dining room. He found traces of blood in the crevices between some ten boards, and identified as group O the blood along the edges of three of them. Setty's blood, in common with that of about forty-two percent of the population, had been group O. Underneath the floorboards he found that a considerable quantity of human blood had soaked into the lath and plaster of the ceiling below, and dried there. He also found traces of blood between three floorboards just inside the sitting room.

On November 1 he was back again. He lifted more boards in the dining room and found heavy stains of human blood, group O, on the wood and plaster below them. There was an iron pipe running along one of the joists, and a drip of blood had run across the pipe. At the time of the drip it had been fresh blood and, in Holden's opinion, undiluted. His estimate of the amount of blood found under the boards was about a teacupful.

On November 3 he made a final examination of the flat. He found small splashes of blood on the wall of the staircase leading up from the ground floor. He found traces of blood on the edges and surface of the green linoleum covering the entrance hall. He found slight smears of blood on several wooden treads of the stairs leading up to the bathroom. And in the bathroom itself he found blood on the linoleum—faint on the surface, quite marked at the edges.

So, in the Hume flat, blood had been spilled on the stairs, in the entrance hall, in the sitting room, in the dining room, and in the bathroom. That blood was going to take a lot of explaining. Much had obviously been wiped up. Before then, the flat must have looked like a slaughterhouse.

By now, Superintendent MacDougall and his colleagues might reasonably have been congratulating themselves on a considerable achievement.

Within three days of the finding of Setty's torso they had investigated Hume's flying trail and collected vital statements from airfield personnel.

Because of this work, within five days of the torso discovery they were holding Hume in custody, and were able to obtain a virtual confession that he had been an accessory ex post facto to murder.

They had then gone far, through the negative results of their inquiries, to discredit his story of the Three. They had demolished his attempted alibi for the evening of October 4. They had shown that his financial circumstances would have been a possible motive for murder. They had produced significant evidence that he was in fact the murderer: the wide distribution of blood in the flat, the haste to have a bloodstained carpet dyed, the sharpening of the carving knife, the secret activities in the kitchen.

They had, in short, good reason to be confident that the weight of evidence they had amassed would be sufficient to secure a conviction when the case was heard.

CHAPTER 5

ON JANUARY 18, 1950, AT the Central Criminal Court, Brian Donald Hume went on trial for his life. At that time, death was still the penalty for willful murder. If Hume were convicted of murdering Stanley Setty, he would almost certainly be hanged.

The queue for the public gallery began to form at five o'clock in the morning, and the numbers soon far exceeded the available space. The national newspapers were preparing to devote many columns, indeed many pages, to the evidence. Star reporters were assembling in galaxy strength. For this was a cause célèbre. The public felt, and rightly, that it was going to be a trial of absorbing interest. Not this time because any fashionable name was involved, or because there was any titillating sex angle. The fascination of the Hume case lay in its many unique features. Never before in England had a dismembered body been disposed of by being dropped into the sea from an airplane. Rarely before had there been such an astonishing story as that of the gangster Three. And the accused man himself had aroused great interest. The murder had been sordid—but there seemed nothing sordid about the appearance or known record of the prisoner, mistakenly but understandably described by one newspaper at the time of his arrest as "a Battle of Britain pilot, one of the Few." Was this man a hero-villain? All the ingredients were present for a tremendous drama.

Leading for the crown was the recently appointed senior treasury counsel, Mr. Christmas Humphreys—a man with a cool, analytical mind, an experienced criminal lawyer, and at the age of forty-nine in the prime of his professional life. He was a man of many parts. His interests included ballet and music; the writing, and reading aloud, of poetry; osteopathy and psychoanalysis. He was a slightly built man who, when addressing the court, tended to speak in a rapid monotone. At the Hume trial words sometimes poured from him at two hundred a minute, so that the shorthand writers had difficulty in taking down what he said. To the ten men and two women of the jury it could well have sounded a bit of a gabble.

Humphreys followed the tradition, well established by 1950, that when execution could be the outcome of a trial the crown should present its case with restraint, rather than fight tooth and nail for a conviction.

So there would be no melodramatics from him, no fierce rhetoric, nothing intemperate. He would be a servant of justice, not an advocate; a prosecutor, not a persecutor. If there were any killing to be done, it would be by scrupulous fairness. But this, of course, did not exclude a sharp edge to cross-examination.

Leading counsel for the defense was fifty-six-year-old Mr. Richard

Levy, K.C. He was a commanding figure in court—"with the bearing of an actor," one reporter thought. He had a pleasant voice and an easy-to-get-on-with manner, and his flow of soft, almost soothing words had much jury appeal. He was well known at the commercial bar, but he was far less experienced than Humphreys in major criminal trials, and this would be his first "limelight" murder case. He was to prove skillful and persuasive in argument, well primed in knowledge, and pertinacious in cross-examination.

From Levy, also, there would be no histrionics, no declamations. Neither he nor his opponent would quarrel with the other or bicker with the judge. As far as leading counsel on the two sides were concerned, this was going to be a very gentlemanly trial.

A MAN ACCUSED OF committing a sensational murder can often seem a surprisingly insignificant figure, a mere cipher, in court, as the lawyers and witnesses take the stage. Not so Donald Hume. High up in the commanding dock of the Old Bailey's Court Number One, he was continually the center of public attention, the focus of curious eyes. The visual impression was not unfavorable. He was pleasant-looking and well set up. His black hair, with its long loose curl in front, was combed into a neat part. His clothes—checkered sport jacket, pullover, and flannel trousers—were perhaps a little spivvish; but the Royal Air Force tie he wore was legitimate, if somewhat cheeky in the circumstances. On the whole he seemed a quite presentable young man.

In the dock he occupied himself busily, making many notes in a thick reporter's book and passing down folded messages for his counsel. He had a jaunty, almost a nonchalant air, which—except under cross-examination—lasted throughout the trial. On one occasion he was seen laughing heartily at some joke as he stood on the steps leading from the cells to the dock.

Later in the trial he was to prove an arresting witness in the box, a man of vigorous mind and nimble wit, a man with complete confidence in himself, a man not to be intimidated by anyone. He was glib, talkative, sometimes gaily impudent.

When, in a cross-examination, Humphreys put challenging questions in a hectoring and haughty tone, Hume several times seemed to the impartial observer to get the better of the exchanges. His replies, though somewhat brash, were spirited. "Now *you're* romancing," he said once to Humphreys; and once, with an insolent pouting of his lips, "Absolute baloney!" As the star performer, he seemed to be enjoying his central role.

He was so assured, so ready with his answers, that at one point the judge had to rebuke him for starting to reply before counsel had finished framing the question. And when the cross-examination seemed in danger of developing into a bitter wrangle, the judge pointed out to him that the purpose of the trial was to make a necessary investigation; that there was no need to answer violently, since there was nothing personal behind the questions put to him. To which Hume replied, "But my life is a personal matter to me."

Throughout the trial his demeanor was that of a man contemptuous of the charge, conscious of his innocence of the murder indictment, and confident of acquittal. If it was a performance—and many saw it as that—it was an impressive one.

THE CASE FOR THE prosecution was effectively presented by Christmas Humphreys in a forty-five-minute opening speech. Summarized in a few sentences, it went like this:

Hume and Setty knew each other in the Warren Street car market. Hume was hard up on October 4, when it was alleged he killed Setty. On that day Setty drew from the bank a thousand and five pounds in five-pound notes. On the night of October 4 someone murdered him with five stab wounds to the body from some sort of knife or dagger. Thereafter Hume was found in possession of a quantity of five-pound notes. On his own confession four of them corresponded with notes that Setty had drawn from the bank. One of them was subsequently passed by Hume to a shop. Two days after the murder Hume dropped the dismembered remains of a man he believed to be Setty into the sea from an airplane. "You may agree with the proposition," Humphreys said, "that he who disposes of the dead body of a murdered man is usually the murderer." In Hume's flat in Finchley Road, heavy staining of human blood had been found, much of it of Setty's blood group, and it was clear to the prosecution that the dead body of the murdered man had been cut up in that flat. "You may agree with the proposition," Humphreys said, "that he who cuts up the dead body of a recently murdered man is very probably the murderer." Hume's story of the three men was complete fantasy. These men had never existed outside the fertile imagination of the accused. Hume had had to romance in order to provide an explanation that might save him from the consequences of his act.

That, in outline, was what the prosecution would seek to prove. What the case notably lacked was direct evidence, as Humphreys made clear at the start. There was no suggestion that Hume had made any confession. No one would be called to say he had seen him murder Setty. There was no direct evidence that Setty had ever been in the Hume flat. No fingerprints of Setty had been found in the flat. No one had come forward to say he had seen his car near the flat. All Hume's clothes had been carefully examined and not a single sign of a bloodstain had been found on any of them. No weapon had been discovered that could have inflicted the injuries to the torso, and no tool that could have been used for sawing through the bones. As far as direct evidence was concerned, there was an almost total blank.

In short, the prosecution was relying entirely on circumstantial evidence.

The evidence of circumstances, as prosecutors in Humphreys' position invariably stress to the jury, is not necessarily an inferior form of evidence. An inference of guilt from a number of known facts otherwise hard to explain may be much more reliable than, say, an identification at a police lineup or the recollection of an event by an eyewitness. Humphreys did not quote, though he might have, Thoreau's colorful aphorism, "Some circumstantial evidence is very strong, as when you find a trout in the milk." All the same, circumstantial evidence makes more demands on juries—once defined by Herbert Spencer as "twelve men of average ignorance"—than the witness who says, "I saw him do it." Not every juryman is capable of imaginative reasoning.

ON THE AFTERNOON of the first day, after a number of witnesses had been called, the jury asked if they might inspect the Hume flat. The judge was agreeable, and at five fifteen they were taken in a motor coach to Finchley Road, accompanied by two court bailiffs. Superintendent MacDougall was awaiting them, and conducted them through the flat. From a layout of the rooms, it will be seen that the entrance hall divides the flat into two separate parts. On the left is the sitting room, overlooking Finchley Road—the room of the dyed carpet—where, in the prosecution's view, Setty was stabbed. Back across the entrance hall is the dining room, where the prosecution believed Setty had died. Beyond the dining room is a small scullery, beyond the scullery the kitchen, and beyond the kitchen a large cupboard, described as a coal cupboard, under a sloping roof but in surface area the size of a small room. On the floor above, a few steps up the stairs, is the bedroom, the baby's nursery, and a bathroom.

The jury spent some ten minutes looking over the place, and were then taken back to the Old Bailey.

The first day of the trial had gone smoothly, but that night there was an upset. Mr. Justice Lewis—sixty-eight, old Etonian, fellow of an Oxford college, devout churchman—who had presided at the opening, was taken seriously ill and had to be rushed to the hospital for an operation. Next morning his place was taken by Mr. Justice Sellers—fifty-seven, a North-countryman, educated at grammar school and provincial university, a Liberal politician with a fine military record, bluff and handsome—who explained what had happened. The jury had to be resworn, the dispersed witnesses of the first day rounded up, some of them by police car, and the trial begun all over again. Humphreys said that the jury would be trying the case on the evidence, not on the speeches of counsel, and compressed his second opening into five minutes. The witnesses who had already given evidence were then recalled in rapid succession.

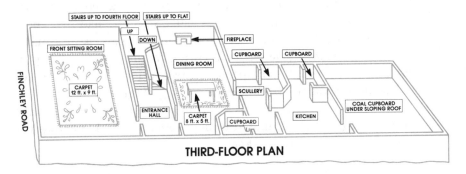

A reconstruction of the lower floor of the Hume flat in Finchley Road, where Stanley Setty was murdered and later dismembered.

IN ANY TRIAL OF GREAT complexity—and the Hume case was a tangle of evidence—matters are often raised by one side or the other which after a few brief exchanges are quietly dropped. These are the matters which, hopefully introduced, are presently seen to be irrelevant or insignificant, or else are so effectively countered that they offer neither side a clear advantage. Other issues grow steadily in importance as the case proceeds, and become the material on which the jury bases its judgment.

Let us first dispose of the probings and skirmishings before moving on to the main battle:

1. The Tentative Alibi

It will be recalled that the Yard men had disproved Hume's claim that on the evening of October 4 he had been in the company of Mr. Douglas Muirhead at the Shepherd public house.

When Hume was questioned at the trial about this exploded alibi, he simply shrugged the matter off. Although, he said, he had told the police that to the best of his recollection he had been with Mr. Muirhead, to the best of his recollection now he had been at home. During the time he had been with the police he had been unable to remember. . . .

Well, it was a point for the prosecution, but not much more than that. Anyone, after a gap of three weeks, might get confused about his movements on a particular night. Anyone could make an honest mistake. The matter was allowed to drop.

2. The Initial Denial

The prosecution made a point of the fact that when Hume was first questioned by the Yard men at Albany Street he had lied about when he had last driven a car and about putting parcels in a plane. Insofar as these lies suggested that Hume might just as readily lie about other matters, they helped the prosecution's case. Otherwise they had no relevance to the murder charge. Hume would presumably have lied about the parcels whether or not he had killed Setty, since he thought they contained human remains and knew that disposing of them was a criminal act.

3. The Missing Evidence

The defense naturally made the most of the lack of direct evidence that Setty had been murdered in Hume's flat. "Where is the knife that stabbed Setty?" Levy asked. "Nobody has yet discovered it. Where is the saw?" And of course there were other gaps. No Setty fingerprints, no bloodstained clothes. But the prosecution had an easy answer. Hume had had slightly more than three weeks to get rid of any evidence of murder before the Yard men had come to his flat. It would have been surprising if by then any fingerprints had remained unwiped, or if a suitable knife one inch wide and at least four inches long had been found, or a hacksaw with traces of bone on it, or bloodstained clothes. Getting rid of the evidence would have been task number one, and indeed would have presented no problem. As the judge was to point out in his summing-up, two parcels dropped by Hume had never been recovered from the sea. Either of them might have contained the missing objects. Humphreys put it more strongly: "Obviously no man in his senses would do anything but put them in the parcel he was going to throw away."

4. *The Last Contact*

Hume said at the trial that he had not seen Setty for almost two years and could hardly remember him. But a witness named Leonard Barker, a motorcar trader who knew Setty well and Hume by sight, said that during the previous summer he had seen the two men talking together outside Setty's garage in Cambridge Terrace Mews, where he had gone to buy a car. If his evidence was correct, it made Hume either forgetful or once again a liar. It threw little light on whether Hume had killed Setty in the flat in October.

5. *The Recovered Fivers*

These would have been of the highest significance if Hume had had no explanation for them. But his story was that he had got them from the Three—and if that story were believed, they were not evidence against him as a killer.

6. *Setty's Car*

Someone had driven Setty's cream-and-yellow Citroën back to the garage at Cambridge Terrace Mews after the murder. The prosecution maintained that Hume had done this. He could drive a car and he knew where Setty's garage was. Hume denied he had done it. He said he would have had the greatest difficulty in finding the garage. As his fingerprints had not been discovered anywhere on the car, there was no direct evidence, only a hypothesis, and nothing more was said about it.

7. *The Question of Noise*

If Hume had murdered a man in his flat on October 4 by stabbing him five times with a knife, Levy argued, the people living immediately below would surely have heard something. The sound of a struggle, perhaps; the sounds of scuffling, of raised voices, of a shout or a scream. And if the sawing-up had been carried out immediately afterward, as the prosecution was suggesting, they would have heard the noise of that, too. Admittedly the sawing could have been of short duration. Dr. R. T. Teare, an eminent pathologist who appeared for the defense and who knew a great deal about sawing bones, said rather surprisingly that it would take an inexperienced person little more than a minute to saw across the thigh of a man of Setty's size. A minute for each thigh, he said. And two, three, or four minutes for the neck, where the bones were more awkward. But, however brief the operation, the noise would have been loud. Loud enough to drown ordinary conversation. "It is impossible to dictate to one's secretary while bones are being sawn," Dr. Teare said, in a memorably macabre sentence.

Well, *had* anything been heard? A Mr. Alfred Spencer, a schoolmaster, who with his wife occupied the flat below, confirmed that he had been at home all evening on October 4. In his evidence he said he could fix the date because his mother had sent him a copy of a newspaper containing the death notice of someone he knew, and he had entered it in his diary. So far, so good. He had been there. And he had heard nothing unusual. Nothing at all. Could a murder and a sawing-up really have taken place just above his head without his hearing a sound? It seemed a little improbable.

However, an effective piece of cross-examination followed, made possible by the Yard's careful research at the house:

HUMPHREYS: You were sitting in a room which was really underneath the large coal cupboard in Hume's flat?

SPENCER: Yes, I was sitting partly underneath the coal cupboard. The flat is not quite the same as the one above.

HUMPHREYS: Can you hear people moving about in Hume's flat at all?

SPENCER: If the carpet is down I should say not.

HUMPHREYS: Did you hear people moving about on that night?

SPENCER: Not more than usual.

JUDGE: What have you in fact heard?

SPENCER: The only thing we have heard is when they have been in the cupboard to get coal.

There was little here for the defense, and the question of noise was not pressed. A glance at the plan of the Hume flat shows that if Spencer spent the evening in a room under the coal cupboard, he was far away from the Humes' sitting room, where the prosecution alleged most of the action had taken place. In fact, he was some sixteen yards away. Naturally, very little would have been audible.

8. *The Staining of the Floor*

On October 6, some thirty-six hours after the alleged murder of Setty in the flat, Hume had arranged for the floorboards surrounding the carpets in the sitting room and dining room to be revarnished with a dark brown stain which he had bought the previous day. The work was done by a man named Joseph Staddon, a painter employed by Saunders garage, in his lunch hour. The prosecution maintained that Hume was trying to cover up marks left by wiped-up bloodstains, and that it was a remarkable coincidence that the staining should have been done on that particular day.

The Humes, however, represented restaining the boards as almost a routine thing with them. Though they had been in the flat for only a year, Mrs. Hume was to tell the court that her husband had already varnished the floor twice himself.

The fact that this time he had brought someone in from outside may well have been connected, one imagines, with his need for help in getting the heavy parcel down the stairs.

In any case, the staining did little to further the murder charge against him. For it had been done *after* the supposed arrival of the Three with the big parcel on the night of October 5, so even if bloodstains had been the reason for it, the blood could conceivably have come from the parcel.

9. *The Felt*

The question arose, where had the felt come from that had been used to wrap around the torso? If it could be shown that it had originated in the Hume flat, this would be strong evidence of his guilt of murder. If not, it would be a point for his story of the Three.

MacDougall was questioned by Levy. "When you were in Hume's flat, did you see any pieces of felt of a similar type to that in which the body was wrapped?" MacDougall replied, "The only felt of a similar type was in the front sitting room under the carpet."

This was suggestive. Perhaps there had been a piece left over when the felt was laid? But Mrs. Hume was to say that she had never seen any large pieces of felt in the flat apart from that under the carpet. Nor, as far as the prosecution was able to discover, had anyone else.

The Yard, early in its inquiries, had issued an appeal through the press. The torso had been wrapped "in a piece of good-quality, brown-dyed, gray wool art felt, machine-stitched, 6 ft. 6 by 4 ft. 6." This felt, or a larger piece from which it could have been cut, might have been sold to some person or persons before October 5 in North London or surrounding districts. The felt, one-fifth of an inch thick, was thought to have been acquired in the North of England, and had probably been used there before finding its way to London or the South. The request for information was particularly directed to furniture dealers, secondhand dealers, and shop assistants. Several people responded to the appeal, and MacDougall himself spent many hours making inquiries among manufacturers. But nothing emerged that pointed to Hume as a purchaser.

Neither side could prove anything, and the origin of the felt remained an unanswered question.

CHAPTER 6

WE COME NOW TO the crucial issues, the pitched battles, which one way or another would decide the outcome of the trial. First:

1. The Blood in the Flat

There was so much of it! Dr. Holden, it will be recalled, had found traces in the sitting room, traces in the dining room (where an appreciable quantity had trickled through the cracks to the plaster below), traces in the hall, traces in the bathroom, and traces on the stairs leading to the bathroom. Considering that this was only the residue after cleaning up, there could be no doubt whatever that a great deal of blood had been spilled in the flat, and very widely spilled. The question the jury would have to decide was how it had got there.

In the prosecution's view, it had resulted from Hume's murder of Setty in the flat. The defense maintained that the blood had seeped out of the large parcel brought by the Three.

If Setty had been murdered in the flat, the quantity and wide distribution of the blood was easily explained. Three of the stab wounds had pierced Setty's lungs, one of them close to the bronchial tubes— which meant he would have coughed up blood. He could have been stabbed in one room and have staggered through the flat afterward, bleeding all the way.

That was the view of Dr. Camps. That was the view of Humphreys, who pointed out that apart from the traces on the stairs leading up to the bathroom and in the bathroom itself, the bloodstains were roughly in a straight line. Setty could have been stabbed in the sitting room before crossing the hall to the dining room, collapsing there, and bleeding to death face downward on the boards.

Levy did not allow this reconstruction to go unchallenged. Would a dying man stabbed five times in the sitting room, he asked Dr. Camps, have had the strength to cross the hall? Yes, Camps said, he would very likely have been capable of taking four or five steps. For what purpose? asked Levy. For escape from his attacker, said Camps. In that case, said Levy, surely he would have made for the front door, the exit, rather than the dining room? "Experience of these cases," Camps replied, "has shown that very often the person attacked is not in a position or condition to recognize doors; he goes away instinctively."

The prosecution's reconstruction remained undented, and it explained both the quantity and the distribution of the blood on the main floor. As to the bathroom, the murderer would obviously have gone up there to wash after the killing.

Hume's explanation of the wide spread of the stains was a much more tortuous affair. His detailed account of what had happened went like this: On the night of October 5, Mac and Boy had carried the parcel up to the flat. They had rested in the dining room (a fact Hume had not mentioned in his original statement to the police) and then put it in the coal cupboard beyond the kitchen. After they had left, Hume "went to the cupboard to move it to one side."

When he lifted it up, it made a gurgling noise and he saw a pool of blood underneath. He was terrified and rushed downstairs after the Three, but they had already gone off in their car. Back in the flat, he noticed blood in the dining room where the parcel had rested. He wiped it up, and also wiped up blood in front of the coal cupboard. Next morning, because he wanted to carry up coal to the cupboard, he got the parcel out and left it by the refrigerator in the kitchen. Later he dragged it as far as the scullery. Later still he moved it again. He told Levy about that. It was one of those strangely phrased colloquies arising from the fact that counsel may not lead his witness.

HUME: I picked it up and started walking through with it. In doing so, I dropped it on the floor.
LEVY: In which room?
HUME: In the dining room.
LEVY: Did it do anything?
HUME: Yes, one end of it opened up and it squirted blood.
LEVY: What did you do then?
HUME: I grabbed it and dragged it into the hall. I readjusted the ropes at the edge of the parcel and went into the kitchen and got a large piece of brown material and tucked it round it. I left it in the hall.
JUDGE: You got what piece of material from the kitchen?
HUME: It was part of one of my wife's frocks torn up.
LEVY: How did the blood get inside the sitting room?
HUME: I cannot explain that.

He had given, at any rate, a partial explanation. If all this moving and dropping and dragging of a blood-saturated parcel had actually happened, some at least of the many bloodstains could be accounted for. But *had* it happened? The jury must surely have been wondering. Once Hume had discovered that the parcel was leaking blood in the coal cupboard, would he not have been more likely to try and deal with it there, to wrap it up in some better way at once, rather than lug it in that condition from cupboard to kitchen to dining room and finally to hall, leaving a bloody trail all the way, which he would have to clean up? Had he not perhaps been forced to invent the movements afterward, in order to explain the wide distribution of the stains?

Another point arises. Just how blood-soaked *was* the parcel? On this we have some independent testimony. Joseph Staddon, the man brought in to stain the floorboards, described how he had helped Hume take the heavy and unwieldy package down the two flights of narrow, winding stairs to the car. Even for the two of them it was an extremely difficult job. After they had carried it about three-quarters of the way down, Hume took a false step and the package got away from them and slithered down the remainder of the stairs. Staddon told the court that at one point Hume said, "Don't put your hands underneath, hold it by the rope," explaining that the parcel was a valuable property.

This suggests that Hume was concerned about the possibility of blood seeping out. But Staddon's evidence was that the gray felt in which the parcel was wrapped had had no stains on it. Was it possible that the parcel could have spilled so much blood through its wrappings while in the flat, and yet have shown not a trace of blood after that slithering journey down?

In his testimony, Dr. Teare said that if the torso had been wrapped in a parcel and moved about, blood would have seeped out, not only from the cut ends but also from the stab wounds in the chest. The amount of leakage would have depended on gravity and on the pressure which was applied to the parcel. If the parcel had been dropped, he would have expected that the impact with the floor would have squeezed blood out of the folds in every direction. "Rather like pressing a sponge?" Levy suggested.

"Yes, like dropping a wet sponge on the ground," Teare said. He took the view that the blood spilled in the flat could certainly have leaked from the parcel. The inference was therefore that Hume's story was true.

Dr. Camps took the opposite view. Closely pressed by Levy, he agreed that there would probably have been about six pints of blood left in the torso, but he could not conceive any way in which a parcel tied up in the felt in which it was found could have made the stains that were discovered in the flat in different places. The amount of blood was consistent with murder having been committed there, but not, in his view, with leakage.

Not for the first time in forensic history, two experts had disagreed in court on a vital matter, and left the jury puzzled.

2. *The Stain on the Carpet*

Round about lunchtime on October 5, the day after Setty's disappearance, Hume had called at a cleaner's shop next door to his flat and asked if they dyed carpets. Mrs. Linda Hearnden, the manager, said that they did. Hume asked how long it would take to get his sitting-room carpet dyed, and was told it couldn't be done in less than fourteen days. He said he would like it done. Mrs. Hearnden suggested sending a man up for the carpet, but Hume said he would bring it down himself. He returned after about ten minutes with a light green carpet, rolled and tied. He asked how much the job would cost. Mrs. Hearnden said if she were to give a proper estimate the carpet would have to be untied and unrolled so she could measure it, but Hume said a rough estimate would do, and this was given. Hume said he wanted the carpet dyed a darker green, and he chose a color from the samples.

At the trial he explained to his counsel why he took the carpet to be dyed on October 5. "It was always arranged that the carpet should be dyed," he told Levy. "It was filthy. I had bought quantities of high-octane gasoline and had attempted in the presence of my wife and others to clean the carpet."

Mrs. Hume was later to agree. "There were stains all over," she said. The fact that it had been taken to be cleaned and dyed on October 5 was, it seemed, just a coincidence, like the revarnishing of the floorboards on the sixth.

However, there was evidence that Hume had been rather more concerned about the state of the carpet on and around October 5 than its known condition would seem to warrant. Mrs. Ethel Stride, the Humes' domestic help, was surprised when she arrived at two p.m. that day to find the carpet gone and to be told by Hume that he had sent it to be dyed because there had been marks on it. In her opinion it had been in remarkably good condition, and this was the first time she had heard any mention of dyeing. Hume said that he had tried to wash the marks out himself, but the result had not been satisfactory. He told her that in doing the washing he had made her mop unfit for use, and he gave her two shillings and sixpence to go out and buy another.

Hume's concern about the carpet did not stop with its removal. Once it had gone to the cleaner's, he wasn't able to rest until he had

got it back. "Frantic" was the word Humphreys used about him. According to Mrs. Hearnden, after nine or ten days he had asked her to "hurry it up." He had said he was going to give a party, as his wife had had a baby and was coming home. (Mrs. Hume had had the baby some ten weeks before.) After that, Mrs. Hearnden said, "he asked about it almost every hour for the last two days." He had been into the shop about eight times, she said.

Hume described this as a gross exaggeration. "Quite likely three times," he said. And once, he agreed, he had phoned up the factory. "You need a carpet on the floor when there is only felt," he said. You also need one, of course, if there is any danger that the police may call and wonder about its absence.

The prosecution had no doubts about the cause of Hume's agitation over the carpet, for this was the carpet that Dr. Holden had taken possession of immediately after Hume's arrest. This was the carpet which, even after cleaning and dyeing, showed a large stain in one corner on the underside—a stain which Holden tested and found to be blood. In the prosecution's view, Hume had taken the carpet to the cleaner's in the hope of eliminating the bloodstain.

The carpet had now become, in the words of the judge, "one of the most important pieces of evidence in the case." For it had been taken to the cleaner's *before* Hume's Mac and Gree and the Boy had allegedly appeared at the flat. So this stain, at least, could not have come from a bloodied parcel. This stain had preceded any parcel. How, then, had it got on the carpet? Was not this almost conclusive evidence that Hume had murdered Setty?

Levy, for the defense, was in a very tight spot indeed. However, he fought back with skill and ingenuity. He was helped by the fact that the techniques of blood-testing at that time were less sophisticated than they are now. The cleaning of the carpet had rendered it useless for blood grouping. Even to prove beyond doubt that human blood was present, it was necessary that a sample should be reasonably well preserved. So the first question Levy applied himself to was, *was* it a bloodstain? Or had it been caused, as the Humes said, by a spilled drink, or by someone being sick at a party? Or by something else?

Levy had, as the saying goes, done his homework on the technical aspects of blood-testing, and he put Dr. Holden through a searching and erudite cross-examination. He would like to know more, he said, of the tests that had been carried out. Holden described them, explaining in detail about the test serums that had been prepared to give a reaction against various types of blood, including that of ox, sheep, pig, rabbit, and fowl, and saying that the only positive reaction obtained had been to human blood.

"What other animals did you include?" Levy asked. "Did you include a dog?"

"No," said Holden.

"Rather a pity," Levy commented.

But that was only the start of his doubt raising. Were there not, he asked, various human secretions, apart from blood, that could have given a positive reaction in the tests? He went through quite a list: saliva, nasal slime, sweat, human milk, semen, human excrement. Holden agreed that, in greater or lesser degree, some of these could have produced a positive reaction.

And were not these, Levy asked, some of the things that might well get onto a carpet in the course of ordinary long domestic wear? Holden replied, "I do not think that most of those things would appear on the underside of the carpet, and certainly not in the quantity indicated by the stain." And he remained emphatic in his conclusion. "I think that a clean-cut reaction such as I got indicates that this was blood. I got a well-defined and well-marked reaction." Other things, he said, would not have given so strong a reaction.

Nevertheless, as a result of the questions and the answers, Levy felt able to say later about the stain, "There has been no evidence that it is even human blood."

He switched now to another aspect of the stain. Had Dr. Holden found any blood on the pile of the carpet? No, Holden said, he had detected blood only on the underpart.

"How do you account for that?" Levy asked.

"It's possible that the pile would clean more easily than the binding underneath," Holden said.

Levy pressed on. "Do you know that the carpet was at all times laid on underfelt? If blood was spilled on that carpet, wouldn't it be inevitable that some would get on the underfelt?"

Dr. Holden agreed that he would expect it. Though it was possible, he said, that the stain had been communicated to the carpet at a later date, when it was rolled up.

It was to be nearly ten years before an answer to that particular problem was forthcoming.

Meanwhile, Levy developed the idea of "communication." He went over in detail the journey that the carpet had made. First to the cleaner's, rolled up; then in a van, where it could have been in contact with many other soiled goods; then put on the floor of a warehouse; finally taken back to the cleaner's by much the same process. Would there not have been ample opportunity for the carpet to collect stains? If the stain *were* blood, could it not have resulted from contact with a bloodstained article—or perhaps from contact with a workman's cut hand? Holden was more than skeptical. Contact with a bloodstained article certainly wouldn't have caused a stain of the kind he had found. The blood would have had to be liquid, and in large quantity. If from a hand, something like half a cupful would have been required.

Levy had moved, of course, into the realm of the purely speculative, almost of the fanciful. Nevertheless, by his arguments and suggestions he had reduced a deadly danger that murder would be seen by the jury as the *only* possible explanation of the stain.

3. The Carving Knife

Before continuing the narrative, let us properly introduce Mrs. Ethel Stride—so far only briefly mentioned—who was one of the most important witnesses on many aspects of the case. She would probably at that time have described herself as a charlady. She was accustomed to working at the Hume flat once a week on Wednesday afternoons, approximately from two to five o'clock. She had been doing this for about four months, since June 1949. She was an elderly woman of impeccable respectability, very intelligent, and solidly independent. As she stood in the witness box, in her best blue coat and wide-brimmed blue hat trimmed with ribbon in the fashion of the day, one hand gloved, fingers tapping together as she listened attentively to the questions asked, and then searched her memory for the answers, no one could regard her as anything but the very epitome of an honest, utterly reliable witness. It was Hume's misfortune that October 5 should have been a Wednesday.

Now, to the knife.

At one p.m. on October 5, Hume had taken a large white-handled carving knife to be sharpened at Saunders garage—which was a small garage in a back lane just behind the flat, accessible in a few seconds through a gate from the yard. Hume told Maurice Edwards, the man who sharpened the knife and whom he knew, that he wanted it to carve a joint.

Edwards put the knife on a rough grindstone while Hume stood by. Edwards then asked if Hume would like the knife finished on the oilstone, to make a job of it. Hume said no, he was quite satisfied with the rough edge.

"He gave me the impression," Edwards said in evidence, "that he was in a hurry to get back and carve the joint." His urgency caused Edwards no surprise. "It's his nature," he said, in a phrase not too happily chosen about a man on trial for his life, "that he's here today and gone tomorrow."

Later the knife was found in the flat, blunt.

There was no suggestion, of course, that this was the knife that had killed Setty. It was quite the wrong size and shape. This was the knife, the prosecution believed, that had been used to cut up Setty's body—and used again, after sharpening, to complete the job.

Hume elaborated to his counsel about the sharpening. He had been helping, he said, to get lunch ready that day, "laying the table or something like that." It was at his wife's suggestion that he went to have the knife sharpened. "She was always getting on to me about it," he said. He had had other knives sharpened at the garage before. "I was always flitting in having something or other done."

The reason he hadn't waited to have a proper edge put on the knife was that they had a joint that day, and he rushed in and out again. Very likely the joint was on the table, and his wife had been in a hurry to get the meal over and feed the baby. A marginally plausible tale, one might think—though the judge did comment later that one o'clock was "a most inconvenient time" to get a knife sharpened.

Unhappily for Hume, there was Mrs. Stride to reckon with. Between two and five p.m. she had cleaned all through the flat, and she had seen no sign of a joint that day, either in the larder or anywhere else. If there had been a joint, she felt sure she would have seen the remnants. "I suppose," Levy asked hopefully, "you did not *look* for a joint?"

"No," she replied, "it would have been most noticeable these days!" There was a ripple of laughter from the meat-starved public in court—one of the rare moments of light relief in the case.

There was the bare possibility that the joint had been finished at one meal and utensils and plates washed and all traces cleared away before Mrs. Stride's arrival.

On this aspect there was a brief but effective exchange between Humphreys and an apparently unalerted Hume.

HUMPHREYS: Did your wife wash up?
HUME: No, I think she went straight up to feed the baby.
HUMPHREYS: Did you wash up?
HUME: No.
HUMPHREYS: Mrs. Stride said that when she arrived the washing up had been done.

To this Hume made no reply.

In the end, he bowed to the wind of the evidence and adjusted his story. He said, "I either had the carving knife for the joint, or I had an Alsatian which consumes large quantities of horsemeat, which needs a fairly sharp knife to cut. . . . I cannot remember whether we did have a joint or not that day. But it was one thing or the other."

It could, of course, have been the prosecution's third thing. The jury must surely have been wondering not only whether there had been any joint that day, but whether there had been any lunch in the Hume household at all. Whether, in fact, there had been anything to wash up. Whether, perhaps, Hume had been too busy with the knife on other joints.

4. Peculiar Behavior in the Kitchen

As we have noted, it was about two p.m. on October 5 when Mrs. Stride arrived at the Hume flat to do her weekly cleaning. Hume met her in the hall and they had a chat—partly about the carpet. Mrs. Hume, who had been engaged with the baby upstairs, presently came down and joined briefly in the conversation. Sometime between two thirty and two forty-five she took the baby out for a walk, and had not returned when Mrs. Stride departed at five thirty.

After Mrs. Stride had been in the flat for about forty-five minutes, Hume told her he was going to tidy up the cupboard beyond the kitchen to make room for coal, and that he didn't wish to be disturbed. "On no account and in no circumstances" were the words he used. He would be "tidying things up to take them away," he said. It wouldn't require more than an hour, so he wouldn't be interfering with the cleaning. If the telephone rang, Mrs. Stride was to say he was not at home. He then shut himself up in the kitchen—well removed, as the floor plan shows, from the rest of the flat—and remained there for about fifty minutes. Shortly before four o'clock he emerged and asked Mrs. Stride to make him a cup of tea. As soon as he had drunk it he said he was going out. He left the flat with a bulky parcel under each arm, wrapped in brown paper. Mrs. Stride closed the door behind him.

In the light of Hume's own story that he was expecting Mac, Gree, and the Boy to call around and see him that day, and on their account had booked a plane for the afternoon, his choice of time for clearing out the coal cupboard could only be considered remarkable. The prosecution, of course, didn't believe it. "What was he doing in the kitchen for fifty minutes?" Humphreys asked. "Not cutting up Setty— that had been done the night before, shortly after death—but the parceling up of little parts of Setty, that would take time; and sure enough, when he comes out fifty minutes later from the work—so important and secret that he must not be disturbed even for the telephone—he has two parcels with him, and off he goes."

The exchanges at the trial about this kitchen episode were notable chiefly for Hume's extraordinary—some must have thought hastily improvised—answers to the questions that were put to him.

Asked by Levy why he had not wanted to answer the telephone, he said, "On the Monday or Tuesday previous the police had been to me. I had had a license up to then for a twenty-two rifle and had been given about three days to hand it in. It had not arrived up to that time. It was coming from Hereford, where the gun was. I thought the police might ring about it."

Asked by Levy whether he had been doing anything in the kitchen besides clearing out the cupboard, he replied, "Not necessarily, but I had a deed box and I had insurance policies due and I think I sorted them out."

Asked by the judge if he wanted to exclude Mrs. Stride from the kitchen, Hume answered, "Only when I was working in the coal cupboard," and then added by way of explanation, "I was wearing some short white trunks. I had taken my other clothes off. They were running or football trunks. I didn't want to be seen walking round the flat in them."

Humphreys' comment on this was devastating. "The absurdity of his keeping Mrs. Stride out of the kitchen while he turned out the coal cupboard struck even him, in the witness box, and produced possibly the crowning lie of the case—that he put on white shorts to clean out the coal cupboard!"

Of course, if Hume had been engaged in butcher's work in the kitchen, shorts might have been quite a good idea. Like an apron, they are easily disposable.

5. *The Question of Motive*

The prosecution in a trial is not normally required to show a motive for a crime. All it has to do is to prove the fact. Many men have been convicted of apparently motiveless crimes, and some have been hanged for them. However, if a motive can be shown, the prosecution's case is obviously strengthened.

In the Hume trial, the suggested motive was money. Setty had had over a thousand pounds in cash on his person when he disappeared. At that time, Hume was hard up. He had recently pawned some of his belongings: a suit and a three-stone ring. He was somewhat behind with his rent. At his bank he had an arrangement for an overdraft of seventy pounds, but he had exceeded it, and just prior to October 5 several of his checks had not been met. On the morning of the fifth—*after* Setty's disappearance but *before* Hume claimed to have received any money from the Three—he had visited his bank and paid in ninety pounds. That was the financial case against him.

The defense contested the motive vigorously. One telling point it made was that on October 3, when the Humes' doctor, Dr. Keith Blatchley, had called at the flat because the baby was ailing, Hume had settled an outstanding account of thirty pounds without being asked to do so. It was also able to show that during 1949 some largish sums had been paid into Hume's bank account, amounting in all to about two thousand pounds—though, as the judge dryly observed, "paying in is one thing, drawing out is another."

Hume denied that on October 3 he had been hard up—at least, he said, "not to that extent." The pawning was of no significance—he regarded it as just another form of selling. He had money which his father-in-law had given him—seventy-five pounds in five-pound notes. On October 3 he had actually had about two hundred and eighty pounds.

"Where did you keep it?" Humphreys asked.

"I kept it in my pocket," Hume said. "I walked about with two hundred and eighty pounds." For a man of Hume's proclivities, there was nothing very surprising in that.

Levy declared Hume's finances to be irrelevant to the case. There was no evidence whatever that his financial position had been causing him any serious concern. Many people with money occasionally had overdrafts.

Humphreys did not press the matter very strongly, and indeed it was not a very strong one to press. Of course, men had been known to murder for much less than Setty had been carrying, sometimes for only a few shillings. But Hume had shown that he could make a lot of money very quickly, as well as spend it very quickly. Would it have been worth his while to kill Setty in his own flat, messily and bloodily, with all the problems and difficulties that were bound to follow—for a thousand pounds? Even if he had somehow known that Setty had had the money on him . . . It all seemed rather unlikely.

Humphreys had already hedged his bets. "For all I know," he said, "it may have been a chance quarrel, it may have been a dispute arising on some contract, upon some business they were doing together. They may both have been drunk, for all I know."

Well, we shall see.

6. *How Many Murderers?*

It was clearly in the interests of the Hume defense to show reasons why the Setty murder was more likely to have been the work of several men (e.g., the Three) than of one acting alone (e.g., Hume)—and on this it worked hard.

The defense argument was that a man stabbed frontally by a single assailant, with blows that were not instantly lethal, would try to protect himself. Even if stabbed five times in quick succession, he would have some power to fight back—or if not to fight, at least to get his arm up to ward off the weapon. The expected result would be protective injuries, particularly to the arm—for instance, bruises. But no such bruises had been found on Setty's arms, and even after immersion they would have been detectable if they had been there.

The conclusion seemed to be that Setty had not resisted. Why not? The defense explained it this way. If two or three men had been involved in the murder, he could have been restrained by one or more from behind while another man stabbed him from the front. In these circumstances he would have had no chance to resist. And the restraint could well have left no marks. Various holds were known, Dr. Teare said, which caused no bruising.

Dr. Camps, for the prosecution, by no means dismissed this scenario as absurd. He, too, would have expected to find defense wounds if a big and reasonably strong man were attacked from the front by one assailant with a knife. His experience of cases of knife wounds—he had dealt with five in the past year—was that the first thing the attacked man tried to do was to get the knife away. Perhaps, he said, as though thinking aloud, Setty's hands had not been free? But there had been no sign that the hands had been tied—and if the wrists had been held, he would have expected bruising. Perhaps Setty had had his hands in his pockets and had been unable to get them out in time to defend himself. Or perhaps the shock of the repeated stabbings had been so great that resistance was impossible.

Humphreys asked Camps how quickly the five blows could have been delivered, and the doctor gave a dramatic demonstration. The jury watched him as, with his right hand, he made five quick imaginary blows downward and to the right against his chest.

Humphreys looked at his watch. "About three seconds," he said. The jury could imagine that there might have been little opportunity for self-defense.

Camps's final view was objective and fair. "I think," he said, "it is impossible to say whether Setty was murdered by one person or a number."

Dr. Teare, the opposing expert, was only a little less cautious. Replying to Levy, he thought for almost half a minute before he said, "I think the absence of marks of defense upon the body renders it more likely that he was killed by more than one person."

Levy developed the gang theme strongly in his final speech to the jury. "Do you think," he asked, "it would have occurred to anybody but a madman to take a man to his flat for the purpose of murdering him and cutting him up . . . ? On the other hand, it would be easy for a gang to cut up this man and take the body to Hume for him to dispose of. . . . These people presumably have at their disposal places which are more convenient for the purpose of murder and cutting up than Mr. Hume's flat. . . . I submit to you with every confidence that Setty was murdered not by one man but by several."

Some telling points had been made, and in his own final speech Humphreys recognized the fact. "It has never been the case for the prosecution," he said, "that Hume must necessarily alone have murdered Setty. He may have brought some other man to the flat with him. Some other man may have been waiting when Hume brought Setty back. Some other man may have come in by arrangement, or not. I know not."

On balance, the defense had had a clear advantage from this particular encounter.

7. *The Rug*

When Mrs. Stride went to clean the Hume flat on October 5, it wasn't only the sitting-room carpet that had gone. A rug in the hall was missing. The hall where traces of blood were later to be found. And the rug, like the carpet, had gone *before* the alleged arrival of the Three with their parcels. A week later it was back in place. Why had it been taken away, and what had happened to it? Another cleaning?

On this, there is no one to quote but Mrs. Hume, giving evidence later in the trial.

HUMPHREYS: Do you remember what sort of rug there was in the hall?
MRS. HUME: A normal rug; green with a floral pattern.
HUMPHREYS: Mrs. Stride said that when she came to the flat it had gone. Do you know what happened to it?
MRS. HUME: No.

A surprising answer, most housewives would think.

8. *The Three—Did They Exist?*

This, of course, was the crux of the case. If the jury could be persuaded that Mac, Gree, and the Boy were no more than figments of Hume's lively imagination, an invention designed to shift the blame onto others, his conviction was likely to follow automatically. Humphreys' unenviable task was to try to prove what he believed to be a negative.

He had already referred in his opening speech to the strenuous but unsuccessful efforts of the police to trace the Three: to the widespread questioning of traders in Warren Street; to the enormous press publicity, which had produced no result; to Hume's abortive search through the photographs in the rogues' gallery, where one at least of the three men might have been expected to appear. What else could he do to impress the jury?

What he did was put into the box the two co-directors of Mansfield Autos Ltd., William Mansfield and Roy Salvadori. They had been trading in Warren Street for some years; they knew most of the people who frequented it; they had known Setty well; and they had been on friendly terms with Hume. It was actually on the steps leading from their office that Hume had said he had encountered Mac. Who, then, would have been more likely to have heard or known of Mac and the rest of the Three, if they existed? Humphreys read out to them in turn the descriptions Hume had given of Mac, Gree, and the Boy. "Do you know anyone of that description?" he asked. The answer was no in each case. The descriptions and the names were alike unfamiliar to the witnesses.

Predictably, Levy derided their negative evidence as worthless. "I could bring before you," he told the jury, "a thousand or ten thousand people who will tell you that they have never heard of the names Gree, Mac, and the Boy. It does not follow, does it, that they don't exist?"

He was scathing about the characters of the two witnesses, who had been "defendants in a very serious case alleging conspiracy, in the high court." It was to do with inducing people to break their motorcar contracts. "Was one of the findings," Levy asked Mansfield, "that you induced Hume to break his covenant?"

"Yes," said Mansfield.

"Was one of the findings that you were a person ready with untruthful answers?"

"I was not there when judgment was given," said Mansfield.

"Are these the sort of persons," Levy asked the jury, "on whose evidence you could hang a cat, let alone a man?"

Levy offered his own explanation of the witnesses' apparent ignorance of the Three—that they might be too scared to tell the truth. "Suppose," he said, "those three men did exist, and Mansfield and Salvadori knew it well. If they knew that, they also knew that the three men had murdered Setty. Do you think that men of the caliber of Mansfield and Salvadori would risk their necks by giving information to the police about people they knew to be ruthless murderers?"

Levy had had an easy task with Humphreys' negative witnesses. Now he sought to produce positive evidence of his own that the Three existed, and he did less well. He called Cyril John Lee, a highly respectable ex-artillery officer, tall and rigid, with a long, fastidious face, who had lived for three years in Cambridge Terrace Mews close to Setty's garage.

Lee said that Setty had had a brisk trade in the mews. At first the garage had been used mostly by local business people, but then a different sort of person had started appearing. "Not the sort of people I would like to see around my doorstep. I should say spivs." During the summer of 1948 he had heard the names Maxie and Boy called out in the mews outside his flat. He couldn't give any descriptions of them. But he had since seen a detailed description by Hume of the man Green, and on one occasion he had seen someone of that description in the mews.

Under cross-examination Lee agreed that Max, Mac, and Maxie were common enough names. Boy, too, could be shown to be not unknown. "Would it be any use to you if I produced the Boy?" Humphreys asked. "There is in this court a man with that name, and his name is Baker."

Lee replied, "I might recognize him as having been there."

At that, a youngish dark-haired man in a smart black overcoat was called, and stood on the left side of the dock, facing the judge. He didn't speak. "Have you ever seen him?" Humphreys asked Lee.

"No," was the answer.

Humphreys fired a last, effective shot. "Do you know that Setty's brother has another garage next door in the same mews, and that he is called Max?"

"No," was the answer. The defense had not been greatly helped by Mr. Lee.

At the very end of the trial, and on the same theme of the Three, Levy produced what the press called a surprise witness. This was an attractive young man named Douglas Clay, who described himself as a free-lance journalist and scriptwriter and, having read the press reports, volunteered his testimony in the case. Clay said that in February 1948 he had been in Paris and came across a gang there who were engaged in the smuggling of arms into Palestine and motorcars into Britain. He particularly remembered two strong-arm men attached to the gang. One was known as the Boy and the other as Maxie. He had met the gang in the nightclubs of Paris and they had offered to cash checks for him. He had collected a good deal of information about them, and had sent a report on their activities to the Sûreté and the British embassy. So perhaps Max, Gree, and the Boy did exist. But had they been *Hume's* Max, Gree, and the Boy—or had he just picked out three names he had heard, three gangster-sounding names, and applied them to his own invented characters? To the jury the issue could still have seemed in doubt.

9. The Three—The Timing Problem

If it were true that the Three had called on Hume on the afternoon of October 5 with two parcels containing bits of Setty, just when had the call been made? How had the visit fitted into Hume's busy afternoon schedule? At one o'clock, it will be remembered, he was having the carving knife sharpened for the joint. He then, according to his account, had lunch with his wife. By two o'clock Mrs. Hume had retired to feed the baby, and Mrs. Stride had arrived, and Hume was talking to her about the carpet. A little later Mrs. Hume joined them, before going out around two thirty with the baby. At three or thereabouts Hume shut himself up in the kitchen and was there till three fifty. At four ten he left the flat with two parcels. Into what interstice of that tight-packed afternoon had this major visit been fitted?

For it was a major visit, not just a casual dropping in by a friend to say hello. If Hume was to be believed, it had been more like a gangland eruption. Three men suddenly arrived at the house. They passed the shop door of the greengrocer's—who said later he hadn't noticed them—rang the bell, were admitted by Hume, and made their way up the steep and narrow stairs carrying their bulky packages. The Boy, a stranger to Hume, had to be introduced. The contents of the parcels had to be described—presses for forging petrol coupons—and the requirements of the Three made known. At some point, threats were uttered and a pistol or a revolver was produced. There was argument about whether the packages should be dropped in the sea, or whether hiding or burying would be better. There was argument about whether Hume could be trusted. There was argument about whether one of the Three should fly with him to make sure the parcels were safely dropped. There was some lengthy haggling about the terms of payment for the job; there was the counting out of money. There was the arrangement made that the Three would return in the evening—but without approaching the house—to pay the balance. Only then did the men go back down the two flights of stairs and depart—once more unnoticed by the greengrocer. It had been, on Hume's showing, a quite protracted visit, with a lot of footsteps, a great deal of talk, even some raised voices.

So—when did this lengthy and far from silent visit take place?

In his original statement to the police, Hume had said between two and three o'clock. That statement had been made only three weeks after Setty's disappearance—and since the delivery of bits of a body by menacing gangsters is, to say the least, an unusual event, one can suppose the details of the visit would have been deeply etched in Hume's memory.

At the trial, the judge questioned him. "Could you tell me what time you think the men arrived?"

Hume replied, "It may have been two forty-five p.m."

With or without this small adjustment, Hume was soon in deep trouble, and the cause of his trouble, once again, was Mrs. Stride. She had been in the flat from two p.m. till after five—and she was emphatic that during that time no one had called.

The defense suggested that she might not have heard the bell because she was upstairs using a vacuum cleaner. But the bell, which rang in the hall, was an exceptionally loud one. It made "a frightful noise throughout the flat." And Mrs. Stride had no doubts at all. Vacuum cleaner or not, if anyone had called while she was there, she would have known. And no one had called.

Hume, in Humphreys' words, "now saw the red light" as the result of Mrs. Stride's evidence and radically changed his story. He couldn't remember, he said, whether the Three had come after the arrival of Mrs. Stride or not. They might have come before two o'clock. But now he was getting ever deeper into the morass. Before two o'clock he had been lunching with his wife—who was soon to say she had seen nothing of the Three. "There was not time, was there," Humphreys said to Hume, "for the three men to come and do all that arguing and arranging before two o'clock?" And patently there wasn't. Quite apart from that, if the parcels had been handed over to him before two o'clock, and the deal settled, would he—with a plane waiting for him at Elstree and a misty night in store—have then spent nearly an hour cleaning out the coal cupboard?

Trapped by the timetable and the evidence, Hume fell back on total vagueness. "I don't know about the time," he told Humphreys, "but these men definitely did come on that day."

Levy did his best to explain away his client's uncertainty. "If you think," he said to the jury, "that in some respects in the course of the cross-examination Hume may have been tripped up on this point or on that point, that may have been due merely to fallibility of the human memory and nothing else."

Well, it was a point of view.

10. *The Three—A Credible Story?*

Let us consider, on the basis of Hume's story about the Three, just what the jury were being asked to believe.

In some room, some building, some unknown place, Setty had been stabbed to death. The Three were almost certainly the murderers. Since even a hundred-and-ninety-pound corpse would have presented no transport problem to three men, they could have disposed of the body themselves, without much danger or difficulty, in a variety of ways. Instead, they dismembered it, spilling a great deal more blood, which they would have to clean up. They then took the head and legs in two parcels to Hume's flat. They had made no appointment with him for any particular time. They had no idea who might be at the flat, or what curiosity might be aroused about the contents of the parcels. They made no attempt to check that the visit was safe before producing the parcels; they were carrying them when Hume let them in. They rejected Hume's obviously sensible suggestion that hiding or burial would be the best method of disposal, and insisted that he should fly them out to sea—a plan bristling with all kinds of hazards, as events were to show. They knew almost nothing about Hume; he was no more than a casual acquaintance they had met only a day or two before. They knew very little about his flying skill and even less about his reliability as an accomplice in crime. Yet they were prepared to trust him with what, if things went wrong, could be their lives.

Moreover, they took the same risk twice. They could easily have brought the torso as well, that first time, and got the business over. One flight instead of two, halving the chance of detection. But inexplicably they kept the large package as a second installment. When they met Hume with it that evening they rejected his second sensible suggestion, that they should drive him to Elstree and put it straight into his hired car. They insisted it should be kept overnight in his flat. It was in a condition, as Hume was later to make clear, to drip and spatter large quantities of blood wherever it was taken. It could have splashed the road that had to be crossed, the sidewalk outside the flat, the stairs the Three had to negotiate. Morning light could have shown a trail of blood. Yet they carried it up and dumped it unconcernedly. It was so heavy that they knew Hume would have the utmost difficulty in getting it down the three-foot-wide stairs to his car in the morning. Furthermore, they brushed aside his suggestion that they should come back and help him, saying airily that he would have to find assistance somewhere else. *Their* necks were at stake, but they were quite content to leave him on his own with this monstrous parcel of flesh and spurting blood—a parcel that Hume had twice said might be too big to go into an airplane—and with all the problems involved in its disposal.

Was it credible? "Of course," the judge said in his summing-up, "improbable stories do happen!"

An analysis made at leisure long after the event is one thing. The factors influencing a jury at the time are quite another. In common with most of their fellow citizens, the Hume jury could be presumed to have read the press accounts of the Setty disappearance. They would have seen headlines about the gang of three that were supposed to have been responsible for the murder. So their minds were already prepared. And Hume's story, as he told it, seemed in many respects remarkably plausible. It fitted perfectly the murky Warren Street scene. Hume's descriptions of the spivvish Three, of their wads of notes, of the way they argued about payment, of the criminal argot they talked, of their crudely menacing behavior in the flat, of the dark threats to wife and child, of their constantly changing plans, of their stupidly obstinate decisions, of their very irrationality—all these things seemed absolutely right for small-time gangsters of low intelligence. The corroborative detail, too, was persuasive—like Mac polishing his flamboyant ring, like Boy putting on his steel-rimmed spectacles to count out fivers, like Gree carving his name as he talked. If the story of the Three was fiction, it was brilliant fiction, for it undoubtedly succeeded in bringing them to life.

11. The Evidence of Mrs. Hume

Although there had been only occasional references to Hume's wife, Cynthia, in the earlier part of the trial, she was clearly a key figure in the case. No one, apart from Hume himself, was in as good a position to know the truth or otherwise of the crown's indictment. For the greater part of the relevant time, she had been in the flat where the drama was supposed to have taken place. She was there all through the evening of October 4, when Setty disappeared and Hume was alleged to have murdered him in the front sitting room and subsequently cut him up. She was there all through that night. She was there, as far as is known, all through the morning of October 5, when Hume was supposed to have taken a phone call from one of the Three, and thereafter was busy ringing the Elstree airfield to book a plane, and hiring a car, and taking the carpet to be cleaned, and getting the carving knife sharpened for the joint. She was there with her husband all through lunchtime. She was there to feed baby Allison at two p.m., and to have a word with Mrs. Stride about the carpet. She went out for several hours in the afternoon, but by six thirty or thereabouts she was back with the baby, feeding her and putting her to bed. If, as Hume said, the Three had brought the heavy parcel, the blood-leaking parcel, to the flat at about nine p.m., she had presumably been there when they arrived. Most people would consider it was quite impossible that in all that time she should have been wholly unaware of what, if anything, was going on in the flat. It was not, after all, a spacious mansion with an east and west wing.

So—what did Mrs. Hume know?

A hush fell upon the court as, toward the end of the trial, Levy called her to the witness box. All eyes were turned on her, and the impression she made was a good one. It has been said already that many people thought her a lovely girl, and a studio portrait of the time confirms their view. In the photograph she is shown as having luxuriant wavy hair, dark eyes, a classically oval face, a full, shapely mouth, and an attractively amused expression. In court she wore a becoming blue suit and a close-fitting blue-ribboned hat over her dark curls. As she entered the box to start her fifty-five-minute ordeal by question, she smiled across at her husband in the dock. Her bright red lipstick only accentuated the pallor of her face.

Her evidence was given in a low, clear, cultured voice that sometimes dropped to a whisper. She seemed, as Levy was later to say, "a gentle little woman."

What she told Levy can be summarized as follows:

She had been in the flat all through the evening of October 4. She couldn't recall whether her husband had been at home or not. She had been listening—she thought in the sitting room—to a BBC radio program, a documentary entitled "Justice in Other Lands," which that night had featured the case of Henri Désiré Landru, the French Bluebeard. She had no other reason to remember that particular evening. She had never met Setty. She had seen photographs of him, but she hadn't recognized him as a man she had ever seen. If her husband had brought Setty to the flat that evening, she would have remembered it. She shared a double bed with her husband, and though she couldn't say for certain that he had come to bed with her that night, she thought she would have remembered if he hadn't.

Levy put a succession of key questions to her:

"Would it have been possible, do you think, for your husband to bring anyone to that flat in that period, sometime between six and eleven that night, and murder him in the flat, and murder him without your knowing anything about it?"

In a scarcely audible voice Mrs. Hume replied, "Quite impossible."

"Did you hear any sound or any commotion or anything that could possibly suggest any such happening while you were in the flat?"

"No," said Mrs. Hume.

"During the whole of the morning, October fifth, from six a.m. when you fed the baby until you had lunch, do you think it would have been possible for your husband to be cutting up the body of a man in that flat without your knowing about it?"

"No," said Mrs. Hume.

"Did he in fact do anything of the sort to your knowledge?"

Mrs. Hume shook her head.

"Did you, during the whole of that period, see the slightest sign of anything unusual, such as I have suggested?"

"Nothing at all," said Mrs. Hume.

"Did you see any signs of blood? Did you smell anything? Did you see any bloodstained knives or anything?"

"I saw nothing," said Mrs. Hume.

Under cross-examination by Humphreys, her replies consisted almost entirely of monosyllabic negatives. They amounted to a plea of total ignorance about practically everything.

She didn't know much about her husband's private life. She didn't know how he got his money. He had told her he was earning his living by flying airplanes. She didn't know that various parcels had come to the flat on October 5 and 6, and had been taken away by him. She hadn't heard the front doorbell ring, though she agreed it rang very loudly. She didn't know that human blood in quantity had been spilled in different places in the flat. She didn't know that three men had come to the flat on October 5. She had had lunch with her husband that day, but she didn't remember sending him out in a hurry to get a knife sharpened. She didn't remember whether there had been a joint for lunch or not. She didn't know much about the carving knife; she had been rather worried that day about her child, and was busy making arrangements for her to go into the hospital.

So that was it. She knew almost nothing of what had happened. She might almost as well not have been there.

No wonder the judge said to the jury, "You may think Mrs. Hume doesn't help you."

Levy, in his final speech, praised her for the meticulous care with which she had given her evidence. "Mrs. Hume is as honest a witness as you could ever have seen," he said. He pointed out that if she had wished to lie, there were many things she could have said in her husband's support. Such as, for instance, that he had been at home all evening, listening to the radio with her. But she hadn't done that. She had kept to the facts as she remembered them.

He used challenging words to the jury. "If Setty was murdered in this flat, he was murdered in the presence of Mrs. Hume. . . . If she is not telling the truth, she is a party to this murder. It could not have been done without her knowing."

Humphreys, in his final speech, was equally forthright. His words stay in the mind:

"I am not prosecuting Mrs. Hume. I am not defending her. She is first and foremost the wife of the man she loves. There is a law older than the law of England or any other man-made law: a man and wife who love each other stick together.

"I do not say that Mrs. Hume had no part in this murder. I say I have no evidence whatsoever she had any part in it.

"I certainly do not agree necessarily that she had no part in the cutting up of the body and the tidying of the flat. That is a matter entirely for you to consider if you wish."

The jury considered it—and what an anxious task it must have been! There was so much evidence against Hume, but Cynthia Hume hadn't looked like a perjurer. She hadn't sounded like a perjurer. Even less had she looked like an accessory after the fact of murder. She had seemed an attractive young wife and mother, telling the simple truth about a quiet evening at home and her worries about an ailing child. Was the prosecution's picture credible? The fat man, ferociously stabbed with five blows of a knife. Staggering away. Coughing blood over the sitting-room carpet. Coughing blood in the hall. Falling on his face in the dining room. Bleeding to death, untended. The shambles in the neat flat. The corpse to be dealt with. The gruesome horror of cutting and sawing it up. Right, that's the head, dear. Put it in the box. Now for the legs. Blood everywhere. The whole place awash with blood. And Cynthia Hume, this "gentle little woman" so preoccupied with her baby, lending a hand, helping to clean up the mess. Was it conceivable?

CHAPTER 7

FOUR WOMEN QUEUED outside the Old Bailey all night in below-zero January temperatures to make sure of getting into the public gallery for the seventh and climactic day of the Hume trial. The first in the queue arrived at eight p.m. She wore two sweaters and a woolen dress, a cardigan, a heavy overcoat, and fur boots, and she had a plaid blanket wrapped around her. She nursed a hot-water bottle, which she refilled at intervals from a nearby café, and she entertained herself with a portable radio. Shortly thereafter she was joined by three other women. As the freezing hours went by, the queue steadily lengthened. The final act in the drama was going to be played to a full house.

Hume, when told about the all-night vigil in the street, was reported to have said, "Anyone can have my place if they wish!"

The following day Mr. Justice Sellers completed the three-hour summing-up he had begun the day before. By the legal men it was held to be a masterly review of the evidence in an exceptionally intricate case. Naturally it sought to maintain a balance between the pros and the cons, and nothing that could be said in Hume's favor was overlooked—but in its total effect it was a summing-up against the accused.

Two matters were particularly stressed. One was the question of Hume's movements on the day that Setty disappeared. "It may have struck you," the judge said, "and struck you very forcibly, that although in this case one has had evidence of September thirtieth and the intervening days and again of October fifth and sixth about the activities of Hume, what evidence is there from him or any other witness as to what he did on October fourth . . . ? You have the fact—notwithstanding that he has made a statement and has given evidence on oath in the witness box—that he has not vouchsafed to you any indication of his movements on the vital day. . . . October fourth is practically a blank."

The judge also dwelt at length, and with obvious disbelief, on the story of the Three bringing bits of a murdered man in broad daylight to Hume's flat, and more bits again at night, and on the grave risks that these and other of their supposed activities would have involved. "You have to consider whether it is a credible story. . . .

"In this trial, as in all trials," he said, "we must ensure as best we can that an innocent man is not found guilty; and in the administration of justice it is desirable a guilty man should not be acquitted because of skillful and sustained lying."

But as he finally put it to the jury, "Even if you completely disbelieve Hume's story, does the rest add up to a certainty?" Had it been proved that it was Hume who had inflicted the stab wounds on Setty?

At twelve thirty the jurors retired to try to answer that question.

They were back in court just two and a half hours later. At four minutes past three Mr. Justice Sellers resumed his place. The black cap, traditional headwear of a judge when sentencing a prisoner to death, was conveniently to hand. Hume, tight-lipped but outwardly calm, stood erect at the front of the dock, hands clasped behind him. Three warders and a prison doctor were in the dock with him. Mrs. Hume was not in court. She was awaiting the verdict at the flat, with her father.

The judge said to the foreman of the jury, "Have you any communication to make?"

The foreman said, "We are not agreed."

Next the judge asked him if there were any likelihood of reaching an agreement.

The foreman said, "I feel doubtful that we shall reach a unanimous verdict."

The judge thereupon discharged the jury. Those were the days when only a unanimous verdict was acceptable.

At seven minutes past three Humphreys rose. The possibility of a disagreement, he said, had naturally occurred to the prosecution, and instructions had been taken from the director of public prosecutions to decide the right course to pursue. After full consideration, the view was that it was not necessarily in the interests of justice that there should be a retrial on the indictment. "Therefore I respectfully ask that a jury should be sworn, and then no evidence will be offered on this indictment."

Hume looked around the court, his expression a mixture of delight and bewilderment.

The delight faded as Humphreys went on. "But I ask that a jury be impaneled in connection with another indictment."

Levy requested, and was granted, a five-minute adjournment so that he and other advisers could discuss the new situation with Hume in the cells.

The tension broke in court, and there was a hubbub of voices. Over it came the sound of new jurors answering to their names.

The sitting resumed. The judge explained to the new jury that Hume had been charged with the murder of Setty and that the prosecution now offered no evidence. He directed them to return a verdict of not guilty, which they formally and dutifully did.

The clerk of the court then read out the new charge—that Hume had been an accessory after the fact of murder, "knowing that a certain person or persons unknown, on October fourth, 1949, murdered Stanley Setty, and then on October fifth and sixth assisted and maintained those persons or person by disposing of the body of the said Stanley Setty."

To this charge, in a shaking, high-pitched voice, Hume pleaded guilty.

There were legal men in court who were surprised he should have done so, since it seemed out of character. The probability is that he very nearly didn't. But, on the facts, it would hardly have helped him to do otherwise. Humphreys, perhaps foreseeing the outcome of the murder trial, had elicited some damning admissions from Hume during his long cross-examination. Asked about the contents of the big parcel, Hume had said, "I thought it might have been part of a human body." Asked about the Three, he had said, "They could have been murderers." And in his statement to the police he had said the thought had crossed his mind that the big parcel might have contained part of Setty's body. In the circumstances, a plea of not guilty could only have postponed the inevitable decision—and after a full-dress contest in court, might have attracted a heavier sentence.

In a final intervention, Levy put the case for leniency. He recalled the pressure the gang was said to have put on Hume, the production of the revolver, the threats that had been made. He felt entitled, he said, to ask the judge to assume in favor of the accused that at least a number of the members of the jury had accepted Hume's explanation in regard to the first indictment.

The judge said dryly he was bound to assume they had not rejected it!

He then pronounced sentence. "You have pleaded guilty," he told Hume, "to a grave crime for which the law fixes a maximum punishment of imprisonment for life. . . . I sentence you to twelve years' imprisonment."

Hume was removed—first to Brixton, then to Wormwood Scrubs. He had seemed momentarily stunned by the sentence, but in the cells below, according to reports, he quickly recovered his customary equanimity. The black cap, at least, had not been required; and in law he had been acquitted of the murder of Stanley Setty forever.

Levy, understandably elated by the success of his defense, but cautious in words, said to reporters, "An unprecedented case? Perhaps. Shall I call it unusual?"

The view of the press went further. "The most surprising trial in a century" was the verdict of one special writer. And that was the general opinion of the newspapermen who had sat through those seven sensational days.

On the following morning one paper carried a banner headline, WHO *Did* KILL SETTY?, and reported that Scotland Yard were renewing their inquiries into the murder. It may well be they were doing just this. An acquittal, after all, is not necessarily the same thing as innocence.

ONCE THE PRISON gates had closed behind him, Hume's name was dropped quickly from the headlines. One of the few further items of interest recorded by the newspapers was that, not very long after the trial, Cynthia Hume divorced him. The ground was cruelty, and the suit was not contested.

Little is known, and perhaps little is worth knowing, about Hume's years in jail. He served part of his sentence in Wakefield; the bulk of it in the grim surroundings of Dartmoor. By his own later account he became friendly in Wakefield with Dr. Klaus Fuchs, the atomic scientist who had spied for Russia, and on release carried a message to Fuchs's father in East Germany. In Dartmoor, where Hume continued his study of electronics, he appears to have been popular with the other inmates. Putting as good a face on things as possible, he talked about "the Moor" to one visitor almost as though it were home away from home. His behavior in prison must have been reasonably satisfactory, for he earned the maximum remission; and on February 1, 1958, having served eight of his twelve years, he was once more loosed upon the world. There was no sign that he had been in any way rehabilitated, no trace of any regret over his part in the Setty affair. He emerged from prison in a nervous but highly rebellious state of mind.

Apart from making arrangements to change his name to Donald Brown by deed poll, almost the first thing he did after his release was to try to sell his story to a newspaper. And what a story he was offering!

It was nothing less than a full confession that he, alone and un-aided, *had* killed Stanley Setty. He was the man who had Got Away With Murder, and had lived to tell the tale.

He knew, of course, that under English law he could never be tried again for a crime of which he had been acquitted. On that score he was quite safe. There was, however, the little matter of perjury to consider. In court he had sworn his innocence. Now he was about to admit guilt. But on reflection he decided there was no danger there, either. If necessary, he could always say that his confession was un-true, that it was an invention, that he had made it solely for money. So the way was clear.

The first two newspapers he went to turned him down. The asking figure at that stage was rumored to be ten thousand pounds, though this was never publicly confirmed. He went on to the *Sunday Pic-torial*, which finally bought his story.

It was a very long story, starting with his childhood and going right through to his release from jail. In the form in which it was originally taken down it ran to some twenty-two thousand words. Here we summarize, from the account the *Pictorial* published, only matters relating to Setty and his murder.

1. The Association with Setty

Hume first met Setty in December 1947 in connection with a car deal. Later, after Hume's Herefordshire factory had been wiped out by fire, he encountered Setty again in London. "On the creep for a shady deal, I drifted into the Hollywood Club, near Marble Arch. Propped up against the bar was the sinister, bearlike figure of the unofficial banker of Warren Street." There was some guarded con-versation as the two men sized each other up. Then Setty produced a roll of fivers and invited Hume to have a drink. "We soon realized we could be useful to each other. He told me he was in a syndicate which supplied war-surplus trucks to the Iraqi army. That night I sold him a gross of American nylons at one pound a pair, and ar-ranged to see him again. We met about two weeks later at his garage. He let me buy some forged petrol coupons from him at two shillings and sixpence a unit to flog for what I could get. This made me about forty pounds a week." The business connection was now well estab-lished. "My wife was with me when I met him next, in a nightclub.

He appeared most impressed with her. He warmed toward me and we got down to discussing skulduggery. He was buying up wrecked cars just to get hold of the logbooks, knowing that if I could snatch cars of the same type for him, they could be passed off as the originals after a little expert respraying. I was out of a job. The ball wasn't bouncing for me anymore. So I went to work for Setty. I snatched six cars—two of them Jaguars—and received three hundred pounds each time from Setty."

2. The Breach

One afternoon in August, 1949, Hume turned up at Setty's garage. As usual, the dog, Tony, was with him. "I quite liked Setty until that afternoon. But he kicked Tony, who had climbed into a car and scratched the paint. Tony yelped with pain. It was the worst thing Setty could possibly have done. For Tony meant more to me than did my wife, or even our baby daughter. Nobody could do that to my pet dog and expect to get away with it. I kept my ears open and heard a few things about Setty. There were whispers that he had done time for fraud some years before. But there were other whispers. . . . I heard stories that Stan had taken my wife out drinking a couple of times in the afternoon. I was fast getting the needle with Setty."

3. The Fatal Night

"It was just getting dark as I arrived home at my flat about seven thirty-five p.m. on October 4, 1949. I had knocked back a few drinks. I was surprised to notice Setty's cream Citroën outside. What was going on upstairs in my flat? As I climbed the stairs I could feel the tension mounting inside me. I burst open the door and went into the front room. There I saw Setty sitting on the sofa. Something snapped inside my brain. I boiled with rage."

Hume told Setty to get out. There was an exchange of insults and threats, a mounting quarrel. Hume rushed out to the landing, where a collection of war souvenirs hung on the wall, and jerked a German SS dagger from its sheath. He returned to the sitting room, brandishing it. "I planned to frighten the living daylights out of him. But I reckoned without myself—and my own mad rage." There were more sneers and insults. "Then Setty took a swing at me with the flat of his hand. He towered above me, tall and powerful." They grappled, and rolled onto the floor. "My sweaty hands plunged the weapon frenziedly and repeatedly into his chest and legs. I had to hurt him."

But Setty continued to struggle. "He was as strong as an ox. The more I stuck the dagger into him, the more he tried to push my head back and break my neck. . . . He wouldn't release his grip. It was like a vise." Finally Setty slumped down, coughing blood. "With a feeling of triumph at winning the fight, I watched the life run from him."

4. The Car

Hume dragged the corpse to the coal cupboard beyond the kitchen and covered it with an old piece of felt. He wiped up some of the bloodstains in the flat. Then he drove Setty's Citroën to Cambridge Terrace Mews, wearing gloves to avoid leaving any fingerprints. He returned to Golders Green by taxi.

5. The Felt Under the Carpet

Next morning Hume finished cleaning up the flat and wiped everything over to remove any telltale prints. He rolled up the blood-stained carpet. There was blood on the felt underneath. He cut off a strip that was stained and threw it away. Then he tugged the felt at each end to stretch it. "I managed to stretch it a good two feet, so that it looked like the original length." No one at the trial had thought of that answer to the problem.

6. The Fivers

"I was alone in the flat. I locked the front door. Then I went to the coal cupboard where I had left the body overnight, and dragged it out. I picked up the tools I thought I needed. They were a hacksaw and a sharp two-shilling-and-sixpence lino knife. . . . It was only when I came to rip the bloodstained jacket off the body with my knife that I felt a large bulge. It was a bundle of five-pound notes—a thousand pounds' worth. When I found them they were smeared with blood, so I had to cut away the stained edges with scissors. Many were ripped by the point of my dagger, but I managed to rescue about ninety pounds' worth. . . . The rest of the notes were useless, so I burned them."

7. The Cutting Up

"I felt no squeamishness or horror at what I was about to do. . . . I knew nothing about surgery, but I worked swiftly. Already it was one o'clock and I knew that the daily help was due to arrive in about ninety minutes. . . . I sighed with relief when it was all done." He wrapped and roped the headless, legless torso, with several pieces of lead as weights, and put it in the coal cupboard. Presently he left the flat with the head and legs, done up in two parcels with various bloodstained clothes. "I managed to clear up and get out of the flat before the daily help arrived." In his raincoat pocket he had the dagger, the linoleum knife, and the hacksaw, wrapped in paper.

8. The First Flight

Shortly after taking off from Elstree, Hume crossed the south coast and headed toward mid-Channel. "Some of the flying types I knew at Elstree will be skeptical when they read this. They knew I had no special ability as a pilot, or as a navigator for that matter." He kept going for about ninety minutes and presently spotted the faint outline of the French coast and what appeared to be an island—"probably one of the Channel group." That was far enough. He flung out the weapons and the parcels and flew to Southend "to make the log entries look accurate in case inquiries should follow."

9. The Second Flight

"I flew steadily on roughly the same course as the day before—toward the southwest." When he thought he could see the French coast, he throttled down and prepared to jettison the large parcel. "I tried to open the door against the slipstream, using the weight of the torso bundle to force it open. To have both hands free I held the control column between my legs. But I just could not shift the bundle." He tried to gain height for a second attempt. "I banked the aircraft steeply, hoping that the parcel would slip downward to the plane door and force it open with its tremendous weight. With one hand I was holding Tony back. He was barking furiously. I was scared that he would fall out if the door burst open. With the other hand I shoved. . . . Suddenly there was an enormous bang as the door whipped open and then slammed shut. The torso had gone. . . . As the plane soared upward I became horror-stricken. I had not noticed that the rope wound around the bundle had become slackened by too much handling. It had looped onto a hook in the cabin and had come undone. The fierce slipstream had whipped off both the slackened rope and the outer blanket wrapping. The outer blanket and the lead weights . . . were clattering and flapping on my tail elevators." Hume fought to control the plane. Suddenly the tail elevators became free. "The kite was trim and level again. But as I circled and peered below, my heart almost stopped. The torso was floating on the water, covered by only the inner wrapping."

10. The Three

"I concocted a story which I suppose was almost as fantastic as my crime. The three mysterious names were real enough, but the descriptions were based on the three officers from the Yard. . . . It was as simple as that."

These were the salient points in Hume's account.

AS EVERY POLICEMAN—and by now many a layman—knows, a confession is not necessarily the same thing as the truth. People confess to crimes they haven't committed for all sorts of reasons. Sometimes

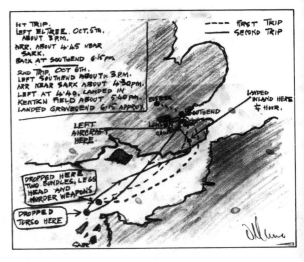

A sketch map prepared by Hume showing where he claimed to have dropped various parts of Setty's body from the plane.

they do it for money, sometimes to protect another person, sometimes from a perverse sort of vanity, sometimes from more obscure psychological motives. And even if a confession is true in substance, it may not be true in every detail. Omissions, evasions, and discreet adjustments are not unknown.

Hume's confession invites particularly careful scrutiny, since by nature and by habit he was a facile and extravagant liar. He lied for the smallest advantage, he lied instinctively if it would show him in a better light, and sometimes he just lied, for no good reason at all. He lied to his business associates, as when he told Salvadori he had trucks for sale, to gain his interest. He lied to his wife, as when he led her to believe he earned his living by flying airplanes. He lied, as the saying goes, "off the top of his head," with no regard for consistency. He embroidered and embellished as a matter of course. On occasion he could manage a lie within a lie, which is no mean feat. The story of the Three, on his admission, was a lie—yet according to his testimony in court he deceived this wholly mythical Three both about the cost of hiring an airplane and about where he had dropped the parcels. This kind of lying requires not just aptitude but an artist's dedication. Hume was a gifted inventor. One of the truest things he ever said was in connection with his story of the Three: "The lies rolled off my tongue." So, regarding his confession, a certain selectivity is in order.

There is no reason to doubt the truth of his central admission— that he murdered Setty, and cut up his body, in the flat. This accords with the weight of evidence produced at the trial. But what about some of the details he gives?

His account of his various illicit transactions with Setty may or may not be true. There is no independent testimony, and Hume is not a reliable witness. His account of why he "got the needle" with Setty may or may not be true. His account of his homecoming on the fatal night, October 4, may or may not be true. If it is, there remain unanswered questions. Who let Setty into the flat? Was he alone there when Hume burst in? The reader will have to form his own opinion on this.

The story of the quarrel and the fight is one man's story. If there was a quarrel, who knows whether it was Setty who aimed the first blow? Hume presents himself as a man provoked beyond endurance by an unwelcome visitor in his home, and then as a doughty fighter defending himself against a formidable opponent who tried to break his neck. But it was Hume who had the dagger. There must have been fairer fights.

Hume speaks of Setty "towering above him." This is a typical self-justifying flight of fancy, for Setty was only five feet six in height and Hume was marginally the taller.

The time given for the cutting up of Setty's body on October 5 cannot be squared with other evidence. "Already it was one o'clock," Hume says, "and I knew that the daily help was due to arrive in ninety minutes." Also, "I was alone in the flat." What about the lunch that Mrs. Hume told the court she had shared with her husband that day? Is it not much more likely that Dr. Camps and the prosecution were right, and that the body was cut up the previous evening, soon after death?

The confession contains a flagrant lie about the time of Hume's departure with the first two parcels. "I managed to clear up and get out of the flat," he says, "before the daily help arrived." But the evidence in court, including Hume's own, was that he had talked to

Mrs. Stride about the carpet, and told her not to disturb him in the kitchen, and asked her to make him a cup of tea before he left. Presumably this lie about an earlier departure is not unconnected with the next one, the biggest whopper of all—his account of his flights "over the Channel" to within sight of the French coast and the islands, taking ninety minutes each way. Here the romancer is in full spate. The known timetable of his takeoffs and landings, vouched for by numerous airport witnesses, would not have permitted it. Hume followed the Thames to Southend Pier and flew a few miles beyond it, which navigationally was all he was capable of. The rest is bragging. In court he had been forced by the known facts to deny his instincts and tell the truth. "I was four or five miles from Southend Pier," he said, "when I dropped the parcels."

THE PUBLICATION OF Hume's confession in the *Sunday Pictorial* brought a storm of criticism and censure from other, more sedate organs of the press, and started a fierce controversy on television and in the correspondence columns. There were those who approved the publication; there were those who denounced it as sensation mongering. Because of the jury's disagreement and the law's virtual abdication, the Setty case had ended in a most unsatisfactory way, with no solution. Who *had* killed Setty? The answer, when it came, was undoubtedly news. Though open to question in some of its detail, the Hume confession went far toward clearing up what would otherwise have remained a baffling mystery. It also shed much interesting light on Hume himself. Because of the very features most deplored by the critics—the boasting, the gloating, the self-exculpation, the lack of contrition—it was fascinating source material for the psychologist and the criminologist.

Most important of all, it came as a reassuring vindication of Scotland Yard. The detectives who had worked so patiently and so efficiently on the Setty case had been sure all along that Hume's story of the Three was fiction; they had been certain he was guilty of murder. They believed they had produced all the evidence necessary for a conviction, and—though policemen learn by hard experience to be philosophical over the vagaries of juries—the outcome of the trial must have caused them some chagrin. Now their view of the crime was shown to have been right in every important respect. In the light of Hume's confession, it wasn't the Yard that had failed in the Setty case. It wasn't the prosecution that had failed. If anyone had failed, it was the jury.

This, surely, the public had the right to know?

APART FROM THE time when Hume was working on his story for the *Sunday Pictorial*, there is a gap in our knowledge of his activities until May 1958—some three months after his release from prison. What can be said with certainty is that the confession had brought no catharsis. He had made it for money, and he now had money. But he wanted more. He wanted "a bundle." And he was going to get it, if he could, by any means—criminal or otherwise. He had finally turned his back on society.

Hume had saved his neck—but saved it for what?

On May 20 he obtained, by forgery, a false passport in the name of John Stephen Bird, company director, of Liverpool. He was to have several other aliases, but this was the one he would now mainly use. As Stephen Bird he traveled to Zurich, which henceforth was to be his hideout and his base.

Shortly after his arrival he met an attractive twenty-nine-year-old Swiss girl, Trudi Sommer, who ran a hairdressing salon in the town. She was sitting in a restaurant with a girl friend; Hume asked the waiter to take a flower to each of them. Trudi was shy of the approach at first, but conversation followed, Hume's taxi driver acting as interpreter. Hume said he was a test pilot with the Canadian forces. Trudi was smitten, and thereafter the relationship developed rapidly. In a matter of days Hume was saying he wanted to marry her. Trudi thought him crazily impulsive, but she was fascinated by him. She had never met anyone like him before.

From now on, when Hume was around, they were constantly together. However, he was not around all the time. In his chosen role of employed pilot he had to appear occupied, and he did quite a bit of traveling. He visited, among other places, the United States and Canada, spending lavishly as he went. But he always returned to Zurich, where Trudi, deeply in love with him, eagerly welcomed back her dashing young hero, her "Johnny Bird," who looked so handsome in the uniform of a Canadian flier.

Presently there was talk of an engagement, of wedding plans.

Hume visited Trudi's parents and was approved. He gave Trudi a diamond engagement ring. In November 1958 their formal engagement was announced in the *Zurich Gazette*. The plan was that they should marry on Saint Valentine's Day—February 14, 1959.

Poor Trudi!

CHAPTER 8

THREE INCIDENTS NOW to be recorded may seem at first sight to have little relevance to our story.

Just before midday on August 2, 1958—a Saturday—a man walked into the Midland Bank in Boston Manor Road, Brentford, on the outskirts of London. The bank was about to close for the weekend, but the man was remembered as having called earlier about opening an account, and he was allowed in. There were no other customers. Almost at once he produced a gun and fired at the cashier, wounding him in the chest. Then, behind closed doors, he forced the staff to tie each other up, and rifled the tills. He left the building with about twelve hundred pounds in notes, and got clear away before the alarm was raised.

On November 12, 1958, the same bank—now removed to different premises—was robbed again, and in similar circumstances. Just before the three-o'clock closing hour, a man ran up the steps from the crowded sidewalk and slipped through the door as the last customer left. At once he produced a .22 and another gun. "Okay," he said, gangster fashion, "I'm taking over." The cashier dived under his counter and pressed the alarm signal.

The manager, Edward Aires, opened the door of his office and looked out. He saw the gunman standing behind the counter. He went back to his desk and grabbed the phone to call the police, but the line wasn't switched through. He went out again and tiptoed toward the robber, keeping a pillar between himself and the man. As the gunman jumped back over the counter, Aires, with great courage, tried to tackle him. The man shot Aires at point-blank range, wounding him severely. He then made his escape, but with only three hundred pounds.

A girl clerk had recognized the robber as the man who had raided the bank before, and she was able to give a detailed description of him. A dapper man, aged thirty-five to forty, five feet six to five feet eight in height, of stocky build, ruddy-complexioned, full in the face, and bluish about the upper lip and chin.

On January 30, 1959, a man entered the Gewerbe Bank in Zurich with a gun concealed in a cardboard box and shot the cashier. Before he could snatch more than a few coins, the alarm bell sounded and he took to his heels. He was pursued along the street by bank clerks and other citizens, not least by a tenacious sixteen-year-old youth who managed to keep him in sight. At some point the robber's way was barred by a fifty-year-old taxi driver named Arthur Maag. The gunman shot him dead. Almost immediately he was seized and held.

At the police station, he said he was a Pole named Stanislav, attached as a civilian to the U.S. air base at Wiesbaden. This was quickly disproved, and with the help of Interpol records the gunman was identified. For the second time in his life, Brian Donald Hume faced a charge of murder—and this time he couldn't romance himself out of it. The Furies had caught up with him at last.

Hume continued to draw freely on his imagination until his final removal from the public scene. In his cell, while awaiting trial, he occupied himself with bringing the story of his life up to date and adding some chapters to a gangster-type novel he had started. Other tales were reserved for the court. One of his claims in Switzerland was that he'd had colorful adventures in the world of espionage. His leanings, he said, were toward communism; he had once been a member of the Young Communist League, and during the Spanish Civil War had tried to join the International Brigade. After his release from Dartmoor he had acted, he said, as a Soviet intelligence agent and had received some twelve hundred pounds from the Russians for his services. While working as a spy he had taken pictures of an American air base in Maine and passed copies to the East Germans. He had buried the photographs, he said, together with a camera and a passport, in a field near Lake Constance. The Swiss police turned over most of the field but found nothing. They also followed up another of his stories—that he had hidden a passport and revolver in a hotel bedroom in Zurich. A search of the bedroom produced nothing. The lies were still rolling from Hume's tongue.

The trial opened in a château at Winterthur, near Zurich, on September 24, 1959, eight months after his arrest. By British standards the court arrangements were informal. There were no traditional ceremonies, no robes or wigs or gowns. There was no raised dock for the prisoner. But there was nothing informal about the watchful guards, who stood with machine guns at the ready. Hume was potentially violent, and they were taking no chances.

His behavior in the Swiss court was much worse than at the Setty trial in London. At the Old Bailey he had shown some outward respect for the authority of the law. At Winterthur he showed none. From the start his manner was defiant and contemptuous. He constantly interrupted the proceedings with insults, sneers, and wisecracks—lolling across a bench or straddling a backward-turned chair. He called the court interpreter Buster and referred to the president of the court as the old guy and that bum. "Tell him to get lost," he said once; and "Tell him if it comes to a slanging match I'll rip him to bits verbally as well as I could physically." The orderly Swiss could hardly believe their ears.

He admitted, for the first time in a court of law, that he had murdered Stanley Setty. He admitted, after consultation with his lawyer, that he had been responsible for the two raids on the Midland Bank at Brentford. He explained why he had gone there a second time: he had meant to take revenge on a cashier who, he said, had misled him the first time about the contents of a safe. (Fortunately the cashier had not been around.) He said he had intended to do the job on November 5, Guy Fawkes Day, but because of the bank's change of premises he had had to postpone it for a week. It had been planned, he said, like a military operation. One recalls such military operations! As more questions were asked about the raids he became irritated. "I have pleaded guilty to shooting someone," he said. "What more do you want? Do you want me to take my teeth out for you?" He said he had no regrets over what had happened in England. "I don't give a damn about what happened over there." He wasn't worried that a cashier had been seriously wounded. As for the shooting of the bank manager, he himself was really the injured party because the manager had jumped on him. There should be protection, he said, for men like himself who got attacked by bank managers!

He described the raid on the Gewerbe Bank in Zurich in ready detail, demonstrating on a diagram just how he had gone about it.

But he said he knew before he went to the bank that the raid would be a failure.

"Then why did you do it?" the judge asked.

"I didn't want my conscience to call me a coward," he replied. Describing his attempted getaway, he said, "Someone got on my back. There was a man who pulled my hair. I was pretty glad when the police arrived." Magnanimously he added that if anyone deserved the reward for capturing him, it was the sixteen-year-old youth who had followed him all the way from the bank. "The others only joined in afterward," he said.

It was all conscious public acting. The image now was of a nonchalant killer with a wry sense of humor. It was bravado, a final piece of self-presentation while the limelight lasted.

A Swiss psychiatrist, Dr. Guggenbuhl-Craig, who had examined Hume in prison several times, spoke in court of shivers down his spine as Hume had talked to him of his acts of violence. He recalled the savage expression on Hume's face when telling of the Setty fight. This man, the psychiatrist said, showed a complete lack of any human feelings toward his fellow beings. He was incapable of genuinely loving anyone—even his fiancée, Trudi Sommer. He could only hate. "He is only really and truly himself in the part of a criminal."

The conclusion? Hume, though in the legal sense completely responsible for his actions, was a psychopath. It was impossible to say whether his psychopathic symptoms had resulted from past illnesses, such as the meningitis he had suffered while in the RAF.

Before the jury retired, the prosecutor voiced strong criticism of the way Hume had been allowed to escape the consequences of his first murder. It was a failing in the laws of England, he said, that a man found to have been incorrectly or insufficiently sentenced could not be brought to court and tried again. After his release from prison Hume had been able to tell the world, "I am a murderer." In such a case under Swiss law there would have been grounds for a retrial.

The Swiss jury were out for a little longer than the Old Bailey jury—about three hours—having five counts in the indictment to consider. The verdict was guilty on all counts, and Hume was sentenced to imprisonment with hard labor for life.

So—to our final view of this extraordinary character.

He was, first and foremost, a show-off. He was a crude, brash, superficially attractive man of no moral or intellectual substance but with great drive and an enormous ego. He was a little man who wanted to be big. He longed to stand out, to be noticed, to shine and impress.

Conceit was his downfall—in the first instance, literally. His flying crash would probably not have occurred if he had not been overconfident, if he had not thought he knew better than his instructor. He consistently overrated his ability and his cleverness.

The two-day flying operations, conducted in full public view, were unnecessarily risky. No doubt the enterprise appealed to Hume as a daring and original method of disposal, a romantic venture, but he would have done better to take the parcels off in his hired car and bury them quietly in a wood. He had a lot of initiative but no wisdom.

One returns, with a layman's proper humility, to Hume's mental state. He was clearly unbalanced. He had a vicious and uncontrollable temper. Any interference with his criminal plans could provoke a wild outburst of rage and threats of physical violence. He was erratic in his swiftly changing moods—euphoric when successful, ferocious when crossed.

His behavior at the Swiss trial was unstable and seemed to mark an even further deterioration in his personality. Was he, one can't help wondering, the victim after all of that wartime crash in the RAF trainer plane?

But the last word must be this. Against such men, whatever the cause of their derangement, society has to protect itself. The Swiss, watching in bewilderment Hume's extraordinary antics and mindful of his record, did what was necessary.

Donald Hume was held in Switzerland's Regensdorf Jail for seventeen years. He had few visitors there, and lived virtually as a recluse in his one-man cell. He listened a good deal to the radio. For a time he did some painting, mostly of animals. He exercised regularly and remained in good physical shape. But mentally his condition steadily deteriorated. He became more and more intractable, with outbursts of savage and uncontrollable violence that kept his around-the-clock guards under constant strain.

In the mid-1970s the Swiss approached the British government and asked to be relieved of their burden. What was required for this dangerous man, they said, was an escape-proof psychiatric establishment, and they had no suitable place in Switzerland. After lengthy discussions a course of action was finally agreed upon, and in August 1976 Hume, escorted by two Swiss policemen, was flown to London, chained from wrist to ankle. Following an examination by two doctors, an order was made for his compulsory detention under section 26 of the Mental Health Act of 1959, and he was removed to Broadmoor—the special hospital in Berkshire intended to provide treatment, in conditions of maximum security, for the dangerously deranged.

THE
WEMBLEY JOB

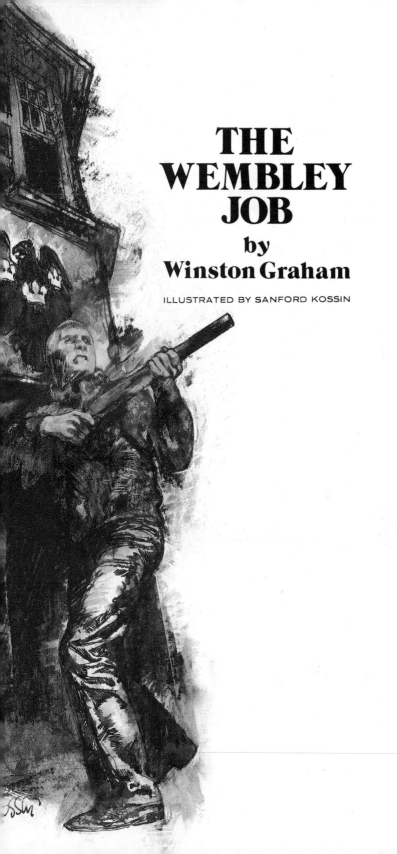

THE
WEMBLEY
JOB

by
Winston Graham

ILLUSTRATED BY SANFORD KOSSIN

On the morning of August 10, 1972, seven masked men armed with shotguns burst into Barclay's Bank in the London suburb of Wembley, fired a blast into the ceiling to frighten the staff, and in a matter of ninety seconds sledgehammered their way into the bank's vault. It was an operation of lightning speed and amazing audacity. Obviously professionals, with getaway cars placed in position the night before, the gang was gone moments later and so was £138,000 of the bank's money.

London had recently been stewing in an epidemic of such raids. The annual rate of bank robberies was climbing alarmingly, and now Scotland Yard was under intense pressure to deal with the situation. Finally a special Wembley Bank Robbery Squad was set up. The chore of figuring out the identity of the bank raiders was as fascinating as it was laborious, but within a matter of months not only had they caught the ringleader but they had also induced him to peach on all his buddies.

Novelist Winston Graham, author of such suspenseful tales as *Marnie*, *The Walking Stick*, and the highly successful "Poldark" books, recounts this incredible tale of the slippery Wembley robbers and the dogged men of the Yard who finally brought them to book.

CHAPTER 1

ON AN EVENING in March, 1969, six men sat drinking in the Cabin
Club in Paddington. The club was no more than two rooms in a
basement, with a bar, a record player, tables with red plastic tops,
bamboo chairs, a bead curtain separating the outer from the inner
room, and an ex-bruiser barman with scar tissue under his eyes.

The group were in the inner room, and the man presiding was the
owner of the club. Broad-set, with a solid fatness that sent the scale
needle over the two-hundred-pound mark, he had a sallow skin, an
inquiring nose, and a slant to his small, dark, active eyes. His black
hair was lank and thinning at the back, and when he spoke, which he
did with a thin cockney accent, a cigarette moved up and down on his
heavy bottom lip. He looked a jolly, friendly, self-indulgent, sly man.
His name was Smalls. Fond parents in North London thirty-three
years ago had given him the names of Derek Crichton, but his friends
called him Bertie.

The others around the table were Johnny Richards—or Vodka
Johnny, as he was known—Tony Edlin, Micky Green, Jimmy Jeffrey, and Lenny Jones. They were expecting a seventh man, and
after a while, all being said that could be said, silence fell among
them except for the clink of glasses and the swirl of liquor. So they
sat until the expected guest arrived, a thin, balding man of forty-
nine in a polo sweater and patched blue jeans, who blinked ner-
vously, like a ferret surprised by the light.

"This is Clem," said Bertie Smalls heartily. "Clem Eden. Clem, meet the boys. Vodka Johnny you know. Sit down. Get him a drink, Micky. What's your poison? That's right, sit down, make yourself at home. This is liberty hall."

Clem sipped tentatively at his drink, held a cigarette to the flame of Micky's lighter, hollowed his cheeks to the pull of the smoke.

Smalls said, "I've told them what they need to know, Clem. How you've got this cleaner's job at Ralli Brothers, how I went round this morning at six thirty all smartened up like a city gent, how you let me in and showed me round before anyone else was there—so I saw the safe behind the counter and the offices upstairs and downstairs and the alarm switch and everything. I was in there upwards of ten minutes, wasn't I, and got a clean picture of all the whole place. And I've told them you'll do the same for them any day they please so they can get the lie of the land, too. Right?"

"Right," said Clem, and coughed bronchially through his cigarette.

"Any questions?" Smalls asked.

The others had been examining Clem Eden intently, for on his reliability their freedom would depend.

"You employed by the bank?" Jeffrey asked.

"Well, no. I come from the Acme Cleaning Company. Bank has a contract for having the rooms cleaned, see. I get there at six thirty every morning. Thorne, that's the caretaker, he lives on the top floor, he comes down and switches off the office alarms and lets me in. Then I have the run of the place for two hours before anyone else shows up."

The group digested this information. "Pretty casual," said Micky Green. "Anybody can walk in, help themselves, then, is that it?"

"No one walks in unless I let 'em. And when they get in, there's nothing to pinch, see. It's all in safes and vaults, and they're protected by these other alarms."

"What other alarms?"

"The A.F.A. Central Station alarm system," said Smalls approvingly. "With air-pressure differential detectors. Very good system. Very safe. You can't get in by what they call forcible entry, I can tell you. But you don't need forcible entry when you know how to switch 'em off, do you?"

"How many staff?" asked Edlin.

"Fourteen. They go to their offices when they come. It's a merchant bank, see. And not quite like an ordinary one at that."

"How not like an ordinary merchant bank?" asked Micky Green. "There's money, isn't there?"

"Course there's money," Smalls interposed. "But this bank accepts precious stones and jewelry against loans. Diamonds and suchlike. It's Hatton Garden, you know. There'll be stones *and* cash."

"Jewelry's not so good," said Micky Green. "By the time you've fenced it you're lucky if you draw twenty-five percent."

"What time does the staff start coming in?" Tony Edlin asked.

"Soon after nine. But this postman comes around eight thirty and I have to sign for letters. You can't tie me up before he's gone."

"We can do for him as well," said Smalls genially.

"No, you can't, he's got a mate in his van."

Vodka Johnny grunted his annoyance. "You should've told us."

"Well, he's telling you now," said Bertie Smalls. "It makes no difference. Postman comes eight thirty. Staff come around nine. Time enough. Wrap you up in five minutes, we will, Clem." He lit a cigarette from the butt of the old and dropped the damp end in the smoldering ashtray.

"I'll go over tomorrow," said Jeffrey, "see for myself. You come, Micky. Can't be too careful."

"Suits me," said Clem Eden. "But early, mind. And watch who's about. I'll leave the front door unlocked. Just walk in casual. If there's anyone in the street, they won't know which office you're going to."

"We'll need tools," said Tony Edlin. "I'll bring in Ronnie Dark. He's got shotguns and handguns. Micky, can you fix the cars?"

"I reckon," said Green. "I reckon."

Smalls took a long gulp of beer; it seemed to go down his throat without visible sign of being swallowed. "Well, that's it, then. When you've all been over we'll have another meet, fix the day."

"Sooner the better for me," said Edlin. "I'm running short."

MESSRS. RALLI BROS. Ltd., an old established firm of merchant bankers, occupied at that time numbers 63-66 Hatton Garden, E.C.1., which is at the north end of the street near Clerkenwell Road, and is part of a seven-story modern building put up after the blitz, with its own drive-in parking lot beside it. The premises have since been occupied by Discount Bank (Overseas) Ltd., a Geneva-based company, and the entrance of double swing doors flanked on one side by a travel bureau and on the other by an empty shop.

A casual stroller down Hatton Garden would be excused for supposing himself in some cut-rate district of a duty-free seaport, for the shops vie with each other in advertising large discounts on all the jewelry they display, and the jewelry they display would not tempt any self-respecting burglar even to turn over in his bed. But this should not deceive the casual stroller, for behind this unappetizing façade, locked away in "burglarproof" vaults, lies some of the finest jewelry in the world, particularly in the form of uncut stones.

Ralli Bros. occupied the ground floor of this building, with a basement underneath containing the strong room and the vaults. On the first floor were the administrative offices, and the rest of the building was rented to various companies connected with the jewelry trade.

March 26, 1969, was a fine day but very cold, with an occasional flurry of snow drifting in the wind. Stray bits of paper and other litter stirred from time to time and blew across the empty street. This is not quite the City of London, but it wakens just as slowly, and no one took particular notice of the two cars, a Ford Cortina and a Corsair, that found their way early to strategic parking meters within strolling distance of the bank, nor of the six men—for Dark had joined them—who got out and sat in a third car until it was time. Four of them—Bertie Smalls, Tony Edlin, Jimmy Jeffrey, and Ronnie Dark—at casual intervals walked up the steps and through the doors of the building, then discreetly into the bank. There, while Eden went about his floor mopping, they crammed themselves into the ladies' lavatory and waited for the arrival of the postman.

At this point things began to go a little wrong. The postman was late, and two of the clerks and a middle-aged bank messenger called Davies arrived early. They were all men, so the robbers' hideout was as yet inviolate, but tension mounted with discomfort. Jeffrey was for cutting it out and trying again another day—nothing had yet gone beyond the point of no return; but Tony Edlin, who was always notably cool, sided with Bertie Smalls in electing to stay. At eight forty-five the postman arrived; Clem Eden accepted the mail and signed for it. As he passed the ladies' on his way to the main office, he gave the door a couple of sharp raps. A few minutes later, on his return, he was confronted by two men in stocking masks and carrying sawed-off shotguns, who motioned him toward the lavatory, where their companions were waiting with a rope and a gag.

Davies, who was sorting the mail, was the next to be set on, and then the two virtuous clerks were surprised at their desks. None made any effort to argue with the great mountain of a man—made stouter than ever by the pullovers he was wearing—or with the gun he carried. Jeffrey and Dark tied them up and gagged them, and the wait began for the chief clerk.

As each member of the staff arrived, he was confronted by the gun of Bertie Smalls and a threat to blow his head off if he uttered a word. Then he was grabbed by the arm and thrust toward Edlin, who held a gun over him as he was tied up and bundled beside the others in a corner. Only one woman, quicker to size up the situation, took the risk of making a sharp dash for the door, but Jeffrey was there to grab her and stick a cloth in her mouth. As soon as the chief clerk came, he was recognized from Clem Eden's description, and dragged into the center of the main office and his keys demanded. By now Vodka Johnny and Lenny Jones had come into the bank from the waiting car and had joined forces with the others.

"They're useless," the chief clerk observed as he handed over the keys, "without Mr. Crafter."

"Who the hell's Crafter?"

"One of my clerks. I only hold the A keys. It's a security measure so that no one man can open the safes on his own. He holds the B keys."

"Which of this lot is Crafter?"

"He's not here yet. I can't do anything without him."

Cursing Eden for not knowing this, the robbers settled to wait.

Mr. Crafter was a little late. His train had been held up by frozen points. While they were waiting, the last of the staff arrived, and then one or two early customers came in. When Mr. Crafter reached the bank, eighteen men and women were strewn about the floor, hands and feet bound and mouths gagged, while two of the gang held guns over them. Two more waited at the bank door to receive any other customers who walked in, while Smalls and Edlin forced the two key carriers at gunpoint to the foot of the stairs, where the alarms were, and then, those switched off, down into the vaults to open the big safes. Each safe had a combination and each had two locks, and when they were open, Jeffrey joined Smalls and Edlin with two canvas grips. While they filled these, three more customers arrived at the bank and were summarily dealt with.

The contents of the vaults were more than they expected, and they grabbed up two extra bags belonging to the staff; then with bags bulging and tin boxes under arms they shoved the two clerks into the vault and ran back up the stairs. Here their friends waited tensely, watched by the captives on the floor.

"Right," said Smalls. "Just leave ordinary. Just like we was customers ourselves."

To the door, their backs to the captives, off with the masks, guns under coats, grips, bags, and boxes as casually in hand as possible, one by one they slipped away. Outside, the world was now awake. Buses were beginning to fill the streets, cars knotted at traffic lights, the thousands of black-coated workers streamed through the narrow canyons of the city. The chief cashier, a Mr. Cyril Preston, had been wriggling himself free while the robbery was progressing; as soon as they left, he struggled to his feet and staggered through the double doors after them. They were just getting into a car fifty yards down the street. Since he did not know how trigger-happy they were, he chose not to shout, but took down the color and license number of the Corsair they drove away in and rushed back to give the alarm.

Around the corner, in St. Cross Street, Traffic Warden Andrews, out on her early prowl, had noted the number of a Cortina parked at a meter, and finding it still there at nine twenty-three and the time expired, she was just writing out a parking ticket when four men came up hurriedly, carrying two canvas bags and a tin box, and piled into the car. So much in a hurry were they that they almost brushed her aside. Breath coming sharp with annoyance, she told the driver to wait while she finished writing his ticket. He grinned at her and said, "You send it to us, love," and drove off. On hearing of the raid, Mrs. Andrews reported the incident to the police but unfortunately could not give an accurate description of the men.

AFTER A HEARTY breakfast and a few stiff brandies to calm the nerves, the gang came together again at Vodka Johnny's house, in Finchley, to examine the spoil. In the tin boxes was sixteen thousand pounds in notes. The rest was in stones, packets of them, carefully graded: diamonds, emeralds, rubies, sapphires, many of them uncut—a massive haul. Ralli Bros. valued their loss at about four hundred thousand pounds.

None of this was recovered, nor were any of the thieves caught. The vehicle Mr. Preston had seen was found abandoned in Bisham Gardens, North London, ten days later. The license plates were false, and it had been stolen from the parking lot at South Ruislip station. Nor was Traffic Warden Andrews' number any more useful. That car was found in Lupton Street, also in North London, on the day of the robbery. It had been stolen in Brixton the day before.

The robbers faded into the background, unrecognized and unknown. The police inspector in charge of the case reported that in his view the thieves were not completely expert: two of them had not even worn masks but only mufflers over their faces. They had not known about the double keys to the safes; they had brought sufficient rope but not enough bags. It all suggested a ruthless but ad hoc group, with some inside knowledge but not a lot, who had been lucky to get away with it.

Clem Eden, the cleaner, was examined and reexamined, for it was found that he had a record; but he maintained that he had been overpowered at the door and bound up like the rest, and no one could shake or disprove his story. It was reported that the gang paid him ten thousand pounds for his part; after living very quietly for a while he disappeared and has not been heard of since. The police would still very much like to find him, for they believe he had a hand in setting up other robberies. But he may well be dead. Once a man becomes inconvenient or a possible risk to bigger men in the criminal world, anything may happen to him.

As Micky Green had predicted, the rest of the robbers did not do so well out of the stones. A "color" man—that is, an expert on colored stones—had to be called in, an elderly man from Brighton called David Kozak, to assist in the valuation and the disposal. Nevertheless they netted about one hundred thousand pounds among them and were able to live it up in discreet but royal style: holidays abroad, good cars, gambling, drink, and women. It had come easy and it went easy. In a few months, having learned from their mistakes last time, they began to look for fresh worlds to conquer.

CHAPTER 2

WHILE IT MAY BE unfair to say that a country gets the crime it deserves, changes in society, changes in the mores of society, seem to
produce criminals to match an emergent mood or to take advantage
of a shaken social structure. The public has its own personal morali-
ties, its own sense of what is and is not justice. The existence of these
beliefs, alterations in these beliefs, spark off latent material in the
delinquent subculture of civilization.

Britain emerged from World War II an exhausted but a united
nation. Crime was kept in check by a police force which, although
scientifically and organizationally antiquated, was run by men with
a sense of mission and a knowledge of almost total public support.
Criminals as a class tended to run to type; and that type engaged in
a lifetime contest with the law during which both sides observed
unwritten conventions of behavior. The idea of carrying weapons of
any sort was anathema to them.

By the early 1960s, however, a change had come over British society. The refusal of large numbers of the new generation to conform
within the existing social framework, the proliferation of new and
irritating laws, even the immense increase in motor traffic, all
brought the police into abrasive contact with the public as never
before.

The widening gap between the law enforcers and the public became most apparent in 1963, the year of the Great Train Robbery.
The sheer skill and effrontery of this robbery, with its haul of
£2,300,000 in used and largely untraceable bank notes, set England
laughing and talking. Indeed, news and views were flashed all over
the world; it became the sensation of the season. The fact that most
of the robbers were later caught did not detract from the original
vicarious thrill of seeing the operation so successful.

The change in general attitude, however, showed not so much in
the public's admiration for the skill and daring of the achievement—
which would have occurred at any time—as in its ability to overlook
the one serious flaw in the operation: the brutal iron bar that felled
Mills, the engine driver, when he showed fight. A new pattern of

robberies was emerging. Now the public tolerance of violence—at least at second hand—set the scene for the appearance of the gun and the blackjack.

After 1963 there was a steady increase in robberies of this kind. Banks had to introduce bulletproof counter grilles. By the late 1960s, when Bertie Smalls and his companions decided to move in on the scene, bank robberies and payroll snatches backed up by guns were becoming so common that the press, which less than ten years earlier would have given them two-column headlines, now noted them as casual items at the bottom of the page.

BERTIE SMALLS AND his friends had realized very soon that ventures like the Ralli Bros. raid were all right in their way, but from an orthodox bank you pulled in *cash,* readily spendable cash, that didn't need any fence or jewelry smart boy to be called in to grab a lion's share of the proceeds without risk to himself. Cash, that was the idea, and if you'd the nerve, first-rate information, and split-second timing and a couple of guns to back you up, it was all there for the taking—bags and bags of it everywhere.

For their operations these men carried revolvers and sawed-off shotguns. Their view, not unreasonably, was that the more obvious the violence threatened, the less likelihood of its having to be used. Sometimes, as an extra warning, they would fire into the ceiling of the bank being attacked just to impress and terrorize the more. No wonder they were called the Frighteners.

Yet they were also known in some quarters as the Laughing Robbers. The whole group were never without a sense of humor. It was grim, rough, callous humor, but it showed even in the disguises they wore: the false mustaches, the red wigs, the nose spectacles. It showed in the audacity and styling of some of the crimes. It was as if a circus clown had turned roughneck bandit.

Their first major raid on a bank had in fact been carried out six months before that on Ralli Bros. It was the most notable robbery of 1968, and took place in Brighton on October 2, when they stole seventy thousand pounds from the National Provincial Bank. For the event the robbers had driven down to Brighton with their wives and families for a jolly holiday picnic—a typical cockney group, out for the day with their beach gear, their beer cans, and their buckets and spades. Then the men, with many a laugh and joke, left their families on the beach and attacked the bank. An hour later, having dumped the stolen money in a prearranged flat, they rejoined their families on the beach and lazed the rest of the autumn sunshine away while the police scoured the countryside for them.

The following March came Ralli Bros., and soon after, in May, a raid on the Skefko Ballbearing Co. Ltd. of Luton, when fifty-seven thousand pounds was taken in a payroll snatch. An attempt to rob Barclays Bank, Wanstead, was a failure, but in February 1970, Barclays in Ilford was raided, with an immense haul of £237,736.

By this time substantial robberies of one sort and another, almost always by armed men, were averaging one a week. The police, particularly Scotland Yard, had no real leads to go on. In London, special flying squads existed to block the main escape roads when an alarm was sounded; routes to and from banks thought to be at risk were kept under special surveillance; often squad cars were on the scene of a robbery within two or three minutes of the raid. But the robbers vanished without trace.

The Yard, however, began to recognize the trademarks of the most successful robbers even if they could not identify them personally. They were now able to distinguish between the experts and their imitators: raw youths, trigger-happy and dangerous, who tried their hand at the same game, often with disastrous results to themselves and to those who got in their way.

Here and there a man was caught, but the Yard was aware that it was only plucking at an occasional branch from a tree that continued to grow and flourish in spite of all they could do. The big men—these were what they were missing all the time. Big in stature as well as importance, for almost invariably the thieves were described as tall, burly men—not surprising, since in addition to their three sweaters apiece they all wore built-up shoes to give themselves height.

Early in 1970 the Yard's Criminal Investigation Department (CID) began to pay some attention to Derek Crichton Smalls. He had "form" —a criminal record—but it was all small-time stuff. When he was twenty-two he had been fined ten pounds for possessing an offensive weapon. The same year he'd got three months for loitering with intent to steal; the year after, eighteen months for living off prostitution. At twenty-seven he had had another three months for loitering with intent, and at thirty another three months for attempted shopbreaking. The following year he'd been fined thirty pounds for receiving stolen goods, and in the past year he'd served a further three months for assault. The police find that people in their misdeeds run surprisingly to a pattern, and this was not the stuff of which real villains are usually made.

He lived with his common-law wife, Diana Whates—known behind her back as Slack Annie—in Selsdon, Surrey, and they had three children. There was one suspicious circumstance—he lived rather too well without enough visible means of support—but he had answers to everything when questioned. Didn't he have this club at Paddington, and all sorts of other interests?

Then in August 1970, "Mrs. Smalls," together with a man called Donald Barrett and another called Danny Allpress, drove to Bournemouth and rented a flat at 30 Talbot Road for a two-week holiday. They gave the name of Johns, and took Smalls's children down with them and were presently joined by Bertie Smalls. It was all very jolly again—another of those happy summer picnics. Allpress, who this time went under the name of Teale, was a car dealer who lived at Barnet on the Great North Road. A man still in his twenties, he did very well for himself, essayed some automobile racing in his spare time, and somehow contrived a better house and smarter cars to drive than most of his age and kind. At Bournemouth, the party met with Robert King, an active robber known to the police.

On February 2, 1971, four masked men raided Lloyds Bank on Poole Hill. Because one of the guns went off prematurely this raid was a failure, and all that the thieves were able to snatch was £2226 from the bank tills. But, expertly driven, they got clear away.

The Bournemouth police moved in on Mrs. Smalls and arrested her on a charge of conspiracy to rob. By this time Daniel "Teale" had disappeared and Bertie Smalls was living innocently at home in Selsdon. He denied ever having been to Bournemouth, and the police could not prove that he had. But they charged both Barrett and King. At the trial, early the following year, Barrett, who had pleaded guilty, got twelve years. King and Mrs. Smalls, who had pleaded not guilty, were acquitted.

In December 1970 the Midland Bank in Harlesden, North London, had been raided and seventy thousand pounds stolen. In July 1971 occurred the mailbag raid on bank money being transported to Portsmouth from the Isle of Wight. Nine of the ten bags were stolen, and the thieves got away with a hundred thousand pounds in cash. The postal workers and guards were held up at gunpoint and the bags snatched while the alarm bell rang continuously and drew crowds of people, who stood and watched the robbers drive away. In the same month the Allied Irish Bank in Kilburn was plundered of a hundred and thirty thousand pounds, and in October of that year Lloyds Bank, Wood Green, lost twenty-eight thousand pounds.

In the first half of 1972, Lloyds Bank, Stoke Newington; Barclays banks in Acton, Newington Green, Wood Green, and Harringay; National Westminster Bank, Palmers Green; Midland Bank, Erith, Kent; and Lloyds Bank, Wood Green—a second time—were all successfully raided; and on August 10, £138,000 was stolen from Barclays Bank on High Street, Wembley.

At this time police morale was low. The force was full of honest and hardworking men who found themselves chasing shadows, grasping at masked men who disappeared before they could be touched, plodding always in the wake of armed robbery, and seldom, it seemed, catching up. The police, though always ready to make use of new inventions, were organizationally behind the times. Members of the Flying Squad operated in collaboration with the Regional Crime Squad and whatever local officers were involved at the scene of the crime, but each branch operated to some extent independently. Along with collaboration there was often rivalry. The top men in Scotland Yard, particularly Assistant Commissioner Crime Colin Woods and Deputy Assistant Commissioner Bob Halliday, began to argue for a reorganization and a total reassessment.

So far—and this was 1972—they had reached some fairly clear conclusions about the robbers and the methods they used. The Yard was convinced that this was not a tight group but a series of groups that formed and re-formed as opportunity or fancy took them—probably around one or two of about a quartet of leaders. Usually with the help of inside information, the gang would select a target. Weeks of careful observation would lead to a selected time for the raid, in which seconds counted; two or three getaway cars would be stolen and parked at a distance of perhaps two hundred yards from the target. (Stolen so recently that in most cases they were recovered by the police before the owners knew they were gone.) The raid car was usually a van, with license plates changed and rear windows blacked out, so that no curious person could look in while the van was stopped at traffic lights. There would also be a cardboard sheet behind the driver. This van would drive up to the target, possibly onto the sidewalk, and the masked and armed men would swarm out and make their grab. As soon as they were through they would come out and split up, running to their waiting cars with the bags of money. As the escape cars drew away, the men tore off their masks. The distance the escape cars went was usually very short, hence the futility of the roadblocks when they were set up. At first the police thought the robbers changed to their own cars and filtered through the net that way, but more recently they had concluded they were using "flops"—that is, flats or apartments belonging to accomplices—where money and weapons could be stored until it was safe to move them.

(One of the most useful accomplices of whom Scotland Yard did not then know was a London taxi driver called Tommy French, a small, dark-haired man of thirty-odd, with tattoos on his hands and wrists, who for one hundred pounds a time ferried the robbers about London in his irreproachably mundane cab, deposited them wherever they wanted to go, and then clicked up his FOR HIRE flag in the normal way.)

The Yard kept careful watch on a number of known villains and many characters on the periphery of crime for evidences of sudden wealth and extravagant spending. But the robbers were careful; and the early 1970s, when credit was easy and money cheap, was a difficult time to check high living. Almost anyone of relatively blameless character could get a loan from a bank and live above his means.

Also, it would seem that the robbers were dispensing with small men, men with not too much to lose, whom the police might hope to bribe for the confidential whisper. Reliability and total involvement were insisted on, and anyone not coming up to the required standard was not invited again and was warned what would happen to him if he opened his mouth even to his dearest friend.

But by 1972 the police were onto Bertie Smalls again. On Monday, May 22, just before the raid on the National Westminster Bank in Palmers Green, a Mrs. Irene Harrington, returning to work after her lunch, noticed a bronze Ford parked in Lightcliffe Road. There were four men in it, all casually dressed and wearing sunglasses, and she thought them sufficiently unusual to wonder if they were making a film. As she passed by, a man crossed the street and leaned on the door of the car, talking to the driver. Almost as soon as she had reached her place of work, she heard the alarm bells going and ran out again, to see the same car abandoned and straddling the sidewalk outside the bank. She told the police she thought she would remember the man who had come up and spoken to the driver. They invited her to the Yard to look at some photographs, and she picked out Derek Crichton Smalls.

Three days before this an airport detective constable was passing the National Westminster Bank in Palmers Green. He saw a red Jaguar pull up and two men go in and later emerge and drive off. His suspicion aroused, he reported the incident to the police, together with the license number of the car. The car belonged to Smalls.

On May 26, Detective Inspector Fitzgerald called to see Smalls, but his wife said he was not at home. The house was searched, but no evidence to implicate Smalls was found. Three days later Smalls rang up Inspector Fitzgerald and asked why the police wanted to see him. The inspector said he wanted his help in inquiries that were being made into the Palmers Green bank robbery, so Smalls promised to come the following day and bring his lawyer. He did not turn up.

Nor did he return home. Diana Smalls said she had no idea where he was and thought he might have left her forever. This was considered unlikely, as the ill-matched couple were known to be devoted to each other, and Smalls was a great family man. But again the scent went cold.

CHAPTER 3

THE LATER ROBBERY, of August 10, 1972, when Barclays was again the target, came to be known as the Wembley Bank Robbery. Because it provided a breaking point for the police and at the same time the first breakthrough in favor of the police, it came to have an importance, both in the underworld and in the annals of the Yard, greater than the event itself, which followed the familiar pattern with the familiar outcome.

As early as May of that year Smalls had met Jimmy Wilkinson and Brian Reynolds at the Royal in Ealing—known to them as Slogger's pub—and Reynolds had said he had been making friends with a clerk who worked in Barclays Bank, Wembley, and had a spare-time job as a disc jockey two nights a week at Tabbie's Club, Ealing. Name of Holt. Youngish—twenty-five or so—lived with his mum and dad still; discontented, vain, weak. The sort of bloke you could flatter into doing something, and if he tried to draw back at the last minute, equally the sort of bloke you could lean on. Properly cultivated, there was nothing he wouldn't tell you. Just at the moment Reynolds was leading him along, half serious, half joking. It was like playing a salmon; you knew when to pull and when to give him a bit of leeway. But soon he'd begin to wind him in.

Already Holt was talking of the pickups of money from the bank by security vans, the days it happened, the time of day, and how it happened. Often there was a hundred and fifty thousand pounds in the bags. When the security guards went in, the bags of money were brought up in an elevator from the vaults below. It took the guards less than five minutes to take delivery of the bags, sign for them, and put them into their van. There were steps leading down to the vaults. Robbers, if they ever did try it on, could probably get down those steps and intercept the money at the bottom before ever it was put into the elevator.

"I reckon," said Bertie, "that your fish is all but landed."

"Give me another two weeks. Then I'll bring him round and you can see him for yourself, can't you?"

Two weeks later Smalls met Anthony Holt in the parking lot behind Marks & Spencer's in Ealing and okayed the venture. But this was to be one of the big raids and most of the big men would want to be in on it. First there was Philip Morris. He was thought by Smalls to be a bit trigger-happy, but as a special friend of Wilkinson's, he could not be left out. A tall, fair, rugged man of thirty-six, Morris most of the time nowadays lived the life of a country gentleman at his farm at Carwinnen, near Camborne. (Of course he'd been a bit of a wild shaver in his youth: put on probation for stealing a car, a two-pound fine for stealing a horse, a day's imprisonment for housebreak-

273

ing, absolute discharge for assault on a policeman, three months at a detention center for attempted theft, four months' imprisonment for breaking a window with intent to steal—all before he was twenty-one. And unfortunately there were a couple of things later, including six years for robbery with aggravation.)

But that was all long behind him now. Except for the idiosyncracy of having guard dogs and floodlights around his farm, he was liked and respected by the local Cornish people; he rode to hounds, was friendly with the local justices of the peace, and was noted for his generosity: no charitable organization went away empty. He was kind to animals and to people—except of course to the milkman he accidentally shot dead when helping to steal £125,000 from Unigate. (This was the one black spot on the group's policy of violence against the person intended as a threat not to be carried out.)

Second to come in was Bruce Brown, a heavy, genial man of thirty-eight, who lived in great respectability with his wife, Glenys, in a detached house called the Crossways, at Heston. He was known to be in the business of property development. A man who bought expensive clothes and looked good in them, well-spoken and easy of manner, he, too, was a popular figure in the solid middle-class society of his district. He had recently become captain of his local golf club, the Ashford Manor, and was friendly with bank managers, solicitors, financiers, and had as his special chum both for golf and for holidays Detective Chief Superintendent Saxby of Q Division, which has its headquarters at Wembley.

Third, and heaviest, and perhaps the most important of this trio, was Brian Turner, aged thirty-five, who lived at Folly Close, Radlett, with his wife, Rose, and three children. Brought up on the Burnt Oak Council Estate, Edgware, he had been known as Tubsy Turner when he ran a grocery shop in Kilburn, and he had been less successful than the other two in shaking off the traces of his upbringing. A smart dresser who always looked less at home in his modish clothes than Brown, he was a man who had a fancy for fast cars and fast women. Yet he was also a lover of antiques and crystal glass, considered himself a connoisseur of food and wine, and was a first-rate bridge player. He owned property in the neighborhood and ran a small supermarket in Kilburn, and these were assumed to keep him in the style in which he lived. His next-door neighbor was a Barclays

Bank manager, which seemed cynically appropriate, since Barclays was the bank most frequently hit.

This trio, together with Wilkinson and Reynolds, Smalls, Lenny Jones, and Danny Allpress, made up the party to do the bank. Allpress was to be the driver, the getaway man. A few days before the job they all met at the Thatched Barn, a motel in Borehamwood, and concerted their plans. Meets, as they were called, were kept to a minimum, since there was a risk in being seen together. Brian Turner and Bruce Brown said they would bring their own guns, and Philip Morris would supply the rest. Morris always had plenty of guns. Brian Turner, who knew the Wembley area intimately, said he would provide the flop. He had a Jamaican girl friend called Maria Mercedes Dadd, whose flat they could use. Two cars would be stolen for getaways—as it turned out, a Triumph and a Ford Cortina. Two vans for the raid were bought. The bank was inspected several times and security vans were watched as they drove up and collected the money. The raid was fixed for August 10. Tony Holt, the bank clerk, was becoming increasingly nervous as the time drew near. They told him to lie down when they came in and no hurt would come to him, and they silenced his scruples with a promise of ten thousand pounds in cash. To a young man restricted in his life-style by a salary of fifteen hundred pounds a year and with aspirations to become a full-time disc jockey, it was a fortune.

The night before the job the stolen Cortina was parked behind the Marks & Spencer store at Ealing, the Triumph was parked in front of some flats off The Broadway, and a van and another Cortina in the parking lot of a public house just off Western Avenue. These were about a mile and a half from the next day's objective.

Bertie Smalls, who since leaving home had been living in a succession of small hotels under a succession of names, decided to spend the night at the flat of Philip Morris' girl friend, where the country gentleman from Cornwall was also staying.

In the morning Tommy French arrived in his unobtrusive taxi and conveyed Smalls and Morris and the guns to Jimmy Wilkinson's flat, where Allpress and Reynolds were waiting for them. Reynolds went off to pick up the getaway van and take it to Wembley, and Smalls, Allpress, and Wilkinson collected the Triumph and one of the Cortinas. Smalls was very irritated when he got into the stolen Cortina to find it had clutch trouble; it was disgraceful the way people did not look after their cars. In the end he abandoned it and joined the others in the Triumph. In the meantime Philip Morris picked up the raid van and drove it to the Green Man public house at Wembley, where the others assembled and were joined by Brian Turner and Bruce Brown in the other Cortina.

Now came the tense time of waiting. The security van usually arrived at the bank at nine forty-five. The robbers drove around and parked in the road leading up to the bank at nine twenty. It was too far away, but they must not draw attention to themselves too soon. They had all, as usual, taken pep pills to give themselves the necessary zip for the moment of action. Twenty minutes later Allpress pulled the van out and slid into a place that had become vacant about three hundred yards from the bank. Brian Reynolds was not with them. He had got out half an hour ago and was loitering by the bank. His job was to go into the bank just after the security men and walk over to the foreign-exchange area; from here, Holt had told them—and they had later verified—you could see when the bags of money came up onto the ground floor. Once the money was up, all Reynolds had to do was walk out of the bank and walk away. It was the prearranged signal for the attack.

In the back of the van the breathing was heavy under wigs and mustaches and stocking masks. Of the five men waiting there for the moment of explosion, only Philip Morris was naturally tall, but Smalls, Turner, and Brown were big men, and they must all—even Wilkinson—have looked enormous in their raiding gear.

A tap from outside told them that the security van had arrived; minutes later two taps told them that this was it. Their van lurched out into the traffic—causing a chorus of protesting horns—accelerated down the street in a scream of first gear, and bounced and jerked to a stop behind the security van.

Allpress, who had driven that distance in his mask, was a moment ahead of the others; following him through the door of the bank came Philip Morris and Brian Turner, with Bertie Smalls and Bruce Brown just behind, and Wilkinson bringing up the rear. Guns were suddenly thrust at the security guards and at the staff; customers stared in horror; Morris and Turner fired over the heads of the people, glass shivering and shattering; guards raised their hands;

people all around collapsed to the floor as they were instructed to do, or else; Wilkinson and Allpress brought sledgehammers to bear on the intervening inside door; Smalls stood by the outer door, covering both ways. Brown, Allpress, and Wilkinson dashed through the broken inner door and returned, dragging the trolley containing the bags of money. Out they went to their van and flung in the bags while passersby, caught up like twigs in a blocked stream, accumulated and stared. An ambulance crew appeared from nowhere and made to intervene until Morris swung his gun on them.

The money was all in; Smalls alone remained in the bank, covering the cowering staff. A toot told him to leave, and he jumped in beside Allpress as the van lurched out again into the traffic, twisting and turning crazily between the buses and cars. It had all taken less than two minutes.

It was not far to the Green Man, but it seemed a long way that day. Still in full regalia, they flung themselves out of the van and piled into the two waiting cars, the bags of money and the guns slung carelessly into the trunks, then off they went again. Brown, Turner, and Allpress were in the Triumph with most of the money, Allpress, of course, driving. The rest followed in the Ford Cortina, driven by Wilkinson. Somehow Wilkinson kept up with the expert Allpress. As they drove they pulled off their masks and disguises. Presently, beginning to breathe easily for the first time, they turned into the Chalkhill Estate, where Maria Dadd had her flop, and were able to carry their bags and gear up the stairs to her flat and dump them there. The two escape cars were driven a few hundred yards farther on and abandoned. With thousands of people living in the small area of the estate, there was little chance of the police being able to make much use of the information when the cars were found.

Later the men left unobtrusively by the back door and took a subway to Baker Street, from where a couple of taxis could convey them back to Ealing. The following day they met to divide the loot. Five thousand pounds was pulled out for expenses, and ten thousand pounds for Tony Holt; the remaining £123,000 was split equally among the seven men who had taken part in the raid, a share-out of about £17,500 per person. As Bertie Smalls said, it always paid to go for cash.

Altogether it had been one of their most successful operations.

THE FOLLOWING WEEK A CONFERENCE was called at Scotland Yard to which all chief superintendents and commanders were summoned. It was presided over by Assistant Commissioner Crime Woods and Deputy Assistant Commissioner Halliday.

With a politeness which did not disguise his anger, Commissioner Woods pointed out to the assembled company that in the past two years there had been a total of fifty-eight major robberies, involving losses of money amounting to over three million pounds, and that in the course of all the police investigations there had not been more than half a dozen substantial arrests. Often, suspected men had been pulled in and then released because there was not enough evidence to proceed. They were confronted with a blank wall of failure. This Wembley job must surely be the last straw. Yet so far Detective Inspector Wilding, in charge of the Wembley investigation, had come up with nothing new.

"Gentlemen," Commissioner Woods said, "you see in this room the cream of the detective force of the Criminal Investigation Department of New Scotland Yard. Most of you have had twenty or twenty-five years' experience in the force. I believe you to be intelligent and dedicated men. But fifty-eight major robberies have occurred over the past few years—all this money has been stolen and no one important has been arrested. What are you being paid for?"

A long and tense discussion followed. Then Woods said, "Let's for the moment forget location, opportunity, clues, evidence, suspicion; let's altogether ignore the necessity of proof. Let us not work from the inside out, as it were, but from the outside in. Tell me, who is there at present out of jail who has, in your view, the *potential* which could lead him into committing crimes of this nature? Tell me, who *is* there? We know all the reputed villains, we've checked them and rechecked them. So this is a man, or men, either with no record at all or moving out of his previous class into the big time. Or someone who for a considerable number of years appears to have been going straight. Think it over. I give you five minutes."

A long pause was followed by one or two tentative suggestions, which were dismissed almost as soon as they were put forward. Then a detective chief superintendent called Neesham got up. "There's a man, Brian Turner. He'll be—what? I suppose about thirty-five now. He got a ten-year stretch in 1962 for robbery with violence. Two payroll cashiers from Rootes were robbed of about thirteen thousand pounds. He only served five. It's about the right timing."

"Where is he now?"

"As far as we know he's been going straight for several years. He hadn't got much of a record before. I think he lives in Radlett."

"Well, look into him—thoroughly."

"And there's Bruce Brown," Neesham went on. "He got three years for office breaking in 1963 and a couple of small things before that. He seems to have turned over a new leaf. Very respectable now. You

can't go on harassing a man if he sincerely tries to live it down. But if we're asked to look for *potential* . . ."

Another detective chief superintendent got up, a man called Mooney. "Rather strange, sir. I'd begun to make a list on my pad. So far I've only got two names on it. They're Turner and Brown."

"Then let's first investigate Turner and Brown—in a big way."

(Even at this conference Bertie Smalls's name was not mentioned. Of course he was already on the wanted-for-questioning list. Yet, even though expressly invited to cast their net wide, the experienced police officers in the room were to some extent still deceived by the triviality of his record. Perhaps it is hard to see an armed bank robber in the person of a stout, genial petty crook whose worst offense in eight convictions has been living off immoral earnings.)

THEREAFTER EVENTS MOVED quickly on all fronts. Woods, in consultation with Halliday and two others, decided to make a long-overdue reorganization of the teams who were to combat the criminals. All groups—the Flying Squad, the Regional Crime Squad, and such other CID officers as were needed—were for the first time in the history of Scotland Yard welded together under a single head and were called the Wembley Bank Robbery Squad. The man chosen to head this squad was called James Marshall.

Marshall, a fresh-complexioned, dark-haired, brisk and cheerful man in his mid-forties, had had an unusual career. The son of a post-office official, he had joined the merchant navy after leaving school and then had become a brass-instrument polisher for Boosey & Hawkes. Moving later to Southampton, and being unsatisfied with his job, he saw an advertisement inviting recruits to the police force and decided to try his luck. After a promising start in Hampshire he moved to London and became a detective in the CID. In ten years his rise was what the press are fond of calling meteoric, and at the time of his call to lead the Wembley Bank Squad he was already a detective superintendent. A tough man, dedicated to his job, willing to rise to any challenge, totally determined to track his criminals down, yet quite without rancor. In the course of his relatively short career his car had been wrecked, he had been caught in a dark alley and beaten up, and he had been awarded the British Empire Medal for bravery in foiling an attempted bank raid. Under his command were Detective Chief Inspector Eist, also a winner of the BEM, Detective Chief Inspector Dixon, and Detective Inspector Wilding.

But without the directive from Commissioner Woods or the drive of Superintendent Marshall's newly constituted force, Detective Inspector Wilding had already, and quite independently, been closing in on one of the two men named by Neesham at the meeting. Every crook not dead, jailed, or hospitalized had been rounded up and investigated and, if necessary, brought in for questioning after the Wembley job. It was a tremendous undertaking, but this time something had to give, and presently one small-time crook under relentless questioning croaked the answer: "Why me? I'm not one of the Frighteners. I cultivate me own patch, see. Go and look up—"

"Look up who, Joe? *Look up who?*"

"Go to Heston, Radlett, Selsdon—that's where *they* live, don't they. Turner, Brown, Smalls, that lot . . ."

The police moved cautiously. Whispered confidences of a petty thief were one thing—proof was quite another. The houses of all three men were kept under the closest surveillance. There was still no sign of Smalls. None of the neighbors had seen him for months. Brian Turner, people said, was on holiday in Spain—but on his own, not with his wife and children. Bruce Brown, on the other hand, had been about recently. He had played a round of golf on August 20. A letter from him to the golf secretary had been posted in Heston on August 23. His car was in the garage, but the house was empty. His wife had told the neighbors that she was taking the children to Wales for a holiday and that Bruce would be joining her "in a few days."

Inspector Wilding stared at the modern, detached, bow-windowed house, with its lawn sprinklers and its pretty, small garden, and did not quite believe it. Something was wrong. Brown had got wind of the suspicion, but was he truly away? At seven on the morning of August 30, Wilding, armed with a search warrant, had the house surrounded and went to the door. No answer. With a neighbor as a witness, the inspector forced an entry through a back window. The house was tidy, deserted. Mr. Brown was not at home.

Then as Wilding sat quietly in the living room talking to the neighbor, a detective constable came in and said, "Beg pardon, sir. There's a loft."

They went upstairs, and presently Bruce Brown was discovered crouching behind the water tank in his pajamas, whither he had fled at the first knock on the door. He showed no fight, indeed seemed in a state of nervous collapse. It was as if he had come not merely to live two lives but to separate them within his own personality. That crude reality in the form of Scotland Yard should bring about a fusion in which the respectable Bruce Brown faced retribution for the sins of his other self was more than he could stand.

Of course he denied everything, even in such a state, and for a time Wilding feared that substantial evidence would again be lacking. Although every room in the house was searched from floor to ceiling—every lining investigated, every jar emptied, every book shaken out, every cranny probed—there appeared to be nothing. Only Mr. Brown's key ring was not entirely satisfactory. There were two keys on it whose purpose he said he had forgotten. It could well have been true. Few people remember to discard keys when their purpose has gone. Inspector Wilding thought this out, then drove to Ashford Manor, Brown's golf club. One of the keys fitted his locker. Inside the locker, in the depths of his golf bag, was another key, and on the key a tag marked SAFE DEPOSIT.

It was not difficult to trace the key to the London Safe Deposit Company, in lower Regent Street. Wilding called there and opened the box. In it were notes to the value of £14,940. Some of the notes had marks on them made by cashiers at Barclays Bank, Wembley. Characteristically, when he was charged, Bruce Brown said, "My reputation has gone, my good name at the golf club, everything. . . ."

CHAPTER 4

A GOOD BEGINNING, BUT only a beginning. Of the two men mentioned at the top-level conference at the Yard, one had now been arrested independently, and with strong evidence against him. But what of all the others? Was Brown one of the organizers, one of the big fish, or merely one of the minnows? He would not say. In fact he said nothing, and his lawyer reserved his defense.

Superintendent Marshall's newly organized Wembley Bank Squad, thirty in number, took over the whole floor of the big Wembley Police Station. They soon became known in the underworld as the Heavies. Every robbery committed over recent years was carefully reexamined for evidence of similarity of style, location, method, opportunity. Every crook under the least suspicion was subjected to surveillance, in which the most sophisticated equipment was used. Helicopters were employed, using men with high-powered binoculars; rooms were taken overlooking other rooms, meetings photographed, conversations taped.

After weeks of concentrated work the police moved in on Maria Dadd. The abandoned cars had pointed to one of the eight thousand people living on the Chalkhill Estate. Elimination had slowly reduced the number. Then a pretty, coffee-colored girl was seen briefly in the company of one of the suspects. Miss Dadd was the only one who fitted the bill. In a small locked cupboard in her flat was a moneybag such as had been used at the time of the raid; in the flat itself, elastic bands were found which are used to secure money, and an expensive radio tuned in to the police wavelength. Maria Mercedes Dadd was induced to admit her part in the robbery but not to give names away. The police next brought in one David Williams, who was Bruce Brown's brother-in-law, on a charge of conspiring to handle stolen property.

Meanwhile, Forensic had turned up more evidence. Vacuum sweepings—the official police term for dust and debris samples—from Bruce Brown's house matched others that had been taken from the security van and the bank itself after the raid on August 10.

On Monday, November 27, Brown, Williams, and Maria Dadd appeared before the magistrates at Harrow and were committed for trial on charges connected with the Wembley bank raid.

Marshall and his squad of tough, seasoned detectives were sure now they had caught one big man in Bruce Brown. The other two were not important. Where were the rest of the big ones? The country had been scoured for Turner and Smalls, and Interpol's help sought for overseas. It seemed likely that they had both slipped away on false passports and were in relative immunity, perhaps in Tangier or southern Spain. It was becoming increasingly evident that Bertie Smalls had been underestimated throughout. Facts the squad had turned up showed that he now had a case to answer in six robberies. It was of paramount importance to catch him and Turner.

Newspapers splashed full-page photographs of Brian Turner and extensive reports of his alleged double life. These photographs and all relevant details had circulated through Interpol to the police forces of the Western world. But for four months there had been nothing. The two men had completely disappeared. They might indeed now be back in England, under other names, planning a new raid. It was intolerable.

Marshall had a hunch that Bertie Smalls was back—if he had even ever been away. Mrs. Smalls's indignation when questioned was just too good to be true.

When the break came, it was so simple, so easy, that that also seemed too good to be true. They traced a girl who at one time had acted as au pair to the Smalls's children. No, she hadn't seen Smalls for years, but she'd heard a whisper from a friend of a friend that he was at present hiding in a house at Rushden in Northamptonshire, where his brother, Kelvin Smalls, lived.

At seven a.m. on December 23 the Northamptonshire police, with Scotland Yard detectives attached, closed around the house. A Christmas tree could be seen in one window; decorations festooned the hall. To avert suspicion a local constable went to the door first, but there was no trouble. He was admitted without resistance, and the CID, following close behind, found Bertie Smalls just climbing out of bed. At first he tried to bluff them, saying that his name was Woods, but when he found they could not be bluffed, he took his capture philosophically. After he had been cautioned, he remarked, "I've been expecting you lot for some time. In a way it's a bit of a relief, like. You can't live like a rabbit in a hole forever."

Here there was a marked difference between him and Bruce Brown, and indeed between him and most of the robbers. Brown lived a split existence and had hypnotized himself into believing he could continue to do so. The front was more real to him than the occasional savage forays that made that front possible. Philip Morris, the country gentleman in Cornwall, and Danny Allpress in his garage, though perhaps not so self-deceiving, saw their respectable identities as a protection which might last for years. Brian Turner, until his front was blown, had no doubt felt the same.

Smalls cynically saw the end ahead; he knew the tentacles of the law were closing around him and that he operated and lived within ever narrowing limits; so, like a senior executive taking out a large insurance policy, he had prepared a safeguard against retirement. It was a dark and disreputable safeguard, which he had envisaged perhaps from the day he moved up into the higher levels of violent crime. Some years before, he had known a man called Gilbey, who, having been caught red-handed by the police, had bought his freedom by turning Queen's evidence and "grassing"—informing—on his associates; and this inspired Bertie to attempt the same.

To betray your comrades in the world of crime is the ultimate sin. Perhaps it is in all worlds. All men abhor the squealer, the traitor to his cause, however misguided that cause may be. Even in the police world he is looked on with contempt, though it may gratefully use him. Derek Crichton Smalls was a commonplace, ordinary small-time thief who deliberately moved into bank robbery as a way of life. His one distinguishing feature was a clear-eyed detachment in which he weighed the risks and took them deliberately, and as deliberately spent the proceeds. He loved and wanted all the luxuries of life and saw only one way of obtaining them. As he enjoyed himself he was always conscious that it was too good to last, and calculated how, if it ended, he was to come to terms with the future. The crimes he had committed, if brought home to him, would earn him probably a twenty-year sentence, which, even with parole, would be likely to run to fifteen. Now thirty-six, he would be fifty-one when he again emerged into the world. All his life he had been a gross eater, drinker, smoker, sedentary, overweight. At thirty-six his expectation of life, he may have thought, was not likely to be much more than fifteen years. To go to prison for that length of time was only a little better than going to the gallows. It was better, far better, to run the risk of being killed by his colleagues.

While Smalls is perhaps one of the least admirable men of this century, one has to acknowledge his cold, cynical courage. As soon as the car was moving on its way to London, he began to make his overtures to Superintendent Marshall. At first they were properly ignored as being conventional ploys to get a lighter sentence for himself—a name here and there, a few small fry roped in: attempted bribery of the police as surely as the drunken motorist trying to slip a tenner into someone's hand.

"Come on, can't we make a deal?" Bertie said in his friendly way. "I don't mean just bail, I'm thinking of outers. I'll give you every robbery in London. I will straight. I'll even stand up in court and give evidence."

"They'll kill you," Inspector Wilding said.

"They won't find me. I'll be away," said Smalls.

Nothing further was said then; but on January 9, at the Magistrates' Court in the North London suburb of Harrow, when he was formally charged, he made certain more explicit statements to Marshall which made that alert officer sit up. This was not "bribery" of the police that he was offering on a small scale; this was a deal, and a deal in the biggest possible way imaginable.

Bertie Smalls wanted "outers" in return for a complete confession covering two score of robberies, with hauls totaling £2,400,000, and giving full and factual details of everyone concerned in them. Everyone. It was a fantastic offer. Marshall took it at once to his senior officers, and from there they went to see Sir Norman Skelhorn, the director of public prosecutions.

At first the director was quite against any such deal. It was the natural reaction. How could justice be done if a leading robber, perhaps the most culpable of all the robbers, having been caught with fair evidence against him, were to be allowed to go free? It seemed to make a mockery of justice and to bring the law into disrepute.

But the laws of evidence in England are so strictly laid down, in the interests—rightly—of protecting the innocent man from injustice, that many a known criminal has been able to slip out of what seemed a certain net, smiling derisively at the police as he leaves the court with his successful lawyer and resolving that next time he commits a crime he must work at it a little more carefully so that he doesn't have all this bother at the end.

And he has obtained his verdict in spite of what had seemed at the time like conclusive evidence. Against how many people could the police proceed with anything like conclusive evidence in all these bank robberies? Those who had been committed for trial, perhaps, plus Smalls and maybe Turner, if he could ever be found. One or two others, perhaps, with endless, patient watching; maybe after another bank raid someone else would slip up; in a month or two, or a year or two, half a dozen more might be behind bars. Smalls offered the names of and detailed evidence against *thirty-one* criminals and promised even more to follow. It was an offer that Superintendent Marshall was in no doubt about accepting.

Nor were some of his superiors. But still the director hesitated. His yardstick had to be: What would benefit the public most? Would it now be in the public interest to see Smalls properly charged and properly locked away, or could this man be allowed to go free of his many crimes in order to catch all the others? In the two famous cases that had broken the Kray and Richardson gangs, *minor* crooks had been forgiven their crimes in order to catch the big men. That was reasonable. All police forces do it from time to time. But accepting Smalls's offer was excusing a *major* crook, perhaps the biggest of them all. Ever since last August the newspapers had been shouting about Brian Turner and calling him Mr. Big. Did not the police at this moment have the real Mr. Big in their hands?

At length the director gave way. What Smalls had to offer was more valuable than the conviction of one robber. It could smash these gangs irretrievably—and diminish the scale of bank robbery at least for some years. *That* was the greater public good. Bertie should be encouraged to talk. So the deal was struck, and by March 1973 a "contract" had been drawn up and signed. In return for his giving evidence for the crown where and when required, Smalls was granted complete immunity from punishment for the crimes he freely confessed he had committed. His immunity ran to all offenses except murder, piracy, treason, and perjury. (This was why, when they were in the dock, some of his colleagues accused him of murder; if they could pin that on him, he would be dragged back on their side of the rail, where he belonged.)

In April Bertie began to talk. Indeed he began to sing. The first of the eight statements he made ran to ten thousand words. He talked almost without a break for three days. He had an excellent memory and a sharp eye for detail. Everything he said carried the conviction of firsthand experience. "I wasn't well for a week after the Wembley job; I got a boil, see, and I went into the outpatients' department and had it treated. Then after that I went on the Saturday to Spain with Bobby King and eventually met all the people I've been talking about there, except for Philip Morris and Bruce Brown. Turner didn't leave England straightaway because he had another job the following week—about forty thousand pounds—with Jimmy Jeffrey, Tony Edlin, Bruce Brown. . . . Brian said this was planned with a security man who was Jimmy Jeffrey's man. They cut it up. . . ." And so on. As a Yard man put it, from the moment Smalls began his statement the sun really began to shine.

Of course the police could not accept everything Smalls said without corroborative evidence (no judge would consider it sufficient on its own), but this they began to collect. A girl called Susan Mattis was arrested and persuaded to turn Queen's evidence, and she confirmed that her flat in Sidney Road, Hornsey, had been used as a flop, as well as another, when she moved to Denmark Grove. She spoke of the guns being assembled there and of one going off acci-

dentally; she spoke of coming home one day and finding Jimmy Wilkinson and another man counting out stacks of money spread on her bed. Diana Smalls—now taken into protective custody with her children—also bore out minor parts of her husband's statement.

The police swooped, and within forty-eight hours of the completion of Smalls's statements, people all over the country were finding the houses of their apparently respectable neighbors raided at dawn and this or that model of middle-class society borne away in a police car. A unit of the Devon and Cornwall police called at Bodryval Farm, Cornwall, and took away not only Philip Morris but Tommy French, the London taxi driver who had driven Morris three hundred miles back to Cornwall.

When the extent of Bertie Smalls's betrayal became known, the fury of the underworld was unrestrained. Most of the men in his circle had felt reasonably safe, and as one successful robbery followed another this confidence had grown. Even if one or two here and there were unfortunate—such as Brown, and now Smalls, where substantial evidence had been built up against them—this was the luck of the game. It was like breaking your leg skiing; you always hoped it would happen to the other chap.

But Smalls's betrayal altered all that. Instead of there being no evidence to connect you with the crimes, here was a man making a definitive statement and prepared to stand up in open court and swear it to all the world. And not just recent crimes either. The Ralli Bros. theft back in 1969; the Skefko Ballbearing Co. the same year; Barclays Bank, Ilford; the Midland Bank, Harlesden; the Allied Irish Bank, Kilburn; and so on and so on. One after another they were going to come out. And every man and woman concerned in them, the big fish and the small. Every sort of circumstantial detail. Shotguns and revolvers had already been found in a briefcase belonging to Brian Turner, bank accounts were being investigated. Now that they had the first firm evidence, Marshall and his men were turning up more to corroborate it every minute.

In the end, seventeen hard-core robbers were remanded in custody and nine more were charged but released on bail.

"That bastard Smalls," some of the hard core were saying, "has killed us." He must be stopped. Grave damage he had done, but it was not irretrievable. If when the case came off the police found their principal witness no longer in a condition to stand up in court, all would be altered. One knew how severe judges were on wicked policemen who invented stories to put innocent people behind bars.

Smalls, however, was not to be found, even though this time he was being sought by the other side. He was, after an initial period in prison, living with his wife and children in the top flat of a high-rise apartment house in North London, wearing dark glasses and trying to grow a heavy beard; twelve armed detectives in relays of four stood guard over him every minute of the twenty-four hours.

This was necessary. Rumor had it that a top-rank Belgian killer had been retained, and waited at Ostend for news of Smalls's whereabouts before he crossed the Channel. The price he was to have been paid has been variously estimated, but the most commonly accepted figure is thirty thousand pounds.

Committal proceedings presented a difficulty. There was no Magistrates' Court in London big enough to house such a crew, together with all the assembled lawyers, counsel, police officers, witnesses, and members of the public. Someone eventually suggested the gymnasium of Wembley Police Station, and the Harrow magistrates gave permission for this to be converted. It was an event unique in British criminal history and was a job attacked by the police with peculiar pleasure. A dais was built for the magistrates, with the coat of arms above it; a witness box; a public gallery; and, of course, an enormous dock. Tables, benches and chairs, and microphones were brought in.

Since the work of assembling the necessary proof against the accused men was an even more laborious business than building the court, committal proceedings were long delayed, and since a magistrate may not under British law hold a suspected criminal in custody without trial for a longer period than eight days at a time, they appeared in force every week at Wembley, conveyed to and from Brixton Prison in two Black Marias escorted by police cars. They murmured and muttered together in the dock, sneering at the policemen while their counsel appealed, on every conceivable excuse, that they should be released on bail until committal proceedings were complete. Watching, too, from the public gallery were many of their none too savory friends, friends who were free, free to go out into the streets and do their bidding. It was a nasty thought. How many witnesses were really going to come forward against them in the end?

This way things dragged on through the early summer of 1973, and then the robbers got tired of having their appeal for bail turned down and took things into their own hands.

BRIXTON PRISON IS A couple of miles south of the river, in the parish of Lambeth. It was built in 1850 and is not listed as a top security prison. Nor does it look it, resembling as it does a sprawling workhouse of Victorian brick, just off the busy thoroughfare of Brixton Hill. Its back gates lead out onto Lyham Road and it is surrounded by narrow streets of small, respectable terraced houses. It is now used purely as a remand prison, where accused men, after having been brought before a magistrate and enough evidence produced to show that there is a serious case to answer, are held in custody until their trial takes place. Or it is where, if the magistrate refuses bail, men await committal proceedings, as was the case with the hard-core robbers. It is always grossly overcrowded.

It has in fact a security wing—D wing—which is equipped with electronic aids and where high security risks such as IRA prisoners are held. There is also an A wing, which is reserved for those who are considered moderate security risks, and it was here that the robbers were detained. (Although they had committed robbery with violence, none had made any attempt at all to resist arrest.) Because they were remand prisoners and not yet officially guilty, they were allowed to wear their own clothes and have their own food, radios, and newspapers. Friends could visit them without a separating barrier, and the prisoners could mingle in the various cells. Although there were fewer than thirty such A-category prisoners, there were some two hundred and fifty others with whom they could mix between nine a.m. and five p.m.

On Wednesday, May 30, two rented cars—Ford Escorts—were quietly parked in Clarence Crescent, about a mile from the jail. They were stage two. Both were left with ignition keys in, full tanks of petrol, and newspapers draped over the steering wheels to aid in hurried identification. At ten that morning a white Ford Transit Rent-A-Van was left in Lyham Road directly outside the main rear gates of the prison. This was stage one. At ten thirty a Lambeth district sanitation truck with hydraulic tipper was admitted through the rear prison gates and began to pick up the refuse bags waiting to be collected. At ten fifty a warder opening a cupboard door was suddenly confronted with three prisoners, one of them holding a gun and demanding his keys. The gun was in fact made of soap, painted black with shoe polish and covered with bits of silver paper to imitate the working parts. It was quite a clever model, seen at a distance, and wisely the warder did not demand to see it work. Then Bruce Brown, the mild-mannered golf captain, led the way to let himself out, followed by Philip Morris and half a dozen of the other bank robbers. They unlocked the doors and raced out toward the truck.

It was here they made a first error, for they did not relock the doors behind them, and a batch of other prisoners, seeing the way open, decided also to have a go.

Two trash collectors were out gathering the bags; the third was dragged from the driver's seat and flung into the yard. Morris grabbed the wheel and swung the truck around; as he turned, the rest jumped aboard and were followed by a dozen more, climbing on and clinging as the truck roared toward the gate. By now the alarms were screaming and a thin line of warders were assembling outside the gates. If the truck had gone right through the gates, they would have been mowed down. But it hit the wooden gates with a resounding crash, and they splintered and staggered and burst open. The hydraulic arms of the tipper were in their raised position, and they jammed in the overhead frame of the gates. A mob of escaping men scrambled, cursing, over the hood of the truck and fanned out into Lyham Road, to be met and chased by the warders.

Thereafter a running battle, with fists, chair legs, and broom handles against truncheons. Brown and his friends raced directly for the Ford Transit Rent-A-Van and scrambled into it, switching on and ramming it into gear as the engine revved; but warders leaped onto the hood and smashed the windshield with their truncheons. Four other prisoners got in the way of a passing car—a Toyota—pulled the driver into the road, and piled inside. A warder jumped on the hood of this car, too, but before he could smash the windshield he was thrown off as the car swept away.

By now more warders had arrived and were fighting hand to hand with the escapees, some rolling over in the road, the blood streaming everywhere. A police dog cornered four men, who immediately gave

up, but others dodged away into the narrow streets leading west and ran for their lives; and others, though cornered, still gave fight. With the Rent-A-Van undrivable, Brown and his friends jumped out again and split up. Two were caught, and then two more. Brown, wielding a club, was felled by a truncheon and slid unconscious into the gutter. This seemed to take the fight out of the rest of the robbers and they gave themselves up. Those who had stolen the Toyota drove it a mile and then jumped out, hailed a passing taxi, and went off in that. But they had been followed by a police helicopter, which diverted a police car to block their way in Bedford Road, Clapham, where another fierce fight took place before they were recaptured.

As the result of all the battle of the day, only two prisoners got away, and they were not part of the group who had planned the escape. Twelve warders were injured, one with a broken wrist, and the following day Superintendent Marshall—at the scheduled court appearance of the accused men, when another week's remand was formally requested—had to apologize to the magistrates for the unavoidable absence of five of the men, who were detained in a South London hospital, Bruce Brown himself with a suspected fractured skull. Marshall asked that the name of the hospital not be disclosed in open court, lest a further attempt be made to rescue them.

CHAPTER 5

ON JUNE 29, AT THE Old Bailey, Maria Mercedes Dadd was sent to jail for twelve months for handling stolen property.

On July 12 Bertie Smalls made a brief appearance at the Old Bailey, when the prosecution offered no evidence against him and he was formally discharged. Just before this, on July 9, the long-pending committal proceedings began in the Magistrates' Court at Wembley Police Station, and here the twenty-six accused men and women were arraigned in two rows for eighteen days. The villains—among whom there were still two notable absentees in the form of Brian Turner and Tony Edlin—did not appear at all downhearted even then. Perhaps in spite of their failure to break out they still believed in their luck. Perhaps numbers gave them courage. And a formidable group they looked, like a platoon of overweight paratroopers being charged before a civil court for rowdy behavior. They laughed and joked among themselves, as they had often done while on their raids. They glowered at the magistrates and exchanged pleasantries with their friends still faithfully following it all in the public gallery.

When Smalls first came in to testify against them, pandemonium broke loose. Whistles, curses, catcalls. "Doing the Royals, eh, Bertie?" "Supergrass!" "Can't you squeal a bit louder, Bertie, we can't hear you!" "Wait for us, Bertie, we'll make you squeal!"

Smalls, described at that time as "a stocky, two-hundred-and-ten-pound man with thinning hair and a dense black beard," glanced once at his old companions and then, one shoulder hunched as if to ward off the evil eye, proceeded to give his evidence without looking at them again. Mr. Michael Worsley, for the crown, listed Smalls's previous convictions and described him as one of the worst characters who had ever gone free of his crimes. At this there was loud applause from the dock.

Mr. John Buzzard, the prosecutor, said he had been instructed by the director of public prosecutions to offer no evidence against Smalls. "Derek Smalls," he told the magistrates, "is required as an important witness against a number of these men charged with bank robberies. It has been considered with great care and, balancing the interests of justice in this case against the interests of justice as a whole, it is considered that this is the right course to pursue."

The sight of Smalls in the witness box was a constant and enduring goad to the robbers, and it seemed they were prepared to turn their half-humorous fury and derision upon anything in sight. They poked fun at the policemen because they were armed with Smith & Wesson .38s. They had a particular thing about Superintendent Marshall, who had loomed large in their world of late. Marshall wore down the outsides of the heels of his shoes quickly, so he had steel pieces fitted to prevent this wear. Moving around the court, he did not put his heels down, in order not to create undue noise when someone was speaking. The gang soon cottoned on to this, and whenever he started moving in or out of court they would begin to sing "Tip-Toe Through the Tulips." The atmosphere in the court was electric, dangerous, and yet sometimes farcical.

After the hearing each day Smalls was whisked away in a police

car, which took care to see it was not followed. Marshall, Inspector Eist, and others were indeed tracked each night, in the hope that they might lead the way to Smalls. Nor were other avenues of escape neglected. A bribe of thirty thousand pounds was offered if a flaw could be found in the committal proceedings, which would enable the top men to be discharged.

The police have friends in various walks of life; they have to have. One day a man Marshall had known on and off for some years rang him and invited him round to a pub for a drink that evening. Marshall went and they had a pleasant enough conversation, but gradually the Yard man was aware that talk was drifting around to a subject he was not prepared to discuss. To save his "friend" from committing an indictable offense Marshall said, "You know this job I'm doing at present? I wouldn't change my opinion or change my tactics on it for a million pounds." Talk continued on safer levels; they had another beer together and then separated. A couple of days later, when Superintendent Marshall entered the courtroom, all twenty-six prisoners in the dock began to sing "Who Wants to Be a Millionaire?"

It was a sultry July in London and trying on the nerves, but everyone bore up well. Shortly before the end of the magistrates' proceedings, when all the prisoners in the dock were committed to stand trial at the Old Bailey, a document was smuggled into court which was headed Press Release and read:

Mr. Bert Smalls, the famous solo singer, who recently broke away from the Home Counties Choral Society, is about to give up the singing side of his career. Apparently Mr. Smalls feels that the singing may affect his throat—permanently. When interviewed on Wednesday Mr. Smalls refused to comment.

WHILE ALL THIS was going on, Interpol was still trying to trace one of the last two big men at large: Brian Turner. In spite of all the publicity—from September 1972 onward—no one had come forward who knew anything of his present whereabouts. Watch for a time had been kept on the Duke of Wellington, an English-style public house at Torremolinos, on Spain's Costa del Sol, which was run by two of his friends. But it had not so far produced any results.

Then one day a call was made to the police by an Englishwoman called Jean Mathers, wife of a retired army officer. She played bridge at a club called El Candado, about three miles from the center of Málaga, and had over the past few months been partnered frequently by a man called Barry Thomas, a cheerful, sunburned, stout man in his mid-thirties—not quite her style, for he wore clothes that were not in the best of taste and his accent suggested he hadn't been to a good school; but he was a first-class bridge player and a pleasant partner, who never got annoyed when he lost. They understood each other's bidding, and in fact had hit a winning streak together with a bridge system of his personal devising. She thought him young to be retired, but did not query it until he dropped the words Folly Close into his conversation. They were words that had stuck in her mind since reading accounts earlier in the year of the wanted man and where he lived. Next day she telephoned Scotland Yard.

In the past months there had been many false trails followed, but as it happened, two CID men were already in Málaga, trying to persuade the Spanish authorities to extradite another man wanted for a crime in England. Marshall telephoned Detective Inspector

Keane and Detective Sergeant Glass to stay in the sunshine another few days and make contact with Mrs. Mathers to see if her hunch was any better than all the others.

What she told them appeared to tally, so that night they went along to El Candado, accompanied by three armed Spanish police. Having warned the owner of the club and made sure that the rear exits were secure, they waited in the shadow of the palm trees at the main door of the club. Presently Mr. Barry Thomas arrived with a twenty-six-year-old girl friend, and they followed him in. It was the last game of bridge he was to play at El Candado, and he gave in without resistance. He carried a forged Australian passport.

Mrs. Rose Turner's comment when news of her husband's arrest reached her in England was, "Oh, sure, he's been on the run all right. From *me*. Girls! He's girl crazy. But as for bank robbery— that's rubbish. He wouldn't hurt a fly!"

However, it was one thing to have Turner identified and arrested in Spain; it was another to get him extradited to stand his trial in England. It was to be four months before they could bring him home.

In the meantime, due to "information received," the last of the big men was picked up. This was Tony Edlin, who was found to be living a respectable life under the name of Weaver, in Glasgow. The expensive fifth-floor bachelor flat in Whittingehame Court looked out on the house of Glasgow's chief constable, Mr. David McNee. The villains in this case seem to have had a talent either for getting friendly with, or living near to, eminent police officers.

Bertie Smalls was moved from his flat to a small hotel in Bayswater and thence to another hideout in northeast London. He was being paid twenty-five pounds a week by the police, and his two elder children were escorted by armed detectives to and from school each day. Bertie took it all in his stride. After all, it was little worse than being hunted by the police, except that *these* hunters, if they found him, would not just detain him for questioning. Naturally an indolent man, he took his time indoors stoically. And perhaps he derived some moral comfort from the feeling that this time, at least, he was on the side of law and order. The strain was showing more obviously on Diana Smalls. She knew what the robbers' friends would do to her or her children if they found her. And the ordeal was not yet nearly over. Brian Turner had still to be brought back from Spain.

The crown's case had to be laboriously and astutely assembled; it would not do to see the villains escape on some overlooked point of law. Months of this tense, claustrophobic living stretched ahead—perhaps another year. She began to be irritable, quarrelsome, sulky, or liable to fly off the handle at the least thing.

On August 8 the Spanish authorities finally agreed to Turner's extradition, and Superintendent Marshall and Inspector Eist flew out to bring him home. On the way back Turner said to Marshall, "I'm innocent, I've done nothing. You've got Mr. Big already: that chap Smalls, who's pretending to inform against us."

But when Turner came before the magistrates in September and Bertie Smalls had to make another appearance, Mr. Michael Worsley, prosecuting, asked the magistrate if Turner could remain handcuffed throughout the proceedings, since "there is a grave security risk in this case and a risk of violence." So throughout the hearing Turner remained handcuffed to a policeman.

The problem of keeping Bertie Smalls alive until the following year, when the Old Bailey trials began, was not eased as the months progressed. It was five people, not one, who had to be guarded. Twice again they moved. Twice Diana Smalls threatened to leave with the children. If she left, the police said, she would be charged and taken into protective custody. There was no way out now for "Supergrass" and his family.

Nor did the villains relax their efforts to help themselves by bribery and intimidation. They still boasted through their representatives outside that anyone going into the witness box against them would "suffer for it later" and that no jury—men and women with families of their own at risk—would dare commit them.

And, of course, the gunman, they said, was still waiting for Smalls. And always would wait, they said, as a man would be waiting for anyone else who grassed. Even if they were convicted, they said, there'd be plenty of money to retain him until Smalls came out of his rathole and the police withdrew their protection. Couldn't go on forever, they said. At the most he'd only got a few months to live.

A trial began at the Central Criminal Court of the Old Bailey on January 11, 1974, when just two men pleaded guilty. One of these was Philip Morris, who, while being questioned, had admitted to the accidental killing of the milkman, and who was now prepared to plead guilty to the Wembley Bank Robbery also. He was sentenced to seventeen years for manslaughter. His confession to the Wembley robbery did not endear him to the others, and afterward he was heard to declare that he did not give much for his chances of survival if he were put in the same prison.

But the other two dozen were all prepared to fight for their freedom to the last gasp, and as a result, Mr. Justice Eveleigh decided to split the indictment into three. Twenty-four people were too many to swallow at one gulp, and no one jury, he felt, was capable of grasping all the many issues involved.

The first trial proper, therefore, began on February 5 and went on until May 23. The second began on June 10 and finished on July 8. The third began on September 3 and finished on September 27. The first of these trials, which ran for seventy-eight days and cost three hundred thousand pounds, was the most important one, and included all the major criminals with the exception of Edlin, though several of the Ralli Bros. raiders were included in the third. Brown, Turner, Wilkinson, Allpress, Reynolds, Holt, and two characters called William Sherville and David Delaney were a considerable group to be accommodated in the dock at the Old Bailey. And all, as has been said, were prepared to fight for their freedom to the last gasp. No holds barred.

They turned the heat on Superintendent Marshall once again. Since bribery did not work, perhaps intimidation would. The Marshalls lived in a modest, pleasant house on the outskirts of London. It had a carport, not a garage, and one afternoon in March Mrs. Jessie Marshall was in her kitchen watering her window plants, and as she turned away to switch on the six-p.m. news, a high-velocity bullet smashed through the window and hummed past her head, showering her with glass and disappearing through the open back door. The police were at once called, and searched the neighborhood, but no one was found.

It so happened that Marshall had not on this particular day used his car but had gone to the Old Bailey by train and bus, so it would have been a reasonable assumption that he would be in the house. Whether Mrs. Marshall was mistaken for her husband or whether it was an attempt to kill or intimidate her will never be known. Since the murder of a high-ranking police officer, or still more his wife, would have so alienated police and public against the accused men, and since high-velocity rifles are very accurate, intimidation with the threat of more to follow was the more likely intent. But one can never be sure, and neither could the Marshalls.

Because a report of this incident if it reached the judge would have muddied the trial, it was hushed up. Because no one had actually been injured, it was thought that the defense might even have made capital out of it, suggesting it was another ploy on the part of the conspirators of Scotland Yard to prejudice opinion against the innocent men in the dock. As it was, a few days later Mr. Justice Eveleigh suspended the trial for the best part of a day while a complaint from a juror—that he had received a threatening telephone call—was investigated.

For this first trial Bertie Smalls had to be dug out of his dark corner once again, and he appeared before the accusing glares of his comrades to substantiate his statements against them. For seven days Supergrass, blinking a little as if from too much cigarette smoke, gave his evidence, while six armed detectives guarded him against attack or assassination. It is a short distance in the Old Bailey between the witness box and the dock, but it is the great divide. In this case it was the divide between almost certain conviction and "a sort of freedom."

By this time more than one hundred and fifty people had been arrested and were awaiting or undergoing trial as a result of Smalls's testimony. It was as if, knowing that no mercy would ever be extended to him now by any member of the underworld, he was determined to give the police full value for his acquittal. No one was spared. When he could not remember a name he would describe the man or woman in detail, with painstaking particulars to help in an identification. And it all had the ring of truth, that veracity which is so hard to come by for the purely inventive mind.

An innocent man was even released as a result of his testimony. Arthur Sanders, serving a fifteen-year sentence for being involved in the Ilford bank robbery, was freed on Smalls's testimony that he was not on the robbery at all. "There was me on it," said Smalls, "and Turner, Brown, Edlin, Jeffrey, Green. Not Sanders. Don't know him." So the prison gates opened for one man just as they were about to close on so many more.

At long last the first trial came to an end. The all-male jury was out for three days, including two nights carefully guarded at a Bloomsbury hotel.

Bruce Brown was sentenced to twenty-one years and Brian Turner the same; James Wilkinson and Daniel Allpress each got sixteen years, William Sherville fourteen years, Brian Reynolds thirteen years, and David Delaney twelve years. Anthony Holt, the twenty-seven-year-old bank clerk and disc jockey, had his sentence deferred for a social report, but later he was sentenced to five years. In his absence, already in prison, Philip Morris received twenty years, to run concurrently with his earlier sentence, the judge pausing a moment to acknowledge his courage in pleading guilty to both crimes. In the second trial a robber called Salmon, and Allpress again, were found guilty and sentenced; in the third, Richards, Edlin, Jones, Jeffrey, and King. At this trial David Kozak was found guilty of receiving stolen goods.

Two last men, Green and Dark, who were both serving eighteen years' imprisonment for the robbery at Ilford, appeared in the Old Bailey on October 18, but no evidence was offered against them because there was only Smalls's unsupported testimony that they had been involved in these crimes. The charges were directed to remain on the file but not to be proceeded with except on leave of the court.

SMALLS'S USE TO THE police had finally expended itself. It was time for him to go. "They'll kill you," Wilding had told him eighteen months ago.

"They won't find me," said Bertie. "I'll be away." But where was away?

One of the terms of the deal was that the police would provide him and his family with a completely new identity and allow him to disappear. Part of that identity would include passports in the new name, so that in principle there was nothing to prevent the family from going to live anywhere in the world.

But his true identity, and the reason for his change of identity, would have to be made known to the immigration department of the country of his choice. (Scotland Yard could not attempt to cheat the police force of another country.) And immigration people, like other people, sometimes talk. He no longer had any profession or trade and for fifteen years had lived almost entirely off his earnings in crime. He had a common-law wife, two daughters, and a small son to keep. And he had no money, or swore he had no money, left from his crimes.

So he disappeared, and so far his disappearance has succeeded. The chances are that, in spite of all his protestations to the contrary, in spite of the extravagant way he lived when he had money, such a clear-sighted crook, traveling frequently abroad after a raid, would make his caches in bank accounts somewhere; in Switzerland, perhaps, or in Luxembourg, or in Spain. His confident remark, "I'll be away," seems to bear out this hypothesis. His view also was that, with all the major robbers inside, even if they had money salted away, none of them was likely to go on spending it over the years in a vain search for the man who had betrayed them. And even if there were one or two with the determination to settle with him when they got out, the earliest they were likely to be able to do anything personally would be 1985—and 1985 could take care of itself.

Of course, even if he has money tucked away, it will not last forever. What then? Will so self-indulgent a man ever settle to the trials of becoming an honest laborer?

THE WEMBLEY BANK Robbery case was important in three respects. It created a sort of legal history, in that never before had so important a criminal been allowed to go free in order to catch so many more. Heads have been shaken in the higher echelons of the law at the disagreeable precedent thus set. Yet the majority of such opinion is that the end in this case justified the means. Since Smalls grassed, the police and the Department of Public Prosecutions have had many other offers from crooks anxious to take the same way out, and the offers have been politely turned down. "For the greater good" must be the one criterion.

But "honor among thieves"? Has some permanent injury been done to this old principle of trust? Now and always in the future it must lurk in the criminal mind that betrayal can sometimes pay off—if what you have to offer the police is big enough. It could become a corrosive element in any crooked operation, breeding suspicion between friend and friend. It could destroy some enterprises before they have begun, for loyalty to one's partner is perhaps more essential in a criminal operation than in any other. By sowing this seed Derek Crichton Smalls may have done more for the police and for law and order than he ever intended.

The second importance of the Wembley Bank Robbery is that it provoked Scotland Yard into forming the Wembley Bank Robbery Squad—a squad which, its immediate work done, formed the nucleus of a much larger crime-fighting unit that has grown out of it under Commander John Lock. The largest of its kind in Europe, this strike force now employs two hundred detectives and uses many of the new and sophisticated techniques first worked out in tracking the Wembley robbers down. The formation of the Wembley Bank Robbery Squad removed forever partitions within the police force, once sensible enough but now out of date, and rivalries and inhibitions between group and group can no longer exist in the same way. Indeed it began a number of reorganizations of Scotland Yard, under Sir Robert Mark, which have given it a new image and a new prestige.

Third and finally, the Wembley Bank Robbery marked, so far, the peak of this form of crime in England, and the success of the CID squad was evidenced by its decline. In the Greater London area the number of major bank robberies had risen by 1968 to twenty-eight a year. By 1972 it was sixty-five. In 1976 the number was down again to twenty-eight.

SCOTLAND
YARD
PAST AND PRESENT

Prior to Scotland Yard,
London's police were the Bow
Street Runners, whose total
never exceeded ten in number.

The Charlies, early watchmen
named after Charles II,
announced the hour but were
ineffective against crime.

Scotland Yard's first officers appeared on the streets of London in 1829 sporting side-whiskers and top hats.

THE YARD'S BEGINNINGS

The first headquarters of the London police was at the site of an ancient palace used by Scottish royalty on state visits. Though police headquarters has moved twice, the force has kept the original name, which dates back to its founding at old Scotland Yard.

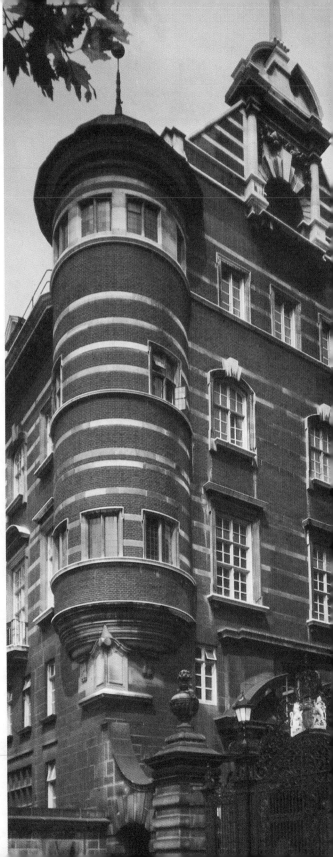

Until 1967, the headquarters of Scotland Yard for over seventy years.

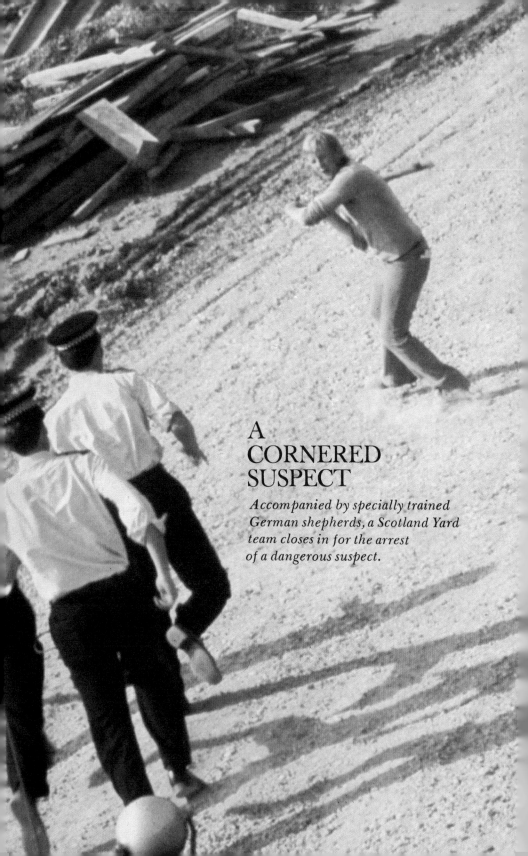

A CORNERED SUSPECT

Accompanied by specially trained German shepherds, a Scotland Yard team closes in for the arrest of a dangerous suspect.

THE SEARCH FOR CLUES

1. At the scene of a murder, a mobile unit controls the initial investigation.

2. Police dogs stand by to search surrounding area for the murderer's scent.

3. Frogmen prepare for a dive into the pond to look for possible murder weapon.

4. The scene is recorded by an official police photographer from Scotland Yard.

5. An inspector briefs local officers about interviewing neighbors and friends.

6. A Scenes-of-Crime officer with a murder bag looks for forensic evidence.

7. The detective chief superintendent of the local division is in charge of the case.

8. A radio-equipped patrol car from the nearby police station assists as needed.

9. Motorcyclists from Scotland Yard's Traffic Division also stand by to help.

10. A local patrol car is positioned to

THE MURDER BAG

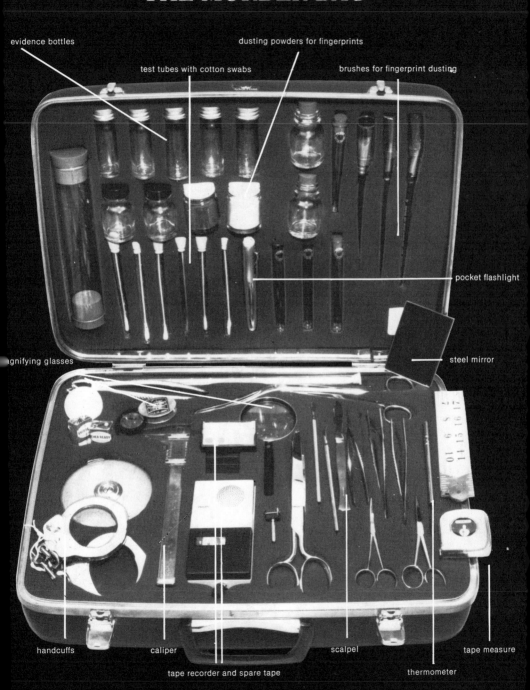

evidence bottles

dusting powders for fingerprints

test tubes with cotton swabs

brushes for fingerprint dusting

pocket flashlight

magnifying glasses

steel mirror

handcuffs

caliper

tape recorder and spare tape

scalpel

thermometer

tape measure

*One compact case contains all the essential
equipment for on-the-spot murder investigations.*

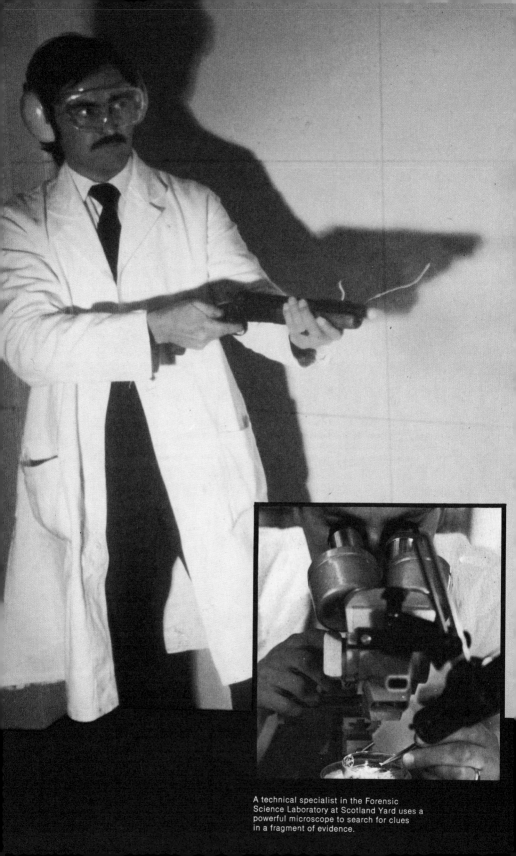

A technical specialist in the Forensic Science Laboratory at Scotland Yard uses a powerful microscope to search for clues in a fragment of evidence.

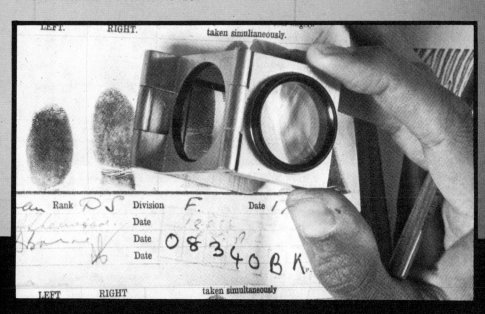

ANALYZING
THE EVIDENCE

*High-speed photography reveals
the behavior of a bullet in flight
in Scotland Yard's ballistics lab.*

The fingerprint classification system most commonly used by police throughout the world—including the U.S. Federal Bureau of Investigation—was developed in 1901 by Edward Richard Henry, who later became commissioner of Scotland Yard. The Yard's files now contain almost three million sets of fingerprints.

The present headquarters of Scotland Yard is
in this new, modern building on Victoria Street.

THE PORTLAND
SPY CASE

КАК-ТО ЧИСТО ПО-ОБЫВАТЕЛЬСКИ РАССУЖДАЮ

PORTLAND
SPY CASE
by
Ludovic Kennedy

At first Peter and Helen Kroger seemed different from the other residents of Cranley Drive in the suburban community of Ruislip, England. They were Canadians, not British, and he had an unusual job selling old books. But they were pleasant enough and in time became accepted members of the town. In this case, however, first impressions proved correct. The Krogers *were* different from their neighbors in Ruislip. They were Russian spies, and they were involved in the leaking of secrets from the sensitive underwater weapons area at Portland Naval Base.

Scotland Yard was informed of the leak, and almost at once Special Branch agents were dispatched to gather the facts. Slowly, inexorably, these facts led to Cranley Drive. What were the Krogers up to? What went on almost every Saturday when they received a visit from the mild-mannered Canadian gentleman known as Lonsdale? For months authorities at Scotland Yard watched, waited and carefully planned the capture of what they now knew to be a highly skilled band of foreign agents and homegrown traitors, a group they called the Portland five.

Ludovic Kennedy, author of *Ten Rillington Place*, a factual account of the ghastly *Evans* v. *Christie* case, and of *Pursuit*, the much acclaimed book about the chase and sinking of the battleship *Bismarck*, now details his exciting version of this notorious British spy case.

Author's Note

THE DETAILED TRUTH of all the events in the Portland spy case is impossible to obtain; firstly, because the intelligence reports are not available, and probably never will be; secondly, because the numerous accounts of it, including those by two of its principal participants* (both of them proven liars), contradict each other at numerous turns. This book, therefore, is simply one author's version, based on his imagination and all the available evidence, of what he thinks most likely happened.

All previous books have referred to the Russian master spy as Gordon Lonsdale, for until recently his real name, Konon Trofimovich Molody, was not known. I have referred to him as Molody almost throughout, not only because it was his born name, but because to continue to call him Lonsdale suggests that he was still somehow partly Canadian. In fact, he was no more Canadian than Leo Tolstoy or Joseph Stalin.

—Ludovic Kennedy

*Harry Houghton, *Operation Portland: The Autobiography of a Spy* (Rupert Hart-Davis Ltd.); Gordon Lonsdale, *SPY: Twenty Years in Soviet Secret Service* (Hawthorne Books, Inc.).

PART ONE
The Spies

Moscow, 1954. There was light snow falling as the chunky, handsome man in his early thirties, wearing a black coat and fur hat, crossed Dzerzhinsky Square. On the far side he ran up the steps that led to the Moscow Center, the huge gray stone building that housed the country's external intelligence services. At the entrance he showed a sentry his pass. "MOLODY, Konon Trofimovich, Major," it read. The sentry gestured for the visitor to go in.

Major Molody went through the glass doors and crossed the big hall to the main elevators. Clearly he was a man who didn't have to ask the way. The elevator was a long time coming, so that when he and others got in, it was full. "Why don't they build us a new elevator?" said a voice at the back, and another answered, "Because they're building rockets to the stars," and one or two laughed, but not much.

Major Molody got out at the fifth floor, walked down a bare corridor to a door marked 514, knocked and entered. A pretty, dark-haired girl in a simple gray dress was sitting at a desk typing.

"Major Molody?"

"Yes. And your name?"

"Anna."

"That is a nice name." He took off his hat to reveal black curly hair and gave her a winning smile. "And Annoushka is even nicer."

She smiled shyly, took his coat and brushed off the snow. "Wait, please," she said, "and I will say you are here."

He picked up a newspaper and glanced at the football scores. Anna went through an inner door, presently reopened it from the other side.

"Please!"

She stood in the doorway, waiting for him to go through. Deliberately he brushed against her as he passed. "I beg your pardon," he said, and smiled. The door closed behind him.

"Konon Trofimovich!"

A big man in military uniform, with grizzled white hair and steel-rimmed glasses, came forward to greet him. "Do you never stop flirting? What would Galisha say?"

"Oh, she doesn't mind. She knows it's not serious."

"Cigarette?"

"No, thank you, Colonel."

They sat in two chairs by the window and watched the snowflakes falling on the city.

"Have you enjoyed your leave?"

"Very much. It's been good to be with Galisha and the children for so long."

"Yes, we've left you in peace. But after the last assignment you deserved it." He paused. "And now, as I expect you have guessed, we have another assignment."

"Yes, I thought so."

"A very *important* assignment."

Molody said nothing. The colonel shuffled some papers. He would tell him in his own good time.

"Let's see now. You first went to America when you were a boy?"

"I was ten."

"Why did you go there?"

"My parents were very poor. My aunt Tatiana was emigrating to America to start a new life, and offered to take me with her."

"How long were you there?"

"Until 1938. When I was sixteen."

"And you lived at 2634 College Avenue, Berkeley, California, and went to school there?"

"Right."

"During your time there, did you ever go to Canada?"

"To Canada?"

"Yes."

Molody thought. "No," he said, "we never moved from Berkeley, so far as I can remember."

"And when you were sixteen, why did you come home?"

"Because my aunt Anastasia, who had also emigrated, decided to return herself. She said I had to choose between becoming an American citizen or remaining a Russian one. So I chose."

The colonel laughed. "You should have stayed," he said. "By now you would have been a rich sanitary engineer in Berkeley, with your own Cadillac and swimming pool, instead of all this cloak-and-dagger stuff."

Molody himself had often reflected how different his life would have been if, like his aunt Tatiana (now director of a French ballet company), he had stayed in the West.

For one thing, he would have had a quite different sort of war—the war in which he had learned the rudiments of his trade. Being parachuted behind the enemy lines; working as a courier for the Polish underground; transmitting and receiving coded wireless messages from secret hiding places; posing as a Russian traitor to infiltrate himself into Gestapo headquarters; working for the first time with the man who was to become every spy's hero—the legendary Colonel Rudolf Abel.

And then the postwar years; first at the university to read law, then at the school for espionage; later the four-year appointment, recently completed, of acting as Abel's number two man in the United States.

It had been an interesting time, with visits to Florida and California (Berkeley had changed out of all recognition), Chicago and Tallahassee, leaving and picking up packages in dead-letter boxes such as holes in walls and the cisterns of lavatories, transmitting and receiving wireless messages to and from the Center, piecing together information not only of American military intelligence but of political planning, especially that directed against the countries of the Eastern bloc.

"When you were in the States this last time," asked the colonel, "did you ever visit Canada?"

Canada again, thought Molody. Where was all this leading?

"No."

"How good is your American accent?"

"Very good, I'm told."

"Could you pass as a Canadian, do you think?"

"Outside North America, certainly. In the United States, probably. In Canada—perhaps!"

"Well," said the colonel, "we will have you tested, and see. The linguistic tests they do nowadays are quite amazing. Then we can iron out any flaws."

There was a knock at the door. Anna came in with coffee.

As she put down the tray she gave Molody a quick, shy look; but he was too preoccupied to notice.

When she had gone, the colonel said, "Rudolf has recommended, and our superiors have agreed, that you should go to England as resident director."

"To England? But—"

"You have no English accent, you were going to say. No, but you have, or soon will have, a Canadian one. And in England the Canadians are treated as brothers. There are many things happening over there that we want to find out more about: the bacteriological establishment at Porton Down, the Polaris base in Scotland's Holy Loch, the American air force bases and their stocks of bombs, aircraft tracking systems and so on. But there's one task that is to take priority over all these."

The colonel paused, seeking the right words. Molody wondered what was coming.

"Our navy, as you know, has a big submarine fleet, many with nuclear missiles. Admiral Gorchkov's policy, we understand, is to build many more of them. What we do not yet know is how strong are the enemy's countermeasures."

"Sonar?"

"Yes, and other things. There have been important developments since the war. The range of detection is said to be much longer, and it is now possible to ascertain accurately depth. What we have to know are the details. The most advanced progress in this field is being made at a place called Portland, a naval base on the south coast. We have a contact there who's been supplying us, but it's scrappy and we want more."

The colonel took a long gulp of coffee and said, "We're arranging for you to go to Canada, where you will assume the identity of a Canadian of your own age. Spend as long a time in the country as you think necessary to familiarize yourself with its customs, politics, dialects and so on. When you are confident you can pass as a Canadian anywhere, then book a passage to England, and we will withdraw our present man."

"Has he got cover?" He meant, in the jargon of the Center, did the present man have a London embassy or trade delegation job.

"Yes."

"Will I have?"

"No, you will be illegal, as you were in New York. If you had cover, you would be automatically followed everywhere, which is not what we want. Try and get some introductions before you leave Canada. Then infiltrate yourself into English society—get a flat, find a job, lead the life of a normal person. You should have no difficulty making friends."

"How do I transmit?"

"We will tell you later."

"When do I leave?"

"Next month."

"And how long is the assignment?"

The colonel shrugged. "Who can tell? You know how little time matters to our way of thinking. Two years, perhaps. Maybe five. Until the job is done."

"And leave?" This was a sore point with Molody, for during his four years in the States he had not been allowed home once.

"Annual. And possibly the occasional trip for consultations. With a Canadian passport there will be no trouble in moving about. But, as you know, with an illegal posting, there can be no help from us if you are caught." He smiled. "When you've been in prison a few years, Konon Trofimovich, we may dream up ways and means of getting you out. Of course, by then you may not want to come home. They say English prisons are nicer than ours."

He got up. "Tomorrow at eight you must report to Branch Five for a refresher course in photographs, radio codes, microdots and all that. And then on Monday you will go down to Clifton for a two-week integration course."

"Oh, not Clifton again," said Molody, laughing.

This was a place near Vinnitsa, in the Ukraine, a sort of mock-up, like a Hollywood film set, of a North American small town. It was staffed mainly by American nationals, some of them deserters from the United States Army. It was here that spies destined for America lived as though they were in America. Here they learned how to order a drink, interpret a menu, make a telephone call; were taught who the country's political leaders were and what they stood for, what plays and films were being talked about, who was who in the world of sports and art and television. There were similar mock-up towns located throughout Russia for all the countries where spies were going to be sent, and the message of all was the same: how not to make mistakes.

"But I did all that five years ago," said Molody, "and anyway, I've been living in America these last four years."

"Ah, but times have changed," said the colonel. "Now we have a brand-new *Canadian* section, and by the time they've pushed you through it, you'll be as Canadian as any true-blue Mountie." He held out his hand. "Good luck. I envy you."

Molody opened the door and went out. Anna had been prettying her face in anticipation, hoping for a word or a smile, perhaps even an invitation. But he walked through the room as though she weren't there, picked up his coat and hat and walked out. He was thinking of Galisha and the children—Liza, Dina and Trofim—and of his old mother, and how long before he would see them again.

Ruislip, England, December 1955. In many ways the middle-aged couple who had recently moved into 45 Cranley Drive were different from the other white-collar workers—engineers, accountants, civil servants—who lived in the street. For a start, they weren't British but Canadian. Then, the husband had an unusual job. He was an antiquarian bookseller. His card said that he had a bookshop at 190 the Strand and specialized in literature about the Americas "from the North Pole to the South." He also kept a stack of books in his house, which in some rooms stretched from floor to ceiling.

Their names were Peter and Helen Kroger. He was a tall, rather distinguished-looking man with a high forehead and cheekbones and a mass of graying hair. He was a quieter person than his wife, though people who got to know him said he had a fascinating mind and could talk on a variety of subjects.

Helen Kroger was made of coarser stuff; she had bright red finger-nails, wore trousers, and had a rolling gait like a sailor's. Between her top front teeth was a wide gap, and, said one neighbor, she had a two-finger whistle that could stop the traffic a mile away. She was more emotional and garrulous too, and sometimes at parties Peter was heard saying to her, "Honey, don't you think you've had enough?" Often Helen told neighbors how sad she was not to have had children of her own, and perhaps because of it she was especially kind to local children, giving them presents and sweets.

In time the Krogers became an accepted part of the community. They received invitations to people's parties and occasionally gave one of their own. Peter's hobby was music, and he would spend many hours listening to Beethoven, Tchaikovsky, Verdi.

Helen was an amateur photographer, and sometimes blacked out the bathroom window facing the Kemps' house next door so that she could do her own developing. But she always joked she was a lousy photographer, and those to whom she showed the results agreed.

Although there was a big lawn, and flower beds at the back of the house, neither Peter nor Helen was much interested in gardening; in the summer, when they were on holiday, Mr. Kemp would come around and cut the grass. Mrs. Kemp was surprised at what late

Major Konon Trofimovich Molody (alias Gordon Lonsdale), a master Russian spy, is shown at left. American-born Peter Kroger (center) was ostensibly an antiquarian book dealer, but he and his wife, Helen (right), worked hand in glove with Molody.

hours they kept; a poor sleeper herself, she would sometimes wake at three or four a.m. to see a light in 45 still burning. Other neighbors noted that at weekends, when most neighborhood socializing took place, the Krogers were rarely free.

The family they knew best were the Searches, who lived almost opposite, at 1 Courtfield Gardens. Wilfred Search was a gas-turbine engineer whose work took him mostly to London Airport. His wife, Ruth, was secretary of the Ruislip Art Society, and several of her still lifes hung on the walls.

The Searches had two children, Philip, twelve, and Gay, ten.

In the background is the Krogers' home in Ruislip, England, an ordinary-looking building that was in fact a house of secrets.

Mrs. Kroger took to Mrs. Search, and several times a week would drop by the side door for coffee and a chat. She used to enjoy watching Mrs. Search cooking, especially mince pies, which she called "those quaint little English pastries." Sometimes when she was expecting Peter back from work and he hadn't arrived, she would run over to Mrs. Search and ask if she thought anything had happened to him, and Mrs. Search would comfort her.

The only time that Mr. Search saw Peter really angry was when he took Helen for a driving lesson in his black Ford Zephyr and they arrived back much later than intended. "Peter was really upset," said Mrs. Search. Mrs. Kroger had a soft spot, too, for Gay (who called her Auntie Helen). She allowed Gay to come over to 45 and play with her makeup on the dressing table, and often gave her presents of half-empty bottles of nail polish, as well as sweets and other things.

Such were the impressions the Krogers' neighbors had of them—that of an odd but agreeable couple, he with an unusual job, she with a kind heart for children. But it was not a wholly true impression. For the Krogers were not Canadians but Americans, and their real names were not Helen and Peter Kroger but Lona and Morris Cohen. Furthermore, Peter Kroger's book business was not his lifework. It was a cover for other, more devious activities. The Krogers were Russian spies.

Peter Kroger was born in 1910 in the Bronx, the son of poor Russian-Jewish immigrants who ran a greengrocer's shop. He was a clever boy, and after high school he graduated first to Mississippi State College and later to the University of Illinois, where he gained a bachelor of science degree.

But Kroger grew up to hate the American capitalist system, became a Communist, and in 1937 joined the Abraham Lincoln Brigade in Spain to fight Franco in the Spanish Civil War. On return to America, his Communist leanings increased when he found he could only get a job as a waiter. Later he obtained employment with a Soviet trade organization, which noted his name and political sympathies for the future.

It was about this time that he met his future wife, Lona Petka, a child of Polish-Jewish immigrants. She was working as a domestic servant, and he found that she shared his Communist beliefs. They married in Norwich, Connecticut, in 1941. The same year he joined the U.S. Army and served in Alaska and Canada, while she worked in an aircraft-production factory. After the war he got a job as a teacher, but soon was approached by Soviet intelligence officers, who had no difficulty in enlisting his services as a Russian agent.

The middle 1940s was a time of intense activity on the part of Soviet intelligence in the United States, Russia being desperate to possess the secrets of the atom bomb. Under the direction of the brilliant Anatoli Yakovlev, given cover as Russian vice-consul in New York, a network of spies was set up. They included Julius Rosenberg—a U.S. government weapons inspector—and his wife, Ethel; Ethel's brother, David Greenglass, who worked in the atom-bomb workshop at Los Alamos, in New Mexico; and Morton Sobell, an engineer working on secret material in the General Electric laboratories. Contact agent for the group was Harry Gold, a Swiss-born American research chemist. The climax of his efforts came in 1945 when the German refugee and brilliant physicist Klaus Fuchs came to Los Alamos from Britain and handed over to Gold full details of the working of the atom bomb.

Fuchs returned to England in 1946 to become head of the theoretical physics division at Harwell, but under Yakovlev the activities of the American traitors continued, and the Cohens were enlisted as Gold's couriers. Although Fuchs's name was discovered among the documents taken by the Russian cipher clerk Igor Gouzenko when he defected in Ottawa in 1945, it wasn't until five years later, when Russia was about to explode her own bomb, that the FBI and MI-5 (Britain's counterintelligence service) caught up with him; and in 1950 Fuchs was arrested by Superintendent George G. Smith of Scotland Yard.

In custody, Fuchs betrayed Gold, and Gold betrayed the Rosenbergs, Greenglass and Sobell. In time the Rosenbergs were executed, the others sentenced to long terms of imprisonment. Yakovlev left hurriedly for Moscow. The Cohens would have been caught too, but by this time they were also working for the illegal network of Rudolf Abel, recently arrived in New York. He was able to warn the Cohens in time, and, staying only long enough to withdraw their money from the bank, they abandoned their apartment on East Seventy-first Street and headed west.

They stayed in California for a while, then, on instructions from the Center, moved to Canada to assume the role of Canadian nationals, just as Molody was to do.

Later, on forged Canadian passports, they sailed for New Zealand and settled down in the Gisborne area of North Island. Here they obtained important information on underwater defenses at the Auckland naval research station, SEATO exercises and nuclear tests in the Pacific, sending it by various means to Moscow. In all that time no one in New Zealand suspected them.

In 1954 they were instructed to come to Europe for a new assignment. Before leaving, they found in the files of the local newspaper office the names of a couple about their own age, by the name of Kroger, who had been killed years earlier in a car smash. They obtained copies of their birth and marriage certificates, and a month later presented them to the New Zealand embassy in Paris with a request for new passports. They were told that these would take two weeks to prepare, and during that time they traveled extensively—on their Canadian passports—first to Vienna, where they stayed at the Hotel Sacher, then to the Far East, Singapore, Hong Kong, Tokyo. On this trip they met Molody, who was en route to Vancouver, and discussed plans for the new assignment.

And now the assignment had begun, and here they were in Ruislip, Middlesex, like any other respectable middle-class suburban couple. And none of their neighbors had an inkling of their nefarious activities or that their very ordinary house was in fact a house of secrets. The guests who came to the Krogers' occasional evening parties would have been astonished to learn that in the base of the cigarette lighter in the sitting room was a secret cavity containing radio codes; that attached to the phonograph in the corner was a seventy-four-foot aerial that ran to the loft; that inside a book on the shelves called *Book Auction Records* was a list of radio transmission procedures; that behind a Bible in the bookcase was special film for recording microdots (i.e., the reduction of a full-size page to the area of a pinhead); that inside a harmless-looking tin of talcum powder in the bathroom was a magnifying lens for reading microdots; that in a hip flask in the bedroom was a cavity containing iron oxide for making invisible Morse recorded on magnetic tape; that beneath the floorboards of the kitchen, where Mrs. Search sometimes chatted with

Helen Kroger, was a radio transmitter that could reach Moscow; and that in various hiding places all over the house were large sums of cash in sterling and dollars.

Nor could the guests have known that every week when Peter Kroger, in pursuit of his legitimate business, sent a parcel of books to the Continent, one or more microdots were concealed among them; or that every weekend in the dead of night, while all the neighborhood (except sometimes Mrs. Kemp) slept, the radio transmitter was hauled out of its hiding place beneath the kitchen floor, linked to the seventy-four-foot aerial at one end and to a tape recorder at the other, and short bursts of high-speed transmissions (unintelligible to anyone except the receiver) beamed to the Moscow Center.

Mrs. Search came back to her house from a Saturday's shopping. Her daughter, Gay, said, "Auntie Helen was over when you were out, Mummy. She gave me this present. Look!" It was a shell necklace.

"Goodness!" said Mrs. Search. "*Isn't* Auntie Helen kind."

Portland Naval Base, England, 1953. In a small room in the Admiralty Underwater Detection Establishment the telephone rang. A little man with small, crafty eyes answered it. He was one of the clerical officers, Harry Houghton.

"Is that extension 245, please?" The voice had a strong Slavic accent.

"That's right."

"May I speak to Mr. Houghton, please?"

"Houghton speaking."

"You don't know me, Mr. Houghton, but I am a friend of a friend of yours in Warsaw—a lady friend, Mr. Houghton."

Houghton laughed—clearly nervous. "Oh, Christina," he said. "How is she?"

"She is fine, Mr. Houghton, and sends you her greetings and love. I was seeing her just last week, and she has a message for you she wants me to give. Do you sometimes come to London?"

"Yes."

"Could you come next Sunday, do you think? I am sure it will be worth your while. Do you know the Dulwich art gallery?"

"I know where Dulwich is."

"Well, ask anyone in Dulwich where the art gallery is and they will tell you. Shall we say two thirty in the afternoon outside the main entrance? Now, how shall I recognize you?"

Before Houghton could reply, the caller went on. "I tell you what, Mr. Houghton. Could you carry a copy of *The Times* newspaper in one hand and a pair of gloves in the other?"

"A pair of gloves?"

"Yes. Then there will be no mistake. Two thirty, then, on Sunday, Mr. Houghton. Good-by."

The line went dead. Harry Houghton replaced the receiver. It had been a funny sort of call, friendly enough on the surface but with disturbing undertones. But then Harry Houghton was a man who was used to being involved in some very funny businesses.

HARRY HOUGHTON WAS born of a poor family in Lincoln, England, in 1905, went to school there·and sang in the cathedral choir. There weren't many jobs going in Lincoln after the First World War, and in 1922, when he was sixteen, he walked into the local naval recruiting offices and signed on for long-term service.

After training, Houghton was posted to the China station, where one of the duties of British warships was to stop the profitable opium-smuggling trade.

A few of the older enlisted men went in for smuggling themselves, despite the risks of being caught, and Harry Houghton didn't need much persuading to join them. "I've never been one," he said years later, "to shut my eyes to a good racket." Greed and the lack of any scruples in satisfying it were to be two of his most prominent characteristics from now on.

By 1939 Harry Houghton had risen to be petty officer, and in Gosport met a Lancashire girl, Peggy, some years older than himself, with a teenage daughter, Margaret, from a previous marriage. They were married in the local register office just before the start of the Second World War.

During the war Houghton saw active service in various theaters, and by the end of it had become master-at-arms—the highest non-commissioned rank in the navy—at a naval rest camp in India. In 1945 he came home, left the navy after twenty-three years' service, and with his record had no difficulty finding a job in Portsmouth dockyard, first as a clerk, later as established clerical officer.

For the next five years the Houghtons lived in Gosport, but more and more unhappily. There were frequent rows between them and, occasionally, even blows. In addition Houghton was beginning to drink heavily, and often his wife had to plead for housekeeping money.

To escape from the drabness and disagreeableness of his life in Portsmouth, Harry Houghton began studying the foreign postings vacancies on the office bulletin board and put in applications for two, one as clerk to the naval attaché at the Warsaw embassy, the other in Singapore.

Houghton was called to the Admiralty to be interviewed for the Warsaw job, and to his great surprise got it. He and Peggy (Margaret by this time was married) sailed for Gdynia in the *Baltavia* early in 1951.

But domestic life for the Houghtons was no better in Warsaw than it had been in Gosport. For a start, most of their colleagues at the embassy moved in a different social climate from the one they were used to. Then, the living accommodations they'd been given were quite inadequate, with the minimum of furniture and little prospect of obtaining more.

And the rows, though the Houghtons put on a brave enough face in public, went on as before. Once, coming home from a party drunk, Houghton pushed Peggy, and she fell awkwardly and broke her leg. Later, when it was in plaster, they had a further row. Peggy accused Harry of deliberately breaking her leg, and Harry said if she didn't look out, he'd break the other bloody leg too. When she had recovered sufficiently, she decided to fly home and stay with her daughter, Margaret.

Houghton, however, had found compensations in other ways. Firstly in the local black market, which provided rich pickings for the unscrupulous. There was a desperate shortage of consumer goods in Poland at this time, and by ordering things from England (which came tax and duty free), Houghton and others were able to reap huge profits. Cosmetics, liquor, tobacco, suits, stockings and fur coats were all much in demand. Coffee, which Houghton bought at around two pounds, he sold for over forty. He paid seventeen pounds for a Hoover vacuum cleaner and sold it for nearly three hundred and fifty. During his stay in Warsaw he made four thousand pounds.

With this income Houghton was able to lead the sort of life he had always wanted, having as much to drink as he could take, offering hospitality and attending numerous parties given by others—Britons, Americans, Poles, many in the same racket as himself. He took a great liking to the strong Polish vodka, and often after office hours was to be seen somewhat the worse for wear.

Such behavior did not go unmarked by the Polish authorities, who, with their Soviet masters, were always quick to notice weaknesses in the personnel of diplomatic missions—and which, exploited, might produce dividends in the future.

Then one evening at a party Houghton met a ravishingly pretty blonde called Christina, who seemed as attracted to him as he was to her. He took to seeing her regularly, gave her presents from England through the diplomatic pouch, and she began helping him find new buyers for his black-market goods.

After Peggy had gone, he would put a lighted reading lamp by his window to show he was alone; and Christina would climb the narrow stairs to his flat and there, for love of her country and, who knows, perhaps for Harry Houghton too, gave the Englishman the pleasures he sought.

By the summer of 1952 the British ambassador and the naval attaché, Captain Austen, concluded that while Houghton's work was beyond reproach, his general conduct was not that expected of an embassy official, and he was posted home. Christina seemed distraught to see him go, and he was miserable at leaving her. They even talked of her going with him to England and their getting married. Before he left, and on instructions from her superiors, she gave him the address of a Pole called Tadeusz, who lived in London and who might cooperate in getting through to Poland, at inflated prices, goods that were in short supply. The long rein on Houghton was slowly shortening.

Although Houghton's social conduct had been unsatisfactory, Captain Austen saw no reason why this should prejudice his chances of future employment. In the papers recommending his recall it was simply stated that the post of clerk to the naval attaché no longer required a clerical officer of his grade; and so no hint of his Warsaw drinking habits, and therefore vulnerability, ever reached the ears of the security people in Whitehall.

As a result, Houghton was appointed in November 1952 as clerical officer in the Admiralty Underwater Detection Establishment at Portland—one of the most secret naval research organizations in the world. It was to be a fateful posting.

He and Peggy took up the thin threads of their marriage and lived first in a council house in Weymouth, then at a cottage on the edge of the Downs at Broadwey, just outside Weymouth, which he bought with his Warsaw black-market profits. He also bought a small Renault car and in this went up to London to see Christina's contact, Tadeusz.

Tadeusz told him that he needed certain types of drugs for smuggling into Poland, and through a friend in this business Houghton was able to arrange it, with a generous commission for himself. He wrote and told Christina of his meetings with Tadeusz, also where he was living and working. This information she immediately passed on.

But the rows with Peggy grew worse, and increasingly she went away for visits to her daughter, in Portsmouth. This suited Harry admirably, as he himself had a new girl friend. She was quite different from Christina—a thirty-eight-year-old spinster by the name of Ethel Gee, who also worked as a clerk in the Underwater Detection Establishment. She lived in a red brick terraced house in Hambro Road, Portland, with her mother, Lily, her bedridden aunt Elizabeth, both aged eighty, and Elizabeth's husband, Uncle John, aged seventy-six. She had a small private income left to her by her grandparents and father to supplement her pay of ten pounds a week.

Ethel, whom Harry called Bunty, had led a very sheltered life, and at first hesitated to go out with a married man. But when he explained that his marriage was on the rocks anyway, she began to accept occasional lifts in his car to and from the dockyard. At lunchtime they would often leave together for a drink and a sandwich at one of Portland's many pubs, the Breakwater down in the Castletown area, or the Clifton up on the hill.

Later, when Peggy was away in Portsmouth, they would drive in the evening to country pubs like the Crown at Puncknowle and the charming Elm Tree Inn at Langton Herring, overlooking the sea. She didn't drink much herself, but was quite happy to sit with Harry while he swapped rounds and gossiped with the locals. The evenings became bright spots in her otherwise rather dull life.

HOUGHTON ARRIVED AT THE Dulwich art gallery well on time, and took up position outside the main entrance as instructed, with a copy of *The Times* in one hand and a pair of gloves in the other. A man approached. He wore a long overcoat and a wide-brimmed hat.

"Mr. Houghton?"

"That's me."

"Shall we go somewhere and talk?"

They went to a tearoom, took off hats and coats and sat down.

"You know my name," said Houghton cheerfully, "but I don't know yours."

"Call me Nikki," said the man. "Why not? It's my name."

"How's Christina, then?" said Houghton.

"Christina is not good. She has been doing bad things. We are finding she is not politically reliable."

"What things?"

"Many. For instance, we know all about the little businesses that she and you were up to in Warsaw. And we know about her introducing you to Tadeusz, and what you have been doing for him. Things your superiors would not like to know."

Houghton said nothing. This wasn't the sort of conversation he had imagined at all.

"That drugs business is finished, by the way," said Nikki, "so you can forget about it now."

And forget about the cash that went with it, thought Houghton.

"Your friend Christina," said Nikki, "is in trouble. Would you like to help her?"

"How?"

"I'll tell you." He reached for his pocket. "But first your expenses for today." He counted out four five-pound notes. "I think that should cover it."

Houghton eyed the fresh notes greedily. He ought to refuse, tell Nikki to go to blazes, take the next train home. But the thought hardly occurred to him. There was nothing wrong in taking expenses. And twenty pounds! More than triple his actual expenses! He folded the notes and put them in his pocket. Nikki watched with satisfaction. Thanks to Christina and Tadeusz, Houghton was now almost hooked.

"How can I help Christina?" asked Houghton eagerly.

"Christina," lied Nikki, "wants to come to the West. If you agree to what I propose, we may allow her to come. You would like to see her, yes?"

"What do you want me to do?"

"Where you work, there are things of great interest to us—"

Us, thought Harry Houghton. Who is *us?* But he knew as soon as he asked.

"We want you to supply us with information on a regular basis, and we will pay you on a regular basis. We will welcome everything you can get for us, even quite small things like local newspaper reports."

Newspaper reports, thought Houghton, just as Nikki meant him to. Maybe I can get away with this by just sticking to newspaper reports.

"Well," said Nikki, "what do you say?"

This was the moment when Nikki expected some conscience pricking, when Houghton might say he couldn't do a thing like that, not betray his country. And then Nikki would say to him, So Christina goes to prison and your superiors will be told of your black-market activities in Poland and smuggling drugs for Tadeusz. But Houghton, who had left his conscience in the cradle, was one step ahead of him. He said, "How much is it worth?" It was the only show of resistance he could make.

"For routine reports, fifty pounds a month. For anything special, a hundred pounds, or even more."

God, thought Harry, just think of the life I could lead on that. Booze unlimited. Regular trips to London.

Before Houghton could say anything further, Nikki said, "Good, that's agreed, then. Now, listen to me." He took two packages from his overcoat pocket.

"This," said Nikki, pointing to the smaller packet, "is a Minox camera for general work. Photographs of buildings and ships, radar installations and so on. As you can see, it's hardly bigger than a cigarette lighter and quite easy to work.

"This other one is an Exakta, and is for photographing documents. It requires more skill and special lighting, but if you follow the instructions inside, you should have no difficulty.

"As regards subject matter, we are particularly interested in asdic and sonar, homing torpedoes, exercise areas, ships in harbor and their equipment. But as I say, even very small things may be of help, so don't omit anything because you think it's no good."

"What do I do with the stuff?"

"Once a month, at the weekend, you will be required to come to a rendezvous in London. The first time will be when you receive an ordinary Hoover brochure through the post. When you get that—"

"Wait a minute," said Houghton. "Where will you send it?"

"To your cottage. Eight Meadowview Road, Broadwey."

"You know where I live, then?"

"We know a lot about you, Mr. Houghton. We even know about your friend Miss Gee."

Houghton stared at him, unbelieving.

"When you get the Hoover brochure, you are to go to the saloon bar of the Toby Jug public house on the Kingston bypass at six p.m. on the following Saturday, bringing with you anything you have. Hold a newspaper in one hand and a drink in the other. A man will say to you, 'Is that the evening paper you've got there?' You will say, 'No, I'm afraid it's a daily.' He will reply, 'I wanted the racing results.' Then you will go with him to his car and hand over your package, and he will give you instructions about the next monthly meeting, and, of course, your money."

Houghton took out a pen and a scrap of paper.

"No, don't write anything. I'll go through it again for you."

Houghton began to realize he had got into much deeper water than he intended, and that now it was too late to go back.

"Good," said Nikki. "I look forward to much useful cooperation."

Nikki paid the bill; they put on hats and coats and went out.

"Good-by, Mr. Houghton."

"Bye-bye, then," said Houghton obsequiously.

And Nikki Korovin, counselor at the Soviet embassy, went off in one direction, and Harry Houghton, ex-master-at-arms in the King's Navy, in another. Events with as yet unforeseen endings would now take their course.

So HARRY HOUGHTON sold himself and his country to Soviet intelligence and continued to do so for the next seven years.

When he arrived back home that day, he opened a file and started putting into it cuttings from local newspapers and other snippets of information about naval affairs that he thought might satisfy his new masters without compromising himself. As usual, his object was to give as little for as much as he could get. He assumed the Hoover brochure would arrive soon, and he wanted to be ready with material when the summons came.

But week after week went by, and there was no sign of it. Why not? Were the Russians taking him for a ride? Had the brochure got lost in the post?

There was no means of finding out, for Nikki had left no address or telephone number. Houghton felt angry and frustrated, thinking of the riches he had been promised and which now seemed to be slipping from his grasp.

The ending of the Tadeusz deal made it all the more aggravating, for until he could get started, there was no spare cash for evenings in the pubs with Bunty, or for trips to London.

This, of course, was what Nikki and his friends had anticipated. The longer that Houghton was kept waiting, the more eager he would be to start.

When at last the Hoover brochure arrived, Houghton was overjoyed. He put his file beside him in the car, drove to London, met his contact in the Toby Jug public house and exchanged packets and information.

On the way home Houghton opened the packet he had been given, and found fifty crisp new pound notes. The next evening he and Bunty went out to the Elm Tree Inn, where he stood several rounds of drinks.

So began his monthly visits to various London rendezvous. Each time, his contact told him where his next rendezvous would be, and the method by which he would be summoned to it. On one occasion it was on receipt of a brochure from the Scotch House in Knightsbridge; on another, of literature from the Sun Alliance Insurance Company.

Once, on receiving advertising matter from the Renault car company, he was instructed to hold the pages up to the light to see if he could detect a pinhole piercing the center. He did, and there was. This meant that on his next visit to London he had to call in at the left-hand lavatory of the public lavatories in Alresford, Hampshire, at two p.m. precisely, pick up a package that he would find hidden behind the door and take it to his contact in London.

His contacts were various. Sometimes it would be Nikki; at other times a man whom he got to know as Roman, who, unlike Nikki, dressed carefully and spoke fluent English; sometimes men whom he didn't know. Most of his rendezvous were in the southwestern area of London, in places like the Maypole pub at Hook, off the Kingston bypass, or the Worcester Hotel by Worcester Park Station.

Once, at a rendezvous near the Marquis of Granby public house near Esher, Houghton observed his contact driving past with two men. When he met the contact, he asked who the men were, and was told curtly that they were friends having an evening drive. Another day he was instructed to leave a package in a lavatory in a pub. He found the pub shut and had to wait about until he was approached in person.

As time went by, Houghton was amazed at how satisfied the Russians seemed to be with what he was sending them, and how promptly he was paid. He had taken a few general shots of ships and installations with the Minox camera, but these could have been taken by anyone.

He hadn't dared use the Exakta camera, firstly because he didn't think he really understood it, more pressingly because in that tiny cottage he was afraid Peggy might find out.

So he made up parcels of cuttings from papers, daily orders at the base (which weren't confidential and wouldn't be missed), what ships had visited Portland and for how long, charts showing the general exercise area (which could be obtained from any good map house), local tide tables and other trivia.

When his contacts asked him for information about the army's training areas for artillery and tanks at Lulworth Cove and Bovington Camp, he sent a report that anyone could have obtained from chit-chat in local pubs.

Houghton would have felt much less happy about the satisfaction he seemed to be giving his masters had he known how their minds worked. For, unknown to him, he was being softened up.

If they tried to put pressure on him now to obtain more secret information, he might panic and pack up. But the longer they waited, the more surely was Houghton trapped; the more he became conditioned to a new style of living and regarded his new income as a permanent fixture, the less in the long run would he be able to give it up.

PEGGY HOUGHTON WAS friendly with Houghton's immediate superior in the office, Bob Connolly, and his wife, and one evening when Harry was out with Bunty, she went to a party at their house. Toward the end of it he sat down with her.

"How are things, Peggy?"

"With Harry? Much the same. Bastards like him never change. I hope I've managed to cover up yesterday's black eye."

"Oh, not again! Why do you go on with it?"

"What else would I do, Bob? Where would I go? I've got no money."

"Wish I could suggest something. But I've got no complaints. He does his work well. A different man at home, it seems."

"Bob, I want to ask you something, but will you get me a drink first? A good stiff one."

"Of course." He took her glass away and filled it.

"Thanks." She took a long, slow gulp and said, "You're going to think this silly."

"No, I'm not."

"All right, then. Does Harry need to bring home office papers?"

"Well, no. Why?"

"Last week I saw him putting a brown paper parcel into that little cupboard we've got beneath the stairs. It was the way he did it. He looked so—well, furtive somehow. Anyway, my womanly curiosity was aroused, and when he'd gone to work, I got out the parcel and peeked into it. I'd better be honest with you, Bob, and say I thought it probably contained a present for our darling Bunty Gee. And if it had, you can be sure I would have let my little Harry have a piece of my mind."

"It contained papers, you mean? What sort of papers?"

"I didn't look too closely. When I saw it wasn't something for one of his lady friends, I lost interest somehow. But office papers, you know, naval things and all that."

Bob stared at her and said nothing.

"You don't believe me, Bob, do you?"

"It's not that, Peggy. I'm puzzled. I can't imagine what sort of papers Harry would take out of the office that anybody would want. He doesn't have access to classified stuff. The papers he handles are not worth a damn."

"Well, I'll tell you something else you may not believe. When Harry was in the toilet yesterday morning, he left his wallet on the table. It seemed to me much fatter than usual."

"So you had a look-see."

"Oh, I know you'll think me a proper bitch, but if you had the sort of struggle I have each week to get a fiver's housekeeping money, you'd maybe see it differently. Guess how much was in that wallet?"

"You tell me."

"I didn't have time to count exactly, in case he came back, but there was at least forty quid there. *Forty quid.* On fourteen pounds a week and a five-pounds-a-week pension, a mortgage to pay and a car to run, where the hell does he get forty quid?"

"Did you say anything?"

"Yes. You know me. When he came back, I pointed at the wallet and said, 'You had a lucky win on the gee-gees or something?' "

"What did he do?"

"Snatched up the wallet, gave me this shiner"—she pointed to her eye—"and told me to mind my own business."

Bob said, "Peggy, let me get this straight. Are you suggesting that Harry's taking papers out of the base and selling them to— well, who?"

"I'm not suggesting anything, Bob. I'm just telling you what I've seen. But mark my words, there's *something* going on."

"What do you want me to do?"

"I don't know. I thought you might have something to suggest."

"Peggy, if there's anything in what you say, it's a security matter. It's not my territory at all. If you're really worried, go and see the dockyard security people. Or the police."

After the party Bob said to his wife, "Do you know what Peggy Houghton told me tonight? She thinks Harry is a spy."

"Harry? *A spy*— You must be joking!"

"No, she was quite serious. Thinks he's been stealing naval secrets from the office and selling them for filthy lucre."

"What did you tell her?"

"That Harry didn't have any secrets to sell, and she ought to forget it."

"She hates his guts," said his wife, "and the life he leads her, I don't blame her. But Harry a spy?" She laughed out loud. "Oh, that's rich!"

And five miles away at the Elm Tree Inn in Langton Herring, Harry Houghton, with Bunty Gee and others beside him, pulled his fat wallet from his pocket and shouted, "The last round's on me, fellers! What are you all going to have?"

BUT PEGGY HOUGHTON was certain that her instincts had not betrayed her, and later, after much agonizing, she went to the dockyard police at the main gate of the base in Castletown and asked to speak to the officer in charge.

Sergeant Goldsmith, who was on duty, took her to see the senior officer, Chief Inspector Jack Burnett. He listened to what she had to say and then sent a report to the base security officer, Commander Crewe-Read.

A little before this, another incident concerning Houghton had come to Crewe-Read's attention. A report had reached him that a strongbox in the Underwater Detection Establishment office had been found left open, and that Houghton had admitted to having taken papers out of it. The reasons he had given had seemed quite adequate at the time, and the matter was regarded as closed.

Now Commander Crewe-Read's suspicions regarding Houghton as a result of Peggy Houghton's statement ought to have been immediately aroused. He knew, as did others at the base, of the Houghtons' domestic difficulties, and when Bob Connolly said he thought Peggy's report was prompted by her intense jealousy of Bunty Gee, Crewe-Read was inclined to agree.

The captain of the base, when told of the matter, agreed too. To all of them the idea of Harry Houghton as a spy was absurd, and a report was sent to the Admiralty more or less absolving Houghton from suspicion. But as a precautionary measure Houghton was moved from the Underwater Detection Establishment to a civilian organization in the dockyard called the Port Auxiliary Repair Unit.

Soon relations between Houghton and Peggy had become so bad that they at last agreed to separate. Peggy stayed on in the cottage and obtained a job in a Weymouth hospital. Harry bought a trailer, which he parked in the grounds of the Pennsylvania Hotel, high up on Portland Bill, between the Verne Prison and the borstal, and close to the network of quarries that supply the famous Portland stone.

Paradoxically his transfer to the Port Auxiliary Repair Unit had the opposite effect to that intended. In the Underwater Detection Establishment, Houghton had had no access to confidential material. But as sole clerical officer of the Auxiliary Repair Unit he handled and distributed Admiralty fleet orders and other material of possible interest to an enemy.

For Houghton the move came at just the right time. His masters had for some time been prodding him to produce more worthwhile intelligence, and here was a ready-made source.

Furthermore, the privacy of the trailer connected to the local electric system enabled him to start experimenting with the Exakta camera and to photograph the documents now coming his way. He would take a bundle of papers from the office when he left work on Saturday, and return them, photographed, on Monday morning. And every fourth weekend he would take what he had photographed to London.

An additional virtue of the trailer was that Bunty could visit him at any time without fear of being disturbed. She was now his mistress, and sometimes accompanied him on trips to London, where they stayed in hotels as man and wife, and went to the theater and ballet (though, not to shock the elderly relatives in Hambro Road, they invented a fictitious couple with whom they said they stayed).

Life for Harry Houghton seemed good. He was separated from his wife, he had a mistress whom he loved, and there was money to spend like water. It was the best racket he'd ever been in. Just every now and again, when surrounded by friends and acquaintances who so readily accepted his hospitality, he wondered what they'd have thought of him if they'd been told its source. But it was too painful a thought to dwell on for long. He wasn't doing any real harm, was he, it couldn't lead to anything, could it, so why fuss?

"What about another drink, boys?"

"Good old Harry!"

By 1958 Peggy Houghton had found another man she wanted to

marry, an ex-airman called Johnson who was a painter in the dock-yard and whose hobby was amateur walking. She brought divorce proceedings against her husband for cruelty, which he did not defend. He moved back into the cottage at Broadwey and, with Bunty's help and Russian money, redecorated and refurnished it.

In that same year Houghton was introduced in London to his new and, as it turned out, last Soviet contact. This was a chunky, handsome man in his mid or late thirties, with dark curly hair and a marked Canadian accent.

KONON MOLODY ARRIVED in Vancouver by Russian grain ship toward the end of 1954. He settled first at a rooming house at 1527 Burnaby Street, moved after a week to 1630 Pendrill Street, and later still moved to Toronto. In both cities he led a quiet life, read all the newspapers, visited theaters and concert halls, talked to all manner of people in cafés and saloons and gradually familiarized himself with the Canadian scene.

Now came the most critical part of his preparations for entering England, the obtaining of a genuine Canadian passport. And here Soviet intelligence, with its huge dossiers on all kinds of people, native and foreign, dead and alive, served him well.

Through his contacts in the Soviet embassy in Ottawa, he was instructed to assume the identity of one Gordon Lonsdale, a man of about his own age, who was born in Ontario of Canadian-Finnish parentage, was taken by his mother to Finland at the age of eight and, according to Soviet records, had been killed at Stalingrad during the war.

To obtain a new birth certificate in Canada presents no difficulties. You go to the register office nearest to your place of birth, give your particulars, show your identity; if these are satisfactory, you are issued a new certificate.

So, well briefed, Molody turned up at the register office in Toronto on December 7, 1954, and stated his business. The clerk reached for a form.

"Your name?"

"Gordon Arnold Lonsdale."

"Present address?"

"Fifteen twenty-seven Burnaby Street, Vancouver."

"Place of birth?"

"Kirkland Lake, Ontario."

"Date of birth?"

"September 27, 1924." (Molody had been born on January 17, 1922.)

"Father's name?"

"Jack Emmanuel Lonsdale."

"Nationality?"

"Canadian."

"Mother's name?"

"Olga Bousu. Finnish."

"Either of your parents alive?"

"No." (This was a risk: Jack Lonsdale was alive and still living
in the area.)

"Do you have any relatives in Ontario who can vouch for you?"

"No."

"Do you have identification?"

Molody drew from his pocket his account card with the Canadian
Bank of Commerce, a driver's license, various letters addressed to
him. The clerk glanced at them, handed them back.

"What happened to your original birth certificate?"

"I don't know. I never saw it."

"How come?"

"My father and mother separated when I was a kid. I guess it
must have got lost. I never had need of it until now."

"Why do you need it now?"

"To obtain a passport. I want to go abroad."

"Okay. Just wait there, will you?"

The clerk went out of the room, and Molody, chewing gum (a
North American habit to which he had become addicted), waited
tensely for his return. He knew the details of his application had
been flawless, but what if there had been some unforeseen hitch?
It seemed an age before the clerk returned, carrying a single sheet.

"Okay, I checked out the details, and we do have registration of
birth of Gordon Arnold Lonsdale on September 27, 1924, with the
particulars you mention. So I guess everything's okay."

"Thank you."

"Just sign here, will you?"

It was fortunate for Molody that he was not asked to undergo a
medical examination. Had he done so, and the authorities made
further inquiries, they would have discovered a feature of his anatomy which failed to tally with Lonsdale's—one, moreover, which
neither Molody nor his clever superiors could ever have foreseen.
Gordon Lonsdale was circumcised; Konon Molody was not.

He signed the paper in front of him. Five minutes later he was
the possessor of a brand-new birth certificate, a month later, of a
brand-new, bona fide Canadian passport. Konon Trofimovich Molody had temporarily died, and the long-dead Gordon Lonsdale was
reborn.

MOLODY STAYED IN CANADA for the early part of the new year. In Toronto it snowed a lot, which made him think wistfully of Moscow, and Galisha and the children. A contact at the embassy told him of the Royal Over-Seas League in London, an organization that helped Commonwealth visitors to England, and he wrote, applying for membership and saying when he expected to arrive. And so as to lead as normal a life in London as possible, he also wrote to the School of Oriental and African Studies, asking to be enrolled in the course in Chinese beginning in October. He had been in China briefly before his American assignment and had been much attracted to the language and the people.

In February he traveled down to New York (flashing his Canadian passport at the immigration people) to see his old friend and fellow spy, Rudolf Abel, now masquerading as Emil Goldfus, photographer, and in overall charge of Soviet espionage activities in the eastern United States. Before a couple of more years he would be betrayed and arrested (with photographs of Morris and Lona Cohen found in his belongings) and his network, like that of Yakovlev before him, destroyed; but not until it had penetrated many organizations and gathered much useful information.

At the end of February, Molody boarded the liner *America* and sailed for England.

On arrival in London he went straight to the Royal Over-Seas League's headquarters off St. James's Street and received the sort of welcome the league traditionally gives to Commonwealth visitors. They not only gave him accommodation until he could find something more permanent, but offered him tickets for test matches and race meetings and concerts at the Albert Hall.

On one occasion Molody visited the House of Commons with a group of fifty league members, and sat on the terrace overlooking the Thames, eating strawberries and cream as the guest of Beverley Baxter, the Canadian-born Member of Parliament. Later, through the courtesy of Sir Jocelyn Lucas, M.P., he was given a seat in the gallery of the House for the foreign-affairs debate on Suez. The man next to him thought he was a Canadian M.P.

References from the secretary of the league also enabled him to find a flat in the White House, near Regent's Park—a big, anonymous apartment house, with its own swimming pool and cocktail bars, whose occupants did little fraternizing. He asked for a flat with a view, and was given number 844, on the eighth floor. During his first few weeks in London he spent a lot of time sight-seeing and tried to familiarize himself with the English scene, just as he had done in Canada.

As his course at the School of Oriental and African Studies did not begin until the autumn, he made arrangements to go on a package holiday tour of Europe.

On July 3 he joined a party of thirty-two people for a fifteen-day coach tour of North Germany and Scandinavia. With his cameras and sunglasses, Molody looked the typical holidaymaker. He soon made friends with the other members of the group, who found him excellent company.

There were two Canadians on the trip, a Mrs. Jones and her pretty daughter, Mary, and he was pleased to find that they accepted him as a Canadian without question. He also got on well with the tour courier, John Schrader, to whom he spoke convincingly of his days as a lumberjack in the backwoods, and of his ambitions to become an antique dealer in London or to start a business in Hong Kong.

The tour went to Copenhagen, Stockholm, Oslo and then back to Hamburg. From here the party were to travel to London, but at Ostend, Molody parted from them to join another coach tour, this time through Central Europe to Italy.

By chance, Mrs. Jones and Mary were also booked on this trip, and the three of them joined the new group together. Once again Molody was the perfect traveling companion, carefree and generous, always happy to stand his round of drinks and gossip in hotel bars in the evenings.

But all this was only one side of Molody's life. There was the other, the principal one, for which he had been sent to England. It was not for the view that he had wanted an eighth-floor flat in the White House, but because the higher you went, the better you could receive foreign radio transmissions.

In the sitting room of his flat Molody installed a powerful radio set (on which he placed a little replica of the *Manneken-Pis* he had bought in Brussels), and in the cold hours of night, while the other occupants of the White House slept, he put on a pair of headphones and listened to coded messages coming through from his friends in the Moscow Center.

His holiday trips abroad, too, had been a cover for more devious activities. John Schrader noticed that whenever a sight-seeing tour was planned, he would say that sight-seeing didn't really interest him, he would stay in his hotel and read a book, or go for a stroll around the town. "Oh, Mr. *Lonsdale*," Mrs. Jones would say to him, "now you're not going to miss the Drottningholm theater this afternoon. They say it's one of the prettiest little theaters in the world, and nothing in it has changed in *two hundred years*." And he would say, "Mrs. Jones, you're very kind, and there's nothing I'd like more than the pleasure of your and Mary's company. But if you'll excuse me, I think I'll just stay back and have a little nap."

In fact, he neither napped nor read nor strolled around the town. In a dozen secret rendezvous he contacted other agents, exchanged information and messages, arranged for dead-letter drops, planned how intelligence from London was to be received and handled for onward transmission to the Center.

Back in London, he was equally busy: digesting information that came to him from a variety of sources, collecting messages concealed behind loose bricks in walls and in contraceptives in the cisterns of lavatories, making telephone calls that would have been unintelligible to any casual listener, receiving microdot equipment and one-time cipher pads and concealing them in secret cavities in objects in his flat, collecting sterling and dollars from abroad—not only for himself but for those on his payroll, hiding them inside a Chinese scroll that hung as an ornament above his bed.

And then, on Saturdays, he would make his way to the only private house in England where he could feel really at home, to the house of fellow Canadians who in fact were no more Canadian than he was—Lona and Morris Cohen, or as their neighbors knew them, Helen and Peter Kroger, at 45 Cranley Drive, Ruislip.

When the Krogers had bolted and barred all the numerous devices they had installed on every door and window of their house, they would pull up the radio transmitter from its hiding place beneath the kitchen floor, run the seventy-four-foot aerial up to the roof, and transmit high-speed coded messages to the Moscow

Center. And afterward, when their work was done, they would sit and talk over a drink, completely relaxed in each other's company, and exchange information about their work and the great cause to which they were all dedicated. Often Molody didn't return to the White House until the Sunday.

The life of a spy is lonely and fraught, his greatest fear that of being discovered. Wherever Molody went in London, he never failed to take precautions, often minute by minute, to throw off possible shadowers. Wherever he walked, he often retraced his steps, turned without warning down an alleyway, stopped outside shopwindows to watch passersby in the reflection of the glass. He jumped onto buses when they were already gathering speed, left them abruptly at traffic lights, ran across the road and jumped onto others. He invariably left underground trains as the doors were closing, sometimes went back a station or two before continuing his journey. And later, when he had a car, his eyes were rarely off the rearview mirror, watching for any vehicle that might be tailing him. On long stretches of road he made abrupt changes of speed; roundabouts he would circle two or three times; often he turned into empty roads, switched off the ignition and waited.

For most of us such an existence would be intolerable. But Konon Molody had been trained for it. To him it was as natural and effortless as breathing.

In October the School of Oriental and African Studies reopened its doors, and Molody began his five-days-a-week course in the Chinese language. His fellow students came from a variety of backgrounds: some were foreigners sponsored by their governments, like the Israeli diplomat Zwei Kadar and the Canadian diplomat Tom Pope, or some, like the American Clayton Bredt, were paying their own way.

Some of the British students were seconded from the services, like Flight Lieutenant Harper, who had been assistant air attaché in Moscow; lieutenants Herschfeld and Parrit and Lieutenant Commander Angel; others from the Foreign Office and from firms whose businesses took them to Chinese-speaking territories.

When Zwei Kadar admitted to having worked as an Israeli agent and told them of his espionage activities in Arab countries, and when a Mr. Elton, ostensibly from the Foreign Office, admitted to having worked for MI-5, Clayton Bredt whispered to Molody, "Listen, Gordon, except for you and me, they're all spies here!"

Someone whom Molody began to see regularly at this time was a Major Raymond Straw of the American air force. He had met Straw and his wife on the Italian coach trip, and when Straw said he was at the American nuclear bomber base at Lakenheath in East Anglia, Molody fostered their relationship. Later his efforts were rewarded by an invitation from the Straws to spend a weekend at Lakenheath.

It was the first of many visits. The Straws took an immediate liking to this intelligent, lonely Canadian and were only too happy, as Molody had intended they should be, to befriend him. The Straws' children called him Uncle Gordon, and on every visit he brought them presents.

Gradually Molody came to know other officers at the base, visited them in their homes, drank with them in the mess. Their confidence gained, his naïve, starry-eyed questions, asked at well-spaced intervals—about the bomber force and its strength and capabilities, the stockpile of bombs, etc.—aroused no kind of suspicion.

Because Molody was a Canadian and therefore a man with whom they partly shared a common language and background, they could be less guarded than with an Englishman. It was Major Straw, too, who introduced him as a member of the Columbia Club off the Bayswater Road, a rendezvous for American airmen in England.

Other matters on which Molody was seeking information were the bacteriological establishment at Porton Down and the names of those who worked there, the Polaris submarine base in the Holy Loch, coastal radar installations and nuclear propulsion for peace and war.

He also kept eyes and ears open for defections of any native-born traitors, those who worked in British government offices and businesses—men like Guy Burgess and Donald Maclean and the yet uncaught Kim Philby—ready to hand over their country's secrets, not for money, like Houghton, but because of their dedication to the Communist cause.

Molody was, and always had been, a man of exceptional energy and stamina, for in addition to his studies at the school and his espionage activities, he had a full social life. Sometimes he invited fellow students and their friends back to the White House for drinks or supper. He was an excellent host and, they found, a born raconteur. He told wild imaginary stories of his life in the Canadian backwoods; his timing was perfect, he used his hands expressively, he knew exactly how to capture and hold an audience's attention. He was well informed too, able to talk on almost any subject, art or music, film or the theater, sport or television. Only on the subject of political ideas and international politics did his friends find he had nothing to say. And, of course, like a good Russian and a good spy, he was an excellent chess player. Few of those who took him on ever defeated him.

He also had time for girls; indeed, girls were a necessary and integral part of his life. He knew how to please them, and because of it and his dark good looks they found him extremely attractive; but he was always careful not to get emotionally involved.

His first girl was the Canadian Mary Jones, whom he continued to see for a time after their coach tours abroad. Then there were Gillian from London, Anne-Marie from Germany and Ulla from Sweden. Another was Carla Pazzini, daughter of an Italian doctor, whom he met on a British Council trip for foreign students at St. Andrews University in Scotland. They spent most of the trip in each other's company, and later saw each other regularly in London.

"He was amusing, very considerate and generous," said Carla. "He was wonderful company."

When another British Council trip was organized, to Torquay, they went on it together. But Carla was puzzled by his sudden absences abroad, often for weeks at a time. Sometimes when he was away he sent her a postcard, but when he returned, he never said where he had been or what he had been doing. In so otherwise open a man she found it surprising.

His next girl was introduced to him by Carla, a beautiful Yugoslav called Zlata Sablic, who worked as a waitress at the National Hospital for Nervous Diseases. She had come to England to improve her English and was studying with Carla at the St. Marylebone Chamber of Commerce. Sometimes Molody invited the two girls out together, and when Carla had gone home, Molody asked Zlata to bring any girl friend of hers to join them for an evening out.

On one occasion Zlata brought a fellow Yugoslav called Gordana, who was also working at the hospital; and when Zlata went home, Molody asked Gordana to bring any of her girl friends to join them. It was as though there were safety in numbers. Often he talked to his latest girl of his conquests with previous ones, even produced photographs. None of them seemed to mind.

"He was," said Gordana, "one of the most interesting people I have ever met. He seemed to have a genuine knowledge of many subjects. He loved music and was proud of his prowess with languages. He could speak a little of several Yugoslav dialects."

These women, and others, sustained Molody in the loneliness of his schizophrenic life. Collectively they meant a lot to him, individually nothing. There was, as always, only one woman in his life: Galisha, in faraway Moscow.

THE MOSCOW CENTER allows its agents abroad much latitude in deciding where and how they live, but insists on adequate cover. A man with plenty of money and no occupation is more open to suspicion than a man with a job.

Molody's main cover, which lasted for two years, was his studentship at the School of Oriental and African Studies. But after a few months he set about preparing a second cover, and a most unusual one. He became a jukebox salesman. This served two purposes. No one in his senses would suspect a jukebox salesman of being a spy. Secondly, he could now start making money on his own account to pay for the way of living he so enjoyed; and for a born Communist, what better way of doing it than by beating the capitalists at their own game?

Indeed, Molody's desire to make money was as powerful a motivation in his becoming a jukebox salesman as the need for a second cover. For the same reason, he started on the football pools. How strained would his loyalties to his country have been, one wonders, if he had won, say, a hundred thousand pounds?

His success in selling jukeboxes (he bought the machines from a wholesaler and sold them at a profit) led him to others engaged in the same line of business. One of these was a man called Peter Ayres, who lived at Broadstairs and was planning to set up a company to make and distribute chewing-gum machines.

They met over drinks in the West End. Molody told Ayres of his success in selling the jukeboxes and suggested he might sell some of the chewing-gum machines on a similar basis. Ayres, impressed by Molody, agreed to give him a trial run. So, a little later, Molody motored down to Broadstairs in his yellow Ford van, picked up a few of the new machines from Ayres's small factory in Oscar Road and took them to London. Within a few days he had sold the lot, at an average personal profit of fifteen pounds a machine.

So began a partnership which for a considerable time proved highly successful. A company was formed called the Automatic Vending Company, Ltd., and Ayres, Molody and a man called Michael Bowers each bought five hundred pounds' worth of shares. They set up two subsidiary organizations: the Thanet Trading Company, which specialized in O Girl chewing-gum machines, and the Peckham Automatic Co., Ltd., with offices in Peckham Rye, which traded in chewing gum.

Molody could now call himself company director, which gave him a useful business status. He traveled widely to sell the machines, and watched his bank account grow to a healthy figure. Ayres and Bowers often visited Molody at the White House, and they went to parties together where they might find new buyers.

All in all, life for Molody seemed good. He was fully stretched on several fronts; he had no shortage of money; he was traveling extensively at home and abroad, including occasional visits to Moscow to report to the Center and see Galisha and the children. He was with her in the autumn of 1957, when she conceived a son, and again in the spring of 1959, when the boy was nearly a year old.

And yet, though he could not see it, a small cloud was about to darken his horizon. His superiors at the Center were not happy at the paucity of information reaching them about underwater weapons. One night in his flat, listening on his headphones to Moscow, he received instructions to assume overall responsibility for the Portland contact. The lives of Harry Houghton and Konon Molody were about to come together for the first time.

FOR HARRY HOUGHTON at this time life seemed equally pleasant. Peggy had met a man at her new job she wanted to marry, and with Bunty now a regular part of his life, he made no objections when Peggy began divorce proceedings for cruelty. He was annoyed that she had taken so much furniture from the cottage, but with money at his disposal he had no problems in refitting it to his own taste.

He ordered a new carpet and chairs for the living room; he had the walls repaneled and the fireplace remodeled; he bought an expensive phonograph and records; and for any guests who accepted his invitation to look in for evening drinks, there was always whiskey and gin.

He continued his monthly trips to London to meet Roman or another contact, hand over whatever information he had and collect his monthly pay packet. It was an admirable arrangement and one which he saw no reason to think would not last indefinitely. Sometimes he took Bunty to London, sometimes he went on his own and met other women. He had always been partial to what he called "a nice piece of crumpet."

One Saturday in the summer of 1958 Houghton drove from Weymouth to an arranged rendezvous with Roman opposite the Maypole public house at Hook. He was there ahead of time and saw Roman drive by in the company of another man. At five thirty p.m. Roman approached him alone and got into his car. They drove together to a nearby sports ground and there exchanged packages.

Roman said, "Tonight I have arranged another meeting for you."

"Oh. What for?" Houghton knew better by now than to ask who or why.

"The meeting is to be at nine tonight at the corner of Edgware Road and Oxford Street."

"You mean Marble Arch?"

"Yes, at the corner. You are to hold a newspaper in your left hand and a pair of gloves in your right."

Same as Dulwich, thought Houghton. They seemed to have a thing about gloves and newspapers.

"A man will approach you and ask if you know what number bus goes to Swiss Cottage. You will say you think it's thirty-seven or thirty-nine. He will say, 'Are you sure it's not forty-eight?' Do you understand?"

"Yes."

"After that, you will be in his hands. Okay?"

Houghton dropped off Roman near the Maypole and went on up the Kingston bypass to London. He was at the rendezvous at the appointed time; so was Konon Molody.

"Excuse me, but do you know what number bus goes to Swiss Cottage?"

"I think it's thirty-seven or thirty-nine."

"Oh, I thought it was forty-eight."

Molody put out his hand. "Mr. Houghton?"

"Yes."

"Gordon Lonsdale."

"Pleased to meet you."

This attractive, assured man with the marked American or Canadian accent was unlike any of Houghton's previous contacts; he was intrigued as to who he was.

Across the road were the empty spaces of Hyde Park, in the summer still light. Houghton said, "Shall we go and talk over there?"

"No," said Molody, at once establishing his authority. "Let's go and have something to eat. I'm hungry. How about you?"

So they walked up the Edgware Road to the Lotus House Restaurant, found a quiet table and ordered a Chinese meal. Molody ordered wine too, but after the bottle had been opened, Houghton noticed—as he was to notice on future occasions—that while his own glass was often filled, his host took only a few sips.

At this first meeting Molody said nothing of the business that had brought them together. It was of his imaginary life as Gordon Lonsdale in Canada that he talked, just as he had talked to his companions on the coach tour, to his fellow students at the school, to the various girls he took out. And as they had fallen under his spell in the telling of it, so did Harry Houghton.

They arranged to meet at Weymouth the following Saturday. Houghton met him at the train at Dorchester and took him to the cottage. They spent the morning touring the area in Houghton's car. (In Portland itself he was quite worried that Bunty might see him, as he had said he would be in London.)

In the afternoon they hired a boat in Weymouth and went for a cruise around the bay. Molody, in holiday gear and using a camera with a telescopic lens, took numerous photographs of the waterfront at Weymouth, of passing sailing ships and other craft; then, with the boatman's suspicions lulled, of various aspects of the naval base from seaward.

In the evening, after Houghton had cooked bacon and eggs, Molody sat up late in the cottage bathroom, photographing documents that Houghton had brought from the office. Before leaving for London, Molody gave Houghton a present of a gold cigarette lighter he had bought at Dunhill's.

This was the second of many meetings between the two. For a time Molody continued the pretense of Gordon Lonsdale, but later, as he and Houghton came to know each other, he made it clear (though without revealing his real name) that he was Russian. He spoke of Russian history and literature, of the Russian way of life, of his apartment in Moscow and how much he missed his wife and children.

Yet so convincing did he appear as a Canadian, so integrated in British society, that Houghton once asked if he were not attracted to the idea of living in the prosperous West. But Molody, unlike Houghton, was fiercely loyal to his country and countrymen. Certainly there were shortages of goods in Russia, but the position was continually improving. Certainly there was inadequate housing, but had Houghton seen the slums of New York? And where else in the world did the workers pay such low rents and have such easy access to the finest in art, music, theater, sports?

It was not only of Portland's secrets that Molody and Houghton talked, but of other naval establishments—Portsmouth and Plymouth, Rosyth and Bath—scattered about the country. Molody was searching in his questioning; no detail, however trivial to Houghton, seemed unimportant for him. Houghton came to admire his stamina and self-discipline, as well as the warmth of his personality, so unlike the robotlike figures that had been sent to him in the past. "However incredible it may seem," he wrote later, "there was a real camaraderie between us."

Camaraderie for Houghton there may have been, but for Molody, despite his ease and affability, it was always assumed. His superiors at the Center were now becoming increasingly concerned at how far ahead the British were in underwater weapons development, and there was pressure on Molody to find out more. But no good spy can ever force the pace. It wasn't until he had gained Houghton's confidence and fully established his authority over him that he was able to take further an idea that had been forming in his mind.

One day he said to Houghton, "Your friend Miss Gee, whom you talk of so much?"

"Oh, yes, Bunty?"

"Why do I never see her? I'm sure we'd get along fine."

"Ah, well," said Houghton, "you don't want to mix business with pleasure."

"Why not? Listen, Harry. Next time you come to London, bring Bunty along too. We can all have a drink, and I'll fix up theater tickets for you after."

Houghton hesitated. "Okay," he said finally. "But how shall I introduce you?"

"Oh, tell her something simple," said Molody. "Say I'm an American naval officer whom you knew in Warsaw, and we've met recently to talk over old times."

"Captain Lonsdale, eh?"

"No, let's not get the roles confused. I'll be Alec Johnson. That's a good, easy name. Commander Alec Johnson of the United States Navy. How about that?"

They met in the Cumberland Hotel at Marble Arch, a stone's throw from Molody and Houghton's first meeting.

"Bunty, this is the friend I was telling you about. Commander Johnson of the American navy."

Molody-Lonsdale-Johnson gave his most winning smile.

"How do you do, Miss Gee? Harry has told me so much about you. What can I get you to drink?"

For half an hour Molody bombarded Bunty with his charms, treating her as though she were the most attractive and important woman in the world. He spoke of the times he and Harry had had in Warsaw, how good it had been to meet up again, what a pleasure it was to make her acquaintance too. She asked him what he did in London, and he said he had an important liaison job with the British navy. And what did she do? Oh, really? Worked at the base down at Portland, same as Harry? Well, who knows, one of his trips might take him to Portland, and then they could have another get-together.

It was a masterly performance, and by the time Molody had slipped Houghton the theater tickets, Bunty had been completely won over.

"I did like that friend of yours," she said as they drove to Shaftesbury Avenue in a taxi. "I thought him a *very* charming man."

HOUGHTON AND MOLODY met twice more in the near future, once for drinks, the second time for dinner. Despite a nagging doubt, Houghton had assumed these meetings to be purely social. After the dinner Molody disillusioned him.

"Harry?"

"Yes, Gordon."

"There must be a lot of classified material that goes through Bunty's office at the U.D.E."

"Yes, there is. Test pamphlets and drawings and so on."

"We must get to see them."

"How?"

"Bunty."

"Oh, no, Gordon. I'm not having any of that. It wouldn't be fair. Anyway, she wouldn't do it." Houghton giggled. "She's not like me, you know."

"No, I can see that. You say she wouldn't do it. But does that not depend on who she'd be doing it for?"

"Not me, anyway."

"No, nor Gordon Lonsdale either. But wouldn't she do it for Commander Alec Johnson and the good old United States Navy? I think she likes Alec Johnson quite a bit."

Houghton said, "You're a cunning bastard, Gordon. Conning old Bunty, eh? I don't think I fancy that."

"No?" Molody was smiling at him. It was a friendly enough smile on the surface, but underneath there was menace. Yet Molody had no need to press things.

"If she could give us what we wanted," said Molody, "we'd obviously make generous adjustments in your monthly arrangements." He was careful to stress the word your.

Houghton's greedy little eyes came to life.

"How much?"

"Double."

"Standard or special?"

"Two hundred."

"A month?"

"So long as we're supplied. And, Harry, you know what you were saying the other day about a new car? I think we can come to some agreement about that too."

Houghton said nothing. Molody knew there was nothing more he could say.

They met at the Mirabelle, one of London's smartest and most expensive restaurants. For Bunty, walking down the richly carpeted stairs with her arm in Harry's, it seemed about as far as you could get from the red brick house in Hambro Road, Portland, and its ailing, elderly occupants.

Molody was already at the table. "Well, hullo there!" He rose, put his hands lightly on Bunty's arms and said, "You're looking real good, if I may say so."

"Thank you, Alec."

"How are you, Harry?"

"Can't complain."

Molody ordered drinks. Then, and later over dinner, he was as always the perfect host, interested in his guests, considerate and generous. Houghton could not but admire, while resenting, the skills he used to charm and flatter Bunty.

At first they talked of general matters; then, as the food and wine relaxed his guests (he as usual took only one glass), Molody steered the conversation in a different direction.

"I want to tell you people," he said, "what a real pleasure it is to be with you this evening. First time I've relaxed all week. God, have I been having a tough time!"

There was a long moment of silence, which Molody and Houghton let ride.

Bunty said, "I can't imagine anyone getting tough with you, Alec."

Houghton said, "What's been the matter?"

"In three words," said Molody, "the British navy. Your old service, Harry."

"What's wrong with the navy?" said Bunty, whose uncle Jack had been a sailor, and who had lived in seaports and among sailors most of her life.

"Oh, the navy itself is okay. Don't get me wrong. It's a great institution. But I know now why it's called the silent service."

"That's because they don't like boasting about what they do," said Bunty. "That's modesty, really."

Molody laughed. "I'm not talking about modesty," he said. "I'm talking about sheer, bloody-minded obstinacy. My job here, as I believe I've told you, is to act as technical liaison officer between our navy and yours. This means, mainly, exchange of information under dual agreement. Well now, in most fields this functions pretty smoothly. I give my opposite numbers details of new developments in our navy; they give me what's new in the R.N. But there's one or two who take everything I give, and when it comes to giving in return, they just clam up and don't tell a thing."

"Who are they?" said Houghton.

Molody seemed to think. "Well, I'll give you one example," he said, "and it might interest you, being as it were on your own doorstep. There's a guy called Rushton at the Admiralty, works in the underwater weapons department, he's a commander like myself. For the last five months I've been telling this guy all the latest developments in our own underwater weapons outfit, and what has he been giving me in return? Little bits and pieces here and there, and all done with very bad grace. Now we know there's a lot of interesting things going on at Portland, where you work, and yet they just will not let us have proper access to it. We've taken it right up to flag level, but even that hasn't produced any results. Well, this is ridiculous. It's bad for me, bad for Anglo-American cooperation, bad for NATO. From a joint defense angle it's more than ridiculous—it's positively dangerous."

Houghton looked at Bunty and saw how impressed she was by Molody's eloquence. He had been pretty impressed himself.

"Oh, hell," said Molody. "We're here to have fun. What am I doing, boring you with my problems?" He looked around the room. "This is a great place."

"What kind of things are they keeping from you?" said Houghton.

"Well, that's a chicken-and-egg kind of question," said Molody. "Until we know what's there, we don't know what we want. But Rushton tells me that underwater weapons experiments are recorded in documents called test pamphlets. Now—"

"Oh, I know about test pamphlets," said Bunty. "I file them in our office. Course, I don't understand what's in them."

"You actually see them?" said Molody.

"Oh, yes," said Bunty. "We've got two files in the office full of them."

"Holy cow!" said Molody. "Here am I, trying to lay my hands on test pamphlets for weeks and months, and here's Bunty who sees them every day. Bunty, how do I get to be a fly on your ceiling?"

Houghton said, "It does seem a shame you can't see them. I mean, after all, in your job you ought to. Don't you think so, Bunty?"

"Well, yes," said Bunty weakly. "I do."

Houghton said, "Why couldn't—"

Molody said, "Why couldn't what, Harry?"

"I was going to say why couldn't Bunty let you have just a peep at one or two? But they're supposed not to leave the office, are they?"

"They're supposed to be kept under lock and key," said Bunty. She giggled. "Not that they ever are."

"Well," said Molody, "I certainly wouldn't want you to do anything you shouldn't do, though if you can think of a way to help— not just me but the whole NATO alliance—we'd be real grateful. Otherwise, I guess I shall just have to keep slugging it out with Commander Rushton."

Molody paid the bill, taking care that his guests should accidentally see it; then they went upstairs. In the foyer, Molody gave Bunty a small package. "Put that in your handbag, my dear," he said, "and don't open it until you get home. It's been a real pleasure seeing you both again. Good night."

Bunty opened the package in the taxi. It was an expensive powder compact from Aspreys. "What a lovely present," she said, fondling it. "I've never had anything like that."

Harry said nothing then, but later in the hotel room: "If you were to bring out one or two pamphlets on a Friday, I could make notes from them over the weekend, you could take them back on the Monday, and nobody would ever know they'd gone."

Bunty said, "Do you think that would be all right?"

"Why not? After all, we're both on the same side. And he'd have got what he wanted long ago if it hadn't been for that Commander Rushton."

"Perhaps Commander Rushton had reasons for not showing them. Perhaps he's been told not to."

"Don't you believe it. I know that type. Keep everything close to their chests. Don't tell a blooming thing to anyone."

"I don't know, Harry. I don't like to."

"In my opinion we'd be doing Alec, and NATO, a great service."

"I'd certainly like to help Alec if I could. Such a nice person he is, so sincere. And as you say, he is an American officer." She laughed. "It'd be different if he were a Russian spy or something."

Houghton worked on her all that week; and on Friday night, when he came to call for her in his car after work, she handed him a shopping bag and said, "Look in there when we get outside, and I think you'll find some of what you and Alec want."

"That's my girl!" he said.

Inside the shopping bag were two test pamphlets. During the weekend Houghton photographed them with the Exakta camera at the cottage and returned them to Bunty when he called to take her to work.

And a little later he not only added considerably to the store of cash he kept in a tin of Snowcem cement in the garden shed, but also put down a hundred-and-fifty-pound deposit in fivers on a brand-new Renault Dauphine. And at the Elm Tree Inn at Langton Herring and the Crown at Puncknowle, the drinks flowed.

IF THE NEW intelligence now coming out of Portland via Houghton and Gee had given Molody's espionage activities an upward turn, his business ventures were being less successful.

For a time the vending-machine partnership with Peter Ayres and Michael Bowers had continued to prosper, and on several occasions had enabled Molody to combine legitimate business with the other. The sale of some of the machines to civil organizations at American bases gave him the opportunity of visiting these bases and picking up snippets of information, small in themselves but of value collectively.

When visiting Ayres at Broadstairs, he made a habit of spending evenings in clubs and bars in Margate frequented by American servicemen from the nearby air base at Manston.

As at Lakenheath, his Canadian-American accent proved a useful

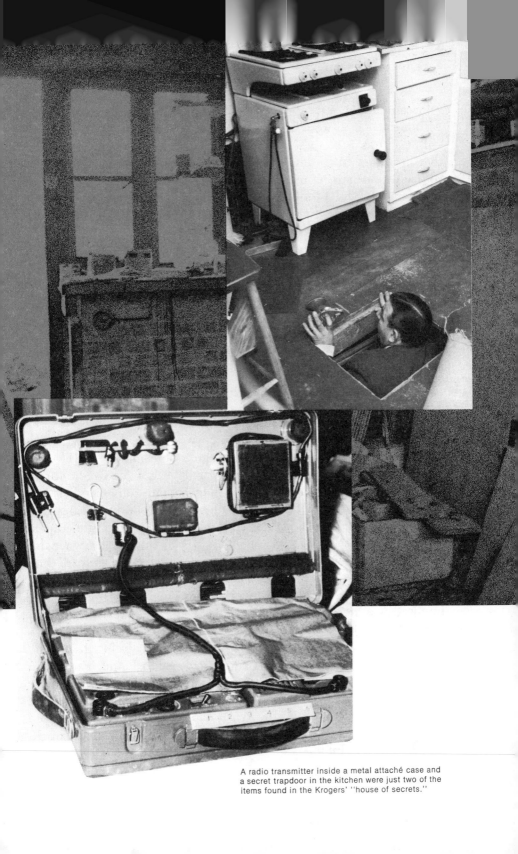

A radio transmitter inside a metal attaché case and a secret trapdoor in the kitchen were just two of the items found in the Krogers' "house of secrets."

lubricant to the striking up of chance acquaintances, particularly with airmen who were drunk.

But it was Molody's desire to profit from the capitalist system that he professed to despise that almost led to his downfall. In the course of business he met a man called Alexander Lester, a veneer importer who did a lot of trading with Italy. Lester bought a few of the machines himself and told Molody he thought there might be a market for them in Italy.

Fired by this cautious suggestion and having no business acumen of his own, Molody told Ayres that the market in Italy was wide open and they should be able to sell over a hundred thousand pounds' worth of machines.

In view of Molody's success in the past, Ayres gave instructions for an immediate rise in production, the engaging of more staff and ordering of more raw materials. But the expected orders from Italy never materialized, and almost overnight the Automatic Vending Company found itself in serious financial difficulties from which it never recovered. Early in 1960 it went bankrupt, with liabilities of over thirty thousand pounds.

Molody himself was also in trouble, with the fear of bankruptcy hanging over him and possible publicity which might well result in his recall by the Center. Not only had he lost his five-hundred-pound investment in the company, and commissions on sales, but he had agreed to become guarantor on various installment sales, and when their payments failed, he had to come up with the unpaid balance. He was in such serious financial difficulties that when his bank manager, Leonard Easter of the Midland Bank, refused him an overdraft (he had given him an earlier one of twenty-five hundred pounds), he asked Alexander Lester if he could borrow four hundred pounds to settle with a finance company that had advanced him money for the installment sales.

When Mr. Lester, on the advice of his solicitors, refused, Molody approached another business friend called Ralph Paton. Paton also refused, but did persuade the finance company to give Molody more time to pay. To economize further, Molody left his flat in Baron's Court (he had moved from the White House a year previously), sold some of his furniture and moved into a more modest flat in St. George's Drive, Pimlico.

By keeping a low profile and strictly limiting his personal expenditures, Molody's finances slowly began to recover, and before long a new business venture presented itself.

With Michael Bowers, who had also lost his capital in the failure of the Automatic Vending Company, he discovered that a switch had been invented that would completely immobilize a car as well as safeguard it from theft. The inventor, a Mr. Samuel Rorke, was dead, but the patent was held by his son, Thomas, and an elderly friend called Albert Warner.

Molody and Bowers persuaded these two that they could market the switch, and early in 1960 a new company was formed, called the Master Switch Company. It later changed its name to Allo Security Products, with a modest capital of a hundred pounds common and a hundred pounds A shares, the names of Michael Bowers and Gordon Lonsdale among its five directors, and offices in Wardour Street, Soho.

In the same year the invention won a prize at the International Inventors Exhibition in Brussels, and Molody and his proud fellow directors were photographed smiling in front of it.

Initially it looked as though Allo Security Products faced a somewhat rosier future than the Automatic Vending Company. But before Molody could share in the success of it, his life had taken a different and quite unexpected turn.

PART TWO
The Spy Catchers

THE BEGINNING OF the end for Houghton and Gee came about on January 13, 1960, in a most unexpected way. On that day a base executive officer by the name of Alfred Watford turned up at the main gate of the dockyard and asked to see the Admiralty constabulary CID officer, Fred Hosking.

Fred Hosking was a portly, pipe-smoking character in his late forties, an ex-naval steward who had joined the dockyard constabulary as police constable on his retirement. His work had been so outstanding, he had shown such a flair for discovering who was pilfering goods from the dockyard and how, that when in 1956 it was decided to appoint the first CID officer to the base,

Hosking was chosen to be trained for the job. In this, too, he had proved outstanding, and would go to any lengths—once dressing up as a workman with pick and shovel—to nail the perpetrators of a crime.

"Well," said Hosking, when Watford had been shown up to his little room above the main gate, "and what can I do for you?"

Watford put down on the table an envelope addressed to him with a swastika on the back, and another with "Dirty Jew" scrawled across it.

"I've been getting one or two like these," said Watford, "and I'd like to find the bastard who's doing it."

Fred Hosking picked up the envelopes and said, "Not very nice, are they?" He puffed at his pipe. "Any idea who it might be?"

"No."

"Got any enemies?"

"No, I don't think so."

"Anyone got a grudge against you?"

Watford thought. "Well, Harry Houghton and I don't exactly hit it off together," he said.

"Why not?"

"Oh, I don't know. I've made one or two jokes in public about how free he is with his money—if it is his money, you know. He hasn't liked that."

"No."

"Have you ever thought," said Watford, "where he *does* get his money?"

Hosking said, "It has entered my mind." He got up. "Well, I'll make some inquiries into this, Mr. Watford, and we'll see what we can find."

After Watford had gone, Hosking sat a long while at his desk, playing with his pipe, staring out of the window at a submarine leaving the harbor, and beyond her, to the hazy outline of Weymouth town. What Watford had said about Houghton's spending seemed to confirm something that had been in and out of his mind for years—the belief that Harry Houghton was a Russian spy.

He had first met Houghton inside the Underwater Detection Establishment when Hosking was a uniformed constable doing guard duty there. He had observed what a dapper little man Houghton was, punctilious in arrival and departure, talkative, gregarious, quite popular.

He had met Bunty Gee too—she also always nicely turned out, but rather stuck-up, he thought, a bit toffee-nosed.

He had seen the two of them come together, and after that watched the years of lavish spending, the drinking, the cars, the visits to London. He knew of the allegations that had been made about Houghton in 1956, and the fact that the Admiralty had decided to take no action. He accepted their verdict—as any man in his position would—and yet the thing continued to nag at him; he couldn't get it out of his mind.

It all boiled down to one simple question. Where *was* Houghton getting the money from?

Some people had thought he might be nicking things from the dockyard, but he knew this couldn't be true from regular checks on cars. He knew, too, that if Houghton had won the football pools or inherited a legacy from an aunt, he would have said so, because he was that kind of person.

So, in the end, it came back to what had been suspected four years before—that he had been selling naval secrets for money and was continuing to do so. So strong was Hosking's belief that he once sent one of his own men, Constable Coleman, who lived at Broadwey, to take a look at the roof of Houghton's cottage to see if there were transmitting aerials.

It was only a few days after Watford's visit that he observed Houghton and Gee come bowling into the dockyard in a brand-new Renault Dauphine. The combination of the two seemed ample confirmation of his beliefs and at last triggered him into action. He spent a full day at his desk writing a report on Houghton and his spending, yet emphasizing—as a good policeman should—that while he believed his suspicions to be well founded, there was little hard evidence on which to base them. He did not mention the matter of the obscene envelopes, as he considered it irrelevant (and indeed, soon after, the sender of them was found).

Hosking's report was typed out, submitted to his senior officer, with whom he had discussed the matter, and sent by him both to the Admiralty and to Detective Superintendent Bert Smith, the head of Dorset's CID.

From there, as an internal security matter, it went to MI-5, at their headquarters in Mayfair.

And in MI-5 it finally reached one of their senior men, Jim Skardon. He read it with increasing excitement, then called for his secretary. "Anne, get me the Goleniewski report, will you? And then put a call through to Admiralty civilian personnel."

When she'd gone, he dialed an internal number on another phone. "Yes?"

"Chief, I'm not sure, but I think we've got a lead on Portland."

JIM SKARDON HAD spent his early career as a CID officer in the Metropolitan Police, but had transferred to MI-5 during the war. He investigated several spy cases with great success, and when peace came, accepted an invitation to stay on. He was a dark-haired, very dapper man, who gave the impression of being smaller than he was because of a rheumatic shoulder and neck which made him move his whole body, instead of just his head, when turning to address anyone. He was often in some pain because of this, but was never heard to complain. He was very modest, highly intelligent and immensely painstaking and, because of his flair for winning the confidence of suspects, one of the most brilliant interrogators MI-5 has ever had.

His big success to date had come ten years earlier, in 1950. Following the explosion of Russia's first atom bomb, word reached London from the FBI in Washington that America's atomic secrets had probably been betrayed by a foreign-born scientist who had worked on the early Los Alamos experiments. Many names were put forward, among them that of Klaus Fuchs, who, it will be recalled, had first come to the FBI's notice when the Russian cipher clerk Igor Gouzenko had defected in Ottawa, and was now head of the theoretical physics division at Britain's Atomic Energy Research Establishment at Harwell.

When it was also discovered that Fuchs's name had been on a prewar Gestapo list of German Jews with Communist affiliations (Fuchs had fled from Germany to Britain in 1933), Jim Skardon had at once contacted Harwell's head of security, Wing Commander Harry Arnold, a former chief of security of the RAF). A few days later Skardon traveled down to Harwell and interviewed Fuchs in Arnold's room.

It was a long and most skillful interrogation, at the end of which Skardon, having completely won Fuchs's confidence, drew from him a full confession—not only of having sold America's atomic secrets to the Russians but of continuing to feed information to Russian contacts in London pubs (much as Houghton was doing) during his time at Harwell.

Soon after, Fuchs was brought to the Atomic Energy Authority's headquarters in the Strand, where Skardon's friend, Superintendent George G. Smith of Special Branch, arrested him.

One matter, though, on which neither MI-5 nor Special Branch had been able to help the FBI occurred seven years later, when Molody's old friend and boss, Rudolf Abel, alias Emil Goldfus, was betrayed by a colleague and arrested in New York. Among his possessions was found a photograph of Morris and Lona Cohen, who, it will be recalled, fled from New York when the Yakovlev network was broken up. Was there any trace of them in Britain? asked the FBI.

After exhaustive inquiries into immigration lists and criminal records, MI-5 and Special Branch had to report that there was none. Nor can one blame them, for Peter and Helen Kroger, leading their respectable suburban lives at Ruislip, had covered their traces well.

By midmorning of the day that Skardon had received Fred Hosking's report, the first pieces of the jigsaw were being put together. The Goleniewski report had come from the American CIA, and it concerned a defector from Polish intelligence named Michael Goleniewski; under interrogation he said he believed they had a contact at the Portland naval base, but he did not know his name.

By the time Skardon had finished reading this, Houghton's personal file had arrived by special messenger from the Admiralty. Skardon, flicking through it, could hardly believe what he read. Houghton had been clerk to the naval attaché *in Warsaw* in 1952. In 1956 allegations had been made on two occasions that he had been taking papers out of the base; the matter was not thought to have any substance, but as a safety measure, Houghton had been moved soon after from the Underwater Detection Establishment to the Port Auxiliary Repair Unit.

Skardon went to the chief, and the chief said, "Well, we know what we have to do now, Jim. Watch him. Watch him twenty-four hours a day. And let Commander Evans-Jones at Special Branch know right away."

When Evans-Jones heard the news, he picked up the telephone. "Get me G. G. Smith, will you?" he said.

SUPERINTENDENT GEORGE G. SMITH was a man with an interesting past. He had been born in 1905 in the little Wiltshire village of Bratton, son of a farm laborer who maintained his wife and five children on a wage of little more than sixty pence a week.

After education at the village school, Smith became a pantry boy in one of the local big houses, but soon left for London in search of something more promising. For a time he worked as a general handyman, but jobs in the 1920s were scarce, and, attracted by the security and prospects of promotion advertised in their posters, he joined the Metropolitan Police.

His early career was spent as a uniformed officer on the beat, much of it in some of London's toughest areas; later he transferred to the CID. He proved to be a shrewd, capable officer, and just before the war he was invited to join Scotland Yard's Special Branch, who were then investigating the first of the Irish Republican Army's terrorist attacks in Britain.

Smith stayed in the Special Branch throughout the war, and worked closely with Jim Skardon and other MI-5 officers interrogating suspected German spies. With his gentle yet resolute manner he was extremely successful.

"His invariable practice," said a colleague, "was to ask the suspect to tell his story over and over again; if the story was false, there would sooner or later be contradictions which Smith would be quick to exploit."

Most CID officers transferred to Special Branch for the war returned to their former duties afterward. But Smith loved the work, and just as Skardon had been allowed to stay on in MI-5, Smith was allowed to stay on in Special Branch.

His main job was keeping surveillance on subversive elements, foreign and British, that might be harmful to national security. He rose rapidly—became chief inspector, then superintendent, and first came to national prominence when working with Skardon on the Fuchs case.

Smith's colleagues knew him as G.G., his initials. He was a large, cheerful man with a moon face, round glasses and a ready smile. He spoke with a soft west-country burr, was polite and considerate to his juniors, yet inside was tough as steel; he was not someone, as some of his colleagues testified, to cross swords with. He was a deeply religious man who rarely missed church on Sundays; yet he had a fund of barroom stories which he would tell on the slightest provocation.

So FROM NOW ON, and quite unknown to himself, Houghton was watched; watched by Jim Skardon's men in MI-5, watched by G. G. Smith's men in Special Branch, watched by Bert Smith's men in the Dorset CID.

In Weymouth, so as not to arouse suspicion, a dozen plainclothesmen, in rotating watches, had him under constant surveillance. He was followed when he picked Bunty up for work, and followed when they went home again. He was followed when he took Bunty to the pubs at lunchtime, and at any other time when he went to or from the base.

No attempt was made to spot-check his car when leaving the dockyard, for at this time MI-5's greatest need was to find out who else was involved. But his mail was examined before it reached him, and his telephone calls were tapped.

He was followed in the evenings, too, when he took Bunty to their usual pubs. He would have been surprised to know that the big, balding man sipping a pint at the bar of the Elm Tree was Superintendent Reg Smith; that the man in the funny Tyrolean hat with whom he played darts one evening was Detective Sergeant Leonard Burt; that the young couple sitting near him who seemed to have eyes only for each other were in fact watching his every move. And he would have been even more surprised to know that from dusk to dawn a car with two men in it was parked not two hundred yards from his cottage, just in case he decided to meet a contact at some secret rendezvous in the night.

But the days and weeks went by, and although it was now clear to everybody, professionals as well as amateurs, that Houghton was spending on drink each week at least half of what he was earning, not a scrap of evidence had emerged to show that his activities were anything but harmless. Were they barking up the wrong tree? the Dorset CID asked themselves. Had it all been a false alarm?

On the evening of Friday, July 1, 1960, their questions were answered for them. As Houghton and Gee were leaving the Elm Tree that night, their watcher heard Jim Crouch, the landlord, say, "Be in tomorrow, then, Harry?"

"No, not tomorrow," said Harry. "Going up to town tomorrow. Bunty and I are taking in a show."

"Well, enjoy yourselves," said Jim Crouch. "See you next week. Nighty night."

NEXT MORNING HARRY HOUGHTON was seen by a CID man disguised as a street sweeper to leave his cottage, carrying a suitcase and a blue shopping bag. He opened the doors of his garage, and a few moments later the Renault Dauphine was observed coming out of it. It turned right at the end of the lane, and a Ford V-8 came out of a side street and followed it. At the main road the Renault turned left for Weymouth.

The Ford followed the Renault into Weymouth, over a bridge and up the hill at the west end of the town, and across the Chesil Bank causeway to Portland. At a bus stop near Hambro Road a nondescript-looking man who had been keeping an eye on Bunty Gee's house for the past hour saw the Renault draw up at her door. Almost immediately Bunty came out, carrying a small case. She got into the car, which then turned back toward Weymouth. Followed by the Ford, Houghton drove the Renault to Weymouth Station and parked in the station lot. He and Bunty, with their cases and the blue shopping bag, went to the ticket office, where another man heard them buy two first-class tickets to London. This man bought himself a ticket, followed them into the train and sat down in the next compartment. In the Ford a radio message went to Dorset CID headquarters: "Contacts on eleven-thirty train Waterloo, arriving two forty." And from Dorset CID this message was at once passed to Jim Skardon at MI-5 and G. G. Smith at Special Branch.

The train arrived at Waterloo punctually. Houghton and Bunty had spent most of the journey in the dining car. The agent who had been in the train with them walked just behind them to the ticket-collection barrier, so his colleagues might recognize them.

Houghton and Bunty went first to the baggage lockers, where they deposited the blue shopping bag. An agent in a taxi outside waited to follow them, in case they took a taxi themselves. But they went to the underground instead, and booked tickets to Marble Arch. Now a scruffy-looking teddy boy and a beatniky girl friend took up the trail.

At Marble Arch, they made their way to the Cumberland Hotel, booked into a double room and went upstairs. Half an hour later they came down and returned to the underground station.

This time they were followed by a middle-aged couple. When the man heard them book tickets for Waterloo, he thought something must have gone wrong. Having just come from Waterloo, why were they going back there? Did Houghton think he had been spotted? The man said to his companion, "Get in touch with the office and tell them what's happening. I'll stay with them as long as I can."

At the Waterloo ticket-collection barrier, the agent heard Houghton say to Bunty, "Let's go to the main-line station, then we shall know where we are." The agent thought they would be returning to the baggage lockers, but instead they walked down the tunnel into Waterloo Road. There he heard Houghton say, "This is the way we took last time."

Houghton and Gee walked down the Waterloo Road. The agent who had been with them in the tube had dropped out now, his place taken by a man in a dirty yellow mackintosh; another agent, in workman's clothes, followed him.

Outside the Old Vic theater, Houghton and Gee were greeted by a third party, a chunky, dark-haired man wearing a blue gabardine mac. The three, said the agent in the yellow mackintosh later, "seemed to be well known to each other." He was quite right; they were. He watched them walk over to a small park and sit down on a bench. There the stranger gave Houghton a white envelope, which he put in his inside coat pocket.

It was now a little after four o'clock. Houghton got up, left the other two on the bench and went down Waterloo Road to the station. He was followed by the man in workman's clothes. He was seen to retrieve his blue shopping bag from the baggage locker, then return by the same route to the bench. Here he handed the bag to the stranger. They continued chatting for quite a time, with Gee and the stranger dominating the conversation, the agent noted.

At five p.m., exactly one hour after they had first met, the stranger left. He was shadowed separately by two agents, who observed that at every corner he turned as though to see whether he was being followed.

He walked around the area for some ten minutes and then came to his Standard car, license number WCV 700. The agents noted that it was only a hundred and fifty yards from the park bench, and that during the ten-minute walk the stranger had passed the car once already. The Standard moved away from the curb, and at the next corner a van pulled out and followed it.

That evening Houghton and Gee were followed to the Albert Hall, where they saw the Russian ballet, and followed again the next day when they returned to Weymouth.

On the Monday afternoon there was a conference at MI-5. The chief of MI-5 was there, and Commander Evans-Jones—the head of Special Branch—G. G. Smith, Skardon, the director of naval security and several others.

"Well, Jim," said the chief, "what have you discovered?"

"The man's a Canadian," said Skardon, "called Gordon Lonsdale. We followed him to a block of flats called the White House in Regent's Park. He used to live there when he first came to London five years ago, and has recently moved back. We've checked with the immigration people and with Canada House, and it seems his passport was issued in Toronto in 1955. Born September 27, 1924, near Cobalt in Ontario. Father Canadian, mother Finnish. Passport renewed here in 1960. He has a job with a firm that has offices in Wardour Street called Allo Security. Apparently they make antiburglar devices for cars."

There was a murmur of laughter around the table.

"Anything else?"

"Yes. About half an hour after he got back to the White House he came out again, got into his car and headed west. We tailed him as far as the White City station, but he was using the usual dodges to throw people off—turning down side streets and back onto the main road, that sort of thing. If we'd have gone any further, he'd have spotted us. Next time we'll arrange more cars."

Evans-Jones said, "It looks as though we're on to something big."

The chief said, "Yes, and we've got to take our time in finding out how big. Don't forget he's a professional. One boob on our part, and he'll have gone."

The director of naval security said icily, "And meantime, how many more secrets are you going to allow out of Portland?"

"I fear that's a risk we've got to take," said the chief.

Evans-Jones said, "What we have to find out is what he's doing with the stuff that Houghton's handing over. Whether he's operating alone or has other contacts, and if so, who they are and where."

"Exactly," said the chief. "And that's going to mean time and men. It means from now on, not only watching Houghton twenty-four hours a day, but watching Lonsdale too. We've got the time, at least a bit of time, but have we got the men?"

He looked at Smith and Skardon.

"We'll find them," said Smith.

"Between the two of us," said Skardon.

So THE MEN (and women) were found, and Lonsdale was watched and followed to the extent that his methods of work allowed. As with Houghton, his mail was examined at the G.P.O. sorting office, and his telephone conversations both at the White House and elsewhere were monitored.

In Wardour Street there is a pub called the Falcon, and the day after the conference, one of Smith's men called on the proprietor, Major Bryan Mattocks, to tell him that detectives wished to keep observation on the offices opposite, and the best vantage point seemed to be the window above the door. In the heart of Soho such a request seemed perfectly reasonable. The room was the bedroom of Major Mattocks' eleven-year-old son, Scott, who, having been sworn to secrecy, was thrilled to find himself caught up in a real live detective drama.

Two women agents moved into his room each day, bringing with them a pair of binoculars to observe any new contacts that Molody might make, and a two-way radio to report to the Yard his movements in and out of the office. Farther down the street was a parked car (a different one each day, containing different agents and parked at different places) ready to trail Molody if he left in his own car.

The manager of the White House was also contacted and sworn

to secrecy. From him the agents obtained skeleton keys to enter Molody's present flat, number 634, while he was under observation in Wardour Street; should Molody decide suddenly to return, the two-way radio system would give the "burglars" plenty of warning. The flat was searched most thoroughly, but apart from the headphones for the radio set and a length of aerial in a cabinet (neither very unusual), nothing of interest was found.

That was how Molody intended it. He knew, as every spy knows, that one day agents or police might come to his apartment and search it; and if they did, he wanted to ensure that they went away empty-handed. That was why Molody had hidden nearly two thousand dollars in cash inside the Chinese scroll that hung above his bed; hidden a set of radio signal plans in a secret cavity at the base of a table lighter; hidden a microdot reader and more signal plans in the false bottom of a tin of Yardley's talcum powder.

And Molody was right in his assumptions; the searchers found none of these things.

Indeed, apart from a Telex from Toronto stating that the man Gordon Lonsdale had given as reference for his passport application had never heard of him, nothing further emerged against him. Nothing in his mail aroused suspicion, nor in his telephone calls, which were mostly about business matters and to girls. He met no new contacts in the Wardour Street office or anywhere else.

As the hot July days dragged by, the watchers and their bosses, who had started off in such high spirits, felt somehow let down; they had expected so much more. But lack of success only strengthened their resolve; a clever spy he might be, and therefore a hard man to catch, but they would surely catch him in the end.

MI-5 HAD NOTED that the first meeting between Houghton and his contact had taken place on the first Saturday in July. Would the same thing happen on the first Saturday in August?

Because of this possibility, the watchers outside Houghton's cottage on the morning of Saturday, August 6, were more alert than usual. Nor were they disappointed. At a little after noon Houghton emerged from the cottage, backed the Renault out of the garage and headed toward Weymouth.

The waiting Jaguar gave him a hundred yards' clearance, then followed. The two men inside expected Houghton to go on to Portland to pick up Bunty Gee, but instead he drove straight to the station and parked his car. There he was observed boarding the twelve-thirty train to London, arriving at three forty. He was carrying a large brown leather grip.

At Waterloo there were seven agents waiting for him in a variety of strange clothes. They observed him do exactly what he had done before—walk down the tunnel to the Waterloo Road and make his way to the Old Vic. The previous meeting there had been at four p.m., and so was this one.

Molody appeared from nowhere, and the two men at once started walking down the road, not this time into the little park but toward the Lower Marsh district.

They stopped once briefly when Molody was seen to hand something to Houghton, then made their way to a workmen's café called Steves Restaurant, sat down at a table and ordered a pot of tea.

Two apparent workmen came in and sat at the next table. The watch one of them was wearing was not a watch but a disguised tape recorder.

When the tea had come, Molody pointed to Houghton's leather grip and said, "You seem to have plenty in there."

"Yes," said Houghton with a knowing smile, "I have more than my sleeping and shaving kit."

They talked about two American code clerks who the papers said had deserted to the Soviet Union. Molody wondered if the report were correct, and Houghton said he thought it was.

Then Molody said, "We can now arrange our future meetings if that suits you. Neither of us wants wasted journeys because of misunderstandings over dates."

"Okay," said Houghton, taking an envelope from his pocket. "I'll make a note of them, because they'll be difficult to remember."

Molody said, "Make a note of the first Saturday in each month, especially the first Saturday in October and November, at Euston. The driver will stay in the car, but I don't know where yet. I'm ninety percent certain I'll be there." (Molody said this because he had been told by the Center that he might have to make a trip to the Continent.)

They finished their tea and paid the bill: one shilling ninepence.

As Houghton picked up his grip, Molody looked at it again and said, "It's certainly fat. I see I'll have plenty of work to do tonight."

"Oh, yes," said Houghton, laughing. "You'll be burning the midnight oil. By the way, that room at the hotel is expensive."

"That's okay," said Molody. "That will be taken care of."

They went into the street. The two agents continued to sit at their table; they knew there were others outside.

Molody and Houghton walked down several streets until they came to a telephone kiosk in Baylis Road. Molody held the door of the kiosk and Houghton went inside. Molody handed Houghton a newspaper. Houghton opened his grip, took out a parcel, wrapped it in the newspaper and handed it back to Molody. Then they walked back to Waterloo Road and parted.

That evening Houghton went to the Cumberland Hotel, where he had a date with a piece of crumpet from South Africa.

Molody went back to the White House, then headed west again in his car. Now there were several cars available to follow him. They kept in touch as far as Hanger Lane, Ealing, on the A40 to Oxford; but a second time, to avoid arousing his suspicions, they called off the chase.

ONCE AGAIN THE hot summer days went by; once again Molody was watched without result; once again there was a top-level conference.

This time there was a full admiral present, and when Skardon and Smith had made their reports, the admiral said, "On behalf of the naval board and the chief of the defense staff, I have to say how deeply concerned we are at the present situation. On two occasions now, Houghton is believed to have handed over information from Portland to the agent of a foreign power—at any rate, he has been observed handing over *something*. I don't have to remind you that at Portland we are conducting the most advanced experiments in underwater weapons warfare anywhere in the world. The Russians—and the director of naval security will correct me if I am wrong—are still nowhere near us."

The DNS looked at his papers and nodded.

"If we continue," went on the admiral, "to allow information from Portland to be passed over—and we don't know what has been passed already—we are in danger of nullifying all our own work, imperiling our safety and that of our allies. To allow this sort of thing to go on seems to us sheer madness. Can we have a firm assurance that next time Houghton is observed handing over papers to this man Lonsdale, they will both be apprehended and arrested?"

The representative from the Prime Minister's office said, "The Prime Minister is also extremely concerned. I have to report to him immediately after this meeting. The matter will come up in Cabinet tomorrow."

The head of Special Branch said, "Please don't think that we are unaware of your concern, nor that MI-5 and we don't share it ourselves. But let me explain the legal position. Lonsdale is a highly professional spy. He is a man who leaves no traces. We have searched his flat, examined his mail, monitored his telephone calls and followed him practically everywhere. But of all this not a scrap of evidence has emerged against him. All we have at the moment are the two meetings with Houghton. If, as the admiral suggests, we arrest them at their next meeting, they may or may not have incriminating material on them. Even if they do have, it may not be sufficient to convict on its own. If they don't have—it's not a certainty—then we shall have nothing to hold Lonsdale on, or Houghton either. We shall have lost two spies."

"But kept our secrets," said the admiral.

"There's another thing," said the chief of MI-5. "We're convinced that Lonsdale has other contacts in this country, but because he's so cunning, we don't yet know who they are. For instance, at last time's meeting, Houghton was seen to hand a parcel to Lonsdale. We followed Lonsdale back to the White House. Later that evening he went out in his car. We followed him as far as Ealing, but he uses so many dodges to mislead pursuers that we had to call the chase off so as not to alarm him. While he was away, another search was made of his flat. There wasn't a trace of the parcel. Now where was it? We think he may have been taking it to some other contact for duplication and inward transmission. Where is this contact? Somewhere off the A40, we believe. Each time we've been able to get a little nearer. Next time perhaps we'll find out."

"Perhaps," said the admiral, "and then perhaps not."

"Please don't think we underestimate the importance of Portland," said the chief. "We're only too aware of it. But for all we know, Lonsdale may have contacts in just as vital fields—nuclear weapons, experiments in germ warfare, anything. If he does, we feel we must give ourselves a chance to find out."

The head of Special Branch said, "It's a very finely balanced affair, as you can see, but I do give you my assurance that as soon as it's possible to move, we shall do so."

As the meeting broke up, the admiral said, "I can't say I like it."

The chief of MI-5 said, "None of us do. But what's the alternative? Let's hope something turns up next time."

AND SURE ENOUGH, something did turn up, although not quite as expected.

At one thirty p.m. on August 26, the watchers outside the White House saw Molody come out carrying a brown attaché case and a gray-looking metal box. He put them on the front passenger seat of his Standard car, then drove by a roundabout route to his bank—the Midland—at 159 Great Portland Street. He took the case and the box into the bank, and was heard telling the clerk that he wanted them kept in safe custody while he was abroad. The clerk took possession of them and gave Molody a receipt.

Forty-eight hours later, Molody left Heathrow for an extended holiday in Prague with Galisha and the children. With his property still in the bank, MI-5 had few worries about his not returning. But what was in the property he had left? What was so important that it needed the protection of a bank?

Superintendent G. G. Smith went to the magistrate at Bow Street and applied in private for a warrant to search "a brown attaché case and a gray metal box, the property of Gordon Lonsdale, at present in the Midland Bank." He added, "I have reason to believe that this man may be engaged in activities prejudicial to the safety of the country."

From the bank's manager, Mr. Leonard Easter, who was sworn to secrecy, Smith collected the brown case (which was marked SKYWAY) and the metal box and took them to Scotland Yard. There they were placed on a table side by side. A photographer was present, and a man with skeleton keys. The man with the keys opened each of the cases. The photographer took several pictures of the inside of the case, then of each object as it was removed, and again of the inside of the case after it had been removed. In this way all the objects would be returned to the positions in which Molody had put them.

It was an important if not a wildly exciting find. Inside the attaché case were a black bag for changing films, a Praktina camera with a number of lenses, a magnifying glass, a silver table lighter, two cassettes, some keys and—most significant—a piece of paper listing various street names in southwestern London.

To Smith and his men there seemed no reason for any of these things to be placed in custody at the bank except perhaps the table lighter. And the table lighter turned out to be the most valuable thing indeed; for in a secret cavity in its base was a list of coded radio signal numbers. The metal box contained nothing but Molody's false papers—that he was Gordon Lonsdale, a Canadian by birth and a sales manager.

WHILE MOLODY WAS holidaying with his family in Prague, what was Houghton doing? Did the pattern of first-Saturday-in-the-month meetings continue as before or, now that Molody was out of the country, were they in abeyance?

This is Houghton's version of events.* The first Saturday in September, when he claims to have met two of his previous Russian contacts—Roman, and a man called John, who with his wife had once visited him at Broadwey. Roman drove John to a rendezvous with Houghton at the Chessington zoo:

> On this occasion I gave John an envelope containing documents and films, and he asked if I'd be going on to London after our meeting. I said I planned to see a friend in town later that evening and he asked for a lift as far as the Robin Hood Gate. . . .
> We had a 'business' discussion in the car, made arrangements for our next meeting, and drove off to the Robin Hood Gate. On arrival, John said he was a little early, so we had a drink together and then left the pub at 9 pm. . . . I . . . watched him leave in a car, not the same one which he'd had on arrival at Chessington—but again driven by Roman.
> The arrangement we had made was for me to meet John at the

---

* *Operation Portland: The Autobiography of a Spy.*

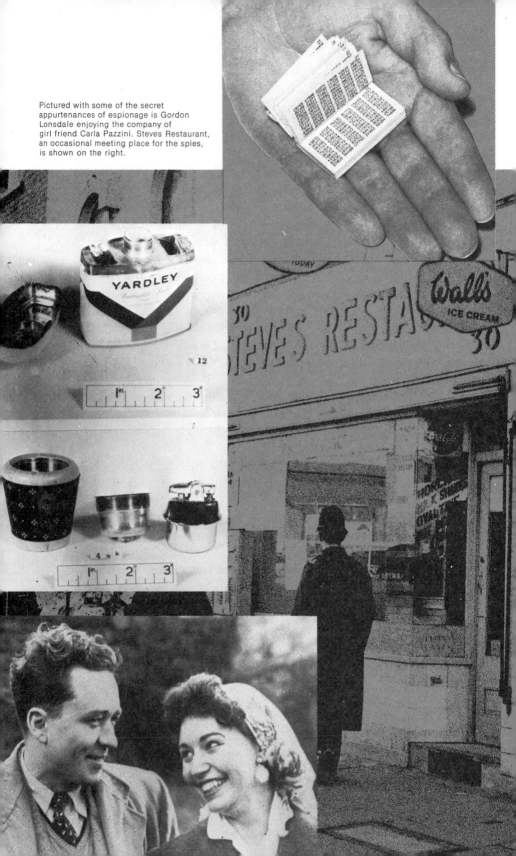

Pictured with some of the secret
appurtenances of espionage is Gordon
Lonsdale enjoying the company of
girl friend Carla Pazzini. Steves Restaurant,
an occasional meeting place for the spies,
is shown on the right.

back of Selfridges the next morning, Sunday, when he would return the envelope and supply more films. After a night in London, drinking with some friends in the Players Club and then sleeping at the Victory Ex-Services Club, I picked up John and drove him round a couple of blocks to make sure we weren't being observed before I took back the envelope.

And his account of events on the first Saturday in October—a day, it will be recalled, that one of the agents in Steves Restaurant heard Molody arrange for a rendezvous at Euston:

Arriving at 4 pm I found Roman himself near the station, and after checking as far as possible that we were not being observed— no mean task in the Euston bustle—we walked a few hundred yards to his car. Roman was the driver mentioned by Gordon in the café and duly recorded by the eavesdropper.

We drove off and eventually headed north on the Al. When I queried this change of stamping ground, Roman said we had been meeting on the south side of London too frequently, and in any event he personally was more familiar with the north side. Leaving the Al, we drove down several side roads, finally drawing up near a gate into a field. We strolled in this field and conducted our business there, keeping the car in view. . . .

By this time it was almost dark. Having settled all outstanding points, Roman drove us to a pleasant country restaurant where we had dinner. Over the meal I remarked that, apart from catching a glimpse of him a couple of times last month when he drove John to meet me, or to pick John up, I hadn't seen him for some time. What had he been doing with himself? . . .

He explained that he had been home on leave. I must have looked incredulous—him, and now Gordon? He assured me that secret agents on foreign service had what we in England would call a leave entitlement. . . . He had been to Yalta, and in view of his dangerous occupation was given an extended stay. . . .

After this leisurely dinner he drove me to Wembley, where I got a train to the West End. Next morning he picked me up in Seymour Street at the bottom of the Edgware Road, gave me back the documents he had photographed, and dropped me near Waterloo. I got the train to Salisbury, picked up my car, and was back in Weymouth at about 2.30 pm.

Although Houghton is a great fancifier, there are two reasons for thinking his accounts of these events are true. Firstly, the first-Saturday-in-the-month pattern had been already established and could be expected to be repeated. Secondly, as regards the Euston meeting, MI-5 themselves had reason to believe from their own agents that this would take place. Why, then, was Houghton not followed on either occasion?

There are two possible explanations: one, that he was followed but on both occasions lost; the other, that MI-5, knowing that Houghton's contact was out of the country, assumed there would be no other contact to take his place. Either way it would seem as though they erred, and that if they hadn't, then, in Houghton's words, "they could have put Roman, John and possibly John's wife in the bag as well."

IT WAS ON OCTOBER 23 at Heathrow airport that Molody, clutching his bogus Canadian passport, was observed by Special Branch returning through passport control. Word was immediately flashed to Scotland Yard, and the watchers outside the White House, in Major Mattocks' pub and elsewhere, took up their stations again.

Next day Molody was trailed to the Midland Bank, where he picked up the brown case and the gray metal box and with them walked down Great Portland Street and along Oxford Street to his office in Soho.

The watchers in the Falcon saw him enter and an hour later saw him leave. He walked to the Piccadilly underground station, now carrying only a briefcase, and the woman behind him in the ticket-office queue, wearing a head scarf and carrying a shopping basket, heard him ask for a ticket to Ruislip. When he was on his way to the escalators, she moved out of the queue, walked swiftly to the nearest telephone booth and put through a call to the Yard.

Meanwhile, two men behind her in the queue, one wearing a bowler hat and carrying a rolled umbrella, the other a spotty, unshaven youth, had also booked tickets—one to Ruislip, the other to Uxbridge, at the end of the line.

The spotty youth got into the same coach as Molody, so as to trail him should he suddenly get out at any station before Ruislip; the businessman entered the coach ahead.

But Molody, behind his *Evening Standard,* must have felt secure, for he remained in his seat for the whole of the thirty-five-minute journey. At Ruislip, the spotty youth stayed where he was; the businessman in the next coach alighted and followed Molody through the ticket barrier. He kept with him along Station Road, leftward at the main road and over the bridge. There he branched off to the left, knowing that the man in overalls on the other side of the road was about to take his place.

As usual, Molody made a detour of the area, doubling back on himself frequently as a matter of routine, often glancing behind him to see if he were being followed. But agents in various shapes or forms kept up with him until he reached Willow Gardens, where a little footpath runs through to the cul-de-sac end of Cranley Drive.

The first house on the right was the Krogers', the first on the left the Searches'; but to have followed the suspect along the footpath might have seemed too obvious, and so once again, and this time on the Krogers' very doorstep, the chase was called off.

AT SCOTLAND YARD, G. G. Smith had recently been joined by Chief Inspector Ferguson Smith, who in September had been away on leave. "Fergie" Smith was an Aberdonian who had gone south in 1934 to join the Metropolitan Police, had later transferred to Special Branch because of his interest in politics and languages (he spoke French and German) and, apart from the war, had been in Special Branch ever since. During the war he had flown in Bomber Command, jamming the German night-fighter controllers, and for this he won a DFC and Bar. He had already worked with G.G. on the Fuchs case.

"Fergie," said G.G., "you know those street names and numbers we found in Lonsdale's case in the bank?"

"Yes, sir."

"Well, there's a lot of pressure building to get results, and we've taken a decision to watch them. It's a pretty long shot, but it's possible something might turn up. It might lead us to other contacts."

"But there are a dozen street names on that list."

"I know."

"With respect, sir, where are we going to find the people? With the White House and Soho, and now Ruislip to keep an eye on, we've just about got everyone tied up."

G.G. thought for a moment. Then he said, "What about the wives?"

"Wives, sir?"

"The wives of our people. They know what their husbands do, and the need for discretion. All we have to do is place them in various vantage points overlooking the streets in question, ask them to keep a lookout for Lonsdale and anyone he meets, then let us know immediately."

"It's a bit unusual, isn't it?"

"It's an unusual situation, and a pretty urgent one. Why don't we sound them out and see if they're willing?"

Without exception, the wives proved more than willing. And so a small female army was recruited and sent to various carefully chosen locations in southwest London where householders had agreed to let them keep observation from front rooms.

The watches were kept in rotation, one or two days a week for each wife. Some wives with small children were so keen to be included that they persuaded neighbors to look after the children for the day. In prospect it seemed an exciting venture; in reality it was a long and tiring business, sitting at the windows of unfamiliar rooms, knitting or listening to the radio to help pass the time, forcing themselves to keep their concentration on the comings and goings in the street. Only once was their patience rewarded, when Houghton was observed on his way to a meeting at the Maypole. But he was already under observation from a trailing car.

Came the first Saturday in November—the fifth—and near Houghton's cottage in Meadowview Road the watchers waited for him to follow his now established pattern. But the morning rolled by and he remained indoors.

The watchers were beginning to reconcile themselves to a blank day when soon after one p.m. Houghton came out of the cottage, got into the Renault and drove off. A Rover parked by the railway bridge let him pass, then followed. The two men inside expected him to turn left at the main-road T junction, either to go to Portland to pick up Bunty or to drive to the station. Instead, he turned right, toward London.

For ten miles the Rover followed, keeping in touch with headquarters by radio. Then came a message: "Base to X-2."

"X-2 to base. Over."

"X-5 is behind you, will shortly overtake. Then return."

"Roger."

A couple of minutes later, a Ford station wagon, driven by a man wearing a tweed cap and smoking a pipe, shot past the Rover and closed on the Renault, now half a mile ahead. The Rover slowed down and at the next side road reversed, turned back toward Weymouth.

Ten miles farther on, the same maneuver was repeated.

"Base to X-5."

"X-5 to base. Over."

"X-3 is in B3390 at junction with A35. When you go by, he will pull out and overtake. Then return. Over."

"Roger."

And so a succession of cars and vans of varying ages and descriptions kept doggedly on Houghton's tail. At Ringwood, he parked outside the St. Leonard's Hotel and, just before closing time, entered the saloon bar. While one man kept an eye on him by the door, the other strolled over to the Renault and noticed on the back seat a cardboard box and a black leather briefcase. He returned to his own car and presently was joined by his companion. Soon after, Houghton climbed into the Renault and the pursuit was renewed.

At Alresford, Houghton stopped outside the public lavatories and went inside. Naturally, his watchers assumed his visit had only one purpose, but according to him he had had instructions to pick up a packet there, as he had done before; this was one reason why he was motoring to London instead of going by train. He picked up the packet, the size of a tobacco tin, from behind the door, put it in his pocket and returned to the car.

On arrival in the London area, Houghton was seen to go first to 39 Aylward Road, S.W., where he arrived at five p.m. and left just before six. He was visiting a cousin. He then drove to the scene of previous meetings, the Maypole pub at Hook, which he reached just before six thirty. Here he was seen to walk up and down as though waiting for someone, and a minute or two later Molody appeared on foot, carrying a briefcase. The two men got into the Renault and, after driving in what one of the agents called "a wide circle," eventually stopped in an unlighted part of South-borough Road.

Here, unseen by the agents, they conducted their business. Hough-ton handed over the black leather case, containing documents and film; Molody handed over his briefcase, containing Houghton's money and documents now ready to be returned to Portland. There were also instructions for further meetings.

By the light of the lamp on the dashboard Houghton wrote down, "Seven or eight next meeting. Next meeting place on Saturday or noon Sunday. If torn, seven or eight next day or same day. If lose contact first Sunday each month, noon and 1 p.m. Punch." Punch meant that Houghton should carry a copy of *Punch* in his hand, so that if Molody were unable to come, any new contact would recog-nize him.

At about seven ten p.m., after remaining stationary for half an hour, the Renault was seen moving again, and was followed back to the Maypole. The two men went inside, stayed a further half hour drinking, then reentered the car and left. After about half a mile the Renault stopped and Molody climbed out.

Now that the two hunted ones had split, which should the hunt-ers follow? An urgent request for instructions was passed by radio, and the reply was swift and unequivocal: Lonsdale. Houghton had done his work for the day, Lonsdale's life and other contacts were still largely a mystery. Undoubtedly the decision was correct; and yet, had Houghton done his work for the day? According to him he traveled on to London, and later that evening, unobserved by any agents, visited the Bunch of Grapes pub to hand over to a differ-ent contact the packet he had collected that afternoon in the lava-tory in Alresford.

With Molody the watchers had better luck. Soon after leaving Houghton he was observed entering another car. This was a big Canadian car—a Studebaker, license number ULA 61, which he had recently bought in part exchange for his Standard at a garage in the Harrow Road. It was a suitable car for a Canadian but, being large and distinctive, less so for a spy. The pursuers had a further advantage in that it was a night of driving rain, which reduced visi-bility and clouded over rear windows.

They kept on his tail, and soon it became apparent that he was not heading back to the White House but somewhere out of London to the west. At the Chiswick roundabout, he took the North Circular to Hanger Lane; at Hanger Lane, he turned left along the A40 to Oxford.

At Scotland Yard, G. G. Smith, listening to the message coming in, said, "It looks like Ruislip again. What's the name of that place we lost him last time?"

"Willow Gardens, sir. Footpath leading into Cranley Drive."

"Well, have somebody stationed in Cranley Drive in case he pops through again."

"Rawlinson and Baker are on their way, sir. We're putting them in Courtfield Gardens, which leads out of Cranley Drive. Baker's got a dog."

"So have I, and about half the population."

"Excuse for an evening stroll, sir. Taking Bonzo out for walky-walkies."

"Oh, good!"

And it happened almost as planned. Molody parked the Studebaker in Willow Gardens, then, carrying Houghton's leather case, cut through the footpath to Cranley Drive. Twenty yards up the street a man in an old tweed coat was strolling slowly, holding on a leash a dog of indeterminate age and origins. Molody didn't notice the man, but the man saw Molody turn sharp right at the end of the footpath, walk up the little drive that led to the front door of number 45, all the time glancing furtively around him. When he reached the door, it was opened for him; and Molody, with another batch of secrets for Russia, disappeared quickly inside.

Now that his pursuers knew where their quarry had gone to ground, it was necessary to see how long he would remain. Clearly the best vantage point for observing the house was 1 Courtfield Gardens. This information was passed to MI-5, who telephoned Mr. Search, just home from Birmingham, to say that a man engaged in a certain case would soon be arriving at his house, and please to give him any facilities he asked.

A few minutes later, an agent did turn up and asked if he could keep observation from a front window—though observation on what he did not say.

The lights burned late in 45 Cranley Drive that night; the Studebaker stayed put in Willow Gardens. At eleven a.m. on the Sunday morning a man was seen approaching the house with a batch of books, and left at one fifty p.m. At two ten Molody, refreshed by a long lie, was observed going to his car, once again looking around him. In a few minutes he returned to the house. He didn't leave for London until the evening.

And that same evening, at 8 Meadowview Road, Houghton said to Bunty Gee, "I saw Alec Johnson in London yesterday and gave him that last lot of stuff."

"What did he say?"

"Oh, he was tickled pink. Sent you his love and asked me to give you all his grateful thanks."

"That's nice, isn't it? Seems a shame he can't get what he wants from those people in the Admiralty. Still, it's nice to think we're able to help him, isn't it?"

"He said something about giving you a present."

"He gave me a present, don't you remember, Harry? That nice powder compact."

"This is something different. A cash grant or something. It seems they have a special fund for this sort of thing."

"I don't want paying, Harry. I'm only too pleased to be of use."

"I think he might be offended if you refused. And anyway, you don't want to look a gift horse in the mouth, eh, Bunty?"

"Oh, well, Harry, whatever you think is right."

And a little later, three hundred pounds was paid into Bunty's account at the Midland Bank, Weymouth.

WITHIN THE NEXT forty-eight hours a number of things happened.

At a Cabinet meeting the Prime Minister said, "Now that the security people have found out what they think may be the center of a large network, they strongly recommend keeping a watch on it, so as to see if anyone else turns up."

He turned to the Minister of Defense. "I don't suppose your people will be too happy about that?"

"They're getting pretty worried, Prime Minister, and last week's events haven't made them less so. Of course, we're keeping any really vital material out of Gee's hands, but there's a limit to what we can do without her getting the wind up. And even then we can't be certain. We'd like to see it wrapped up."

"So would we all. But my advice from the intelligence services is that we must hold on a bit longer."

In Mayfair, the chief of MI-5 said to Skardon, "What do we know about the occupants of Forty-five Cranley Drive?"

"Not much. Name of Kroger. Middle-aged couple, both Canadians. He's a secondhand bookseller, used to have an office in the Strand, doesn't any longer. No children. They've been there five years. Nobody seems to know their history before that."

"Any gen on them from Canada House?"

"Not a thing. They've never heard of them."

"We must get photographs. The FBI may be able to give us a lead. And, Jim, we've got to keep that house under constant surveillance."

"We've already had a man in the house opposite. People called Search live there. He's a gas-turbine engineer. Married, with two teenage children. I suggest we put a permanent team in."

"Are they reliable?"

"Hard to say yet, but I would guess so."

"It may be a long watch, Jim. And we shall have to have relays of people. If the Searches aren't to get suspicious and start blabbing to the neighbors, we shall have to put them in the picture."

"All right, sir."

"Why don't you and Charles go down there and ask them out to lunch? I'm told the food at the Bull at Gerrard's Cross is very good."

So over smoked salmon and lamb cutlets at the Bull, the two men from MI-5 gently broke their news to the Searches.

"Mr. Search, how well do you know the Krogers who live opposite you?"

"We've known them since they came to live there. My wife really sees more of them than I do, being away such a lot."

"I see Helen two or three times a week," said Mrs. Search. "She's always popping over to the kitchen for coffee and a chat. She seems very fond of my daughter, Gay, too, and gives her little presents of nail varnish and sweets and so on. Auntie Helen, my daughter calls her. She has no children of her own, you know." She broke off to look at the faces of her two hosts. "But why do you ask about the

Krogers? These inquiries of yours are to do with drugs, aren't they? Or so I've been told."

"We had to tell you that initially, Mrs. Search," said Skardon, "because we were very pressed for time. No, they're not to do with drugs. They're to do with the Krogers."

Mr. Search said, "What are the Krogers supposed to have done?"

MI-5 had thought out very carefully what they were going to tell the Searches, and Skardon said, "They are not supposed to have done anything. But we're afraid they may be—quite unknowingly—being used by foreign agents."

"You mean Russians?" said Mr. Search.

"We don't know."

"Used in what way?"

"We don't know that either. But we have to know who are coming to see them." Skardon produced a couple of photographs of Molody, taken in the Wardour Street office by telephoto lens. "Have you ever seen that man before?"

"No," said Mr. Search. Mrs. Search shook her head.

"What do you want us to do?" asked Mr. Search.

"We'd like to have two men in the house during daylight hours. If it won't be too much of a nuisance for your daughter, we'd like to put them in that little room of hers overlooking Cranley Drive. They'll have binoculars and a special telephone to talk to us. And they'll bring their own food."

"How long will this be for?" said Mrs. Search.

"Impossible to say at the moment. But probably several weeks."

"Several *weeks!*" said Mr. Search.

Skardon's companion said, "We do realize how much this is going to inconvenience you. But I promise you we wouldn't be asking you if it wasn't something absolutely vital to the national interest."

"What do we tell the children?" said Mrs. Search.

"Just continue with the drugs story," said Skardon. "That's something they'll understand. And don't say anything about the Krogers. Say our people are watching that big block of flats behind your house. And of course not a word about any of this to anyone. I can't stress how important secrecy is."

Mr. Search nodded. Mrs. Search said, "What happens when Helen comes over unexpectedly? What shall I say to her?"

"Just behave as you would normally. It's very important."

"Well, I'll do my best," said Mrs. Search, "but I can't say I look forward to it."

On the way home Mr. Search said to his wife, "Good heavens! To think of Peter and Helen mixed up in something like this. What an extraordinary business."

THE AGENTS CAME IN two by two—two in the morning, two at midday, two in the afternoon. They set themselves up in Gay's little bedroom, with their binoculars and cameras and special telephone sets, thermos flasks and packets of sandwiches.

After a few days it was felt that so many men turning up regularly at the house might lead neighbors to wonder if the Searches had started a house of ill fame, and it was decided to switch to women instead. If people asked questions, they were to be told the women were new members of the Ruislip Art Society, come to see the secretary, Mrs. Search.

They were all pleasant, ordinary young women in their late twenties and early thirties, with names like Pat and Joyce, and after the novelty had worn off, the Searches became accustomed to their presence. Even Gay and Philip, who had been quite excited by their arrival (but sworn personally by Jim Skardon not to breathe a word to anyone), came to regard their presence as perfectly normal. After a time the women did most of their watching from the kitchen window.

Once Mrs. Search asked one of them if she liked her job, and she replied that it was better than some they got, like hiding in the backs of trucks. Mrs. Search wondered why she had to hide in a truck, but felt it would be improper to ask.

Although Mrs. Search had dreaded her first visit from Helen Kroger, she had prepared herself mentally for it, and it passed off better than she expected. One advantage was that, as usual, Helen did most of the talking, and she had only to respond. All the same, she did find it hard to look Helen in the face.

Despite what Skardon had said about the Krogers being used, it was hard to believe they were not involved in some way. Had Skardon deliberately played down the Krogers so as to make things easier? Could it really be possible that Helen and Peter were quite different people from the couple they thought they had known over all these years? She didn't really know what to think; it was better not to look farther than the end of every day.

IN MAYFAIR, THE chief of MI-5 said to Skardon, "Jim, do the names of Morris and Lona Cohen say anything to you?"

Skardon thought. "Not off the top of my head, they don't."

"Remember what they found on Rudolf Abel when the FBI arrested him?"

"Of course. Their photographs. The same pair who skedaddled when the Yakovlev ring was smashed."

"Right. And guess where they are now."

"You tell me."

The chief passed over two sets of photographs, one of the Cohens found on Abel, the other of the Krogers taken from Gay's bedroom window.

"Good God!" said Skardon.

"That's where they are now," said the chief. "Forty-five Cranley Drive."

ALTHOUGH THE SECURITY people were fully expecting Houghton to travel to London on the first Saturday in December, the third of the month, he and Bunty remained that weekend in Weymouth. This was the first time in nearly six months that he had broken the pattern. Had he got the wind up, cottoned on to being followed? Had his contact Lonsdale warned him to stay away? MI-5 spent an uneasy week hoping they had not missed the bus. Relief did not come until a week later, Saturday, December 10, when once again Houghton was followed to Portland to pick up Bunty, trailed to Weymouth Station and the London train.

As soon as this news reached G.G. and Skardon, men in various disguises were sent out into the Waterloo Road and the area of the Old Vic.

At three twenty p.m. Molody's Studebaker was observed going past the Old Vic. A quarter of an hour later it was seen doing the same thing, this time, said the agent, "with the driver appearing to look for someone." At three thirty-eight Molody was seen walking north along Waterloo Road, holding a shopping bag which, said the agent, "seemed to be well filled." He entered the station, where another agent saw him studying the arrivals indicator. This showed the Weymouth train running half an hour late. Molody then left the station and walked back down Waterloo Road.

The train finally arrived at four thirty. Houghton and Gee walked down the tunnel to the Waterloo Road and turned right toward the Old Vic. Molody meanwhile had returned to the Old Vic himself, hung about there for a few minutes, then began walking south on Waterloo Road. Houghton and Gee were temporarily lost sight of. When next observed, all three were walking together up Waterloo Road and eventually entered a pub near the Festival Hall.

The three sat down at a table in the corner: Houghton, who knew Molody as Lonsdale; Gee, who knew him as Johnson; and Molody, who alone knew he was Molody. From his shopping bag he produced a square box which contained a special camera for photographing documents (this was before the days of the Xerox copying machines). Did Houghton think he would be able to use it? Houghton, who had some time previously lost the Exakta camera with which he had photographed earlier documents, said he thought he could, and the box was handed over. Molody also handed over an envelope containing a questionnaire which he hoped Houghton and Gee between them might answer.

"Our people will be real grateful," he told Gee, "if you can help us out with this one."

Houghton went to the bar to buy a round of drinks, and when he came back, Molody was asking Bunty if she knew the differences between American asdic sets and British ones. She replied, truthfully, that she didn't.

Later Houghton and Bunty went for an evening on the town; Molody took the Studebaker down to Ruislip to transmit to the Center the latest intelligence, then spend a relaxing weekend with the Krogers.

AT MIDNIGHT, UNKNOWN to the occupants of 45 Cranley Drive, two apparently innocent-looking furniture vans were parked in two side streets, one half a mile to the north of the house, the other the same distance to the west. There was no furniture in either of the vans. There was, instead, a crew of post-office engineers and some ultrasensitive listening equipment; and from the roof of each van, invisible in the night, rose a long aerial. A day or two earlier these same engineers had listened to a series of dot-dot-dash-dash call signs on 17,080 kilocycles, followed by short bursts of coded high-speed transmissions. Half a dozen listening posts all over the country had fixed the source of the transmissions as Moscow.

Now the equipment in the furniture vans was tuned in to the same frequency. The crews had been listening since eight o'clock that evening, and all they had heard so far was static and crackle. They had spent the time reading paperbacks, doing crossword puzzles, drinking tea; they were about as bored as men could be, but their orders were to stay listening until dawn.

Suddenly, and so loud they were almost deafened, came the dot-dot-dash-dash call sign, the answering call from Moscow, and a twenty-second burst of transmission. As the message went out, the receivers in each van were turned to the bearing that gave maximum strength.

Later, when the two bearings were plotted, they intersected precisely at 45 Cranley Drive.

This time the anger of the Admiralty Board could scarcely be contained. It had been known that Houghton had been spying for the Russians for at least six months, maybe longer. Meetings had been allowed to take place, secret after secret allowed to be handed over. It was all very well talking of enticing other fish into the net, but what other fish had emerged? (They hadn't for security reasons been told about the Krogers.) How long was this lunacy to continue?

There were comings and goings, conferences and telephone conversations embracing MI-5, the Admiralty, the Home Office, and once again reaching the Prime Minister and Cabinet. And finally a decision was taken. If the watch on the Krogers produced no new results or fresh contacts before the next expected meeting between Houghton and Lonsdale on Saturday, January 7, then at that meeting they would be arrested.

In her room at Hambro Road, Portland, Bunty Gee was studying a copy she had made in her own hand of the typed questionnaire given by Alec Johnson to Houghton at their last meeting (Harry had asked her to destroy the original after making a copy, and this she had done). The questions, about antisubmarine detection gear, were very technical; Bunty couldn't make head or tail of them.

Nor could she have been expected to, for they had been written by a Russian with imperfect knowledge of British naval terminology. The word radiator occurred frequently. To Bunty, radiator meant either an electric heater or a part of a car. She was not to know that the Russian word for transducer was *izluchatei,* whose literal translation was "a radiation source." She was puzzled by the phrase "duration of pulses for different regimes of operation," as well she might be, for an English naval document would have referred to "methods of operating." The word station was equally incomprehensible; she was not to know that its British equivalent was "set," or that the rather flowery phrase "basic units of hydroacoustic stations" meant quite simply asdic sets.

Yet even if the questionnaire had been worded correctly, Bunty Gee would have found it impossible to answer, for as a clerk she had no technical knowledge of underwater weapons at all. However, to oblige nice Commander Johnson, she asked her colleague Mr. Hutchings to explain some of the terms about asdic sets that she came across in her work. What, for instance, was the difference between an oscillator and a hydrophone? An oscillator, said Mr. Hutchings, worked outward and a hydrophone worked downward. And the difference between an oscillator and a transducer? None, said Mr. Hutchings, they were the same. Later she wrote down what Mr. Hutchings had told her and put it in her bag.

Houghton, however, over in the Port Auxiliary Repair Unit, had had a stroke of luck. An envelope addressed to the Underwater Detection Establishment, marked SECRET, was delivered to his office by mistake.

He slipped it into his pocket and took it home. That evening he steamed it open and inside a further envelope found a drawing of Britain's first nuclear submarine, the *Dreadnought,* with details of her antisubmarine gear. He took the drawings into the bathroom and photographed them with the new camera. Next day, having replaced the drawings and resealed both envelopes, he dropped the outer envelope in the interoffice mail Out tray. As he did so he thought, Gordon will be pleased with that; maybe that's worth another special payment.

And yet there was another side to Houghton. He was doing what he was doing because, through his own greed and unscrupulousness, he now had no other option. He did not like it—not for any moral reasons but because, however much extra cash he had to spend, however congenial Gordon Lonsdale might be, he was trapped, no longer his own master. There were times, perhaps even more than he cared to admit, when he longed to rid himself of the burden, cease leading a double life, become free. Earlier, seeing that the post of harbormaster at Bridport—a sleepy little town along the coast—had become vacant, he applied for it. There, he thought, he would be safe at last, beyond the reach of Gordon's long arm; there he and Bunty could start a new life. Now came a reply saying his application had been unsuccessful.

The fates were not with Harry Houghton; they had decided that his future must take its predetermined course.

CHRISTMAS, FOR THE Searches, was not the happy family occasion it usually was; for while they ate their Christmas dinner, exchanged presents, put on funny hats, the two young women agents kept their watch in the room above. Spies might be expected to take advantage of a time when the rest of the world was sleeping.

The teams of women agents had been coming to the house nearly two months. They had been no bother—they couldn't have been easier or more considerate—but for Mrs. Search the situation generally was becoming intolerable. She knew instinctively that whatever gloss Skardon may have put on things, the Krogers themselves must be actively and deeply involved. It was this she found so hard to bear; that all the things Helen Kroger had told her over the years about her life in Canada and with Peter in England were lies. Was the affection that Helen had shown for her and all the family, and which had been fully and genuinely reciprocated, was that a lie too? She felt betrayed and profoundly humiliated.

Sustaining Helen's visits, too, had become a dreadful strain, because it meant that she, Ruth Search, had also begun to live a lie. She could not be naturally natural with Helen anymore, only pretend natural. Although Helen was always her vulgar, cheerful self, apparently suspecting nothing, Ruth felt weak and sick when her visitor had gone, and had to sit in a chair to recover.

There was the fear, too, that one day Helen would somehow get to know that eyes were watching her from the bedroom window, that the agents couldn't have been coming there for two whole months without her knowing.

Once, when Helen arrived unexpectedly, Mrs. Search saw to her horror that one of the women had left her handbag on the kitchen table. Helen, of course, noticed it.

"That's a real nice bag, Ruth. Is it yours?" She fingered it.

"Oh," said Mrs. Search in exasperation, "I'll murder that daughter of mine. She never puts anything away." She picked up the bag and put it in a cupboard, and Helen changed the conversation to other things.

And then there was the evening when they were all relaxing, and conversation turned to the women upstairs, and Gay said, "Do you really think they're looking for a drugs ring, Mum? They're taking a terribly long time about it."

And quite unknowingly Philip said, because there had been an item about Russian spies in the papers, "*I* think they're looking for Russian spies"; and he got down on his haunches and began dancing a gopak.

The children were bewildered when their mother, usually the calmest of people, suddenly shouted at her son, "*Stop it*, Philip, do you hear! *Stop it, stop it, stop it!*"

MOLODY SPENT CHRISTMAS across the road with the Krogers, and was back there the following weekend for New Year's. Peter Kroger had messages for him from the Center, including three microdot letters from Galisha.

When Molody got back to the privacy of his room at the White House on the Monday, he opened the bottom of the Yardley's talcum-powder tin and took out his microdot reader.

Hello, my darling,

I congratulate you on the past 43rd anniversary of the October Revolution.* We were hoping for letters from you, but now it seems they will come at the end of the month.

---

*This rather stilted phrase sounds as strange to us as "Happy Christmas" does to the Russians.

As far as my work goes, everything is fine. There are two Rumanian girls, aged 7 and 8, among our pupils, and I took on the task of teaching them the Russian alphabet. They have made terrific progress (all due to *them*, of course!) Simultaneously *they* teach *me* Rumanian. During a visit of the Central Committee's Commission, they read so well I was really delighted. And now, every time I come, they implore me to teach them more!

On November 3 we had an evening party at the place where I work, and I sang "The Cranes," etc. It reminded me of our life in Prague, and I felt very very sad. Whenever we meet we have to rush off, and we are left with very little time. I remember the day before our last in Prague. And "The Cranes" particularly disturbs my peace of mind. I find it difficult and sad to sing it.

At home everything goes on as usual. Liza has greatly distressed me this term. For the first time in six years at school, she brought home a report with four 3s [2 means bad, 3 just passed, 4 good] for geometry, algebra, English and P.T. The rest were 4s. You can't imagine how much this upset me, considering that her entrance to the Institute is not far away. Dina had even worse marks, including those for diligence and discipline.

On the 7th I was at Rima's and Igor's. There were fourteen of us including the Tromkins. We drank your health and everyone sent best wishes. They were all so sorry you weren't with us, I especially. Do you realize that for seven October and six May Day celebrations now I have been alone?

Life does seem unfair. Of course I understand you are doing the work you love, and I know you are doing it conscientiously. But I can't help looking at things as a woman and a wife, and I do suffer. Write and tell me that you love me, and I shall feel better.

There was a letter from Liza too.

Hello, dear Daddy,

I congratulate you on the 43rd anniversary of October. How are you? We are all well.

We are going tomorrow to Aunt Vera. Mother has been invited for a visit.

The first term finished badly with three 3s. I'll try and do better next term. The 3s I got for subjects for which I had 4s last term.

Winter has already set in. Aunt Vera fell and broke her leg. It's still painful. Grandma is well.

Daddy, all of us are expecting you. Come home quickly. Trofim recently "wrote" a letter to you and kept on saying, "Dear Daddy, come home quickly."

Many, many kisses,

Your daughter,
Liza

P.S. Daddy, come home quickly, Trofim.

In an earlier letter there was a reference to his mother's being ill. "Can you somehow manage to come home—after all one only has one mother in the world. I suppose it's impossible, coming home before the appointed time."

And there were practical requests too. "If possible, please let me have 2500 rubles a month," and "I ask if it is possible to send me a white brocade dress with white shoes."

MI-5 HAD BEEN following Molody for six months, the Krogers for two. Although they were still convinced that such professional spies in such an elaborate setup must exist to serve others than Houghton and Gee, although telephones had been tapped, mail scrutinized, strangers to the Krogers' house followed wherever they went, nothing further had emerged. If there were others in the ring, then they had been brilliantly kept out of the picture. Now it was time—some said long past time—to act; and on January 5 the decision was confirmed that, should there be a meeting on Saturday, the seventh, the principal participants would be arrested.

MI-5 had done the investigative spadework; now it fell to Special Branch to obtain evidence and execute the warrants for arrest. So on the afternoon of Friday, the sixth, Chief Inspector Ferguson Smith traveled down to Weymouth to join the overnight watchers near Meadowview Road.

It was at six thirty on the Saturday morning that the telephone rang in G. G. Smith's house at Hounslow. It was a message from Ferguson Smith to say that a light had been switched on in Houghton's bedroom window. An hour later there was a further message, that Houghton had left for Portland in the Renault, and at eight forty-five, that he and Gee were on the road to London. By that time G.G. had reached the Yard. At ten he briefed his detectives.

MOLODY, UNAWARE OF ALL these activities, rose, breakfasted in his kitchen, then sat down at his desk to reply to the letters from his wife.

My beloved Galisha,

Just received your mail. I am very happy to have three letters from you in one lot. Many thanks for remembering my requests.

I will write this very day to V.M. that 2500 rubles should be handed over to you—or more correctly 250 rubles. I saw photographs of the new currency a few days ago, and to me it's a great improvement.

As regards the white brocade dress, this is very difficult. In "other countries" brocade is not worn. How to post it on to you and when? A dress and a shoe cannot be put in a pocket. But I will do everything possible.

You write that you have celebrated seven October anniversaries without me. Of course this is true. But don't forget that I have celebrated them without you and without the children and my people. When we were in Prague, I did try and explain things to you.

I hope you don't think I am an entirely hardhearted man who gives no thoughts to anyone else. But I have only one life, and not a very easy one at that. I want to spend it so that later, when I come to look back on it, I shall feel no sense of shame.

I know too what loneliness is. During the past twenty-nine years, that is since I was ten years old, I have spent only ten years with my own people. I didn't want it and I didn't seek it, but that's how it's turned out. It wasn't ever really my choice—it all started back in 1932 when Mother decided to send me to the nether regions [i.e., America]. At that time she couldn't have foreseen the consequences of such a step, and I can't blame her.

I'm not complaining but even you cannot imagine how sad I feel in general and especially at this moment. I feel all right, sleep badly, live in a new flat of one room of approximately ten square meters, bathroom and lavatory, and kitchen which is so small there's no space even for a chair. This is the eighth new year I have celebrated without you. I spent it with a fellow named Kroger. *Such is life.* (I know that expression in so many languages I feel sick.)

For the last twenty minutes, I have been pacing the room, and I simply cannot continue this letter. "I am weary and sad and there is no one to shake hands with" [from a Russian poem].

Many kisses to my beloved wife and children.

(P.S. I will be 39 shortly. Is there much left?)

THE WEATHER THAT DAY WAS bitterly cold and the roads were very icy. The cars following Houghton noticed how cautiously he was driving, and so had no difficulty in keeping a reasonable distance behind. But this put him behind schedule, and when he reached Salisbury Station, he and Bunty had to run for the eleven-fifty train. They bought round-trip tickets, then raced for the platform where the train was waiting.

Ferguson Smith and one of his colleagues were close behind, and in the general scramble to catch the train he and Houghton almost collided. They were all too late. As they reached the platform the train was pulling out.

The next train was at twelve fifty p.m. Houghton and Gee, carrying a shopping basket, went for a walk in the town.

AT ABOUT THE SAME time, Molody met Helen Kroger in Selfridges department store in Oxford Street. He handed her his letter to Galisha, also the three microdots, enclosed in glass slides, that contained her letters to him. Peter Kroger would reduce Molody's own letter to a microdot for transmission to the Center, and burn Galisha's microdots in his boiler.

Molody looked at his watch. In just over three and a half hours he would be meeting his Portland contacts at their usual rendezvous. He hoped they would bring an answer to his questionnaire.

HOUGHTON AND GEE were back at the station in good time to catch the twelve fifty when it pulled in. Ferguson Smith and his friend kept well out of sight until the two of them had boarded the train, then slipped into a coach just ahead. And from the radio car parked in the station parking lot a message was sent to the Yard that the train carrying the two suspects would arrive at Waterloo at two fifteen p.m.

By then G.G. and his team of watchers had posted themselves at Waterloo and its approaches.

At his briefing to them earlier he had said, "If things go as I expect, they will meet near the Old Vic between three thirty and four thirty. As already agreed, some of you will take up position on one side of them, some on the other. Keep your eyes on me. As soon as I see anything passing between them, I'll pull my handkerchief from my pocket. That's the signal for the cars to draw alongside and for you to move in. Look out for them trying to destroy anything, and see in particular that Gee doesn't open her handbag. With luck the whole thing will be over within seconds."

As usual, great care had been taken with disguises. Several detectives were dressed as teddy boys; others wore shabby suits; one was dressed as a porter, another as a match seller; there were two girls in slacks who might have been mistaken for students. (At the final briefing they had all had a good laugh and made rude jokes about each other's disguises.)

G. G. Smith himself, waiting by the ticket barrier, wore a black beret and a continental-style raglan. To his amusement he was importuned, while waiting, by a homosexual (who, after being arrested later that afternoon, was astonished to see Smith at Bow Street next day).

The wait was longer than expected, for the train was delayed by a landslide near Basingstoke and was thirty-five minutes late. Smith saw Houghton and Gee approaching the barrier, Gee still carrying her shopping basket, in which he noticed a parcel. Ferguson Smith followed a few steps behind.

They walked down the steps into York Road, were seen to exchange a few words and then walk to a bus stop near the Union Jack Club. As they reached it, a number 68 bus arrived and they boarded it. This was unexpected, and Ferguson Smith had to run quite fast to board it too.

Houghton and Gee had arrived ahead of schedule and so had time to kill before meeting Molody at four thirty. They left the bus at East Street, Walworth, and strolled slowly through the market, which was full of Saturday shoppers.

Ferguson Smith and his friend, following not far behind, hoped they didn't look conspicuous; for stall holders and others in that area have a knack of spotting a copper a mile away, and the last thing Ferguson Smith wanted at this juncture was a cry of "Here come the heavies!"

At four fifteen Houghton and Gee left the market, boarded another 68 bus, this time without Ferguson Smith and his colleague, but with another detective in their place. They alighted near the Old Vic, walked along the Lower Marsh, then retraced their steps to reach the outside of the theater at exactly four thirty p.m. A minute later, Smith saw Molody approach them, and noticed the Studebaker parked some fifty yards away. As Houghton and Bunty saw Molody, they turned and began walking southward down Waterloo Road.

Molody followed them, caught up with them, took his place between them, putting one arm around Gee's shoulders and the other around Houghton's. After a few steps he changed position so as to be on the outside of Gee, who then gave him her shopping basket. This was the moment of truth. G.G. took his handkerchief from his pocket. The teddy boys and the others moved in, the cars drew alongside.

G.G. went up to the trio and said, "I am a police officer, and you are all under arrest."

Bunty, totally perplexed, said, "Oh!" Houghton said, "What?" Molody, who from earliest days had been conditioned to expect this, said nothing.

G.G. took the shopping basket from Molody, said to him, "It's Scotland Yard for you, my boy," and bundled him into the first car. Detective Sergeant Anne Winterbottom took hold of Bunty and guided her into the second car; Ferguson Smith propelled Houghton into the third.

As the convoy moved swiftly off, Molody heard G.G. say into the car's radio microphone, "Lock, stock and barrel." It was the code phrase for reporting that the operation had gone off as planned, that all three were in the bag.

On arrival at the Yard the three prisoners were taken to separate offices and searched. In Bunty's shopping basket were found four Admiralty test pamphlets and a tin containing undeveloped film. When processed in the laboratories, the film was found to contain three hundred and ten photographs of warships taken from the confidential publication *Particulars of War Vessels*. In Molody's pocket were found one envelope containing one hundred and twenty-five pounds in Bank of England five-pound notes, in another, three hundred American dollars in twenty-dollar bills. Nothing incriminating was found on Houghton.

G.G. then cautioned each prisoner individually. "I am going to detain you here on suspicion of having committed offenses against the Official Secrets Act. This is necessary because I have inquiries to make. You need not say anything, but I must warn you that anything you do say may be taken down and used in evidence."

Houghton said, "I have been a bloody fool," which was perfectly true. Gee said, "I have done nothing wrong," which she had deluded herself into thinking. Molody said, "To any questions you may ask, my answer is no, so you need not bother to ask"—and from that moment on, as a true professional, he was as good as his word. He added, "Since it looks as though I may be here some time, I should be pleased if you could find me a good chess player"—a request that was later granted.

THAT SATURDAY MORNING the Searches were told that the Krogers were to be arrested that evening. The news was naturally a shock, and a shock made much worse by an unexpected visit from Helen in the afternoon. She was in a dissatisfied mood, complained about the cold weather, said that she and Peter were thinking of making a trip to Australia.

Mrs. Search felt dreadfully torn between loyalty to her country and to her friend. Afterward she told her daughter, "I felt like saying to Helen, Run now, while you still have the chance."

At six thirty that evening—roughly the time when the Krogers would have expected Molody to arrive with the intelligence he had collected from Houghton and Gee—G. G. Smith (without his beret), Ferguson Smith and others arrived in Ruislip. Detectives were discreetly placed in Willow Gardens, Courtfield Gardens and at the back of 45 Cranley Drive, in case the Krogers should attempt a getaway. The two Smiths went up to the Krogers' front door and rang the bell. They heard bolts being drawn back and a lock unclicked. Peter Kroger opened the door.

G. G. Smith gave him his best smile and said, "I am a police officer making certain inquiries. May I come in?" and, before Kroger could reply, put his foot firmly inside the door.

Peter Kroger said, "Certainly." He led the two officers into his book-lined sitting room at the back, sat down in an easy chair and invited the officers to do the same. But they remained standing.

G.G. said, "I would like to see your wife as well."

At this moment Helen Kroger came into the room. G.G. said,

"I am a police officer, and I wish to ask you the name and address of the gentleman who comes and stays with you each weekend, particularly the first Saturday in each month." The Krogers looked at each other briefly and said nothing. Smith said, "Would you care to tell me?"

Kroger ran his fingers through his hair and said, "Well, we have lots of friends." Pressed again, he mentioned several names, but not that of Gordon Lonsdale.

Smith then told the Krogers he was going to arrest them on suspicion of offenses against the Official Secrets Act and take them to Scotland Yard; and he showed Peter Kroger a search warrant, which Peter read aloud to his wife. Smith told Mrs. Kroger to get ready, and she went to her bedroom to put on a coat.

Detective Sergeant Anne Winterbottom, who had also entered the house, followed her into the bedroom and noticed Helen Kroger, with her back to the door, slightly bending over a chair. When Mrs. Kroger returned to the hall, she said to G. G. Smith, "As I am going out for some time, may I go and stoke the boiler in the kitchen?"

Smith noticed that she was holding something under her coat. He said, "Certainly, but may I first see what you are holding inside your coat?"

Helen Kroger produced her bag, then was allowed to go to the kitchen. Inside the bag were found a sheet of coded numbers that made up a message, the list of streets in southwestern London that Smith had already seen in Molody's case at the Midland Bank, the three microdot letters from Galisha to Molody, and the manuscript letter to Galisha from Molody that he had written that morning and handed to Helen Kroger in Selfridges. It was a damning indictment.

Helen Kroger seemed suddenly to have lost interest in stoking the boiler. She and Peter were put into a police car and taken to Hayes Police Station.

In the morning Jim Skardon, on his way to look at the Krogers' house, called in at 1 Courtfield Gardens. "We won't be bothering you now anymore," he told Gay and Philip. "We arrested the Krogers last night." The young people were shattered.

Gay went upstairs to her room, now for the first time in two months empty of agents, and burst into tears. Then she collected every little present that Helen Kroger had given her, took them downstairs and threw them all into the trash can; for her they had become as contaminated as their donor.

DURING THE NEXT few days teams of detectives with search warrants spent hours examining every floorboard, cavity, piece of furniture, ornament, cupboard, garden shed, and any other place that might hold secrets in the houses of the five defendants.

In Gee's house at Hambro Road they found her own handwritten copy of the questionnaire given by Molody to Houghton, and a list of numbers of eighteen test pamphlets from the base; some were struck out, and there were crosses marked against others. In a handbag were found three hundred and sixteen pounds in fivers and one-pound notes, and savings and share certificates to the value of some four thousand pounds.

At Houghton's cottage, in a bureau in the sitting room, was found a paper with the word Keep, followed by three lots of three-figure numbers, and the word Gone, with four lots of three-figure numbers. All referred to test pamphlets to which Gee had had access. The four sets of numbers after "Gone" were the numbers of the test pamphlets in the shopping basket handed by Gee to Molody just before their arrest, and the three numbers marked "Keep" were of test pamphlets found hidden in Houghton's phonograph.

Also found in the cottage were the camera Houghton had been given by Molody, and three charts with penciled markings on them. The first chart included installations in the dockyard, the second chart showed submarine exercise areas of 1957, and the third showed up-to-date secret exercise areas, as well as details of Admiralty property in the Weymouth area.

In Houghton's bedroom was found a Swan Vestas box of matches, with a false bottom containing the message about future meeting places and ending with "Punch." In Houghton's car, recovered from Salisbury Station, was a map of London and a year-old copy of *Punch*. In addition, five hundred pounds in premium bonds were discovered, and six hundred and fifty pounds hidden in a tin of Snowcem in the garden shed.

In Molody's flat at the White House they found eighteen hundred dollars in the Chinese scroll that hung above his bed; a type-writer that had typed coded figures found in Peter Kroger's *Book Auction Records;* one-time cipher pads in a cavity of the lighter taken to the bank; the microdot reader and signal plans (duplicates of which were found in Cranley Drive) in the base of the Yardley's tin of talcum powder; and a Canadian passport and birth certificate showing Lonsdale's age to be thirty-six, a contradiction of what he had written to Galisha: "I will be 39 shortly."

At 45 Cranley Drive, in the course of a three-day search, they made the biggest haul of all, though they almost had to take the house apart to do it. In the table lighter, the talcum-powder tin, the hip flask and a torch casing they found microdot readers, the black oxide for making invisible the Morse recorded on magnetic tape, one-time cipher pads and a variety of signal plans. One batch of signal plans covered the period April 14, 1960, to January 26, 1961, and listed various transmission times—some marked "Transmission Blind," others, "Transmission on orders of the Center." Various code signs were listed: *Lena Ya Amur, Volga Ya Azov, Rosa Ya Fielca.* In the loft were found two cameras, one of which Molody had temporarily deposited in the Midland Bank while away in Prague; and behind the fiberglass insulation in the roof, over twenty-five hundred American dollars and American and British traveler's checks. In the bedroom they found a microscope with glass slides for containing microdots, and in a black handbag, two hundred pounds in five-pound notes and two New Zealand passports. They leafed through every page of literally hundreds of books, and in *Book Auction Records* found the list of coded figures typed in Molody's flat; behind a Bible they found the special film for making microphotographs.

It took them nearly a week to find the radio transmitter hidden beneath the kitchen floorboards. In the same pit they found poly-ethylene bags containing the automatic keying device for high-speed transmission, a reducing lens for microdots and six thousand American dollars, all in twenty-dollar bills.

Yet thorough and painstaking though the Special Branch search had been, it had not been thorough enough; for when Molody's fellow director in Allo Security Products, Michael Bowers, was em-powered by the Krogers to sell the contents of 45 Cranley Drive to raise money for their defense, he was told by them to be sure not to sell a pair of bookends and a leather writing case. At home, Bowers examined these objects and found four thousand dollars in the bookends, and in the writing case, two Canadian passports. One had been issued at Ottawa on June 15, 1956, for Thomas Wilson, described as a storekeeper, born in Toronto in 1911, now five feet nine inches, with brown eyes and gray hair. The other was issued in September 1956 for a secretary called Mary Jane Smith, born in Montreal, 1915, with blue eyes and brown hair. Both passports showed the holders had traveled extensively in Belgium and Holland in 1956. Both were forgeries, and were being kept for emergency in case the Krogers had to make a quick getaway.

A FEW DAYS AFTER experts had sorted out the various transmission times and call signs, radio engineers working for MI-5 sent out the dot-dot-dash-dash of the call sign at one of the fixed hours. Back from the Moscow Center came immediate acknowledgment.

There is a story that the British operator then sent the following message: "Scotland Yard here, old cock. Just to let you know we have got all your people in the bag." But if such a claim was ever made, it was on flimsy evidence. For long after the arrest of the Portland five had been made public, the engineers heard the messages from the Moscow Center still being broadcast on 17,080 kilocycles at the usual times. This could only mean one of two things: that the transmissions were a bluff, designed to alarm our intelligence services into thinking that there were other agents in Britain, as yet uncaught; or that there really were other agents to whom it was necessary to send urgent instructions. But instructions to do what? Lie low, perhaps, or escape to the Continent? Assume a new identity? Note new operating and transmission procedures? Who could tell, for the cacophony of high-speed coded Morse was beyond unscrambling. Only the agents, if there were any, and their masters at the Center knew.

THE DAY AFTER his arrest Houghton volunteered a statement to Superintendent G. G. Smith, in order, he said, "to protect Miss Gee, as I have dragged her into this mess." The motive was fine but the statement ludicrous. In essence it said that not only Bunty but he, too, had believed all along that Lonsdale was Commander Alec Johnson of the U.S. Navy, and that he had put pressure on Bunty to produce documents for Johnson "because we were all working for a common goal." Not knowing of the many occasions on which he had been followed, he concluded by saying that he hadn't handed over any documents until the day of his arrest.

A little later, having decided that this account wasn't going to wash, he tried a different tack. From Brixton Prison, where he was on remand, he sent word to G. G. Smith that he would like to see him. G.G. went there that afternoon.

"Well," said Smith, when they had sat down in the interrogation room, "what is it?"

"I'd like to make a proposal," said Houghton hesitantly.

"And what are you proposing?"

"Well, there were times before I met Lonsdale," said Houghton, "when I met others. One or two from the Soviet embassy, and I think one from the Polish too."

"Yes."

"Well, I was thinking, if you could show me photographs of the people at these embassies, I might be able to identify them."

"Go on."

"Well, it's obvious, isn't it?"

"Not to me, it isn't."

"Well, then, I could appear for the prosecution."

"Oh, I get the message now," said G.G., who had got it all along. "You want to turn Queen's evidence, is that it? Shop your girl friend and the others and get yourself off the hook? No, my friend, we're not having any of that. And if that's all you wanted to see me about, I'll bid you good-day."

The British government had decided that the world should know to what lengths the Soviets were prepared to go to obtain the secrets of other countries, and so the trial of the Portland five was given maximum publicity. It opened in No. 1 Court at the Old Bailey before Lord Parker, the Lord Chief Justice of England, on March 13, 1961.

The press of the world (save the Russian agency Tass) were there, come to see and describe this ill-assorted collection of spies for themselves. Among the more perceptive correspondents were Patrick

O'Donovan of the *Observer* and Rebecca West of *The Daily Telegraph*. Molody, still masquerading as Lonsdale, made a favorable impression on both.

"Now that the rumour was out," wrote Patrick O'Donovan, "he looked Russian, but the nicest kind of Russian . . . fit and chunky and ready for a party." Rebecca West spoke of "a suggestion of physical self-respect . . . after weeks in prison he looked as if he could have walked out of the Old Bailey to the nearest tennis courts and played a good, hard game." She was impressed by his turnout. "He had managed to shave carefully that morning . . . his gray raglan coat was beautifully tailored and shaped." She added, "Mr. Lonsdale chews gum, steadily, ceaselessly."

The Krogers, too, made something of an impression. "They looked the pair of fanatics they were," wrote Rebecca West, and suggested that the intensity of their beliefs in Communism gave them "distinction of a religious sort." She spoke of Peter Kroger's white hair "winding round his head like a glistening bandage"; he reminded her of a figure in a Stanley Spencer painting. To Patrick O'Donovan, Kroger looked like "the tall suave manager of a chemists' shop, a round, decent man who took pleasures gravely." Rebecca West described Helen Kroger as a handsome "Rubenish woman," but O'Donovan thought her "a bit tousled . . . hard to place . . . but bright, with a hint of more than suburban authority."

To Miss West, Bunty Gee appeared as the most sympathetic of all the prisoners, "a brave woman . . . to attract the attention of counsel she rapped the pencil on the edge of the dock with a gesture full of fierce, unexpended power." In contrast, Patrick O'Donovan thought her "a dumpy little woman with a sensible hair-do who in a few years would be a nice English Mum." Houghton he described as "small and wizened and balding with a wily face dominated by a tremendous nose . . . looked the sort who knew how to look after officers and men . . . he seemed at ease and bowed too elaborately to the judge."

The prosecution was opened by the Attorney General, Sir Reginald Manningham-Buller, Q.C., a burly, pipe-smoking Conservative lawyer known to Fleet Street by his nickname, "Bullying Manner." A fascinated public and press heard him relate for the first time the background to the charges; the various rendezvous between Lonsdale, Houghton and Gee; Lonsdale's furtive visits to the Krogers'; the searches of their houses and the secrets within. He read out Houghton's statement, and one of Gee's too, proclaiming injured innocence.

Then the witnesses appeared: first the anonymous MI-5 agents, Mr. X, Mr. M, Mr. A and so on, whom Patrick O'Donovan described as "almost indistinguishable, nice, clean ordinary young men who knew their jobs but were frightened of the witness-box." Next came Mr. Leonard Easter of the Midland Bank, Superintendent G. G. Smith and Chief Inspector Ferguson Smith, Mr. Michael Bowers and Detective Sergeant Leonard Burt. A naval electrical officer, Mr. James Adam, gave evidence about the radio transmitter in the Krogers' house: neither the set nor any of its components were of British make; with the automatic keying device it could send messages at a speed of two hundred and forty words a minute; it could reach Moscow "and beyond."

Various naval experts testified to the importance to national security of the documents found in Houghton's and Gee's possession, and then Bunty Gee went into the witness-box. She stuck to her story that she knew Lonsdale only as Commander Johnson, and that she had only handed over documents to help him, and because Houghton had suggested it. Asked if her original statement to Superintendent Smith that she had done nothing wrong was true, she replied, "Well, in the light of what transpired, I had done something terribly wrong, but at the time I did not feel I had done anything wrong criminally." Rebecca West was impressed by what she called "her short, pursy dignity," but Patrick O'Donovan took a different view. "She spoke in a soft, rather silly voice. She laughed, mostly at herself, and looked delighted when the court snickered at one of her perky answers. She had a butterfly mind . . . and was at once shy and garrulous."

Then it was Houghton's turn. His evidence was a mixture of lies, false dramatics and self-pity. He admitted the four-thousand-pound black-market deal in Warsaw, and said that he had been living on it ever since (the six hundred and fifty pounds in the garden shed, he said, was what remained of it). He asked permission not to give Christina's other name, "because we are talking about an iron-curtain country." He put forward the Dulwich art gallery meeting by four years—to 1957. Twice Nikki had asked him to supply naval information, and twice he had refused. (Asked by counsel, "Information on what?" he replied, "I cannot disclose that in open court," to which the Attorney General said he had no objections!)

As a result of refusing to disclose information, said Houghton, two London thugs had visited him, once at his trailer and later at the cottage, and given him with fists and feet "the biggest hammering of my life." There had been threats, too, to beat up his wife in 1957 and Miss Gee in 1960, to send him bombs through the mail and put poison in his tea. The effect of all this was rather spoiled by Molody, sitting next to him, putting his face in his hands and shaking helplessly with laughter.

Houghton said he had never given any information of use until the day of his arrest. Like Miss Gee, he had always thought the man Lonsdale to be Commander Johnson of the U.S. Navy, and saw no harm in letting him have a glimpse of one or two test pamphlets. He explained his photography of the pictures in *Particulars of War Vessels* by saying he had deliberately taken them out of focus. He hadn't received a penny from anyone for any information he had supplied. All in all it was a contemptible performance.

Neither the Krogers nor Molody chose to enter the witness-box, but their counselors announced that they wished to make statements from the dock. Molody went first, and as he rose to his feet there was a quickening of interest in court. For the past week the sight of this square, handsome, dark-haired man, sitting silently in the dock, had been a center of attraction. Now he was about to speak. What would he sound like? What was he going to say?

To Rebecca West and others his voice was a disappointment, "commonplace . . . lost him much of his distinction." She added, "He spoke English as Slavs do who have studied it in their own countries with American teachers, as a foreign language they have had to learn." She was not to know that it wasn't from American teachers

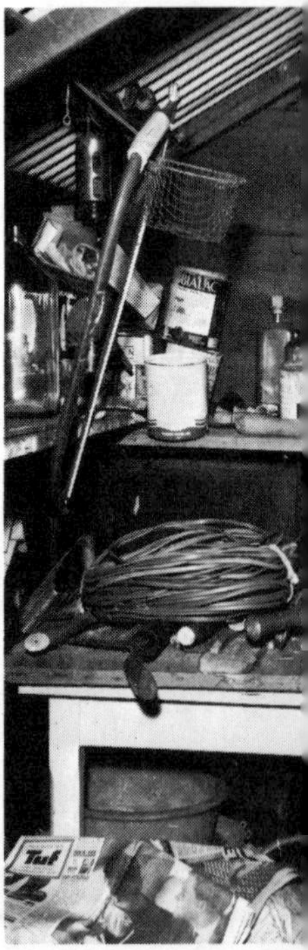

In from the cold, the Krogers and Harry Houghton say good-by to prison life. Behind them are mementos of their spying days: a microdot enlargement, and a canister of cement in Houghton's garden shed where six hundred and fifty pounds was found.

in Russia that Molody had learned his English, but from his childhood in California.

Nor did what Molody had to say help to increase his stature. The Krogers, he said, were personal friends who let him stay at their house on their frequent trips abroad. All the incriminating articles he had put there while they were away—the false lighter, the false hip flask, the cameras, the microdot reader, the false passports, the money, the transmitter under the kitchen floor, the signal plans—the Krogers knew nothing about them at all. "I realize," he concluded, "it is too late to make amends, but I feel the least I can do in the circumstances is to accept full responsibility for my actions." For so intelligent a man it was a preposterous statement, and as he sat down, many people in court wondered what possible good he could have thought it would do for either him or the Krogers.

Kroger's statement was no less absurd. What Lonsdale had just said, he declared, was true. He and his wife had first met him in 1955. "Attracted by his effervescing personality and stimulating comments on literature, I invited him to my home." Later, as they got to know him better, "he would drop into our home during the week and on weekends, liking my wife's cooking and even pitching in with the preparations and a bottle of wine." He knew nothing of what was in the bookends, powder tin, etc., or even of the existence of the Canadian passports. He explained the headphones to the radio set by saying he liked listening to the early morning news and didn't want to disturb his wife. Neither he nor his wife had ever engaged in spying "or other irregular activities."

And to round off the farce, Mrs. Kroger stood up and said, "Lonsdale has been a good friend of mine for over five years. I have always found him helpful in the house, bringing in the coal, helping me with the dishes and even going shopping. On several occasions he helped me with my photography."

She explained the incriminating things found in her handbag by saying that Lonsdale had lunched with her that day and given her an envelope, saying, "Will you please look after these till I see you?" She explained a long length of electric cord used to light a way to the transmitter, by saying it was for inspecting apples stored in the loft under the roof.

THE JURY WERE OUT FOR an hour and twenty minutes, and on return brought in verdicts of guilty against all five.

To Molody, Lord Parker said, "You are clearly a professional spy. It is a dangerous career and one in which you must be prepared, as you no doubt are, to suffer if and when you are caught. Moreover I take the view in this case that yours was . . . the directing mind. You will go to prison for twenty-five years."

To the Krogers he said, "I take the view that I cannot distinguish between you. You are both in this up to the hilt, you are both professional spies. The only distinction I can make between you and Lonsdale is that, if I am right, yours was not the directing mind, and you are older than he is. You will each go to prison for twenty years."

To Houghton he said, "In many ways you are the most culpable, because you betrayed the secrets of your country. I have considered long what to do with you. You are, however, now fifty-six, not a very young fifty-six, and it is against all our principles that a sentence should be given which might involve your dying in prison. But for that I would give you a longer sentence. You will go to prison for fifteen years."

And to Gee he said, "I have reluctantly come to the conclusion that I cannot distinguish between you and Houghton. You were in a position of trust because you were thought honest and trustworthy, and you betrayed that trust. I am quite unable to think it a possibility that you did what you did out of some blind infatuation for Houghton. Having heard you and watched your demeanor in the dock and in the witness-box, I am inclined to think yours was the stronger character of the two. I think you acted for greed. You will go to prison for fifteen years."

Bunty Gee followed the others down to the cells, about to pay the price for her efforts to avoid a lifetime of spinsterhood. Now the dock was empty. The court rose, the Lord Chief Justice departed, conversation broke out like a swarm of bees. The most notorious British spy case of the twentieth century had finally reached its end.

FOR THE BRITISH security services the conclusion of the Portland spy case was both a brilliant success and a partial failure. It was a success in that it was the fruits of the most painstaking and patient detective work, in which pressures to act prematurely were bravely resisted, in which always a delicate balance was preserved between keeping constant watch on Molody and the Krogers, and yet ensuring that they remained unaware of it.

In his memoirs, written long after the event, Molody tried to diminish the role of his captors, like his claim that when he recovered his case from the Midland Bank he knew at once it had been tampered with. Had he known, he would have left the country immediately, before the authorities could arrest him. In fact, he knew nothing; not that his flat was watched, his movements followed, his mail scrutinized, his telephone tapped; and for this, much credit is due to the agents and detectives of MI-5 and the Special Branch, and those like Skardon and G. G. Smith, who directed them.

And yet, despite their vigilance and caution, the long months of waiting and watching were to some degree in vain. The only fish to surface in what was hoped would be a big haul were the Krogers. Were there no other fish? It is hard to believe it—to believe that the Krogers and their armory of intelligence devices existed only for Molody, or that Molody existed only for Houghton and Gee. Certainly before, and probably during, the surveillance of Molody and the Krogers there must have been other Houghtons and Gees— British men and women in government offices, aircraft factories, military bases—who had sold or were selling their country's secrets for Russian money; some who had passed out of the picture, their usefulness over; others who, because of the Krogers' and Molody's superb wariness, had yet escaped the vigilance of Smith's and Skardon's men. It is a sobering thought that some of them, at least, and perhaps other, newer recruits are still among us today.

As first offenders the Portland five should all have served their sentences in the first offenders' wings of prisons such as Wormwood Scrubs, Wakefield and Maidstone; but because they were regarded as high security risks (i.e., liable to escape), they were sent to orthodox prisons to mix with the ordinary run of criminals: Molody to Birmingham, Peter Kroger to Manchester, Houghton to Winchester. All three complained bitterly through their M.P.s to the Home Office against this and other discriminations (none was allowed to attend evening education classes), but all in vain.

Gradually conditions relaxed a little, and the five occupied their nonworking time in various ways. Molody read widely, including the latest copies of *Pravda* (every prisoner is allowed a copy of his local paper), and took to translating English books into Russian. They included *The Man Who Never Was, Popsky's Private Army* and *Beyond the Chindwin*. He was approached at intervals by British intelligence (including his old friend Mr. Elton from the School of Oriental and African Studies days) who were hopeful of making a deal with him for reduction of sentence in return for information supplied.

But Molody was too strong a character and too well trained even to be tempted by such an offer. If he had to serve a sentence of twenty-five years, then he would serve it; he had always known that, if caught, there would be a price to pay. In prison he was as liked and respected by the authorities and fellow prisoners as he had been by men like G. G. Smith and Ferguson Smith, who had been instrumental in sending him there.

Peter Kroger was also a model prisoner— "a good example," wrote someone who knew him, "of the power of inner resources." He was a natural teacher who loved both acquiring knowledge and imparting it. As a result, fellow prisoners were always coming to him for advice on a variety of subjects, and he was always ready to give it. "He was patient and enduring," said another who knew him. "I have yet to discover the man who found him less than amiable."

For Mrs. Kroger, in Holloway with Bunty Gee, and without her husband's intellectual resources, life was more irksome. She was always complaining, and when toward the end of her sentence Gay Search visited her, she said sourly, "Tell your mother I shall never forgive her." Bunty Gee found her coarse in her habits, and said she often ate food with her hands.

Bunty herself, always a shy person, mixed with others as little as possible and was happy to take on the job of prison librarian.

In Winchester, Houghton's thoughts were centered on seeing Bunty again; and though both of them made repeated requests through the Home Office, it wasn't until the autumn of 1964, or three and a half years after the trial, that they were allowed a half-hour meeting in Holloway. Thereafter similar meetings were allowed at three-month intervals.

Apart from this, Houghton spent much of his time making a

tapestry bedspread. "There are more than 120,000 stitches in the finished article," he wrote. "How do I know this? Because, having little else to do, when I'd finished the job I counted them."

PERHAPS MOLODY'S MORALE remained so high because of what the colonel had told him at the Moscow Center in 1954—that if ever he found himself in prison, they would in time find ways and means of getting him out. First indications that this was a possibility came when Molody's old friend Rudolf Abel, sentenced by a U.S. court in 1957 to thirty years for espionage, was exchanged in 1962 for the American pilot Francis Gary Powers, also given a long sentence by a Soviet court when his U-2 reconnaissance plane was shot down in 1960 while spying over Soviet territory.

In 1963 the British businessman Greville Wynne was given an eight-year sentence in Moscow for collaborating with the Russian traitor Penkovsky in bringing out intelligence to the West. After this it occurred to many people, both in Russia and Britain, that a similar exchange might be arranged with Molody. There were no further secrets for either to divulge; neither could do any more harm to the society that had imprisoned them; both were looked on as uninvited guests.

Accordingly, an exchange was arranged, and on April 21, 1964, Molody was taken from Winson Green Prison in Birmingham to Northolt airport and put on an RAF transport plane to West Berlin. At five thirty next morning he was driven to the Heerstrasse checkpoint in the German Democratic Republic. A man got out of a car and walked toward Molody's car to satisfy himself that it contained Molody. As he neared, Molody recognized him as his old friend, the colonel from the Center. They smiled but said nothing. Then a British intelligence officer walked over to confirm that Wynne was Wynne.

The two men got out of their respective cars. Molody thought that Wynne looked ill (which he was after eleven months in the Lubyanka Prison), and said to his guard, "I sure hope he doesn't choose this moment to kick the bucket!" Then the control officer said, "Exchange," and Wynne was bundled into Molody's car and Molody into Wynne's.

That afternoon Molody reached Moscow and soon was entering

his own house, to be greeted enthusiastically by his family—Galisha, Liza, Dina, Trofim and his youngest child. And later that evening, to complete his happiness, his old friend Rudolf Abel, whom he hadn't seen since 1955 in New York, looked in for a drink and to share their latest experiences.

At long last Molody had come in from the cold.

Two YEARS LATER, in 1966, the notorious British double agent George Blake, sentenced to an unprecedented forty-two years' imprisonment for espionage, made his brilliant escape from Wormwood Scrubs to Russia. Afraid that this portended similar action by the Krogers, Houghton and Gee, the Home Office panicked. Houghton was bundled out of Winchester prison in the middle of the night, driven at top speed to the security wing of Durham Prison (usually reserved for murderers and other men of violence), made to wear a shapeless uniform and put into solitary confinement. Transferred to Parkhurst, on the Isle of Wight, Peter Kroger was made to wear the same clothes and also put into solitary confinement. Bunty Gee was whisked from Styal open prison in Cheshire—where she had been more or less free to come and go—returned to Holloway and forcibly removed to the borstal wing. She was put in a filthy cell, and for weeks the light was kept on all night so that the authorities might see she was still there! "I am worse off now," she wrote to a friend, "than at any time during the past $5\frac{1}{2}$ years."

Gradually, as time passed without any further attempted escapes, the authorities relaxed these restrictions and conditions again returned to something like normal.

Next to leave were the Krogers, who in October 1969 were exchanged for the Russian-held British lecturer Gerald Brooke, sentenced to five years for espionage in 1965. Their fear had always been that they would be deported to the United States, there to stand trial for their activities in both the Yakovlev and Abel networks. But the United States government had no wish to reopen the wounds of cases they considered closed.

Before his departure Peter Kroger's fellow prisoners gave him a farewell dinner; and Helen Kroger told Gay Search that she had at last forgiven her mother. The next day the Krogers, with Helen clutching an outsize teddy bear, boarded a plane to Poland. They traveled first class, and spent most of the journey drinking champagne and talking to the accompanying pressmen.

Last to leave were Houghton and Gee, who were finally released in May 1970 after just over nine years' imprisonment. Bunty returned to her house in Portland; Houghton went to a neighboring hotel. It might be thought that after everything Bunty Gee had endured at Houghton's hands—his conning her into believing that Molody was American, his offer to the crown to turn Queen's evidence against her, the long, wasted years of imprisonment—she might not have wanted anything more to do with him. But in fact she needed him as much as he needed her. For several weeks the pair were pursued relentlessly by the press, but at last escaped their attentions long enough to travel to Poole and be married at the local register office. It says something for both that though they had betrayed their country, neither at the end of the day betrayed each other.

In October of that year three of the principal participants in the Portland spy case died. Molody collapsed from a heart attack while picking mushrooms in a field outside Moscow. He was still only forty-eight, and undoubtedly his death had been brought on by the accumulated strain of nearly twenty years' espionage in his country's service. Later that month Mrs. Search and Superintendent G. G. Smith also died, both on the same day.

Of the rest, the Krogers have never been heard of again. Wilfred Search lives alone in 1 Courtfield Gardens (the owner of a handsome set of cutlery, presented by a grateful MI-5). His daughter, Gay, is a free-lance journalist; the Kemps still live at 43 Cranley Drive. Jim Skardon and Ferguson Smith are in retirement, and Mr. and Mrs. Harry Houghton live in a comfortable house on the outskirts of a south-coast town. For all of them the Portland spy case now is but a memory of the distant past.

DOCTOR
CRIPPEN'S DIARY

DOCTOR CRIPPEN'S DIARY

by
Emlyn Williams

Even today, nearly seventy years after the event, the name Hawley Harvey Crippen, M.D., is still likely to evoke cries of "monster" and "fiend." Ironically, however, most people of the time knew Crippen as a pleasant, inoffensive gentleman who couldn't hurt a fly. And certainly when Inspector Dew of Scotland Yard uncovered the ghastly secret of Crippen's cellar, the good people of Hilldrop Crescent were unprepared to believe that their neighbor was capable of anything so horrendous.

It is true that his marriage was unhappy, and true that his wife had been unfaithful. Then along came Ethel—sweet, tender, trusting—and once love had entered the picture there was no turning back. By the time Inspector Dew had made his grisly discovery, the doctor and his lady were one step ahead of him—on a ship in mid-Atlantic, fleeing to Canada. But there was a new invention, the ship-to-shore wireless. . . .

The distinguished author-actor Emlyn Williams, of *Night Must Fall* and *The Corn Is Green* fame, re-creates this hair-raising but strangely touching story in the form of the doctor's intimate diary, complete with his erratic punctuation and spelling; and while the diary is an ingenious fictional device here, it is based solidly on the facts.

PART ONE
TOWARDS THE YARD

CHAPTER 1: THE GUY NOBODY NOTICES

HOSPITAL COLLEGE, CLEVELAND Ohio, March 13 1883.

This is me, Hawley Harvey Crippen & what do you know, Im 21 today! (The 13th, but Im not superstitious). And since theres nobody in this sleazy rooming house to tell the big news to, heres me telling it to myself.

And in a Diary!! What am I doing with a Diary? (A thick one at that, as Diaries go) Because it's my only Birthday Present, thats why. When you're on your ownsome & dont mix, even your 21st B. can pass unnoticed.

Except by Mr Melton my English teacher in high school—he has kept up with me ever since, with birthday cards & now this, he's a kind fanciful soul. His note says, Make sure you keep this Diary up—put your thoughts in, you never know where it might lead.

The reason old M. got the idea I could be a writer & keep a Diary was that he once gave us a Composition to do, the *Adventures of a 5-Cent Peice*. Well, I was only 12 but I took that Coin all over town—out of the till into the purse of a rich lady covered with jewelry, then its stolen by 2 burglars who fight over it & one kills the other & old M. said that was farfetched & better stick to facts.

But he did say, in his blunt way, Crippen youre nothing to look at & not blessed with a pretty name & never open your mouth, but stick a pen in yr hand & youre off. So here I am, back to the same ruled paper. Try anything once. (I do know one thing this writing will show up—faulty puntuation & certain spellings not what they might be.)

What shall I put? Born Coldwater Michigan, father dry-goods merchant. Cold & dry, thats me. Not a v. good start in Life.

Well, I've got to the bottom of that first page and starting another, what do you know?

You could call me the guy nobody notices.

They dont even look right through me, they just bend to left or right to see who's behind me, like I was a lamppost. A short lamppost at that, 5 ft 5 (just), bulgy forehead, thick moony steel-rimmed glasses, weakish mustache, (sandy, walrus variety) & losing my hair, on my 21st birthday.

But theres more going on under that hair than meets the eye. For one thing, I face facts—how many guys aged 21 will own up that theyre never going to make their mark in the world?

But my intelligence is average, I worked hard at my medical studies & got my M.D. here. Off to London (England) any minute, to perfect them (expenses paid by Uncle Otto, with intro to Hospitals so I can watch operations etc, I'm looking forward to it)

Funny how I came to see myself as Doctor—when I was 12 in Coldwater, Uncle Otto was doing well with his barber's shop & I liked to watch the shaving & haircutting. I thought, I'll be a Barber when I grow up, & he gave me lessons in Haircutting after hours (& if I had friends at this moment, I could cut hair for them).

Then comes the day when one of his assistants is drunk & slips while shaving a customer with cutthroat razor & the razor lives up to its name, blood all over the place, my Uncle faints & I rush up with towels & basin & bind up the poor guys neck, tight, they said afterwards I had saved his life.

My Uncle said how brave I was to face the blood, I said it was just like any other mess, he said I was meant to be a Doctor & here I am, training to be one.

Only not on a big scale, my plan is to be an eye-&-ear man, with Dentistry thrown in, as a boy I used to fiddle with gadgets & things & enjoy getting them to go right, like a Singer sewing machine one time. And I'm on my way.

My, my wrist is tired already—thats the beginning, and end, of my diary! What that guy Rousseau must have felt like at the end of those

Confessions—but from the hints you get, his wrist got pretty tired other ways, but thats sly talk & only for this ruled paper.

Which I'll be burning anyways. But it has helped my temper.

17 HANDEL ST, BLOOMSBURY, London, 8 wks later, May 12, 1883.

What do you know, I somehow didnt burn it & here I am, having just found it bottom of baggage!

So here I go again.

I have a poor room not too spick-&-span, but I do like this City. After those Middle-West shantytowns & that terrible twang—I seem to be sensitive to sounds, particularly ugly voices—I'm American too but the rare times I open my mouth I am careful to speak nicely. My landlady remarked, O Mr Crippen I like the way you say Good Morning, so quiet & pleasant.

Then theres the Police, the Yankee tourists are right. Coming out of Westm. Abbey & strolling round the corner, I said to a Bobby, Excuse me, could you direct me to Cleopatra's Needle? And instead of just pointing in a surly fashion, he took trouble to say, Go across the road, round Scotland Yard there, & along the Embankment.

I said, To us across the Herring pond, a yard is like what you call a garden here, & I dont see a garden. Then he laughed & said, You wont see Scotland neether, then explained it's some sort of Police Headquarters. I was conscious of his courtesy.

I enjoy the lectures & demonstrations of operations at St. Thomas & Barts. In secondhand shop in Charing Cross Rd, bought old copy of a manual on *Dentistry*, also Cunningham's *Manual of Practical Anatomy*, I'm told a good Surgeon can really strike it rich. With luck this manual could take me quite a way.

Then for pleasure I bought a ragged old *Dracula*—I like to dip into those made-up horrors, farfetched but take you out of yourself.

Walking through Camden Town up toward Hampstead, I took a wander through the residential part, lovely solid houses in wide curving streets with names like Place & Crescent—gentlemen's houses, respectable, everybody keeping to themselves. I must have London blood, for my heart is set on having one of these, on a lifelong lease.

It seems crazy writing to myself like this—things I know already—but it puts it together, like framing a picture. Maybe it's a habit I ought to take up.

2347 MADISON ST DETROIT, March 13 1885, 23rd birthday.

Well, I didnt. (Didnt take it up I mean, its been 2 yrs to the day) But then this last yr Ive been hard at it studying for my Diploma, thats what I'm going to NY for, to take it at Opthalmic Hospital.

2347 M. ST, DETROIT, 3 mths later, June 28.

I passed! And I'm Doctor Crippen, for life!

Passed with Credit, & the Credit said, This Candidate gains special mention for hygienic state of hands when at work on sore gums, & for their soft delicate touch so appreciated by a patient. I never thought of that, must be second nature to me. I'm going to keep my hands up to scratch with that Velvet Lavender they advertise in the NY subway.

Yes, on my way, & that tall house in the curved London street is that one step nearer. Mind you, theyre all big family houses. Doctor & Mrs Crippen!

SALT LAKE CITY, 3 yrs later, March 13 1888, 26th birthday.

What do you know, 3 yrs since I wrote that, & with Detroit behind me (Asst. to Dr Porter) here I am, married with baby! Shows you dont know yourself as well as you thought you did. Whats the story? Oh, it just happened.

Charlotte Bell, daughter of a waterworks engineer—well, between me & me—a Plumber. Not pretty, not plain, poor complexion. Taller than me, but what could I expect, I wasn't looking for a wife in a circus.

A nice girl who respects my wishes, cleans and cooks well. I dont love her, leastways I dont think so—I wouldnt know, as I cant imagine loving anybody. Liking some, yes. But even then, not enough to make a friend.

The bedroom business I manage all right, but it doesnt bother me. From the way I overhear other young fellows talk, I must be pretty undemanding in that area. And I'm glad, saves a lot of wear & tear. And money. Enough of that.

And like a lot of married men who dont drool over kids, I was presented with one within a year. A boy, Otto Hawley Crippen if you please, Charlotte wanted him named after me & I let it go.

I still think of London, & that curved road with the trees. Itll come.

SALT LAKE CITY, 3 yrs later, Feb 21, 1891.

Charlotte passed away 5 days ago, while I was out of town on business trip (Pneumonia, sick 2 weeks).

That sounds as if I'm writing this because I'm upset. But it's not so, I'm writing to put on record—between me & myself as usual!—a funny thing.

It's rare for a doctor to be able to say he's never seen a dead person, but people dont die of earache or a wisdom tooth. So this was my first time.

I walked in & found 3 neighbors (women of course) who had come in to view. They hadnt known her except to nod to, but they all 3 had the same look—& I guess what they call in books <u>awe</u>—ie, fear of a Dead Person.

And they feel this <u>awe</u> because theyve been told to, since they were born. And theres no sense in it—what is so mysterious about stopping breathing, when you think, its one of the few prospects weve all got in common?

The mortician had done an A.1 job, & I could hardly credit it was Charlotte. She looked far cuter than she ever had in life. More repose. None of those second-rate thoughts flitting through her head—in fact it looked better empty.

He had worked on that poor complexion & she looked downright pretty, like a waxwork—so like, in fact, that I had to pinch one cheek to make sure it wasnt.

Call me a cold fish if you like, whats the use of me pretending, when I'm telling something <u>to myself</u>? I realized today that not only the mouth & ears, but the whole human body is just an object, and when dead is no different than a clock thats stopped ticking & can never be started again. Doesnt that make sense?

P.S. A telegram just got to me, from Charlotte's father, saying theyll see to little Otto. A relief.

The funeral was frugal. But rubbish was spoken, from up in the pulpit & by the graveside. They kept referring to <u>Poor Mrs Crippen</u>, as if I hadnt ever given her a cent for housekeeping.

HICKORY HOTEL, BROOKLYN, 13 months later, March 13 1892, 30th birthday.

Here I am again! (I can understand people who keep track of

themselves by writing everything down, starting off with <u>Dear Diary</u>, I nearly did then) Working for Dr Jeffery, & doing the best yet—well liked for courtesy & efficiency.

30! I dont mind Middle Age getting nearer, it will suit me better than being young, I think.

Getting a bit sick of eating houses & sour-faced waitresses & having to do my laundry at the sink. Wont write again unless I can put down the name of a new wife.

That makes me smile over my pen, sounding as it does like that British king Henry the Something, that made a hobby of beheading them, & then on to the next—hardly my line of country!

HICKORY HOTEL, BROOKLYN, NY. A month later, April 14 1892.
  <u>Cora Turner!</u>
  Isnt that a good-sounding name?

CHAPTER 2: CURIOSITY, INDIFFERENCE

NOT A WIFE of course—and no Charlotte neither—Mercy no! I'm confused, and writing in this may straighten me out. Met her 3 nights ago, when I'd been in Brooklyn 7 months, in the Eldorado Vaudeville Theater on the corner. A fleabag.

Well, watching a waltz I got a whiff of strong perfume and turned to look (I had discouraged it with Charlotte) and there was this woman staring at the stage with her lips not together. Perfect teeth (& I ought to know). Then she turns to me & says, Aint that <u>beautiful?</u>

Then when we got up to leave she said, Pea-nut? & offers me one, which I courteously took & partook of. She was two or three inches taller than me, but now, seeing her in the light, I realized she wasn't an older woman, but a young one, 26 at the most (She was actually 19—ie, 11 yrs younger than me)

She had 2 things I was face to face with for the 1st time—& me aged 30! A fur coat, & makeup. Not only that pappier-poudry stuff, but rouge & lipstick, the whole kit & caboodle. She looked (at best) like an actress, & at worst—well. But it takes all sorts.

But her voice was low and ladylike, when she said, My husband being out of town, could I trouble you to walk me to my house on the next street?

I raised my hat, With pleasure. Glancing sideways as we walked, I noticed she did not pull her veil down in the street. I saw a man give her a good stare, then another. She was certainly an eyeful. I felt proud of myself.

Her house was just a rooming house, she asked me in, I hesitated and she said, O only the parlor, & gives what they call in storybooks a throaty laugh. The parlor was v. shabby but she didnt seem to mind.

She threw back her fur & I saw she had a full bust, a bit too full for me, & nearly as low cut as the actresses on the stage. She was wearing a reddish sort of brooch, I asked what it was, she said, Only a garnet but I do love jewelry. Then she brought two small glasses out of a sideboard & poured, it was port. Her eyes very dark & soft, like molasses.

Then she talked, in that quiet voice. Daughter of a Professor in an upstate College, good Catholic family, she carrying out her Dad's ambition for her to be a singer—& her husband working hard as the Head of a Travel Agency to provide her with the essential training.

Ive never been within a mile of a female like this one. We're meeting next week. I'm puzzled what she sees in me. We'll see.

HICKORY HOTEL, BROOKLYN, 5 weeks later, May 22 1892.

After that first night we have met once a week. Before proceeding to the Eldorado, we met in neighborhood drugstore (coffee, I paid) & after the show the glass of port in the parlor. The 3rd time she told me she expected her husband back next week.

And the 4th time, she confessed she didnt have a husband at all, & that the man she was expecting back in town (by the name of J. Lincoln) had taken advantage of her 3 yrs back, when she was 16. He had bought her the fur coat & the garnet, but after that gave her only just enough to live on. He'd promised to pay for her voice lessons but he was a rat, she was through with men.

Then we had 2 more ports, walked over to my (Hickory) Hotel and went quietly up to my room, where intimacy took place.

(What is good about a Diary, you can put in things like that, which you would not dream of uttering out loud)

It wasnt anything to write home about. I was scared I might not be up to it (if I may so put the problem) & of course that means you havent much of a chance.

But good enough for her to give me a nice kiss, then squeeze my hand. She did say I looked funny without my glasses, I had hoped she would pay me a compliment.

And she did giggle at me insisting to keep my pajama top on—I reckon I just didn't fancy being in my birthday suit as you might say, we all have quirks.

Then I told her I had prospects, & proposed. She said Yes. We are to be married in 3 months, Sept 1st.

Its confusing, because I still cant see what she sees in me, I think she thinks Im cleverer than I am. I seem to amuse her in some way, like I was some weird young kid. Youd never think I was 11 yrs older.

Dr. Crippen's ill-fated second wife was Cora Turner, née Kunigunde Mackamotski.

And what do I see in her? I certainly dont love her, any more than I did Charlotte—not the way they carry on in the storybooks. I guess that (on my part) its just Curiosity.

I guess I want to go on like I was doing that first night when I walked her home. I want to show her off.

1754 BURGOYNE ST. ST LOUIS, 22 months later, March 13, 32nd birthday.

After we got married (in Jersey City) we came down here, where I am doing well as consulting physician to an Optician, Mr. Hirsch on Olive St. Was able to give Cora a Xmas present. A diamond ring. Small, but good.

V. small house but we have got to be patient. Cora a bit slapdash with cooking & cleaning but with more life than Charlotte, & her singing is pretty. And will get prettier with the lessons I'm paying for.

In our private relations, I'm afraid she gets kind of carried away, so I guess its only fair that I should perform a husbands duty once a week.

Also, again with her youth & temperament, I can see she craves for company & so I have cultivated 2 or 3 married couples from the local church (Catholic). I'm not religious but it's a stylish atmosphere & churchgoing is a good respectable habit. She wants me converted but I've ducked that.

It's a dull day-to-day life, but that suits me. No more pen-to-paper till further notice.

1754 Burgoyne St, St Louis, Feb 10 1896.

Well, heres the Further Notice, 2 yrs on—no, its not the 10th, its the 11th.

It's taken all this time for the balloon to go up, but it had to come. All these phenomenons are gradual, & then—boom!

Little things, week to week. Smoking, which I dont hold with in a wife who calls herself a lady. First 3 a day, then 6, then 12, then 20. Me getting back after a hard day to dirty dishes piled up, laundry basket spilling soiled linen & her sitting back with feet up, cigarette glued to her lip & in the sulks.

Some evenings she beats me at my own game and wont speak! I try to cheer her up with a glass of her favorite port, no good. The house was small to begin with, but it's shrinking by the day.

Then she starts going to the toilet, every hour on the hour. I ask if theres something wrong with her bladder, she says, Dont talk to a lady like that, I say I'm not only her Husband but a Doctor, & so we go on.

Then I start noticing her getting v. flushed, & with her putting on weight she looks more like 40 than 23. Then (all of a sudden) she starts jabbering again, & I take note of her voice—that soft purring carry-on in the Eldorado was a performance, & I know too well how ugly noise affects me. The worst Bronx twang, like a buzz saw with a nose.

Going on about how she misses her Dad the College Professor. College Professor!

One day in the desk I came across her Birth Certificate—he was a college man alright, a Yonkers college where he was janitor. And I saw she's no more Cora Turner than I am, she had to come clean then—Ma was German, Pa a Russian-Polack immigrant, and she's Kunigunde Mackamotski! Sounds like something written up on the wall of a subway W.C.

When I first met her, the only true thing she said was, that she was a Catholic.

Well, on such evenings I used to think (with her gabbling on)—she's hystirical. Then, only last week, I wised up—it wasnt the toilet she was making the trips to, it was the bathroom cabinet. I was looking for some Enos Fruit Salts, when behind the medicines I found a half-empty bottle of Gin.

Well, we come to tonight. The worst yet. I was sitting with the St Louis paper & having a quiet read, about those terrible goings-on in London a while back—my nice respectable London—with this Jack the Ripper thats a maniac who murdered these women in the East End, terrible to think there are such people about, & they say hes supposed to be a Doctor—(a libel on my profession!).

Well, I happened to mention this & she says, What sort of women did he murder? And I say (joking), No better than they should be. Then she gives me a glassy look, then snarls through the smoke from that damned cigarette—Say that again! I did, adding, You know—prostitutes.

Then she said, going up into a screech—I know prostitutes? Are you telling me I'm a person that knows prostitutes?

Then I knew there was no arguing with her, and I said, What you need is another date upstairs, with the toilet. What you mean, she said, & those eyes that had once looked so melting, now they were a pair of blackberries on fire—what you mean? Then the balloon goes up.

Good-for-nothing small-town quack, youre nothing but a little stick-in-the-mud—and whats more, you've got me stuck in the same mud, up to here you have! Then she screams—Mr P.T., Mr P.T.! I said, What that mean & she said, It's what I always call you to myself! (Referring to my quirk already mentioned)

Well, I could have killed her then. But I can keep my temper.

Then she had to stop for breath, so I jumped right in & asked her why she'd married me. She said, Because I was at my wits end. She told me it had been either having to go be a waitress, or me—so it had to be me.

Well, I get her up to bed & into a stupid sleep, then I sit & take stock. It's a funny thing, I should be shaking all over but I'm not, I'm as cool as a cucumber.

And I said to myself, Tonight has done the trick. 3½ years of a marriage that was like sitting in a miserable little room with the window sealed, and all of a sudden—an explosion & fresh air right through.

That sounds as if I'm walking out. I'm not.

Because I'm the plodding sort, that tends to want to stop wandering and stay put. For instance, though Charlotte wasnt that big in my life, I never thought of wanting to get out of it, and the same with this situation.

Oh yes, till tonight it's been a miserable one—because I was scared of her. After tonight—no. Because I know now she's scared. Bored with me, yes, but scared—scared that she may (one of these days) be left in the lurch. Thats why she's been hitting the booze.

She's dependent on me. To outsiders I'm the henpecked hubby and her the big boss. Well, it's more like the other way round. No, I'm not walking out.

I suppose it's like a boxer feels, going into the ring. A challenge.

One thing for sure. It's going to be a long match. The longest ever.

34 STORE ST, TOTTENHAM Court Rd, London, 5 yrs later, March 13 1901, 39th birthday.

Ashamed to report that the only event in the 5 yrs is this move to London last yr, when the 20th Century (can't get used to saying it!) brought me luck. With my diploma, a British doctor (Newton) in Philly got me fixed up here as Manager for *Munyon's Remedies* (Patent Medicines) in Shaftesbury Ave. Modest little business, poky flat too, but it's London at last.

One office boy, and my promised Secretary turned out to be a mousy 17-year-old girl with long straight hair that looked as if it was just going to get in her inkwell. By the way, she turned up last week with her hair up for her 18th birthday, and I didnt recognize her! (Not much of an item for a Diary!)

On domestic front, nothing to report (after that rowdy night all those yrs back!) The gin was never in the bathroom again (moved into sideboard) but not overindulged in since except when on show, so she can go on bubbling & flashing & showing those healthy teeth. I'm a bit balder, her coal-black hair a bit fairer, to do with a bottle (not the gin one).

The future Music Hall star Mrs Cora Crippen has not yet made the grade (she's putting on more weight) & Agents not helpful, she gets mad at them.

But her private life is OK, although (since that night) I never performed the Husband's Duty. Now I know her well enough to know—to put it in a coarse manner—that she has to have it. Or there'd be hell to pay.

Well, one married couple we met at her Catholic Church in Kentish Town includes a well-built baritone. He may well sing of a Sunday—solo—but (during the week) isnt above a duet on the side.

Suits me. I'm a peaceful man.

39 HILLDROP CRESCENT, Camden Town, London NW, Sept 27, 1905, 4½ yrs later.

Now this is an address!

Moved in last week. It's come true! She agreed that the Store St flat was getting more poky, and I walked about and saw this house TO LET. Just as I had dreamed of it—bay windows, three storys without the Area (basement part) & 2 trees in front garden, thick with leaves. Road dips down in graceful curve, with a slight slope, hence the name—Hilldrop Crescent. Omnibus to work, but worth it.

A big house, for 2 people. 2 sitting rooms on 1st floor with bedroom & sitting room on floor above that, 2 bedrooms & attic above that.

In basement, kitchen & maids room (which will use as dining room) next to cellar (for coal & rubbish) under front door & front steps.

Quite a mansion, but I fancy a roomy home. And for an extra reason. For the first time since married, I'll have my own room, & my own single bed. (I bet it suits her too.)

The Landlord Mr Lown, very pleasant, he said he would be relieved to have a Doctor for a tenant, 52 pounds 10 shillings a year per annum for 3 yrs. To celebrate move, will buy her a small diamond brooch to match bracelet I gave her last year. Makes me feel good, & I can afford it with spending nothing on myself.

Being handy with my hands, I'm going to wallpaper right through. Green I thought (restful) but she gives a shriek & says, With my Irish blood I'm superstitious & green would be a Hoodoo on me in a house & bring bad luck.

I thought to myself—Irish? No kidding, I never knew Dublin was in Poland.

Pink! The place will look like a whorehouse, but if I insisted on the green & she so much as broke her little finger, she'd blame me.

She's a muddle of a woman—spends money like water on clothes—my friends call me a Bird of Paradise—but over Housekeeping watches the pennies like a refugee from where her Dad came from, hates servants (& they hate her) she'll do the shopping & cooking & washing, which means she'll half do it, hit or miss, & thats where I'll come in.

Anything for a quiet life.

She's got Bruce Miller's photo by her bed. Music Hall Artist, a Bass this time, with a Musical Saw. She tells me he's American, tall & strapping, & she goes to him & his wife for duets. It's the one thing she seems to work at, is the duets. I asked her what the wife was like, & she said, Hard to describe. I bet. I expect the wife turns the music pages for them.

Saw a letter on her dressing table, Dear Brown Eyes, Tuesday usual time, Bruce. He calls them Brown Eyes, I call them Blackberries. Depends how you look at it.

Thank God for Bruce, for theres nothing doing for her in the Profession, I guess she's not loaded with talent (& lazy). She did a sketch she wrote herself, at Balham Music Hall, but faint applause, a Flop as they say.

I am amused to look at the program—Acting Manager, H. H. Crippen. Do I manage her? Her friends wouldnt think so, but she needs me more than she thinks.

She wasnt helped by the name she billed herself by—*Macka Motski*, if you please (made up from Mackamotski). I might just as well go on the Halls as Crip Pen. (Sang song called *An Unknown Quantity*. Judging by her figure—she's still putting on weight—if she goes on like this, *An Unknown Quantity* will just about describe her.)

I feel if she is to get anywhere she must have a name which will look well across a marquee, and have got her to turn into *Miss Belle Elmore*. Hello Belle, So long Kunigunde.

I notice when she goes for the duets, she puts on all my peices of jewelry.

39 HILLDROP CRESCENT, 6 months later, March 13 1906, 44th birthday.

Nothing to report. Business not so good—& its one business after the other—its not that I cant settle to one job—I am reliable—but no job seems to be able to settle to me.

And not my fault, take the Drouet Institute, Regents Park, some months ago.

I worked hard for them, then I began to smell a rat—the man keeping the accounts had (to me) a shifty eye. Then both eyes got shifty, & it ended in the Police Court.

I had to give evidence, about seeing him practicing signatures—and being a moral man, I hated the prospect of that! Sleepless nights, so she had to put something in my nightly Dr Tibbles Vi Cocoa, to make me sleep at all.

Then the Sovereign Remedy Ltd—the Sovereign turned out to be less than solid gold, went bankrupt. Then the Aural Clinic—failed last week.

Am in middle of reading *Diary of a Nobody,* life in the London suburbs. V. amusing.

A Nobody with a Diary, thats me. Better news next time.

39 H. CRESC, 2 YRS LATER, March 13, 1908, 46th birthday.

I seem to be settled at last—my own little Office in a big block of Offices, Albion House, New Oxford St, where I work still for Munyons Remedies but also I work in partnership with 2 pleasant Doctors, Rylance & Masters *(Yale Tooth Specialists)*.

I even had a <u>Dental Mechanic</u>, Bill Long who has worked with me on and off for several yrs, then theres young Taylor the Commercial Traveler who comes in and out, a bright willing lad that wants to be a Doctor, but unfortunately—like my Uncle Otto—cant stand the sight of blood, & in our profession, that is a serious handicapp.

We are all in harmony, & they seem to like me & my ways. I even cut their hair for them at times! (the Doctors & Bill Long) & sometimes (in fun) they give me the nickname of Sweeny Todd the Demon Barber of New Oxford St. All friendly, though we are formal together, its always Dr Crippen & Mr Long etc.

And of course theres my Sec & Bookkeeper, thats been with me since the early Drouet Institute days. Since I work hard, thank God for her, she is so good you dont know she's there. Quiet as a mouse & smooth as a machine.

A mouse machine, that just about describes Ethel Le Neve.

CHAPTER 3: LOVE

39 H. CRESC, 2 WEEKS later, March 27 1908.

Something extraordinary has happened.

I don't know where I am. I'm 46 yrs old, & I just don't know. All of a heap.

This afternoon I was in the Office in Albion House—the usual business afternoon, wax-in-the-ears, filling come loose etc. Rain, across New Oxford St a regular pea-souper of a fog, so you could hardly tell an ear from a mouth, when—a knock at the door.

A telegram.

I do get the odd business telegram & was just opening it when I saw it was for my Sec. I doubt if she'd ever had one in her life & opening it her hands were trembling. She looked like a scared child.

I knew why too—I'd overheard Taylor the Comm. Traveler chatting to her.

The family live in a bad part of Camden Town—quite near Hilldrop Cr.—but the one she's really close to is her father. The telegram is to say he's been run over & dangerously ill in Hospital.

Well, she went dead white, looked across at me—she's the same height, & her face crumpled up like paper, & the next minute she'd flown over to me & her head on my shoulder & sobbing like a baby. There was a funny nice smell like of wild flowers somehow, it was the eau de cologne which on hot days I'd seen her dab some on a little handkerchief.

Then she babbled something, twice—I couldnt get it, she was kind of hiccuping. And holding me tight.

It was a bombshell. I'd never so much as shaken hands with her, just Good morning Miss Le Neve, Good morning Doctor, & here I was with my arms round her.

This wasnt a mouse, nor a machine neither, it was a person.

Well, I said, There, there, or words to that effect—nothing that sticks in the memory—sat her back at her typewriter & poured a drop of brandy from the emergency cupboard. I said she must go back to her lodgings (Constantine Rd Hampstead) & offered to see her to her omnibus but she insisted she was all right. I gave her money for her fare up to the Hospital & she went.

And left me in the Office. Alone. And I'd never been in it, ever, without her there. In her quiet corner.

A minute ago, as I was writing down the above, I heard Cora's voice behind me—Hawley, what the bloody hell are you writing, your life story?

I said, I'm working on a treatise (as well I might be). But in future I'll confine my scribbling to my private bedroom.

She's sitting there in one of her trailing negleeges or whatever, manicuring her nails. When she's not on show, her voice gets more and more of a rasp on it. And to think I have got no idea what my Sec's voice sounds like, except for Good morning Doctor, yes Doctor no Doctor.

(Ive got to the end of the Diary, would you believe it. Because it is a Diary now, & Ive got kind of addicted)

N.B. buy another tomorrow. A thicker one.

And I wont refer to my better half (!) as anything but B.E., her name suits her less every day. Belle my eye.

39 H. Cresc, next evening March 28 1908, 9 pm.

Didnt sleep last night. And today, alone in the Office, not a stroke of work—I just sat looking at the corner where her typewriter was sitting, with a black hood over it like it was in mourning.

What does she look like, I thought to myself—and (after 8 yrs) I couldnt remember. Slim, brown hair parted in the middle, tied in a neat bun, large eyes—but what color? Neat ankles in black stockings—I had noticed that, and when she put her typed letters in front of me, small delicate hands.

Then in the middle of the afternoon, still staring at the typewriter, I got up, went to it, and under it pulled out a little drawer. I felt like a criminal or something.

Pencils, little bottle of our Liver Pills, old postcard from her Dad, a copy of the *Sunday Companion,* then the eau de cologne. I sniffed at it—& with the scent, that short minute with her comes back to me, the babbling of it as well. What was it she said, twice? And I remembered.

She said, <u>You</u> are my father now. Twice, she said it.

And I could have been too. When checking insurance I had once glanced at her Birth Certificate, & she was born in 1883, when I was all of 21.

Thank God for pen & paper. If I hadnt got into the run of this Diary, I'd this minute burst.

39 H. Cresc, 2 days later, March 30 1908, 6 am.

Couldnt sleep.

Last evening La Belle came back from another audition.

Blast them—she said—they wouldnt even let me finish my 1st chorus, & the Sods were only touring managers at that, that Mr Didcott has the cheek to call himself an Agent, he wont be mine much longer. (I knew there was more to her bad temper than that—Bruce Miller's gone back to U.S.A.)

I looked at her where she was standing in front of the mirror, taking the hatpin out of her showy best (audition) hat with all that glitter on it (all that glitters dont mean contracts) glaring away at herself & fiddling with that dyed hair with the false curls. And I thought, Who is she?

A stranger.

And that slip of a ghost of a girl, who I only know from her typing, is close to me. She belongs to me, I'm her father and her—

Her what?

I feel as if Ive been run over or something.

39 H. Cresc, later same day, 11 pm.

Today endless in Office, me doing my own typing, like a crippled person stumbling around on a sheet of paper. I went & sniffed the eau de cologne, twice.

Whats the matter with me?

39 H. Cresc, 3 nights later, April 2 1908, 10 pm.

This afternoon, with me typing in Office, she walks in. A dark wisp of a thing, tired out & no color.

I thought, She's come from the Funeral and said, like a dumbell, Youre back, how did it go, as if she had come straight from a wedding or some such.

She said, He nearly died but now off the danger list, thank you, then she comes right over to me.

I sat right back—what did I expect?—& she takes the heavy typewriter up, then back to where it belongs on her little table. She looks at my typing, tries to bite back a smile, takes up an eraser, puts it down again, rolls out my letter, and starts typing from it. She retyped the other letters as well.

As I said Good night and she said, Good night Doctor back, I dont think Ive ever called her anything. Not even Miss Le Neve.

I know I'll be awake again tonight. This cant go on.

39 H. Cresc, next evening, April 3, 1908, 10 pm.

On way to Office this morning—walking down to New Oxford St from omnibus—I bought a bunch of daffodils. Funny, all these years, with all the jewelry & new fur & such, I never once took home flowers.

I was putting them in the jug we have in the Office for hot water for the tea—I like English tea—when she arrived, still in her black. Good morning Doctor—then she saw me put the jug next to her typewriter. From pale she went quite red & said, Nobody ever brought me flowers before, thank you Doctor.

I said, I think by now you can stop calling me Doctor. Then I thought, I don't want her to call me Hawley.

And then I had a somewhat odd idea but didnt hesitate. I said, What's your father's name? Peter, she said. I said, Would you like to call me Peter? She thought a minute, then, Yes I would.

Then we got to work as usual, me filling prescriptions etc & her fetching them to be typed. And I thought, I'd like to sit in this shabby room, just the 2 of us, right through tonight and all tomorrow, and so on. I dont want to go home.

What sort of a home could you call it?

39 H. CRESC, NEXT evening, April 4, 1908, 12 pm.

I know I wont sleep, so here I am.

Tonight she gave a dinner party, celebration, the great Belle Elmore entertains her select group of friends (helps to make up for Bruce M. having gone).

With not landing an engagement, she's been keeping in touch with the Profession by taking stage paper *The Era* every week, & via that, enrolling as a member of the Music Hall Ladies Benevolent Guild (also through my old friend Dr Burroughs being its Hon. Physician).

And so met this couple Mr and Mrs Nash (he manages her, she performing under name of Lil Hawthorne, a Variety Turn as they call it) then (through them) Mrs Eugene Stratton, wife of a blackface comedian (American) who they say is famous.

Quite pleasant people, well spoken for Theatricals—& the celebration was because she's been put on the Committee, fancy that.

Well, B.E. was straining herself to please, & that meant talk, nonstop, nobody could get a word in edgeways, the conceit oozing out of her like persperation. Laying down the law about some poor actress married to an Irishman who had asked him to divorce her, & what a sauce on her part, she must know he's as staunch a Catholic as I am, & of course, he wont hear of such a thing.

I didnt say anything.

After dinner, she obliges with usual Song at Piano—the one she gave at last stage Appearance (early last year, Bedford Music Hall, 3 nights). *Down in the Old Cherry Orchard.* (But not wearing the short spangled dress she wore on the stage.)

It was never a big voice, but with the rest of her getting bigger the voice has got smaller. And wetter, quite a bit off the note.

Then whist. And the gin was out. She got fairly blotto over the cards, I always know because she doesnt bother (in front of guests) to hide her feelings for me, ie contempt. I'm in a draft Hawley, how many times do I have to tell you—

You'd never guess it was <u>my</u> jewels she'd got on! The others dont seem to mind, but that voice goes right through me. I look at her & I think of that slip of a girl bent over her typewriter. This morning she called me <u>Peter</u>—<u>good morning Peter</u> she said.

She was wearing a costume with coat over hips, trimmed with braid and braid buttons to match, blue serge she said it was, matches her blue-gray eyes. The other one she has is a costume in what they call gray shadow-stripe. She dresses very plain & ladylike, just needs a little flash of jewelry to set it off.

She's 100% perfect.

As they left Stratton says to me, quite jovial, Doctor what about getting the Christian names going. I'm Gene what are you?

Without thinking—Peter I said, like a shot. When theyd gone she said, Whats this Peter business? I said it's a third name & I'm sick of <u>Hawley</u>. Every time she hears Peter now it'll make her mad & she'll be flashing the old blackberries. I don't mind.

39 H. Cresc, 11 months later, March 13, 1909, 47th birthday.

Still 100%. One Saturday 6 months ago now, (since we close the Office at 12:30 on that day) I asked her to lunch at the Holborn Restaurant. It's got to be a habit by now and every Saturday, my excuse to No 39 is that I'm at the B. Museum Reading Room, brushing up my Medicine.

My Dearest (Ive taken to always calling her my Dearest, in my mind, & will henceforth refer to her as such, ie my D) is no easy talker, but Im not one to mind that—& when she <u>does</u> talk, its to the point. Sensible, wise & quite a sense of humor & she seems to appreciate mine, what there is of it.

She always loved her father of course, but with him being strict with her (& unreliable) she was always frightened of him—thats whats made her timid & not sure of herself. She says nobody ever did anything for her before I did. She already has confidence in me.

Plain, shy Ethel Le Neve worked as Dr. Crippen's secretary and bookkeeper for several years before their romance bloomed.

Like me, she's never made friends, so this getting together (like two magnets) was meant to be. I count the hours till that Saturday lunch.

And Sundays are horrible. I sometimes curse Bruce Miller for leaving the country, he was able to keep the lady on a fairly even keel but she's getting worse & worse—she's missing it badly. Gin isnt enough.

39 H. CRESC, 10 DAYS later, March 23 1909, 11 pm.

But whats more occupying my thoughts tonight, by a long shot, is what happened in the Office this afternoon. After 6 months!

The coldest day yet, this winter, & I saw her stop typing for a minute & rub her fingers, they were quite blue. I got up, doctorlike saying, We'll soon get the circulation back, & went & rubbed her hands together, quite hard, till they got good & warm.

Then I did something I still cant credit. I took her hands—palms up—& I kissed both palms.

Then I looked at her—there was such a beautiful look on her face that before I know it my glasses are in my hand & weve got our arms round each other, & kissing. Properly.

Well we stared as if we'd never seen each other before—like in a panic. Except I couldnt really see her, without my glasses she was just a fuzz.

She said, First time Ive seen your eyes, theyre nice. I said, Ive seen yours, theyre nice too. She said, You should put your glasses on again. I did. Then I said, You don't mind the glasses? She said, No, theyre a part of you. Well (I said) I have a few false teeth as well. She said, quite natural, with a smile—I know, Ive seen you cleaning them, through that glass door.

I said, I would have thought youd have liked young Taylor much better than me (the young Commercial Traveler). Then she says, He doesn't need glasses & I'm sure he's got all his own teeth, but I dont like him the same.

Then we stare at each other again. Luckily it was near time to go home, so I snatched at my bowler hat & coat & said something like, This wants some thinking over, & went.

And I never spoke a truer word. Ive been thinking it over ever since.

39 H. CRESC, NEXT morning, March 24 1909, 7:30 a.m.

I realize now, that all my life Ive been kind of drifting—letting things happen, easy come easy go, line of least resistance. And what makes me realize that, is that although I'm sitting here in my slippers, & pretty well shivering with cold—in spite of such a handicapp, for the first time in my life, I am sure of something.

And that something is—that I have got to have her—not just in the crude manner, I wouldn't speak of her in such a way—but to have her with me, for the rest of my life.

(I stopped writing just then, to sniff the eau de cologne, perhaps I'm going off my head.)

Yes—at long last—& about time too—I understand what all the poetry & ballads & stuff have been going on about these hundreds of years—*Drink to Me Only With Thine Eyes . . . I Want You for My Very Own . . . Cuddle Up a Little Closer*, all that stuff.

In my humble view now, all that doesnt go far enough.

39 H. CRESC, NEXT EVENING, March 25, 1909, 11 pm.

In the Office today, nothing more said—just a warm feeling in the cold air, Whats the word—closeness, that's it. We understand each other.

An hour ago I was sitting staring into the fire, with her (the Other One) opposite in one of those negleege things—stained & frumpy by now & the old glass of gin in her hand, when she says, all of a sudden, Youve changed, youre thinking of something else all the time. I said it was Anno Domini & she said, Oh no, if anything youre more sprightly than you used to be, nipping up & down those stairs.

I said to myself, My friend youre on thin ice. But felt complimented just the same.

39 H. CRESC, A WEEK later, April 2 1909, 11 pm.

Nothing more said in Office, but my mind's working.

After leaving Office this afternoon, I called at the big Walpole Hotel in Tottenham Court Rd, to see a Mr Jesson who runs it. Last year (as a sort of extramural medical activity that I got into through another patient) I was able to help him over a situation where discretion was needed—viz venereal disease, & I know he's been grateful to me since.

Last evening I asked him for a little discretion in return—viz, the use of a room in his hotel, every Sat afternoon, 2 till 4.

Its booked for this Sat. Provisionally. I wont bring it up till lunch at the Holborn. But I have got a feeling she wont get up & leave the Restaurant.

39 H. CRESCENT, 5 WKS later, May 5, 1909.

She didnt.

At least, when she did leave, she left with me, we took a cab to the Walpole Hotel.

And have every Sat aft since.

Last time was our 5th.

That hotel room, with no picture nor ornament, is a home to me such as 39 H. Cresc has never been. Because these afts. are, from the start, so easy & peaceful—I never dreamed I would gain such happiness & I dont know what Ive done to deserve it.

I suppose its because (unlike some) she doesn't make demands nor sarcasms that would frighten even Casanova off—she just loves me being close to her, & of course that leads beautifully to the rest of it. And no pajama top neither!

I'm a new person. At 47!!

CHAPTER 4: HATE

LIFE AT No 39 IS strenuous. With Mrs Lucas only coming once a week, theres a lot of work & I have to get down to it before the Office, cleaning boots, making breakfasts, then the beds.

But I'm up early anyway with my thoughts, & the chores keep me from brooding.

And Sunday is less of a nightmare—I play cards with the lodgers, makes life easier.

39 H. CRESC, 4 WEEKS later, May 31 1909, 11 pm.

Miss Belle Elmore, Hon. Treasurer of Music Hall Ladies Benev. Guild, has persuaded the Guild to move their premises to Albion House, just above my Office & Drs Rylance & Masters, Committee Meetings every Wed. She's got a nerve.

Is it to keep an eye on me?

39 H. CRESC, 2 MONTHS later, July 27 1909, 11 pm.

No, just to tease me—she never comes near my door before or after a Guild meeting. Thank God, couldn't bear to see her face to face with my D.

39 H. CRESC, 5 WEEKS later, Sept 1st 1909, 11 pm.

Thank God for the Saturdays.

Same feeling, only stronger. The only part I cant bear is when I look at my watch on the bedside hotel table & it says 1/4 to 4 & I see the look in her blue-gray eyes.

And I dread seeing her on to her omnibus to Hampstead, to her digs—but its a comfort to know that her landlady Mrs Jackson is fond of her & treats her like a daughter. I dont blame her. We love each other, for ever.

At No 39, she snaps at me now & then, but not as bad as before.

Jack the Fireman seems to have done the trick. Hes welcome to all the grunting & perspiring.

Tonight, she had the Nashes to dinner. My Lady alright till she gives a big sigh & says what she needs is a change. I nearly said, What about our Jack isnt he a change? but she meant a holiday & I knew why. The Nashes had just come back from a week in Paris. Oh I would like to see the Continent, she said.

I reminded her that Mr Nash had just been left money by an uncle & I hadnt—but as to the Continent, I might scrape together enough for a day trip to Dieppe.

Quite neat, I thought.

I notice in the paper they are advertising this stuff *Harlene for Hair*, supposed to cure baldness. Must get some, try anything once.

39 H. CRESC, 2 WEEKS later, Sept 15 1909.

Back to the rows & hystirics. She vomited last night. I go to bed worn out, disgusted.

39 H. CRESC, 6 WEEKS later, Oct 28 1909.

Life goes on, nothing worth writing down, no plans to work out on paper. I live for Sats, but I worry about my Dearest fretting about the future—its no life for a young person of 26, & I know her mother has been writing her about getting married.

Life at No 39 worse & worse. Thank God for the Nashes, & now the Smythsons & the Martinettis, these last a retired Act (him a juggler, fancy a Retired Juggler)—she had met them through the Guild of course, a quite sprightly couple that seem to be amused by her, & that makes her take to them.

I just sit there while they talk Shop, the Rag was down (meaning the Curtain), arguing about which Comic has the best gags, getting the Bird, Front of Cloth—it's double dutch to me. I just sit there.

Not that I dont like the Music Halls—last week I invented business dinner & took my D. to the Palace Th. and there was Julian Eltinge, a clever American chap, quite hefty, dressed as a woman with evening dress and ospreys. Now my D. and I never mention la Belle Elmore by name, but I could not resist whispering to her, Thats the woman I married.

It was so sudden & comic that she laughed right out loud.

39 H. CRESC, 1 WEEK LATER, NOV 2 1909, 6 pm.

I knew it would happen, sooner or later.

Because of which, I have now got to face a 2nd talk with B.E. when she gets home from a Fitting or whatever it is. Just got home to find she's left a paper on my desk.

DEAR MRS. C., HE IS CARRYING ON WITH HIS SEC, WELLWISHER.

I'll now get my answers ready by writing down what I should say. It'll help me—

Now be sensible dear, every man with a Secretary he appreciates is accused of this sort of thing, its a joke by now, anyway I'm not the philandering sort, you should know.

(Thats a good one, remember to use it.)

Here she comes—

39 H. CRESC, 6 WEEKS later, Dec 15, 1909.

Tonight usual drunken abuse, & on top of that something new, & she better watch out.

The evening of the anon. letter, she didnt know what to believe—well, tonight she brings it up, shouting—one of these days I'll walk down from the Ladies Guild to your Office & face her with it, the brazen bloody trollop.

That from her!!

I hate the ground she walks on.

I hate her.

I hate her.

H. CRESC, 2 WEEKS later, Sat Jan 1 1910.

New Year's Day & what a New Year's Party we had! She got drunk, behaved herself till they'd all gone, then went berserk, smashed a chair & 3 glasses.

I cant stand it—Ive got to give her something in her drink to calm her down.

Call at Lewis & Burroughs Chemists.

Burroughs?

Same name as my old friend Dr John Burroughs! The coincidence may bring me luck.

39 H. CRESC, 2 WEEKS LATER, Fri Jan 14 1910.

Another row tonight, & of course my D's name dragged in the muck, top of her voice.

Then vomited.

I hate her—
I hate her
I hate her
I hate her
I hate her
I hate her
I feel better after that.

39 H. CRESC, 5 DAYS later, Wed Jan 19, 7 am.

She was quite perky beginning of last evening, had heard a rumor at the Guild that Bruce Miller (her American Bass) is coming back to try his luck once more in London. (I sure hope he makes it.)

Calling today Lewis & Burroughs to sign for Hyoscine & pick it up.

Hadnt heard of Hyoscine here, but thank God I remembered it's used in the States, by the people who know, in cautious amounts to calm patients down who have problems of temper due to Alchohol & sudden sexual urges.

(NB Bear in mind that correct procedure is to reduce crystals to a liquid, then to be used in v. small tabloids. Prescribed dose, one 150th of a grain, watch that)

Mr and Mrs Eugene Stratton to dinner tonight, with him being famous she'll get excited & the gin will be out.

Memo for plan, each time she needs calming down. Slip up to bathroom, slip bottle into my jacket pocket, back downstairs again, carefully slip exact dose into gin.

39 H. CRESC, NEXT morning, Thurs Jan 20, 7 am.

And last night it worked!

I saw all the bad signs on her when the Whist came out, slipped upstairs—and in 15 mins its working like a charm, she stops arguing with me and gets drowsy. Not enough to draw attention, from the Strattons, just mild and kind of lazy.

And once theyve gone, she just yawns & goes up to bed like a lamb. Thanks, Lewis & Burroughs.

39 H. Cresc, 3 days later, Sun Jan 23, 10 am.

Yesterday, at our Holborn Rest. lunch (oh how I long for Sats!) an important moment.

I was making light of having to get my own breakfast & clean my own boots, even after the lodgers have gone—when she says, But Peter dear, doesn't—isnt your breakfast prepared for you? (As I said, We never mention her name)

Oh no I said, the lady of the house is <u>not</u> an early riser.

And then I said, Except on Sundays, of course, when she goes to Mass in Kentish Town.

I could have kicked myself. Too late. She said, She's a—Catholic?

Yes, I said, I go to church with her sometimes, to keep her quiet.

She talked of something else, quick, but I knew what she was thinking.

For the first time, there was something a bit sad in the Saturday afternoon.

And it set me thinking. Hard.

39 H. Cresc, same day, Sun Jan 23, 10 pm.

This is an important entry, the most so far. And it gives me a big kind of relief to write it down.

By this evening she was drunk, & sour from a letter from the Teddington Music Hall canceling her 3 trial nights in March.

Well, she was sitting there sipping & trying to read a book, when she asks me—or orders me, more like it—to refill her glass. When I relieve her of it I realize she hasnt had a bath since yesterday morning, ie attention to personal hygiene is no longer an important factor. Like many doctors I am squeamish on that, wont go into details even to myself.

Then, just to say something, I suggest asking the Burroughs to dinner (old friends) I havent seen him for a long time. Oh no, she snaps, Ive turned against the both of them & I wont have them in my house. Then she sits picking her teeth & skipping through her Marie Corelli.

Then I thought, its <u>not</u> her house, how dare she call it her house, I want her out of it, I hate her I hate her—

And then, with her turning a page with a sniff, I felt something click in my head—like a watch starting to tick which isnt going to stop ticking, neether. And I said to myself, so clear in my mind I thought for a minute Id said it out loud—I said, she's got to go.

And inside myself—slower—I said it again. In those couple of seconds while she turned that page, little could she guess what big seconds they were.

She's got to go.

CHAPTER 5: I'VE ALWAYS BEEN TIDY

39 H. Cresc, next eve, Mon Jan 24, 11 pm.

From now on, this is a Secret Diary.

(I ought to give it up—but too late now, I need it)

In front of me Ive got a small strongbox, bought it to keep my Diary under lock & key. (I'll destroy it when the time comes, dont worry) Ive always been methodical in my work, all the small items catered for, & I'm going to be methodical now. Plan of campaign. Means telling fibs to my D, I dont like that but it's got to be done.

Let me think. A little sea trip necessary. Dieppe. Didnt I make a joke about maybe a little holiday there, one of these days?

Tomorrow Ive got to get the thing started, & got to word it right. And as Ive done before, I'll use this Diary for a quick practice of suggestions & explanations I may have to make next day. A sort of Memo of Future Talk.

Memo of Talk, tomorrow at Office. Since my D opens all my letters to Office—Good morning my D I got a letter this morning to No 39—from a Monsiur (cant spell it) Larive in Dieppe, big patent-medicine firm, suggesting meeting with view mutual arrangement, wants me to pop over on night boat this Thurs, will be back (of course) for our secret Sat.

Report same to No 39, only careful to say letter arrived at <u>Office</u> & I left it behind <u>there</u>.

39 H. Cresc, Fri Jan 28, 1910, 5 pm.

Back from Dieppe, where I half expected my Frenchman to meet me! Had quiet morning in a little cafe. Even had a glass of red wine, since my little job was done.

And the little job had been, to stroll carefully round the boat at about bedtime & take stock. Railings everywhere, of course, but right at the back—the Stern I think they call it—right next to the railing a little steep stairway, up.

Now if you were told that if you stood halfway up the stairway you could see the lights of Dieppe miles away, you might be tempted to have a look. Quite slippery, those stairs, & there's quite a noise from some machinery nearby, goes on all evening, thats why its so deserted.

It'll be February of course & could be a rough night, but with any luck it wont be, Dover-Calais is the rough crossing & I believe in luck. I enjoyed the wine. She's not home yet from the Guild, so I can now get my speech ready.

Memo Talk, at 39. Yes dear, excellent business deal, & what do you think—Monsiur Larive has asked us both for next weekend, the only thing is there was money & jewelry missing on the boat, the Steward said its common on those night crossings, so they strongly advise ladies not to travel their jewelry on those trips.

On 2nd thought Monsure suggested a midweek visit—next Wed to Fri (so as not to cut into my Secret Sat, Feb 5)

39 H. Cresc, later that eve, 10 pm.

She got back grumpy as usual, but flattered about Dieppe though wont admit it. All arranged. (Was miffed about leaving jewelry at home, but saw the sense of it)

Martinettis coming dinner and whist Monday, she'll be telling them all about her invitation to the Continent.

Everything going according to plan.

39 H. Cresc, 3 days later, Mon Jan 31—or rather Tues Feb 1, 1:45 am.

Worn out.

All fine through dinner, she had just enough gin for her to sparkle, then dinner over we get the usual rendition at the piano—this time my least favorite of the Repertoire, as tried out at Camberwell Music Hall—*She Never Went Farther Than That.*

Then all of a sudden Paul Martinetti (in all innocence) mentions that the Smythsons have heard from her Bass (Bruce Miller) that he is not coming back after all.

Her face goes from red to black & back again, they couldnt help notice, & she didnt speak for 5 minutes. (I was thinking, Cant he send a pal?) Then Paul M. asks to be excused (to go upstairs) & 5 minutes later we hear a crash & he comes limping down. It had slipped my memory (a) that the gas mantle on the landing was out of action & (b) that the lav. window was open (on a winters' night, & Paul M. delicate). He had missed his footing in the half-dark & was wheezing (a bit of a self-coddler if you ask me) & only a twist of the foot, not even a sprain—& he did say, it's nothing Peter nothing.

Well, she turned on me & screamed. Wheres your bloody manners, letting a guest go upstairs by himself, there are times when you disgust me Mr P.T. & you know it, etc. Well, Paul (trying to make light of things) said, What does P.T. stand for, & then I (to stop her telling them it meant Pajama Top)—said it means Mr Pete.

Which (I must say) was quick of me, considering that (inside) with her bringing that up, I was seeing red. The gin started flowing again & I knew I was in for a bad night.

I ask to be excused—Paul M. calls out, in fun, Dont you fall over— I go up to bathroom, grope at back of cupboard shelf for bottle, get it into jacket pocket as usual, go back down, take her glass for refill & slip into it required dose. Thank you Lewis & Burroughs.

At 12:45 I went looking for cab for Martinettis, which took time & she blamed me. When they left they looked sorry for me. (Her friends like me, I dont know why)

Well, once theyd gone she really let me have it, picked up an ashtray & it whistled past me, could have gashed my face. Then she rampages upstairs stumbling & muttering, What youve done is give me a splitting bloody head, get me my headache pills.

I was hoping her muttering meant my medicine was beginning to work. But I was fed up, & said, Get your pill yourself & went to my room to write this.

I hate her. I h. h. I h. h. I h. h.

First I took out the eau de cologne & sniffed it like it was a drug. My D., everything going according to plan.

3 HOURS LATER, 5 am.

No it's not. When I wrote I was in for a bad night, little did I—
What do I do now? Tell me what to do—

449

To think out how I stand, I must write it all down, carefully, it will steady me—

Was woken up an hour ago, she'd called out shrill, twice—I thought, Oh God she's going to vomit again—put on my robe, ran in to her, lit gas & looked down. She hadnt bothered to get into night-dress & was sprawled naked on the bed.

But she wasnt wanting to vomit, there was that dry rattle in the throat.

I rush back to my room, light gas, take jacket off chair & take out bottle of hyoscine tabloids. It isnt the hyoscine, its her headache pills—& I remembered that with the gas low in bathroom, & the mantle outside broken, it was hard to see—Id felt for the bottle in back of medicine cupboard, & taken the wrong one.

I'd put headache pills in her drink, & she had staggered into the bathroom (in the dark, sozzled) & taken the hyoscine. Probably 100 times the safe dose.

I run back to her. You just know when somebodys dead.

She was dead.

Then my thoughts start going flash-flash. First flash, is like when I saw Charlotte on that bed—it's an object, like furniture, like a big doll left lying about waiting for a kid to dress it.

Then another flash—she's gone, and me and my D. are all right, for ever & ever—

Then another flash—but it's here, in my house—I wasnt even calling it she, I was thinking, it.

And Im responsible.

Im confused and yet not. Must get it right. Of course taken one way its just an accident—but if it hadnt happened, this body—by Thursday, with luck—this same body would be rolling about in the English Channel & I would have got it there. So I cant feel anything different from feeling this is my doing just as much as Wed would have been. It's like planning to catch a train on Wed and finding yourself already on it.

The difference being—Ive got a problem here that I wouldnt have had on Wed. What do I do with it now?

Do I go round to the police station & tell the truth—nothing but?

How could I prove the accident? Even if her fingerprints are on the bottle of hyoscine as well as mine—but whos to prove I didnt advise her to try it, knowing what was good for her, being a Doctor my-self? Then they find out about my Saturday afternoons—they always do—no, I couldnt bear my Dearest to be dragged thru all that.

No, here I am in the middle of the night with the whole of London asleep all around, & only me awake. In a desparate situation.

Desparate remedies.

An hour later, after thought.

First, work out tomorrow—no my God it's 6 am. it's today—

Gen. plan. Must (at all costs) turn up regular at Office, and keep regular hours within reason—everything as normal as poss, for future reference, if ever necess.

The work at No 39 to be considered as a nasty spring-clean job to be done as quick & neat as poss. Like when a roof's fallen in & you have to clear away the rubbish & then sweep up.

Work at No 39, 6 pm to 11 pm, and then knock off (Light in kitchen wld be suspicious any later). Up again soon as it's light. Wear only underdrawers. Move hip bath from bedroom down to kitchen.

Details for today. Lunch hour, walk down to 1 King Ed. Mansions Shaftes. Ave, to ask how Paul Martinetti's cold is. And tell them that when I left No 39, she was still in bed. Never a truer word.

Throw hyoscine away. Wash & dry her glass. Check there are enough candles for lantern for cellar.

Get out of bottom of trunk *Manual of Practical Anatomy* I bought (all those yrs ago!) Take it in briefcase to Office, for close study during day.

Second thoughts—must only be in-and-out at Martinettis, spend rest of lunch hour shopping. That will make me late at Office, will tell my D that Martinettis kept me.

Shopping list. (Already have spade for clay from garden—NB, Not more than one Item from each shop) small axe, saw, pickaxe, big waterproof sheet, quicklime (2 sacks).

(NB, Before each shop, take off glasses. Dump parcels of shopping in Albion H. basement lumber room, to be picked up on way home)

In No 39, sharpen carving knife.

Food. Theres fruit & vegetables in larder & I'll shop for more. (I most likely wont be hungry, but if I do get peckish, I wont be fancy-ing anything cooked—I'm not squeamish but only natural)

Must keep going. Grueling, but I'm stronger than I look. Whats got to be done, got to be done. And any time I get tired & fed up with it, I'll think of my D, she must come to no harm. The future is ours, & thats all that matters.

I'll put my head in at the bedroom door so to make sure everything's OK, put a sheet over it, make myself a cup of tea.

Give hands & fingernails final scrub before putting on stiff collar & frock coat. Brain clear. Off to Office.

39 H. CRESC, SAME day, Tues Feb 1st, 6 pm.

Just peeked in bedroom door, its still as I left it (where else, but you have to check). Under the sheet, like in the mortuary.

Then I had a funny impulse. I telephoned my D (she was still at Office, working late) & told her I loved her. Oh she said, quite worried, Are you sure youre not being overheard?

Quite sure, I said.

All went to plan during day, was only ½ hr late from lunch. Just going to unpack shopping.

But first, before its dark & while Im fairly fresh, remove it down to kitchen. All those stairs!

½ hour later. It was good idea doing that while fresh—the weight! Like a sack of potatoes, had to roll it down the stairs & along passage. Never realized stairs & passage so dirty.

One v. bad moment—rolling it down the stairs I slipped, my glasses fell off & rolled under it, I thought I had broken them & that would have been terrible. But God was on my side.

Memo—must bring spare pair tomorrow from Office.

Was quite out of breath, made myself tea, and did refresher study of *Manual of Practical Anatomy*. Funny how these things come back. Now's the hard part.

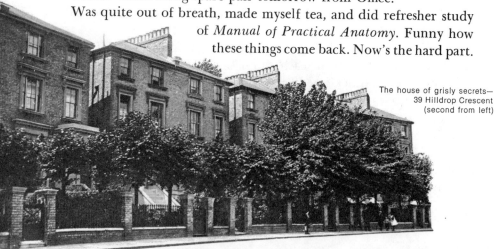

The house of grisly secrets—
39 Hilldrop Crescent
(second from left)

39 H. Cresc, next morn Wed Feb 2, 8 am.

Worked till 11 pm, was so dead I slept till 6. Woke up with light, worked. Its laborers work at that, yet here I am, fresh as paint, & preparing my Memos for the day!

Something is keeping me on the go, like some sort of clock inside me is wound up & driving me.

A minute ago, a bit of a scare. A knock—milkman. And me in my underdrawers, & not presentable besides (ie not clean)

I nip into cellar, he knocks a couple of times & leaves the bottle. I was glad of a glass of milk, though of course I am making tea quite a bit, also Bengers Food, v. nourishing. (Cellar floor being made of broken bits of street paving, plus bricks, makes things easier.)

Memo for talk with my D. in Office, this morning.

My D, I'm afraid I have got some news.

When I got home yesterday eve (Tues) I found she had packed a bag & left me, for America.

You see, the night before, we had had the final blazing row & she said she was leaving for good, to join Bruce Miller—you know, her old flame the American Vaudeville chap. I wasnt sure if she meant it so didnt mention it to you yesterday, but shes gone alright.

She must have packed in tearing hurry, didnt take half of her things. Train to Liverpool I suppose, I dont even know what boat.

Did you ever know of anything so mad, Im upset with the humiliation of course but the house is so quiet you wouldnt believe—

N.B., today being Wed, she'll be missed at the Music Hall Ladies G. Committee Meeting, so 2 notes for my D. to take up to them. One to Sec Miss Melinda May, 2nd to Committee, in my writing, signed Yours etc Belle Elmore, per H.H.C.

Dear Friends, Please forgive a hasty letter, but—

No, I cant give <u>them</u> the idea she's walked out on me, make me look a fool, how can I go out of my way to be the laughingstock of all those Guild gossips? I'm made of better stuff than that—

Dear Friends, I have just had news of the illness of a near relative & at only a few hours notice I am obliged to go to America. Under the circs I cannot return for several months, & therefore beg you to accept this as a formal letter resigning my Hon Treasureship. I am enclosing checkbook & deposit book for use of my successor, etc. I hope some months later to be with you again, & in the meantime wish my good friends & pals to accept my sincere and loving wishes for their own personal welfare.

Believe me, Yours faithfully, B.E., pp HHC.

I'll tell my Dearest that the reason the letters are in my writing is she was in such a tearing hurry she asked me to write them for her.

For a chap whos never done it before, Im getting to be quite a good liar.

39 H. Cresc, evening, Wed. Feb 2nd, 11 pm.
Work OK, worst over.

Tomorrow eve will be mostly clearing up before Mrs. Lucas's day next day (Fri)

I'm tired already—its the digging that takes it out of you—yet cant stop writing.

And perhaps helped by what I have in front of me. A glass of her gin!!

Tomorrow morn, pack her big empty suitcase with stained clobber, pickaxe etc plus (most important) the head, which I have ready in cupboard under sink wrapped in towel. (I remember what a surgeon told me that first London trip, that a head seems to weigh as much as the rest put together, and golly it's true).

Place suitcase in back of attic, to be disposed of in good time. (Luckily, attic temperature v. cold).

All went well at Office today, except my D gave me quite a turn. After she read the 2 letters which she was to take to the Guild, she looks up at me, in the eye, quite quiet, & says, Peter why cant you tell the truth?

I looked at her, thinking for a minute she meant—but of course she meant about my wife walking out on me. I couldnt make her see that I couldnt tell anybody (but her) that I had been humiliated. Women are funny.

39 H. Cresc. Fri Feb 4, 7:30 am.
Finished.

CHAPTER 6: OVER AND DONE WITH

LAST EVE (THURS), swilled at everything, then went over house as if with microscope. And basement clean as new pin for Mrs Lucas today. But I wouldnt be a butcher for anything.

Strange that I was more disgusted by her vomiting than by anything in the last 3 days. Over & done with.

Being a thoughtful man, I am considering how I am feeling at this moment, & am relieved to note that the cellar is not going to be that much on my mind. To put it bluntly, to me it is no different than her having been put to rest yesterday, Thurs Feb 3 1910 at 6:30 pm (exact time!) in Kensal Green Cemetery, Dearly Beloved Wife Of. Only less expense, no tombstone etc!

I expect if anybody read all that—they wont, by the time I've burned it!—they would think I was mad. I'm not. They might do things I thought were mad—people just dont understand other people.

At Office yesterday, a mother brought a child with infected tooth, poor little girl was crying herself sick, with pain & of course frightened of me. I got my D. to hold one hand, I held the other, for a minute (it works wonders).

She soon calmed down, & the mother said (which I'd heard before) Doctor what a soft touch you have. Then my D said, Peter why do you look amused at that? And of course I couldnt tell her.

Re the whole operation in No 39—one funny thing. By the end, with all the tidying & washing, as well as using up all the old newspapers for soaking, I had run out of towels, & with contents of hole in cellar ready to be covered in (lime, & clay from garden all ready) I wanted something to use as towel to wash my hands when finished.

So went upstairs to pick out an old shirt from my chest of drawers, & what should be the first thing I fish up, but a Pajama Top!

I had to smile, & nothing could stop me from taking it down to the cellar, looking down into that hole, & then I said out loud, This is from Mr P.T., & dropped it down & then covered the whole thing over with the clay & lime, & the bricks over that.

Childish, I know, but everybody does something childish sooner or later.

Which reminds me—must spread coal dust & bits of coal back onto disturbed part of cellar floor, also that filthy broken chandelier thats been down there since the first yr here. Over the dining table, it was. And crashed down the first night. Pretty grand ideas we had in those days, didnt we?

39 H. CRESC., SAT Feb 5, 7:30 am.

Yesterday eve, as I got in at the gate Mrs Lucas was leaving, I explained that the lady of the house had been called back to U.S. on business. She said she'd never seen the kitchen so tidy.

Slept like a log. And today lunch, Holborn Rest.

(Rest. for Restaurant, but it does mean <u>Rest</u> to me!)

And then Walpole Hotel. I feel Ive deserved it.

39 H. CRESC. WEEK later, Sun Feb 13, 9 pm.

God what a long empty day, too cold out, tried to read, but couldnt even carry on with Edgar Wallace. And my D sitting in those dingy digs in Constantine Rd, Hampstead, it isnt right.

Ladies Guild Meeting tomorrow, Albion House, so Martinettis will be popping over to my Office, any news of our dear Belle?

Memo of Talk to them etc, Got a cable, her sister pretty sick & she'll be there some time, would I send over clothes etc which she was in too much of a hurry to take.

39 H. CRESC., NEXT eve, Mon Feb 14, 9 pm.

I was right, over they came, Can't <u>think</u> why she didnt leave a note for us. Then Mrs Eugene Stratton looked in, Do let us know how she is. They all seem quite fond of her. But you never know with these Stage Folk. They didnt even notice my D at her typewriter. She was relieved.

I asked Dr Rylance if he did not notice I looked lonely, he remarked that he did.

Memo of talk to my D. at Office.

Tomorrow being our Anniversary you & I are going to have an Evening Out, early dinner in West End, then Seymour Hicks in *Captain Kidd*.

And I have a present for you—or rather, presents. Jewelry, plus fox fur & a muff.

Then go to safe & get them out—ring with 4 diamonds & ruby.

Gold brooch (with points kind of radiating from each point set in brilliants, diamond at center) All for you my D.

No, they do not belong to Somebody Else—didnt I give them, over the yrs, out of money I was earning? They're mine, that's why I stopped her taking it all with her—they're mine, for you to have—with her vulgarity they looked a bit showy on her, but on you they will look lovely.

H. Cresc, two days later, Wed Feb 16, 8 am.

The dear girl started off saying no no no, she was quite startled at the idea, but I persuaded her in the end, saying that it was a 1000 to one chance nobody we knew would see us in the West End, then she said, no again & finally we compromised on the fur & brooch.

Well, we both changed at the Office, she looked lovely with brooch, she was still not sure if it was right but being a woman had to enjoy it a bit.

And after the little dinner, walking down Shaftesbury Ave, who do we run into (a 1000 to one chance!) but those damned Martinettis, also off to a theater. I barely introduced my Secretary, they gave her a funny look—Mrs M in particular, she seemed to give the brooch quite a stare. Then we moved on.

Impertinence.

Proceeding to theater, my D. was quite taken aback by this incident & it was hard to cheer her up. But the play did, so all was well. Seymour Hicks very polished.

But I did hate seeing her off on the omnibus to her Hampstead lodgings. My D, you belong in No 39.

39 H. Cresc, next morning, Thurs Feb 17, 8 am.

Memo talk to my D. I see that on this Sunday Feb 20, the Music Hall Ladies Guild is holding their Benev. Fund Charity Ball—now I think we deserve a real night out, (not just a theater) & I can get tickets through Annie Stratton, ½ a guinea each, and you can wear my favorite Princess robe I gave you with the gold sequins, will match the gold in the brooch on your bodice.

But my D, the brooch is yours, from me, & anyway Clara Martinetti already had a good look at it & isnt going to keep her trap shut, what does it matter anyway? I insist.

39 H. Cresc, 4 days later, Mon Feb 21, 8 am.

It was a beautiful ball. Plain sailing.

Well, not all plain sailing, she had really jibbed at wearing her brooch with the Martinettis & Nashes etc recognizing it. I said, That is just why I want you to wear it, to make me proud of you. And however they pretend to have liked her, she did leave me, didnt she?

Then she said, But Peter they dont know that, you wrote she'd gone to America because of family illness, why didn't you tell the truth, it would look so much better for us now!

And of course she was right—but we all make mistakes. I told her I didnt like to think of her as a coward, & she gave in.

And as to the Ball—I was no Fairy Prince of course but Cinders looked a treat as the Londoners say, every inch a lady, & I loved to watch the admiring looks. A couple of dirty ones as well, but that's life. Mrs Smythson asked (my D. out of earshot at the time) if I had heard lately from Belle. I said, Oh yes, shes right up in the wilds of the mountains of California.

39 H. Cresc, week later, Tues March 1, 8 am.

My Goodness, the house is empty! Not empty of what was living in it before—empty of my Dearest.

Memo, of talk to her. She will be shy of the idea.

My D, the Saturdays are lovely but it is in No 39 that you belong & I cant rest till youre beside me in that double bed bought by me & which I left years back.

How do you mean, a haunted house? Dont you talk like one of those novelettes, theres nothing of her in the house except all those trashy clothes & Ive piled them out of sight in one big cupboard. (I must gently remention her moving in, every other day)

Yes, but Ive got to think about it too. We want to get married, We are going to get married. But by the law we cant until desertion has gone on for 7 yrs & then person assumed dead. This calls for thought.

39 H. Cresc, 2 days later, Thurs March 3, 10 pm.

I was right, shes like a frightened bird at the idea of moving in, but every day I make progress.

Memo of next talk. My D, you'll be my housekeeper, what does it matter what gossips might hint at?

39 H. Cresc, 3 days later, Sun March 6, 10 pm.

Memo of Talk. My D, next weekend Sat 12th, lunch at Holborn Rest, but not the Walpole Hotel, lets make it the house, & for good! And that means we'll wake up, in No 39, on my birthday!

And in the evening, a quiet home dinner with wine & you can give me a taste of the cooking you boast about—no my D, Im wrong, you never boast—I wouldnt like that.

39 H. Cresc, week later, Sun March 13, 48th birthday.

What happiness.

She did move in. (Had never seen the house, of course) On the doorstep, Welcome home I said, picked her up & carried her over threshold, I really surprise myself these days.

And a beautiful dinner just as planned, & her a good cook, she'll soon get used to the kitchen being in basement. Nervous of course, & kept looking round at everything but will soon settle down.

Doesnt mind the pink. And for the first time in No 39, I slept in the double bed. A special night.

She has belonged to me now for best part of 2 yrs, & will, for ever. Memo, tomorrow buy a bangle for her birthday.

39 H. Cresc, week later, Sun March 20, 10 pm.

Tomorrow early will take cab to my D's old lodgings, 80 Constantine Rd Hampstead, with suitcase full of clothes etc for that nice landlady of hers Mrs Jackson—shoes, long cream coat, mole coat & skirt, black voile blouse, hair combs, 3 nightgowns almost new, pair pink shoes, black feather boa etc etc. She deserves them, for having been like a mother to my D.

Since Mrs Lucas is only once a week, my D. will do only 4 days in Office so as to run house etc. Shall miss her sorely on her non-Office days, but the thought of her settled in my house will more than make up. Now plans, I like plans. I wrote that something calls for thought, and it does.

First—Dr Masters has a married daughter in NY & gets cables from her, Xmas & birthdays etc, & pins them over his desk—last week I saw him put old ones away in a drawer. Slip in there tomorrow lunch hour & take one from drawer.

Draft letter to Martinettis.

Dear Clara & Paul, Please forgive me for not running in during the week, but I have been really so upset by very bad news from Belle that I did not feel equal etc. She is so ill that I am considering if I had not better go over at once. I do not want to worry you with my troubles—I will try & run in, etc.

With love & best wishes, Peter.

We had a beautiful Sunday today, more like summer than March, fine & dry so I get to digging at flower bed in front garden like a countryman, my D has shopped for some bulbs.

Memo. Talking of summer, <u>must do something about suitcase in attic</u> before warm weather.

39 H. CRESC, NEXT evening, Mon March 21, 10 pm.

Funny I should have written that re warm weather—the matter has got more urgent.

Tonight I was complimenting my D on the house being in apple-pie order—the way she's switched things round & bought nice things at Caledonian Market etc.

Oh, she said, Peter I am glad, now I can start on the attic & clear out the rubbish.

I didnt say anything.

Memo Talk. My D, I dont want you to go up yet, theres stuff that I pushed up there, so you wouldnt be upset seeing it lying round the bedroom etc, wait till Ive got rid of it.

39 H. CRESC, NEXT morning, Tues March 22, 8 am.

Ive got a good idea.

Memo of Talk. My Dearest, with Easter coming up a change of air will do the trick & youll come back to the house, a different girl—you remember my business trip to Dieppe, well I thought then what a nice place to take you too, we'll pack a couple of suitcases, Easter Thurs till Tues—what do you say?

And, my D—talking of packing, Ive got an idea—since you want to clear the attic out, I'll travel that nasty suitcase full of her rubbish—Ive never been able to fancy opening it—& when nobodys looking I'll tip it overboard.

Good riddance.

39 H. Cresc, that evening, March 22, 10 pm.

My D was home today, I arrived back at 6 & said I'd had a cable. I took it out of my pocket (the Dr Masters cable) & read out, Belle dangerously ill with double pleuropneumonia, Otto, then put cable back. My D was upset, she has a really kindly nature.

39 H. Cresc, next evening, Wed March 23, 10 pm.

This morning, at big entrance into Albion House, ran into Clara Martinetti and Mrs E. Stratton on way down from Committee Meeting, Ladies Guild.

They buttonholed me of course, though could see I was in a hurry. I took the cable from my pocket & read it out to them, explaining Otto was my son & that I had a feeling there might be worse news later, in which case I would be going to Dieppe for Easter.

People are strange—they stared at me as if Id said I was going to throw myself off the top of Albion House, & said, Oh Peter, why? I said, for a change of air. They stared even more, & I said, Because I shall be so upset I will have to get away & pull myself together. They said, Oh dear & went. I was polite, as always. People are strange.

39 H. Cresc, next evening, Thurs March 24, 5 pm.

Home early from Office, so my D. can pack, she's at it now upstairs, excited, we're off to Dieppe tonight, for Easter. In 10 mins a cable will arrive which I'll take up & read to her (same Dr Masters cable again)—Belle died this evening six oclock Otto.

(My D, we can't cancel Dieppe now, it'll help me forget)

Then send (from Victoria) telegram announcing news to Martinettis. Belle died yesterday 6 pm, please telephone Annie Stratton, shall be away a week Peter.

Telephone stage paper *The Era* to have Obit on Sat. ELMORE, March 23, in California, U.S.A., Miss Belle Elmore (Mrs H. H. Crippen). Mail 1/6 Postal Order to *Era*, to pay for Obit.

N.B. Order black-edged mourning cards, plus writing paper.

39 H. Cresc, 5 days later, Tues March 29, 8:30 pm.

Back from Easter in Dieppe, lovely holiday, my D was distressed (over my son's cable) for rest of Thurs, but the sea trip brought roses back in cheeks.

Sat in same cafe I was in before.

Then we got into conversation with the waitress, a nice plain girl (spoke quite good English, as Dieppe people can do) who told us her dream is to go into service in London (as maid) but the type of day-tripper that comes over doesnt offer that sort of chance—anyway she wants to go into a house which her mother would know beforehand was respectable.

Then my D. said jokingly, Wouldnt it be nice if she came to work for us & I'd get so I could speak French—I ought to, with a name like Le Neve!

Well, I put it to the little Mamselle & she jumped at it. And next day her Maman comes over & she seemed to take to us, saying she would be relieved to know that *ma fille* will be with a Doctor *comme il faut* (respectable).

I take that as a sizable compliment. Her name is Valentine, I call her our Easter Valentine.

Will come to us in about a week, will explain to Mrs Lucas we need a maid to live in. Showed V. (from my wallet) a snapshot of No 39, she was impressed.

Then we joked about us going to have a French maid, like in those farces with Charles Hawtrey etc.

(PS—Suitcase disposed of on trip out, Newhaven-Dieppe, no problem)

Lovely holiday.

39 H. CRESC, NEXT morning, Wed March 30, 8 am.

Today will be Music Hall Ladies G. Committee Meeting, so must be ready for the condolences—what a shock, cant believe she has gone from us, etc.

39 H. CRESC, THAT evening, 9 pm.

I was right, those very words! Also the Guild want to send an Everlasting Wreath, & I explained that my son would know what the Guild meant, no point. Was your son with her when she died, Yes I said. I thought they would never go, I wish people would mind their own business.

I told Dr Rylance I hadnt let him know before, so as not to spoil his Easter.

39 H. Cresc, a week later, Wed April 6.

Black-edged writing paper arrived. Draft letter to her sister in Brooklyn—

My dear Louise, I hardly know how to write to you of my dreadful loss, the shock to me has been so dreadful that I am hardly able to control myself. A few weeks ago, we had news that an old relative was dying, and to secure the property, it was necessary for one of us to go. On the way my Cora caught a severe cold which has settled on her lungs (etc, about the pleuropneumonia, then—) and now the dreadful news that she has passed away—imagine me nevermore to see my Cora alive nor hear her voice—

(Wait—I have just had what they call here a brain wave. Last yr, when her mother died in Calif., the ashes were sent to No 39—I remember how she carried on sobbing about it—& the box is in the safe right now)

Well Louise, she is being sent back to me, & I shall soon have what is left of Cora, here in No 39. Of course I am giving up the house, it drives me mad to be in it alone.

Love to all.

Valentine is a treasure & loves my D.

At the Office my partners Dr Masters & Rylance & even William Long pull my leg about my French maid—they just wont believe she's as respectable as I am!

Home & front garden lovely. And I'm sleeping so well.

39 H. Cresc, 2 weeks later, Thurs April 21, 10 pm.

A very nice thing. Dr and Mrs Masters have asked me to dinner with my D. (I dined a couple of years back, saying my wife wasnt well, I liked them & they liked me)

Now it is really kind of them, & a snub to the gossips—I know they will both like my D.

39 H. Cresc, 2 weeks later, Sat May 7, 11 pm.

Nice dinner party at our home this time, with Dr & Mrs Masters. My D. a delightful hostess, shy & friendly. Party only marred by last night's shocking news of the Kings death, the end of the Era of Ed. VII.

But it did lead to us getting on to subject of medical etiquette— ie the fact that any doctor gets wind of all sorts of scandals & has to keep them to himself—from Mrs Masters telling me that Dr. M. was for a yr or 2 assistant to a big Physician by appointment to the King. Then she hinted that her husband got to know details which would be v. interesting in yrs to come. I was taken with that.

Very pleasant evening, a glass of wine each.

39 H. CRESC, 2 WEEKS later, Thurs 19 May, 10 pm.

The Nosey Parkers are back.

Who should I run into, in Maples Emporium (Tottenham Court Road) but Mrs Nash & Mrs Smythson—me with my D. on my arm.

Whilst I was raising my bowler, they stared quite rudely at my D, & I'm afraid she was so timid she just walked on. Then we chat stiffly—so sad the King dying like that, poor Queen Alexandra—then Mrs Nash says, Did you get news of the funeral?

I was at sea for a moment, & said, The Kings funeral? Well they gave me a v. cold look but I hadnt said it as a joke. No, they said, another funeral. Both ladies sticking out bustwise, & glaring at me from under those big hats, like a couple of haughty hens.

Oh, I said, the funeral went satisfactorily, all was over very quietly, & I have her remains at home. (I didnt mean it to come out like that, but it did—then I explained about the box)

So if anybody wants to see the ashes, theyre welcome.

Our evenings at home get even nicer, more and more cozy. Valentine adores my D & even the cat next door comes in every other evening by the kitchen window to say hello to her & ask for a saucer of milk.

The two of us dont seem to be parted for a moment—she said once, Peter, wouldnt it be nice if you sat with me in the kitchen reading the paper while I get our dinner ready. So now we make quite a habit of it, I even fetch & carry salt pepper etc & watch the oven. Let me write down how delicate & pretty she looks sitting there, with her brown hair like a sort of halo against the lamplight.

And we talk by the hour, in such an easy manner. Like when she told me her real name is Neave, but when she was 14 she thought it was too ordinary & when she heard there might be French blood in the family she turned into Le Neve.

We tell each other everything. Plain sailing.

39 H. Cresc, a week later, Wed May 25, 10 pm.

Funny I should have written <u>plain sailing</u>, thinking of this evening. Not that it was a storm, just a breeze really.

I had a little extra desk work & was a bit late getting to her down in the kitchen as we had arranged, & found her sitting at the table kind of knotting her hands & then unknotting them.

I said, I tell you what, this Sat we'll have a night out West End style, what do you say to *Dr Jekyll & Mr Hyde,* with H. B. Irving?

Oh no, she said quite sharp, something cheerful. I said what about Gertie Millar at the Gaiety, *Our Miss Gibbs,* & dinner before at the New Gaiety Rest. next door, you can wear the Princess robe etc?

Then she blurted that she would be relieved <u>not</u> to wear the jewelry or white ermine.

Well, I was quite took aback & said, Why on earth not, theyre <u>yours</u>, with my love!

I know, she said—I know, but—Peter how can I explain—I have a feeling—that Im being watched.

I stared at her. She said—I suppose it's because she's dead, but every time I put them on, I can feel her eyes on me—

Then she started to sob, & of course I took her in my arms like she was 10 yrs old, then she gave in & will wear presents.

She loves me, but also respects me. Women get superstitious & I must humor that. This has given me an upset stomach, & I have been feeling so well.

39 H. Cresc, 5 weeks later, June 28, eve, 10 pm.

It was such a lovely evening, after day in Office my D. & I sat in our bit of back garden, near the roses, you could smell them. She has green fingers.

Then a knock at the front door, could just hear it. Mr Nash if you please. Bluff, friendly, but a bit—what's the word—Yes, <u>furtive.</u>

The impertinence of some people. Just a social call—then he says, My wife was wondering, have you heard any further from California? (Oh these women!)

I said, No, not since I had a letter from my son, after the funeral. Then he said (I could hardly believe my ears) Have you got the letter here?

I said, No, at the Office, but the ashes are here, Mrs Nash must have told you about them.

(Then I quickly had to turn to my D and explain the ashes had arrived at No 39 on a day she was at the Office & that I'd put them away without telling her, so as not to upset her with such a gruesome matter)

Then I said to Nash, Would you like to pop upstairs & see the ashes? (Quite polite) He went quite red & said, No thank you.

He went quite soon after. What I didnt like, was that he had quite spoiled the evening for my D.

Impertinence. What news from Calif. indeed, what did he expect when somebody's been dead for 3 months—Spirit Messages?

I just want to be left alone by such people.

39 H. CRESC., WEEK later, Tues July 5, 10 pm.

V. sad evening, for both of us. Big upheaval at Office.

Poor Dr Masters (always delicate) had been home with the flu for over a week, then it turns to pneumonia. A daughter telephoned the Office in tears, he died early this morning.

Such a nice man to have gone so suddenly, so cruel. My D wept into her hanky which made me feel worse, I had to pat her hand.

Funeral on Sat the 9th, I told her we'll shut the Office for whole morning & go to pay our respects. Such a devoted family.

39 H. CRES, NEXT eve. Wed July 6, 9:30 pm.

Well well well—

Feel all stirred up again, must write it all down—

Today was my D's day at No 39 going to wash curtains while V. cleaned out basement. In the Office, I had just finished work on a lady patient (a stopping) & thinking of my D at home, hanging curtains on clothesline in back garden—well, the patient was hardly out of the door when there was quite a scurry of feet on the stairs & the Office door burst open.

It was her, quite out of breath. I jumped up and said, What is it? Scotland Yard, she said.

PART TWO
YARD V. CRIPPEN

CHAPTER 7: JUST ROUTINE

GOT TO WRITE IT all down fresh, like those statements criminals make, so I can examine and sort out.

When she said, Scotland Yard, my mind flashes back—how the mind does dart about, when called upon—I hadnt heard <u>Scotland Yard</u> (except written down, as in E. Wallace) since I was a young chap come here from U.S. to watch operations etc, when the policeman remarked that it wasnt a Yard & not in Scotland.

As she said it, behind her I see two bowler hats coming up the stairs.

Then the two gentlemen in the doorway, one my age with clipped mustache, the other a young fellow. Says the older one (v. pleasant) Excuse the intrusion Doctor, I am Chief Inspector Dew, Metropolitan Police Office, New Scotland Yard. Quiet, quietly dressed—not quite a Gent of course, but well spoken. Then he said, This is Sergeant Mitchell. A well-behaved Cockney lad.

(My D told me afterwards that at 10 am she had been upstairs taking down curtains when V. comes up to say 2 gentlemen to see her. My D. explained to them she was the housekeeper, the Insp told her they had called to make inquiries about a Mrs Crippen.

I asked her if they had the cheek to examine my desk or start wandering around, she said no, they just sat with the Insp chatting to her. She did notice the Insp had a good look at her brooch.

She tells him of the sick relative in U.S., then the 3 come down to the Office on the omnibus. And here we are.)

Insp. Dew says, Doctor could we see you alone?

(It was nice that the Insp called me by my title)

My D. looked quite flustered, but I pressed her arm & said, Im sure its nothing.

She takes her work over to Dr Masters office, I ask the gentlemen to sit down.

And gentlemen they were too, in behavior, when you think of the cops in the States. These 2, in their bowlers & stiff collars, might have been 2 other Dentists come to ask me if I was qualified to address a Conference or some such.

I wasnt scared. And not scared now, I just want to straighten out. The Insp takes pipe from waistcoat pocket.

DEW—Mind my Navy Mixture, Doctor?

(I said I didnt, he lit up)

DEW—Last Thursday a Mr & Mrs Nash called on us at the Yard.

(I guessed theyd talk, but never thought theyd have the sauce to go as far as this.) The Insp read their statement, We have been v. worried about Mrs Crippen etc. Then about noticing the brooch on my D— a lot of busybody stuff.

One bit struck me as funny. Something like—Belle must have written us her address—& if she did, & then didnt hear from us, she'd have been quite cut up.

It was an effort not to smile.

DEW—This is just a routine inquiry of course, & we thought you could help us to ease their minds—

ME—Theyre all nice people Inspector, but Im afraid they love a bit of gossip—

DEW—Quite quite. At the Yard, we have to deal with a lot of such well-meaning people, for our sins. And now, if you dont mind, a Statement from you. And the usual preamble—just routine you understand—if you wouldnt mind writing down, I desire to make a voluntary statement to clear the whole matter up.

First, of course, the account of the death. I described my son's 2 cables & his letter after the funeral.

DEW—Could I see them?

ME—I'm sorry, but theyre in my desk at home.

DEW—And now, if you dont mind, your particulars. Just routine.

So I talk, with Serg Mitchell taking it down in shorthand.

From the beginning, born in Coldwater etc etc, the Story of my Life—(having kept this Diary helped me to remember a lot of the details!) After a ¼ of an hour, a knock at the door—William Long my dental mechanic, announcing a patient for an extraction.

I said I was busy, but the Inspec said, No no, I dont want to interrupt your days work. So we stopped & I got on with the extraction, later on it was lancing a gumboil, then another extraction, with my Life Story in between.

(It was a specially busy day with poor Dr Masters patients to see to as well)

They seemed really interested in the work, & I was quite pleased to be seen at it. I felt the Insp respected me for my job, as I respected him for his.

We hadnt got halfway through when it was One pm & the Inspector suggested lunch, in the corridor I put my head in at Dr Masters to call to my D we were out for lunch & would be back, they took me to a little Italian place I knew round the corner, nice roast beef.

It was kind of him, but at same time I knew he didnt want me out of his sight in case I got together with my D & made up a story about California.

At the lunch table (now that the notebook was put away) we really chatted. About the Coronation next June (George V)—my D and I must get into the sidewalk crowd for that—then the Archer-Shee Case (the boy thats supposed to have stolen the 5/- postal order) then about how Scotland Yard works, the files they keep, the finger-print collection, how they have to go to Police College first & the tough Detective training, wrestling & all that, it was very interesting to the layman as it were.

The Inspector looked like somebody sitting in his club, with his pipe puffing away & eyes twinkling. He told me he had a son same age as Otto, the son studying to be a doctor. I didnt tell him I hadnt seen my son since he was 4, I thought he might think it kind of un-feeling.

He told me he was something of a gardener & I told him about me digging the flower bed so as to get the bulbs in for Easter. Then—kind of out of the blue—he shot out, quiet & pleasant—

DEW—For Easter you and Miss Le Neve went to Dieppe?

Well I didnt expect that. But no good saying no, he must have got it out of the Nashes.

Then I thought, in a flash—that suitcase I took away on the trip & never brought back—could Valentine have told them—no, V. didnt see us off, we hadnt even met her yet—

Then, re me and my D, I saw my way clear, & went to work on the Insp. And looking back, I think I did a good job.

ME—Inspector, I can see youre a man of the world & I'll speak freely in front of Serg Mitchell. My wife & I had not shared a bedroom for 5 yrs, & you know what that could do to a man in good health.

(That gave him quite a twinkle of the eye)

ME—As you could both see this morning, my Secretary is an attractive young person, a lady, & with me not getting on with my wife we naturally formed a close bond. Now that I am free she is my fiancee & we plan eventually to marry.

DEW—I can understand that, she is such a charming young lady she deserves to be happy—if I had a daughter Id want her to be like Miss Le Neve.

Now that pleased me. And the little confession had been a wise move on my part, cleared the air.

Well, back to Office & on with my Life Story. Ending at last with the Martinettis coming to dinner Jan 31 & the details of my wife being called back to the States. (He must have seen the Martinettis as well, he knew she was rude to me at dinner over him going to bathroom etc.)

It was a slow business, particularly with the Serg at the end reading it all back to me, then me writing down, This statement has been read over to me. It is quite correct, without any promise or threat having been held out to me.

It was 5 pm before the notebook was put away, then some chat. I was just answering a query from the Insp about—is there much connection between ear & mouth troubles, when—again out of the blue—

DEW—What about the jewelry & fur?

ME—What jewelry & fur?

Which, come to think of it, was a slip, what other jewelry & fur could there be? I should have just said what I said next—

ME—I gave them to my fiancee.

(Which was the truth—though I was glad she was out of the room for this.)

DEW—Why didnt your wife take the stuff with her?

ME—I wouldnt let her. I explained to her it was jewelry & fur I'd given her, so they were my property.

For the first time—now I come to think of it—the Insp gave me a sharp look, just as the Serg looked up at me from his scribbling. Then they gave a quick look at each other. (Ive just remembered it—thats why its good to write things down.)

DEW—When you told your fiancee that the presents to your wife were your property—did she accept the explanation? (sarcastic almost)

ME—I persuaded her to see that my way of looking at it is right. (And it is)

Then I offered the Insp a cigar & we chatted. Then, just as sudden as the times before—he remarked, casual like—

DEW—Could I trouble you & your fiancee to join us in a cab for a short visit to your residence?

Well, I was quite taken aback. Theres a British saying, An Englishman's Home is his Castle, & I'm as good as English by now. But I suppose he has to do his job. I said, very polite, I invite you to look round the house & do whatever you like.

Then I called my D. in. She looked a bit keyed up & I was pleased to see the Insp get up & give her a really nice smile, I felt he was thinking of her as his daughter, & the smile made her easier at once.

We walked to the cab rank and went up to No 39, chatting easy all the way. About dentistry, false teeth being mislaid—Dentists always raise a smile just being Dentists, but they can get their own back with a couple of stories of their own.

Well, once home I gave them a glass of sherry, then I started taking them on the Grand Tour, (leaving my D in sitting room, naturally not looking v. happy). In the bedroom the Insp very struck by the big cupboard full of fancy clothes & ostrich feathers. Also examined my D's jewelry & fur. Then he said, Don't bother to come with us for the rest, we'll just have a look round.

First thing I do when they are gone, is to unlock the cupboard in my study & whisk the locked strongbox (containing this Diary) in among the ostrich feathers they had finished with.

Then back into sitting room where the Insp. joins us to finish his sherry. Then he remarked, casual again—

DEW—If only we could get on to the doctor who signed the Death Certificate—

ME—Of course—Inspector, one minute—

I walk over to the safe, then see that my D has got up, quite sharp. I say, if you wait in the bedroom I'll come for you, & she goes. I unlock the safe & plonk it in front of him.

Me—I knew this would have upset her—you see, these are my wife's ashes, my son sent them on & I put the box away so my fiancee wouldnt see it.

Dew—May I open it?

He did, and there they were, her mothers ashes, with printed on the box—Burbank Funeral Co. That was a stroke of luck, her mother having died in the same part of the world.

Just a small neat pile, like the Insp.'s cigar ash. I couldnt help thinking—My, those crematoriums do a thorough job.

He shut the lid, quite reverent, said, Very sad, & I took the box & locked it back in the safe. Then I fetch my D back in, then the Serg comes in, from downstairs, & asks if there is a lamp or something to see into the cellar with.

I told him the lantern was in the cupboard by the sink, with a candle in it, the Insp got up and they went down together. I made an excuse to my D that I had some papers to look at in the study, to avoid sitting there with her, waiting. They were down there 12 mins by my watch. It felt longer.

They come back up, a second glass of sherry, chat, then—

Dew—Oh, by the way—you said your son's letter & the cables were here—could I have a squint at them?

I go to the desk, but cant find them anywhere.

Me—I am stupid, I just remembered they are at the Office after all, in the safe.

Dew—Never mind—

Then he gets up & thanks me for giving him so much of my precious time. Then a joke about the next time he gets toothache, he'll come calling on me again.

They shake hands with my D (the Insp giving her the same nice smile, & saying, Good-by my dear). I saw them to front door, they left. About 8.

I went straight down to basement, opened cellar door & lit a match.

Nothing much disturbed, the old chandelier moved over in case there was something in small pile of coal under it. What they call a routine check.

Walking up to sitting room, it occurs to me that theres a fairly bookish word for the Insp's demenour right through this visit—cant think of it though, itll come to me.

But I am pleased to say I felt calm & satisfied. When I think how jumpy I got when the Bobby called to interview me about that mess the Drouet Institute got into—well, times have changed.

I've got some confidence in me.

Mind you, I did find myself feeling in trouser pocket for keys, which include key of strongbox (Diary) & of cupboard where I keep strongbox.

My D says it was the longest day she'd ever spent. What she was most anxious about, of course, was her own position & how far it could embarass me—I think she had an idea, poor innocent pet, that we could get into trouble with the Police for not being married yet.

Then I laughed at her & said about the Inspect being a Man of the World, then I explained it had just been a routine call, adding that those meddlesome Nashes had made a suggestion, which made Scotland Yard want to search around for a letter in the ladys handwriting giving the idea she might be going to commit suicide, which she never would do.

That seems to satisfy her, then she says, He's a nice gentleman—when he said <u>Scotland Yard</u> I quite expected to be afraid but he has a kind face. (That's good)

Though she did say, I would have thought he'd have taken your word about the cremation, once youd told him about your son's letter. I said its the Routine Business again, anyway he's got the truth now & I dont think he'll bother us again.

(As I said it, I almost said, I'll miss his company, because in a way it was what I felt. I liked him calling her <u>my dear</u>, & me <u>Doctor</u>.) At the same time—

Inscrutable—that's the word I was looking for. Right through, he was inscrutable.

39 H. Cresc, LATER same night, 12 pm.

But on the other hand, he could be putting that on.

You might say that these Scotland Yard chaps are on the easygoing side—I dont see them getting the upper hand of these violent cases you read about.

Now my son's letter.

MEMO—yank old discarded typewriter from back of attic. Now write draft of letter to be typed on it—

> 1473a Jones, San Francisco, or some such,
> Fri March 25, 1910.

Dear Dad,

Here is a letter as opposed to usual Xmas Greeting, but you will have had my sad cable by now telling you of my stepmother's death (they got into touch with me as next of kin) 2 days ago (23rd) from double pleuropneumonia.

Im afraid its the climate here if youre unused to it, cold evenings on top of hot days. I am glad to say she did not suffer too much, mostly unconscious. Death Certificate enclosed. (Cremation, the ashes will be sent to you).

I am very sorry to have to write this. All well with me as I hope you are. Moving to Denver next week.

> Your respectful son,

Then copy signature (from old Xmas card,) Otto H. Crippen.

(NB Remember not to give his real address, 1427 N. Hoover St, Rural Delivery, L.A.)

In morning, must leave home early, shop at stationers not too near house for thin wodge of plain typing paper, return house, ask my D. to telephone Office to say I'll be $\frac{1}{4}$ of hour late through tidying up some business at home, fetch old machine from attic, type letter, take it in pocket to Office.

39 H. CRESC, NEXT morning, Thurs July 7, 8 am.

Couldnt sleep, sat up reading a Sherlock H. tale in an old *Strand* Mag. I was struck with this one, in it a chap who has (by all accounts) a v. nasty wife, gets rid of her in quite a clever manner—& straightaway the author labels him as a criminal.

I suppose because the last couple of days have brought certain matters back to my attention, I dont see the Authors point of view.

Ive never diddled a soul out of a penny, all my life Ive been a model citizen, I am no criminal. And I dont see that the unusual event of this year turns me into one. I feel quite touchy about this.

Come to think of it, its funny too that while Ive never got any special pleasure out of being the model cit. mentioned above, all these years, I do feel personal satisfaction with having achieved my independence through my own unaided enterprise. I've dealt in a bold manner with a very tight spot, & able to say (like in the Army)

The manouvers were 100% successful. I'm well aware I'm in the minority in this, & the great thing is that my D must never know. The idea of her being hurt or worried over me—no, it mustnt happen.

Memo of Talk to her when I get back at 6—

My Dearest, I've done a stupid thing. Left my old briefcase on the omnibus.

No, no important papers in it, but in the Office this morning I remembered the letter there from my son enclosing the Death Cert., I put them in the briefcase to bring home for safety. Plus the 2 cables I read out to you.

Oh wait a minute, I have got the letter, I must have put it in my pocket, here it is—but we must try and track the Certificate and the cables, we'll try the Lost Property, & only hope that if the briefcase turns up, the contents wont have been thrown away out of spite & itll be empty.

Yesterday at the Office everybody must have been curious about the 2 bowler hats shut up with me for so long. Memo—happen to say to Miss Curnow of Munyon's Remedies (she's a talker) that they were making inquiries concerning the burglaries round about Hilldrop Crescent.

39 H. Cresc, Thurs eve July 7, 11 pm.

This evening arrived home about 6, without briefcase. (I had left it on the omnibus, empty) & explained it all to my D. She said she'd go to the Lost Properties tomorrow & try to track it down.

Then I go into study, Valentine knocks & comes in. She looked somewhat sureptitious.

Val—(in her funny English) Two gentlemen today.

Me—The ones that called yesterday?

Val—No. I look out of window to see if it starts to rain, and I see them.

Me—Where?

Val—In garden.

Me—What were they doing?

Val—They look.

Me—What at?

Val—The round part of garden.

ME—You mean the flower bed.

VAL—*Oui.* Pushing the ground with their feet, then they bend & look close, I think for a minute they will pick flowers & I think I must go out & say to them that this is private garden, & I go out.

ME—What did they say to you?

VAL—That they are Police, then they go.

ME—*Merci* Valentine, itll be those burglaries down the road, I expect they were looking for footprints in the garden. Dont tell Miss Le Neve, these things make her nervous.

I go back to the sitting room, a knock at front door.

The Bowler Hat Bros, Inspector & Sergeant. Interview yesterday v. satisfactory, just a couple of routine questions. Im getting used to that word routine.

When I took them up into the sitting room I noticed my D seemed much better after me soothing her down last evening. She had changed into her gray shadow-stripe costume, quiet & plain, I am always proud of her quiet ways.

I wasnt a bit put out by them arriving, if anything quite pleased, for I told the Insp the whole story about the mislaid briefcase, & handed over my son's letter.

The Insp read it carefully, then said, I am sorry, its very sad, & put the letter in his pocket. (All plain sailing)

Then I asked him if he'd like my fiancee to leave us—no no he said, I wouldnt want to turn Miss Le Neve out of her own sitting room—& that was a very nice way to put it. Even after what was to happen in a minute, you have to like the man—behind that smile & polite voice, theres a brain ticking. Tick-tock. Ive got a brain as well. He and me, we're a couple of clocks.

Well, we sat down, I pored sherry & we chatted, about whether Mrs Keppel etc would be at the Coronation next year, etc, then the weather.

It was a balmy summer evening, trees green & shining in the sun. And the room spotless, once again I was proud of my D.

Id almost forgot what he had come about—now I must get this all correct—when he fired a question at me—not fired, no, too strong, it was like the one about Dieppe, kind of casual but sudden. He said, Could you help me, Doctor, about the Death Certificate?

I said, The Death Certificate, yes?

Then he took my son's letter from his pocket. He took it out—v. carefully—I don't see why it's so important.

DEW—Would you oblige us by writing to your son asking for confirmation that he sent it?

ME—As you read in the letter, by now he'll be in Denver. My son's pretty restless, always changing jobs—when he last wrote, he was in Los Angeles—

DEW—When he last <u>wrote</u>, you said?

ME—Thats right.

DEW—But Doctor he says here—I quote—<u>as opposed to the usual Xmas greeting</u>. And that seems to imply he wasnt in the habit of writing you letters?

I had to think, quick, and then be just as quiet spoken as him. No bluster, Crippen, no bluster.

ME—Im sorry Inspector, I didnt say anything about a letter, I said, when he last wrote, which was last Christmas. On the back of his Christmas card.

(At this point I felt pleased with myself, though I was careful not to show it)

DEW—Would you have the card handy?

ME—Im afraid not. You see Inspector, being a man of method I throw my Christmas cards away on the 7th of Jan, a habit I learned here.

DEW—(a smile) My wife does the same, says they start cluttering the place up.

Then he said, very crisp—

DEW—Any possibility of anybody else close to her or you being concerned with the Death Certificate—

ME—Well, I feel there is a strong possibility she met up with a variety artist by the name of Bruce Miller that was sweet on her some years ago, he is somewhere out there & she may have got together with him & he could have arranged the funeral.

The Insp then thanked me, then some more chat, he seemed to pay particular attention to my D, asking her about her cooking, he's a bit of an amateur cook himself, of a Sunday.

Then he got up, brisklike. You'd never have thought he had another card up his sleeve. An ace.

DEW—Thank you again, Doctor, and you too, my dear—very nice

brand of sherry you have here, I look forward to sampling it again sometime.

ME—A pleasure, Inspector—anything I can do to help.

Well, they were just turning to go when—

DEW—You think Bruce Miller may have been in charge of the funeral arrangements?

ME—More than likely—

DEW—Your good wife attended Sunday mass at the Catholic church in Kentish Town?

ME—Yes, regularly—

DEW—You may not be aware that Miller was a staunch Catholic too?

ME—No, I didnt know that. (They do their homework, down at that Yard)

DEW—Since they were both staunch Catholics, how did she come to be cremated?

CHAPTER 8: YARD NOT QUITE SO FRIENDLY

AND IN THE SILENCE after that, I remembered—too late—the fuss she had made when her mothers ashes arrived. Not so much grief—she didnt like her mother that much—as shock that her stepfather, a non-Catholic, had gone against family wishes & had her Mom cremated.

All I could say was, I just dont know, unless—as one has heard—cemetery space in the big cities on the Coast is at a premium—

DEW—True, one has heard of cemeteries getting more & more congested, cremation is so much more civilized—

ME—I agree.

More small talk, & they went. Polite as ever.

But I dont feel as confident as this time last night.

39 H. CRESC, SAME evening.

Quite perturbed, & wont sleep well. It's like this.

My D seemed fine after that talk, & went down to kitchen to prepare dinner—I didnt go down with her like I usually did, as I had some tax papers to deal with.

It wasnt nighttime yet, but dark & close & stormy, & it started to thunder. I didnt bother because one time in the middle of the night it had thundered & it hadnt frightened her—then I heard, coming up the stairs—a shriek almost it was—Peter—Peter—

I raced down the stairs, thinking, she's burned her poor hand. At the first I couldnt see her in the kitchen, the light was so poor—then I spotted her in the corner by the little window, her back flat against the wall, pale and breathing hard. I rushed to her & she rushed to me, I had my arms around her, what is it my Dearest, what is it . . .

Well, she didnt know. She tried to tell me, but she just didn't know.

She told me (like a child she was) that for several weeks now she'd noticed she had a funny feeling as soon as she got to the bottom of the basement steps, & it got worse outside the kitchen door, then a bit better in the kitchen, but not much. That was why she'd suggested me being with her in the kitchen as much as possible.

What sort of feeling, I said. Peter I know its silly, she said, but it's like—a sort of smell.

That gave me a bit of a jolt but only for a second, because there is no smell, I check every week.

She took hold of a potato she had nearly peeled, & went on with it. How do you mean, I said, a real smell, like drains?

Oh no, she said, its as if it was inside my head—just a bad feeling, oh I know I'm silly—

Then she makes a sharp turn towards the kitchen door, & I see her go dead white. From where we were, I could see the dark passage & the cellar door opposite, closed of course. I said, My Dearest, what is it? Then she said, in a whisper—she could hardly speak—Peter I just heard something—like a cry, not human—

I thought she was going to faint, & all I could think of was to get her back to normal, so I walked to the open door & looked out into the passage.

There was something there. Moving. And just then, there comes a great clap of thunder & something flashes past me & into the kitchen.

I heard my D. behind me give a shriek, & turned just in time to see the next-door cat—terrified by the thunder—streak up to the open window & out.

Well, I put my arms round her & start to laugh, & then she laughed as well, with relief—hystirical to start with, then calmed down. Then she looks down at her hand, and we see that in her fright she had clutched the little knife she had been peeling the potatoes with, & there was blood all over her hand.

I was upset & rushed her to the sink, she said, Oh its a small cut, she was less concerned than me. And she was right, the blood made it look worse than it was, I bandaged her hand with a clean dishcloth & she went on getting the dinner ready.

I shut the window after the cat, in case of rain. She remarked that she had often noticed the cat prowling around in the passage, outside the cellar.

Then I sat down to shell the peas for her, then she said, Once you are down here with me, I'm alright. Then she kissed the top of my head, very light, a way she has.

But I had been real upset. Upset at seeing her upset, I mean.

And she was scared—thats the worst of being a timid young creature thats too imaginative. But now she's told me, & got it out of her system, she'll be alright.

And I think the cat helped.

39 H. CRESC, NEXT morning, Fri July 8, 7:30 am.

No sleep.

Im not even wondering if he's coming back. Just wondering when.

And Ive got to be ready. Knowing him, he'll only come back if he's got a couple of questions. Strictly routine.

Questions about something new he's got on to. What things?

Suppose it's something I won't be able to answer? Because there'll be no answer?

If that happens, Ive got to make up my mind as to what would be my plan of action.

When in a tight corner—no, thats putting it too high, lets say— when faced with an embarrasing dilema (cant spell all that)—the truth can have its uses.

But not here. Oh no.

If only that trip to Dieppe (Dr & Mrs Crippen visiting the Frenchman) had happened, & been a success—me & my D. would be married by now. But no use thinking on those lines.

The truth can have its uses—that keeps running through my head. Looking back, theres something on my mind that I dont enjoy dwelling on, because it could be another if only.

And here it is. The night she had that accident, was I too over-wrought & full of the Dieppe scheme (and of my 100% intention to carry that scheme through)—ie, should I have wiped that thought completely off the slate? Instead, should I have said to myself, This thing tonight being an accident that could happen to any husband (even a loving one) with a difficult hystirical wife, I must leave everything as it is & telephone the Police <u>now?</u>

From what Ive studied of the man Dew & the police attitude & methods, I have a feeling they would have believed me, & by now—

No, that <u>is</u> an if-only, & no good tormenting myself with it, whats done is done. Whats dead cant be brought back to life.

Wait a minute. Yes it can.

<u>M</u>emo Talk (assuming that Dew <u>may</u> somehow corner me)

Inspector, <u>I</u>ve been thinking this over, & the moment has come for me to make a clean breast of it, & Im only sorry to have wasted your time—as you may have guessed during our talks, I wasnt always tell-ing the truth, & in a minute I'll tell you why.

<u>Firstly</u>, my wife is not dead (not, at least, as far as I know) & <u>sec-ondly</u>, she did not leave to see to a sick relative, she walked out on me for good, to join her fancy man Bruce Miller in California.

Then Dew will ask—

Dew—Why did you pretend about the relative?

Me—I didnt want to be talked of as a fool by all her friends.

(True)

Now suppose then he asks—

Dew—But <u>why</u> did you want to make out she was dead?

Now this will be my strong card—this is where the truth, & nothing but the truth, will hit strong & hard.

Me—Inspector, I happened to know via a patient of mine, a Mr Matheson in Golders Green, whose wife deserted him 4 years ago & never been back—just disappeared—& who wants to marry again, that you have to wait 7 yrs—7, Inspector, <u>7</u>—before you can marry again. I know you like my fiancee Miss Le Neve, & you must have seen that I just worship her—

(It's TRUE, TRUE!)

Well Inspector, put yourself in my place, as a happily married family man—suppose <u>you</u> had been in my shoes when you were hop-ing to marry your wife—7 <u>yrs!</u>

I must sit down & try to get that by heart.

Memo—this morning take this (ie Diary) to Office—luckily strong-box just fits into my attache case—& in future store it at back of my one locked drawer.

Take no chances.

OFFICE, NEW OXFORD ST, same day, Fri July 8, 12 noon.

Good thing I brought Diary here, I just couldnt fix my mind on business—between patients I feel a bit jumpy & this steadies me.

Plenty to write about too (my D out delivering prescriptions, so isnt here to notice me scribbling).

I somehow wasnt too surprised to see the shadows of the 2 of them on the glass of the door. Almost expected it. 10:30.

My D answered the door, & when she said, Oh come in Inspector—if she felt any aprehensions she certainly managed to hide it. I really think the dear girl is getting the better of her fancies.

Insp not quite so friendly. Good Morning, I have just a few questions. (Not Good Morning Doctor)

And that damn Serg Mitchell with him again. Now there's a poker face. Part of his job I suppose.

They sit, my D takes her work into Dr Masters office, Insp asks if he may smoke his pipe, then remarks that the weather's changed, not quite so sunny as yesterday—all as per usual. But I know his tactics well enough by now to say to myself, you never know the minute.

When the Serg put down a gladstone bag & brought that notebook out, I made out not to notice.

I didn't like it.

But I kept my smile on. Then the talk. And no small talk.

Just inscrutable.

DEW—My first question—

And then he remembered something & took an old envelope from a pocket, with some scribbling on it.

DEW—Excuse me—while I remember, Mitchell, re the Copleston Case, this note should go to the Assistant Commissioner today—(then to me) would you allow the Sergeant to type it out for me—no, not on your Office paper, just a plain sheet.

I said, Of course, & the Serg went to my D's typewriter. While he typed—it was only three or four lines—the Insp talked about the Copleston Case, how theyre trying to prove that when she married him she did know he had a wife already & is not the innocent party she passes herself as, it was most interesting.

Then Dew took out my son's letter, as before. I thought, I'm getting a bit sick of that letter. I was getting ready for a question from him about it, but he was just looking down at it.

Then the Serg comes up with his typed notes, puts them down, & goes back to his shorthand book.

Wait a minute. His typed note, to the Commissioner, typed on my D's typewriter. Nothing of the kind, it was an excuse to have something typed on this particular machine, on a blank sheet from my desk, in case one or the other matched my son's letter. Well, theyll draw a blank on that. But—

MEMO. Remove old typewriter from back of attic, walk it to Regents Park Canal & dump it. Must keep ahead of him.

(One thing occurrs to me & it interests me. When he mentioned the Copleston Case theyre working on and the important note to the Assistant Commissioner, at first—of course—I didnt tumble to what he & the Serg were up to, I thought the note was a genuine message. And what did I feel, as I recall now? Jealous. Plain jealous, because he was interested in any other case but me. I just felt like I shld be the only one. Not that Im a case, of course.)

Then we had a bit of small talk. I'm getting wary of the small talk by now, thinking, what's this leading to, and I was right.

He's just mentioning that yesterday after his pleasant glass of sherry at No 39, he took the wrong omnibus for Waterloo Station. I put him right on that, then he weighs in.

DEW—Talking of omnibuses, yesterday when you left your briefcase on the omnibus, were you downstairs or on the open top?

ME—On the top, it wasnt raining after all & since I rarely travel by omnibus, I sat on a front seat, to get the view.

DEW—And very pleasant it can be. Oh, by the way—

And cool as you please, he looks at the Serg, & the Serg opens the gladstone bag. Then the Insp bends down & fishes something out of the bag. My briefcase.

ME—Good gracious, thats quick work. And is the Death Certificate inside?

I asked that so quick & eager, I give myself full marks. But wait.

DEW—Im afraid not. Empty.

ME—Well, thats natural isnt it? The thief found nothing of value and in temper threw it away—

DEW—It was never thrown away, the conductor found it on the bus, upstairs on your front seat. Empty.

ME—There was a suspicious-looking man opposite me, I remember wondering afterwards if he might take a fancy to it—

DEW—But he didnt, here it is—

ME—I mean what was inside—

DEW—You mean, he went off with a strange Death Certificate & 2 cables?

Still smiling. But for the first time, he'd got me.

And I said it, in those words—Inspector, you've got me! Then I start to ask him about the Copleston case, man to man.

But the game isnt over, hes got another card to play.

The trump card. He takes something out of his pocket & hands it to me. A cable.

I can remember it pretty well word for word.

NO TRACE IN CALIFORNIA FILES OF REGISTER OF DEATH OF PERSON YOU INQUIRED OF STOP WE CONFIRM THAT SINCE EVERY DEATH IS AUTOMATI-CALLY FILED HERE SHE CANNOT HAVE DIED IN CALIFORNIA STOP REGRET CANNOT ASSIST YOU BUREAU OF VITAL STATISTICS IN SACRAMENTO

I said to myself, How right I was to work out what to say, if I'm ever caught out. Because here I am, caught out.

Then I thought of my D—she would have to know it all later any-way, & it will have more effect if she hears it with the 2 of them present. I must fetch her.

Then something happened that I didnt like too much.

I get up, v. calm & alert & take a step to the door. It must have looked a bit sudden, because (out of the corner of my eye) I saw the 2 of them—exactly together—they shot up from their chairs like a pair of jack-in-the-boxes, streaked past me, swung round & barred my way to the door.

You have to take your hat off, it was the neatest bit of drill you ever saw. They were looking at me, very steady, nothing more. I thought, they look as if the handcuffs will be out any minute.

Then I thought, dont be a damn fool.

DEW—Did you want something?

(No calling me Doctor)

ME—Well yes Inspector, I want Miss Le Neve to come in.

The Inspec looks at the Serg, & seems to loosen up.

DEW—Fair enough. Sergeant, get her, will you?

And we sit down again, the Serg comes back & holds the door open for my D.

She didnt look too alarmed, she told me after that she thought I wanted her to type something. I took her arm gently & said, Sit down, my dear. She looked a bit aprehensive then, but I was behaving as reasuring as I could.

And when we were all seated, the interview went exactly as I had prepared it, I might have seen it in a crystal ball—Inspector I'll make a clean breast of it, my wife is not dead etc.

The only thing was of course, I hadnt prepared for my D being present, & when I said, My wife is not dead, she gave quite a cry & sat staring at me with her hand to her mouth.

I said quickly, Let me finish & you'll understand. Then, as I turned to the Insp again, I thought—good thing they saw her do that, because it proves she believed in the Death Certificate, no girl could have acted that.

Then everything went through according to plan, with the Sergeant's shorthand scratching away.

Then, when the Insp got to his question about, Why did you want to make it look as if she had died—then I let fly, about me having waited 3 long years. I said, For the past 3 yrs she has been my only comfort.

Then, from the look on her face, with the surprise and the pain giving way to a look of love, & her lips trembling, I heard my voice break & felt my glasses steam up, it was heat from tears.

And I could tell that the 2 Scotland Yard men believed me, every word. They had to.

Then the Insp said, Of course, I shall have to find Mrs Crippen, to clear this matter up.

I said, Can you suggest anything, Inspector, would an Advertisement be any good?

He said, An excellent idea. And then I drafted one, Will Belle

<u>Elmore communicate with H.H.C. or authorities at once. Serious
trouble through your absence, 25 dollars reward.</u>

Then the Insp gets up, quite sharp.

DEW—Well, I'm off on the Copleston Case, you dont mind if Sergeant Mitchell waits in the office across the corridor, I may want to phone him about that, if you dont mind—thank you very much.

And he went, then my D showed the Serg into Dr Masters office opposite, luckily his Sec was at the house seeing to the funeral on Sat, she would have thought it funny to see the Serg sitting opposite her in her office with the door open so he could keep an eye on my door.

In case I left.

But thats only natural.

Now I recall something. When the Inspect said, Thank you very much, & went, there was a look in his eyes that wasnt there before. What was it?

It seems to me Ive seen it somewhere else, though never on people talking to <u>me</u>, or looking at me.

I remember—I saw it once when caught in a crowd at Liverpool St Station & the Stationmaster etc were greeting the King, & Queen Alexandra, on arriving from Sandringham. He & the group were looking at the K and Q with respect.

The Insp looked at me with <u>respect</u>.

Once my D & I were by ourselves, I turned to her. She looked kind of bewildered, I said, What is it?

MY D—Peter I don't understand—whats happened—why did you tell him shes still alive when you had a letter from your son—you <u>showed</u> it to me—telling all about it & enclosing the Death Certificate that I tried to trace—what is it all about?

Then, telling her now the details of all that—typing the letter myself, copying my son's signature, leaving the briefcase on the omnibus—I realized that when I had made a clean breast to the Inspector, she had been completely at sea because she could not <u>believe</u> I had not been telling the truth all along.

MY D—Peter you had been telling lies.

ME—But I <u>had</u> to tell him lies, don't you see, so we could get married sooner—

MY D—But you had lied to <u>me</u>—

ME—But what would be the point of telling you any different? If I'd let you know from the start that I was misleading him & that she is alive, from what I know of you it would have worried you to death. Youd have been awake all night, afraid he might find out there was no Death Certificate etcetra—you do see that my Dearest dont you?

And once again that was dead easy for me, to say all that, because it was the truth—100% what I felt.

But coming out with all that to her, about making up the Death Cert—what were my feelings?

Well, quite different from with the Insp—with him it had been like a game, a fight almost. With her I was like a schoolboy whos been caught & has to own up. Almost as if I was in the witness box, like a criminal.

E.g, when—I remember—when I told her how I had copied my son's signature, she interrupted, quite sharp for her. Forged, she said, you mean forged.

Well I had to say, Yes if you look at it like that—but she didnt seem to understand, kept remembering things— But the Obituary Notice you put in *The Era*—the memorial cards with the black edge you sent out—

I said, My Dearest, you must remember that I did it for you—for us, for our future! I know, she said, I know— (She just had to believe that)

Then—oh yes, I made a mistake.

ME—Did you notice the look he gave me just now when he left?

MY D—Yes I did.

ME—It was a look of respect.

MY D—Respect?

ME—For me, for having planned all that & within an ace of getting away with it.

She just looked at me.

MY D—Getting away with what?

For a second—it was like—yes, I know—like being on thin ice and hearing a crack. Get off the ice.

ME—Well, getting away with convincing him she's dead, and getting that nearer to you-and-me being married.

MY D—There may have been respect, Peter, but I saw something else as well—I did—

Me—What?

My D—Suspicion.

Well, I stared at her, and I gave quite a chuckle. Suspicion, I said, why my Dearest, you sound like one of those Sherlock Holmes things—suspicion of what?

My D—I don't know—I just felt . . . (I dont think she knows how she feels, poor pet). You dont think . . . they might report you—or whatever they do—for fraud—no, I don't mean fraud—sort of misrepresentation of facts, like perjury—

Me—Perjury, my dear, is when youre in a court giving false evidence under oath, now just calm yourself & get on with those prescriptions, theyre badly needed & we dont want patients dying on our hands— I was trying to jolly her along like a dutch uncle, & I think I managed it pretty well. I must continue the good work.

She's typing at the minute, quite herself. She just couldnt bear for me to get into any sort of trouble—the same as I think of her. I still sometimes take a sniff at the eau de cologne, she has teased me about it. We love each other.

A sandwich, then both back to work. After 10 mins, to cheer her up, I repeated what the Insp had said at lunch that first day. I told her his exact words—She is such a charming young lady she deserves to be happy, if I had a daughter Id want her to be like Miss Le Neve.

Well, normally she would have blushed from the pleasure of such a compliment, but she just looked at me, sort of hesitating & said, Did he? & went back to her typing.

And that funny look meant she was thinking, Is it true, did he hear the Inspector say that, or is it all made up like the other things?

Me who have never told a lie unless absolutely necessary. I cant bear to think she doesnt trust me.

A minute ago, ran into Dr Rylance on my way to W.C. He said, Peter you look worried, I said, its these policemen, they keep on pestering me about that Drouet Institute trouble years ago, as if I was to do with it. Sounded alright.

I can hear the Insp outside calling, I'm back Mitchell—

Office, later same aft, 4:30 pm.

Steady steady. A good think.

When the Insp came back into Office, the Serg behind him, his appearance was different. Somehow not so spick & span as before—grubby almost.

He asks my D if she minds leaving us alone, she goes, then he asks if I mind him washing his hands at the washbasin. I said, Make yourself at home.

I ask them to sit down, quite calm, but I knew something was coming & braced up for it. I said—in my mind—over & over again—I am an innocent man, I am an innocent man. Just as well I did.

DEW—I'm afraid you wont be very pleased with what I'm going to tell you.

ME—Oh? I'm sorry to hear that, Inspector—

DEW—Ive spent the afternoon up at your house.

(I am an innocent man, innocent)

ME—Youre right, Im not at all pleased. Isnt that against the law?

DEW—Im afraid not, I have a search warrant.

ME—May I ask what you were searching for?

DEW—Anything that might help us to trace your wife.

ME—(And this took some asking) And did you find anything?

DEW—About that old typewriter in the attic—is that the one you wrote your son's letter on?

I had pushed that typewriter into a dark corner behind a lot of stuff. He's thorough. Is he trying to break me down? I'm tougher than I look.

ME—Thats right, I thought it would be too risky to use this one.

DEW—Quite right.

Then he takes a handkerchief from his pocket, lays it on the desk, takes tweezers from pocket, unfolds handkerchief with tweezers.

Inside handkerchief is something with dried blood on it.

It was the dishcloth I had tied round my D's hand last night when she cut it peeling the potatoes.

I explained that to the Insp—the cut's still not quite healed, I said, she can show it to you, in the other room—I remember throwing that into the rubbish bin under the sink. Where did you find it?

SERG—Under the sink. Half behind the bin.

DEW—(quite genial) You must have missed your aim.

ME—Must have.

Old typewriter, dishcloth, he's been through the house with a microscope.

And found <u>nothing else</u>.

Thank my stars I moved the Diary out. Just in time.

Then what happened? I asked them how business was—we all three had quite a chuckle about that—then the Insp said they were catching a train to Leeds, for a big forgery trial.

Now I come to what's on my mind.

We were chitchatting about No 39—that it was a big house to run & how clean it was kept (they ought to know).

ME—You see, Inspector, with all this coming out about me being stupid & pretending that my wife was dead, & all the discussion about that, Miss Le Neve has been feeling more & more uncomfortable in the house—

DEW—Thats very understandable—

ME—And I'm thinking of buying a flat. (It had been an idea, for a minute)

Then he talked about him & Mrs Dew having bought their own house, then about which house agents are the best, then (for something to say) I asked—let me get this straight—

ME—When you buy a property through a house agent, does the buyer pay the commission to the agent?

Then the Insp says something about the commission being split, or something—then he says (looking straight at me) he says, <u>In the cellar</u>.

I stared at him.

The cellar? I said.

He smiled then, as if he was puzzled, & he said Yes, I was answering your question, I have an idea the commission is usually split <u>between the buyer and the seller</u>.

(He had swallowed the word <u>and</u>, so that it sounded like <u>in</u>, ie buyer in the seller)

ME—Oh yes of course—

What else could I say? I was so knocked off my perch I cant rightly remember what happened then.

Yes—he & the Serg looked at each other.

Theyll be coming back to the house. Not now, nor tomorrow, they wont be back from Leeds till tomorrow eve.

But they'll be in there the next day, Sun the 10th.

Got to get away.

39 H. Cresc, later same day, 7 pm. Fri July 8th.

Brought strongbox home, diary in it.

(NB Must burn diary)

Sent my Dearest to Mrs Masters, for condolences before funeral in the morning, so she wont notice me humped over blank page. (Which I have been since I slipped down to have a look at cellar. The old chandelier has moved again, coal disturbed, but must have been v. casual, bricks not tampered with.)

Oh dear, I dont like what happened just before she left for the Masters house.

She was sitting at sitting-room desk sorting out household bills, when I heard a sharp tearing noise, looked round & she was tearing something into small peices, then she threw them into the wastebasket almost as if she was angry.

While she was upstairs getting my bedroom slippers, I got up and looked in the basket at what she had torn up. Her eyes had caught two or three cards left over in a cubbyhole of the desk. I saw a strip of black. Memorial cards.

I did all that for the best. She's got to see that.

Steady steady. Think.

Theres a lot to work out, one thing at a time.

Out of the country, & her with me.

Dieppe. (I know it, & it doesnt know me) Night boat tomorrow night, July 9, 11 pm.

First, my D will be back from Mrs Masters any minute. Memo of talk with her, & a difficult one too.

My Dearest, I dont know how to break it to you, but earlier today the Yard showed themselves in their true colors, having the impudence to come up here & ransack the house, I said How dare you, what were you looking for?

Papers, they said, anything which would help us to trace her whereabouts in California. And of course they found it, at the back of my drawer. I'd forgotten it—you remember when I told you she'd written a note asking for the rest of her things. Well theyve got her address from that, & they hinted they'll be cabling her to pay her fare here. To give evidence.

My D don't carry on so. I'm here to protect you—the fact is that when you were afraid I might have done something unlawful in stating to 2 Police Officers that she was dead, & I said Nonsense—<u>well I was wrong</u>.

It is a misdemenour & I can be prosecuted, then it would all come out in the papers about you living in here, & I cannot watch your good name having mud thrown at it—now listen carefully.

For you & me, the only hope of happiness is to get out of the country, tomorrow night. And then sit & work out how we can travel somewhere & start life 100% fresh, you & me, & get married . . .

Never mind about bigamy, nobody will ever know & in a case like this <u>nobody</u> with any human feelings would ever look on it as even a misdemenour.

(And I feel thats true, <u>with all my heart</u>) & now, my D, shall we think about packing? (NB Pack haircutting scissors.)

4 HOURS LATER, 11 pm.

Well, the female sex is extraordinary.

I expected hysterics at the least. But to my amazement, sat almost calm, her hands together in her lap, didnt speak until I'd finished.

Then she said, Ive been expecting something like this almost without knowing I was—just a vague pressentiment—and now its on us & we can do something . . . I feel better. Peter, I have a feeling we shall be alright, because I love & trust you with all my heart.

I nearly cried when she said that. She will make me a wonderful wife.

Get my D. to sew 4 rings, 2 brooches into lining of one of my vests.

<u>About tomorrow</u>. My D will be home, going through everything & packing & waiting for funeral.

Get to office at 9 am. First, make request to William Long my dental mechanic to go straightaway & shop for articles for boy aged 16—2 shirts (guess at size & tell him) 2 collars, brown suit, buttoned boots, flat cap.

(He will not think it so strange, a year back I asked him to shop for some down-and-out youths at hostel run by a clergyman patient)

Then a note to be left for him.

Dear Mr Long, Will you do me the very great favor of winding up my household affairs. There is £12/10 due to my landlord for past quarters rent. I cannot manage about Valentine the French girl, she should have enough saved to get her back to France. Kindly leave keys with landlord etc. Thanking you with best wishes for your future success & happiness, Yrs faithfully—

Then note to be left for Dr Rylance. Good thing I told him that Scotland Yard has called on me to find out if my wife had any estates to pay taxes on. I can use that. <u>Dear Dr R . . . I find that in order to escape trouble I shall be obliged to absent myself for a time.</u>

Then explain to him that I have already paid Goddard & Smith £10/12/0 rent, in advance up to Sept 25, also that there will be several paid bills to enter into file on my desk, and that he will find key of desk in upper drawer of little cabinet in Coulthard's office.

At 10 am. to Bank, withdrawals. 11 o clock, Masters funeral.

39 H. CRESC., HOUR later, 12 midnight.

Now this <u>is</u> a quandary.

We had done quite a bit of packing & I sent my D to bed (pretty tired, poor pet) & told her I'd light a fire in the study to get rid of some old papers. (Gave her something to make her sleep, thats the good thing about being a doctor).

And here I am, sitting with the fire lit, & staring at it, & then at the two thick books in front of me.

This Diary's come to be a part of me. And I cant bear to destroy it.

And yet nobody—<u>nobody</u> must get hold of it.

And yet—imagine in a hundred years time . . .

I must think. Wait a minute. Yes.

That dinner party, when the Masters came to us, some weeks back, when Mrs M. hinted that the Dr. had knowledge of people in high places that could be of great interest in years to come.

Thats it. Get a plain piece of paper & paste. Wait, pigeonhole of letters . . .

Yes, Ive found one from him to me, signed S. T. Masters. Write on the plain paper, in capitals—IN DEFERENCE TO ROYAL FAMILY. NOT TO BE OPENED TILL 50 YEARS AFTER MY DECEASE.

No, TILL 65 YEARS. Cut out lower part of Masters letter to me (the part with his signature on it) paste it under the above.

I recall well that his desk is in a sort of study, like mine, bathroom just outside. After the funeral, with the sitting room full of the mourners, I will pick up my attache case in hall, nip up as if to bathroom, get to desk, deposit strongbox at back of a bottom drawer.

Knowing Dr Masters wife & family, that wish of his will be respected.

Let me see, we're at 1910. Add 65 yrs.

1975. Looks funny on paper. I dont like to think of my D as old, but she wld be 92. Me, 113, & too far gone to bother about.

But I hope therell be a certain amount of interest.

Fire is nearly out. Glad I didnt feed it. I'm tired. (Put out black tie for morning—mourning—both!!)

39 H. CRESC, NEXT morn., Sat July 9.

My D. slept, of course—so did I, in snatches, but too excited to go right off. Filled with love & admiration for her, so sensible & prepared for hardships.

Oh, but I cant stand to part from writing things down, the relief of it.

I know what I'll do—I'll keep it up, but must be careful not to put anything down which might be awkward in case of my privacy being invaded. In view of that, must be careful to establish my innocence by making statements in regard to said innocence—will do so IN CAPITAL LETTERS.

A new life!

CHAPTER 9: THE NEW LIFE

HOTEL DE LA GARE, Dieppe, next eve, Sun July 10, 1910. 10 pm.

Excellent crossing, calm moonlight night. Lucky for me, I had work to do on the boat.

(Thanks to the UNWARRANTED PERSECUTION OF ME BY SCOTLAND YARD CONCERNING MY MISSING WIFE)

Unusual work. I had to sit my Dearest down in our cabin, in the middle of the night crossing, unpin her lovely brown hair, & cut it to the shape Ive been used to cutting William Long's hair, & the others. (I did that in another existence, because already Albion House is far away, & No 39 does not exist)

Sad to see those gleaming tresses on the floor, & then to sweep them into a newspaper & pitch them through the porthole—but it was nice (somehow) to be bending over her with my waistcoat brushing her shoulder, & to see her in the little mirror, turning from young lady into little boy. A loving feeling, quite pleasant.

And she makes a nice little boy, about 15, William Long had made a good job of his shopping—the brown suit fitted well on her hips—rather tight—& the boots just right, a little big. She had been very nervous of the idea of course, but it was funny—once it was in the process she got interested & amused, as if we were dressing up for a fancy-dress do. Looking in the glass after she'd put on the Eton collar, she said, I look like *Tom Brown's School Days!*

Then I shaved off my mustache, shortened my straggly hair, & though I couldnt see too well what I looked like without my glasses, she said it made a lot of difference. I made her practice walking up & down with longer strides, & crossing her legs after sitting down. Quite a pantomime.

Mr John & Master Robinson. Father & Son. I think of the day she said to me, Youre my father now & I feel quite a lump in my throat. Little would I have thought of this.

Standing in the crowd waiting to disembark at Dieppe, 8 am, I whispered to her that in mid-Channel I had lost a Future Wife & gained a Son, it made her smile. I could tell she was thinking, anythings better than that uncertainty.

Hotel de la Gare, Dieppe, next eve, Mon July 11. 10 pm. Waking up this am, I got quite a shock turning & seeing this head on the pillow next to me, cropped so close. For a moment I thought I was in the wrong room.

For their escape, Crippen successfully disguised Ethel Le Neve as a boy.

It's awkward without my glasses—long sight, not too bad, but cant read except in bedroom, but outside I can always get my D to read things to me if necess.

HOTEL DES ARDENNES, Brussels, 3 days later, Thurs July 14.
Registered as *Robinson, Merchant* & *Robinson, Fils.*
Have made inquiries here, earliest Atl. sailing is for Canada, in 6 days time, Antwerp to Quebec, SS *Montrose.*
Suits us, I dont fancy the States much anymore, with memories I dont care for, plus the fact WE MIGHT RUN INTO A CERTAIN PERSON, stranger coincidences have happened & I would hate my D to be subjected to meeting her.
Ive booked a cabin, & we must make these next few days a bit of a holiday. We can sit in the sun, Dad can have his glass of red wine & Master Robinson will have his lemonade—no, this is the Continent, they think nothing of schoolboys drinking wine, he can have a glass too.

HOTEL DES ARDENNES, 2 days later, July 16.
Nothing to report. Exhibition v. interesting. Had to scold Master R a couple of times for sitting with fingers locked together under chin—Ive coached him to sit with each hand holding a knee. He is v. willing to learn.

HOTEL DES ARDENNES, Brussels, 3 days later, Tues July 19.
Nothing to report indeed!
Strolling round on my own this morning (my D. doing bit of washing in the room).
I happened to pass a big newsagents & glanced at the stand. I stood & stared, couldnt believe my eyes.
Looking me straight in the face was an enormous photo of my D.
My favorite photo of her, but enlarged to cover the whole front page of the (London) *Daily Mirror.*
I bought it, folded it over so the front page was hidden, & walked back to the Hotel in a trance. In the room (thank God) I find a scribble from her that she has gone for a stroll too, to get the benefit of sea air & sun. I sit down, reach for my glasses, & settle down to a read. A special sort of read.

Daily Mirror, Fri July 15. (4 days ago, & 6 days after we got away)
Under her dear face—*Miss ETHEL LE NEVE, missing in connection
with Camden Town Mystery, may be describing herself as Mrs Crippen, wanted by Scotland Yard.*

Inside—BODY IN CELLAR MYSTERY. *Since on the 13th Inspector
Dew discovered the remains believed to be Mrs Crippen, the house
has been closely guarded—last night it was in complete darkness except for a light in the basement.* etc. etc.

This terrible thing is in front of me, & out of window I can see the
sun on the sea, I cant believe it. Everything goes swirly.

Then I turn over, & heres a full page again—B.E. underneath, and
the top half a huge picture of myself, staring at me.

My first feeling is as if all my clothes have been blown off me & I
am standing on a platform in front of a crowd, in the nude.

To somebody whos never seen their name in print—except in a list
at a charity dinner or when I got my Diploma—to see yourself in a
headline gives you a very strange feeling. Like being drunk.

Its as if you are reading about somebody else & then it hits you—
it's you!

And the thought of all those people taking the trouble over you—
the newspaper reporters, the printers up all night, the newsboys—all
to tell the world about you—Heavens above!

Then my second thought is—what a terrible enlargement of my
Photo, newspapers must do something to them to make them look
worse, those pebble glasses glaring at me, enough to frighten a grown
person—

And my name underneath, in thick print. CRIPPEN, THE WANTED
MAN.

MY GOD THIS IS UNBELIEVABLE, A BODY IN NO 39 BUT THEY CANT
THINK IT'S TO DO WITH ME, THEY MUST TRY AND TRACE THE FORMER
TENANT, THIS IS TERRIBLE—HOW CAN I PROVE IM INNOCENT—

Once the shock has worn off a bit, I study the small print. My goodness, the things they can put together in the paper, you only realize it
when your own turn has come.

Mrs Crippen's stage career (4 photos, in costume)

Mrs Crippen's Stage Career (Thats a good one!) 4 Photos in costume. *Daughter of Polish nobleman* (Thats better still) *The woman
has been seen in Edinburgh* (Thats good, but I dont like my D de-

scribed as <u>the woman</u>.) *Crippen described as being seen in various seaside resorts, Brighton, Bournemouth, Ramsgate.* (Thats good.) *Neighbor heard 2 terrible screams from No 39, during Easter* (But we were in Dieppe, with house empty!)

Then—*Mr Crippen was rather a short gentleman, somewhat stout & bald, who said he had felt his wifes death acutely.* Now that description is just rude. (Not even <u>Dr</u> Crippen)

Then words like <u>ghastly, grisly, horrifying details, fiendish</u>—I'll now tear the ghastly grisly *Daily Mirror* up into small peices & drop it in the wastebasket.

Thank Heaven my D wasnt with me when I saw it. We're off to Antwerp 1st thing in the morning, & not a minute too soon.

S.S. *Montrose*, NEXT DAY, Wed July 20.

Steaming out of Antwerp, what a blessed relief! My D & I stand watching the Quay creeping away—good-by to the Old World, to the old life! My first sea trip since NY 10 yrs ago, & my D's 1st ever—I will see she enjoys it.

A nice boat, not too grand, not too small & fairly empty for this time of year—nice cabin. Master Robinson behaving well, helped by only slight roll of ship.

SS *Montrose*, NEXT EVENING, July 21, 10 pm.

Got *The Four Just Men* (E. Wallace) out of Ships Library, far-fetched as usual but passes a couple of floating hours agreably. Its about a murderer whos got a warrant out for him, & £1000 reward. Now thats a lot of money.

Yesterday evening, an awkward moment. But amusing.

My D walks out to go to the toilet, opens a door marked GENTS, walks in & there are 3 men with backs to her, standing at the urinal. She gave one look & scuttled out, & off to a proper WC.

I had to laugh, the poor dear confessed she had no idea that men <u>stood</u> on such occasion, & she'd even been wondering what the men in the Dieppe streets were doing behind those metal circular partitions with their feet showing. She was quite the blushing schoolboy, I told her that one of these days she'd be the blushing bride. We had a laugh over it.

SS *Montrose*, NEXT EVENING, JULY 22, 10 pm.

My D asleep in the Upper Berth.

Beautiful weather, Herring Pond living up to its name, you almost feel youre on a cruise. Moon last night, my D & I walked round & round, then sat in a secluded part behind the lifeboats, where I could hold her hand & we could watch the beautiful silver lights the moon put on the water.

We're not bothered by people, as everybody seems to keep to themselves on a trip like this. That suits us. We got talking to one Canadian, I said I was a widower & that my boy & I were going to settle in Canada, the man said it was a country full of opportunities.

And I believe that. I intend to work hard as a Doctor, & I still have the knack of being liked by patients. We are going to be alright.

SS *Montrose*, NEXT EVENING, Sat July 23, 10 pm.

Something happened this afternoon that gave me a real shake.

The 2 of us were on one of our little strolls in the sun, & got to the very quiet back of the ship as usual. I was pointing out something in the water some distance off, & wondering if it was another boat, & in pointing it out I put my arm round my D's shoulders (no more than that, I am naturally v. careful in public) & then she (as has often done in the past) takes my hand & gives it a little squeeze.

Well, suddenly I hear behind us (the wind carrying the sound) a man say (quite distinct), I wonder if those 2 <u>are</u> father & son. And he gives a kind of chuckle & moves on.

It was a minute before it dawned on me what he was getting at, thank God my D didn't latch on, she just said, What did he say? & I said, He said something about the <u>sun</u>, & we walked on.

But I felt sick to my stomach. The idea of a stranger taking me for one of those filthy pederasts you read about in the Sunday papers!

I'm still v. angry.

And more so, through having noticed that strolling with this fellow was the Captain himself. I would not like to have him thinking there could be such a person on his Passenger List.

SS *Montrose*, NEXT EVENING, Sun July 24, 10 pm.

My D already asleep, & I can hardly keep my eyes open, its this splendid sea air.

The SS *Montrose*, on which Crippen and Ethel Le Neve
fled to Canada, was equipped with the new Marconi "wireless."

A very nice thing has happened.

The Captain (Capt. Kendall) cannot have taken any notice of that fellow's remark, because lo & behold, a message from him to say he is asking a few passengers every day for sherry etc at 6, & could Mr & Master Robinson call on him tomorrow.

Now Ive always understood that this is quite an honor aboard ship, & I feel gratified. My D is nervous of course, but by now she has so trained herself in her <u>role</u> (as they say in the Theater) that she will pass muster, & anyway (as practically a schoolboy) she will not be called upon to converse.

Every happy day, we stand at the back of the ship & watch the old sea move away from us and the new sea approach, all the old things moving farther away back into the sky (my long sight as good as ever). Then we stroll to the front (my dutiful son holding my arm) and the New Life nearer & nearer.

S.S. *Montrose*, 2 DAYS LATER, July 26, 6 pm.

The little party went off splendidly, only three other guests & the Capt a v. genial chap, handsome, clear-cut, telling good jokes.

Sherry for me, lemonade for the Youngster. The Capt seems to take a real interest in me (not just polite) & asking how long we will be in Canada etc.

I told him I was a Doctor (who had been stuck in the North of England) looking for opportunities. He was another who told me I'd be sure to find them in Canada.

A very interesting thing happened—a Junior Officer came in with a typewritten message, one of the others asked what it was & the Captain showed it to us—quite proud he was. A message to say would he contact a firm in Quebec re supplies to be shipped back to Antwerp next trip.

Somebody said, in a joke, how had he got the message—had a fish jumped aboard with the message in his mouth, yet the paper wasnt wet! The Capt explained its this new wonder they call Wireless Telegraphy, meaning they can send a message to a ship with no telegraph poles.

It is what they call a Marconi Wireless Short Distance Installation, & I was introduced to Officer Llewelyn Jones, who is called the Marconi Operator.

Just through what they call the Air Waves. Beats me. Uncanny. But what a boon to Civilization!

The Capt has asked us in again today at 7.

Dipped into *Pickwick Papers*, always liked that, wholesome fun & educational into the bargain, & now must smarten up for the sherry (and merry) hour with the Capt. He likes us.

A v. nice trip, I dont like to think of it ending.

SS *Montrose*, AT FATHER POINT, off Quebec, 5 days later, July 31, 8 am.

Writing this on deck, on my knee, in the sun. Ship at standstill. My D. not up yet, a little tired after being kept awake by hooting of foghorns during night (beautifully clear now).

Quebec only 12 hours off. Have just been lent binoculars to see glimpse of Promised Land across St Lawrence River, land just near enough to see big crowd at quayside, the Canadians must have very little to do to be having a look at a ship this time of the morning.

Everything packed, (not much to pack) The Capt calls out that we dock this evening, weve halted here for mail & formalities. He even stopped for a chat with me, I must say he has been v. attentive.

I like these formalities aboard ship, hes standing at attention next the gangway, waiting for some official.

My D. looks rested & with roses in her cheeks, better than for a long while. I ordered a glass of sherry, & she's taking a sip from my glass for us to drink to the future. And heres to it—to the Future.

S.S. *Montrose*, SAME DAY, 12 noon.

Can it be the same day?

Well, the Official arrived up the rope ladder (peaked cap & papers). I heard somebody say he was the Pilot. He shakes hands with the Capt. looks round to see everything's OK with the ship, & as they go off to the Capt's cabin to see to business, my Master Robinson comes round from behind some lifeboats & nearly barges into the two of them. The Pilot gives Master R. a look, lifts his cap & goes on.

An Officer comes up to mention to me that the Capt would like a word. I follow him. In the Capt's cabin, the Capt & the Pilot.

Then, just as I was thinking—I know that face, even without my glasses—the Pilot says, Good Morning Doctor.

Published less than two weeks after Dr. Crippen's arrest aboard the *Montrose*, this artist's conception captured the drama of the scene, but it erred in several major details.

Inspector Dew.

All I could think of was, that in London that last day, (& me waiting for him to) he never called me Doctor, not once. And here he is, calling me Doctor.

I answered him with, Good morning Mr Dew. Then he said, Very sorry to do this Doctor, but I have to arrest you for the Murder & Mutilation of your wife.

Well, that word Mutilation (even nicely put by the Inspect) quite offended me, since it is a word foreign to a medical man. Then he handcuffed me.

I said, Cant she & me be together, the Insp said he was very sorry, against the rules. Which means that the next time we will see each other will be in—what do they call it—the Dock. I dismiss it from my mind—

So here I am in one empty cabin, & her in another, while they search our cabin.

To keep me company, I have got a hefty keeper, in case I try to jump overboard or something.

(When I took this Diary from my pocket & said I wanted to write in it, the keeper looked at me very puzzled, I guess it was a funny thing to want at a moment like this, but he didnt stop me.)

I asked him if he had known about the Insp & he said, Of course, the whole crew knew he was on his way across on the *Laurentic*, & (thanks to the Wireless Telegraphy between Capt. & Insp) so does the whole world, every newspaper has been full of it for 10 days, didnt you see that crowd on the quay at Father Point, the neighboring town of Rimousquee (cant spell it) is bursting with journalists etc, you are more famous than King George V or General Tom Thumb.

When the Insp comes in, he will take this Diary from me, but I would like to finish it off. (I have always been tidy)

Now, recalling those words in the *Daily Mirror*—ghastly, horrible, grisly, fiendish—words which are in a million mouths at this minute— I have an odd thought on this, which—BEING INNOCENT—I can write down as the Man in the Street, also as a realistic medical man, with a Degree.

In the same way that the Unknown Person who did this will be famous when they catch him—in that same way I am (at this minute) famous all over the world, because they think I did it.

503

And what they mean by it, is not the fact that in my house some woman met her death at the hands of a man (these things happen all over the world, dozens every day, & they hardly get into the papers at all)—by it, they mean that the man (whoever he is) tried to dispose of the body in this way.

And that's where the cheap sensationalism comes in, all over the world—sheer vulgar horror at the gory details which any Surgeon goes through & thinks little of, working on a body that can feel nothing. I speak with common sense. But what is important is—HOW CAN I PROVE IM INNOCENT?

And yet you have to come back to one thing—thinking of my meeting with the Insp earlier on—when he said Good Morning Doctor— it sounds strange this, but its true—behind the official nature of the thing, it was almost like two old friends meeting unexpectedly—hard to believe what the whole thing was about.

And that look I'd seen on him before, only this time more marked. Respect.

And I feel the same respect for him. Tracking me down like this, you have to hand it to them.

Come to think of it, when they took me here from the Capt's cabin, there was quite a crush of passengers outside—these things spread like wildfire—and they give me the same look. Respect, with a bit of fear thrown in, like for a tiger out in the Zoo on his way from one cage to another. Or the Royal Family.

People used to say, There goes little Crippen, he'll never get anywhere, poor chap. And now that THEY THINK I DID THIS TERRIBLE THING OF WHICH I AM INCAPABLE, Im Royalty. Thats funny.

I'LL HAVE A TERRIBLE TIME PROVING MY INNOCENCE, but I am determined to do it, because my D must be protected at all costs.

And we'll be together once its over—we will we will. I'll never forget that last look she gave me, the love in it, & fear & shame. But most of all, the love.

Until then, I'll be in a series of cells just like this—when Im not in that dock, fighting for my life, & hers.

So until she and me will be together again, theres nothing more to say.

Signed, at Father Point, Sun July 31, 1910.

H. H. Crippen.

AFTERWORD BY THE AUTHOR

ON THE AFTERNOON of Saturday, July 9, Inspector Dew had called at Albion House to find that Crippen had not returned from lunch; he and Ethel Le Neve were already on their way to Dieppe.

Dew and Mitchell spent Monday, July 11—two days later—going through 39 Hilldrop Crescent with a fine-tooth comb. It turned out to be an exhausting and fruitless day's work; they found nothing.

But—almost as if drawn by a subconscious afterthought—Dew returned later with Mitchell and concentrated on the cellar. That was July 13—beyond a doubt, Crippen's unlucky day.

Studying the bricks left clear of coal dust and rubbish, Dew saw that one brick looked almost loose. He straightened up and fetched, from the adjacent kitchen, a small poker, and was able to prize up the brick. Underneath he found a layer of clay and lime; on disturbing this, he was overpowered with a stench which drove him and Mitchell up into the summer air for a moment's relief.

There can have been few moments in any man's life when acute physical revulsion can have been so mingled with the intense excitement of success.

Three days later, on July 16, Scotland Yard issued a warrant, WANTED FOR THE MURDER OF . . . The inspector had lost no time; the police bill which was circularized immediately included a detailed description of the couple, their possible wardrobe and a full account of the jewelry.

There was, however, no mention of the strong possibility that the wanted lady was dressed as a boy; fortunately for the fugitives, William Long, the "dental mechanic" (possibly from fear of being suspected as an accomplice), had not yet vouchsafed to Dew the story of his shopping trip.

All ports were to be watched; but again fortunately for Mr. John and Master Robinson, Antwerp was clearly not as vigilant as it might have been. Four days later, on July 20, they boarded the SS *Montrose* with no trouble.

But their luck ran out. Captain Kendall would appear to have been not only an amateur sleuth, but (judging by his immensely long mes-

sage by wireless telegraphy to Scotland Yard) a sharp-eyed and resourceful one.

After studying the police bill, which had arrived on board with his
papers, on the stroll mentioned by Crippen he *did* register that
Master Robinson had held his father's hand and "squeezed it immoderately." (Since that historic message, how often—in a cable—has
the word *immoderately* been spelled out over the telephone?)

He also noticed that the lad's trousers were "very tight about the
hips, and split a bit down the back and secured with very large safety

pins." He then proceeded to challenge comparison with Sherlock himself: recalling that the official description of Crippen had included mention of glasses and false teeth, he observed (while entertaining the couple) that "the mark on the nose, caused through wearing spectacles, has not worn off since coming on board"; next he proceeded to tell Crippen "a story to make him laugh heartily, to see if he would open his mouth wide enough for me to ascertain if he had false teeth. This ruse was successful." Did it cross his mind that "this ruse" was being played on a professional dentist?

When the *Montrose* arrived in Quebec, Scotland Yard's Chief Inspector Dew (light coat, center) escorted Dr. Crippen ashore in handcuffs as throngs of people jammed the quay for a glimpse of the sensational suspect.

THE PRISONERS WERE TAKEN from the SS *Montrose* to Quebec, and then extradited to England on the SS *Megantic*, arriving at Liverpool on August 28.

The Crippen trial, at the Central Criminal Court, Old Bailey, London, opened on October 18, 1910, and lasted five days, closing on October 22.

The accused, in the face of glaring evidence, pleaded not guilty and maintained, to his last breath, the demeanor of courteous and kindly forbearance which had characterized him through life—except, needless to say, during the week of Monday, January 31, 1910, when, at number 39, he found himself cornered into a program of industrious physical activity which was to miss complete success only by a hairsbreadth—or rather by the breadth of a very thin poker fetched from a kitchen.

At Pentonville Prison, London, at 9 a.m. on November 23, 1910, he was hanged.

From that day to this, his name has maintained a steadily permanent life: a legend evoking two incongruous figures. The Little Man and the Monster.

CRIPPEN'S LAST LETTER to Ethel Le Neve, written on the eve of his execution after the news that there was no hope of a reprieve, is a remarkable document, for more than one reason. First, for its sudden and unconvincing appeal to the Deity; second, for its moving bravery in the face of inevitable official annihilation (it is noteworthy that Major O. E. M. Davies, the then governor of Pentonville Prison, is the only such official in British prison history to have called personally on the Home Secretary to request a reprieve); third, for its proof of unimpaired and selfless devotion to the love of his life; and last, for his assumption of his own innocence. It is an assumption unequivocal and unshakable.

"God indeed must hear our cry to Him for Divine help in this last farewell. . . . The Governor brought me the dreadful news at about 10 oclock. He was most kind, & left me with, God bless you! Good night. . . .

When he had gone I first kissed your face in the photo, my faithful devoted companion in all this sorrow. . . . How am I to endure to take my last look at your dear face? . . . I know you will be

the only one to mourn for me—but do not, dearest, think I expect you to put on mourning—that I leave you to decide on. . . . I feel sure God will let my spirit be with you always . . . & after this earthly separation will join our souls for ever. . . ."

The rest of the letter (that is, the bulk of it) consists of an intricate and fairly unintelligible examination of the medical evidence at the trial regarding the remains found under the cellar.

"Now it is plain to everyone that . . . the fact that no navel was found on that piece of skin . . . is proof beyond any possible doubt that the remains found at Hilldrop Crescent were not those of B.E. . . . I write these things in the hope that the unreliability of the case brought against me, may be understood by thoughtful people. . . ."

It is true that Crippen knew the letter would be scrutinized by the authorities; but it is extremely unlikely that he hoped that such a protest might raise doubts, and at the eleventh hour persuade the Home Secretary to change his mind. The alternative theory is even more untenable: that Ethel Le Neve had known the facts, and that this was an attempt on his part to convince the authorities that she hadn't. No, she believed him innocent; and he was not going to make her crippled future even more of a ruin by a confession.

Chief Inspector Dew as he gave evidence in the murder trial of Dr. Crippen in October 1910

How *could* SHE BELIEVE HIM innocent, after sitting in that court, hour after hour, and hearing the evidence?

It is true that her mind must have seized on one argument completely in favor of the accused: that is, the unacceptability of the theory that a murder by poison had been carefully planned. For it would have appeared incredible, in a court of law, that a medical man would proceed openly to a well-known pharmacy, sign his own name to a lethal purchase of poison, and then, twelve nights later, commit a premeditated murder *in his own home,* so ensuring either immediate discovery, or the ghastly prospect of disposal. Crippen disliked his wife, but he was far from stupid.

Ethel Le Neve must have realized, however, that even if she urged that argument upon the prisoner's counsel, the point could never be mentioned in court; it was inconceivable that the defense should suggest that the death itself was, as I believe, caused by an accidental overdose—a calamity leading on Crippen's part to shock, panic, and the fatal disposal of the body—for the simple reason that the accused had, from the beginning, committed himself to maintaining that the remains found were *not his wife's.*

Dr. Crippen and Ethel Le Neve in the witness box. She was later acquitted and disappeared into obscurity until 1954.

And since that was his defense, how could Ethel Le Neve have imagined that, during the few hours a week when number 39 was empty, a stranger had smuggled into the house the remains of an unknown human being and buried them under the cellar—when (a) a Dr. Pepper had testified to the presence of hyoscine in the recovered tissue and (b) a Dr. Willcox had identified the garment found with the remains as *Crippen's missing pajama top?*

The answer is that when subject to one of the two emotional forces which rule our world—sex and religion—a human being will believe anything.

From the moment when Scotland Yard coaxed that first brick out of a cellar floor, life for Crippen's mistress was to become a personal hell, and her only chance of survival was to have faith. To believe the unbelievable.

FOUR DAYS AFTER Crippen was sentenced to death, Ethel Le Neve was taken from Holloway Prison, tried (in the same court) for having been an accessory after the fact, defended by F. E. Smith (later Lord Birkenhead), and acquitted. She then disappeared into an obscurity which, by 1954, forty-four years later, would have appeared to be complete and permanent.

In that year, during which the *Sunday Dispatch* (London) was serializing Ursula Bloom's "factual novel," *The Girl Who Loved Crippen*, its editor, Charles Eade, was visited by an irate Mr. Neave: "I am Ethel Le Neve's brother, and how dare you . . ."

Miss Bloom went out of her way to meet him, and tactfully suggested that he might help her with the rest of her book. A week or two later she received a letter, signed "Ethel Le Neve," suggesting that the brother was unsuitable as a consultant, and that Miss Bloom would do well to write to Miss Le Neve "care of Mrs Smith," at an address in Addiscombe (a South London suburb), from which Mrs. Smith would presumably forward the letter.

Miss Bloom did not write, having decided on a bolder move. She took a train to Addiscombe and walked to Mrs. Smith's home, reaching it at between five and six on a fine summer afternoon—a semidetached little house in the usual endless row of identical dwellings. The door was opened by Mrs. Smith.

Although the photographs extant of Ethel Le Neve had been taken a good forty-six years before, when Crippen's secretary was twenty-five, the visitor recognized the seventy-one-year-old lady facing her. She was Ethel Le Neve.

Miss Bloom said quickly, "Please be reassured, I promise I am not here to invade your privacy." Mrs. Smith asked her in, and in the typical little front room they sat facing each other.

With what must have been admirable sensitivity, the writer ventured into questionable territory with the caution of a good doctor dealing with a special patient; starting as the tolerated visitor, she was to end up as the trusted friend. (Throughout the relationship she never set eyes on Mr. Smith; she gathered that he worked at Hampton's, a big West End furniture store, commuted, and physically resembled Crippen. His wife had borne him two children, a boy and a girl.)

Mrs. Smith, of her own accord, talked freely of the past. On November 24, 1910, the day after Crippen was executed, she left the country, under the name of Ethel Allen, on the SS *Majestic*, he having previously arranged for this to be financially possible; at his express wish, her destination was Canada. For her, this Atlantic

After he was found guilty of murder, Dr. Crippen was
executed at Pentonville Prison, London, on November 23, 1910.

crossing—her third within four months—must have been unbearably poignant.

At some time during the First World War she returned to London to be with a sister who was dying of consumption, and stayed with her old landlady, Mrs. Emily Jackson, who was still devoted to her. Then came marriage, and retirement to Addiscombe.

Her only social activity of any kind seems to have been to befriend a neighbor, a delicate little boy named Rex Dunning, whom she nursed through an illness; he was to become as close to her as her own children, and when he had grown up she told him her secret.

By the end of 1966 the old lady was very frail, and on the point of admittance to the hospital; one day she asked Rex Dunning to take her, that afternoon, for a London car drive to two places she had known.

It was with some trepidation that he consented. Outside each of the two buildings, she sat in the car for several minutes, very upright, without speaking, then asked to be driven back home. The buildings were both prisons: Holloway and Pentonville. There had been no mention of Hilldrop Crescent.

Shortly afterward, near the beginning of 1967, Mrs. Ethel Smith died in Dulwich Hospital, London, S.E. 22, at the age of eighty-four. Thanks to Miss Bloom's persistently loyal refusal, sometimes under pressure, to disclose her friend's married name or whereabouts, the death passed unnoticed.

Poor Ethel Le Neve. And poor Crippen. She loved him, he loved her. As a step toward diminishing the legend of the Monstrous Little Man, it would be fair to remember that.

THE SHEPHERD'S
BUSH CASE

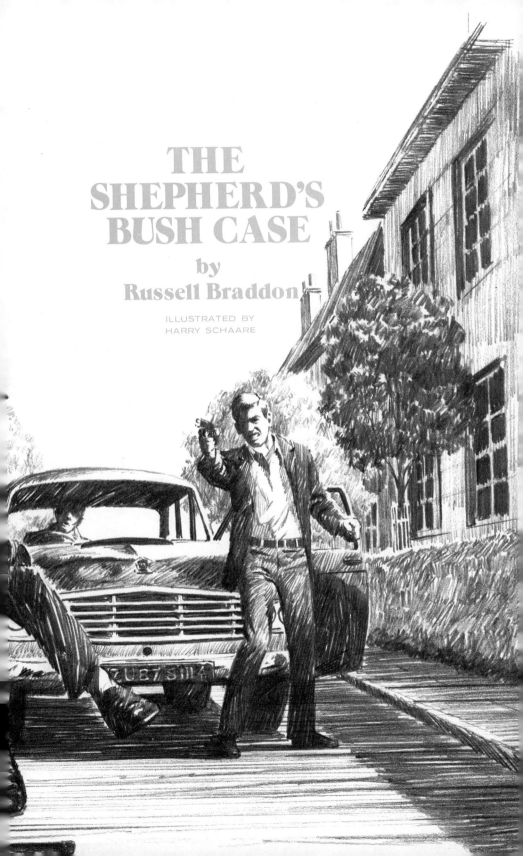

THE SHEPHERD'S BUSH CASE

by
Russell Braddon

ILLUSTRATED BY
HARRY SCHAARE

It was August 12, 1966, a sunny summer afternoon.
Three British policemen stopped to investigate a
suspicious-looking small car dawdling on Braybrook
Street in London. Minutes later all three policemen
were dead, ruthlessly murdered in front of the
shocked eyes of children playing on the grass
alongside the road.

The men of Shepherd's Bush Police Station were
used to murder; it was an inevitable part of their job.
But no other murder compared with this one. The
dead policemen had been their colleagues; more than
that, they had been their friends. A team of sixty-five
detectives was organized for the sole purpose of
finding the murderers, and for the first time in his
twenty-seven-year career, Detective Superintendent
Chitty gave the order to arm the ordinarily unarmed
policemen of Britain. Thus began Operation
Shepherd, one of the longest and most grueling
manhunts in the annals of British crime.

Australian-born British writer and TV personality
Russell Braddon, author of the best-selling thriller
The Thirteenth Trick, captures all the excitement
and tenseness of this extraordinary story.

CHAPTER 1

FOR THE BRITISH, the weather and the time of day added a cruelly ironic dimension to the shooting of three London policemen on August 12, 1966. British criminals infrequently murder British policemen, and not since 1911 had they dared to murder three at once. That they should have done so for the second time on a singularly beautiful summer's afternoon, before the eyes of a dozen incredulous children, and for no apparent reason, stunned the entire nation—not excluding most of its criminal fraternity.

Yet events had conspired pitilessly, that sunny Friday, to bring the three unarmed policemen, in their Triumph 2000 patrol car, across the bows of a dawdling Vanguard and to leave them dead in its wake.

The three officers were plainclothes Criminal Investigation Department (CID) men at Shepherd's Bush Police Station in London's F Division, which encompasses the borough of Hammersmith and its population of about one hundred thousand.

Shepherd's Bush Police Station—known simply to locals as the Bush—was a new building which looked more like an annex to a hospital than what Londoners call a nick. And it had been frantically busy for months seeking an unknown murderer who, on six separate occasions, had deposited the body of a naked prostitute on an open London site.

By August, however—the chief suspect having died and the murders having ceased—the case had been closed. Christopher Head, one of the sergeants investigating it, had returned to normal CID duties, but had been switched from his desk job to patrolling with two others in a Q car—an unmarked patrol car.

He had particularly asked his detective inspector, Kenneth Coote, for David Wombwell and Geoffrey Fox to make up his team, and these three had thus become the crew of the fast but inconspicuous sedan code named Foxtrot One One.

Head, the leader of the team, was thirty-one years old, powerfully built and extraordinarily conscientious, having chosen to become a policeman for the wholly uncomplicated reason that he detested criminals.

Wombwell, who was twenty-five and a temporary detective constable, was there to assist Head. Tall, slim and soft-spoken, he had become a policeman because he had tired of selling cars. Like Head, he seemed destined for success in the force. Unlike Head, he was married and had a son aged three and a daughter aged one.

Fox was a uniformed forty-two-year-old constable whose role it had now become to don civilian clothes and drive Foxtrot One One. For this task he was marvelously equipped, having a vast knowledge both of West London's geography and of its criminals, and being as well the pleasantest of companions. Off duty, he was a dedicated fisherman. At home, he was a genial host, constantly bringing young policemen there for meals with his wife, his two teenage children and his baby daughter.

On the morning of August 12, the crew of Foxtrot One One had set off on a normal patrol.

Prior to their departure they had received no unusual orders from Coote, and Coote himself had left the Bush shortly thereafter to give evidence at Marylebone Magistrates' Court against five would-be escapees from the prison at Wormwood Scrubs. Unhappily for Christopher Head, David Wombwell and Geoffrey Fox, that evidence consisted largely of three tea chests full of such damning exhibits as grappling irons and steel cable, all of which, after the hearing, would have to be transported back to the Bush.

AT THE SAME TIME that Foxtrot One One left the yard of its station, John Witney kissed his wife good-by and drove off (to work, she thought) in his small car—a battered blue Standard Vanguard.

A pale, skinny thirty-six-year-old with wispy fair hair, Witney had failed as a soldier, failed as a civilian, and was currently—as five convictions attested—not exactly succeeding as a criminal. Nor, as his wife supposed, was he driving his Vanguard to work; rather, he was driving it to the home of another failure, a Scot called John Duddy, so that the two of them, accompanied by a mutual friend called Harry Roberts, could go thieving.

Duddy, thirty-eight years old, soft-spoken and stocky, had a shock of graying hair, was the father of two teenage daughters and the son of a policeman. With convictions against him both as a boy and as a man, he must have been a disappointment to his father; but his friendship with Harry Roberts, and their endless talk of "big, easy money," were so alarming to his wife that ten days earlier she had left him.

But if Duddy and Witney were dismally inadequate, to a degree that made them instantly forgettable, Harry Roberts—who waited with Duddy for Witney to arrive in the Vanguard—was fascinatingly complex.

A trim thirty-year-old with a good army record, he was a skilled bricklayer, a reliable long-distance lorry driver, an amateur artist and a considerate husband. But he was also violent.

When he was sixteen, for example, and his mother had dragged him away from the company of a man she considered less than honest, he had punched her in the mouth for her pains.

As well as that, she knew that he had been taking money from her handbag, or out of the till at her restaurant, for more than three years. But because he wanted to become a policeman she had reported neither his stealing from her nor his assault upon her. Her marriage having broken up, she had always worked hard to ensure that her son, whom she called Robin, got a private education; and she was determined that that policy should continue.

He had repaid her devotion by becoming a habitual thief, for which he was sent to a reformatory.

A week after his release he had been conscripted into the army, where he had revealed a liking for its orderliness, an aptitude for the rigors of jungle training, and a marksman's skill with a rifle.

Discharged from the army, he had become a van driver and married a blond stripper. "We didn't hit it off," his wife, Mitzi, subsequently confessed. "Then I lost my baby after a seven-and-a-half-month pregnancy, and that finished us." She left him in 1959 and was never to see him again; but he, in the meantime, had been fired from his job, for stealing, and jailed.

And it was while he was in jail that the police discovered (thanks to his wife, he believed) that he had also broken into the house of a seventy-eight-year-old man and nearly murdered him with a whiskey decanter.

For that attack Roberts was sentenced to seven years' imprisonment and dispatched to Wormwood Scrubs. There, though tidy by disposition, he refused to clean his cell; though indifferent to the quality of food, he ate prodigiously; though fond of cards, he was too impatient a player to be a popular partner; though a good student (he became proficient in bricklaying and plumbing and attended classes in French), he was violent in argument; and though he boasted of his sexual prowess, his drawings and paintings revealed a distrust for women that amounted to nothing less than sexual aversion. All his females were either as sexless as Disney's Snow White or as predatory as his wicked Queen. Roberts' main artistic obsession, in fact, was not the female form but an exploding ship sinking into a sea of flames.

His mother had visited him regularly at Wormwood Scrubs; and when, after serving four years and eight months of his sentence, he was released, she had bought him a smart new wardrobe. In return, he had promised to go straight and had indeed taken a bricklayer's job in Bristol and worked at it very hard. His employers had found him honest; Mrs. Perry (the redheaded woman with whom he lodged, and the wife of a former policeman, from whom she was separated) had found him home-loving and generous; a big secondhand Daimler had been his only extravagance; James Bond novels and wrestling on television had been his favorite pastimes; and crime had seemed the thing farthest from his mind.

At the beginning of 1966, however, he had moved back to London and taken Mrs. Perry with him, having convinced her that the Labour government had so destroyed business confidence that the building trade was doomed. With her as his platonic mistress, he had become the lodger of married friends called the Howards, and thereafter had lived on the proceeds of crimes committed with the help of Witney (whom he had met in Wormwood Scrubs) and Duddy (whom he had met at a London club).

Worse than that, Roberts had bought three revolvers. "Just as frighteners," he had assured his landlady.

"Then why the bullets?" Mrs. Howard had demanded.

But he had persisted in his explanation that he had begun to carry revolvers with him—as he, Duddy and Witney stole metal from builders' yards, raided betting shops late at night, and preyed on unaccompanied rent collectors—just as frighteners. "Although," he had somewhat inconsistently admitted to Mrs. Perry, "I'll never let myself be sent back to prison. I'd rather shoot it out than be sent back there again."

Then had begun a series of visits to the homes of Witney and Duddy—visits that Mrs. Witney dreaded and Mrs. Duddy loathed. Conspiratorial visits, where endlessly the talk was of money. Big, easy money.

So Mrs. Witney had begun to keep the curtains drawn and, when Roberts arrived, to swear that her husband was out; Mrs. Duddy had begun to threaten that if Roberts' visits continued, she would leave; Duddy had begun to look nervous, his incessant nail chewing belying the bold tattoo on his right forearm (a pierced skull and heart) inscribed *True to Death;* and Witney's sharp features had begun—as daily he lied to his wife about going to work—to look more furtive than ever.

Only Roberts, with his hooded eyes, arched eyebrows, jaunty walk and confidence in his frighteners, had seemed happy. But then Roberts—for all his kindness to his landlady's children and his willingness to redecorate her flat—had always been insensitive to the feelings of others.

In fact, having agreed with Witney and Duddy that they must steal another car to take the place of the battered and all too recognizable Vanguard, he had even pointed to his three revolvers and told his nervous companions, "If we *have* them, we must be prepared to use them."

When Witney arrived at Duddy's flat in Treventon Towers that glorious morning of August 12 to find Roberts carrying a shopping bag, he was not therefore deceived by the fact that all he could see of its contents was an old pair of overalls. But he said nothing as Duddy got into the back seat and Roberts sat in front, dropping the bag behind the front seats. He simply started the Vanguard and headed for the nearest railroad station parking lot.

OVER THE PAST twelve weeks they had similarly sallied forth time after time and by now were all convinced that Witney's small car, with its ungainly shape, faded paintwork and constantly trailing exhaust pipe, was far too conspicuous. Their next job was to be the holdup of a rent collector, and for that they were determined to steal a blue Cortina.

Hoping to find their Cortina that morning, they were carrying with them a set of false license plates bearing the number of a blue Cortina they had seen parked in Shepherd's Bush. Let any witness of their proposed holdup take the number of their getaway car, the police would trace as its owner an innocent motorist. Let a witness catch sight of them in Witney's decrepit Vanguard, on the other hand, and the hunt would soon be up.

Unfortunately none of the parking lots they visited that morning contained a suitable blue Cortina, so they stopped off at a pub called The Clay Pigeon and drank some lunch.

Ten miles away, at The Beaumont Arms in Shepherd's Bush, the crew of Foxtrot One One, having finished their morning patrol, were also having lunch.

The Vanguard left The Clay Pigeon and drove to Acton Station, whose parking lot contained no such Cortina as they required. Although it was only three o'clock, the would-be but by no means industrious thieves decided to call it a day.

At that moment Detective Inspector Coote (whose evidence against the recaptured jailbreakers had concluded) found himself stranded at Marylebone Magistrates' Court with three tea chests full of exhibits and no transport to take him and them back to the Bush.

He therefore rang his station and ordered that Foxtrot One One be instructed by radio to collect him. Head at once telephoned the Marylebone court from an Acton call box and assured Coote that Foxtrot One One would pick him up in about twenty minutes. Coote, a patient man, lit his pipe and waited by his tea chests.

A few minutes later Foxtrot One One headed back from Acton toward Coote in Central London.

Witney, meantime, was dawdling along Du Cane Road toward the grassy stretch that separates Braybrook Street from Wormwood Scrubs jail. Unable to go home, because his wife would ask him why he was back from work so early, he was in no hurry. Nor were Duddy and Roberts, whose only employment was thieving. They planned to lie in the grass in the sun and talk.

Tragically, even before they turned into Braybrook Street their Vanguard was spotted by Head and Fox—to whom a dawdling vehicle, occupied by three men in the middle of the afternoon in Braybrook Street, was highly suspicious. Long experience told the policemen that its occupants were almost certain to be planning either to spring a prisoner from the adjacent jail—or to steal a car—or to collect a car they had previously stolen and left in the nearby public housing development lot.

So Fox accelerated, and as Foxtrot One One passed the Vanguard, Head flagged it down.

Witney promptly drew into the curb, and Fox pulled up the Triumph 2000 about ten yards ahead of him. Wombwell got out of the back seat of the Triumph and walked slowly, as policemen do, back to the Vanguard. Head got out of the front seat and followed him. Both stopped by Witney's window and loomed over him.

"We're police officers," Head announced, lest Witney had mistaken them, in their civilian clothes, for anything else. "Mind telling me what you're doing, running round three-handed in a vehicle like this, this time of day?"

Witney's nervous explanation did nothing to lessen Head's suspicions. "This *is* your vehicle?" he persisted.

"Yes."

"Got a road fund license?"

"No."

"Why not?"

"Well, I can't get her taxed until I get a Ministry of Transport certificate of fitness, can I?"

"Then perhaps you'd show me your driver's license and your insurance certificate."

Glumly, Witney produced both, and having examined them, Head commented, "This insurance certificate is three hours out of date. It expires," he said, pointing, "at noon on August the twelfth. It is now a quarter past three on August the twelfth." And passing the two documents to Wombwell, he prowled suspiciously around the back of the car. Wombwell began to copy Witney's name and address into his notebook.

"Give us a break, guv," Witney pleaded. "I was nicked for being unlicensed only a fortnight ago."

Wombwell went on writing—and Roberts reached back into the shopping bag, thinking, If they find the guns I'll get fifteen years. Beyond Witney's frightened face and Wombwell's unsympathetic shoulders he could see the gloomy structure of the jail to which he had vowed he would never return.

Head appeared at Duddy's window and, bending down, peered inside. "What's in the bag?" he demanded.

Bluffing desperately, Duddy displayed the overalls, and thought for a moment, as Head stood upright again, that they had got away with it. But: "I'm not interested in them," Head snapped. "I want to know what's underneath them."

Convinced that he was trapped, Roberts leaned across Witney, shot Wombwell under the left eye, killing him instantly, leaped out of the Vanguard, shouting, "Come on," to Duddy and Witney, and fired at Head—missing him.

"No!" shouted Head. "No, no"—running toward Foxtrot One One, seeking cover in front of it.

Some of the children playing on the grass thought they were watching the filming of a sequence for television. Others sensed something less innocent. None moved.

Duddy stumbled out of the Vanguard, a pistol in his hand, and ran toward the Q car—which Fox, going on the offensive, was reversing at Roberts.

Roberts shot Head in the back, dropping him on the road in front of the Q car.

"Shoot!" Roberts screamed at Duddy, pointing at Fox. So Duddy fired twice, almost wildly, then a third time, very deliberately, through the front window and into Geoffrey Fox's forehead.

Fox slumped leftward, knocking the gear into forward drive and depressing the accelerator. Foxtrot One One bounced over Head's thickset corpse—which jammed under the chassis, raising it just enough to deny the madly spinning rear wheels any traction.

Roberts and Duddy raced back to the Vanguard, where Witney was busy removing Wombwell's incriminating notebook.

"*Drive!*" Roberts snarled.

"You must be bloody potty," Witney yelped.

"Drive, unless you want some of the same," Roberts ordered.

At which Witney reversed at full throttle thirty yards down Braybrook Street, swerved wildly out of it, just missed a car that had halted at the junction, and sped away from the scene of the crime, sparks flying from his trailing exhaust pipe.

Leaving a dozen or so children to stare sickly at David Wombwell, who lay on his back, legs straight, with ankles crossed, pen in hand; and the defiant corpse of Christopher Head underneath a roaring, stranded Q car, inside of which slumped an apparently weary Geoffrey Fox.

CHAPTER 2

"GET HIS LICENSE number," shouted Bryan Deacon, the driver of the car with which the Vanguard had almost collided. "It may be a jailbreak."

"PGT 726," his wife told him, and went on repeating it as he turned into Braybrook Street and headed for a butcher's shop from which he knew he would be able to telephone the police.

Almost at once they came upon Wombwell's body, lying, it seemed, at attention.

"He's dead," Mrs. Deacon reported.

Deacon stared at the car beyond Wombwell, puzzled by its bellowing engine and smoking rear wheels. Then, just as he noticed Head's body jammed underneath it, a man ran to the car, leaned through its window, switched off its ignition, and yelled, "Get the police, get the police."

Deacon sped to the butcher's shop, dialed 999 on the telephone, and scribbled PGT 726 on a piece of butcher's wrapping paper as he waited for an answer.

"The incident has already been reported, thank you, sir," Scotland Yard advised him.

So, ignoring the fact that his wife was not only very pregnant but also somewhat hysterical, Deacon sped back to Braybrook Street to give what help he could. There he found two carloads of policemen —the first driven by Police Constable Sidney Seager, at whose wedding Fox had been best man—and more arriving, or so it seemed, by the second.

Realizing that there was nothing he could do, he walked to the nearest police car and handed its driver the piece of paper on which he had scrawled PGT 726. The policeman picked up his radio and broadcast the number—and Witney's arrest became inevitable.

REPORTERS RACED TO Braybrook Street, which the police were already cordoning off, but the bodies and the bullet-shattered window of the Q car told their own story, and a growing crowd of children and housewives were all eager to provide extra details.

A policeman posted to control the traffic spoke for the many officers already prowling Braybrook Street. "I can't talk," he told reporters. "I'm too choked. They were my mates." Then he burst into tears.

As details of the triple killing were broadcast by the BBC, the British public reacted with that same sort of numbed incredulity as had greeted the sudden death of King George VI and the assassination of President Kennedy. Only twenty-seven policemen had been killed on duty in the past fifty-six years; now, for no apparent reason, three had been murdered in ten seconds.

Harry Roberts' mother, for example, was at Camden Town that afternoon, visiting a friend. When they heard the news she said, "What a shocking thing. What's the world coming to?"

Mrs. Perry, Roberts' woman companion, was having a drink with a friend when she heard the news. "Oh, golly," she said, seeking, as a former policeman's wife, to explain the inexplicable, "someone must have had a grudge."

In Torquay, Christopher Head's mother was having afternoon tea with a neighbor and listening to a radio concert when the music was interrupted and an announcement made that three Shepherd's Bush policemen had just been shot. Even though none of the murdered policemen was named, Mrs. Head heard no more of the resumed concert. As soon as it had finished she made her excuses and went to see her grandchildren by her older son.

Harry Roberts himself was sitting in a Euston café with Witney. "You look as if you're going to keel over," Roberts said contemptuously. "You wouldn't squeal, would you?"

THE POLICE MACHINE that would soon ensnare Witney was already in top gear. The killing had taken place at three seventeen; Scotland Yard had received the first phone call about it from a housewife at three nineteen; and by three twenty, three top investigators had been assigned to the case.

Of these, the most important—because he was to lead the inquiry throughout—was Detective Superintendent Chitty, who was called into Commander Millen's office at the Yard and told, "Three coppers have been shot at Shepherd's Bush. I want you to take over the investigation."

Chitty protested that he had only wound up his last case that morning, that he was therefore not on call, and that anyway he needed the leave due to him to help his wife move into their new home in Kent.

"I'm sorry," said Millen.

"How are they?" asked Chitty.

"The coppers? Dead," said Millen. "I'll see you at the Bush."

A quiet man, who liked to take his wife an early morning cup of tea each day, and watch ballet and variety shows on television, and garden during weekends, Chitty departed at once for Shepherd's Bush. There he was to spend nearly every waking hour for the next ninety-six days and nights.

Detective Inspector Jack Slipper, on the other hand, was in a Flying Squad car when he heard over its radio that "a very serious assault had taken place in Braybrook Street, London W12," and that the "three occupants of a Standard Vanguard," probably numbered PGT 726, were "to be approached with the utmost caution if seen or stopped."

Almost at once a second message came through on Slipper's radio. "All Flying Squad units," it said, "are to telephone in immediately."

Slipper telephoned from the first nonvandalized call box and, having been told the facts, was ordered to report to Shepherd's Bush to "assist in every way." A tall, powerfully built man with a ready grin and a deceptive look of wide-eyed ingenuousness, he was in fact as confident as his fierce little mustache, and sufficiently cunning to have earned himself the nickname Slippery Jack.

At the same time exactly, Detective Sergeant Ron Lawrence, a Scenes-of-Crime specialist, heard that there had been a shooting in Braybrook Street and decided to drive there in his own car to see for himself.

On the way he told himself that it was probably a hoax. When he reached Shepherd's Bush Green and found it as quiet as ever, he decided it definitely was a hoax. But approaching Braybrook Street, he was caught up in a frenzy of racing police cars and screaming ambulances, and he knew that whatever else it was he was about to inspect, it was not a hoax.

"What's happened?" he asked a young uniformed constable.

"They're all dead," the constable told him incredulously.

"Who's all dead?"

"The law. Someone shot up the whole crew of a Q car."

What had been a good-natured gesture of cooperation on Lawrence's part thereupon became his specific responsibility. He was the Scenes-of-Crime expert for No. 1 District, and this crime had taken place in F Division, which was part of No. 1 District. Instantly, therefore, he began organizing the ritual of cordoning off, taking photographs, getting statements from witnesses, searching for bullets and cartridge cases, looking for fingerprints, and shrouding the dead policemen in plastic sheets—of which he had only two in his car, so that he had to radio for a third.

BY WHICH TIME Detective Inspector Coote was no longer patiently puffing his pipe as he stood beside his three tea chests and waited to be picked up by Foxtrot One One. Far from pleased, he rang his station and snarled, "Where the bloody hell's my transport?"

"Haven't you heard, sir?"

"Heard *what?*"

"The crew of Foxtrot One One have all been killed."

"How?" he asked, thinking there must have been a collision on the way from Acton. "Was there an accident?"

"No, sir. They were shot."

"Right. Obviously you'll need all the transport you've got. Don't worry about me. I'll get back as best I can."

He rang Paddington Police Station, where they knew what had happened and told him, "We'll send Sergeant Miller with his car. You've got him for as long as you want."

Miller found Coote stunned. "Three wiped out at one hit," he kept saying. "What the hell can have happened? They were doing a normal run-of-the-mill job."

Once back at the Bush, however, he showed no sign of confusion. Advised that almost every CID officer from each of the divisions in No. 1 District was already at Braybrook Street, Coote first ensured that someone had gone to break the news to Mrs. Fox, Mrs. Wombwell and Mrs. Head, then decided to stay at the Bush and set up an inquiry headquarters. The rest of the afternoon he spent ringing Scotland Yard and other stations in No. 1 District for filing cabinets, typewriters, trestle tables, typists, index cards, logbooks and an authorization for the installation of extra telephones.

Between making calls he answered calls—from other police stations in every district in London and most of the regions outside it.

"Can we send down a coachload of officers?" one regional station offered. "Twenty-five have volunteered."

"I'm on a fortnight's leave in London," a Nottinghamshire officer advised. "I'll do anything."

"We're sending our Flying Squad. Anything else you need?"

"How can we help?"

Then Chitty arrived from Scotland Yard, followed almost immediately by Millen, who now assigned Detective Chief Inspector John Hensley and Detective Inspector Slipper to assist Chitty. And around this nucleus a team of sixty-five detectives, five of them women, was swiftly to coalesce—a team whose sole task it became to find the men who had killed their colleagues Head, Wombwell and Fox.

CHITTY HAD WASTED NO time getting to Braybrook Street, where he found a bevy of detectives doing all those things that the initial investigation of a murder demands. Though he wore his soft felt hat —which looked two sizes too small for him—at its customary jaunty angle, he was anything but happy as he surveyed the three bodies, then ordered them to be laid on the grass strip.

Why, he asked himself, had the Q car stopped the Vanguard? And what possible crime could the Vanguard's occupants have been caught committing, to escape the penalty for which they were prepared to slaughter three policemen? The answers eluded him. For the moment they were known only to the three shrouded bodies lying on the grass strip, and the men who had shot them.

But other equally vital questions (such as how many men had there been in the Vanguard, and what did they look like, and what exactly had transpired?) had been and were still being answered with great enthusiasm—and varying degrees of inaccuracy—by a score of witnesses.

The man who had reached in across Geoff Fox's body and turned off the motor had, for example, been resting in the cab of his lorry when he heard shots and thought a film crew must be at work.

A ten-year-old boy who had been out looking for his two friends saw the whole sequence of events, described them in starkest detail, and concluded, "It was horrible. It made me cry."

"One of the men was wearing a blue suit," declared another child. "He looked a bit scruffy and he fired a small gun. There was another man in a white coat, a bit fatter, with brown hair parted on the side."

"A man got out of the blue Triumph," related a third, "and walked to the car."

"And someone hit him on the head and shot him when he fell. And another man was shot as he ran away. Then a man broke the window of the blue car and shot the man inside."

The constant childish use of "man" to describe both the three killers and their three victims tested the patience of the policemen interviewing each youthful witness, but they persisted—and were rewarded with descriptions of the killers that were inaccurate as to almost every detail—except for the observation made by a fourteen-year-old girl that one of them had looked like Bobby Charlton, the idol of England's football fans, who had thin, fair, receding hair.

While conflicting descriptions left the police with little idea as to what their suspects looked like, they were left in no doubt at all that the vehicle in which they had fled was a small car.

"It shot round the corner and made me skid and fall off my bike," complained an aggrieved eleven-year-old.

"I saw these two chaps kneeling beside a car and heard what sounded like shots," a local housewife reported. "I thought they

were fooling about. Then I heard two more shots and both the men reeled over and I realized they weren't fooling about at all. Then this green car pulled away like mad and belted off down the road. So I rang the police."

Who had instantly radioed—of all the Q cars available—Foxtrot One One to go and investigate. That sort of irony Chitty and his colleagues could well have done without.

CHAPTER 3

ALL THIS, AND THE crime less than two hours old. But already Coote's hastily assembled inquiry headquarters—on the first floor of the station—was hard at work as typists began to type out the witnesses' statements, and the newly installed phones began to ring, and the search began for the owner of Standard Vanguard number PGT 726.

Meantime the station and welfare representative, Detective Constable Alastair Dent, an ex-heavyweight boxing champion of the Royal Air Force, who was known locally as the Gentle Giant, had been telephoned at his home—to which he had just returned to celebrate his birthday after working from six till two.

"You'd better come back," he had been told. "Three of our lads have been shot."

"Who?"

"Not sure yet."

Dent had driven back to the station in his old car, found everyone too sick to talk, gone to the communications room, learned the facts, and having ensured that someone in Torquay would visit Mrs. Head, prepared to visit the two widows.

Though he was good at his job—helped by his obvious sympathy for anyone bereaved and by his comforting resemblance to John Wayne—he hated it. F Division had for too long been known as the murder area, and with each of its murders—not to mention its traffic fatalities and suicides—he seemed to have inherited the unenviable task of breaking the news to the victim's mother, or wife, or family. It never got any easier, it always terrified him, and it still depressed him. But none of the ordeals of the past compared with this one. Not only had the dead men been his brother officers and friends; Dent also knew how pitifully inadequate would be the pensions on which Mrs. Wombwell and Mrs. Fox would henceforth, with their children, have to survive.

He found that both widows had already received the news and that Mrs. Wombwell, who was twenty, had only one immediate request—that her mother-in-law be telephoned before she learned that her son had been killed when she watched the news on television.

"It isn't true," sobbed Mrs. Wombwell senior then. "It just can't be. This only happens to other people." But it was true, and it had happened; and not only to her but also to her daughter-in-law, to her grandchildren and to Mrs. Fox—who had been making tea for her infant daughter when the doorbell had rung and her life had been shattered.

As for Mrs. Head, when the doorbell rang at her older son's home, where she was playing with her grandchildren, and her son returned to the drawing room and sent the children outside, she did not need to be told that Chris was dead. In a way she'd known it ever since the broadcast of the concert was interrupted; but that made the confirmation of it nonetheless appalling.

EVEN THE MURDERERS, it seemed, were appalled. Roberts returned to the Howards' flat in Wymering Mansions, where he lodged, looking flushed and breathless and complaining that he had a headache.

"Never mind," Mrs. Perry said. "I've got some nice rock salmon and chips for your tea."

"I can't eat anything," said Roberts, who normally devoured whatever she set before him. "I'm sick to here"—pointing peevishly at his throat.

Ignoring his petulance, she continued to prepare his meal. Then asked, "Did you hear about the three policemen?"

"Shut up," he snapped. "It was us."

For the moment, though, he was safe, because it was not Wymering Mansions that armed police were surrounding but the block of flats wherein lived the hapless original owner of PGT 726.

Five hours later this unfortunate man was released, having convinced Detective Superintendent Chitty of his innocence. He had sold the Vanguard to a dealer, he told Chitty. No, he had not notified the authorities that he'd sold it to a dealer. Yes, he could tell

Chitty the dealer's name. And yes, he thought the dealer had sold it—to a man in Kilburn.

"Find the present owner," Chitty ordered then, Scotland Yard itself having already issued a statement saying, "Just after the shooting, a green van reversed past the police car. . . . If the owner was not involved, he must know exactly what happened and it is essential that he come forward. . . ."

Though it was a Friday night, the police had no compunction in calling upon the dealer.

Yes, he had bought the Standard Vanguard—which was blue, not green—in October 1965, and sold it a month later for fifty-five pounds and a Ford Anglia in part exchange.

To whom? To a John Witney, who lived in Paddington.

At nine p.m. Chitty dispatched a detective inspector and a sergeant to question Witney in his basement flat.

"We're making inquiries concerning the owner of a small blue Vanguard, PGT 726, which we understand is yours," said the inspector.

"Oh no, not that," Witney responded.

"What do you mean, not that?"

"We've just seen on the telly about the coppers being shot," Witney explained.

"Well, they can't mean our car," Mrs. Witney interposed. "Where is it, dear?"

"I sold it," Witney declared. "Today."

"You didn't tell me," she protested.

Witney thereupon told his wife and the police an elaborate story. He had left home that morning, met some friends, left them, and driven alone to The Clay Pigeon. There he had a drink in the saloon bar, which he described in great detail, and had seen a salesman who, he remembered, was smoking a cigar. He'd spoken to no one until he returned to the parking lot, where a man in a small blue car, an Anglia, he thought, had called out, "What'll you take for the old banger?"

"Gimme a score," Witney said he'd replied, "and you can take it away."

"I'll give you fifteen quid," the man had said.

He'd thought the man was joking, he told them; but, to his surprise, the man had given him ten pounds then and there and promised him a further five pounds when he received the logbook the following day. Then, having arranged a rendezvous, the man had driven him two miles down the road to Hayes, whence, Witney explained, he'd caught a 207 bus to Acton Vale, where he'd visited a betting shop, which he named.

"Did you place a bet?" the detective inspector asked him.

"No, I only popped in."

"And what time was that?"

"About a quarter past three," said Witney innocently.

To which Mrs. Witney unhelpfully retorted, "You told me you'd been to work! And you didn't tell me you'd sold the car! What's going on?"

"I haven't been to work for five weeks," Witney confessed. "I had to get you some money somehow."

"And you let me get up every morning thinking you were going to work," she complained.

Advised of Witney's alibi, Chitty found it improbable, but an alibi nevertheless. So he sent his colleague Hensley to search Witney's flat for guns and to question him further.

A big, smart-looking man with carefully combed hair, rimless glasses, a polka-dot bow tie, and a pipe clenched perpetually between his teeth, Hensley clearly unnerved Witney, who constantly mopped at his forehead with a towel that he kept clutched tightly in his hand. Though Hensley found no guns, his suspicions remained sufficiently strong for him to say, in the curiously stilted language of the police, "I believe that men using your vehicle were concerned in the killing of three police officers, and I must ask you to come with me now to Harrow Road Police Station for further inquiries."

At which Mrs. Witney fondly embraced her shaken husband and begged him, "Please, darling, tell them the truth." And then, perhaps remembering all those visits from Harry Roberts, added, "What have you been doing? Tell them who you were with."

"I daren't," Witney told her. "Get me a solicitor."

Arrived at Harrow Road Station, however, he stuck stubbornly to his story of the man at The Clay Pigeon who'd bought his van that very afternoon and how he'd "had to sell the car to get Mum some money."

"Bring him over here," Chitty instructed when Hensley rang him and told him what had happened. "But don't let anyone see him"— this lest any subsequent identification of Witney be invalidated by even a prior glimpse, let alone press photograph, of him arriving as a suspect at the Bush.

Lying on the floor of a police car and covered with a blanket, he was driven through a large crowd into the yard of Shepherd's Bush Police Station and taken inside.

There Lawrence, the Scenes-of-Crime specialist, who was collecting his exhibits together, saw him, and was surprised to find that he felt no emotion at all—the more so since he had just returned from the postmortem on the three murdered men. The chipped bullet that had passed through Fox's brain, fractured against the interior metalwork of the Triumph 2000, and dropped to the floor was one of his exhibits.

Chitty likewise had no difficulty controlling his emotions as he confronted the man he was certain had been one of the killers. Though he had known Fox for years, admired Head, and been responsible for Wombwell's transfer to the CID, he was conscious of the fact that several lurid, recent scandals had tarnished the reputation of Britain's policemen, and was determined that nothing should go amiss in this investigation, where natural vengefulness could so easily induce a violation of a suspect's rights.

He had even hesitated before taking the very un-British step of arming his detectives. But with three dead already, and their killers believed to be both armed and ruthless, he had decided that arms and ammunition must be issued. Public opinion was soon to swing wholeheartedly behind him.

Indeed, public opinion, only a few hours ago tolerant at best, at worst downright critical of the police, had by now become uncompromisingly partisan.

The crowd outside the station was there not to witness the arrival of suspects but to express its mute sympathy. Already the foyer of the station was full of flowers. Already the letters and cards of condolence were pouring in. And already donations by the hundred were being delivered by hand to help the families of the men who had been killed.

As if to acknowledge that this was no fickle, popular whim, a television van was parked outside the station to record the story for as long as it might run, and newspapermen had arrived by the score, to depart only when relieved, and the next day to return again.

Not only that, but the commissioner of the Metropolitan Police, Sir Joseph Sampson, visited the Bush; the Home Secretary, Roy Jenkins, spoke briefly to the television cameras from the steps of the station; and the Queen sent a personal message of sympathy from Balmoral, where she was on holiday with her family.

Witney, however, refused to alter his story, so Chitty detained him for the night, without charging him, and turned his attention to the acquisition of more radios, the allocation of a special channel on which they could transmit and receive messages without interference, and the issuing of descriptions of the three wanted men.

Not surprisingly, since they were wrong in almost every respect, these descriptions were to yield no results; but Chitty was not really much concerned about descriptions based on the shocked or over-stimulated memories of children. He was convinced that Witney—with his Bobby Charlton–type hair—was one of the killers, and that Witney would crack.

Which is not to say that he simply sat back and waited. On the contrary, the entire Flying Squad—a hundred and ten officers driving in fast but inconspicuous cars and innocent-looking vans, and known unlovingly to the criminal fraternity as the Heavy Mob—sped purposefully to every known villainous haunt in London throughout the night. If any gang was sheltering the killers that night of August 12, it could expect no peace until it handed them over.

Thus ended the first day of Chitty's investigation, which he had already code named Operation Shepherd. Neither he nor any of his team returned home that night, nor were they to do so for the next seventy-two hours.

In the detention room, Witney slept not at all that night.

In Treventon Towers, Duddy slept with two of the murder weapons at his feet and one under his pillow.

In Wymering Mansions, Roberts, having watched with Mrs. Perry a television news report of the shootings, decided to sleep alone; and when his landlady returned late with friends, who loudly discussed the afternoon's murders, he shouted, "Shut up with your theories. I'm trying to sleep."

CHAPTER 4

"I KNOW THIS VANGUARD is *some*where," stated Chitty, for whom its discovery had been made no easier by the fact that some of the witnesses in Braybrook Street had given him registration numbers at odds with that provided by Mr. Deacon, "and I must find it. It must have been used prior to the killing. I want to know when, why and where—and also where it was garaged. A van doesn't just disappear into a row of streets without someone seeing something!"

It was a provocative and clever statement, which Chitty concluded by asserting, "This inquiry has got to be successful."

"Look out for a tatty old van," his colleagues and subordinates urged all and sundry. "With its wishy-washy blue paint and broken exhaust pipe, it'll stick out like a sore thumb."

But there were other things to be found as well as small vans colored a wishy-washy blue. For one thing, Lawrence, the Scenes-of-Crime expert, wanted the fragment of the bullet that had killed Fox. So the dawn of Saturday, August 13, found seventy-five policemen crawling shoulder to shoulder along the grass edge of Braybrook Street. Later, soldiers arrived with mine detectors, which would reveal the presence of anything metallic concealed by the grass. Thus relieved, the policemen moved to the other side of the road and crawled through the narrow gardens in front of the houses instead.

Eventually the bullet fragment was found and handed to Lawrence. Now all that remained to be found was the van, the murder weapons and the killers.

Police swooped on likely hiding places for all three in Greenford, Acton, Islington, Paddington, and London Airport, and began to drag the river Thames and a number of sewers as well.

Nothing relevant to Operation Shepherd was thereby unearthed, but by turning over so many criminal stones, the police were driving the denizens of London's gangland almost frantic.

For once, though, the press was less concerned with the trivia of a murder inquiry than with the sheer enormity of the crime itself and the public's reaction to it.

"A net of vengeance is slowly tightening," one journalist observed.

"The worst of gangland Chicago has come to a sunny English street," lamented another.

THE BIGGEST MANHUNT EVER, one headline proclaimed.

DAZED INCREDULITY, reported another.

And all the time, for armchair detectives as well as the professionals, there remained the tantalizing questions: Why had the three policemen been shot? And why had they not reported that they were about to investigate an obviously dangerous situation?

Neither armchair nor professional detectives, of course, considered for one second the ludicrous possibility that Foxtrot One One had stopped simply to question a dawdling van in which three petty criminals were planning nothing more lethal than another installment in their endless saga about how to make easy money.

But neither Duddy nor Roberts could stop thinking or talking about it; and on Saturday morning Duddy lost no time crossing to Maida Vale and consulting with Roberts in the flat he shared with Mrs. Perry and the Howard family in Wymering Mansions.

"God, what a hell of a mess we've made of everything," Roberts complained.

"I wish it'd never happened," Duddy told him, gnawing at his fingernails.

"We should've burned the car," Roberts nagged.

"Why?"

"The flames would have destroyed our fingerprints. We should go and do it now."

"It's too dangerous," Duddy countered. And Roberts didn't argue with him, being happy to have made his point while indulging once more his fantasy about flames.

The police who sought to capture him had their feet firmly on the ground, however. No one at the Bush doubted that the case would be solved, and everyone on Chitty's team was prepared to work around the clock until the case was completed. The fact that the station was flooded with armed plainclothes officers was a constant reminder that this was a unique case, which, as Chitty had said, *had* to be solved, because if the police couldn't track down those who killed their own, what protection could society expect in the future from criminals who would assume that by killing witnesses they could avoid conviction?

Perhaps, subconsciously, society was also aware that this case would invite murder were it to remain unsolved. But consciously the only reaction was one of outrage that three men should have died protecting the public and that the dependents of the three officers must suffer hardship as well as grief. The instant desire to help was spontaneous and staggering.

A car-rental firm offered its fleet of chauffeured Rolls-Royces for as long as Chitty's team might need them.

A vast conglomerate offered all the facilities of its Xerox copying unit.

An aircraft operator offered his planes, and a manufacturer of bulletproof vests offered as many of his products as there were policemen to wear them.

The houses of Braybrook Street left their front doors open all night so that the police could refresh themselves with a constant supply of tea and sandwiches.

Every chief constable in the land offered assistance for any task, no matter how menial.

Two coachloads of Hampshire police arrived without waiting to be asked—and had to be sent back lest an invidious precedent were created for subsequent murder inquiries.

The entrance and foyer of Shepherd's Bush Police Station were brilliant with flowers—gladioli, roses, chrysanthemums, carnations and even cacti.

Hotels sent hampers of food, and the Territorial Army and the Girl Guides and the Boy Scouts offered their complete cooperation. Officers from the Bush were greeted by solicitous strangers every time they left the station; five-pound notes were pressed into their hands; a Liverpool schoolboy pushed a ten-shilling note across the counter of his local nick and said, "This is for the families of the murdered bobbies"; and from all over the country people sent letters and money.

At Shepherd's Bush Station there was a queue four deep and fifty yards long for weeks on end—waiting to hand money over the counter to a police clerk who was so hard pressed that he had time only to say thank you, drop the money in a bag, greet the next visitor, and when the bag was full, send it off to Scotland Yard—which had to set up a special department to receive and handle the donations.

"Get a thing like this," explained a policeman at Uxbridge Road Police Station, "and in they come. Mothers with their kids, the lot, bringing in cash. Odd, isn't it? I don't know why."

The mayor of Hammersmith, focal point of F Division, launched an appeal for two hundred and fifty thousand pounds, as a fund for policemen's dependents. A wealthy manufacturer contributed one hundred thousand pounds. A widow instantly sent her weekly pension. A numismatist instantly sent his George III penny.

Detective Constable Dent, the Gentle Giant, was delighted that at long last something was being done to care for the families of officers killed while on duty. Officers were not insured by their employer, the police force, and to insure themselves privately had always been, and would forever remain, in view of the risks they ran, so costly as to deter all but the extraordinarily provident. Now, as he visited Mrs. Wombwell and Mrs. Fox, dealing with dozens of forms, from death certificates to their claims for pensions, and returning to them the pitiful personal effects left in their late husbands' lockers, Dent knew that, for the first time, penury need no longer be the lot of a copper's widow.

And still it was only Saturday—the first full day of Chitty's inquiry. Above the station, the Union Jack hung at half-mast; and outside the station, the Member of Parliament for Hammersmith was advocating the restoration of capital punishment to a receptive crowd.

"I warned M.P.s at the time the no-hanging bill was pushed through the Commons that something like this would happen," he raged. "I was the only M.P. on the Labour benches who opposed it. Now this slaughter takes place right in my own constituency."

Indifferent to such emotive rhetoric, the uniformed police at the Bush continued to function normally on the ground floor, and Chitty's team—making full use of Coote's organizational skills—continued to collect and collate evidence on the floor above.

Two small lost girls were brought in to the ground floor by the couple who had found them. "They've told us where they live," one of the pair said, "and it isn't all that far from where we live, so can we take them home for you?"

"Madam," said a relieved desk sergeant, "if you'd give me their names and then take them home, I should be much obliged. We're rather busy!"

Upstairs, as the telephone calls began to flood in, in response to Chitty's appeal for news of the Vanguard, they were more than busy. Every call had to be logged, with entries as to its time, the name and address of the caller, and the nature of the information. The coherent had to be sifted from the incoherent and the relevant from the irrelevant; the degree of urgency had to be assessed; and everyone had to be handled with the utmost diplomacy. Yet during a sleepless night nothing went amiss. Everywhere were the opened packs of cigarettes, brimming ashtrays, dirty cups, half-eaten sandwiches and stubbled chins of a team obsessed with its unfinished work. And in the early hours of Sunday came the break Chitty had prayed for. A man telephoned to say that there was a "wishy-washy blue Vanguard," like the one the police had described, in a garage under the arches of the railway line at Vauxhall.

A detective sergeant was dispatched to investigate, and shining his torch through a crack in the padlocked door, saw the back of a small blue car. He could not, however, see its license plate, because a spare wheel had been leaned against it.

More detectives were rushed to the grimy cul-de-sac. Using steel cutters, they severed the padlock; and when they rolled aside the spare wheel they beheld on the license plate the letters and figures PGT 726.

Men from the Murder Squad swept in, floodlights were set up, photographers and fingerprint experts went to work, and every inch of the van was searched. Dozens of fingerprints were rushed off to the Criminal Record Office for identification. A pair of license plates (JJJ 285D), three .38 cartridges (all recently fired), part of a nylon stocking and some overalls were found. And by dawn it was established that not only were some of the fingerprints Witney's (which was to be expected, were he guilty or innocent, since the car had been in his possession at least until lunchtime on the twelfth) but also, and more significantly, that the garage had been rented in Witney's name.

Chitty went down to the detention room and told Witney that the Vanguard had been discovered. More than that he did not reveal, leaving Witney in an agony of doubt. Refusing to be drawn, however, Witney said nothing. Chitty pondered what a court would make of the evidence that a car allegedly sold on the afternoon of a triple

murder, and subsequently observed by a dozen or so witnesses to have been used by the murderers, had finally been discovered in a garage rented not by the alleged purchaser of the vehicle but by its alleged vendor. Leaving Witney alone in the detention room, he ordered Slipper, of the beaming smile and ingenuous stare, to break Witney's alibi.

Sunday morning's newspapers gave full vent to the nation's fury. "An outrage," declared the *Sunday Mirror*. "There are moments in the lifetime of every generation when a single terrible incident reaches out from the headlines and rocks the British people on their heels."

Widely quoted also was the secretary of the Police Federation, who warned, "London and other large cities are in danger of being dominated by gangs of organized criminals . . . desperate men who will stop at nothing."

The abolition of hanging, proclaimed the advocates of hanging as a deterrent, had proved "a license to kill."

"Let all who agree," exhorted a prominent Tory M.P., "speak up. It is not enough to be shocked."

Americans read the story on the front page of their newspapers that morning and were shocked not so much by the triple killing as by the fact that no British policemen carried firearms and that, this being the case, so few as thirty of them had been killed in the past fifty-six years.

British readers found more significance in the fact that, of those thirty, seven had been murdered in the past *four* years, and four of them in the year since the abolition of hanging. And one Briton at least was shocked to read in his Sunday paper that a man called Witney was being detained at Shepherd's Bush Police Station to "help the police with their inquiries."

"That's it!" Roberts exclaimed to Mrs. Perry. "They've got Jack. If only Duddy had helped me burn that car, we'd all be in the clear."

Duddy arrived shortly thereafter, just as alarmed as Roberts, and the two of them at once drove to a remote part of Hampstead Heath and buried their three incriminating guns.

The Home Secretary visited Shepherd's Bush Police Station for a second time, and stood on the steps facing the television cameras, journalists, photographers and a crowd of three hundred. An owlish-looking, somewhat patronizing man, he looked nervous, as a woman armed with nothing more dangerous than her shopping bag shouted at him, "You should bring back hanging."

"And why not the cat-o'-nine-tails as well?" a second woman demanded.

"I want to speak to the policemen on the job here," Mr. Jenkins responded, thereby answering neither remark, "to express to them my support and sympathy in the struggle they are waging against criminals who are threatening the whole basis of civilized life in this country."

Referring then to the statement of the secretary of the Police Federation, he assured his listeners: "I can well understand the reaction and feelings of policemen at the present time; but it would be quite wrong for me to make a major policy decision in the shadow of one event, however horrible that event may be."

The police replied to the Home Secretary not with words but with a gesture. They paid one pound a head into a fund from which a reward of one thousand pounds could be offered to anyone providing evidence leading to the capture of any of the murderers. But, they warned, "don't have a go at capturing them yourselves. Send for us. They may shoot you if cornered. If you think you know where they're hiding, don't go near them. Have them watched and call us immediately."

That Sunday afternoon the two killers still at liberty decided to flee London. Duddy made his way to Glasgow, where he had relatives and friends; Roberts told Mrs. Perry to pack a suitcase and meet him at Paddington Railway Station, whence he took her by taxi to the Russell Hotel.

Having checked in as Mr. and Mrs. Crosby, they went to dinner in a small restaurant, and after the meal returned to the hotel. Mrs. Perry lay on one twin bed, and Roberts, who felt sick, lay fully dressed on the other, staring at the ceiling and smoking incessantly. They hardly talked all night, and when Roberts did speak it was to express not regret or remorse but only dismay at the situation in which he found himself.

"What a mess I've made of things," he brooded. "What a bloody mess. If only that copper hadn't decided to inspect the car."

Already the responsibility for the killings had ceased to be his and become that of "the copper." Already his two victims had merged into one—one who had caused his own death by deciding to search the car.

As Monday dawned he turned finally to Mrs. Perry and said, "I've got to get away, pet." He did not say where, but a plan was forming in his mind. "Perhaps we'll be together again in a few months," he comforted her; but if he really thought so, he was deluding himself.

CHAPTER 5

EARLY ON MONDAY MORNING, Roberts and Mrs. Perry checked out of the Russell Hotel and walked to Euston Station, where Roberts checked his suitcase into the baggage room and tore up the ticket. Now at least no one would find his clothes and trace him to Euston. Or if, in three or four months, they did, it would be a red herring they found, not a clue.

Because next he went to an army-surplus store, where he bought a rucksack, some combat clothes, a tent, a Primus stove and a sleeping bag. Thence to a grocer's shop, where he bought a small stock of canned food. And finally, with Mrs. Perry, by bus to Epping Forest, on the outskirts of London.

"I'm on my own now, pet," he told her then. "I'll have to make my own way from here."

"But where will you go?" she asked.

"I don't know," he confessed. "I haven't really made up my mind"—and began to cry.

Mrs. Perry hugged and consoled him until he pulled himself together and said, "You'd better go before I get any worse." Pulling six pound notes and some silver out of his pocket, he gave her the coins. "For your fare home," he explained. "Sorry it's so little, pet, but I'm going to need it more than you." So Mrs. Perry caught the bus back to Central London, and Roberts, rucksack on back, strode off into the depths of the forest.

JACK SLIPPER, MEANTIME, briefed by Chitty to break Witney's alibi, had gone to the betting shop in Acton Vale into which Witney had claimed to have popped at exactly the time when Wombwell, Head and Fox were being murdered. The manager and the staff were all happy to make statements to the effect that they knew Witney well, so if he had popped as much as his head into their premises that Friday afternoon, they would have seen it. On the contrary, however, they had seen nothing of him at all.

Witney, though, stuck to his story—but, confronted by the man who had rented the garage to him, he began to look more agitated than ever, despite the fact that the man had declined positively to identify him. Once again Chitty left him in the detention room to ponder his likely fate.

While frogmen searched the waters of the Thames by Lambeth Bridge—which the Vanguard had been seen crossing en route to its garage—and the Flying Squad swooped on more clubs, pubs and houses known to be frequented by criminals, the commissioner and Chitty discussed the legality of continuing to hold Witney without charging him, and speculated about the nature of the crime into which the crew of Foxtrot One One had stumbled and for which they had paid with their lives.

High on the list of possibilities was the theory that the men in the Vanguard had been about to spring from Wormwood Scrubs the Russian spy called George Blake; and had Sir Joseph and Chitty known at that time that one of the three murderers was Harry Roberts, whose tutor, when he had studied French in Wormwood Scrubs, had been George Blake, they would have taken their theory even more seriously.

As it was, they eventually dismissed it and came down instead in favor of a new theory, that Foxtrot One One had somehow been caught in the cross fire of a war between rival gangs of racketeers. Overtaxed though Scotland Yard's resources were, they therefore decided to provide all their witnesses with police protection.

As he left the station, Sir Joseph agreed to speak to the television cameras before the now customary crowd. "Like most sticky murders," he told them, "this is obviously going to be a difficult one, but I have no doubt we'll get to the bottom of it." And then, with perfect timing, he appealed directly to the underworld, whose life-style had been so grievously disrupted of late by the activities of his Flying Squad. Referring to the gunning down of unarmed policemen, he remarked, "Some of the most persistent criminals don't stand for this sort of thing, and sometimes we get much help from them. I would *welcome* it now."

At which the underworld began loudly to protest its innocence. So loudly, in fact, that Scotland Yard's experts began also to doubt the theory that the killers were well-known gangsters. But if not that, and not parties to a proposed jailbreak either, then what were they? Indeed, what could they be?

Whatever they were, the demand that society in general and the Home Secretary and Parliament in particular respond to their crime by restoring the death penalty grew stronger by the hour. Some even advocated arming the police.

As to which Lord Justice Parker forthrightly declared, "There is no room for sympathy for criminals who are out to make war on society. It is war in cold blood."

The Home Secretary, however, equivocated. "Today we have a real menace to society, both in organized criminal conspiracies and in individual acts of violence," he admitted. "Unless we can control the momentary crime wave, we shall get a climate hostile to individual liberty. Therefore, the battle against crime must have first priority. The present position is terrifying a lot of people. . . ."

Neither of these statements did much to soothe Britain's now savage breast, but Scotland Yard's assistant commissioner at least made no attempt to shirk the questions many Britons were asking. Admitting frankly his belief that the abolition of hanging *had* had an effect upon the criminal mentality, he added, "But if the crew of Foxtrot One One had been armed, some of those children playing in Braybrook Street might have been caught in the cross fire—and they would have died too."

As if F Division had not already grieved enough since Friday, a fresh blow now befell it. Police Constable Seager—the officer who drove the first patrol car to Braybrook Street and there discovered the body of his best man, at whose home he had met the girl he married—was on traffic duty when a trailer truck overturned and killed him.

Refusing to be distracted, Chitty charged Witney that, with others, on Friday, at Braybrook Street, he had murdered Christopher Tippett Head, David Stanley Wombwell and Geoffrey Roger Fox. His evidence was more circumstantial than conclusive, but he was certain that the strain of being the one man charged, of having to bear the guilt alone, would break Witney.

To hasten this process he allowed Mrs. Witney to visit her husband, and then asked Coote to go down to the cell to which Witney had been transferred from the detention room and there, accompanied by another officer, take his fingerprints and antecedent history.

"This is a terrible mess," Witney kept assuring Coote, but just as constantly proclaimed his innocence. His task completed, Coote returned upstairs—surprised on the way to observe that, despite the hour, a large crowd had once again assembled outside the station—and told Chitty, "I wouldn't mind betting he'll want to see you soon. Another half hour and he'd have been talking to *me*."

Shortly after midnight, as Coote had foretold, Witney rang the bell that summoned his jailer and asked to see Chitty. "Witney's put his hands up," the word flashed through both floors of the station. It was the break on which Chitty had gambled. Confronted with the statements Slipper had elicited from the staff of the Acton Vale betting shop, and for some hours worried by what clues might or might not have been discovered in his Vanguard, Witney at last wanted to talk. And even though Chitty had not been home for more than three days, he acceded promptly to his prisoner's request and had him brought upstairs.

"This is a terrible mess," Witney said once again. "But I honestly didn't shoot the coppers, guv'nor. I know you must've found out a lot about what happened, so I'll tell you the whole truth. As God's my judge, I had absolutely nothing to do with the shooting of any of those three coppers."

As usual, Chitty said little while allowing his prisoner to believe that he knew everything.

"I'm frightened for my family, not for myself," Witney insisted. "I know I'll be going away for a long time, but it's for them I'm frightened. And as God's my judge, I had nothing to do with the shooting. I just drove into Braybrook Street, where a car pulled up alongside and two men got out, and one asked if it was my car."

Then followed the whole squalid little story—not of a coup to release a master spy, not of ruthless gangsterdom at war with itself, but of one petty villain acting as chauffeur to two other petty villains, each of whom he named, and to both of whom he attributed the entire responsibility for all that had transpired.

Unable to remember either Roberts' or Duddy's exact address, Witney offered to guide the police to their homes.

As soon as he had written and signed his statement, therefore, Hensley—immaculate still in his bow tie, pipe clenched as firmly as ever between his teeth—put him on the floor of what looked like a normal London cab, covered him with a blanket, and unremarked either by the press or the waiting crowd, but followed by Flying Squad crews, dogs, dog handlers and a tear-gas marksman, drove first to Wymering Mansions in Maida Vale and then to Treventon Towers in North Kensington.

At dawn the Flying Squad burst into each flat. At Wymering Mansions they found only Mrs. Perry, Mrs. Howard and her two children; and at Treventon Towers they found only Duddy's two teenage daughters. But by then Witney was sleeping like a baby (guarded, at Chitty's insistence, by an officer from another division), and Chitty knew that to close the case he had only to find John Duddy and Harry Roberts.

Seventy-seven hours after the killings, the first charge had been made. Eighty-two hours after the killings, Chitty returned home for the first time since Friday morning. Eight hours later—having given his wife her customary early morning cup of tea—he was back at the Bush, sustaining the momentum of Operation Shepherd.

CHAPTER 6

THE PUBLIC AND THE POLICE, summarized one of Tuesday's headlines, CLOSER PERHAPS THAN EVER BEFORE. Below the headlines a photograph showed uniformed officers, men and women, arranging bunches of flowers at the Shepherd's Bush Station—into which had flowed no less than three thousand pounds in donations as well.

Each day now the Shepherd's Bush murders were front-page material for all of London's newspapers, and Chitty's jauntily cocked felt hat had become the story's trademark.

"He's a wonderful governor," said the men who were his subordinates. "He works, works and works."

"He's a lovely man," said the women on his team. "As courteous and considerate as possible."

Mavis Brown was one of the typists sent from Scotland Yard to help him. A blond, cheerful girl from Wales, she had known Chris Head well and worked with him often. She felt bitter about his murder and that of his crew. "They were so young," she lamented, "and they were mercilessly killed."

So she begrudged no one the long hours she and her fellow typists were spending at the Bush, and minded not at all when Chitty—calling her by any Welsh name that came to mind—dropped statements on her desk at ten o'clock at night and said, "Can you do this bit for me, Blodwin, please?"

At ten twenty that Tuesday morning Witney was formally charged at West London Magistrates' Court. Slightly stooped, doubly handcuffed, hair sparse, eyes red-rimmed, and wearing the casual clothes and red carpet slippers he had had on four nights ago when the police first visited him at his home, he was asked had he anything to say in reply to the charge, and answered, "No, sir, nothing."

He was remanded for a week and taken away. His wife, who had sat dumbly in court behind him, could do nothing but watch him be led out.

Mrs. Perry, on the other hand, was talking freely about Roberts, telling one of Chitty's detectives how she had left him at The Wake Arms in Epping the day before, and listing all the goods Roberts had previously purchased at Euston.

Scotland Yard was thus enabled both to issue a photograph of Roberts—the hooded eyes somewhat baggy under their thick arched eyebrows—and to advise that he would probably be dressed in combat clothing and carrying a sleeping bag and a rucksack.

At eleven thirty that morning a man telephoned the *Daily Mirror* and said, "This is Duddy. If I didn't do the shooting, do I get done just the same as the others?"

The journalist to whom he was speaking suggested that he speak instead to the paper's lawyer. The caller countered by suggesting a rendezvous—on the cricket field at Turnham Green, in an hour's time. "But if there's a smell of a copper, I'll be away," he warned.

"I understand," the journalist acknowledged. "Do you want me to bring a lawyer?"

"No. I just want to speak to one man. I dinna want anyone else. Just one man."

The journalist informed Chitty of the rendezvous, and Chitty, even though he suspected a hoax, staked out the whole of Turnham Green. Twelve thirty came, and Duddy did not.

After so grueling a morning's work, Chitty's team adjourned in shifts to The Beaumont Arms, across the road from the Bush. It was a genial session, which the innkeeper (who had recently broken his leg) enjoyed as much as the officers in his bar. Enjoyed, that is, until he propelled himself upstairs on his crutches and there discovered a burglar.

"Thief! Thief!" the innkeeper bellowed. At which half the men of Scotland Yard stormed upstairs and flung themselves upon the terrified intruder.

Duddy and Roberts, though, remained at large, the one having fled to the bosom of his Glaswegian clan, the other skulking somewhere in the dense thickets of Epping Forest. Chitty, therefore, had already rung Glasgow's police and asked them to assist by looking for Duddy, and demanded a sweep through Epping Forest the following day in the hope of unearthing Roberts.

Wasting not a second, the Glasgow police visited a Vincent Duddy, who soon agreed to take them to the hideout of his brother John. Following Vincent up three flights of rotten tenement stairs, they allowed him to knock on a door and say, "It's all right, it's me, Vinny." Then they burst into the room—and found a scared, paunchy Scot lying dejectedly on a crumpled bed.

At Glasgow's Central Police Station, Duddy said, "I was in the car, but I didn't do the shooting. I'd like to see my father. He's the only man I can talk to."

Instead, Chitty decided that Duddy would see Slipper and Hensley. Having flown to Glasgow, they found short, thickset Duddy wearing a cardigan and an open-necked shirt. He was abject, and visibly stunned.

"You're to be taken to Shepherd's Bush Police Station for questioning about the murder of three police officers in Braybrook Street last Friday," Hensley advised him.

"Yes, sir," said Duddy quietly, his Scottish accent muted by years of life in London. "I understand."

At Glasgow airport, a huge crowd had collected, anticipating Duddy's immediate transportation to London. Handcuffed to Slipper, and concealed under a plastic raincoat, he was driven right onto the tarmac, hustled up the steps of the aircraft, and installed in a curtained section at the rear of the plane.

"I'm hot," he complained when the plane had taken off, "and these handcuffs hurt."

"Sit low, then," said Slipper, "so none of the press boys can photograph you"—and removing the raincoat, he unlocked Duddy's handcuffs.

"I must tell you what happened," Duddy said then.

"You're under caution," Slipper reminded, lest Duddy had forgotten that henceforth anything he said could be taken down and used in evidence.

"I don't care," Duddy retorted, and Slipper opened his notebook. "It was Roberts who started the shooting. He shot the two who got out of the car and shouted at me to shoot the other one. I just grabbed a gun, run to the police car, and shot the driver through the front window. I must've been bloody mad. I wish you could hang me now."

At Heathrow airport, in London, they ran a gauntlet of hundreds of journalists, and it was late at night when they reached the Bush, where Coote took Duddy's fingerprints and questioned him.

"I didn't mean to kill him," Duddy protested. "I just wanted money. Quick money, the easy way. I'm a fool."

When all the formalities were completed, and Coote was about to leave him to sleep what was left of the night, Duddy looked at him perplexedly. "I expected to be treated rough," he said. Coote didn't answer. "After what I done to your mates, I mean, I expected to be treated rough."

Having admitted, though, that he had used a Webley .45 to shoot Fox, Duddy had no cause to fear reprisals from individual policemen. In Detective Sergeant Lawrence's possession was a .45-caliber bullet that would put Duddy away for years. The police were perfectly content to leave his punishment to the courts.

Yet, having started to talk, Duddy seemed unable to stop, never ceasing to confess to the murder of Fox, everlastingly denying the murders of Wombwell and Head, shamelessly seeking to shift the blame from himself to Roberts and Witney, and garrulously relating the story of an outing intended only to provide a blue Cortina and ending instead in a mindless shoot-out.

Now at last Chitty knew why the crew of Foxtrot One One had died, and could see for himself how insignificant were two of the killers. But the third remained at large. And the third was the one who had, without warning, leaned across Witney and cold-bloodedly shot Wombwell dead. Such a man had to be different from the other two; and the two hundred policemen who at dawn began scouring the densely wooded six thousand acres of Epping Forest were armed and wary.

CHAPTER 7

THOUGH THEY THRESHED systematically through the thickest undergrowth, though their dogs sniffed, scampered and growled, though detectives darted—pistols outstretched—from one likely place of concealment to another, the two hundred beaters found nothing but infuriated lovers and a youthful pair of bemused hitchhikers.

"Motorists are advised *not* to offer lifts to any hitchhiker wearing an army combat jacket," Scotland Yard warned. "It could be Harry Roberts."

His name now as well known as the Prime Minister's, Roberts betook himself from Epping Forest to another wood some six miles away and there, with the skill and cunning that the army had taught him in the jungles of Malaya, began constructing the hideout in which he would live for the next three months.

Unaware of this, the police swept Epping Forest a second time, using five hundred officers on this occasion, one of whom was the Scenes-of-Crime expert, Lawrence, to whom, in the middle of the forest, a message was brought, asking him most urgently to ring his home. Anticipating every conceivable kind of family disaster, he ran miles to the nearest call box and, as soon as his wife had answered, blurted out, "Ron here, what is it?"

"We've been *burgled*," she wailed.

"Is that all?" he snorted, and returned to the sun-dappled depths of a forest resounding to the baying of dogs and the trampling of

men armed with radios, truncheons, revolvers, rifles and canisters of tear gas—men in uniform and men in city suits, and all of them in pursuit of an ex-army sniper called Roberts.

They found a campsite and a fire over which was suspended a saucepan. The camp had just been abandoned and the saucepan contained the unappetizing carcass of a squirrel. It looked a promising lead. And when the dogs began to bark excitedly, it sounded promising too.

They followed the dogs eagerly and were led to a forest hut—a good defensive position for a desperate marksman.

Approaching it with infinite caution, and no less courage, they stormed inside. And found themselves face to face with a horse. The search continued.

"The forest," one journalist wrote that night, "is Roberts' only friend." Had it occurred to him to speculate in which *other* forest Roberts might be seeking asylum from the prying eyes, not only of the police but of an alert and vengeful public as well, the case might have ended much earlier. But it didn't occur to him, so another journalist was obliged to admit that "fifty million detectives can't find Roberts."

Fifty million detectives could, on the other hand, rejoice in the capture of Duddy, at whose hearing in the West London Magistrates' Court, on the nineteenth of August, Lawrence had to produce a series of exhibits. Chitty sat in the body of the court, watching Coote hand the exhibits one at a time to Lawrence.

The exhibits were in cardboard boxes, and as he took one from Coote, Lawrence noted the bullet that had killed Fox lying loose. It was exhibit 13.

Having handed him exhibit 12, Coote began to rummage in the box while Lawrence gave his evidence.

"I can't *find* it," Coote muttered.

Lawrence continued with his evidence.

"*I can't find it,*" Coote repeated.

Lawrence glanced at him and realized the problem. "*I've* got it," he murmured.

"You *bastard!*" Coote hissed.

Whereupon, from the rear of the court, came a derisive growl from Chitty. "Made a right muck-up of that, didn't you?" he observed. It was the kind of imperturbable good humor, even when things were going badly, that made him so easy a man for whom to work.

The new relationship between the police and the public also facilitated Operation Shepherd. Britain's ordinary citizens were angry to learn that police widows like Mrs. Wombwell and Mrs. Fox were ineligible for payments from the Criminal Injuries Compensation Board; its underworld had just advised Scotland Yard that they would surrender Roberts the second they laid hands on him rather than endure another minute of the activities of the Flying Squad; and its television viewers had just responded with fury to the pontifications of a panel of pop and folk singers, one of whom had said about policemen, "They smash people over the head who are demonstrating perfectly legitimately." The company that had broadcast his words was compelled to apologize and explain that the program had been filmed months previously.

As the search through Epping Forest continued, Roberts telephoned a woman friend in London. "For God's sake, help me," he begged, and asked her for money.

Refusing to send him any, she rang the police, who by then, convinced that he had left Epping Forest, were wondering whether Roberts might not be holding a family of campers hostage somewhere. Because they were not convinced that he might not return to Epping Forest when the hue and cry had subsided, they decided to resume their search of it every now and then. Wherever else he was, Roberts would soon learn that Epping Forest at least was not his friend.

"Wherever you are, Harry," his estranged stripper wife, Mitzi, now publicly pleaded, "give yourself up. You've nothing to lose and everything to gain—maybe even your life. Please, please don't hurt anyone."

Because he believed her responsible for his stretch in Wormwood Scrubs, there was no one whose exhortations were less likely to influence him than hers; but if she left her husband cold, she was receiving more attention from other men than ever before, the tragedy that had inspired a nation's generosity having also made her the most popular stripper in the North of England.

"Good evening, music lovers—and Harry Roberts!" quipped a

master of ceremonies with ineffable bad taste. "A big hand, please, for Mitzi Roberts."

"We've had to boost her fee," a club manager complained; and the more intense the subsequent search for her murderous estranged husband, the greater the desire of men who were complete strangers to her to pay to watch her take off her clothes.

If no one in Britain was inclined to comment that publicity for a stripper was hardly a healthy by-product of murder, Radio Moscow lost no time in asserting that the murders themselves were symptomatic of a sick society. "Look at the number of Western and gangster films shown in Britain's cinemas and on TV, most of them of unmistakable American origin," scolded one of its English-language broadcasts. "Look at the orgy of killings that goes on in cheap thrillers. Look at the way crime is sensationalized in large parts of the British press. There lies the root cause of the trouble."

Whatever and wherever the root cause of the trouble, Harry Roberts was the latest exponent of the trouble itself, and no less than eighty thousand policemen were scouring Britain for him as thousands of calls were made to police stations all over the country by people who were sure they had seen him. In London alone, on a single day, thirty raids were made by armed policemen in response to alleged sightings of him. Yet still he eluded capture.

Perhaps, speculated the press, he had dyed his hair? Or grown a beard? Or a mustache? Though well intentioned, such speculations did not help. The photograph of Roberts issued by Scotland Yard had, through no fault of theirs, not been a particularly good likeness. Further to confuse the public by superimposing upon this photograph conjectural dyed hair and a hypothetical mustache was to make their recognition of Roberts virtually impossible.

Despite which the public continued, with the utmost sincerity, to recognize him—in Foyle's huge bookshop in Charing Cross Road, for example, obliging the police to seal it off and search it for thirty-five vain minutes. At Victoria Station, where he was swiftly apprehended and turned out to be a Spanish boxer called José Valesco, who had come to London to fight Johnny Prescott. In the restaurant of a Glamorgan hotel, from which he was extracted, and discovered to be an innocent diner, whose meal, when he returned to it, was cold.

Five times in one day he was seen hitchhiking on the road from Dartford to Canterbury, and was picked up on each occasion. He turned out to be a singer called Alfred Hancock, who wailed, "Why do I have to look like Harry Roberts? Why can't I look like Mario Lanza, or Beniamino Gigli, or Enrico Caruso?"

He was seen scuttling into the Sadler's Wells Theatre, into which fifty policemen poured after him—and found only an opera company industriously rehearsing Offenbach's *Bluebeard*.

And he was seen and detained in a London street—where he turned out to be one Martin Wiener, an American artist preparing an exhibition whose theme was a protest against violence!

Conversely, a Leeds hitchhiker got one lift after another by the simple expedient of attaching to his rucksack a sign that said: I AM NOT HARRY ROBERTS. And a hoaxer got all the publicity he needed by ringing the *Evening Standard* and saying, "My name is Roberts. If you give my mother two thousand pounds, I'll give myself up."

That same night, on radio and television, Roberts' mother appealed to her son. "Robin," she faltered, "I ask you from the bottom of my heart to come into the open and give yourself up. If you make an appointment with me, I will come with you. The whole thing is killing me. Please do as I ask before there's any more bloodshed. I've given this a lot of consideration, Robin, and I'm doing this on my own. I'm sure I'm advising you correctly."

Neither she nor the police were greatly surprised when her son ignored her suggestion; but Roberts himself would have been surprised, had he heard it, by the accuracy of the latest police speculations about himself. He must by now, they were saying, have run short of cash. He would be compelled thereafter, they suggested, to resort to theft. They had described his predicament precisely.

CHAPTER 8

ROBERTS HAD INSTALLED himself in a trackless corner of Thorley Wood, some six miles from Epping Forest. Having found a patch of thick undergrowth, he had crawled into it, dug a shallow hole, and pitched his tent over it. Next he made a kind of breastwork with the excavated soil, carpeted the earth floor with plastic bags, and camouflaged his tent with more plastic bags painted green and brown. Then he wove a screen of light branches over the whole, installed his sleeping bag, the Primus stove, a lamp and two radios, set up an elaborate warning system of trip wires, and dug drains so that his tent would remain watertight even when it rained.

He had, of course, been obliged to steal both the paint and the radios, and he was regularly obliged to steal money (either by breaking into a house or by breaking open the coin box of a public telephone) for the purchase of food.

Every day he listened to the BBC's news items about himself, and most days he bought and read a newspaper. He had kept his camp and cooking utensils spotlessly clean, and he was growing a beard. He was comfortable enough in the warm summer weather and had not so far been disturbed, even though there was a Gypsy caravan a few hundred yards away in another part of the wood.

Realizing that he must steal cash to survive, he returned to the spot on Hampstead Heath where he and Duddy had buried the three guns. Disinterring two of them, he left behind the pistol with which Duddy had murdered Fox, and returned to Thorley Wood.

Then, from local stores, he bought leather (with which he made himself a holster for his Luger) and cans of food, paying for them with handfuls of small coins stolen from the telephone box. Politeness not only prevented those who sold him his purchases from commenting on such unusual legal tender, but a reluctance to look foolish in front of friends caused at least one suspicious villager to hold her tongue.

"Gosh, he looked like Harry Roberts," said the lady in the general store after his first visit; but when her assistant and a customer laughed at her, she felt that she must be wrong and never mentioned it again.

Day succeeded day, and Roberts' hideout, never easily detectable, merged more and more into the surrounding undergrowth. The raw earth of his breastwork mellowed, broken branches healed, and trampled grass sprang up anew. Only occasionally did intruders come his way, and when they did they were only boys, who noticed nothing, though Roberts saw them as they hunted for rabbits. After two weeks in the open his face had lost much of its puffiness, his complexion had freshened, his confidence in himself was growing, and

Britain's persistent policemen had resigned themselves to a prolonged search.

They were not in the least discouraged, however. Even though the Bush had received 3714 phone calls and 521 letters in the fourteen days since the triple murder, and dealt with twelve hundred sightings of Roberts in the ten days since issuing his description, there was no sense of defeat or futility in Chitty's operations room.

Nor was there any feeling that the inquiry had lost its momentum after so early and promising a breakthrough. Policemen are more accustomed, in fact, to wars of attrition than to swift campaigns of annihilation. Detectives rely not on flashes of brilliant intuition but on the patient, jigsaw assembly of a hundred unspectacular facts into an invincible case against the accused. And Chitty's case against Witney, Duddy and Roberts was already well-nigh invincible, lacking, as it did, only their guns and Roberts.

Even had Chitty's team begun to weary, continued public interest would have sustained them. Flowers were still being delivered to the station. A card of sympathy had arrived "From the housewives of Braybrook Street." Donations to the fund for dependents had topped a hundred and fifty-seven thousand pounds. And as a kind of inverted compliment to the indefatigable Flying Squad, London's crime rate had decreased dramatically.

ON AUGUST 31, CHRISTOPHER Head, David Wombwell and Geoffrey Fox were buried. Their funeral was organized by the commissioner's department itself, and Chitty and his team stopped work for the first time in nineteen days to attend it.

The service was held in the Church of St. Stephen and St. Thomas, almost opposite the Shepherd's Bush Police Station and not a mile from Braybrook Street. Though the morning was wet and the wind strong, crowds stood five deep as six hundred policemen lined the route, and flags flew at half-mast from every shop.

Fourteen funeral cars drew up outside the church at ten fifteen to the tolling of bells. The commissioner himself delivered the eulogy. Six police officers acted as pallbearers to each of the coffins. And the air was sweet with the scent of hundreds of wreaths.

The hearses departed; Chitty and his team went back to work; and the inquisitive remarked that conspicuous among the many floral tributes were one from the Royal Canadian Mounted Police and a second—of gold and white chrysanthemums, the card inscribed "With deepest sympathy"—from Mrs. Margaret Roberts junior, better known in the North as Mitzi.

AUGUST ENDED AND September was greeted with a new notice on the board outside Shepherd's Bush Police Station. To the familiar collection (offering ten pounds for the return of a dog, appealing for information about the recently closed case of the nude murders, offering rewards for information about stolen jewelry, furs and postal orders, and giving solemn warning about the ruinous habits of the Colorado beetle) was added a poster promising that "a reward of up to £1000 will be paid for information leading to the arrest of Harry Maurice Roberts, wanted for questioning in connection with the murders of three police officers on 12th August 1966 Braybrook Street Shepherd's Bush."

The reward was offered not because the public's desire to see Roberts in custody was waning but because the police—from whose contributions of a pound each the reward would be paid—were determined to match the generosity of the public. The offer of a reward made no appreciable difference to the public's eagerness to report sightings of the elusive killer. He was seen so frequently, so ubiquitously and so mistakenly, in fact, that Chitty decided to appear on television and attempt to describe him more accurately.

This was a move dictated as much by the demands of economics as by those of efficiency. Coote, for example, had been filled with apprehension as he telephoned the Wiltshire police to advise that Roberts had been sighted in Savernake Forest.

"How genuine do you think this caller of yours was?" demanded a senior Wiltshire officer, whose force, like all provincial forces, could not afford to waste a penny.

"He said," Coote cautiously recited, "it was definitely Roberts."

A massive—albeit reluctant—sweep of the Savernake Forest was therefore mounted by the Wiltshire police, whose costly and exhausting search was followed step by step, and hour after hour, by an equally costly television unit. Not surprisingly—since he was a hundred miles away in Thorley Wood—Roberts was not discovered. Neither the Wiltshire police nor the television company blamed anyone at Shepherd's Bush for that, but Coote was glad when Chitty went on television in an effort to make its repetition less likely.

Looking exhausted, but speaking lucidly and compellingly, Chitty showed Britain's viewers various photographs of Roberts, and drew attention to his large, bulging eyes, the heavy eyebrows and the thick hooded lids. Appealing for help in finding Roberts, he exhorted those watching his broadcast to take no risks. "Contact either Scotland Yard or your local police station," he advised any who might think they had seen Roberts, because the missing man was rightly believed (though for the wrong reasons) to be armed.

The wrong reason was a curious one. Ever since his arrest, John Duddy had been talking. In his cell, on the way to and from the Magistrates' Court, to all and sundry, he had talked and talked and talked. Yet not once, as he unburdened himself of every other guilty detail, or sought to attribute all the guilt to Roberts and Witney, had he admitted that he and Roberts had buried their guns.

He had made no attempt to deny that it was he who had shot Fox, nor to conceal from Chitty the kind of gun—a Webley—he had used. But he had consistently refrained from revealing the whereabouts of either that gun or the other two—which had led Chitty wrongly to assume that Roberts must have taken all three into hiding with him.

It was typical of Chitty's extraordinary capacity to master and retain small details that he was as determined to retrieve these guns as he was to capture Roberts. From Mrs. Perry and Mrs. Howard he had learned that Roberts had bought the guns for ninety pounds from a Cypriot he'd met in a triangular-shaped restaurant somewhere in London; and even as he bent his mind remorselessly to the hunt for Roberts, he never forgot that Operation Shepherd would be wound up only when the guns had been seized and the anonymous Cypriot, as well as Roberts and his two incompetent friends, had been sent to prison.

Two days after his broadcast, Chitty took time off from his investigations for the second and last time. A memorial service for Head, Wombwell and Fox was being held in Westminster Abbey, and Chitty and his team were determined to be present.

The day was sunny, quite unlike the day of the funeral, and into the abbey flowed a blue wave of serge-clad policemen and policewomen—two thousand of them—the men in gleaming boots, carrying their helmets, the women trim in hats and black shoes. Also there were scores of VIPs—from the Prime Minister to peers of the realm, from senior politicians to distinguished lawyers, from the Home Secretary to foreign delegates attending a conference of the International Police Association in London.

The chief mourners, of course, were Mrs. Head, Mrs. Fox and Mrs. Wombwell; but *their* grief seemed no less than that of the massed ranks of police officers within the abbey or of the overflow of civilians sitting in the cloisters outside.

"And there shall be no more death, neither sorrow, nor crying, neither shall there be any more pain," the commissioner read from The Revelation.

The dean of Westminster Abbey expressed the hope that the murder of Head, Wombwell and Fox might precipitate a revulsion in society against all forms of brutality and violence.

The congregation sang "Abide with Me"; the police choir sang "God Be in My Head"; and many wept. Nor were their tears stilled by the tolling of muffled bells as the service ended and the congregation filed out of the abbey's gloom and into a sunlit crowd of more than a thousand.

"I knew my Geoff would get killed someday," Mrs. Fox confessed. "But he always wanted to be a policeman—was so proud of his job, and so was I—of his job and of him. I had nineteen happy years with him. What made him happy made me happy."

The youthful Mrs. Wombwell was no less composed. Slim, graceful, fair-haired and astoundingly clear-eyed, she said, "Although my children are still so young, it's for them I must live now."

Chitty drove back to the Bush from the abbey and was advised that during his brief absence there had been seventeen reports of sightings of Roberts. But the memorial had marked the end of the first phase of Operation Shepherd. The dead had been honored and two of their three murderers were in cells. Now, with minds purged of grief or any other emotion, Chitty's men must apply themselves to the relentless routine of the hunt for the third.

Though Witney, the next day, asked, "How are the wives of the policemen who got killed? I can't bear to think about their kids. Roberts and Duddy must've been mad," his words moved no one—

not to pity for Mrs. Fox or Mrs. Wombwell, not to grief for the dead, least of all to compassion for a repentant killer. Immune at last to emotion, those who heard Witney's whine merely noted that yet again he was attempting to shift all the blame to Roberts and Duddy.

"You've got the impression Witney was *forced* to drive away after the shooting," Duddy retaliated. "You take it from me, Witney was the brains of the outfit." But no one cared about Duddy's retaliation, because he and Witney had become little more in the inquiry than garrulous ciphers. What mattered now—all that mattered—was finding Roberts.

Sensing this, the public also curbed its emotions. The crowds outside the Bush at last went home. The flowers in the foyer slowly died, leaving nothing but a few cacti to remind of the recent profusion; and only the unaccustomed bulge of revolvers on the hips of Chitty's industrious detectives indicated that a manhunt had yet to trap its prey.

CHAPTER 9

THOUGH PUBLIC DISPLAYS of mass emotion ceased with the memorial service, acts of individual charity persisted. Money continued to flow into the fund for dependents at the rate of almost four thousand pounds a day. Mrs. Wombwell's neighbors cleaned and polished her flat when friends took her away with her children for a holiday. And Harry Roberts' mother was showered with gifts after her appeal to her son to give himself up.

"I don't like it," she protested, weeping. "I don't want them. I don't think it's right"—and sent all the flowers and fruit to a hospital, and all the cash to the police orphanage. Nevertheless, the public's sympathy for her was both genuine and justified. Mrs. Roberts was a hardworking, well-spoken woman, with whose anguish it was very easy for thousands of parents to identify.

But that in no way ameliorated the public's antipathy toward her son—now being sheltered by former members of the National Organization of Cypriot Fighters (EOKA) living in London, according to gangland rumors. Chitty took note of the rumors, and of the names of the Cypriots with whom Roberts was alleged to have consorted in the past, but concentrated mainly on reports that he had been seen skulking in Piccadilly, eating at Euston, drinking in Camden Town, walking in the Elephant and Castle, and even sleeping in St. James's Park.

The next rumor—an inspired leak from the underworld, whose nerves were so frayed by the Flying Squad's unremitting attentions that it was prepared to try anything—was that Roberts was dead, wasted by a professional killer! But having briefly considered this convenient suggestion, Chitty and his colleagues decided that there was no reason why they should believe it. Even a suggestion that Roberts was masquerading as a woman was more convincingly corroborated. At least, a girl in a beauty salon was prepared to swear that she had dyed the hair of a masculine-looking lady with a forelock like Roberts'. In support of the Roberts-is-dead story, the underworld had produced nothing. Nor, unfortunately, had a search for the masculine-looking lady. And neither did several hundred further swoops, which by September 24 had taken the total of sightings investigated to fifty-three hundred.

Accordingly it was decided to attempt a better description of the wanted but elusive man. He had a jaunty walk, it was announced, and was a big eater. He had slightly protruding teeth and a passion for suede shoes. He needed to shave only occasionally, and, like Duddy, he bit his nails.

Not content with describing him, the police even filmed an actor made up to look and walk like him, and the film was shown on television. But all it did was to provoke reports that Roberts had been seen in Wales, in Ireland and in the Isle of Man, all of which had to be investigated and none of which bore fruit—unless the brief detention at the Cork Film Festival of Eddie Byrne, a well-known actor unfortunate enough to have eyes like a well-known murderer's, can be deemed fruitful.

In spite of this fiasco, the rumors that Roberts was either in Eire or heading for it were so strong that Chitty flew to Dublin. He soon returned. But to ensure that Roberts did not enter the Irish Republic by its back door, he ordered that every coffin being airfreighted to Belfast be examined at London's airports. All, regrettably, to no avail.

After six thousand false sightings, Britain's newspapers began to lose interest. To print the six thousand and first would hardly be a scoop, even for a local rag.

It was a clairvoyant, therefore, who gave the journalists their next real story. Roberts' corpse, the clairvoyant revealed, lay in a certain unfrequented part of Epping Forest.

The police followed the clairvoyant's directions more cynically than faithfully, and were astounded to find the promised corpse. It was five weeks old; but it was not Roberts'. And even while a dental check was identifying the body as that of a missing man who had committed suicide, fresh reports were flooding in that Roberts had been seen in an airplane, a train, a lady's bedroom, a women's public lavatory, in a car heading west, in other cars heading toward every other point of the compass, in the Lake District, in Soho and—inevitably—in one of the two thousand flats of Dolphin Square. No matter what the major crime or scandal in London, somehow, at some time, someone allegedly concerned is almost invariably traced to a flat in Dolphin Square.

OCTOBER CAME AND the nights grew cooler. Not only that, but soon the leaves would start falling. If Roberts was living rough, the police reasoned, the likelihood of his being discovered would grow by the day as trees and undergrowth shed their lush summer foliage, and damp wood smoked on every outdoor fire.

It was his character, however, rather than the season that was beginning to imperil Roberts. Having concealed himself in Thorley Wood with a degree of skill and cunning for which his army instructors would have awarded him the highest marks, he had begun, after six weeks, to behave carelessly.

Compelled to forage each night, he had begun to raid houses too close to Thorley Wood for his own security; and deprived of human company, which he minded a great deal less than most, he had begun to read at night by lamplight. Both habits were cardinal sins for a fugitive in hostile territory. The first had sooner or later to draw the attention of the local police to Thorley Wood; the second could at any time betray him to any of Thorley Wood's occasional nocturnal prowlers.

Forever self-indulgent, Roberts persistently broke the rules of the game he was playing. Yet reading the newspapers he bought each day by the light of his reckless lamp, or listening to one or the other of the two stolen and potentially treacherous transistor radios he kept inside his sleeping bag, he must frequently have felt immune to detection, even though he wore, on his daily visits to the store, the most highly publicized face and combat jacket in Britain.

Snug inside his tent in Thorley Wood on October 10, he read that because someone had found a rucksack in the area, police frogmen were searching a reservoir in distant Cheltenham. They searched it for three days.

On October 11 he read that Chitty and his sergeant had flown to Dublin a second time. There the Irish police had collaborated with Chitty and, by scouring the city and every possible hideout and haunt within a thirty-mile radius of it, had thrown Eire's underworld into a state of vociferous uproar. But they had found no English murderer.

On October 12 Roberts read of a malicious phone call to his mother. "I've some bad news for you," a husky voice had told her when she picked up the receiver at three o'clock in the morning. "Your son has committed suicide."

"Oh, dear, oh, dear," she had sobbed. And when the caller sought to elaborate, had begged, "No, leave it for now, please. Ring me later."

On October 22 he read of the escape from Wormwood Scrubs of his onetime tutor in French, the spy George Blake. Though the headlines left him in no doubt that Britain regarded this as an outrage (Blake had been sentenced to a record forty-two years' imprisonment, of which he had served only five and a half), it never occurred to him that there would be renewed speculation in Scotland Yard as to whether he, Harry Roberts, had not after all, on August 12, been casing the Scrubs with a view to springing George Blake some ten weeks later.

Superintendent Chitty left the problem of the Blake escape to Inspector Coote—who had also to deal with the discovery of a racket in wood alcohol inside the prison from which the escape had been made. Chitty let it be known that he now believed Roberts to be hiding in England, not in Ireland, and as an armed murderer, not as a Russian Pimpernel.

IN THORLEY WOOD IT was late afternoon and raining, so the murderer lay in his tent, reading. The sound of raindrops falling on his tent was agreeable and reassuring.

Indifferent to the rain, three boys scouted through the wood, eyes alert, hunting for rabbits. "Hey," said one suddenly, pointing to Roberts' hideout. "Look at that."

Curious, because no one but the Gypsies called Cunningham lived in the wood (and they lived in a caravan some distance away), the three boys crept up on the elaborately concealed and apparently deserted tent. They were about to peer into it when a radio began to play. Lest they be accused of intruding, the three boys stole away.

"I wonder if it was Harry Roberts?" one of them suggested when he got home.

Angry with him for getting wet when he had a cold, his mother doused his childish enthusiasm with adult contempt. "That's impossible," she snapped.

Once again Roberts had escaped detection; but this time through no fault of his own. Far from becoming warier as autumn made him vulnerable, he was growing more complacent than ever, having added a small stolen stove and a makeshift chimney to the comforts of his already too comfortable home.

Even so, the announcement in his October 21 newspaper that Witney and Duddy were to go on trial on November 14, and that the Attorney General himself would conduct the crown's case against them, should have set his antennae aquiver. Instead, taking comfort from a ludicrous report that he had been seen on the nine-thirty morning coach from London to Birmingham, dressed as a woman and wearing a gray wig, he carried on exactly as before.

Several nights later John Cunningham, the youngest of the Gypsy family, was prowling the woods, looking for game to shoot with his slingshot. When he saw a chink of light shining deep inside the undergrowth and then, creeping forward, heard the rattling of a spoon in an enamel cup, he returned to the family caravan and told his father that someone else was camping in Thorley Wood. A nomad himself, the arrival of yet another nomad was of little consequence to Cunningham senior.

The following day Chitty's team dealt with a further twenty-seven sightings of Roberts in London alone.

CHAPTER 10

ACCUSTOMED AS THEY were to the long, slow slog of almost all crime detection, Chitty and his team were not unduly depressed by their failure to track down Roberts. Witney and Duddy, though, were another matter. Not forever could they go on being remanded in the hope that soon Roberts would be captured and that the three of them could then stand trial at the Old Bailey together. Ten weeks having elapsed since Witney and Duddy were arrested, it had been decided they should go on trial without Roberts on November 14.

They were assigned two of the bar's most eminent lawyers for their defense against the crown, whose case was to be conducted by the Attorney General. And while they instructed their counsel, Chitty and his colleagues ensured that no detail of the case against them had been overlooked.

Thus Lawrence prepared his multitudinous exhibits, from photographs of the bodies to bullet fragments and cartridge cases; Slipper checked the statements that had demolished Witney's alibi on the one hand and would establish Duddy's guilt on the other; Coote made sure that every document required was readily available; and Chitty descended constantly upon his ever willing typist, Mavis Brown, saying, "Would you do this bit for me before you go home, Taff?"—or Blodwin—or Gwynneth—or even, occasionally, Mavis.

Meantime, mistaken but well-intentioned sightings of Roberts continued up and down the land, reaching and then surpassing the staggering total of seven thousand. And the Hertfordshire police arrested the Gypsy, John Cunningham, charging him with all the break-ins and thefts committed by Harry Roberts.

A twenty-one-year-old farmhand, Cunningham sported a pencil-thin mustache, looked more like a Hollywood Gypsy than a Romany, and seemed hopelessly lost in the face of a mass of circumstantial evidence. Indeed, he would almost certainly have been convicted had not a police dog handler decided to question his father; his father would almost certainly never have mentioned the chink of light and the clatter of an enamel mug his son had heard in the depths of Thorley Wood two nights earlier had he not been desperate to shift

to anyone else the blame for the crimes of which his son was being accused; and the police officer would almost certainly not have bothered reporting so unlikely a story had he not instantly thought of Harry Roberts, whose two colleagues in crime found themselves early the next morning heading in a police van for the Old Bailey.

"I'll never forget that Friday," Duddy began at once to babble to his escorting officer, disregarding every warning that even now anything he said could be taken down and used in evidence. "Never," he insisted. And then, quite gratuitously lying, added, "Roberts must still have the two thirty-eights and a Luger."

Convinced that all three guns were still safely buried, he was probably trying only to shift the blame for everything related to the Braybrook Street killings to others, although why he should have considered it more blameworthy for Roberts still to possess the guns than for Roberts and himself to have buried them is not easy to fathom. But Duddy's was a very woolly mind, and self-exculpation was ever his dominant instinct.

"You've got the impression Witney was forced to drive away after the shooting," he gabbled on, reverting to one of his favorite themes. "Well, like I told you, he was really the brains of the outfit. He even said we should go back to the garage, clean the van down, and then cut it up."

The idea of three men first cleaning a van and *then* cutting it up (into presumably unidentifiable pieces) is so ludicrous that one is forced to wonder why Duddy bothered to invent it. It can only be assumed that Duddy, whose policy it seems to have been to distort every truth in the hope that it would thereby be annulled, was attributing to Witney his revised version of the desire expressed by Roberts to destroy the Vanguard with fire.

"I appreciate the way you chaps have treated me," Duddy concluded, ingratiating as ever. "I'd expected to be treated real rough after what I done to your mates."

Brought up into the dock, Duddy and Witney were indicted on ten counts before a jury of nine men and three women, and pleaded not guilty to each charge. The Attorney General then opened the case against them, explaining lucidly—but at the law's pedestrian speed—the sequence of events that had left three policemen dead in Braybrook Street one sunny afternoon in August. "Members of the jury would be told," the Attorney General explained; "members of the jury would hear . . . members of the jury would see for themselves. . . ." No effort, it was clear, was going to be spared to convince members of the jury that what the crown maintained was true. From the well of the court, Chitty, Coote, Slipper, Hensley and Lawrence listened intently. To all these wordy allegations of the crown's they must shortly lend the substance of their own patiently amassed, precisely documented and impassively presented evidence.

The Attorney General waxed righteously eloquent while his supporting counsel sat attentively self-effacing. The jurors absorbed the catalogue of horror he recited, glancing from time to time at the two accused: the one, pale, skinny and thin of face and hair; the other, stocky, fresh-complexioned and shock-haired. The gallery was packed but silent. A corps of reporters scribbled furiously. The judge, alert as an eagle, made constant, careful notes. The day passed.

THE NIGHT PASSED too; and at first light the police dog handler, accompanied by other officers, cautiously approached the thicket in Thorley Wood wherein—according to Mr. Cunningham senior—a stranger lay concealed.

At first, though standing almost in front of it, they failed to notice Roberts' hideout. But a second look established that behind the apparently innocent mound and beneath the apparently natural foliage was a cunningly camouflaged tent.

Pouncing upon it—thrusting their way into it—they found a small cast-iron stove, a neatly stacked pile of faggots, a Primus stove, a sleeping bag, two army blankets, some cooking utensils, some kerosene and a bottle of denatured alcohol, two clean shirts and some handkerchiefs (all neatly folded), a stack of canned food, some fishing tackle, two transistor radios, a pile of newspapers (the last dated November 2), a holster (but no gun) and a bottle of whiskey.

They did not find Roberts, who had fled in advance of their onslaught and taken refuge in the adjacent wood, in a barn he had earlier stocked with a small Primus, a jar of denatured alcohol, a sleeping bag, a torch and a revolver. But his pursuers were not unbearably disappointed. A large force of policemen had already encircled the whole of Thorley Wood and begun to converge upon its center, examining every bush, tree and shrub as they did so.

AT THE OLD BAILEY THE jurors, counsel, accused, police officers and reporters rose as the judge entered Number One Court. The second day of the trial of Witney and Duddy had begun.

Its atmosphere, though, was markedly different from that of the day before, because not only had Chitty been advised in advance of the proposed investigation of a tent in Thorley Wood, but he had also requested a massive stakeout of the entire area. If the tent was Roberts', he would not escape again. In the well of the court, therefore, there was an air not only of intense concentration but of suppressed excitement also, as Chitty's team, with one ear on the morning's proceedings, kept the other cocked for any hint of a message from the world outside.

BY ELEVEN THIRTY that morning, though Thorley Wood was crawling with armed policemen, Roberts had still not been unearthed. So two of them—Sergeants Smith and Thorne—decided to take a look in the adjacent Nathan's Wood; and what immediately caught their attention there was an apparently disused barn.

Entering the barn, they found it stacked with bales of straw—between two of which, on the floor, Smith noticed a jar of fluid. Picking it up, he sniffed at it. Denatured alcohol. *Not* what one would expect to find in a barn. So he and Thorne pulled some of the bales aside, and revealed a sort of straw igloo. Inside which they observed a Primus, a torch, and a man in a sleeping bag. Smith prodded the sleeping bag, and a shaggy head emerged which, despite its long hair and ginger beard, Smith instantly recognized as the head of Harry Maurice Roberts.

"Don't shoot," Roberts begged. "Please, don't shoot." And crawling out of his hiding place, he promised, "I won't give you any trouble. I've had enough. I'm glad you've caught me."

MRS. PERRY WAS in the witness box when Coote became aware of the usher beside him.

"Yes?" he said.

"Will you tell Mr. Chitty he's wanted on the phone?" the usher asked him. "The Hertfordshire police want to speak to him."

As Mrs. Perry's cross-examination continued, Chitty left the court. Soon the Attorney General followed him out. They conferred, returned to the court, and left it a second time for further consultations. Those in court tried desperately to ignore these comings and goings, but already there were some who were prepared to swear that someone had been picked up near Basingstoke—someone thought to be Roberts—fingerprints were all that was needed to confirm it.

Chitty returned to the well of the court and picked up his briefcase. "They think it's Roberts," he told Coote. Then turned to Lawrence. "You ever looked after a big murder trial before?"

"No," said Lawrence.

"Well, you've got one now," Chitty told him, and left for the police station thirty miles away at Bishop's Stortford.

Diplomatically, the judge adjourned the trial for lunch.

REMOVING A FULLY loaded Luger from Roberts' belt, the police had handcuffed him, driven him to Bishop's Stortford Police Station, and given him a large, hot meal, which he ate with his usual appetite. They had also taken fingerprints from the holster and the whiskey bottle found in his tent.

Chitty arrived and looked long and hard at the man he had been hunting for ninety-six days. Then he telephoned the Old Bailey, where the trial had resumed. The Attorney General's assistant had just passed a note to Lawrence asking, "Is it Roberts?" and the judge was glancing toward him. Just as Mrs. Perry was saying, "I was very frightened he would come back and shoot me," Lawrence was given a message from Chitty.

"Yes, it's Roberts," he wrote, and sent the note to the Attorney General's assistants, who passed it to the Attorney General, who rose at once and said, "I think it right I should inform you, your lordship, that there is confirmation of information that the man Roberts has been arrested today.

"In the circumstances, I would respectfully request your lordship to adjourn this case until tomorrow morning so that the fullest consideration can be given to the situation which has now arisen."

Nodding, the judge declared that he was adjourning the trial for that day. "Come back at ten thirty tomorrow morning, when we *may* go on with the trial," he instructed the jury. "Or when," he warned, "it may be thought right to discharge you from giving a verdict and to make other arrangements."

As ROBERTS WAS DRIVEN into Shepherd's Bush Police Station, Chitty noticed that typists and other members of his team were hanging out of every first-floor window, that a huge crowd had returned (some of them, in fact, had been waiting for six hours), and that they were booing angrily.

It may have been the boos that made Roberts suddenly defiant; or it may have been his mother waiting there to speak to him, her face taut with misery because she thought he looked like a thin old man; but whatever it was, he refused to talk.

Accordingly, judging his man shrewdly, Chitty did the talking himself, dispassionately reciting the crimes Roberts had committed and advising him, without rancor, that he would forthwith be charged with three murders. As if anxious to talk, then, Roberts abruptly admitted that he had been living rough ever since he left Mrs. Perry on August 15, and that he had survived by stealing food and money.

"I'll tell you the truth," he continued. "I shot the two policemen that Friday afternoon, and it was Duddy [who] shot the driver. I thought they were going to find the guns, so I shot the officer who was talking to Witney, and then I shot the one who was talking to Duddy. I got out of the car when he was running back toward the police car and shot him. Duddy got out and went to the police car and shot the driver. Then we got back into the car and Jack drove to the arches at Vauxhall."

"And what about the guns?" Chitty asked.

"Well, you've got 'em all back now, haven't you?" Roberts replied.

"*Have* we?" asked Chitty, who had only the Luger found on Roberts in Nathan's Wood that morning. Clearly Roberts thought Duddy had surrendered the last gun; and Chitty had no intention of correcting that misunderstanding. "Well, have we?" he persisted.

"Me and Duddy buried them on Hampstead Heath on the Sunday," Roberts admitted, certain that Chitty knew it already. "I dug two of them up a couple of weeks later. The Luger's the one you got when I was caught. The thirty-eight you'll find in the barn."

So the first of the two missing guns was still in Nathan's Wood, Chitty thought; but where was the second?

"Can you remember where exactly you buried them?" he asked, poker-faced and casual.

"Yes."

"Could you *show* us?"—almost challenging him.

"Sure."

Thus did Chitty bluff an unwitting Roberts into disinterring the last exhibit he needed to make his case irresistible. As if to reward his prisoner, he allowed him to see his mother for two minutes.

"Did they hurt you, son?" Mrs. Roberts asked.

"No," he replied. "They've been the essence of kindness."

Next morning, Hensley and Roberts, accompanied by six detectives, traveled to Hampstead Heath in a police van. A second van, in which were two police dogs with their handlers, followed them.

Arrived at the heath, the ten men crunched their way across the frosted grass, the two dogs padding alongside and Roberts leading in his rubber boots.

Halting and pulling aside some bracken, Roberts said, "We buried them there," pointing. And seconds later Hensley was stooping to pick up Duddy's gun. Roberts was stunned.

"Well," Chitty commented happily, when told how shocked Roberts had looked to find himself outwitted, "you've got to play cunning with cunning."

Lawrence was no less happy. Tests had established that the Luger found in Roberts' possession in the barn at Nathan's Wood was the weapon that had killed Wombwell and Head; the Webley retrieved from Hampstead Heath was the weapon that had killed Fox; every single item of forensic evidence a prosecuting counsel could conceivably demand was now in hand; and his work was done.

Mrs. Roberts brought her son a clean shirt and underwear, which he put on after returning from Hampstead Heath and before being rushed to the West London Magistrates' Court to be charged with three murders.

"I have nothing to say today," he told the magistrate, who, having remanded him in custody, granted a voluntary bill of indictment, enabling the police to rush him directly to the Old Bailey.

"Put up Harry Maurice Roberts," ordered the clerk of the court, and straining to catch its first glimpse of a monster, the packed gallery saw a slim, tanned thirty-year-old wearing an open-necked shirt, jeans and rubber boots.

"Well, Harry Maurice Roberts," the judge advised him, "a bill has been signed against you providing for your trial in this court with two other men, Witney and Duddy, and that means the proceedings in the Magistrates' Court will be brought to an end and you will all be tried together."

Roberts nodded, and when asked did he want legal aid, replied, "Yes, please, sir."

Ten minutes later, handcuffed to a warder, he was on his way to prison, there to await trial with Duddy and Witney.

CHAPTER 11

"FOXHOLE OF A FASTIDIOUS FUGITIVE," had been one paper's caption to its photograph of Roberts' hideout. It gave British readers their first insight into the complexities of his character. A determined fugitive can rarely have behaved so inconsistently.

He had hidden like an animal in the forest, yet shopped in the village each day like an innocent housewife. His camp was so sited and constructed as to escape attention forever; yet once inside his tent he had regularly turned on his transistor radio and lit his lantern. Hell-bent on eluding capture, he had bought leather for a quite unnecessary holster from a tanner whose premises were directly opposite those of the local police. Devoid of any remorse for the crime he had committed, or for the families of the men he had murdered, he went to considerable pains, while awaiting trial, to write Witney a letter, the implication of which was that Witney had masterminded the crime itself.

Incapable of compassion, he evoked none; yet Mrs. Perry could not refrain from bringing to the attention of those who questioned her his kindness to her daughter and his readiness always to act as baby-sitter to Mrs. Howard's children. That news should have influenced public opinion of him one way or the other. Either it should have persuaded people that there was some good in the man after all, or it should have reminded them that Hitler and Himmler had been kind to children too. What made Roberts so enigmatic a figure was his effortless ability to alienate others so totally that no one at the time was, or ever has been since, inclined to attempt to understand him.

"I'm overjoyed he's been caught," declared a forthright Mavis Brown, who, in spite of her youth and cheerfulness, was normally unemotional about criminals. As is the case with most people who work with police officers, there was little in life that any longer shocked her. To join Chitty's team, for example, she had been detached from an inquiry into the vicious murder of a homosexual—about which she had effortlessly kept her mind open and impartial. Yet when Roberts was captured she had been overjoyed.

"He'd really made the life of the police difficult," she explained; and it was a good explanation of her attitude, because not only was it honest, it also reflected perfectly the attitude toward Roberts of society at large. He had ceased to be a monster and become instead an antisocial nonentity who had to be locked away. Harry Roberts, in short, was one of the earliest British manifestations of the disease of almost mindless nastiness that was soon to become a plague.

Between November 16 and December 6, when the three murderers finally went on trial, Chitty's massive team was virtually disbanded. Its work was done; its weapons had been returned (with not a bullet fired); Operation Shepherd had fulfilled its every purpose, and all that remained was the administrative task of filling in endless forms, keeping all the necessary exhibits conveniently at hand, and preparing the case papers for a trial against three defendants instead of two. That task was carried out by Chitty, Coote and Lawrence; their secretarial work was done by the smiling Mavis Brown.

It was not only the police who were discommoded by the termination of the November 15 trial and its retrial early in December. On November 29 the Attorney General had to appear for the crown at an inquiry into the huge landslide that had killed most of the children in the local school at Aberfan. His place as leader of the prosecution of Witney, Duddy and Roberts had therefore to be taken by the Solicitor General, for whom an immense amount of preparation was involved.

But the trial, when it finally took place, seemed almost a formality, so foregone was its conclusion. Duddy and Witney pleaded not guilty to all the charges, including that of triple murder. Roberts pleaded guilty to murdering Wombwell and Head, not guilty to murdering Fox, and guilty to possessing firearms in a public place. As the three men stood side by side in the dock, Witney looked defeated, Duddy looked nervous, and Roberts—to the fury of David Wombwell's mother, at least—looked positively cocky.

Once again Chitty and his colleagues sat in the well of the court; but this time Chitty had ordered Mavis Brown to attend the trial and take shorthand notes—which, for him, was a quicker and cheaper process than paying for court transcripts each day. As the trial opened, she found herself so overwhelmed by the pomp and ceremony of the occasion, and by its significance, that her hand shook too much to take legible shorthand.

The nervousness soon vanished, however, as the crown presented its just and irrefutable case. And when all the evidence for both crown and defense had been completed, and the judge's summing-up concluded, it took the jury only thirty minutes to find the three accused guilty of murdering three policemen and of carrying firearms with intent to commit an indictable offense.

Passing sentence, Mr. Justice Glyn Jones told the convicted men, "This is one of those cases in which the sentence of imprisonment for life may well be treated as meaning exactly what it says. Lest any Home Secretary in the future should be minded to consider your release on license, I have to make a recommendation. My recommendation is that you should *not* be released on license, any of the three of you, for a period of thirty years, to begin from today's date."

It's what they deserve, Mavis Brown told herself as the three were led away; and had she shouted it aloud there would have been none in that court, or even outside it, who would have contradicted her. Yet the sentence was not merely severe; it was the heaviest ever imposed in Britain.

"And the irony of it all," commented Slipper afterward, "was that if they'd just let themselves get arrested, instead of shooting it out, they'd probably have got off with six months apiece."

But, misled by his belief that the abolition of hanging meant (no matter what the crime) a life sentence at worst, which had meant—in some cases—no more than fifteen years in jail, Roberts had preferred to shoot, and Duddy and Witney had been too much under his influence even to dissociate themselves from his action, let alone to resist it.

Their tragedy, and that of Roberts (because to go to jail in 1966 with no prospect of release before 1996 *was* a tragedy), was that they had never bothered to read the small print of the act that had abolished capital punishment. Had they done so, they would have realized that also abolished was the crown's need to obtain a unanimous verdict against a defendant before he could be imprisoned; that majority verdicts would henceforth prevail; and that once a prisoner had been found guilty, the judge had the right to recommend that he be detained for a minimum period that might well *exceed* the maximum sentence of the past.

To this extent, the so-called license to kill that flowed from the abolition of capital punishment was a gross misnomer. Unfortunately, in 1966, men like Roberts were too woolly-minded to perceive it; and when, later, bitter experience taught them the truth, the expedient they adopted was even more frightful than the one adopted in Braybrook Street. It gradually became the practice of criminals to shoot not just to avoid immediate arrest but also to remove the risk of identification by any witness. The era of the cold-blooded gunman had come to Britain.

RELUCTANT TO LEAVE even the smallest loose thread untied, Chitty continued his investigation. Though Roberts and his two wretched colleagues had been put away, the man who had provided them with their guns was still at large.

Chitty had few leads to follow except that the man he wanted had probably fought for EOKA, possibly been an associate of a Cypriot known to have been an acquaintance of Roberts, and was almost certainly a habitué of a West End café that was shaped like a triangle.

Meager though this information was, Chitty followed it up with zest. Christmas came and he and his colleagues gave Mavis a dressing-table set, but displayed no such Yuletide goodwill toward the man who had become their chief suspect, Christos Costas, whom Chitty arrested in February 1967, charging him with having sold three pistols to Harry Roberts early in 1966.

Costas was given bail at the Magistrates' Court hearing, and committed for trial. At that trial—where he pleaded not guilty—Roberts was brought from prison to give evidence.

Looking maddeningly complacent (in spite of the three prison officers who guarded him throughout), Roberts blandly declared that he had never seen Costas before in his life. But the jury disbelieved him and found Costas guilty. Totally unabashed when he heard the news, Roberts, who was being bustled into a van for transport back to prison, nodded at nearby detectives and said, "See you when I'm sixty!"

If these were hardly the words of a man who believed passionately in his own innocence and the justness of his forthcoming appeal, Roberts' remarks were substantiated by the outcome of that appeal, which, like Witney's, was dismissed on May 31. With each of the three murderers in a different prison, and the dealer who had sold the murder weapons securely locked up as well, the case was virtually closed.

Still to be settled was the small but vital part played in this drama by the Gypsy, John Cunningham. All charges against him having been dropped, three hundred pounds was awarded to him for his information about a chink of light in Thorley Wood that had led to the arrest of Harry Roberts.

CHAPTER 12

"MERCILESS MEN," SAID a *Daily Telegraph* editorial, commenting on the sentences meted out to Roberts, Witney and Duddy, "deserve no mercy." But for each merciless man there was a guiltless parent, or wife, or child, and no one editorialized about them because the guiltlessness of convicted criminals' relatives is almost as distasteful a subject to the rest of society as the crimes of the guilty. After the Shepherd's Bush murders trial, those who were guiltless had, as usual, to suffer too.

Duddy's father, now retired, fell down some stairs only hours after his son had been sentenced. Rushed to the hospital, he died that night, following brain surgery.

Duddy himself had the decency to offer his wife a divorce, but she refused it, unable then to appreciate that by 1996 she and her husband, if both were still alive, would be elderly strangers. It was nevertheless eleven years before she could bring herself to end formally the marriage that Roberts had virtually destroyed ten days before the shootings in Braybrook Street.

Said Mrs. Witney after her husband's trial, "I love that man. I don't care how long they keep him, he is still my husband and I'll stand by him."

Said Mrs. Perry of Roberts, "I'll wait for him."

Said Roberts' self-righteous father, of the son he had never attempted either to support or even to contact, "I have no intention of visiting him in prison. I disown him."

Said Roberts' loyal and decent mother, on the other hand, "I suppose all I can say now is that I've got peace of mind."

Said Chitty to the commissioner of police, in a memorandum that was a tribute not only to the three men shot dead on August 12 but also to their guiltless families, "It is the wish of all officers of the murder team that they are *not* to be recommended for special recognition." Having duly expressed that wish, however, Chitty felt obliged to say of the many officers who had worked with him, "All were important links, regardless of the duty they performed, and all their efforts are worthy of the highest praise."

And to this day British policemen remember vividly the pointless murders of Head, Wombwell and Fox and the model investigation that brought their killers to justice. But the public—that same public that had responded to the killings with such spontaneous dismay and generosity—quickly forgot them. Which is strange, because the only other triple shooting of policemen in Britain has become part of the nation's history and London's folklore.

What, then, distinguished the Braybrook Street murders from the murders that preceded the historic siege, in 1911, of Sidney Street? Partly it was that the anarchists who gunned down the three policemen in 1911 had killed in a cause, and then had fought to the death, even though hopelessly surrounded by hundreds of policemen *and* by the Scots Guards—whom Winston Churchill, then the Home Secretary, had not hesitated to call out. And partly it was that, after the siege, life in Britain had resumed its normal tenor for three more golden years, and even then had surrendered it only to the insatiable demands of war on a global scale.

Of Braybrook Street's three killers, however, the first had been tamely led away in his carpet slippers, the second had been discovered cowering on a furtive fugitive's bed, and the third had emerged from his lair not with both guns blazing but with both hands held high, pleading, "Don't shoot. Please, don't shoot."

Mr. Jenkins, moreover, was a far from Churchillian Home Secretary. Which is not to say that anything he did or said at the time was less than admirable, but that everything he did was colorless and everything he said quite marvelously unmemorable.

More significant than any of the killers, however, or than the Home Secretary himself, should have been a magnificently efficient police investigation, a period of genuine national grief, and the public's heartwarming response to the mayor of Hammersmith's appeal for a quarter of a million pounds.

As to the first, though, the public soon forgot the details of Operation Shepherd because the good that policemen do is seldom remembered: it is their failures that are unforgettable. It is the murderer, not the detective who brings him to trial, whose waxwork likeness appears in Madame Tussaud's. All the world knows of Dr. Crippen, or the Boston Strangler, or Leopold and Loeb; but almost no one can recall the names of the policemen who tracked them down. Only in fiction are policemen the stars; in reality, the spotlight never leaves the killer.

As to the nation's grief when three of its policemen were shot, it was the grief of those who realized that *nothing* was sacred and no one safe—the grief of those ashamed at their relief that *they* were still safe—and, like all grief, it was transient.

Only the nation's response to the needs of Mrs. Wombwell, Mrs. Fox and Mrs. Head was long-lasting, being spontaneous, genuine and deep-seated. That the fund reached its target is evidence enough of that; that it attracted donations from all over the world, and that these donations included more than fifty-five thousand English coins, from sovereigns to threepenny bits, positively restores one's faith in human nature. Mrs. Wombwell, Mrs. Fox and Mrs. Head received £26,250 apiece; and the five fatherless children of Mrs. Wombwell and Mrs. Fox became the beneficiaries of a trust incorporating the balance of the money raised.

Happily, though, the matter did not end there. At the beginning of 1967 a police dependents' fund was launched—its target a million pounds—its objective to ensure that never again would the wife or children of an officer killed or permanently incapacitated while on duty be left to survive on a scandalously inadequate pension.

"At least," says Detective Constable Dent grimly, "the killing of Chris Head, David Wombwell and Geoff Fox broke through the inertia that'd always stifled any move to organize proper compensation or insurance for police officers' families. The police dependents' fund was a specific outcome of the public's reaction to those three killings."

And what of the three killers? Forgotten men, each in a different prison, they serve out their long sentences. About Witney and Duddy there is nothing of interest to report. Roberts still manages both to perplex and repel. He has become interested in gardening, particularly in roses.

"But," reports his mother, "he's brazen as brass still. He's got no sorrow."

For years before he got into trouble, though, she had known that. A mother's boy who would punch her in the mouth if she crossed him, steal from her handbag if she turned her back on him, and remain dependent upon her until Mother Army took her place, he always had been amoral. Later, when his wife had failed to mother him, his marriage had failed; and when Mrs. Perry had successfully mothered him, he had become almost human—but never, in the smallest degree, moral. Nor even immoral. Simply and incorrigibly amoral. So he had shot two policemen dead, yet had no sorrow. It was something his mother had to accept.

She had difficulty accepting one thing about her son, however. "It's a mystery to me why he didn't turn the gun on himself," she mused; and then faced up to the truth about the boy who once had said that he wanted to be a policeman. "I suppose it's because he was a coward. But I suppose, too, I'll still visit him in jail. After all"— refusing to deny him—"I *am* his mother."

THE SIEGE OF
SIDNEY STREET

THE
SIEGE OF
SIDNEY STREET
by
Julian Symons

They were anarchists and jewelry thieves, and the City Police wanted to know exactly what they were up to in the shabby little East End house at Exchange Buildings in London that blustery December evening of 1910. Characteristically, the police chose to meet the problem directly; they marched up to the front door and demanded to know what was going on inside. As a result, three officers were gunned down, and the thieves fled. Several weeks later they were traced to a nearby tenement at 100 Sidney Street.

Police cordons were quickly drawn around the building, but the hunted men trapped inside met them with such a barrage of fire that marksmen from the nearby Tower of London had to be called in. Despite icy rain and the peril of stray shots, crowds thronged the adjoining rooftops and streets. Shortly, high government officials were rushing to the scene, including the then Home Secretary, Mr. Winston Churchill. Not until the tenement-turned-fortress went up in flames and the firefighters were called in did the siege reach its deadly climax.

Julian Symons, the internationally acclaimed crime writer and author of such thrillers as *The Narrowing Circle* and *The Color of Murder*, re-creates the harrowing siege of Sidney Street through the very eyes of those who lived through the ordeal.

PART ONE: THE MURDERS
MACNAGHTEN

First of all I'll put down a few facts as to what this book is about, then say something about how Melville Macnaghten, ex-policeman, came to turn author. I'm not a practiced hand as a writer, but I suppose the best way to go into authorship is head-on—like taking a plunge into icy water.

My subject is the Siege of Sidney Street, which took place in January 1911. Nothing else like it has ever occurred in British criminal history, and thank goodness for that. Three policemen were killed and others were wounded in the astonishing events that ended at the blazing house in Sidney Street, in London's East End. Mr. Winston Churchill, the Home Secretary, was involved; the Scots Guards were called in to help the police. And a veil of mystery still hangs over some of the participants. Or it has until now. Nine years have passed—I am writing this in 1920—and it is time to draw the veil aside.

Now about myself. I don't want to bore you with a life history. I'll only say that at the time of the siege I'd been chief constable of Scotland Yard's Criminal Investigation Department (CID) for several years. I think it would be generally agreed that I made a success of the job. This was partly because of my memory for names and faces. I took pride in knowing the names, the careers and the qualifications of all the seven hundred men who worked under me. The men liked that. Then I've always been an adventurous sort of fellow, and they liked that too.

I used often to go down to the East End at night. Not in disguise, none of that Sherlock Holmes stuff for me. On the contrary, I took pleasure in wearing my usual clothes, an overcoat with an astrakhan collar and a well-brushed bowler. I took care also always to carry my cane and gloves. These served as a sort of badge of identity. I once went into a club where a knife fight between two gangs was just starting. They stopped, in pure astonishment, I daresay, when I walked in the door. These things are remembered.

I retired in 1913, when His Majesty was pleased to tap my shoulders with his sword, so that I became Sir Melville. But retirement hung heavy on my hands, and I found myself thinking more and more often about the Sidney Street case, which had been the most remarkable affair during my time at the Yard. I was still in touch with some of the principal participants, and it struck me that if I could get them to tell their stories of what happened in their own words, filling up the gaps in between from my personal knowledge, this should make an exciting book. It took quite a time to gather the material together, but I managed to do it in the end. I even persuaded Winston Churchill to write an account of the part he played in the siege. The result is this book.

And that's enough of my prelude. Now let's get to the action.

THIS IS A STORY about anarchists in London—I mean violent anarchists, the sort who want to blow up everything, not just cranks who sit around talking about how wonderful the world would be if everybody shared their worldly goods. I regard men and women of this kind as mere cranks, although I have noticed that the people who are always talking about sharing all worldly goods are those who have none of their own to share. However, they're harmless enough.

The people I mean are far from harmless. In the past twenty years Britain has been inundated with the scum of other countries. Nihilists from Russia, advanced socialists from Germany, communists from France and so on. It is people of this kind that I am talking about. Now, let me make it clear that I don't object to these people professing their ridiculous creeds and dreaming of the day when their ideas will overthrow the British Empire. It is when they rob and murder to gain their ends—or to get money for themselves, as they do quite often—that I say the foot of authority should be stamped firmly down, squashing them like vermin. Wiser men than

I have decided that Britain shall welcome these people. Very well, then. Let them come here and work, if they can find work to do. And let them keep the law. If they do so, neither we nor they have anything to worry about. Some of them, however, have no intention of keeping the law.

A few years ago a Russian was held by the customs at Dover because he had forty-seven automatic pistols in his luggage. And he was allowed to bring them in! When such things happen, it may seem ridiculous that the English police are armed with nothing but truncheons. Yet this is our custom, and I am in favor of it.

Well, this is a story about a gang of these anarchists or social revolutionaries or whatever they call themselves, about the people they killed and wounded and the trouble they caused. We naturally keep an eye on their activities, by means which will be described in detail a little later on.

I used to go down and pay an occasional visit myself to their headquarters, the Anarchist Club, in the heart of Whitechapel. This seemed a cheerful enough place, a meeting ground where all these foreigners could drink their lemon tea, play endless games of chess, and gabble away to each other. I can't say that any of them were impolite to me, and I was prepared to accept the place as a safety valve. After all, many of them were living four, six or eight to a room, and I daresay they needed a little relaxation. I never saw a knife drawn in the Anarchist Club, or even a fight take place there, as I did in many an East End pub. But the fact remains that all of the Sidney Street figures used the club for their plotting.

This particular plot consisted of an attempt to burgle a jeweler in Houndsditch. The people involved rented a couple of small empty houses in Exchange Buildings, a cul-de-sac just nearby; they bought a cylinder of oxygen and rubber tubing, and they planned to drive right through to the jeweler's safe, cut it open, and take the contents. These men, and some of their women, installed themselves in the houses they had rented and began the work of knocking down walls. Every one of these villains, these "idealists," was armed to the teeth with either Mauser or Dreyse pistols. Their names will emerge later on, but the leader of the raid was a man who called himself George Gardstein. He had half a dozen other names, and he was an old hand at robbery. Like most of the others, he was wanted by the police, in this case the German police. Gardstein was a Lett, and a member of some sort of anarchist group in his own country.

And now after this brief introduction I pass on the narrative to a man who was there, and who has put down the events of that evening in his own words.

THE SERGEANT'S STORY

My NAME is Arthur Bryant, and in 1910 I held the rank of sergeant in the City of London Police.

The night of December 16, 1910, was windy and unusually dark. I was on duty at Bishopsgate Police Station, and we weren't expecting a busy night because most of the people living round about were Jews, and it was the eve of the Jewish sabbath, so that the streets were deserted. Little we knew.

It was just after eleven o'clock that young Walter Piper came into the station all out of breath, and telling some tale about heavy drilling and sawing going on. Young Walter was only a probationer, and he was stammering in his excitement. I tried to soothe him down, asking exactly what he'd heard and where it was. "Exchange Buildings," he said. "It's a little street off Houndsditch."

"I know Exchange Buildings. And what did you hear?"

"A lot of hammering and sawing. I tell you, Sergeant, they're cutting through the brickwork in a house there, so that they can get through to the jeweler's in Houndsditch. I tell you I heard them."

"Did you actually see anything suspicious?"

"No, but you can hear the hammering. There's another man heard it, came and told me. You've got to come now. Sarn't Bentley's down there, he sent me back for you."

"All right, son, no need for all the excitement. If Bob Bentley's down there, he won't let 'em get away."

A couple of minutes later I was on my way down to Exchange Buildings with Sergeant Tucker, whom we all called Daddy, and another constable. And Walter, still excited. It's a pity he was so excited, because there was one bit of information that he forgot to give me or Bob Bentley or anybody. It was the fact that he'd called at Exchange Buildings and exchanged a few words with a man there. This meant that the gang were on their guard. Would it have made any difference if we'd known that? Perhaps not. But then again, it might have saved three lives.

Exchange Buildings is a cul-de-sac leading off Houndsditch, and on the corner of it I met Bob Bentley. He pointed to a house on the right. "That's the one." It was one of those houses with a folding shop front, and its windows were covered with green shutters, though you could see a bit of gaslight shining through. It was dark down there in the cul-de-sac, just one lamp flickering in the wind.

"What do you think?"

"No doubt something's going on. I've been down the next-door cellar, heard the knocking. We'll see what's what in a minute."

Then he told me where he was putting men, one by the jeweler's shop in Houndsditch, one on the corner where we were standing, one farther up Houndsditch by a possible way out to Cutler Street. Everything covered. Bob was a real professional. The rest of us would go along to Exchange Buildings, to the house with the green shutters, and if necessary force our way in.

There were seven of us—Bob Bentley, Daddy Tucker and I, who were all sergeants, and four constables, two of them in plain clothes. Too many? Perhaps, though it didn't seem like that at the time. We didn't all bunch together, but stood waiting in the cul-de-sac, ready to stop anybody trying to get out. Would it have been better to send in the plainclothes constables first? I doubt very much if it would have made any difference, because Piper had already put them on the alert.

It was just about eleven thirty p.m. when Bob knocked on the door, a proper policeman's knock, the kind you can't fail to hear. I noticed one or two curtains raised in the house opposite.

The door was opened.

I was just behind Bob, and so you might think I must have got a good view of the man who stood there, but I didn't. It was very dark inside, although you could see a little steep narrow staircase straight ahead.

I could see a room on the right with a big fire burning in it. There were a few shadows flickering on the walls through the open door and I thought, Well, that's cozy.

But the man was just a dark mass with a light behind him. I know

now that it was Gardstein, their leader. Bob asked him a couple of questions, was somebody working inside, who was making all the racket, that sort of thing, and he just didn't answer, so Bob asked if there was anybody in the house who could speak English. The man just stared, then nodded, pushed the door to and disappeared.

The sound of hammering had stopped. Was the man going to try to do a bunk out of the back? Somebody behind me called out, "Tell 'em we'll break down the door if they don't open up." They must have heard it inside. I said to Bob that we should go in and he should open the door. He did so. We were in a tiny lobby, and I pushed open the door of the room on the right.

Cups and saucers on the table, three of them, but nobody there. Where were they? Hammering down below? Or upstairs? There was total silence. Then I realized that in the silence a man was standing on the stairs. We couldn't see his face, just his legs. When Bob asked questions he answered them, but only in monosyllables, speaking with a strong accent.

I shall write first what was said. They were the last words I heard Bob Bentley speak.

"Is anybody working here?"

"No."

"Anyone in the back?"

"No."

"Can I have a look in the back?"

"Yes."

"Show us the way."

"In there."

He pointed to the room with the fire, and we stepped inside. I had time to see a door leading out to the back, and then the room appeared to explode. It was filled with noise, and it seemed to be filled with light. A man came through the back door, and he came through firing. I heard Bob cry out and clutch his shoulder, and then there was another shot that seemed to blow him right out of the room. I could hear more shots being fired from the direction of the stairs.

I don't mind admitting now, looking back on it, that I was dazed and didn't really know what I was doing. We come up against plenty of rough customers in the East End, and I've tackled some with pistols, but generally they use them only if they have to, because you get topped for murder. Here we were just making what was almost a routine inquiry about something suspicious, and the suspects were shooting us down without hesitation, really shooting to kill. I never saw anything like it before, and I hope I never do again.

I saw the man who had shot Bob point the pistol at me, and I wish I could say that I tackled him, but that wouldn't be exactly true; I put out my hands to try to get hold of his pistol, then there was a flash and another flash. Oddly enough, I didn't hear the noise of the shots, but the room was full of blue smoke. Something had happened to my left arm so that I couldn't lift it, and I found it rather hard to breathe, but I wasn't aware of any pain. I looked down at my arm and saw blood, but it never occurred to me that this was a result of the firing. In fact, I'd been shot twice, in the arm and in the chest.

I staggered out of the room and toward the front door. I was aware of firing from the stairs, and as I went out of the house I stumbled over something. I looked down and saw that it was Bob's body. At the same time one of the constables, Woodhams, was saying something to me and tugging away at the body.

Even in my dazed state I realized what he was trying to do and bent down to help him. Then Woodhams' mouth opened suddenly and he gave a high-pitched wail, fell backward, and his helmet dropped off, showing his ginger hair. I turned around and saw a hand—nothing more, just a hand—poked out from the house door holding a pistol. It wasn't fired in my direction but toward the entrance of the cul-de-sac opening out to Houndsditch, where Daddy Tucker and Constable Strongman were moving up toward the house. Looking for a doorway to give a bit of protection, they stepped back. Then Tucker turned around, staggered out into the road and up toward Houndsditch, and fell down.

I've said I was in a daze, but sometimes you see things more clearly in that sort of state, the way you do in a dream. I'd walked away, not knowing what I was doing, and collapsed against a wall. My legs just didn't have the strength to carry me, but my head seemed quite clear, and I was able to see and take in, although purely as a spectator—I couldn't move—the last scene.

The pistol that had been pointed from the doorway became an arm, and the arm turned into a body, that of a short, slim man neatly dressed in dark clothes, dark-haired and pale-faced. This—again, I know it now—was Gardstein. He was followed by two other men, whose faces I did not see so clearly, although one of them, with rather hunched shoulders and a ratlike face, I recognized later from photographs as the bank robber Fritz Svaars. Behind them there came a sight I could hardly believe. It was a woman. I could not see her face in the dim light, but she was very decently dressed. She wore a fur toque on her head and—the thing that seemed to me really dreamlike and unbelievable—she carried a large muff.

The four ran toward the entrance which would get them out of Exchange Buildings, into Houndsditch and then through to back alleys. They fired as they went. And now came the truly heroic act of the evening. Constable Choat, who'd been up at the Houndsditch end of the alley, tackled Gardstein. He caught him by the wrist and tried to get hold of his gun. It was the bravest thing I ever saw or expect to see, because it was not just Gardstein he had to contend with but the two others with him, both of whom had pistols or revolvers. Choat was a very big man, four inches over six feet and strong as a bull, but what use is strength against bullets? It was over in seconds. Gardstein shot him, and then the others came up and shot him too—in the back. He fell, but he didn't let go of Gardstein, and they tried to force Choat to let go. Gardstein was shot too, by one of his friends. We'd have been happy to shoot him, but we had no weapons.

That is all I can say about what happened on the night of December 16, 1910, in Exchange Buildings. After the sight of that last scene, which is fixed in my memory like a photograph, my mind went blank, and I have lost all recollection of what followed. I am told that I wandered around holding my arm and calling for a doctor to look after me and attend to Bob Bentley and the rest, but I remember nothing of that. Indeed, I recall nothing more until I awoke in hospital, and then learned I had been shot twice, in the arm and chest.

I asked also about my comrades, and because of my condition was given evasive answers. It was not until several days later that I learned the terrible truth. Bob Bentley was taken to hospital. He had been shot twice, in the shoulder and the neck, and one of the shots had severed his spinal cord. He died on the following morning. Daddy Tucker had been killed outright. The gallant Constable Choat had been shot eight times. He was taken to the London Hospital, but died within a couple of hours of his arrival.

I have put all this down at Sir Melville Macnaghten's request, and he has asked me to add a note about the other two wounded policemen, Constable Woodhams and myself. Ernie Woodhams was permanently crippled by the shot that shattered his lungs, and I was not able to take up police duties again because of the bullet in my chest, which could not be removed. We were both promoted, Woodhams to sergeant and I to subinspector, and pensioned accordingly, at a higher rate than would have applied to us as constable and sergeant. Later the people of the district, many of them very decent friendly folk, clubbed together and bought me a gold watch.

Sir Melville has also asked me to state my conclusions or opinions. I have one, and it is simply this, that the police should have arms and be trained to use them. Had we been armed, the three policemen killed might be alive today, and Woodhams might not be a cripple nor I an invalid.

MACNAGHTEN

THE NEWS OF THIS outrage infuriated every policeman in London and horrified the general public. The funeral service for the three dead men took place at St. Paul's Cathedral, and it was a deeply impressive scene. The policemen's helmets were placed on their coffins, and Bentley's had a hole in it where a bullet had passed through. All the important dignitaries of the City of London attended the service, including the lord mayor, the sheriffs and the alderman in their scarlet gowns. There was a special police contingent.

In the meantime, the three men and one woman seen by Bryant had got away.

We found a witness who had seen them going down one of the narrow passages at the back of Houndsditch, and had been threatened in broken English by the two who were carrying revolvers and half dragging the third, but after that nobody had seen them—or was prepared to admit seeing them.

That is less surprising than it may sound, for the East End is full of bolt-holes. It is also full of petty criminals, who want nothing to

CITY OF LONDON POLICE.

MURDER OF POLICE OFFICERS.

£500 REWARD

WHEREAS Sergeants Charles Tucker and Robert Bentley, and Constable Walter Charles Choat, of the City of London Police, were murdered in Exchange Buildings, in the said City, at 11.30 p.m., on the 16th December, 1910, by a man who is now dead, and other persons now wanted, whose descriptions are given below, and who were also concerned with the deceased Murderer in attempting to feloniously break and enter a Jeweller's shop, and killed the Officers to prevent arrest.

PORTRAIT AND DESCRIPTION OF THE DEAD MURDERER.

Name said to be GEORGE GARDSTEIN, alias POOLKA MILOWITZ.

Both may be incorrect.

DESCRIPTION:

Age about 24, height 5ft. 9 in., complexion pale, hair brown, slight dark moustache worn slightly up at ends, good physique.

DESCRIPTION OF THE PERSONS WANTED.

FIRST. A man named FRITZ SVARRS, lately residing at 59, Grove Street, Commercial Road, London, E., age about 24 or 25, height 5 feet 8 or 9 inches, complexion sallow, hair fair, medium moustache turned up at ends, lighter in colour than hair of head, eyes grey, nose rather small, slightly turned up, chin a little upraised, has a few small pimples on face, cheek-bones prominent, shoulders square, but bend slightly forward; dress brown tweed suit, thin light stripes, dark melton overcoat (velvet collar, nearly new), usually wears a grey Irish tweed cap (red stripes), but has been sometimes seen wearing a trilby hat; a Locksmith; native of Libau, Russia.

SECOND. A man known as "PETER THE PAINTER," also lately residing at 59, Grove Street, Commercial Road, London, E., age 28 to 30, height 5 feet 9 or 10 inches, complexion sallow, hair and medium moustache black, clear skin, eyes dark, medium build, reserved manner; dress brown tweed suit (broad dark stripes), black overcoat (velvet collar, rather old), black hard felt hat, black lace boots, rather shabby, believed to be a native of Russia. Both are Anarchists.

THIRD. A woman, age 26 to 30, height 5 feet 4 inches, slim build, fairly full breasts, complexion medium, face somewhat drawn, eyes blue, hair brown; dress dark three-quarter jacket and skirt, white blouse, large black hat, trimmed black silk), light-coloured shoes.

The above reward of £500 will be paid by the Commissioner of Police for the City of London to any person who shall give such information as shall lead to the arrest of these persons, or in proportion to the number of such persons who are arrested.

Information to be given to the City Police Office, 26, Old Jewry, London, E.C., or at any Police Station.

City Police Office,
26, Old Jewry, London, E.C.
22nd December, 1910.

J. W. NOTT BOWER,
Commissioner of Police.

The Gardstein poster. The subject was already dead when the picture was taken. His eyelids had to be opened to produce a lifelike expression.

Peter the Painter, one of the anarchists. A smartly dressed occasional house painter known for his violent activity.

do with the police. And to a certain extent, the investigation was affected by the fact that the crimes had been committed in an area just within the jurisdiction of the City of London Police.

The City Police are a body quite separate from the Metropolitan Police, with their own headquarters and their own offices. Somebody once said ironically that if a corpse were found with the head in one area and the body in another, you would have to carry out two quite separate investigations. The City Police are proud of their separate force and I say nothing against them, except that their confounded independence does make cooperation difficult at times. But there, I suppose that is tied up with what we are all proud of, the independence of the English character.

Mr. Winston Churchill, then Home Secretary, played a key role.

Anyway, as a consequence of this, we at the Met didn't have much to do with the initial part of the investigation. It was the City Police who looked at the two little houses in Exchange Buildings where the gang had been living for a day or two, and found the place in the backyard where they'd begun to break into the jeweler's shop, the operation that had made all the noise. They found all sorts of tools, the oxygen cylinder and so on, but nothing that told them who the robbers were. It just so happened that on this point we knew a little bit more than they did.

On the morning after the outrage, I took a stroll down the corridor outside my room in Scotland Yard and across a courtyard and had a chat with Superintendent Patrick Quinn of Special Branch. I could have called him up on the telephone, or sent him a memorandum asking whether he could help us, but I will admit to an old-fashioned liking for talking to a man face to face. Some people might say that my five-minute walk to see Pat Quinn was a waste of time. I can only say that I don't agree. Besides, I always liked talking to Pat Quinn.

Pat was an Irishman with twinkling eyes and a neat little goatee, and he had been with Special Branch for more than a quarter of a century, since it was founded as the Special Irish Branch, soon after the Phoenix Park murders. Since then, the Irish had been dropped, and the Special Branch was concerned much more with the spies, most of them Germans, who had become increasingly active in Britain. It was important to keep tabs on them all, and Pat had his agents among the German community, and also among the Blow-'em-up Brigade, as I called our friends the anarchists.

When I went into Pat's office, he looked at me with his head a little on one side, which was a way he had, and just the hint of a smile.

He said, before I could speak, "The answer is yes. Or probably yes."

"But you don't know the question."

"I think I do. Can I tell you anything about the people responsible for *this?*" He tapped *The Times,* which was open to the page with its heading: ANARCHIST OUTRAGE IN WHITECHAPEL. "One of my little pigeons was in their company not more than forty-eight hours ago. He heard their plans, or some of them." Pat always called his agents his pigeons. He went on before I could speak. "I know what you're going to say. If he heard their plans, why didn't we stop them? Two reasons. First, he didn't know the details. And second, what concerns the Special Branch is treason, not robbery. It's no use looking down your nose at me, you know it's true."

If I did look disapproving, the look reflected my feelings. "I should have thought the least your man could have done would have been to report the facts to you."

"Which he did."

I stared hard at him. "If you had passed on the information to me, three men might be alive today."

"If I'd thought for a moment that something like this would happen, of course I would have. But Nikolai didn't know any details, and you must remember that I hear dozens of these stories. Most of them come to nothing. If you'd pulled in this little lot, Nikolai would have been no use to us anymore. And he had to be protected. If they'd got to know he was informing—" He drew a finger across his throat and made a gurgling noise. Quinn is a good fellow, but there is something deplorably crude about him.

"Nikolai. Another Russian."

"Did you think you could put an Englishman into a gang like that?" What he said was perfectly true, of course, but I am old-fashioned enough to find something distasteful about the employment of a foreigner in this way. "Young Nikolai's been here only three months. He plays the balalaika. That's how he managed to get in with them. He's teaching one of them to play the mandolin." He threw back his head in a great roar of laughter, then wiped his eyes with a colored pocket-handkerchief.

What Nikolai Tomacoff had to say proved important in identifying the men and woman involved, and since the object of this narrative is to tell the story as far as possible in the words of the chief participants, I asked him to set down for me just how he became acquainted with the gang and what they were like. He had learned to speak a little English but not to write it, and what follows is translated from the Russian. I may say that I had to pay him for what he wrote, and that my two meetings with him convinced me that he was an unprincipled scoundrel. He continued to work for the Special Branch as an informant for some time after the events described here. I did not envy Quinn in having to use such people as his tools.

In order that I should not involve myself too much in this part of the narrative—you will have enough of me at Sidney Street, later—I have followed Nikolai Tomacoff's narrative with those of two other people concerned. The first is Nina Vassilleva, the lady wearing the toque and carrying the muff, and the second Dr. Scanlon, who was called to attend a sick man early on the morning of December 17.

THE BALALAIKA PLAYER'S STORY

MY NAME IS Nikolai Tomacoff, and I am a Russian. I left St. Petersburg in August 1910, when I was twenty-one years old, to come to England. I had been told that it would be easy to make money in England, for somebody who plays the balalaika as well as I do. In St. Petersburg I lived with three maiden aunts, which was very boring. Ivan Lebeder, my friend with whom I came here, is a Lithuanian, and he belongs to some revolutionary group who call themselves Liesma, which means the Flame. He talks to me about this all the time, how easy it is to make money in England by robbing banks and shops, because the English police are so stupid. I do not listen much to Ivan, because I am not a revolutionary and I find all this very boring. All I wish to do is to play the balalaika, and make some money, and meet English girls.

But this does not happen. England is not at all like what they have told me. We Russians are all crowded together, along with Lithuanians and Latvians and Poles, in the East End of London. Many of them are Jews, and I do not particularly like the Jews. And the places where we had to live! I shared one room in a lodging house with Ivan, and there were eleven other people living in the same small house. We all had to wash at one tap, and to use the same privy in the yard outside. And we were lucky, for in some lodging houses there were twenty or more people sharing four rooms. This part of the city was badly lit, full of narrow, twisting alleys, and filth lay about in the streets. I did not meet any English girls, and I did not make much money.

There were six of us who formed a group to play and sing. We called ourselves the Slavonics, and we got plenty of engagements to play at parties and weddings and in clubs. But money? For an evening's work we might get ten shillings, which was less than two shillings each. It was not that our patrons were mean, simply that they had very little more money than we had. I had been much better off in St. Petersburg, although in St. Petersburg there had been my maiden aunts. Anything was better than living with my aunts!

When I had a little money I used to go to one of the local pubs. Generally the Three Nuns in Aldgate, where the beer was strong, and in the middle of the day they put free food—sausages and bread and cheese—on the counter. One day a man bought me a drink, a man with a bowler hat which he wore tipped down low, almost over his eyes. That is the way most respectable Englishmen wear their bowler hats. We got into conversation, and he said that he might have a job I could do for him occasionally. He laughed a lot and made it all seem like a joke, so I could not tell if he meant what he said. We met again that evening in another pub, in Tottenham Court Road, outside the East End—I lost my way in getting there—and he told me what he wanted. He had seen me playing the balalaika in the Anarchist Club (I was usually paid there in lemon tea, not money), and he knew of my friendship with Ivan and that I mixed with others of the same group. He wanted me to meet him each week and tell him anything I heard about what they were doing and planning. He put down a gold sovereign on the table between us and said it would belong to me if I was prepared to work with him.

I agreed. I had no hesitation about it. There are people who say that I betrayed some cause or another, but what do they mean? I never pretended to have any sympathy with these people who called themselves revolutionaries but were really no better than criminals. I liked my British friend, Mr. Quinn, much better. For one thing he was always laughing, while most of them were as solemn as tombstones. I looked forward to our meetings every week. Mr. Quinn read Russian but spoke it only a little, and my English at that time was not good, so we talked in French. When he was pleased he would give me ten shillings, or at other times five, and if I had no valuable news he paid only my fare from Whitechapel. Sometimes we would go out together for a shilling dinner of beef and something called Yorkshire pudding, which he said was very English. I suppose Mr. Quinn was some kind of a policeman, like our czarist secret police, the Okhrana. But he was a nice man and I liked him very much. There is nothing nice about the Okhrana.

I have been asked to tell what I know about the plans for the robbery on Friday, December 16, which ended with the deaths of three policemen. On that morning I gave a mandolin lesson to Fritz Svaars. He was a funny fellow, Fritz, or perhaps I should say he was two people. For the one part, he was what he called a revolutionary and I would call a robber. He came from Riga and was full of stories about the things he had done there, the shops he had broken into, the ambush he had shot his way out of, killing a policeman and a shop owner while getting away, and so on. A very fierce character he made himself sound, although he didn't look it. But Fritz was also a gentle and rather sentimental person, who was very fond of dressing up and acting. The Anarchist Club was putting on a Christmas play— one with a socialist moral, needless to say—and Fritz had a part in it. He also had to play the mandolin, and that was why I had been giving him lessons. Sometimes we practiced at the Anarchist Club, sometimes at the rooms in Grove Street which Fritz shared with friends and with his mistress, a miserable sniveling Russian girl named Luba Milstein.

Fritz was a boastful talker, and for a week or more he had been saying that in a few days he and his friends would be rich. On this Friday morning he was very excited. "You know where I was yesterday, what I was doing? I was with Malatesta. You must have heard of him."

Of course I had. Malatesta was the famous Italian anarchist who had been living in England now for some years. "Malatesta works now in his own electrical shop, isn't that so? He doesn't mix with politics."

"Did I say this was political? He sold me a cylinder of oxygen. I told him it was for a magic-lantern show." Fritz twisted his mustache triumphantly. "Of course I did not give him my name. And I did not collect the cylinder myself. I sent a boy to collect it. One must be careful in everything, Koba says."

"Who is Koba?"

"He is a very important man."

"And what do you want the oxygen cylinder for?"

"What do you think?" Fritz plucked at the mandolin. He was a good pupil.

For a burglary, I thought, for blowing up something, or opening a safe. But I did not say so. I said nothing.

"Something big is happening, my friend. Important people are here, people like Koba. We are going to be rich."

"You mean the cause is going to be rich?"

"It is the same thing. We social revolutionaries do not make such bourgeois distinctions. We are the cause. If we starve, the cause starves too. You don't believe me."

Partly because I really found it hard to believe Fritz's boasts, partly to try to learn more, I said, "You say big things, Fritz, but what do you do? Learn the mandolin so that you can be in the Christmas play."

He jumped up and almost threw the mandolin at me. "Look," he shouted. "You look here." He took from his trousers a Browning revolver and waved it at me.

"You had better put that away." They are used to shouting and odd behavior in the Anarchist Club, but people were looking at us.

Fritz muttered angrily, but he tucked away the revolver again in his trousers.

"Are you going to hold up a bank?"

"Not a bank." He said sulkily, "Perhaps nothing at all—I show you this only because you laugh at me, you think I am not serious. Perhaps you would like to join us, eh? Or do you not have the courage? Or don't you need money to live on, like other people?"

"I need the money. I don't like taking risks."

"Life, my friend, is taking risks." Fritz was mercurial. He had recovered his spirits. "We have a little meeting this afternoon. If you like to come, we will perhaps tell you what is happening. Or perhaps not. It is not a matter for me."

When I asked him who decided that, he shrugged.

That afternoon I went around to 59 Grove Street. It was a wretched little place, but no worse than the house I lived in—indeed, a little better, because fewer people lived in it. There were three rooms, one on the ground floor and two on the first, and everything was dirty, as it always is in such houses. At the back on the ground floor there was a copper tub for washing clothes, and outside was a yard with a privy. The staircase leading up to the first floor had no handrail, and the thirteen stairs were very steep. In the dark it would have been easy to pitch down them. I walked carefully up those thirteen stairs.

When I was at the top, Luba—Luba Milstein—came out and stood staring at me. "What do you want?" She was a heavy, dull-looking girl, and I could not imagine what Fritz saw in her. He had told me once that she knew nothing about the ways in which they got money, she was not one of *them*. I asked why he had taken her as mistress, and he gave one of his attractive grins. "Because she loves me. She does whatever I tell her." Looking at Luba, I could believe this was true.

I tapped the mandolin and said I was coming to give Fritz another lesson, and that there were only nine days to Christmas.

"Not now," she said, and pointed to the back room. "They are all in there." I could hear a murmur of voices. "You cannot go in there."

I smiled at her and said they were expecting me. She watched with her heavy cowlike gaze as I opened the door, but made no attempt to stop me.

There were seven people in the little room, and I had met six of them before. One was George Gardstein, who seemed to be their leader, and who had a dozen other names as well—Gardstein, Morin and Mourrewitz were three that I had heard. He was a small, neat man, elegant and almost feminine in his movements, with delicate hands and feet. It was easy to imagine him an aristocrat, although I believe his parents were workers. He had a natural air of command.

Then there was his mistress Nina Vassilleva, an intelligent and determined woman, quite different from the cloddish Luba. There were Fritz and his cousin Jacob Peters, who seemed to me a true revolutionary. He had been tortured by the czarist police, and you could still see the marks where they had torn out his fingernails. There was

Joseph, a tall man with a limp, who dragged his right foot behind him at every step. He was a watchmaker by profession and a thief by occupation. He took jobs with jewelers and then stole their stock, making the theft look like an outside burglary. Then there was the man they called Peter the Painter, because he sometimes worked as a house painter, although he was always smartly dressed. He had sharp eyes that made me feel uncomfortable when he looked at me, and looked rather sharp and bristly altogether. His hair was closely cropped, *en brosse*, his mustache curled up to fierce waxed points, he made jabbing motions with his clawlike hands. All of these people I had met before.

The stranger was a man I hardly noticed at first. He sat in a corner of the room, in the only armchair, puffing away at a pipe. I noticed nothing particular about him except that he had a heavy, pockmarked face and small shrewd eyes.

Gardstein had been speaking when I entered. He stopped, turning to Fritz with his eyebrows raised.

"Nikolai, my teacher. I said he could join us, do something for a change instead of going *tum-tum-tum*." His fingers plucked the air.

"We have enough people already. Too many." Gardstein frowned at me, then began talking again to the rest of them. He spoke in Russian, his language very pure and classical, with no slang or colloquial phrases.

"It is important that our plans should be precise. We shall have thirty-six hours, no more."

"We shan't need half of that," Fritz said.

Gardstein ignored him, but his next words were a reply. "We have first to get into the shop. We have to get through a rear wall, and then break down the wall behind the safe. Then there is the safe itself, we cannot be sure how long that will take. You have looked at it?" He spoke to Fritz, who was a locksmith.

"Only through the window. But with the oxygen cylinder it will be easy." He laughed. Peter the Painter laughed too, and said the great thing was to have got into the house. "And then it will be the sabbath. All those faithful Jews will be praying." He put his hands together.

"It is not so simple," Gardstein said. "It will be difficult to work in the day, and at night we must not make too much noise."

"We can get through from the house to—" Fritz began.

Gardstein cut him short. "We will not talk about the house or what we reach when we get through, if you please."

The woman, Nina, spoke for the first time. "That's right. There has been too much talk."

If I had been one of them—and of course I was not—I would have agreed. I had learned that they were planning a burglary, that they had rented a house from which they were going to break into another house or shop, and that they would be making their breakthrough on the Jewish sabbath, which began that Friday night. But then that is the way with the Slavs—not only Russians, but Poles and Letts as well. We are cursed with agile tongues, and we cannot resist talking about our plans and our exploits. This applies especially to revolutionaries.

I have heard a dozen plans for the assassination of the czar and his leading ministers discussed in minute detail at the Anarchist Club and even in public houses. Then I have known them turn in the next breath to matters of absolute triviality, as they suddenly turned now to talking about the Christmas play in which Fritz, very reluctantly, had agreed to play the part of a policeman. There was to be a lot of shooting in the play, and Peter the Painter jumped off the bed on which he had been sitting, snatched up a Mauser revolver lying on a shelf with cartridges piled up beside it, pointed it at Fritz, and pulled the trigger. There was a click. Fritz put his hand to his heart, staggered, cried, "I'm shot, I am killed," collapsed to the floor. Peter put his foot on the body, twisted his mustache, said, "So die all villainous policemen."

"And what policeman is not villainous?" Joseph asked. "I don't know how you can play such a part."

"It was the only part I could get." Fritz scrambled up from the floor.

"And he plays the mandolin too."

"With Nikolai's help. Our Nikolai is a wonderful teacher." Fritz snatched the mandolin from me and began to play a simple folk dance I had taught him.

Joseph began to hum the tune, Peter the Painter started to dance upon the same spot as though he were marking time, Gardstein put his arm around Nina and whirled her about. Only Jacob, who sat on a stool with his hands on his knees, looked on impassively. Or was it only Jacob? I had forgotten the stranger, who now spoke for the first time.

"Comrades, do we have any idea what exactly is in this safe?"

He did not speak loudly, but the effect was immediate. Jacob Peters nodded, as if to say, Now we're getting down to business. The word comrades marked this man off from the others as well, because it was a word they didn't often use to each other.

Gardstein said, "No, Comrade Koba, we don't know exactly. Money and jewels. We hope for a lot, but it is impossible to be sure."

"You ought to be sure. You may be taking risks for nothing." Koba also spoke in Russian, with an accent I found it hard to identify. Certainly he was not from St. Petersburg or Moscow. "And too many people know about it. Every time another person is told, you double the chance of somebody talking." Jacob Peters nodded again. Koba looked directly at me. "This Nikolai is here because he plays the mandolin. Very nice, but it is ridiculous that he should be present. He must be asked to withdraw."

"Yes, of course you are right," Gardstein said.

I got up. Fritz gave me my mandolin. I opened the door and felt my way down the dangerous stairs. I did not see Luba again.

An hour later I used the telephone and spoke to Mr. Quinn, something he had told me to do only in case of emergency. It seemed to me that this was an emergency, and I thought that he would be excited, but I should have known Mr. Quinn better than that. He did not seem to be interested in the burglary so much as in Koba. He made me give a description of Koba, asked if he had said anything to indicate that he was paying a special visit to England, and how important he seemed to be in the group. When I asked whether he was going to arrest them all, he just laughed. I have said already that he laughed a lot, Mr. Quinn.

"But don't worry, my little Nikolai. If we have to arrest them, we will make sure that you are not suspected. Perhaps we shall have to arrest you too." He laughed again.

I did not think that was funny. So I did my best to help the English police and to stop the crime. I know now that Mr. Quinn did nothing. I do not understand English ways. The Okhrana would have arrested us all and tortured us. I understand that better.

NINA'S STORY

It was in 1906 that I came to England. My father was a chef in the palace at St. Petersburg, but he lost his position because of being a Jew. That was after the revolution of 1905. When this failed, the police carried out a pogrom against the Jews, as well as arresting the revolutionary leaders. My father was not arrested, but he lost his job. It was on his advice and with his help that I left Russia.

There are times when I have been sorry that I came to England instead of to America. The English are all bourgeois, fat, smug and self-satisfied. I had thought there would be the chance to make revolutionary propaganda in England, and perhaps also to start my own business, but for three years I worked as a servant to a family in Dalston, which is North East London. Then one day I heard a man complaining about the price of cigarettes, and thought that I could make and sell them. I am clever and quick with my hands. I used to buy tobacco cheaply and then roll the cigarettes. From this I made a living, although not very much of one. How can a woman make a living in this capitalist society?

I used to go to the Anarchist Club in Jubilee Street, and to other communist and revolutionary clubs. It was in one of them that I met George Gardstein. That was not his name, nor was his real name on either of the passports he carried. Names are of no importance to a revolutionary. When I met him, we both knew that our lives would be joined from that day. The bourgeois word for this would be love, but we never used it. We worked for the same cause, social revolution. I accepted him as my leader, did what he told me to do.

I have been shown what the disgusting police spy Tomacoff has written about the discussion before the planned expropriation of the jeweler's shop in Houndsditch, and it is accurate enough. I put it on record that I never liked the man Koba. He was supposed to have escaped from prison in Russia and to be the representative of a revolutionary committee in Geneva. Everybody listened with great respect to what he said and George thought highly of him. I could not see why. The rest of them were mostly trash.

Fritz Svaars was a lightweight, and the sniveling Luba who went around with him was so stupid that she never realized how we lived—

by expropriations from the rich. Joseph was jealous of George. Peter the Painter was a mere boaster. I could go on, but what would be the point?

The plans for the raid on the jeweler had all been made by George. We rented the two houses in Exchange Buildings (there was very little money, even with what I made through the cigarettes, so that other people had to be brought in, too many people), and Joseph, George and I stayed in one of the houses. George arranged for Fritz to buy the oxygen cylinder and the tubing, and we started the breakthrough. I suppose it is true that we made too much noise. I have already said that most of them were stupid people.

I was upstairs and knew nothing of what was happening until I heard the knocking. I looked out of the window, and the whole street seemed filled with policemen. Then there was the shooting. They tell me that this shocked English people, but what did they expect? In Russia the police would have shot us down as we came out of the house, and naturally enough we shot first. I learned afterward that the police did not carry arms. England is a strange country.

Now George shouted to me that we must get away, and we went out into the street, Fritz, Joseph and George, with me following them. Jacob Peters and another man, named Max, ran out of the other house. One of the policemen, a man twice as big as George, tried to stop us. George shot him, but he still clung on and Peters shot him too. One of his bullets hit George.

When I saw what had happened, that George was unable to walk, so that Fritz and Joseph had almost to carry him through the streets, I could not believe it. That we should get clean away, all unhurt, all except George, the only one who was worth anything.

Our journey through the streets and alleys seemed never ending, but at last we got to Grove Street, where only that afternoon the last conference about the raid had been held. At Grove Street, Peters joined us, having run through the alleys another way. Max had gone off to a friend's house. Somehow, they dragged George up the stairs, with Joseph and I following them. They had to be careful, because there was no rail and at one point I thought he would drop down into the hall. Then they got him onto the bed.

Somebody turned the door handle. I put my back against it, and we looked at each other. We thought, The police! Then there was

Luba's voice whining something, and Fritz called, "Don't come in."

George was still wearing his overcoat. The back of it was covered with blood when we turned him over. He was very pale and his hands were cold. I knelt beside him, trying to warm them.

"A doctor," Fritz said. "We must get a doctor."

George whispered something; I bent over him.

"Papers must be burned."

Fritz repeated what he had said about a doctor. He told me that I must make the doctor swear not to tell the police. He took out his revolver and said that I should show it to him.

"Put that away," I said. "What use do you think it can be?"

"You can make him come here. Then you tell him that if he does not keep silent he knows what will happen to him."

I shook my head and Peters supported me, saying that if the doctor went to the police, that could not be helped; the important thing was to bring him here.

The four of us stood looking at George, lying on the bed, bloody and very pale, when there was a stifled scream behind us. It was Luba. Her fat mouth opened. She looked like a gasping fish. Before she could speak, Peters said sharply that George had been shot and that she must get him a cold compress.

She stared at the figure on the bed. "But what has happened?"

"Never mind what has happened. Do as you are told."

When she had gone, I said to Peters that a cold compress would be useless. He gave his grim smile and replied that it would keep Luba occupied, and that she should come with me to the doctor. Then Joseph said, "And what about us, what shall we do? We must get away."

Peters agreed. "We have killed some of them. The police will start a pogrom tomorrow."

Fritz began to shake. He had been tortured by the Okhrana in Riga, and we all knew that he could not bear the thought of it happening again. He started to sob and said that he would go out now, kill as many of them as he could, and die himself.

Peters told him not to be stupid, if we were careful we should all get away. I know now that there would never have been a pogrom, that is not the English way, but at the time we expected a pogrom by the police.

During this time George lay on the bed as though he were life-
less. I knelt down and put my arms around him. He opened his
eyes and looked at me, but did not speak. When I got up, there was
blood on my coat. Peters took me by the arm and we went outside
the room.

"It is useless to stay with him. Fetch a doctor, then leave. I fear
there is nothing a doctor can do. I think he is dying." I looked at
him fiercely and he said, "I shot him, yes, but it was an accident.
What good do you think it will do for any of us to stay? The police
will catch and torture us."

I believed what he said, but I made up my mind then that if there
was anything I could do for George I would stay with him. Luba
came back with the compress. We put it on the place where most
blood showed, and covered it with a towel. Peters, Fritz and Joseph
stood whispering to each other in a corner of the room.

Luba began to whisper. "What did you want to bring him here for,
why did you not take him to hospital?"

"Be quiet, fool." That was Fritz, and he was shouting. I thought
he would strike her, but he did not. "Go with Nina and find a
doctor."

Policemen were placed in nearby houses. Here two of
them patiently await developments.

"Find a doctor, he says, find a doctor, how can we do that? It is three o'clock in the morning."

Joseph said he knew a doctor who had a service throughout the night. He was somewhere in the Whitechapel Road, and we should know the house because there was a brass plate outside written in English and in Yiddish. He did not know the doctor's name.

When we left, the three men all shook me by the hand. I knew what this meant, that they were going to try to find a safe place for themselves, perhaps to get out of England, and that I should do the same thing. The handshake meant also that they understood my link with George, and knew that I had a personal problem which only I could solve.

I remember those days, after the shooting at Exchange Buildings, as one long nightmare, but these were perhaps the worst hours of all, the time after George had been shot and before I knew whether he would live or die.

Luba and I walked through the bitter night with our heads covered with shawls as protection against the wind and driving rain—down Grove Street and across the Commercial Road, usually so busy but now utterly quiet; along Settles Street, where George had lived

While policemen stand behind, awaiting orders, members of the Scots Guards crouch, ready to shoot.

for a few days until he was asked to go because they did not like his visitors; and through to the Whitechapel Road.

Luba scuttled along beside me—she could never walk straight, but moved a little sideways like a crab, so that she was always knocking into you and then moving away—muttering the whole time about the trouble we would all get into, and how she thought we should go to the police, asking in what sort of accident George had been hurt, and whether I thought Fritz would be sent back to Riga, where he had been badly beaten by the police.

She also said over and over again that she could not come back to Grove Street and that she had nothing to do with the shooting, as though I cared whether she came back or not. She spoke both as though we were all in deep trouble, which was true, and as though we had done nothing to cause it, which she must have known was ridiculous.

But Fritz always swore that she knew nothing of how he got his money, and perhaps she was so stupid that she really did not know. She was the most stupid woman I have ever met.

We did not see more than half a dozen people as we passed through the streets, where in daytime there would have been hundreds. The hope of finding a doctor on duty seemed to me very small. When we found the house with the brass plate there was no bell outside, but a tube for speaking into. I spoke into it in Yiddish and asked for the doctor. The reply was in English and I could not understand it—at the time I had only a few words of English, and I knew that Luba had none. I repeated what I had said, very slowly, but back came a volley of English.

Luba was tugging at my arm, asking what he was saying, as if it was not obvious that I could not understand. Then I said, in English, very slowly, "A man is very bad—at Fifty-nine Grove Street. You must come."

A silence. Then he said, "Two minutes."

It was more than two minutes, but not much more, when the door opened and the doctor appeared. He was not very old, perhaps thirty, very much muffled up, and he carried a cane as well as the doctor's bag.

The doctor nodded to us, nothing more, and on the way back to Grove Street we did not speak. Even Luba was silent.

THE DOCTOR'S STORY

I SHOULD LIKE TO MAKE it clear that I have set down my part in this deplorable affair with the utmost reluctance, and only at the insistence of Sir Melville Macnaghten. My involvement was purely coincidental, and although I acted for the best I was blamed by almost everybody concerned for what I did.

I should explain first that my medical practice is not in the East End at all, but in a far more respectable part of the City of London. A number of my patients are City gentlemen, solicitors and brokers and their clients, and if you ask anybody in the neighborhood of Moorgate, I think they will tell you that Dr. John James Scanlon is an up-to-date man, and one to be relied on.

At the same time Moorgate is near to Aldgate, where the East End begins, and my practice does include some of these aliens, who expect an endless amount of treatment and as often as not leave you whistling for your money. Mine is a very different practice from that of Dr. Bernstein's in the Whitechapel Road, where on the night in question I had unluckily agreed to stand in for him because he was indisposed.

I was reluctant to do it, but Dr. Bernstein pointed out that he had stood in for me on other occasions. That was perfectly true, but mine is a different class of practice. I was the victim of my own good nature.

When I had dressed I found the two young women waiting, and we set off. I took a heavy stick with me, to be prepared for anything that might happen.

Men have been lured into dark alleys by young women, set upon and robbed before now. I did not take much notice of what the women looked like (something the police blamed me for afterward), except that they were young, and much muffled up, and that they talked to each other in a language that I presumed to be Yiddish.

One of them, who walked in a curious shuffling kind of way, seemed to be complaining to the other, and I walked on a little ahead and then called on them to hurry. After all, it was they who had called me out in the middle of a winter night. When I turned, I noticed that the shuffling woman had disappeared. The other explained to me that she was reluctant to see the wounded man. I nodded, and we had no further conversation.

It has been suggested that I should have found out in more detail what was wrong with the man, but why should I have? I was going to see him.

Number 59 Grove Street was a decrepit-looking house typical of its kind. It was pitch-black inside, and I gripped my stick, ready to resist an assault.

The woman stood aside, but I pushed her before me for safety's sake and struck a match. It showed a dingy interior, with moldering walls and a steep flight of stairs lacking a handrail or banister. A dim light was visible in the upstairs front room. I followed the woman up the stairs.

The room was in a state of general disorder, and I noticed no more than that. The police appeared to think that I should have observed such things as weapons and ammunition lying about, but why should I have looked at or for them?

What I saw in the flickering gaslight was a man lying on a bed and groaning. He was fully dressed except for his boots. There was blood on the bed and on the pillow. I asked the man his name, and understood him to say he was George Gardstein. He appeared to understand English, and spoke it a little.

I asked him what had happened. He did not answer me immediately, but talked to the woman, who seemed to be urging him to say something. Then he spoke to me, and I remember his words exactly. "Three hours ago shot—by my friend—shot in the back—by a mistake."

So the facts, or what he alleged to be the facts, were established. I now turned him over, removed his upper clothing, and examined him. The bullet had entered at the back a few inches below the shoulder blades, and had lodged somewhere in the front of his chest. (I may say that later examination proved my diagnosis to be correct, and that it was actually touching the right ventricle.) The man was very weak and vomited blood while I was examining him. It was obvious that he should go to hospital, but when I suggested this he turned, raised himself in the bed, and shook his head violently. The woman then said to me that they could not go to hospital because it would get their friend into trouble.

I had no wish to become more involved than necessary in what I could see must be an unsavory affair, and I made no comment. I repeated that he should go to hospital, and again they refused. The man asked me for something to ease the pain, and I said that I would give him some medicine if the woman came back with me. She moved to the door, and I stopped her. "My fee is ten shillings," I said. Perhaps this may sound heartless. I can only say that my experience is that if you don't get money from these aliens when you are treating them, you never get it. I had no intention of remaining unpaid after being called out in the middle of the night. Gardstein told the woman to feel in his pockets, and she discovered a sovereign. I gave her the ten shillings change.

On the way back to the surgery the woman spoke only once, to ask if Gardstein were dying. I told her what was perfectly true, that I had known men who had suffered such wounds in the Boer War and had lived to tell the tale. I mixed a morphine sedative, told her that I would make a morning call to see how the wounded man was faring, and sent her off. Then I sat down to consider what position I should take.

This was not so simple as it may seem. Gardstein had been shot in the back, and of course I did not believe for a moment the story of the accident. It may be thought that it was my duty to inform the police. On the other hand, if I did so, my name would be branded as that of an informer, and no immigrant in trouble would ever come to me. I could have borne this with equanimity, but there was Bernstein to think of. His practice also would be shunned, and this would have been a serious thing for him.

I decided to sleep on my decision (it was by now five in the morning) and wait until I saw Gardstein later. Perhaps by then he might be better, perhaps he might even have moved or been moved. I will be frank and say that I hoped this might be the case. I have already made clear my distaste for the affair. I snatched an hour or two and went around again to Grove Street, and found Gardstein dead.

That is really all I have to say. To the criticisms of my conduct—that I should have got the man to hospital and should have informed the police immediately—I can only say that my critics do not know the kind of people I was dealing with. If I had informed on them, I might have been subject to personal attack.

NINA'S STORY (CONCLUDED)

WHEN I RETURNED with the medicine George was lying as we had left him, groaning. I pulled him up and forced some of the medicine down his throat. Then he lay back again. "I am dying," he said.

Between two like us there were no concealments. I told him what the doctor had said, but he did not believe it. Neither did I. The doctor was a coward and a weakling and wanted to get rid of us.

"I am dying," he repeated. Then he told me, looking at me all the while, what he wished me to do. "The doctor will go to the police. Tomorrow they will start a pogrom. When I die you must get petrol, pour it over me and on the bed, set fire to it. Then go to Gold Street (which was one place where we had had a room, nearby) and burn all papers there. Then you must find Koba, tell him that I failed but that the cause will not fail."

I had not liked Koba, but I knew how important he was in the movement. "Where shall I find him?"

He said faintly, "Through Jacob Peters. But perhaps he has already got away. He is clever." He smiled and his eyes closed. I did not tell him that I felt sure Peters too was trying to escape. For a few moments I sat looking at his hands. They were small, white, delicate and perfectly formed, the most beautiful hands I had ever seen on a man or a woman. He opened his eyes and started to moan again. I gave him some more medicine. He asked me to swear that I would do what I had said, and I did so, although I knew I should never be able to burn his body.

Then he said, "You must disappear too. Disguise yourself. Remember all I have said."

Blood came out of his mouth and I wiped it away. I tried to give him more medicine, but he refused it, saying, "No good." Those were his last words. I sat beside him until he died, which was just after seven in the morning. I felt nothing but sorrow. I should have had to go out and return to buy petrol, and I could not return there. I kissed him and left the house of death.

I went to other houses where our friends had lived, in Turner Street and Lindley Street, but could find nobody except the miserable

Luba, who spoke of going to the police and telling them all she knew. I went to the Anarchist Club, but nobody there had seen Koba or Peters or Fritz or Joseph or Peter the Painter, or if they had seen them, they would not tell me. Of course they all knew what had happened, and were frightened of the police and what they would do. By that time I was frightened too. I went back to another room George and I had occupied—the one in Buross Street—and then I dyed my hair black. I burned some of the things I had been wearing on that night, and I began to burn some of George's papers. When I looked at myself in a glass the effect of the dye was horrible. Streaks of my fair hair showed through the black. The landlord, Isaac Gordon, who lived below, brought me a newspaper with a description of a woman, as they said, "wanted for questioning": "Age 26 to 30; 5 ft. 4 in.; eyes, blue; hair, brown; dress, dark blue three-quarter jacket and skirt," and so on. I was only twenty-three and they had my height wrong, but I was still more frightened. It was then I burned my blouse and skirt, and my black hat. I could not bring myself to burn the feather trimming on the hat, and I gave this to Gordon. I gave the lining of the skirt to his wife, Fanny. These were very foolish things to do.

MACNAGHTEN

I HAVE MENTIONED already the problem involved by the fact that the crime took place in the City of London, and yet within a few yards of the Met boundaries. The investigation, strictly speaking, was under their control, and although they consulted us, perhaps I may be forgiven for thinking that our resources were greater and the scope of our activities wider, so that we might have got quicker results. As soon as I had talked to Pat Quinn, of course, the information he had obtained through Tomacoff had been passed on to our City colleagues. But now an unexpected turn of fortune involved us very directly in the case.

It was around midday on the Monday after the murders that the telephone in my office rang, and I heard the slow, emphatic voice of Fred Wensley, or, to give him his full name, Detective Inspector Frederick Porter Wensley. Fred Wensley was the finest detective on the

Metropolitan force, which in my eyes means the finest in the world. He was from Somerset, and his voice still retained a trace of the West Country burr. He had served in the East End during the whole of his police life, and his knowledge of it was unrivaled. The criminal fraternity called him the Weasel (foreigners could not get this right, often turning it into Vensel), but with his heavy frame and square, slightly drooping jowls he looked more like a bloodhound. And that is what Fred Wensley was, not one of your fancy Sherlock Holmes characters who smacks his head and says he knows the answer, but a real, human bloodhound who once he got his teeth into a case never let go. Why was he still only a detective inspector and not a superintendent? Well, it isn't always the best men who are in the top jobs.

Now, Fred Wensley was attached to H Division in Whitechapel, bordering the City of London territory where the policemen had been shot. What he rang up to tell me was that a certain Dr. Scanlon had reported to a police station in H Division that he had visited a patient that morning at 59 Grove Street, Whitechapel, and found him dead of a bullet wound. You may be sure we asked Dr. Scanlon later on why he had not reported the wound on the night he'd first seen the man, a question to which we never got a satisfactory answer. If he had done so, a number of the gang might have been picked up immediately.

Dr. Scanlon's report put Fred Wensley fair and square in the middle of the case, and from then on he was fully involved in it. He had called me up to ask if I would be interested in meeting him in Whitechapel, and you may imagine my answer. I called for my chauffeur, Crowther, and had myself driven down there in half an hour.

The house in Grove Street has already been described, and I will say no more about it except that I found the milieu infinitely depressing. Upstairs, in the front room, Wensley was waiting, with an inspector named Thompson from the City Police.

The dead man was on the bed. He looked uncommonly peaceful, and I must say also extremely handsome. Some reporter fellow who said afterward that he looked like Adonis was not exaggerating as much as usual. There was a good deal of blood around, and on a table beside the bed was a tweed cap with a variety of ammunition in it, rifle cartridges and cartridges for a 30-caliber Mauser.

"Have a look at these, sir, they were in his clothing," Wensley said.

There were another fifty or so cartridges of different kinds, some Belgian, some German. "And this. It was under his pillow." It was a loaded Dreyse pistol, with two clips of ammunition for it. For the un-initiated, a Dreyse is an up-to-date and very accurate German pistol with a long barrel. They aren't easily available in this country.

"Several sorts of ammunition, one pistol," Wensley said. "If this was their storehouse, it means the others have got away. Leaving their extra ammunition behind." I nodded agreement. It just emphasized the fact that these were men who would stop at nothing.

"And look at some of this stuff," Thompson said. I looked through a small pile of papers, some of which had been found in Gardstein's wallet, others on the mantelpiece, and some under a sewing machine which stood beside the window. There were letters, some in Russian—which I could not read—some in what was obviously an elementary code, some in French. A couple of these were addressed to the Fritz already mentioned, and some others to Peter the Painter. (The letters in Russian and in code turned out to be for the most part purely personal—greetings from friends and lovers, or complaints about the brutality of the police.) There was a card saying that Gardstein was a member of some Lettish revolutionary group, two passports in the names of Morin and Mourrewitz, and some instructions in French for exploding bombs and for the timing of fuses, as well as a number of detailed gun specifications.

In short, the material in the room made it clear that we were dealing with a resolute and dangerous criminal gang. It did not, however, give us a hint of where they were to be found. I went back with Fred Wensley to H Division, at Leman Street Police Station, and gave him the names Quinn had got from the informant Tomacoff. One or two of these were known to Wensley. He had actually met Peter the Painter, who was, as he said, a man always smartly dressed and with plenty of girl friends. He had often seen Fritz Svaars in the Anarchist Club, and had seen Gardstein there too, with a woman who seemed very devoted to him. He had seen Peters and would recognize him again, but knew nothing of the mysterious Koba beyond having heard his name mentioned. Pat Quinn had already told me that Koba was a Russian, a figure of authority, famous among the revolutionaries for the expropriations (the word they used for their robberies) that he had planned and carried out.

Descriptions of the gang had already been issued, based on what the policemen had seen at Exchange Buildings, but we realized that these were not likely to be altogether accurate. We had a watch on the ports, but men like these often had friends among the foreign sailors and were smuggled onto boats. "We shall get them through the women," Fred Wensley said in his slow way. "Mark my words, the women will give them away."

It was by now midafternoon and we were eating thick roast-beef sandwiches, very different from my usual lunch at the Garrick Club, but still very good, when a sergeant came in to say that a man outside had some information about the murders. Fred Wensley pushed aside his sandwiches and had the man sent in.

He was a fat little fellow named Isaac Gordon, very much in awe of the man he called Mr. Vensel, and frightened by what he was doing. I admired the way Wensley treated him, like a strict but benevolent headmaster. Gordon could speak English, but had an accent you could have cut with a knife. I will not attempt to reproduce it. He was clutching a parcel done up in brown paper.

"I have a very respectable home, you see, Mr. Vensel, but I let rooms in it. I have to do this, you see, to make a little money. There is nothing wrong in my letting rooms, is there, Mr. Vensel?"

Fred Wensley pondered the point as though he were making an important decision, then said, "Nothing at all, Mr. Gordon, nothing at all."

"And you see, when this man, Mr. Morin, he says we must have a key to keep the door locked when he is out, that is reasonable too."

"Yes, that is reasonable."

"And if he has his friend to stay with him, his lady friend, is that my business either? But now, you see, she is burning her clothes. And papers, she is giving me papers to keep for her." He held out the brown paper parcel, saying over and over that he had not looked at it and did not know what was inside. The parcel contained some books—the usual kind of subversive literature, with titles like *On the Revolution* and *On Revolutionary Government*—a Russian passport issued to a woman named Minna Gristis, and a collection of photographs. Among them there was a picture of Gardstein, and Wensley recognized pictures of Peter the Painter, Fritz Svaars, and two other men whom he knew only as Max and Joseph. There was also a photograph of Gordon's lodger, and she was the woman called Minna Gristis in the passport. Those photographs were enough for us.

In six minutes Fred Wensley, little Isaac Gordon and I were in my Daimler and on the way to Gordon's lodging house. I think it must have been the first time Gordon had ridden in a motorcar, and he kept looking out of the windows and shaking his head in astonishment as we sped through the streets. He had been very insistent that we must not say he had been to see us, and halfway on our journey he suddenly realized that he might be seen traveling in a motorcar with two policemen, and begged to be let out. We put him out of the car and continued on our way, stopping just short of his house in Buross Street. Fred was out of the Daimler, had knocked on the door, and was inside while I was still telling Crowther to wait. I found Fred talking to Mrs. Gordon, who was as nervous as her husband had been, and again I admired the way he soothed her, saying that they had done the right thing, and that now he was there they had no need to be afraid. These were words that anybody might have used, but when they were spoken by Fred Wensley, East Enders believed them.

Their lodger opened the door in answer to our knock and stood staring at us defiantly when Wensley introduced himself. She was a good-looking woman in an intense kind of way, but at this moment she looked very odd because she had tried to dye her naturally fair hair black, and the effect had been to produce alternate streaks of black and blond. She must have been expecting Wensley to comment on this, but he merely looked. Then he said in his most solemn voice—and he could be very solemn—that I was Melville Macnaghten, chief of all the British police. At that she was terrified. She retreated to the bed and sat down. I asked her if she spoke English and she said yes, a little, but she spoke French better. I knew, however, that Wensley had no French, and so asked my questions in English, speaking slowly. As in the case of Gordon, I won't attempt to reproduce her atrocious accent.

"What is your name?"

"Nina Vassilleva. Sometimes I am called Lena. I am a Russian. I make cigarettes."

"That is not the name it gives here." I showed her the passport. She looked startled and then shrugged, as if to say that women like herself had many names. I did not pursue the point.

"Are you a member of the Anarchist Club?"

"I have been there."

"And you know other members?"

"Some of them. I do not go often."

"Do you know that some police officers were shot at Houndsditch on Friday night?"

"I have heard it." She gave me one long look, then stared down at the worn rug.

"We think that some of your anarchist friends took part in this." She shrugged again. "Are you saying that you do not know any of them?"

"I know nothing about it."

I could not flatter myself that I was making progress, but even so, I was surprised to hear Wensley beside me say harshly, "We are told you have bullets and cartridges here."

And then she flared up. "It's a lie!"

Of course it was true that we had no such information. But I realized the purpose of the statement when she continued. "You can look for them, if you like." She said it with a sneer, but it gave us the authority to search the room, and we proceeded to do so.

She sat drumming her heels on the floor while we looked in a clothes closet and a rickety chest of drawers, and beneath the mattress and the bed. There was a small fireplace in which papers and clothes had been burned. I sifted them, to reveal only ash, while she watched. We found no bullets or cartridges. What we did find, however, provided overwhelming proof that she was the woman who had been seen hurrying away from the scene of the crime. There were a dark blue jacket and a coat with large stains on the front. When we asked what they were, she replied that she must have spilled something on them. There was also the muff that she had been seen carrying away from Exchange Buildings. It was typical of these careless revolutionaries that she should have burned some things and kept others that were just as incriminating.

She stood up and said, "You want me to go with you?"

Now Wensley produced from his pocket, like a very ponderous conjurer performing a card trick, the photographs given to us by Isaac Gordon. The first one was of Fritz Svaars. "Whose photograph is this?"

"I do not know."

He showed her the other photographs, and each time she said, "I do not know," until he came to Gardstein. Then she put her head in her hands and wept. Fred Wensley repeated, "Whose photograph is this?"

She raised her head. "He was the best friend I had."

"He is the man who lived here with you, in this room?"

"Yes."

"And he was at Exchange Buildings?"

"Oh yes, yes, yes."

"And you saw what happened there?"

"I saw nothing. I had nothing to do with it."

"And you said he *was* your best friend, so you know he is dead."

"It would have been better if they had killed me," she cried. "I wish I could have taken the bullet in my own heart."

"He wasn't shot in the heart, he was shot in the back," Wensley said stolidly. In spite of his great qualities, he was an unimaginative fellow at times. "One more question. What do you know about Koba?"

"I know nothing about Koba."

Wensley put his chin in his hands and looked at her, rocking a little on his feet in a way he had. He had very big feet, Fred Wensley; that old saying about telling a policeman by his feet really applied to him. "If you could help us find any of these friends of yours—"

"I am not an *informer*." It is impossible to convey the venom she put into the words. She said again, "I am ready to go with you."

"Go where?"

"You are not going to arrest me?" She made it sound like two words, "ar rest," in a way that would have been comic at any other time. She sounded astonished, and I was surprised myself.

"Arrest you?" Wensley said, as though nothing had been farther from his mind. "But you've told me, Miss Nina, that you had no connection with what happened at Exchange Buildings." He put on his bowler hat and walked down the stairs, leaving her on the landing, still looking astonished, as well she might.

Out in the street, Wensley stopped to have a word with a man who was lounging on a corner. When we moved on I noticed him giving a sly look at me, and I knew what it meant. I said, "Detective Constable John Holmes, transferred to H Division from E Division last year. Six years' service, commended for bravery in connection with an armed robbery a couple of years ago."

"Wonderful, sir. I take off my hat to you." He lifted his bowler. "You understand the strategy, sir. Miss Nina's more use to us running free than if we took her in. Young John will keep his eye on her, and I'll be putting three other men onto the job as well, so she'll be watched round the clock. I'll be surprised if in a day or two that doesn't bring results."

That was Fred Wensley's prediction, but he was wrong. Nina Vassilleva was followed night and day, and of course soon realized it, although she made no attempt to get away from the detectives. She took a train down to Dover, but when she made to board the boat for Calais, one of our men stopped her.

"What is to happen to me?" she asked him. "If I go to Russia the secret police will kill me, and if I stay here I shall be hanged."

Our man simply said he had his instructions and turned her back. After that she went back to the Gordons, with whom, surprisingly enough, she remained on good terms. She went once or twice to the Anarchist Club, but was never seen speaking to any of the men on our wanted list. The Gardstein poster (the picture taking was gruesome, as may be imagined—his eyelids had to be opened to produce a lifelike expression) did have one result. The landlord of 44 Gold Street recognized it as a picture of his lodger, who called himself a student of chemistry and used the name of Morin. A student of chemistry indeed! His room was a kind of laboratory, in which we found nitric acid, nitroglycerin, books dealing with the making of explosives and the melting of ingots, as well as a Mauser pistol and hundreds of cartridges. A dangerous gentleman, our Mr. Gardstein, and we were lucky to be rid of him.

We had men on the streets dressed as peddlers, bootblacks and street hawkers, but they brought in only misleading rumors.

We tried to gather more information through Tomacoff. He was put into a hotel, all expenses paid; we bought him a lot of new clothes and sent him out to scout around every day to see what he could find. After a few days he told us where Jacob Peters was living. We had a man waiting in Peters' room, and he came quietly. He denied everything when arrested on a charge of murder, saying that his cousin Fritz was a wild character, and that he had no connection with what Fritz had done. He admitted knowing one or two of the other conspirators, but had no idea where they could be found. He said he had never heard of the mysterious Koba.

That was one to us. But we just missed Peter the Painter, after a tip given us by Tomacoff. It took us to a house not far from Grove Street, where Gardstein had died, but our quarry had left just a few minutes before. He went to earth absolutely and totally, and the next news we had of him was a month later, when Pat Quinn informed us that, according to his sources abroad, Peter the Painter was in Paris. So, one to us and one to them. I found it rather cheering to consider the whole thing in the light of a sporting event in this way. And for a couple of weeks after that, nothing happened.

A woman named Luba Milstein, who has already been mentioned, came to us admitting that she had been the lover of Fritz Svaars, but protesting her innocence. It was hard to believe that anybody could have been so close to the revolutionaries and known nothing of what they were doing, but her stupidity was such that this was perfectly possible in her case. She gave us little useful information, but we kept her in custody, partly for her own safety.

Fred Wensley and the City Police had literally dozens of detectives combing every lodging house in the Whitechapel area, but although they pulled in a couple of little fish, there was no news of the ones we really wanted—the limping Joseph, or excitable Fritz Svaars, or Koba. We were still looking for Koba, but we accepted it as likely that after the failure in Houndsditch he had given up the English group and got away to France or Switzerland through the underground channels that these damned people were able to use through sympathizers. It beats me how anybody could sympathize with villains who wanted to kill policemen and rob respectable citizens, but some people did. The rewards we offered brought in nothing at all. Either people knew nothing, or they were frightened to talk.

December 23. The three murdered policemen were buried, and as I have already mentioned, a service was held at St. Paul's Cathedral. Nina Vassilleva attended it. She bought a small memorial card with portraits of the policemen inside. Perhaps, after all, she was not devoid of decent human feeling.

Christmas. I must confess that I spent it in the bosom of my family, at our estate down in Wiltshire, although I had a special line on which I could have been called in the case of urgent news. Unhappily there was none. Fred Wensley and his men, Superintendent Ottaway of the City Police and his men, spent their time searching, searching, without success.

New Year's Day, and still no news. There were some ironic and some savage editorials in the papers, criticizing the inactivity of the police force. And then, quite suddenly on the night of January 1, 1911, came the break. It was sometime after midnight, and I was at slippered ease in my London rooms, considering retiring to the arms of Morpheus, when the special police telephone rang. It was Fred Wensley, and for a man usually so phlegmatic, his voice was hoarse with emotion.

"Fritz and Joseph, sir. We think we know where they are. Information received."

"Splendid work. I'll just slip on some clothes and be with you in—"

"No need for that, sir. There's a lot of preliminary work to be done. If you come down in the morning you won't miss any of the fireworks."

"Very well, Fred," I said. "It's the East End, I suppose. What's the exact address?"

"Number One Hundred Sidney Street."

PART TWO: THE SIEGE
MACNAGHTEN

THE SIEGE OF SIDNEY STREET falls naturally into two parts, the first being the Houndsditch murders and the search for the men involved, the second the siege itself. The heroes of the first part were the policemen who died in the performance of their duty, a duty carried out without the least thought of the consequence to themselves. In the second part there were a dozen heroes, but if there is one who should be picked out, it is Fred Wensley. I am particularly glad that I have been able to get Fred to put down his own account of what happened, in his own words.

THE DETECTIVE'S STORY

SIR MELVILLE HAS TOLD me (well, he suggested it, but his suggestions are like instructions to me) to set down my story of what they call the Siege of Sidney Street. Before I do it, though, I'd like to say that the whole affair wasn't so very unusual. Of course it was unusual for three policemen to be killed and others to be wounded, and thank God for that, but it all fitted in with the fact that the East End was a very violent place. Still is for that matter, although I like to think we've cleaned it up a bit.

When I was first moved to H Division Whitechapel, I'll be frank and say I resented it. I was in L Division, which covers Lambeth, a tough but decent area, and the idea of moving to the worst slum district in London was something I really hated. Later I came to love the East Enders, and I hope a lot of them grew to accept and trust the man they called Mr. Vensel.

Just a few words about what it was like when I first went there, in 1891, soon after the Jack the Ripper business, although I was only involved in that as a fairly junior constable. But in those days, and for ten years afterward, it wasn't very unusual for us to get a report in the morning that a dead man had been found in the area. We would go down and look at him, and find somebody with head and body injuries that might have been caused by the man falling over when drunk, or as the result of a quarrel, or they might have come from his being knocked down by a cart and horse, or even a motorcar—though they weren't too plentiful in the East End at that time. Or the man might have been murdered.

It was hard to tell, hard for the doctors to tell, and few of these cases were classified as murder. What often happened was that a man met a woman in a pub, she offered to take him home with her, and when they got "home" her fancy man would be waiting with a friend or two. If the gull handed over his money, he was probably allowed to leave. If he showed fight, the best he could expect was to be beaten up. If they found they'd been a little too rough and killed him, it was simple enough to carry out the body and drop it in a street not too nearby. Witnesses? No doubt they existed, but they never talked. There were plenty of gangs in Whitechapel, and if you ran across a gang, the best you could expect was broken ribs and a broken head.

A year or two before the Sidney Street business, we'd succeeded in breaking up two well-organized gangs who called themselves the Bessarabians and the Odessans. They were mostly Russians in both gangs, with a few Poles, Armenians and others, and they fairly terrorized the area. Most of their victims were aliens, and they would never talk. We managed to lay them by the heels when the two gangs had a pitched fight one night in a pub and an Odessan was stabbed to death. We got the leading Bessarabians, and they went down for long sentences. After that, we found it fairly easy to deal with the rest of them.

All this may sound tough, and it was, but it was the best possible training for a young detective. It might be dangerous, but it was never dull, and I took risks when I was young that I wouldn't take now. I took some hard knocks too. I must have been knocked on the head half a dozen times, and if one knife in my ribs had been a couple of inches higher, I shouldn't be writing this little memoir. But I loved the life, and I won't pretend I didn't.

It was one of those cases in which I took a bit of a chance—it involved chasing a murderer over some roofs until in the end he jumped into the crowd watching below—that first brought me in touch with Sir Melville Macnaghten. Just after this affair he strolled into Leman Street Police Station, a tall, elegant man with that air about him which belongs only to the English upper classes. It so happened that I was the only CID officer on duty, and he asked my name. I gave it.

"Sergeant Wensley," he said. He thought a moment, then went on. "Frederick Porter Wensley. Joined the Met in 1888, came to the CID in 1895." He went on to a list of commendations which I would blush to repeat. I learned afterward that he was able to do the same thing with every man in the CID.

I am writing this for Mac, which as he very well knows is what we called him behind his back, though not to his face. And he knew very well too that I wouldn't pull any punches in what I wrote. I wouldn't say that Mac was a great detective, or anything like it. He liked to come in on a case, and sometimes his physical presence was a help and sometimes we wished he'd been somewhere else.

But he was a first-class organizer, and he won our respect and affection by the way he handled people. He knew just the right things to say to people, and could put anybody at ease without the slightest air of condescension. Now me, I get on well enough with people of my own class, and I'm on first-name terms with all sorts of crooks, though I make sure they don't call me Fred but Mr. Wensley, or more likely Mr. Vensel. I'll be frank, though, and say that I don't feel comfortable when I'm talking to a man who's been to Eton and Oxford and places like that. Except for Mac, that is; I've never for a moment felt anything but at ease with him.

In the full knowledge that he's going to read this, I should like to say that he's one of the greatest gentlemen I've known.

Now back to Sidney Street. High time too, you may say, but I wanted to give you the background, otherwise you don't get the real flavor of what we had to do. These so-called anarchists, they were just a gang like the Bessarabians, except that they'd got all those arms and were so very ready to use them. The Bessarabians mostly used knives.

When the New Year came, I don't mind saying that all our leads on the gangsters who were still free had produced very little. The ploy of leaving Nina Vassilleva free just hadn't worked—she was a tough one, as tough as any man—and the informants I had out had brought in nothing at all. It was midnight, a filthy night with snow falling heavily, and the only reason why I was still at Leman Street was that I didn't look forward to the journey home. Then the duty sergeant came in and said there was somebody to see me. Who was he? He wouldn't say, and he was so muffled up the sergeant couldn't see his face below the eyes. What was it about? He'd just said the one word, Houndsditch. It was enough to make me see him.

In he came, and sure enough he was covered up like a wife in a sultan's harem. He had on a long blue overcoat, a black hat pulled down right over his eyes, and a scarf wound around his face. There was snow on his overcoat and hat. He looked like somebody out of one of the melodramas like *The Ticket-of-Leave Man* that I'd seen when I was a kid. The sergeant was a bit nervous about leaving us together. I think he had it in mind that our customer might start flourishing a knife, but I told him it was all right. Gangsters don't come into police stations and draw knives.

When the sergeant had gone out, my visitor slowly unwound the scarf. It was Tomacoff the informant. I stared at him and asked what game he thought he was playing.

"It must not be known that I come here," he said. "Or I am a dead man."

I could appreciate what he meant. I didn't feel too warmly about Tomacoff myself. A regular police informant is one thing, but somebody who worms his way into a group and then betrays them, well, he's no favorite with me, although of course I'm prepared to use him. But he was right that if they got to know he'd visited Leman Street, he'd be a dead duck. It must be something important that brought him here.

"If I give you information and you catch them, I get reward. Five hundred pounds. Is that right?"

"Not a matter for me." I wasn't going to make any promises to a man like Tomacoff, who had already been put in a hotel by us and been bought a lot of new clothes, very likely including the overcoat he was wearing. "If you know something, tell me."

"I want to know—"

I got up, came around from my desk, took him by the lapels of his coat, and shook him. "You tell me what you know, understand. Otherwise I'll make quite sure that your friends know you've been here, and you'll be dead. Just as you say." I shook him gently back and forth. Nothing more than that, but when I let him go he collapsed into a chair and stared at me. He was quivering as if I'd given him a beating. That's what I call moral persuasion.

"Fritz Svaars and Joseph. I know where they are."

"And where is that?"

But it isn't possible to get a straight answer from a man like Tomacoff. Like so many of these foreigners, he was a natural playactor, and he also wanted to show me how clever he'd been. So I had to listen to a long tale about how he'd talked to a photographic enlarger named Perelman, who had once been Gardstein's landlord, and how Perelman had told him he had arranged for two very important men to be transferred from one safe place to another, from the care of someone named Betty Gershon to a room in the house of Perelman's cousin, from which they were hoping to arrange transport abroad. They would move one at a time, and the second man wouldn't move until the first had sent back a message saying he was safe. The "safe" message would be in some sort of code. And how did Tomacoff know that these "important men" were those we were looking for?

"I know Betty Gershon." Tomacoff preened himself. He might really have been a bird. "And I know where she lives. At number One Hundred Sidney Street."

"But what is her link with our men?"

"Joseph is her lover. He lives with her. Sometimes."

"And what about Fritz Svaars?"

"Where Joseph goes, Fritz goes. They are always together. Believe me, I know them both. But you must do something quickly. They move from Sidney Street tomorrow, in the afternoon."

I talked a little longer with Tomacoff—and discovered incidentally that he had come to me only because he had not been able to reach Quinn of Special Branch on the telephone—but he knew nothing more. When he had gone, I telephoned Superintendent Ottaway of the City Police. We agreed that although the information—and the informant—left something to be desired, we ought to act on it. I called Sir Melville to tell him what was happening. But first I called Divisional Superintendent Mulvaney, the head of H Division. If I have been making it seem that I was running affairs, well, that's true up to a point, because of my special knowledge of the area. Nonetheless, Mulvaney was my boss, and it was he who made the big decisions. Mulvaney said we should have an immediate conference, and it was then that I called Sir Melville and said we'd be happy to see him—tomorrow. Why did I do that? Because Mac was an administrator, and we were making hard, practical decisions. Mac was splendid on how to cut red tape, but as to how men should be deployed in the field—well, let's say he had very little knowledge of fieldwork.

Mulvaney, Ottaway and I, together with a couple of sergeants, went to have a look at the house, as well as we could see it on a pitch-black night, with snow driving in our faces. It was one of a block of ten, called Charley Martin's Mansions after the name of the landlord who owned the lot. They were flat-fronted, with three upper stories and a basement, quite a bit bigger than most of the houses in the area, and they came out flush to the sidewalk. In one room of one house two desperate criminals were hiding, almost certainly with a whole armory of guns and ammunition. The rest of that house and all the

As others look on, Mulvaney, Ottaway and Wensley confer. They wanted the anarchists but no more dead policemen.

other houses were filled with aliens of all sorts. How were we going to take the men in, without their causing a holocaust among our own police and the population in general that would make the Houndsditch killings look like a picnic?

That was the problem we faced—Mulvaney, Ottaway, another City Police superintendent, named Stark, and I—as we sat down with cups of strong tea at the station.

One thing we all agreed on, and that was the need to have men watching the house, men who must be in place before the morning. It was suggested that, when this had been done, we should wait for the men to show themselves, and take them in the street. But I pointed out that, according to our information, only one man was coming out and that the other one wouldn't appear until he had the coded "safe" message. If we took the first man in the street, the other would start firing. Then there was another snag. We could position our men at night, but in the morning some of them were bound to be seen. Svaars and Joseph would know the game was up and, if they ran true to form, would start shooting.

That was one consideration. Another was the fact that what we were arranging rested on the unsupported word of Tomacoff. He had

Undanted by warnings of possible danger, Home Secretary Churchill dons top hat and coat and arrives at Sidney Street.

been useful in the past, it was true, but as I've said already, he was very much a playactor. He might be exaggerating, or his information might be plain wrong. It was impossible to be sure, and also impossible to check what he'd said.

Stark of the City Police put this point of view most forcibly when he said, "This operation could make us a laughing-stock."

True enough, but it didn't get us very far. I asked him point-blank what he would propose to do. I'd already ordered some detectives out, and they were in and around Sidney Street, shivering in doorways and no doubt cursing Fred Wensley's guts. Ottaway of City had called in all the uniformed men he could get hold of, and they were standing around at the station stamping their feet and trying to keep warm.

"What are we going to do, then? Call the whole thing off?" I asked. "If we do and they get away, they'll be laughing all the way from Bethnal Green to Aldgate."

There was a general murmur of agreement at that, and I went on to push the point home. "If we're going to do this, we've got to do it right. We have to gamble on them being there. They got away at Houndsditch. They mustn't get away again."

Mulvaney thumped his fist on the table and said that force was what we needed, overwhelming force. He was a cautious man, Mulvaney, the sort who always wanted odds of ten to one on his side before he would place a bet. Now he asked how many men Ottaway had ordered up. The answer was a hundred. "Then, by God, we'll have a hundred of the Met there as well. What do you say to that, Wensley?" What I could have said was that the area would be choked with policemen and that half the number would do as well, but as I've said already, Mulvaney was my chief.

With that settled, he sat back as though all our problems were solved, until Stark asked where we were going to put them, and admitted that he didn't know the area well. They looked at me and I said, "Give me some paper and turn up those gas jets and I'll draw you a map."

They crowded around and I drew a map of Charley Martin's Mansions, very much as I've described them here. I marked in Lindley and Hawkins streets, and I then went on to show the peculiarity of this block. Another street, Richardson Street, cut into Lindley Street at one end and Hawkins at the other, and the houses inside these four sections of street formed a kind of square. If you were fanciful, you might say it was like a sort of medieval castle, with all the houses facing outward to the road, and all the backyards inside. The entrance to these rear yards was through an alley that led in from Lindley Street. When I'd made the map I sat back and left them to draw the conclusion.

It was Ottaway who said it. "They're boxed in. They can only get out through the front door or the yards, and we'll have men posted for that."

"What about across the roofs?" That was my chief, Mulvaney.

"With the number of men we've got, we can cover everything, including one other possibility that hasn't been mentioned. They might try to break through into an adjoining house and fool us by walking out of there. Remember, their specialty is breaking through walls, and for all we know they've got the equipment to do it. So we look out for somebody either side, as well as front and rear."

"But the people who live there, will they cooperate?" Mulvaney again.

"They'll cooperate. They don't say no to the police." And that was true. They might not want to help, but they wouldn't hinder. "The rest of the men I suggest should be posted in the other streets. And we should be looking for houses opposite where we can put some men."

There was silence. Then Ottaway said, "Very good, Fred. I like it."

It was Mulvaney, always inclined to be a Jeremiah, who asked the awkward questions. "The idea of putting men in houses opposite is so that they can fire at the house, right?"

"That's right."

"What are they going to fire with?"

It was a good point. In general, I think it is a mistake for police to carry weapons. I have never carried or needed one myself in my whole police career, and I had no wish to encumber myself with one now. But these were exceptional circumstances, and the sad truth was that neither the City Police nor the Met had an armory that could by any stretch of the imagination be called modern. In H Division we had a few snub-nosed bulldog revolvers, some of which were so antiquated that they had to be reloaded after each shot. The best of them would fire five shots in ten seconds, a rate of fire which is perfectly reasonable when dealing with the usual kind of desperado, but not adequate for this particular case. They were also hopelessly inaccurate at any distance over thirty yards, which is again no drawback in relation to most criminals, but placed our men at a terrible disadvantage against men using Mauser and other pistols with a range approaching a thousand yards. The City Police were in a similar position.

Then Ottaway said that they could lay hands almost immediately on a stock of rifles. That was perfectly true, and we had the rifles within a few minutes. What he didn't say, perhaps because he didn't know it, was that they were Morris-tube rifles. I have had firearms training myself, even though I never carry a weapon, and it occurs to me that readers may not know exactly the nature of a Morris-tube rifle. The Morris-tube is an ingenious device. It consists of a small-rifled barrel fixed into an ordinary rifle, so that the tube is smaller than the bore of the weapon into which it is fixed. A sighting device is then fitted, so that when you are firing at a target ten yards away it looks as though the distance is four or five hundred yards. In other words, the Morris-tube is a useful training weapon, but hopelessly inaccurate over distance. It also tends to foul up quickly.

In any case, there were not nearly enough rifles and revolvers of any sort to go around, nor did all the men know how to use them. A good many of them, armed only with their truncheons, were going to have to face men with pistols, as at Houndsditch.

It is easy to say that we should have been better armed, and when the siege was over there was plenty of blame thrown around, some of which stuck to Mac. The eventual result was that we received a supply of modern arms, but of course that did not help us on that morning in early January. Our conference ended at one thirty.

The events before daylight, when the whole thing exploded, can be put best in the form of a timetable:

1:30 to 3:00 a.m. One of my detectives, Sergeant Jacobson, knew this particular patch even better than I did. He took a dozen men and began to put them in the adjoining houses. One experience he had shows the truth of what I'd said about cooperation with the police. In most of these houses the landlord lived on the ground floor, and when Sonny, as we called him, knocked on a door in Hawkins Street the landlady, a Mrs. Rubenoff, opened it. She looked at Sonny and the men with him, saw that they were policemen, and went back to her room without saying a word, leaving the door open. That's the kind of cooperation you get in the East End.

Sonny and four men crept through the house to the backyard and over a low wall. Then they were right at the back of 100 Sidney Street, blocking the rear exit. It was still snowing, and one of the men started stamping his feet. Sonny put a finger to his lips for silence, and the man stopped. It was vital to get them all into position without the men in number 100 knowing anything about it. Sonny then repeated the operation with numbers 98 and 102, putting four men in the yard of each house. He had no trouble; it all went smooth as silk.

The back was now completely covered. At the same time, the rest of us had set about the job of covering the front by trying to get into the houses opposite. One belonged to a pharmacist named Cohen, and when there was no reply to our taps on the door we got in through a woodyard at its side. The woodyard gate was locked, and I had to do a little fiddling with a skeleton key. The same key opened the back door of the pharmacist's. As we went in, a figure in a white nightgown at the top of the stairs called out in a quavering voice, "Clear out now. I've got a whistle, and if you don't go I shall call the police."

A police whistle at that moment would really have given the game away. It was too dark to see any faces, but I said, "Cohen, this is Mr. Wensley, you know me. I'm coming up to talk to you. Put on a light. If you blow that whistle, you'll be very sorry." I didn't raise my voice, but people tell me that I've got a naturally menacing manner. Anyway, it worked. Cohen lit the gas jet on the landing and didn't blow his whistle.

The men with me stayed below while I told Cohen that we wanted to use his front room, on the first floor, which faces number 100 almost directly.

"But it is my bedroom. My wife is asleep there."

"Then you'll just have to wake her up."

"Mr. Vensel, I do not see why you should turn us out of our bedroom, what is it for? I never have trouble with the police, why am I turned out?"

"This is an emergency. You're helping us." He went on complaining, and I had to be firm. "Cohen, we have to use your room for a few hours. Either you and your wife get dressed, or we turn you out, it's your choice. Now, you go and get dressed, and don't show a light. If you show a light or if you blow that whistle, you'll spend the rest of the night in a prison cell."

Ten minutes later Cohen and his Rebecca were out of the room and in the back kitchen, making tea. A few minutes after that, three men had barricaded the window with the mattress which they took off the bed, and had their Morris-tube rifles ready, concealed by the bedroom curtains.

3:00 to 7:00 a.m. So our men were in place, the net was drawn, and, so far as we knew, the men we were after suspected nothing. But what about the rest of the people in the house? They would be in danger of their lives as soon as trouble started, and we had no idea who they were. Mulvaney, Ottaway and I had a conference in the woodyard. The snow had stopped, but the night was still miserably cold, with gusts of sleet and rain, and although you could turn up your coat collar, it tended to seep in and run down your neck. I called over Sonny Jacobson and asked him which had been the most cooperative of the people he had called on. He said Mrs. Bluestein, at 102. I told him to see Mrs. Bluestein and find out what he could from her about the landlady at number 100 and to tell her she might have to offer some hospitality for a few hours. Ten minutes later he came back, laughing.

"Mrs. Bluestein, she don't like her next-door neighbor Mrs. Fleishmann," he said, waving his hands. "Mrs. Bluestein, she says that Mrs. Fleishmann, her nose is in everybody's business. Mr. Fleishmann is a tailor, and she's got no quarrel with him. But Mrs. Fleishmann, she says Mrs. Bluestein is like that with her lodger Mr.

Pankowski." Sonny twined his fingers closely together. "And Mr. Pankowski, he is eighty-two years old."

"Did you tell her—"

"When I say she must have Mrs. Fleishmann in her house, she said that if she saw her she would spit in her face and call her the liar that she was. I said all right, Mrs. Bluestein, close your eyes and you won't see her, and she went back into her room and slammed the door. So the front door's open, and we can put the Fleishmanns in the house somewhere. All sixteen of them."

"Sixteen?"

"That's a joke. They've got three children. They sleep on the ground floor."

"I'm going over to talk to her." Sonny was grinning at me. "What's the matter?"

"She only speaks Yiddish. You'll need an interpreter. Me."

Sonny was the only Jewish detective we had in H Division at that time, which meant that on this night he was an indispensable man. We crossed the street together, acutely aware of those drawn curtains at the second-floor front room. Then we were across. Like most of the houses in the area, this one had window shutters. I tapped on them gently. No reply. I knocked again, more loudly. There was some muttering inside. Sonny answered. More speech from inside, this time much louder, a woman's voice.

"What's she saying?"

"She thought I was the milkman and said no thanks, don't want any. I said it's not the milkman, it's the police. I don't think they believe me." A man's voice, shouting. "They don't."

"Tell them we'll break the front door down if they don't open it. Tell them it's Vensel."

Sonny rattled off some Yiddish. There was grumbling from inside, then he said, "They're coming."

The front door opened a few inches and a thin, bearded face peered out. The door was on a chain, but when Fleishmann saw me he took it off. Sonny and I pushed into the little hall. I stopped Mrs. Fleishmann from lighting the gas, and told Sonny to speak in whispers. "Tell them the situation, find out how many people are living here, and what they know about the men on the second floor."

Sonny gave me an old-fashioned look, as if to say that I was asking him to find out a hell of a lot. Then he went into a whispered chat with them, which I thought was never going to end, while I stood against the wall and tried to exercise patience, which is the virtue every police officer needs. Fleishmann spoke in a whisper, but every so often his wife's voice would rise, and Sonny would pat her on the arm to soothe her down.

All the time I was conscious that just a few feet away in the darkness there was a staircase, and that the firing had come from a staircase in Houndsditch. If they came down the stairs and started shooting, we should be dead ducks.

At last the palaver stopped, and Sonny told me the result.

"This floor, there's them and their daughter Leah, in the front. In the ground-floor back, there's an old couple named Clements, and he's stone-deaf. First-floor front, a man named Schiemann, his wife and four children. First-floor back, two more little Fleishmanns—twins.

"Second-floor front, our Mrs. Gershon, second-floor back's a stockroom. Fourteen of them all told, just about average round here."

"What about the men?"

"They say they don't know about any men."

"Do you think they're lying?"

Sonny shrugged. "They don't know what the word means. If they think you don't want to hear it, they don't say it."

"Put a light to the gas."

"But, boss—"

"Put a light to it."

Sonny did as he was told. The flickering light showed Fleishmann's face, thin and bearded, and his wife, who'd forgotten to put on any stockings. Beyond them was the staircase, hardly more than three feet wide, with a bend in it at the first floor. A man with a gun on that staircase could shoot down a dozen attackers below.

I'd taken the chance of putting on the light because it was necessary to impress the Fleishmanns, and it was easier to do it if they could see me. Now they'd seen me, and I'd seen that staircase. I said, "All right. Put out the light, we'll talk in their room."

In the room, the gas was on already. Their baby daughter slept peacefully in one corner. I said to Sonny, "Tell Fleishmann to go upstairs and fetch down Mrs. Gershon."

Sonny looked at me with his eyebrows raised. Then translated. Fleishmann let out a long wail of protest and started talking twenty to the dozen.

"He says he would not do it for a thousand pounds. If Mr. Vensel is here, there must be big trouble, and he wants no part of it."

I shook Mr. Fleishmann back and forward, as I had shaken Tomacoff. "If there are no men up there, he's got nothing to be afraid of. He's lying." Fleishmann went on shaking his head, collapsed on the bed, and started coughing. I turned to his wife. "You're a respectable woman, Mrs. Fleishmann. I believe Mrs. Gershon's got two men up there in her room. Is that the sort of thing you allow to go on here? Go up and fetch her down."

In the stress of the moment I spoke to her direct, as though she could understand, but of course Sonny had to translate. She refused, like her husband, saying she would not do it for five thousand pounds. At that I fairly lost patience and told Sonny to say I was arresting them on the charge of harboring dangerous criminals.

That did it. She fell on her knees in her nightdress, imploring me not to take them to the police station, they would be disgraced forever. Fleishmann went on coughing. I had a moment of inspiration. "Tell her to go up and say her husband has been taken ill, ask Mrs. Gershon to come down and help."

It worked. With genuine tears in her eyes, tears which came from the thought of their possible arrest but which might have been caused by worry over her husband, Mrs. Fleishmann went out of the door. I heard one stair creak as she began to go up. Fleishmann stopped coughing. The baby went on sleeping. There was silence.

Sonny took out the truncheon, which was his only weapon. He whispered to me, "If they come down with pistols . . ."

If the men came down, our only hope was to take them by surprise. I knew the risk and thought it worth taking. We had to know whether anybody was up there (if not, we would call off the manhunt before we became laughingstocks, for all the reporters would be here as soon as they knew what was happening) and, if so, whether it was one man, or two, or more. As the silence lengthened I thought that Mrs. Fleishmann's nerve had failed her, or that our birds had flown, or—

Then the same stair creaked. Somebody was coming down. Sonny and I positioned ourselves on either side of the door, which was half open. Mrs. Fleishmann appeared, not speaking. Behind her was another figure, and as it entered the door I got an arm around its neck and over the mouth and twisted an arm behind the back. Then I almost released my grip in surprise. The figure was a woman, tall and thin. My surprise came from the fact that she was wearing only a slip and petticoat, nothing more. She gave a squawk of protest and asked what was happening. I was relieved to hear she spoke in reasonable English. I told her that I was a police officer and asked if her name was Gershon. She said it was. I then asked if she had men living in her room, and she indignantly denied it.

Mrs. Fleishmann took a hand, rattling off some indignant phrases to Sonny, who translated.

"She wasn't in the bedroom. She was sleeping in the stockroom opposite."

When I asked why she was doing that, she shrugged and adjusted the pince-nez she wore, which had slipped down when I caught hold of her. She was a tall, skinny female, with a peering look, who reminded me of an ostrich. It was hard to imagine her mixed up with a group of revolutionaries.

"And you say there is nobody in your room?"

"Nobody."

"All right. I am going up to look for myself. If you are lying and they shoot me, you will be hanged for helping them to murder me."

She adjusted the pince-nez again, a nervous trick she had. "My cousin is there."

"You mean Joseph?"

When she said yes, that was a relief, because until that moment we hadn't been certain that we weren't chasing shadows.

"And another man with him?"

"No other man. It is my cousin, and so I sleep in the other room."

"My information is that another man is there with him. His name is Koba."

"Koba has gone, it is not Koba." She put a hand over her mouth as she realized what she had said.

"So there is another man. Who is it? Is it Fritz Svaars?"

"It is a stranger, I do not know him."

It took another ten minutes to make her admit that she knew the man, and that it was Fritz Svaars. Then she said that they had taken away her dress and her boots, so that she should not get away, and told her to sleep in the stockroom. Whether or not this was true—and she certainly had no dress or boots—it didn't seem Mrs. Betty Gershon was of any further use to us at present. "All right," I said to Sonny. "Get somebody to take her to the station."

"But I cannot go like this." She might give shelter to murderers, but she was nothing if not respectable, Betty Gershon.

I asked Sonny to tell Mrs. Fleishmann that she would have to lend her neighbor a coat and some boots. Would you believe it, this was more difficult than it had been to get her to go upstairs. What, lend clothes to a woman who had been keeping men in her room? She would have to burn the things afterward, she could never wear them. But in the end she reluctantly produced an old coat and some shoes, and we packed Betty Gershon off to the station.

I told Sonny to ask if Mrs. Fleishmann had knocked on the bedroom door. She said she had, and there had been no answer. Then Betty Gershon had come out of the stockroom opposite, and they had talked. So the element of surprise no longer existed. The two men must have heard the knocking and the voices. They would know something was up. They were there, stuck up at the top of the house, and what they would do was anybody's guess. It was like having a time bomb up there, without knowing when it was to go off. The only certainty was that at some time it was going to explode.

"We've got to get everybody out of here," I said to Sonny. "All of them, the whole fourteen. I'm leaving it to you."

"Many thanks. Where are you going to be, boss?"

I jerked a thumb across at Cohen the pharmacist's. "Over there. In conference. Trying to decide what to do next."

"Good luck."

He spoke to the Fleishmanns and then said, "They're only too keen to get out and into safety. And Mrs. Fleishmann says she'll do her best with the others. Being neighborly at last."

"Let me know when they're all out. Try and keep it quiet and watch out. We don't want you getting hurt."

"Nobody ever said Sonny Jacobson didn't look after number one."

Sonny didn't do himself justice. It took a brave man to stay there, wake up these people, explain to them, and get them out of the house. We had policemen waiting just beside the door to help get them down the road and to safety. And it took time. The Fleish-manns were only too keen to get their children away (baby Leah slept through the whole thing), and so were the Schiemanns, once they'd been made to understand the situation; but the old couple on the ground floor objected strongly. In the end the old man, who was ninety, had to be carried out kicking and making the hell of a hullabaloo.

The whole thing took over an hour. And on the top floor every-thing remained perfectly quiet. They couldn't have failed to hear the racket the old man made, but there was not so much as a twitch of the curtains from that room.

I'd spent the time in discussion with Ottaway and Mulvaney about what we should do once everybody was out of the house. We stood for most of the time in the archway of the woodyard opposite, under cover but very cold. The men standing out in the open, of course, were colder and very much wetter. Every quarter of an hour we got reports from three sergeants who were making the rounds.

"Begging your pardon, sir, but some of the men are asking when they're going to see some action," one of them said to Superintendent Ottaway.

"We're still getting the tenants out."

"And then shall we go in, sir? Some of the lads are just spoiling for it. They want to go into the house and up those stairs."

"We'll see."

The temptation to try to rush them was strong, but it meant a risk of heavy casualties that none of us was prepared to take. Mulvaney thought that with the dawn the anarchists would realize that their position was hopeless and give themselves up. I didn't believe it, but there was always the chance that he was right. Dawn came, a watery dawn, with an east wind cutting through us, and the snow turned into rain, and the ground slushy underfoot, and we still hadn't decided finally on a course of action.

Then, in the dim light, a tall figure came walking down the mid-dle of Sidney Street (we had police cordons at Hawkins and Lindley streets cutting off the vital sections of Sidney Street), his bowler tilted down a little forward over his eyes, a stick in his hand. He gave first one quick glance in the direction of number 100 before join-ing us in the archway and greeting us.

"Good morning, gentlemen. Although in fact it's a devilish rotten one. They tell me we've cornered our rats and the question is how we smoke 'em out, is that so?"

It was Mac. I have never felt more pleased to see him in my life. And at this point I'm happy to hand over the story to him again.

MACNAGHTEN

I MUST SAY IT WAS very decent of the two supers—Ottaway and Mulvaney—and Fred Wensley to seem pleased to see me at the unearthly hour of seven, when they'd no doubt been expecting me a couple of hours later. The truth is, I couldn't sleep.

As I've said, the excitement of the chase has always been the most fascinating thing about police work for me, and this was a chase in which it looked as though at last we'd found the quarry. I rose just before six, and as I shaved found myself humming a line of doggerel, *"I say what a day we are having, my boys, I say what a day we are having"*—the chorus of a popular song which I'd heard a week before at Evans' Cave of Harmony, the music hall in Covent Garden. I got Crowther out of bed early too and, still humming, had myself taken down to the East End.

My spirits rose further at sight of the police drawn across the road at the corner of Hawkins Street and Sidney Street. They had orders to let nobody through, but although most of the men were City Police, there were a couple from the Met who recognized me. And I need hardly say that I recognized them. When I asked one how he felt, he said, "Very cold, tired and hungry, sir." Then he added, "But nothing that a bit of action won't cure. I'd like to get at those"—and he used an unparliamentary expression that I won't repeat—"who killed my mates."

The supers and Fred Wensley were looking a little blue about the gills, and they didn't say no to a stiffener from the flask that I always carry in my top pocket. I told them what my constable had said and asked what they thought about rushing the place now that all the tenants were out. The front door had been left standing invitingly open.

Ottaway shook his head. "We don't want any more men killed, sir.

Not if we can avoid it. And we couldn't. Inspector Wensley's been inside. He can tell you."

"The stairs go round like this." Fred made almost a right angle with his fingers. "Anybody at the top is pretty well under cover. You try to rush the stairs, they fire, somebody's hit—only one, if you're lucky—and he falls on the stairs, must do. Then he's blocked the staircase and you've got to get over him while you're under fire. It would be suicide."

Mulvaney said, "There's another point. By law we aren't allowed to open fire until we've been fired on first. That means—"

"Quite," I said. Mulvaney was a very cautious, legal kind of man. I'm all in favor of observing the law myself, but I'm in favor of other people observing it too.

If we sent men over to storm the house, and they saw those two villains with pistols in their hands, nobody would be inquiring too closely afterward into the matter of who fired first.

Mulvaney went on. "It's my opinion they know the game's up. Give them a shout and they'll surrender."

"And if they don't?"

Mulvaney shrugged broad shoulders. "Starve 'em out."

"I don't think that's practical. We've got hundreds of policemen around, we can't keep them here forever." That was Ottaway. It was a ticklish question as to who was in control, the City of London Police or the Met, and thank goodness it was one we never had to solve officially. Mulvaney and Ottaway were polite enough, but it wouldn't have taken much to get them at each other's throats. Fred Wensley was going to say something, but he caught a glance from me and didn't.

He had more drive than either of them, but he ranked as their inferior, and at the moment an instruction from him would have been unwelcome. On the other hand, though I had no authority over the City men, it was clear that Ottaway would accept me as a mediator. I asked him what he suggested.

"We've got men up there." He jerked a thumb up toward the pharmacist's first floor. "Tell them to fire a warning volley. See what the response is. Then we'll know where we're at."

I thought a minute. I could see some merit in both ideas. If we could get them out without a shot being fired, it would be a triumph,

Ready to help the wounded, London Hospital
nurses wait with police. Despite heavy
firing, there were few casualties.

but I couldn't see a simple shout doing it. On the other hand, a warning volley was almost certain to start a gun battle.

"Why not gather some men here ready for a rush," I said, "then
try to attract their attention, throw stones at the windows. If they
come out, well and good. If not, we'll know where we are."

A little to my surprise, this was agreed to without argument. Fred
Wensley got busy, and within five minutes we had a dozen men
armed with revolvers ready for the dash across the road.

A thin sleety rain was still falling. It was now completely light.
The house opposite was as quiet as though it were empty. Small groups
of curious sightseers had gathered behind the police cordons at
Hawkins and Lindley streets. Then Fred Wensley shouted, "Come on,
lads, let 'em know we're here." A sergeant named Hallam ran across
the road, beat a tattoo on the open door of the house, ran back.

We waited, standing under the archway, some of the men coming
out from its shelter to stand looking across the road. "Some pebbles in

Members of the Scots Guards stand in a doorway, ready to shoot, while Churchill looks on anxiously.

the yard here," Wensley cried. "Use 'em." And he set an example by gathering a handful of pebbles and starting to throw them up at the second-floor window. The distance across the road wasn't more than forty feet, so it wasn't necessary to get out far to throw the pebbles, which were really more like bits of grit. Some of them spattered against the second-floor window. They produced no reaction at all. I must confess that the thought crossed my mind for a moment that in some way or other the men had escaped.

For a moment, but only for a moment. A sergeant, Ben Leeson, had found a brick. He shouted, "I'm going to let 'em have this to wake 'em up," and moved out into the road to throw it. At the same moment a pane of glass shattered in the first-floor window—not the second—and there was a *snap-snap-snap* of automatic pistols. Shots spurted from the stones of the yard. The brick dropped from Leeson's hand; he shouted, "I'm hit," and started to stagger back toward the woodyard. The other men were running back too. Sergeant Hallam checked himself to help Leeson. From above, in Cohen the pharmacist's, I could hear the sound of our own men firing.

In a few seconds they were all back inside the yard, with the gate slammed to behind them. Leeson was half carried into the Cohens' kitchen, and Wensley opened his coat and shirt. His hands as they came away were red with blood.

"I'm dying, Mr. Wensley," Leeson said. "Give my love to my wife and children."

Wensley patted him on the shoulder and said we'd get him a doctor. This involved a problem. We had the anarchists trapped, but in a sense they had us trapped too, so far as fetching help went. Anybody who went out into the street would be exposed to fire, and there was no way out at the back on our side of the road, so that a doctor would have to be fetched by crawling over the roofs. There were half a dozen volunteers to make this roof crawl, and Wensley picked one of them. Then he turned from Leeson to Sergeant Hallam, who was standing shaking his head, and snapped, "What's wrong with you?"

"Seem to have gone deaf."

Wensley looked at Hallam's helmet, then took it off and pointed to a hole in the rim. A bullet had passed clean through it. "Don't wonder you're deaf. You're lucky to be alive." He patted Hallam's shoulder. "Tea's coming up. Have a cuppa and you'll feel better. You did well."

I went upstairs with Mulvaney to the bedroom where our men were stationed behind the protection of the bedding. We bent low as we moved across the floor to them, and it was just as well we did, because as we reached our sharpshooters there was a loud ping, and fragments of glass showered down on us. A bullet had hit the chandelier in the middle of the room, which was no doubt the Cohens' pride and joy. I spared a moment to feel sorry for them.

The men here were all from the Met, which was why Ottaway was not with us. I asked one of them, Constable Harris, whether he could see the men firing. He shook his head. They saw only the smoke. The anarchists must have put up barricades of their own.

"What about your return fire?"

He looked up and tapped his rifle. He was a slow-spoken man. "These just ain't no good for the job, guv'nor."

One further word about the Morris-tube rifles. From Fred Wensley's account you might think that these were a police issue, but of course they were not. In the Metropolitan Police we had no stock of rifles—and why should we have had? Rifles were for soldiers, and the police had never needed them before in my lifetime. The Morris-tube rifles had been borrowed from a miniature rifle range used by the army, and I quite agree that, ingenious as they were, they were not at all what we wanted. Even firing across the street they were not accurate, and of course the degree of error increased with the distance.

Mulvaney was gloomy as we went downstairs again. "This is what I feared, just what I feared. We should never have alarmed them. There's one man dying now, and God knows how many more to come." I reminded him that Leeson was not dead yet, and that we had the place surrounded. "Aye, but what good's that? It just means more men getting shot." He was a regular wet blanket, Mulvaney. The excitement of the chase meant nothing whatever to him.

Leeson lay on a couch in the kitchen, groaning slightly, Wensley by his side. Ottaway was not there. He had gone scrambling over the outbuilding roofs at the back, to arrange for a man to get into the Mann and Crossman brewery, farther down the street. It was a tall building, and from the upper windows cross fire could be directed at number 100. This was a good idea, except that the chances of a hit with a Morris-tube rifle at that distance were pretty slim.

There had been a lull in the firing. Now it started up again, and a couple of minutes later the doctor arrived, having been shot at as he came over the outbuildings. The doctor's name was Johnstone, and he seemed to know his job. Standing behind him, I could see a bullet wound just beside Leeson's left nipple, in toward the chest.

"I'm a dead man, Doctor," Leeson said. "Isn't that so?"

"Be quiet." The doctor started to probe, and Leeson cried out.

"Not there, it isn't there. The other side."

Dr. Johnstone pulled back Leeson's coat and shirt farther, to reveal another wound just below the right nipple. He turned the man over to see the points of exit. Leeson groaned and fainted. The doctor stood up. I asked him what the chances were.

"If you can get him to hospital, he's got a chance. If he's left here, he'll be dead in a couple of hours."

"Right, then, we'll get him to hospital," Wensley said. "First thing we need is a stretcher, right? I'll get one."

If anything could have increased the respect in which I held Fred Wensley, it would have been his return in what seemed a miraculously short space of time with a stretcher. He had scrambled over the outbuildings and got to the brewery, where Ottaway had sensibly been organizing a headquarters out of the immediate range of gunfire. He had also prepared for the possibility of casualties, hence the stretcher. Unfortunately Cohen the pharmacist had no telephone, so there was no way of talking to Ottaway.

The firing had slackened off, but the weather had become worse. When we had tied Leeson to the stretcher and opened the door into the yard, we were met by icy rain that drove straight into our faces. There was nothing for it but to take Leeson over the rooftops and into the woodyard below, where we had a van used for carrying wood propped up against the wall. Unfortunately it was nothing like high enough to get the stretcher up—the wall was around fourteen feet high—and a ladder had to be tied to the van. Wensley got up to the outbuilding roof from the ladder, and with Dr. Johnstone pushing from below and Wensley pulling from above they got the stretcher up. Then the doctor went up the ladder. On the outbuilding roof they were hidden from the gunmen, although there were bound to be points at which they would be in view.

"Good luck, Fred," I called. Wensley raised a hand to his bowler, in a half salute.

"I hope we shan't need it, sir." As he says, nobody ever called me Mac to my face. Then, keeping very low and pulling Leeson on his stretcher, they moved to the other side of the roof and out of sight. A detective named Corrington crawled after them to give help if it was needed.

"I hope to God they get across," Mulvaney said. He was never one to look at the bright side of things, Mulvaney.

We went upstairs again to talk over the situation with our sharpshooters. The men opposite, they said, were good at keeping out of sight, and at present were holding their fire. However, they shot at everything that moved, especially if it wore a policeman's helmet.

"When they fire, you must get a sight on them," I said.

"Just for a second." Again Harris was their spokesman. "And I ain't a bad shot, sir. If I had a real rifle, I might pick one of 'em off. But with these, it's going to be luck if we're on target, isn't it so, boys? What I mean is, they're not the tools for the job."

There was a general murmur of agreement. And these were the men in the best shooting position! Our other men, in doorways, had these same Morris-tube rifles, or fowling pieces which were not much more accurate, or old revolvers. Another man said, "We're out-matched, and that's a fact."

Harris coughed. "Begging your pardon, sir. Could I just make a suggestion?"

"Why not, Harris? Suggest away."

"If a party was to make a dash over the street, we could give covering fire; and if you got word to some of our other chaps, they could fire as well. It's only a few yards across, and I know a lot of the lads would be ready to try it. I would myself."

Mulvaney was shaking his head, and for once I agreed with him. With luck we might get half a dozen men across the road and into the doorway without any of them being hit—although it would need luck—but inside the house, a man standing in the angle of the stair-way could just pick them off with very little risk to himself. As we talked, a spatter of firing came from the back of the house, but our men in the backyard there weren't in such a good position as us, and weren't likely to have more than nuisance value. And now there was a sustained burst of firing from the house, not in our direction but across toward the brewery.

"They've been spotted," Mulvaney cried, and again I was inclined to agree with him. Our fellows responded, but it was true that they had nothing much to aim at, just the occasional sight of a hand. I told Harris to let me have his rifle. He handed it over, and I lay down behind the mattress.

I used to be a pretty good shot when I was young back in Bengal, and I get a very fair bag even now when the grouse season starts, but when I put the rifle to my eye I understood the difficulty the men were having. There was the window no more than forty feet away. Put the rifle to your eye and the distance seemed to be increased twenty times. I tried half a dozen shots, but they spattered against the brickwork well away from the window, and I gave the damned rifle back to Harris.

"You'll have to do the best you can, lads."

"But what about my idea, sir?"

"Does you credit, Harris, but the superintendent and I agree it's not practical."

Mulvaney and I went out into the yard, and keeping under cover, watched the firing from the house, directed toward the brewery. It would die down for half a minute or so, presumably while they put in a fresh clip, then start again, *snap-snap-snap*. Pretty well half an hour had passed since the party went off toward the brewery, and they should have been there several minutes back. We were speculating on whether to send more men across when Corrington came crawling over the outbuildings. He jumped down to the wood van and came across to us. He was breathing hard, but in the end got the words out.

"We were nearly across, but then they spotted us. Bullet grazed the doctor's forehead, but he'll be all right, he got over. And Sarn't Leeson, he managed to get off the stretcher, rolled down the roof, and they caught him. Leastways, I think they caught him."

"Inspector Wensley?" Corrington shook his head. "What's happened to him?"

"They had him trapped, sir, trapped in a gutter. I got as close as I could and called to him, but he didn't answer. I'm afraid he may be a goner, sir."

THE DETECTIVE'S STORY (CONCLUDED)

I WAS NOT A GONER, but it was a near thing. Here is what happened.

What we had to do was crawl over the outbuildings or sheds, the roofs of which were fairly steeply coved, and then drop down the other side into the yard of Mann and Crossman's brewery. While we were on this other side we'd be visible and exposed to gunfire from the upper windows of 100 Sidney Street. From the first floor we couldn't be seen, but from the top floor we could. It was a matter of chance. And in any case, there wasn't much risk for a single active man who could slide quickly down the roof and then drop into the yard. It was quite a different matter, though, to get a wounded man on a stretcher—and Ben Leeson was no lightweight—across and down.

It wasn't possible to move fast, and the only thing was to keep low and hope they'd stay on the lower floor.

Carefully, moving a few inches at a time, we got the stretcher up to the top of the roof. Then we started to move down the other side. We were as quick as men could reasonably be, but not quick enough. As Dr. Johnstone and I began to move the stretcher toward the brewery wall, I heard a click which sounded a little like hail, and recognized it as bullets striking the tiles. The others didn't realize that we were targets for a few moments—the weather has already been mentioned, but I should emphasize that at this time the rain was really falling in buckets—but then a tile just behind Leeson was struck, and he cried out.

"What are you doing? You're taking me into the line of fire again."

"Needs must, old son," I said, and at that moment Dr. Johnstone clapped his hand to his head and almost lost hold of the stretcher. A thin streak of red appeared across his forehead, was washed away by the rain, and reappeared. He called out that it was just a scratch, and it proved afterward that a bullet had grazed his forehead.

We were now moving down the angle of the roof, and the doctor was near the brewery wall. A policeman's head appeared over it with a helmet on it. He shouted something about being ready for us.

I saw Leeson was struggling with the straps we'd put over him, and asked what he was doing.

"I'm getting off this bloody stretcher."

He managed to get the straps loose and, with nothing to hold him, rolled down the roof, a distance of perhaps twenty feet, and disappeared. The doctor, who had been carrying the lower end of the stretcher, had already reached the edge. Now he vanished. The same policeman's head bobbed up again. He shouted, "We've got him, sir, he's all right!" Then a bullet removed his helmet. He remained there for a moment with a look of astonishment on his face, and disappeared. I heard afterward that, quite remarkably, he was unhurt.

All that remained was for me to get down. Simple enough, you might think. But the gunmen had now got the range, and they were fairly peppering the tiles all around me. I let go of the stretcher and heard it crash in the yard, but with the bullets coming so thick and close, the chances of being hit as I slid down to the wall were high. Instead I crawled onto the gutter of the shed, which was partly shielded by the top of the wall. My bowler fell off, and as it dropped toward the wall I saw it bounce up in the air as it was struck by a bullet. The gunmen seemed to have a better aim for hats than for people, but still this did not encourage me to try to scramble across and down to the wall. So I lay out full length in the gutter, in an inch of sleet and water. I was very wet and very uncomfortable. I lay there for something like half an hour, out of sight. It was at this time that the rumor of my death spread. Special editions of the papers were being rushed out, and I had the pleasure of seeing in the *Evening News* a couple of hours later:

Detective Inspector Wensley's Gallant End
Killed While Helping Wounded Colleague

The most uncomfortable half hour of my life, as I say. The gunmen knew I was there, and fired in my direction every time I made an attempt to wriggle along in the direction of the brewery yard. But my nearest approach to being hit showed me the means of escape. On one of my little expeditions a bullet struck and smashed one of the tiles no more than a couple of feet away from me. A fragment struck me glancingly on the head, so that I was happy to stay where I was for a moment or two.

When I had recovered, I looked down at the space that had been occupied by the smashed tile. There was the shed below me. If I had been thinking straight, it would have occurred to me before that I had only to loosen enough tiles to be able to drop through into the shed, and although I never carry firearms, I do invariably have in my side pocket Wensley's Persuader, which in a policeman's ordinary life is far more useful. Wensley's Persuader is less than half the size of a truncheon, and has a weight of lead shot in one end. A tap with it will knock a man unconscious, or paralyze an arm that's carrying a knife.

It was a matter of five minutes' work with the persuader to break up a few tiles and make a hole in the roof large enough to drop through. The drop might have been a nasty one, but luck was with me, for almost immediately below me stood a big brewer's dray, painted in the Mann and Crossman colors of green and gold. I made one last wriggle, this time out of gunshot, got my legs into the gap.

Lowered myself and let go. I landed plumb in the dray, very wet, but undamaged except for the blow with the tile, which was bringing up a bump on the back of my head. I got down from the dray and strolled into the brewery yard, where colleagues were both astonished and pleased to see me. I learned that Ben Leeson had been rushed to hospital and that his chances were good. I'm happy to say that he eventually made a complete recovery.

MACNAGHTEN

MULVANEY AND I STAYED where we were, in Cohen the pharmacist's, for another half hour. I should like to say we were watching the progress of the battle, but in reality there was no progress. Sidney Street was clear for a hundred yards or so, the distance between Lindley and Hawkins streets, and the gunmen fired at anything in that area. They wounded one constable in the arm and killed a stray black cat. We returned their fire, but it was obvious that, as Constable Harris had said, we were outmatched. Their fire and ours had broken a lot of windows, and there was a great deal of glass lying about in the road.

It was plain, too, that no single individual could control all the proceedings. We were at the front of the house, Ottaway in the brewery was to the side of it, and for us to communicate with each other and with the men at the back of the house meant a long and intricate detour through houses and backyards and over walls. It was said afterward that we might have foreseen this, but I don't honestly see how we could have. We were dealing with a situation quite unprecedented in police history.

In one of the lulls that came in the firing, Mulvaney said to me, "We need help, sir. I don't mean men, we've got enough of them. I mean weapons. Regular army rifles, sir. Lee-Enfields, and men who can use them. I think we need the troops. If we send someone across to the brewery—"

"It's a good idea, Superintendent, but why send somebody? We're doing no good here, let's go ourselves."

I'm not sure that the idea delighted Mulvaney, but he could hardly say no. We told Harris and his colleagues to keep up their fire, and got to the brewery by the route the others had taken, up the ladder, across the roofs and down. There was little risk for an active man, and in fact the gunmen couldn't have spotted us, for they didn't fire a shot.

At the brewery, I was delighted to find Fred Wensley, looking a bit dazed from the knock on the head he'd had with a piece of tile, but in good spirits except that he was annoyed at losing his bowler. I also found Ottaway, who agreed that we should try to find a gunsmith who could let us have something better than those wretched Morris-tubes, and also that the quickest and best way of getting more fire-power was to bring in the troops. Scotland Yard had no authority for this. The order had to come from the Home Secretary, Winston Churchill.

I had a slight acquaintance with Winston, as everybody called him, and although I am a Conservative and he is a committed Liberal, I admired his drive and energy. The brewery telephone was in operation, and within a few seconds I had spoken to the Home Office and learned that Mr. Churchill was at home. I looked at my watch and saw with astonishment that the time was only just after nine in the morning.

The manservant I spoke to sounded shocked by the idea that anybody should want to speak to his master at such a time. "I am afraid Mr. Churchill is still in his bath."

"Then get him out of it."

"I beg your pardon, sir."

"Ask him to come to the telephone. Immediately."

A couple of minutes later his voice, unmistakable in its strange mixture of a subdued growl and a faint lisp, came on the line. "This is Winston Churchill. I understand you wish to speak to me on an urgent matter." A moment's pause and he added, with his characteristic hint of humor, "I hope the urgency justifies my getting out of my bath wrapped in a towel like a Roman emperor—a wet Roman emperor."

I outlined the situation rapidly and without interruption. When I had finished, the Home Secretary said simply, "Tell me what you want."

"Enough troops, armed with modern weapons, to arrest or kill these men."

"You shall have them. I will give instructions at once. If you will send a man to the Tower of London with details of what you want, I will make sure that the men are ready." I started to express my thanks when he interrupted me. "Macnaghten."

"Yes."

"I might come down and have a look myself. Why should you have all the fun?" A chuckle, and the line was disconnected.

I sent Mulvaney to make the necessary arrangements at the Tower, and suggested to Ottaway a little idea that had crossed my mind when I had observed that the men shot at everything that moved, especially if it wore a policeman's helmet. Suppose that we rigged up a dummy policeman and put it into the pharmacist's window, making no effort at concealment. It should draw their fire and might even, when they saw that the figure did not fall when shot, induce the men to reveal themselves.

Ottaway was enthusiastic, and a couple of constables went to work constructing the dummy. His face was brown paper, and his body was a hayfork borrowed from the stable for the horses in the brewery yard, but he looked quite convincing from a little distance. We found that it was easy enough to get him into a house a couple of doors away from the pharmacist's but still very visible from number 100. We put him into a first-floor window there, with what looked like a rifle at his side. A fusillade of shots came at once from the house, half a dozen of which pierced the dummy's straw body and knocked him backward. Just for a moment or two we could see the bodies of two men as they fired from a corner of the window. Then they vanished. The moment had been lost. We put up the dummy again, but this time the gunmen ignored him.

I returned from this sally a little disappointed, to find that Pat Quinn had arrived and that Ottaway and Wensley were excited about a vantage point they had found which overlooked the gunmen's position. This was at the very top of the brewery's bottling storeroom. There were large slatted windows here, which gave complete protection, and anybody firing from this point would command a good sideways view of number 100, away and to the right, although firing through the horizontal slats presented some difficulty.

"Now all we want is the troops," Ottaway said.

Just at that moment a cheer went up from the crowd, and looking beyond them we could see a detachment of Scots Guards marching down the street. They halted at the word of command, and we hurried down to meet them. There were twenty all told—a fresh-faced lieutenant named Ross, a couple of noncommissioned officers and seventeen men. Mulvaney was with them, and he had explained the situation on the way back from the Tower of London, where the guards were stationed. But now Ottaway and I told Ross of the latest developments.

"Put the men where you want. Shouldn't take more than a few

minutes to chase them out," Lieutenant Ross said. In this he was mistaken. At the time I agreed with him and would have wagered that the affair would be over in another half hour.

Ottaway, Mulvaney and Lieutenant Ross settled the placing of the men. Three of them went up to the bottling storeroom from which we had just descended. Another three went around to fire at the back windows, and four to replace our police marksmen in the pharmacist's bedroom. The rest pushed past the spectators—many of whom patted them on the back—and through the police cordon, and lay

In firing position, three Scots Guardsmen lie on the cobblestones of Sidney Street while unarmed police stand at the corner, out of the path of bullets.

down in the street some twenty or thirty yards from the house. They carried with them boards intended to display newspaper posters, on which they lay. Then, with their caps pushed back a little on their heads, the checked cap bands showing distinctively, they started firing on the house. These were the men in position first. The others, of course, had to clamber over fences and climb ladders just as we had done, and this took a little while. The men lying in the road opened the firing with their Lee-Enfields, followed by those from the brewery and then, a few minutes later, the ones from Cohen the pharmacist's and the roof of a pub at the end of the street, named the Rising Sun. When they were all in action—and remember that there were policemen with revolvers standing in doorways and firing too—the noise was tremendous. It seemed impossible that any living thing in the house could survive.

And yet survive they did. Whether the soldiers' marksmanship was not what might have been expected, or whether the gunmen were especially lucky or adroit, spurts of shooting continued from the house. The concentration of fire had one effect, that they moved now from one floor to another and from front to back, so that their chance of actually hitting anybody was much reduced. Whereas earlier on they had evidently taken careful aim, their firing now seemed to be almost at random.

The Scots Guards who lay exposed in the street should have been an easy target, but in fact only one of them was hit, and he suffered nothing more than a flesh wound in the thigh. I went up to the bottling storeroom, from which the soldiers were concentrating their fire on the second-floor front.

"I'm thinking they won't be using that room again," said the noncom in charge of the group. "Now the floor below, boys." They turned their sights to the floor below and put some shots into it. Then the noncom cursed gently but fervently as a couple of defiant shots came in reply from the top floor.

In fact, this barrage had no more effect than to damp down the firing from the house, and the chief danger was to spectators from the bullets that ricocheted off buildings. Even a spent bullet can do some damage.

I was standing beside Pat Quinn at the front of the police cordon by Lindley Street when he exclaimed, "I've been hit!" and dropped to the ground. I bent over him and found that he had been struck on the leg by a bullet that had lodged in his trouser cuff. It must have been a ricochet, for the wound was only slight, and a direct hit would have done far more damage. And who could tell whether it was one of our bullets or one of theirs? It crossed my mind, I must say, that there was a certain amount of poetic justice involved. If Quinn had passed on the first information he received, we might have caught the whole gang, or most of them, at Houndsditch.

It was midmorning. The snow was now slushy, and the later fierce sleet had become mere drizzle, although there was still a biting wind. Above the hum of the sightseers behind me and the sound of the barrage, I heard angry voices raised, and as I helped Quinn to hobble back toward the first-aid station that had been set up, I saw Wensley engaged in an angry altercation with a little knot of policemen. I left Quinn to make his own way—he was not badly hurt—joined the group, and asked what the trouble was.

"We've got a small supply of weapons from a gunsmith, sir, and they've been given to men who are used to handling them." I noticed now that all of the men around Wensley were holding shotguns. "They want to rush the house. I've told them it's no go." Wensley's face was red with anger, and some of the men around him were looking equally furious. Their spokesman was Constable Harris, one of the marksmen in the pharmacist's who had been replaced by the Scots Guards.

"They're doing no better than we were. Why not let us go back there, now we've got these?" He patted the shotgun he was holding.

"Because they're picked marksmen, Harris, that's why."

"Then whyn't they give us covering fire while we make a dash along the side of the street? If those anarchists have to shoot us, they'll need to show themselves. We don't mind taking a chance, do we, boys?" There was a chorus of approval from the others. "Now Sergeant Leeson's copped it, we want to get at them, that we do."

I was startled. "Is Sergeant Leeson dead?" I asked Wensley.

"Not that I know of, sir, he's in hospital. It's just a rumor." Wensley shook his meaty fist in Harris' face. "They were all saying I was dead an hour back. I tell you Ben Leeson's gone to hospital with the doctor. I saw them go off in the ambulance with my own eyes."

"He looked a dead un to me," said one of the other men. "Shall we rush the house, sir? We'll take our chances on getting killed if we can get those—" I omit the expression he used. I had just begun to explain to them that the problem wasn't reaching the house but getting at the men after they were inside, when Harris shouted something incoherent and pushed his way through the police cordon, waving his shotgun. A couple of other men began to follow him until they were stopped by Wensley and myself. Then we stood and watched Harris, holding our breath.

He ran along on the same side as number 100, with the spectators at both ends of the police cordon cheering him on. The windows of some other houses on that side were open, and women leaned out of them, shouting encouragement. As he passed the soldiers lying in the street they held their fire, and so did those at the other end and in Cohen's.

There was a spatter of rifle and pistol fire from the back, no more. Wensley, at my side, murmured, "Never known the police so popular in this area."

Now Harris had reached the house, crouching almost double. He was at the door, kicked it farther open, vanished inside.

The soldiers still held their fire. Even the crowd suddenly became silent. Then there were shots from inside the house, although it was impossible to tell whether they were from pistols or Harris' shotgun. A sound moved through the crowd, a sort of sigh like wind passing through wheat. Harris reappeared in the doorway. He was swaying.

The soldiers in Cohen's opened fire, concentrating as it seemed on the first-floor windows.

Harris took half a dozen steps across the road and then fell down.

The soldiers in the road started firing again.

Harris didn't move.

Two policemen ran over from the woodyard beside Cohen's, zigzagging across the road until they reached Harris. Then they picked him up and ran with him, while the soldiers kept up their covering fire. They got back to the woodyard and safety.

Fred Wensley uttered one loud expletive. I was feeling the same way. One of the men said, "If we'd all been with Harris, sir—"

I cut him short. "Then you'd have been shot just as he was. I'm having no more men killed, you understand? In future you obey orders. Now, go where Inspector Wensley thinks you can be useful."

Mind you, I could understand their feelings. Harris was a brave man, though a foolish one.

A familiar voice in my ear said, "What's been happening?" It was the Home Secretary, Mr. Churchill, a smile on his face and a cigar in his mouth. I leave him to tell his story.

THE HOME SECRETARY'S STORY

I AM HAPPY TO ACCEDE to the request of my friend Sir Melville Macnaghten that I should put on paper a note of the part I played in the Sidney Street affair. Sir Melville called me up on the telephone and asked for troops. I am bound to confess that my pulse beat a little faster, and I instantly determined that, come what may, I would take a personal look at what was going on. I was criticized for this direct participation later on in the House of Commons, and on reflection I agree with my critics. Somebody in my position has no business meddling in things which are really the province of the police, but there it is. My inclination has always been to march toward the sound of gunfire.

After talking to Sir Melville I removed my towel, or toga, dressed, and got down to the Home Office. There I found remarkably little further information awaiting me. Some anarchists were shut up in a house in the East End. Nobody knew how many were inside, but they were said to be firing in all directions. The most recent information we could gather was from a newspaper bought in the street. A new edition was being brought out every hour, and they were sold as fast as the newsboys could hand them out. The paper said that Detective Inspector Wensley had been killed, and that three other policemen were believed to have been shot. That was decisive. I had myself driven down to the East End, and to Sidney Street, immediately.

It was an astonishing scene. There in the middle of the street was what looked like a completely bare space, with the crowds held back by police cordons at either end of it. But the space was not really bare. There were the Scots Guards firing from a little way down the street, and policemen lurked in the shadow of every doorway, crouching with guns and pistols pointed toward one single house, a house identical in appearance to all those beside it. There were army sharpshooters firing from the top of a brewery. And there at the other end of the street, the roof of the Rising Sun public house was crowded with more troops, with Lee-Enfields, which they loosed off at the house.

And the crowds! This must have been the most cosmopolitan assembly ever seen in such numbers in the metropolis. It was as though all East London had crowded into this one small area of Whitechapel. As I pushed through them to get a better view, I heard the language of almost every continental nation spoken, along with a big smattering of Yiddish. There were also, of course, many East Londoners of older vintage. I was recognized, and I cannot say that my reception was friendly. There were shouts of " 'Oo let 'em in?" which referred to the government's refusal to place any limit on the entry of aliens to this country. I was strongly tempted to stop and argue with them, but refrained.

Just to one side a little group of police officers were standing, including Sir Melville and an officer introduced to me as Inspector Wensley, to whom I said that I was glad the rumors of his death—like the rumors of my own in the South African War—had been much exaggerated. But I saw immediately the force of the objections later made by my critics. I had come as a spectator, but now I was there, the police officers inevitably looked to me for a lead. The position was that of stalemate. What was to be done?

"The first thing is to have a look for myself, a little nearer the scene of action."

At that they all appeared horrified. Macnaghten started to say something about my safety being in their hands. I interrupted him.

"I've been in tougher spots than this, and so have you. If I'm to give advice—and it will be advice, mind you, nothing more—I have to see the situation."

"We've just had a man shot when he tried to get into the house against orders."

"I promise not to go into the house. I want to see the lie of the land, that's all."

There was silence. Then Wensley said, "If Mr. Churchill keeps close to the wall on this side and three or four men go with him, it should be safe enough. I'd like to volunteer as one of them." He was a man after my own heart, Wensley.

So it was agreed. Along with a party of uniformed constables, all of them armed, we crept along within a few yards of the house, keeping close to the wall. The locals, sitting at their windows as though they were watching a show at the Mile End Empire, gave us a rousing cheer, very likely thinking that we were going to make an attempt to storm the house.

Glass crunched under our feet. We stood sheltered by a warehouse. A couple of Scots Guards, who had been finding things a bit hot in the road, were in the doorway of the wineshop in front of us, firing occasionally. From the pharmacist's across the road came steady firing, with an occasional reply from the house.

Wensley stood behind me, telling me how the land lay and discussing what might be done. When I said that storming the place from below seemed a possibility, he disagreed.

"I don't say it isn't possible, sir, but the stairs go round like this." He showed with his finger. "We should do it all right, but we're liable to lose several men."

"What about the back?" I could hear the sound of firing at the rear of the house.

"Same objection, sir. They'd have to get in through a window, and they'd just be targets for anybody inside."

"How about going onto the roof, getting in through a trapdoor?"

"No trapdoors in these houses, sir."

I'd been told briefly about Wensley's exploit in getting Sergeant Leeson over the rooftops. "All right, then, what about taking a leaf out of your book, Inspector—getting on the roof, smashing some tiles, and dropping through?"

"I was just dropping onto a brewer's dray, sir, not to a place where a man was waiting to shoot me. I'd be sorry for the first lads through."

"I see. Then how about trying all these methods at once?" Wensley gave me an old-fashioned look, but said nothing. "Damn it, man," I said, "there are only two of them. You're not telling me we can't get them out."

"No, I'm not saying that." He made a gesture with his thumb at the men behind him. "They're all keen as mustard to storm the place. We have to hold them back. We remember that three of our men were killed at Houndsditch and some have been wounded today. We don't want any more deaths."

I felt rebuked, but still I was not satisfied. "How do you see it, then,

Inspector?" At that moment a bullet ricocheted off the roadway and struck the wall a foot away from where we were standing.

"The way I see it, sir, is that we should beat a retreat. If you've seen enough, that is."

On the way back to Macnaghten, Quinn of Special Branch (who'd got his leg strapped up after being hit) and the others, Wensley told me how he saw it. "We've got them boxed up there. Sooner or later their ammunition's going to run out. When it does, we just go in and take them. These riffraff aren't worth dying for."

Very sensible, but it didn't satisfy me. It is part of my temperament that I can never be happy playing a waiting game. I always prefer to succeed by positive rather than negative means. When we were all gathered around a table in the brewery office, with glasses of whiskey which had been procured from somewhere in front of us, I put forward my plan.

"Inspector Wensley has told me the difficulties in the way of storming the house where these villains are installed. I agree with most of what he says. There are dangers, certainly, but with the use of a little ingenuity they can be minimized. Is there a steel foundry in the vicinity?"

"Several, sir, within a mile or two." That was the local superintendent, Ottaway.

"Very well. I propose you should try to find one that has a steel plate of this shape." I sketched roughly an old-fashioned shield. "We shall need say half a dozen of them. Under cover of these, we shall storm the house. Each shield should give protection for two men. If there are no shields, any curved metal plates will do." Nobody said anything.

"Gentlemen, I await your comments."

"It's an ingenious idea," Macnaghten said. "But I don't know what chance there is that anybody will have such a shield in stock. If they have to make them—"

"A plate, then. Surely a foundry must have metal plates."

"That doorway's narrow. If the plates were too wide, they'd never get in," Ottaway said.

"Right, then. The plates must be narrow."

"How about you, Wensley?" I said. "I'd like to hear what you think."

Wensley looks rather like a bloodhound, with small mournful eyes and a droop to the mouth. "It's clever, but I don't think it will work. Our men are going to be shot at from above when they get inside. What are they going to do, hold the shields over their heads? If they do, the rest of their bodies will make a pretty good target."

It has been said that I never listen to what other people have to say. Quite the contrary is true, as I think I showed on this occasion. In a sense it was no part of my duty to take personal control or to interfere with those who were in charge on the spot. Very true. Yet I could see that my presence there made the police officers reluctant to express their opinions, and in that sense the decision had to be mine.

"I take your point," I said to Wensley. "But I am not prepared simply to allow events to take their course, as you gentlemen seem to advise. Since nobody has another suggestion, I shall be glad if you will make inquiries of the local foundries in relation to these metal shields; then, when we have them, call for volunteers to storm the house."

It was apparent to me that this idea did not meet with entire approval, but nobody positively opposed it. Superintendent Ottaway went off to try to find these protective shields. I still believe, in spite of the various objections, that they would have worked, with little or no loss of life. At this very moment a detective came in to report that Constable Harris, who had made the gallant but foolhardy attempt to storm the house, was not badly hurt, and in fact had not been shot. A loose balk of timber from above had struck a glancing blow on his head, and he had suffered nothing worse than concussion.

Whether my view on the usefulness of the metal shields was correct will never be known, for events now moved in a way unforeseen by any of us. We were still drinking our whiskey, and I had just lighted my second cigar of the day, when a police constable came in and said, "The house, sir, the house is on fire."

We left the brewery office and went outside.

Apart from one important further intervention, which I understand Sir Melville will record, that concludes my part in the Siege of Sidney Street.

Upon the whole, I accept the criticisms made of my actions. I think that I exposed myself to personal danger—something which has never concerned me in the least—and also caused anxiety unnecessarily to the officer in charge, which I much regret. I forgot for a few hours that I was a member of His Majesty's government, and therefore should have been wrapped in cotton wool. But I must say that I thoroughly enjoyed myself.

MACNAGHTEN

WE STOOD AND WATCHED the smoke. It curled up thinly, delicately as the smoke from a cigarette, and it looked as harmless. The smoke came from the back, curling out of an attic window, and it seemed at first that its effect might be trivial, because firing continued from the front of the house. Mulvaney put in a call for the fire brigade, because, as he said, a fire of that sort can spread. In the meantime we stood watching, and a strange sound, what I can only call a sob of pleasure, went up from the crowd. One or two voices shouted hideous, obscene comments.

"Watch 'em come out now. Watch the rats come out."

"They're going to be burned alive."

"Best way too, kill all that—scum."

"Anyone fancy roast pork for dinner?"

And now came one of the most extraordinary incidents of the siege. A postman in his red and blue uniform, sack on back, somehow managed to get through the police cordon, walked along to 104 Sidney Street, pushed some letters into the box, and returned the way he had come, apparently unaware of what was going on around him. The crowd gave him a roaring cheer.

Within a few minutes it became clear that the smoke meant fire and that the fire was not trivial, or at least that it was beyond the power of those inside to put it out. There was not much wind, and the roof was now shrouded in smoke, still a delicate blue with no sign of flame, but distinctly thicker. I was standing beside Churchill, and asked him what he thought.

He chewed on his cigar. "If they want to surrender, they can show the white flag."

I asked the other police officers. They agreed that rushing the house would now be not only dangerous, but pointless. Wensley raised a thought which had already occurred to me.

"I shouldn't be surprised if they lit the fire themselves. We'll need to watch out they don't make a break for it."

And now the smoke was much thicker, gathering like a thundercloud around the top floor of the house. Mixed in the cloud were thousands of bits of charred paper, which fluttered slowly to the ground. The soldiers in the pharmacist's bedroom increased their rate of firing, and I could hear that at the back also they were using more firepower. It seemed impossible that anybody could survive in such an inferno, but proof to the contrary was a sudden sharp burst of firing through the first-floor window, the pistol flashes showing briefly in the smoke.

And now, with bells ringing, the fire engines arrived. They got to the edge of the police cordon at Lindley Street, and the men started to unwind their hoses. Mr. Churchill made a growling noise in his throat.

"What are they doing?"

I stared at him. "They're going to put out the fire."

"Let me talk to the officer in charge."

A couple of minutes later the officer, whose name was Davis, stood looking in bewilderment at Mr. Churchill, who pointed with his cigar at the house.

"Anarchist gunmen are shut up there. They are dangerous."

"That's as may be, but the house is on fire."

"If you run your hoses and ladders up beside the house, your men will be shot at."

"What are we to do, then, sir?"

"Let it burn."

Davis looked from one to the other of us. Then Ottaway said, "What about the houses on either side? If we leave the fire unchecked, they may burn too."

"Get the people out of them. But the thing is almost finished now, and we are not risking a single life to save the two villains trapped in there. That is an order, Mr. Davis. As soon as the men have surrendered, or it is safe to do so, you can get your men to work." He put a hand on the man's shoulder and said kindly, "I know it goes against the grain."

"That it does, Mr. Churchill. We're meant to put out fires, not to watch them."

"This is an exceptional case, and you may regard yourself as being under a direct order from the Home Secretary. Now, tell your men to stand ready, but not to go into action yet."

Davis did so, still a little unwillingly.

Mr. Churchill stood staring at the smoke that hung over the top of the house, shrouding it like a dark mantle. His gaze was somber, his jaw stuck out.

The orders were given to evacuate everybody in the houses on either side of number 100, and within minutes the people were out of them, a stream of women and small children, with some men following, carrying their few belongings, among them family pictures and Russian icons. One of the men came over to us and asked in broken English what was to happen to his "fern cheer," by which he meant his furniture. He appealed to Wensley, the police officer all of them knew.

"My fern cheer, Mr. Vensel, what happen if my fern cheer burned?"

"Don't worry, dad, we'll try and make sure it isn't."

"But Mr. Vensel, my fern cheer, if it burns, who pays?"

Wensley, still watching the house, clapped the man on the shoulder and assured him, "It won't burn." There was not much else he could say, and astonishingly the man accepted it. This ruthless decision was justified by events, but I cannot say I was happy about it, either at the time or in retrospect.

I looked at my watch and saw almost unbelievingly that the time was one thirty. I was reminded I had not eaten since early that morning. Many of the police, of course, had last eaten at some time on the previous night, and if I was hungry, they must be ravenous. I was suggesting to Ottaway and Mulvaney that we should try to organize a mobile canteen when there was a gasp from the crowd and a shout of "There 'e is."

On the first floor a dark figure could be seen, apparently clambering out of the first-floor window and standing on the sill outside. Was it intending to make a jump for safety? There was a sharp burst of firing from the soldiers opposite, but although the figure swayed, it did not fall. I saw Mulvaney cross himself rapidly and murmur a prayer. The thought crossed my mind, as it must have done the mind of many another there, that these men seemed to be more than mortal. Then the figure moved again back into the room, and could be seen as nothing more than a torn, burned curtain that had deceived us in the smoke.

In the next moment there was a long-drawn "Aaah" from the crowd as one single tongue of flame came from the attic window. As though to synchronize with this, there was a sudden burst of firing from the first-floor front window, so that the sinister tongue of flame above was echoed by the quick spurts of yellow below. We heard the same sounds repeated from the back of the house, and again somebody fanciful might have imagined that the numbers of the men inside had suddenly been augmented and that, with the evacuation of the inhabitants from the neighboring houses, anarchists had crept up out of cellars or tunnels to join their friends. I will confess that this thought also occurred to me. And then five minutes later rational intelligence dismissed it.

The top of the house was now burning furiously, with flames making a crown of fire over the roof, and a thick pall of smoke hanging over the first- and second-floor windows. The flames leaped from the attic window, and it was plain that the upper floor must now be uninhabitable. All firing had stopped, and there was no sound to be heard except the crackling of the fire, with below it the excited hum of background noise from the watchers.

Then a figure appeared at the first-floor window, no charred curtain this time, but a frightful apparition like something out of a story by Edgar Allan Poe. It seemed for a moment that the figure had red hair, but in fact the hair was wreathed in flame, the face blackened by it. The clothes also were on fire. Yet in its flaming hand the figure held a pistol, and some incoherent shriek of defiance came from its mouth.

The soldiers and armed policemen did not hesitate. There came a terrific volley of fire, fiercer than any during the whole siege. The figure vanished from the window as suddenly as it had appeared. A haze of blue rose from the rafters, a smell of cordite was strong in the air. Again there came that hint of something beyond our human understanding as the sound of two more pistol shots was heard from inside the house. Some of our men fired another scattered volley in response, although there was now no figure to be seen, and they were firing into smoke.

And then came the end. The house literally began to collapse. The crown of flame on the roof disappeared as, with a roaring and sucking sound, it fell in. Then the flames shot up again from the floor below, and this collapsed too. I can say nothing that would put it more vividly than one of the newspaper reports on the following day:

> Blazing timbers were flung into the street, masses of masonry crashed down, fiery splinters like shooting stars were hurtled a hundred yards or more. Broken glass fell upon the pavement again and again with a dreadful sound of destruction. And with all this turmoil and fury there poured a terrific artillery of shots.

This last effect was remarkable. The collapse of the house made it certain that the wretches in it could not have survived. Yet now, as one bit of masonry crashed upon another, and iron girders stuck up out of the collapsed building like great naked ribs, there was firing from every direction. The soldiers in Cohen the pharmacist's fired, and the soldiers on top of the brewery and those on the roof of the Rising Sun fired too. And the policemen fired—the dozens of police who had been huddling for hours in alleys and behind doorways fired also, less in the hope of hitting anything than in celebration, as though they knew that at last this was a moment of triumph.

Then the firing stopped. A detective sergeant—his name was Jacobson, and he had been instrumental earlier in getting the house evacuated—began to walk toward the house, holding a double-barreled shotgun. He was followed by a dozen others, all of them with their guns out. They came up to the empty houses on either side and went into them, in order to make sure that the men had not broken through the walls. Then Jacobson emerged, moved cautiously up to the half-open door of number 100, and gave it a kick. The door fell inward, and he jumped back as tongues of blue and yellow flame spat out at him. Then he raised his hand in a prearranged signal, and the firemen began to unroll their hoses and advance on the house. As the water jets started to spray over the ground and first floor, the flames turned pale, then became hissing clouds of smoke and steam. Within minutes the firemen were inside the building. Soon afterward there was a great shout of warning followed by cries of pain.

The two superintendents and Wensley crossed the road toward the house, and Mr. Churchill started to follow. I laid a hand on his arm.

"Mr. Churchill," I said, "I feel responsible for you. It may be dangerous over there."

At that his nostrils flared. It was far from my intention, but the word dangerous had moved him to action. He simply said, "I am going into that house."

I followed him with Pat Quinn beside me. As we got to the open hole that had been a door, Davis, the chief fireman, appeared, his face streaked with dirt.

"Stretchers," he called. "We want stretchers." Then he saw Mr. Churchill.

"I've got men buried in there," he said. "If I'd been let free to work when we got here, this wouldn't have happened."

Inside, the house was a shell, yet some fragments of it remained. If you looked up, you could see the sky, but you saw also sections of the upper floor leaning perilously inward. Above us a small table still stood, with ammunition on it, upon a part of the floor which looked as though you could walk on it. Beside the ammunition was a glass of water. The flames were all out, but smoke hung thickly, and we put handkerchiefs over our noses and eyes. Men with stretchers came past us and moved to the back of the house, where the firemen had been hurt. Part of the sidewall had collapsed and had brought a section of the upper floor down with it. Five men lay there, half buried in rubble. Two had been struck by a falling beam. We helped pull them out and got them on stretchers, and Mr. Churchill played his part.

Then the fire chief said shortly, "I wouldn't stay if you don't have to. Another wall may come down."

"I understand your feelings," Mr. Churchill said in his slow, emphatic voice, which came muffled through the handkerchief. "But if you'd gone in when you wanted to, those men would have been shot, not injured. Hallo there, what's this?"

We were standing inches deep in rubble, but I saw what he was staring at. Just beside the fireplace was a bulky mass partly covered by debris. As the fireman pulled this away, a body was revealed, or rather part of a body, in a sitting position. The head had apparently been burned away in the fire, and all that remained was the trunk and the arms. It was one of these, sticking up out of the rubble, that caught Mr. Churchill's eye. A little digging in the middle of the room by a fireman revealed the legs, which were separate from the body, and apart from these, a fragment of the brainpan and a skull-cap. The heat must have been intense, for almost all the clothes had been burned off the body, and when a fireman touched the protruding arm, a piece of skin came away in his hand.

The fireman's digging also turned up a pistol. Mr. Churchill picked it up and weighed it in his hand. "A Mauser," he said reflectively. "Better than anything we've got. We must do something about that."

I will confess that the sight of the burned body nauseated me. I stumbled out of the door and across the road, where a nip from my hip flask was a necessary reviver after I had removed the handker-

Flames leaping from the windows while the shooting goes on. Later, when the fire was extinguished and the guns silent, police examined the charred debris. Inside, the burned bodies of the anarchists were found.

chief. Mr. Churchill, however, was made of stronger stuff. He stayed in the house for half an hour, although when he emerged he did not disdain a drink from the flask himself. Then he nodded approval.

"An excellent malt. You'll be pleased to learn that they've found the other body too. He was in the back room. Unrecognizable, of course, but it looks as if he was shot. The doctors will tell us in due course. I wanted to be sure neither of them had got away."

Outside, it looked as though a pitched battle had been fought. Walls were scarred and windows broken all down the street. On both sides, the houses next to number 100 were more or less intact, and it seemed likely that the gentleman worried about his "fern cheer"

would find it little damaged. Uniformed constables and plainclothes detectives were standing around, some chatting to each other, the rest clearing away the spectators, who were now wandering all over the street.

And then an astonishing thing happened. From those spectators there came, slight and sporadic at first, the sound of clapping. It was begun perhaps by no more than forty or fifty people, but it swelled into a chorus, so that all of them were clapping their hands, the rag-tag collection of peddlers and housewives and tailors and seamstresses and out-of-works. They were joined by the people at the windows and those on the surrounding rooftops. Hats were thrown into the air, and a ragged cheer came from the crowd. It was as though they were applauding the actors at the end of a play.

Mr. Churchill looked around with a rather grim smile. "This is our moment of popularity, but what will it be like tomorrow, eh, Macnaghten? Anyway, I'm glad to have been here at the end of a memorable occasion. History will remember the Siege of Sidney Street."

That was the first occasion on which I heard the phrase used.

But it was by no means the last time, and it was far from the end of the affair. The newspapers had a field day, belaboring the government and the police on all sorts of grounds. There was a strong movement to ban all further immigration into Britain, and an equally strong movement to arm the police. This was further emphasized by a statement of Mulvaney's that although there were some revolvers available, these were, as he put it with masterly understatement, "not a type sufficient for the purpose." A memorandum came through from Mr. Churchill saying that we must be provided with "the best pattern of automatic pistols at present procurable, and this should be put in hand *immediately.*"

Very true and perhaps necessary, but it did not take account of the fact that this was the only occasion in my lifetime that weapons had to be used in any quantity. As Wensley had put it, "It needs a very nice judgment to hit upon the exact moment when one would be justified in using a gun. In this country an officer would only be entitled to shoot when his life was in imminent danger. To pull the trigger a moment too early, or because of some misunderstanding, would almost certainly bring about a charge of manslaughter." This is not the rule everywhere, I know, but I like to think that we manage such things best in England.

Much more serious were the suggestions that we had handled the affair incompetently. These suggestions were made at a conference a week later at the Yard, called by the commissioner. For the benefit of readers unacquainted with the Scotland Yard hierarchy, I should explain that the commissioner is at the head of the whole of the Metropolitan Police, of which the CID is of course only one part. The commissioner was not in a good mood. He held up a bunch of press reports.

"You may have seen some of these, gentlemen. They come from the French, German and American press. I will just read one or two headlines. 'The Army Called Out to Deal with Anarchists,' 'A Thousand Police versus Two Rebels,' 'Tragicomedy as British Authorities Muddle Through.' An American paper suggests that a destroyer should have bombarded Sidney Street from the Thames while the police evacuated the whole of the East End population. I trust they were joking. But these reports are typical. Would anybody like to comment?"

Most of the officers chiefly concerned with Sidney Street were around the table—Mulvaney, Wensley and myself, Pat Quinn from Special Branch and Ottaway from the City Police.

Mulvaney said, "There weren't a thousand police. No more than two hundred at the most."

"Even so, Superintendent. Two hundred against two seems long odds."

"It may seem like that, but the overriding consideration was saving lives," I said. "In this whole operation against two absolutely desperate men who shot to kill, one sergeant was wounded—and the news about Sergeant Leeson is good—together with one constable and one Scots Guard. Several civilians were hurt, but they knew the risk they took in being there. I think the fact that the casualties were no worse justified the precautions we took."

"You've forgotten my wound," Pat Quinn said, and roared with laughter.

"You count as a civilian." I looked around the table. "I think everybody here will agree with me that the siege could have been over in half an hour. The cost would probably have been a dozen men killed." There was a murmur of agreement. "I refute entirely the idea that we could have done better. The way it was handled—and I am happy to have had a share in the handling—was a triumph of good sense."

The commissioner turned over the papers in front of him. "I have a number of suggestions here, made mostly by members of Parliament and military men. One or two seem to have some merit. The idea of pumping a nontoxic gas into the house, for instance, to render the men insensible. Was that considered?"

Mulvaney, Ottaway and I looked at each other. Then Ottaway said, "No, sir."

"Why not? One of my correspondents suggests that laughing gas could have been obtained from any nearby doctor."

"Very likely, sir. And the pump would have presented no difficulty. But how were we to get near enough to pump it in?"

"My correspondent, a retired major general"—the commissioner coughed, whether with ironic intention it was hard to say—"suggests that attention could have been held by concentrated fire at the front, while men at the back pumped gas in through the window."

"Two comments on that, sir. They wouldn't have stood a chance in the world of escaping attention, because from what we can tell, the men moved from front to back all the time. And the second comment is that within a couple of minutes most of the windows were broken. For the gas to be effective, they'd have had to be closed. The major general wasn't there. If he had been, he wouldn't have made such a stupid suggestion." Ottaway spoke with convincing calmness.

"Point taken." The commissioner picked up a paper. "There is a suggestion here from an opposition member of Parliament. I think I should read a few lines. 'If the Home Secretary, instead of stopping the operations of the fire brigade, had encouraged them, the siege would have been brought to a quick conclusion. The force of a jet of water is very considerable, and a few well-directed jets would have knocked the men off their feet and ended all resistance within minutes.'" He looked around. "Well, gentlemen?"

I said, "It's ingenious, but I don't think it would have been practical. Again, if the firemen had been near enough to direct the hose, they would have been under fire. If they were to remain in safety, they couldn't have directed the hose with any accuracy."

I may privately admit that I felt there was some force in this suggestion, and, although risky, it just might have been successful, but the commissioner merely nodded, apparently satisfied.

"I now come to a different line of criticism. Namely, that we have killed only two of the conspirators, that there is no proof of their identity, and that the rest of this murderous gang are still at large. What am I to say to that?"

This was Pat Quinn's affair, and he ticked off points on his fingers. "The identification. These men were Fritz Svaars and Joseph—"

"Joseph what? He must have another name."

Pat smiled slightly. I like Pat, but his air of knowing everything can be a little trying.

"His name is not Joseph, but William Sokoloff, a name that I have seen spelled in six different ways. He was a watchmaker and a professional burglar, and as such must have a record in the ordinary criminal files. He was also up to his eyebrows in the affairs of the Liesma group in which Gardstein was important, and that is why he interested me. He was never called anything but Joseph."

"How do we know that one of the men in the house was Joseph?"

"Because he had a limp, and one of the bodies found had an old thigh fracture which would have caused such a limp. We also have the word of Mrs. Gershon, who was living with Joseph. He had been shot, by the way, and he was certainly the man who appeared for a moment at the window.

"And how do we know that the other man was our friend Fritz the mandolin player? Well, the body was too badly burned for identification, but the size was right for Fritz, who was a short man. One of my little pigeons learned that Fritz and Joseph were together for a couple of days before we found them. And although in Mrs. Gershon's presence Joseph mostly referred to him as my pal, just once he forgot and said Fritz."

"And the others? They have got away?" The commissioner's tone had sharpened. I had noticed before that he did not much care for Quinn's self-assurance.

"By no means. The woman Nina Vassilleva was left free because it was hoped that she might lead us to her friends." Quinn smiled at Wensley to show that had been his idea. "She did not, and she is now under arrest. Fritz's lady friend Luba Milstein gave herself up, and has been in our hands for weeks. Jacob Peters, who was in the robbery, has been arrested thanks to information from one of my other little pigeons. And we have two or three others as well."

"What about the gentleman known as—ah—Peter the Painter? I take it he has not yet been apprehended?"

Quinn coughed. "He is now in Paris. So the Sûreté tell me."

"He was one of the conspirators. And he escaped?"

"How big a part he played in the actual robbery I leave to the CID and the uniformed branch to determine. My concern is with his anarchist connections. You must understand that these men have all kinds of international contacts. There is an underground movement in every industrial country—"

"The long and short of it is that he has got away?"

"That is the short of it," Pat Quinn said, unperturbed.

"And the mysterious Koba, who was present when the robbery was planned, according to one of your—ah—pigeons. He got away too?"

"My information is that he left the country within twenty-four hours of the Houndsditch murders. He may even have gone before the robbery took place. He was here only on a flying visit."

"A pity."

"No doubt, although I am not sure what charges could have been preferred against him. None, I imagine, since he took care not to become personally involved. But it is a pity, certainly. The rest of them are small fry, but he is known in four or five countries. A subtle, resourceful, intelligent man. I should have liked the chance of interrogating Koba."

EPILOGUE
MACNAGHTEN

So, OF THOSE SEVEN revolutionaries Tomacoff saw at Grove Street that day, three died—Gardstein, Fritz Svaars and Joseph—two were under arrest and two got away. Naturally we should have liked to catch them all, but in the circumstances I thought we did well. I wish I could say as much about the later court proceedings when Peters and Nina were put on trial with their other friends. I sometimes think that English criminal law is devised especially and exclusively to assist the defendants, and this case might have been taken as an example of that thesis.

On the one hand, it was absolutely clear that Peters and Nina Vassilleva were involved in the robbery up to their necks. On the other hand, it was difficult actually to prove it, or to say exactly who had fired the shots that killed and wounded the policemen. Certainly it was not Luba Milstein, and she was quickly discharged as having been a mere tool of Fritz Svaars. None of the other three men arrested were at Exchange Buildings when the robbery took place, although they were no doubt up to all kinds of other revolutionary mischief which in my view would have justified their imprisonment. However, they were discharged too.

That left Nina and Peters. Nina had undoubtedly been present, but on all the police evidence just as certainly had not fired a pistol, although there were plenty of witnesses to say that she had dyed her hair and tried to conceal evidence. And Peters? Well, it is quite possible that his hand held the pistol that killed Sergeant Tucker and Constable Choat, but the prosecution never managed to prove it. Peters was a very tough customer. I went to see him once in prison, and urged him to confess, on the ground that if he did he might help his comrades. He looked at me with his close-set eyes, grinned, and said in broken English, "Why I confess? In England you do not hang me. I have five years in prison perhaps, and I know Russian prisons. England is better."

What happened must have exceeded his best hopes. The prosecution was bungled, the police witnesses could not identify him positively, and some of the East Enders were afraid to come forward. He was set free, and left the country within a week.

Nina received a two-year sentence for breaking and entering, but this was quashed because the judge had misdirected the jury. She stayed in England, and some time afterward wrote the memoir you have read.

Not much remains to be said. A few weeks after the siege I attended a basement shooting gallery where manufacturers had been invited to submit up-to-date pistols and revolvers for police use. Mr. Churchill was there, and we tested a dozen different makes. In the end, I am happy to say that a British gun was chosen, the Webley-Scott .32 automatic. And even happier to say that there has been little need to use it.

But there is just one final word, and it is a word of some importance. More than six years after the siege the Russian Revolution took place, and the Bolsheviks under Lenin and Trotsky seized power. I had retired from police work, and so knew little more about those appalling events than I read in the newspapers. I assumed, like almost everybody else I knew, that the Russians would return to their senses, throw those villains out, and bring back the monarchy. To my astonishment this did not happen. By early in 1920 the Bolsheviks were firmly installed in power and we were beginning to hear of other names among their leaders—Zinoviev, Kamenev, Stalin. It was against this background that the final scene of the drama was played out.

I was living now for the most part very quietly, but still went twice a week to my club, the Garrick. There one day I lunched with Pat Quinn, still at the Special Branch.

"You remember Sidney Street?" he asked, as though I could ever forget it. "Come back to the Yard with me. I've got something to show you."

Back in the office, he took from a drawer a photograph album. It contained a pictorial record of the siege, and also photographs of the revolutionaries, some of them obtained no doubt through his pigeons. There was handsome Gardstein, arrogant-looking Peter the Painter, narrow-eyed Peters, Nina and the rest. He stopped at the picture of Peters. "Have you heard of the Cheka?"

I had indeed. It was the organization founded by the Bolsheviks to suppress and imprison their enemies.

"Peters is deputy head of the Cheka. He is a powerful man now in Russia."

He showed me a photograph of Peters with Lenin, Trotsky and some of the other revolutionary leaders. Then he turned to the last page of the album, and to a picture with "Koba" written beneath it. Koba was wearing a cap at a jaunty angle, he had the mustache affected by many revolutionaries, and he was smiling in the sly, secret way that people do when they know they are going to get the better of you. He was not a man I would have cared to trust at any time.

"That was Koba in Russia in 1906," Quinn said. On his desk was a Russian newspaper. "Now look at this. It's a special issue of the revolutionary paper *Pravda*, published to celebrate the triumph of the revolution. The two center pages are pictures of the leaders." He opened up the paper, and there in the middle was a picture in which some twenty small photographs were placed, framed in a kind of banner. The writing at the top and bottom was in Russian, and Quinn had to translate.

"It says 'Central Committee Russian Communist Party' on the top and 'Long Live the Third Communist International' below. Do you recognize anybody?"

"Lenin and Trotsky."

"Look at the photograph of Koba in my album, and then at the man below Lenin on the left. Use the glass." I looked through the magnifying glass. He was not wearing the cap, but the sly, secret smile was similar. And yet there seemed something different in the expression. Was that just the effect of the years that had passed, or was it a different man?

"What do you think?" Pat Quinn asked.

"I don't know." I used the glass again, and shook my head. "It's impossible to be sure."

And I have never been sure since. Below was the name, and Quinn translated it for me. It was one that had recently become prominent:

J. V. STALIN

A Historical Note

THIS IS A NOVELIZATION based on the actual happenings in Houndsditch and Sidney Street. All of the historical personages existed, and the narrative is true in general, although not accurate in every detail.

It may be of interest to say a little more about the career of Sir Melville Macnaghten. He was born in 1853, educated at Eton, and was in many ways a typical member of the English upper class in the late nineteenth century. In his early twenties he went out to manage the family estates in Bengal, and remained there for twelve years. Then, with no obvious qualifications for the post, he was appointed to the CID post, and to the surprise of a good many people made a success of the job. He was conservative in his opinions and reserved in his manner, but he had also the streak of adventurousness suggested here. His reminiscences, *Days of My Years*, appeared in 1913. They contain an account of the siege which mentions a mysterious Mr. Nemo as the chief conspirator. I have considerably enlarged his role in the siege.

Superintendent Patrick Quinn was head of the Special Branch. Winston Churchill was there, and played the part I have given him. His presence was strongly criticized in Parliament. Detective Inspector Wensley's heroism in helping to carry Sergeant Leeson over the shed roof to safety is accurately described. Wensley's distinguished career culminated in his appointment as chief constable of the CID.

And the conspirators? Peters was the assistant head of the Cheka, which preceded the OGPU and the KGB. He is thought to have died in the purges of the 1930s.

Stalin was known as Koba, and carried out several "expropriations" in Russia. There have been persistent rumors that he was connected with the Houndsditch robbery, but in placing him among the conspirators I have used a fiction writer's license.

—Julian Symons

ACKNOWLEDGMENTS

Page 313, lines 27-37; page 375. lines 1-6, 12-38: from *Operation Portland: The Autobiography of a Spy* by Harry Houghton, copyright © 1972 by Harry Houghton. Used by kind permission of Rupert Hart-Davis Ltd. and Harry Houghton.

ILLUSTRATION CREDITS

Page 3: courtesy of the Metropolitan Police, London.

THE STEALING OF MURIEL McKAY
Pages 8-9: Rick McCollum. Pages 10, 11, 12, 15, 20, 26, 27, 28, 58, 63: Popperfoto. Pages 14, 61: The Press Association Ltd. Pages 17, 25, 31, 41, 46-47, 50, 51, 59: BBC copyright photographs.

NEILL CREAM, POISONER
Page 68 (left): courtesy of the Metropolitan Police, London. Page 68 (right): London Express News and Feature Services.

THE CASE OF STANLEY SETTY
Pages 205, 245, 254: Syndication International, Ltd.

SCOTLAND YARD: PAST AND PRESENT
All photographs courtesy of the Metropolitan Police, London.

THE PORTLAND SPY CASE
Pages 306-307: Rick McCollum. Pages 309, 316 (left, bottom right), 336, 355 (background, bottom), 374 (top, bottom left, background), 406-407, 407 (bottom left): Syndication International, Ltd. Pages 316-317 (background), 317 (top), 355 (top), 374 (center left), 407 (background, top): Popperfoto.

DOCTOR CRIPPEN'S DIARY
Pages 416-417: Rick McCollum. Pages 419, 439, 495, 510-511: Syndication International, Ltd. Pages 426, 431, 498-499, 509: Popperfoto. Page 452: Radio Times Hulton Picture Library. Pages 502, 513: Mary Evans Picture Library. Pages 506-507: The Press Association Ltd.

THE SIEGE OF SIDNEY STREET
Pages 590-591: Rick McCollum. Pages 602, 617, 652, 653, 664-665, 680: Syndication International, Ltd. Pages 603, 639: The Granger Collection. Pages 616, 638, 681: The Press Association Ltd.